RUTHLESS

# RUTHLESS

## A New History of Britain's Rise to Wealth and Power, 1660–1800

EDMOND SMITH

YALE UNIVERSITY PRESS
NEW HAVEN AND LONDON

Published with assistance from the Annie Burr Lewis Fund.



For information about this and other Yale University Press publications, please contact:
U.S. Office: sales.press@yale.edu yalebooks.com
Europe Office: sales@yaleup.co.uk yalebooks.co.uk

Set in Minion Pro by IDSUK (DataConnection) Ltd
Printed and bound in the UK using 100% renewable electricity at CPI Group (UK) Ltd

Library of Congress Control Number: 2025940615
A catalogue record for this book is available from the British Library.
Authorized Representative in the EU: Easy Access System Europe, Mustamäe tee 50, 10621 Tallinn, Estonia, gpsr.requests@easproject.com

ISBN 978-0-300-27851-4

10 9 8 7 6 5 4 3 2 1

# CONTENTS

*List of Illustrations and Figures* *vii*
*Acknowledgements* *x*

Introduction: For Profit 1

*PART ONE INNOVATION AND EXPLOITATION, 1660–1750*

1 The Spirit of Enterprise: Innovation, Investment and the State 19

2 A Green and Pleasant Land: The Environment, Agriculture and Natural Fibres 53

3 Descent into Darkness: Mining and Metallurgy 91

4 Between Heaven and Hell: Conquest, Colonisation and Slavery 123

5 War Profiteering: Violence, the State and Economic Development 156

*PART TWO INDUSTRY AND EMPIRE, 1750–1800*

6 A Scientific People: Inventing, Stealing and Commercialising Technology 189

7 Masters of Reality: Applied Science and Remaking the Natural World 226

8 Fire and Iron: Power, Metal and Engineering 261

9 Made by Slaves: Colonial Goods, Capital and Networks 298

10 The Empire's New Clothes: Cotton and the Transformation of British Industry 341

Conclusion: Wealth and Power 376

*Notes* *381*
*Bibliography* *412*
*Index* *440*

# ILLUSTRATIONS AND FIGURES

## PLATES

1. Philippe Jacques de Loutherbourg, *Coalbrookdale by Night*, 1801. © The Board of Trustees of the Science Museum, London, CC BY-NC-SA 4.0.
2. Joseph Wright of Derby, *A Philosopher giving that Lecture on the Orrery in which a Lamp is put in Place of the Sun*, 1766. Wikimedia Commons.
3. James Ward, *A Border Leicester Ewe*, c. 1795–1800. Yale Center for British Art, Paul Mellon Collection.
4. George Morland, *Slave Trade (Execrable Human Traffick, or The Affectionate Slaves)*, c. 1788. Collection of the Smithsonian National Museum of African American History and Culture.
5. *A Pit Head*, c. 1775–1825. © National Museums Liverpool / Bridgeman Images.
6. Plate (Chinese, for British market), c. 1723–35. Metropolitan Museum of Art.
7. Plate (Bow porcelain factory), c. 1755. Metropolitan Museum of Art.
8. Brown Bess flintlock musket, c. 1790. Birmingham Museums.
9. Tea casket, c. 1765–70. Metropolitan Museum of Art.
10. Set of wrought-iron leg shackles, eighteenth–early nineteenth century. Collection of the Smithsonian National Museum of African American History and Culture.

11. Joseph Wright of Derby, *Arkwright's Cotton Mills, by Day*, c. 1795. © Derby Museums / Purchased with assistance from the Heritage Lottery Fund, the Art Fund (with a contribution from The Wolfson Foundation), the V&A Purchase Grant Fund, and the Friends of Derby Museums / Bridgeman Images.
12. Bedcover (Indian, Gujarat for British market), early eighteenth century. Metropolitan Museum of Art.
13. Textile sampler, 1784. Metropolitan Museum of Art.
14. Exterior detail view of a frieze on the Town Hall, Liverpool. © Historic England Archive.
15. Roma Spiridione, *The East Offering its Riches to Britannia*, 1778. From the British Library archive / Bridgeman Images.

IN THE TEXT

1. An idealised English farm, title page of John Worlidge's *Systema Agriculturæ*. Image provided by The John Rylands Research Institute and Library, The University of Manchester. 62
2. Bénard after De La Rue, 'A mine: cross-sections of the galleries and miners digging', eighteenth century. Wellcome Collection. 95
3. James Chadwick, map of Liverpool, 1725. Wikimedia Commons. 152
4. Map of Liverpool, 1824. Image provided by The John Rylands Research Institute and Library, The University of Manchester. 153
5. Society for the Encouragement of Arts, Manufactures and Commerce gold medal, designed by James Stuart, die cut by Thomas Pingo, first struck 1758. Image courtesy of Royal Society for the Encouragement of Arts, Manufacturers & Commerce. 200
6. J. Pass after J. Ihle, 'The century plant (Agave americana) flowering stem', c. 1796. Wellcome Collection. 238

7. J. Aikin, 'A description of the country from thirty to forty miles around Manchester', 1795. Wellcome Collection. 255
8. Milk ewer and tea pot, from Matthew Boulton's manufacturer's catalogue of silver-plated ware, c. 1790. Elisha Whittelsey Collection, Metropolitan Museum of Art. 292
9. 'Stowage of the British slave ship *Brookes* under the Regulated Slave Act of 1788', 1788. Library of Congress, reproduction number LC-USZ62-44000. 306
10. Sugar bowl, c. 1820–30. V&A accession number C.14-2023. © Victoria and Albert Museum, London. 337
11. John McGahey, 'Cotton Factories, Union Street, Manchester', c. 1829. Image courtesy of Manchester, Art Gallery. © Manchester City Galleries. 365

## FIGURES

1. GDP and GDP per head in Britain, 1660–1800 (using values from 1700). 6
2. Total economic output from agriculture, industry and services in Britain, 1660–1800 (using values from 1700). 6
3. Number of captive people trafficked from Africa in ships owned by British slave-trading corporations and independent slave-trades from London, Bristol and Liverpool, 1660–1810. 310

# ACKNOWLEDGEMENTS

The roots of this book lie in a project that I began in 2020, funded by the Economic and Social Research Council, that set out to investigate how people invested in innovation and the impact this had on Britain's economic development. While reading about how entrepreneurs work, it was not unusual to find biographies and accounts of leading businesspeople from the past and present that use the term 'ruthless' to describe a key trait that set these individuals apart. Rather than necessarily denoting cruelty, the ruthless streak of prominent capitalists was intended to highlight their single-mindedness, obsessive dedication and a take-no-prisoners attitude in pursuit of their goals that left little time for considering the wider impact of their work. This ruthless mentality resonated in the materials I was working with about the lives of people during Britain's remarkable rise to wealth and power in the seventeenth and eighteenth centuries. This only became more prominent when I was invited to join another project on the legacies of the British slave-trade, supported by the Arts and Humanities Research Council, where I researched the impact of slavery on northern Britain's economic transformation. During these projects, as I collected data on thousands of capitalists active across Britain and came to understand their lives and businesses more deeply, it became clear that it wasn't only the ruthless pursuit of profit that connected inventors in London to slave-traders in Liverpool or miners in Wales, but a much broader and deeper web of relationships that needed to be understood together to understand the economic transformations that took place in Britain during the nation's rise to wealth and power.

While researching and writing this book, I've been privileged to work with many brilliant colleagues who have provided critical feedback, shared ideas, pushed me in new directions, and made the work of completing this volume much more engaging. I am profoundly grateful to the many universities, archives, funders and individuals that have assisted with the project. Thank you to everyone who attended and offered feedback at events at universities in Busan, Cambridge, Chicago, Leiden, Liverpool, London, Lund, Manchester, Newcastle, Oxford, Seville and Sheffield, and to anyone who joined public events related to these projects. Special thanks go to members of the project teams and other colleagues who I've worked closely with during the completion of this work, including Cátia Antunes, Hannah Barker, Michael Bennett, Mariana Boscariol, Catherine Casson, Lila Chambers, Georg Christ, Benjamin Constanty, Helen Corlett, Peter Knight, Sylvie Cunliffe, James Dawkins, Nick Draper, Kieron Flanagan, Shounak Ghosh, Lisa Hellman, Andrew James, Camilla de Koning, Charmian Mansell, Safya Morshed, Nuno Palma, William Pettigrew, Nick Radburn, Alka Raman, Philipp Rössner, Haig Smith, Kimberley Thomas and Nuala Zahedieh. Bringing the book to life wouldn't have been possible without the team at Yale University Press, where Julian Loose, Frazer Martin, Rachael Lonsdale, Robert Sargant, the book's anonymous reviewers, and everyone else I've worked with have been fantastic.

Most of all, I thank Rachel, for supporting me in everything I do, critically reading every word I write, and for making life beyond this book absolutely brilliant.

# INTRODUCTION

## For Profit

'Gentlemen, we are beginning to build a cotton factory for which we shall want a steam engine . . .'

It was that easy. With the opening line of their first letter to a pair of Birmingham-based engineers in May 1797, John Kennedy and James McConnel were on their way to acquiring a mail-order steam engine of their very own. They wrote themselves into the history of Britain's industrial revolution in the process.

Born in Scotland, McConnel and Kennedy had moved to Lancashire in the 1780s to complete apprenticeships with William Cannan – McConnel's uncle, who had grown up in the same village as Kennedy. Here, in the heady days of textile innovation that were quickly transforming Lancashire into Britain's most advanced economic region, they learned not to spin cotton, but to build machines such as spinning jennies and water frames that made it possible for a single worker to do the work of a dozen. When the younger Kennedy finished his apprenticeship in 1791, the two entrepreneurs went into business together in Manchester, investing £250 in their new enterprise alongside £350 from Benjamin and William Sandford. This was the equivalent of more than a skilled craftsman could earn in four years.

The company's inventiveness and technological sophistication quickly set it apart. By 1795, the firm's value was already close to £1,800, and the two Scotsmen had left the Sandfords behind for a factory in Canal Street where they initially focused on building cotton-spinning machinery for mill owners across Lancashire and beyond. This part of the business continued for a few more years, but the two men soon found a better use of their skills. Kennedy devised a way to connect a steam engine more effectively to a spinning mule, and a new process known as double speed enabled machines to produce particularly fine and high-quality thread. In 1797, the partners set out to build a high-tech cotton factory dedicated to producing the best-quality cotton yarn on the market.

It was with this aim that they wrote the simple lines above to the Birmingham-based company of Matthew Boulton and James Watt, which since 1775 had been manufacturing and installing steam engines for industries ranging from ironworks in Shropshire to coal mines in Scotland. Unfortunately for McConnel and Kennedy, Boulton and Watt's vast manufacturing works was overwhelmed with orders, and the 14-horse-power machine they requested was not a popular model. Boulton and Watt regretfully informed the cotton-spinners they would not be able to receive an engine as soon as they hoped, and that it would be quicker and cheaper if they went for a 12- or 16-horse-power model instead. Keen to get started, the Manchester-based businessmen ordered the larger machine at a cost of £821 2d – more than their entire start-up capital only six years before.

The technical ability of McConnel and Kennedy, and that of Boulton and Watt, were vital components for the success of their business, but they were by no means the only ones. Launching a new cotton factory in Manchester depended on global supply chains and sales networks that tied the northern town to a much wider world. Raw cotton was sourced from plantations in the United States, Dutch Suriname, Portuguese Brazil and British colonies in the Caribbean, and it is likely that McConnel and Kennedy's thread (and cloth made with it) was exported to markets just as wide-ranging, with British cotton textiles sold across Europe, Africa, America and Asia. This was an economic system that depended on the conquest and colonisation of land far from home, the exploitation of enslaved labour to harvest raw cotton, and the sometimes-violent establishment of imperial and commercial interests that criss-crossed the world.

When McConnel and Kennedy's steam engine finally made its way to Manchester, the combination of technological innovation, extractive plantation agriculture and exploited labour provided the foundations that pushed their business to new heights. By 1801, they employed over 300 workers in a company worth almost £22,000 – not a bad return on the original £250 they had invested only ten years before! They kept reinvesting, building a second steam-powered mill that could employ more machines, more engines, more workers and more plantation-grown raw cotton. And yet, while McConnel and Kennedy's commercial success was extraordinary, it was still only one factory among dozens in Manchester employing steam engines to power their world-changing machines. This former backwater of north-west England was well on its way to becoming known as Cottonopolis, a city of mills and steam, and among the most productive places on the planet.[1]

## THE TECHNOLOGICAL FRONTIER, AND BEYOND

The machine-powered cotton mills of Manchester were at the forefront of a revolution in how humans exploited technology and power for profit. For the first time in history, productivity would become disconnected from the number of people labouring to produce simply what their own hands could make. Technology provided society with what has been described by historians as a free lunch: that is to say, people could work less and produce more. It is hard to understate just how transformative this was. The latter eighteenth and nineteenth centuries were a period of accelerating and unprecedented technological change and economic growth, when entrepreneurs and inventors like Kennedy and Watt used their creativity and mechanical knowledge to produce new tools that could be employed across an array of sectors. Sometimes new technologies or processes transformed how work was done dramatically and unexpectedly, while others complemented existing technology and contributed to continuous and incremental progress. It was through such innovations, and the scientific and enquiring minds that created them, that some of the economic breakthroughs that brought Britain such remarkable wealth and power rested. In some classic studies of the industrial revolution, Britain's inventiveness and technological advances alone largely explain this transformative period of economic progress.[2]

This, of course, was not the whole story. Inventors did not change the world with an idea alone. They needed partners to invest in and implement their vision, workers to execute it, natural resources to fuel their machines, and a world of customers to buy their products. Creativity and invention were vital, but their impact depended on broader economic systems that were brutal in their approach to productivity as often as they were enlightened. Britain's rise to wealth and power depended on changes in how people exploited land, labour and the rapidly globalising world as well as new technology. At home, more and more workers were released from agriculture to work in cities, mineral wealth was wrenched from the earth in ever greater quantities, and a manufacturing base that had been perfecting woollen cloths for hundreds of years was rapidly turned towards the manufacture of cotton. New centres of wealth emerged in Manchester, Liverpool, Birmingham, Glasgow and elsewhere, with mills built first alongside rivers that powered their waterwheels and later alongside new canals that helped supply them with coal or transported their goods to distant markets. Overseas, Britain violently established its far-flung empire, conquering and claiming lands across the world, and trafficking millions of enslaved people to work on them. These colonies provided raw materials and tropical produce for consumers in Britain, redrawing the map of supply and demand as they did so. Britain moved from a bit player to a lead actor on the world stage, becoming a financial and commercial behemoth that could shape the conditions of trade on every continent.[3]

Understanding Britain's rise to wealth and power demands looking at the full array of economic activities that were taking place and recognising that changes in different parts of the economy were happening simultaneously and in connection with each other. To what extent was Britain's industrial revolution the result of its machines, which produced goods with miraculous efficiency? How much did it owe to the country's natural abundance, which provided coal for its engines, ores for its furnaces and food for its labourers? Or did it stem from Britain's colonies, where a brutalised enslaved workforce produced cotton for its factories?

Answering these questions requires a longer and broader look at the origins of Britain's wealth. Between 1660 and 1800, Britain's economic output grew from around £40 million to over £185 million (using values from 1700, see Figure 1). Generally, economic growth outstripped population growth, meaning that the average person was contributing more to the economy than had been possible for earlier generations. Most of the population remained poor, but wages and domestic consumption increased, and among professionals and propertied society disposable income rose significantly. That upward trend was already well under way by the middle of the seventeenth century and, despite intermittent peaks and troughs, continued to rise throughout the eighteenth. Growth was driven by the physical expansion of the market through colonisation and international trade, increasing regional specialisation and integration across Britain itself, and advances in productivity that had nothing to do with the later development of steam-powered mechanisation. Quite simply, in the century and a half before McConnel and Kennedy ordered their steam engine, Britain's economy was already booming.[4]

Central to this economic dynamism were a group of individuals that we can call capitalists – people who chose to invest their money, their time and their resources for profit. Unlike later proponents of 'capitalism', these were not necessarily supporters of nascent ideas related to free trade or liberal economics and are defined instead through their economic actions rather than any outward ideology. Indeed, for understanding the origins of Britain's economic transformation, capitalists are more usefully understood as people who undertook activities intended to increase profits, exploiting new economic frontiers including land, labour, trade, finance and technology. They were not rentiers or landlords, living off financial investments or rents from inherited land (although some benefited from these opportunities too), but were focused on achieving greater profits by embracing new ways of doing business and entering new markets that Britain's global trade provided. While lacking a single clear social, political or professional definition, it is possible to identify similar behavioural traits in how and why these individuals took part in economic exploitation. Not all of these capitalists were successful, and they were by no means all rich, but through their ruthless pursuit of profit, they would revolutionise Britain.[5]

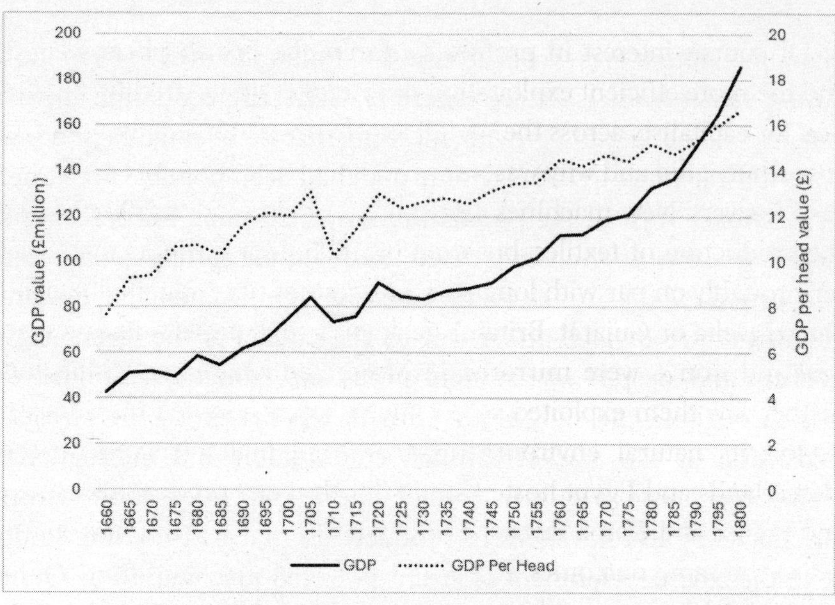


*Figure 1. GDP and GDP per head in Britain, 1660–1800 (using values from 1700).*[6]

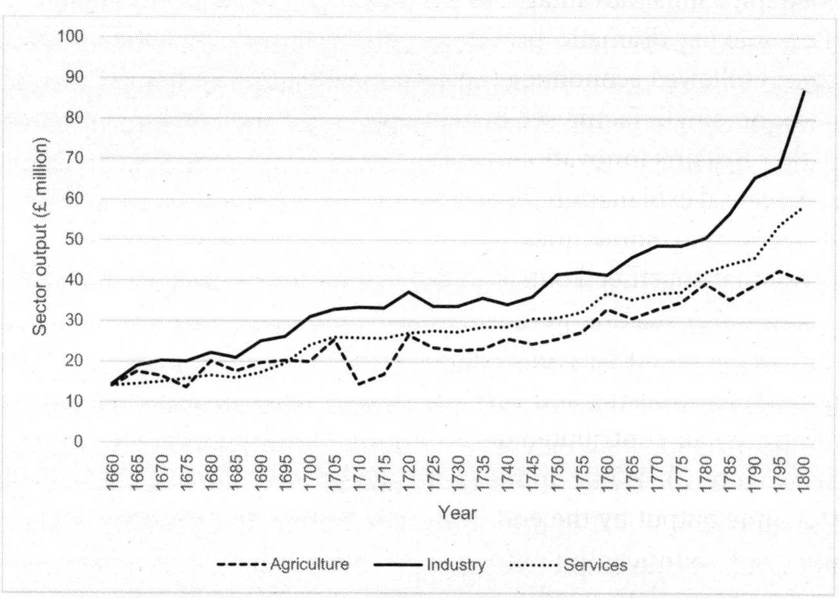


*Figure 2. Total economic output from agriculture, industry and services in Britain, 1660–1800 (using values from 1700).*[7]

Of course, interest in profit was no unique British phenomenon, and the more efficient exploitation of resources was a driving motivation for capitalists across the world. So why, then, did Britain industrialise when it did and why was it the first country to do so? There are no easy answers. New machines and sources of power certainly boosted the production of textiles, but even by 1800 British productivity was only roughly on par with long-standing centres of production like the Yangzi Delta or Gujarat. Britain's geological advantages – its access to coal and iron – were mirrored in Mysore and northern China, but neither saw them exploited so effectively. Japan adopted measures to exploit its natural environments that were highly successful, the Netherlands and Egypt hosted similarly advanced service economies, and France and China saw scientific interest grow – yet none of these led to the same outcomes as in Britain. The exploitation of enslaved people for labour was taking place in Portuguese Brazil and Spanish New Mexico in similar ways as in Britain's colonies, but neither led to the same advantage for capitalists in their home countries in fuelling industrial growth. In each case there were opportunities for capitalists to exploit similar advantages to their British counterparts but, despite often making dramatic profits in particular sectors, none of these regions followed economic trajectories that matched Britain's.[8]

As no single factor set Britain apart from its competitors, then neither Britain's innovation, empire nor geology can supply us with a monocausal explanation. The answer instead lies in the confluence of different, and sometimes seemingly disparate and disconnected, forces that together contributed to Britain's remarkable economic expansion. A starting point for understanding this dynamic can be seen in the broad base of Britain's rising economic output. In 1660, agriculture, industry and services (which notably included finance and trade) all contributed a roughly equal share to Britain's output (see Figure 2). While industry forged ahead to make up half of economic output by the end of the eighteenth century, other sectors also grew significantly: output from agriculture almost tripled and services more than quadrupled. There were plenty of opportunities that were ripe for exploitation beyond those offered by new industrial technologies – and Britain's capitalists set out to seize them all.

Britain's economic transformation depended, then, on what I call 'networked capital': the mutually reinforcing combination and exploitation of financial, natural, human and intellectual capital across different businesses and sectors. The example of McConnel and Kennedy exemplifies these dynamics: they relied on colonial exploitation for raw cotton, international trade to transport it, and mechanical skill to fashion it. This single firm in Manchester depended on a multitude of other capitalists who, over the previous century and a half, had ruthlessly set out to extract more profit from their myriad business interests. Development was a cumulative, progressive and collaborative process and it was the looping of value-added interactions across sectors that allowed Britain to thrive despite the inevitable entropy of any single invention or innovation. A broad economic base enabled one sector to pick up the slack of another as well as creating opportunities for people to take innovation from one area and apply it in the next. Divergent legal systems between Britain and its colonies also meant that capitalists could take advantage of capital-intensive investment in machinery and infrastructure at home while simultaneously employing brutal labour-intensive strategies in plantations overseas, with the two often allied through supply chains, markets and people. Links like these meant that Britain's economic transformation was driven not by a single industry, commodity, invention or regulation, nor by simply taking advantage of new territories, technologies or markets. Rather, Britain's rise to wealth and power depended on capitalists' ruthless efforts to exploit them all at the same time.[9]

Applying a similar single-minded dedication to efficiency and innovation across such a wide array of activities was no simple task. It could not be achieved by any single person, business or even by the state. Instead, it rested on an economic and legal culture that valued and protected the pursuit of profit. Political power was widely distributed, and while the state regularly imposed strict policies to gain an economic advantage over international rivals, it did not excessively favour any particular faction in Britain. The dividing lines between the commercial interests of merchants, craftsmen, landowners, colonisers and others were increasingly blurred, with major corporations, local regulatory groups and business partnerships all welcoming financial and intellectual capital from across these groups. Although many people specialised in one area, the opportunity for people to invest their expertise and cash across sectors created the necessary conditions for sustained and connected growth across the economy. Consequently, institutions developed that made it easier for capitalists to work together. Informal but widely accepted rules about how to conduct business were flexible enough to weather changes in politics, society and attitudes that were taking place during this period, and provided stability and helped make business relationships more predictable. Webs of social and cultural interaction tied capitalists together and provided mutually reinforcing benefits across industries. In turn, opportunities for networked capital to make an impact increased and the transmission of useful knowledge, innovative ideas and market insights flowed more easily. The breadth and depth of personal networks, coupled with widely accepted and predictable tools for business practice, meant that people could work fruitfully across sectoral, geographic and class boundaries in ways that were not seen elsewhere. It was through their networks that Britain's capitalists connected the exploitation of land and people across Britain and its empire with scientific and technological advancements, drawing them together to create a perfect storm for economic growth.[10]

## WEBS OF INDUSTRY AND EMPIRE

Between 1660 and 1800, Britain was transformed by changes that were far more extensive and profound than can be explained by any single sector, commodity or technology. Historians have described these changes as revolutionary in areas including agriculture, science and finance, as well as industry, but none of these took place overnight. To tackle the longer trajectories of development that are necessary for understanding Britain's rise to wealth and power, this book is roughly divided chronologically, into: Part One, which uncovers the deeper foundations of Britain's economic development in the century after 1660; and Part Two, which takes the story right up to the end of the eighteenth century and the steam-powered cotton factories that are so deeply ingrained with how the industrial revolution is pictured. Within this structure, and to highlight the simultaneous development of different sectors, each chapter tackles a distinct factor that contributed to Britain's developing economy while simultaneously exposing how links across different parts of the economy reverberated across Britain and its empire.

*Ruthless* begins by asking how capitalists benefited from invention, technology and the spread of useful knowledge, and vitally how these were commercialised by businesses in the pursuit of profit. Chapter One introduces this theme by considering how a quickly changing intellectual landscape altered how capitalists identified possibilities for exploiting the natural abundance they saw around them. In doing so, it uncovers who these capitalists were, how they were brought together, how they understood the risks and opportunities that novel ventures represented, and, overall, how they came together so effectively to forge new paths in so many different sectors during the century that followed. Some of these developments lent heavily on support from the state, which handed out patents and corporate privileges, as well as providing muscular protection for key industries, as part of a long-lasting strategy designed to help Britain win its economic battle against international rivals. These trends are picked up in Chapter Six. By the middle of the eighteenth century, interest in invention had gripped the minds of capitalists across the country, with many taking part in formal and informal societies dedicated to sharing the newest scientific ideas, and how like-minded entrepreneurs might profitably employ these. Groups like these provided a key conduit through which people could engage with the latest ideas and helped maintain virtuous cycles of scientific advance and business opportunity. As well as local inventiveness, Britain's innovative development also depended on the adaption (and sometimes outright theft) of intellectual property and technology from abroad, and finding ways to substitute imports for domestically manufactured goods was a key feature of Britain's economic transformation. Finally, this chapter considers how businesses converted existing facilities, adding value by bringing together Britain's rich legacies of physical and human capital with the technological advances and global trading networks that were so important for Britain's eighteenth-century growth.[11]

The pursuit of profit often began close to home, and Britain's capitalists ruthlessly set out to exploit the natural resources that were found around them. Britain didn't have the right climate to grow luxurious, tropical crops like sugar, silk or spices, but its temperate climate and varied landscapes were very well suited for cultivating the two most important resources for its burgeoning economy: food and raw wool. The impact of agricultural improvement was boosted by investment in transport and other infrastructure that helped connect rich agricultural regions with Britain's growing towns and cities, as well as increasing connectivity between urban and rural areas through the social and business networks of capitalists involved. At the start of this period, agriculture employed by far the most people in Britain, produced the greatest share of Britain's goods, and was an essential part of everybody's day-to-day lives: after all, everyone has to eat. By 1800, following a series of 'agricultural revolutions', Britain's farms were producing at least twice as much per acre than they had a century and a half before. It wasn't just food that was produced on agricultural land, and raw materials for vital industries were also harvested by labourers in Britain itself and by enslaved workers in colonies overseas. These included, most prominently, the vital fibres for Britain's vibrant textile sector, including the wool shorn from sheep that supported so much of Britain's manufacturing and trade at the start of this period, through to silk and cotton that could only be grown abroad before it was fed into Britain's most innovative textile industries in the eighteenth century.[12]

Chapter Two introduces these themes and explores the agricultural changes that took place in the second half of the seventeenth century that laid the foundations for ongoing development in the following decades. In doing so, it shows how raising crops and rearing sheep together helped landowners maximise their profits, with wool from the latter providing the essential raw materials for Britain's largest industry, producing woollen textiles, that used its access to the nation's natural produce to produce cloths that were sold across the world. Chapter Seven continues the assessment of Britain's exploitation of the land at home and abroad, by looking at how capitalists sought to transform it, whether by transplanting crops and agricultural techniques from one continent to another, or by investing in infrastructure like canals to radically alter the natural landscape to better suit the interests of a new industrial age.

Opportunities for capitalists to exploit the environment were more dramatic still when it came to extracting the fuel and ores, and Britain's machine-made future was intrinsically tied to the natural resources that labour and technology made available. As David Hume put it in 1752, 'steel and iron' in the hands of British capitalists had 'become equal to the gold and rubies of the Indies'. Engines of all shapes and sizes needed metals and fuel to function, torn from the ground by workers in awful conditions to be consumed by Britain's flourishing industries. Increasing the productivity of mines benefited from new techniques and machines, but also from sending workers deeper underground and into more dangerous conditions. The extraction and production of vital commodities like coal, iron and copper all increased dramatically by the end of the eighteenth century. Mining and metallurgy in turn added value to an array of different sectors. Britain's nascent mining industry had several key advantages: large deposits of coal and ore were found near waterways, it was served by a commercially dynamic economy, and it could draw on skilled craftsmen and engineers.[13]

Chapter Three takes these connections as its starting point and interrogates how widespread enthusiasm and mad-cap plans for hurriedly growing Britain's mining industry towards the end of the seventeenth century gave way to dozens of smaller enterprises that set out to profit from the natural resources that could be extracted from beneath their feet. It especially focuses on the importance of trade and links between copper and coal mining to show how integration into the wider economy and broader networks of expertise were essential for the industry's early and rapid growth. In Chapter Eight, the focus shifts to Britain's prominent iron industry, with regional specialisation and technical advancements leading to clusters of metallurgical ability dramatically transforming towns like Birmingham into centres of industry. As well as the booming production of iron goods, it assesses how metal work and new ways of generating power went hand in hand. The first commercially successful steam engine in Britain was used for pumping water out of coal mines, before decades of incremental improvements led to James Watt's design being implemented more widely in textile and metallurgical industries by the end of the eighteenth century.

As conquest and colonisation brought new territories into Britain's dominium, capitalists began to seek wealth not just from their own land but on the frontiers of empire. The final chapters of each half of the book expose how the exploitation of empire, enslaved people and global trade were intrinsically linked to Britain's economic development. Colonisation led to Britain commanding vast new territories, helping make up for its small size relative to nearby competitors such as France, or global ones such as India or China. Even after the United States gained independence, goods from these territories continued to serve the British market. Colonists set out to extract wealth by employing brutal methods for exploiting enslaved labour and developing complex proto-industrial systems that left cash-crop monocultures in their wake wherever the environment permitted. In Britain's colonies, the exploitation of enslaved labour for profit was deeply interlinked with the development of industrial capitalism. Horrific discipline, harsh conditions and high concentrations of labour in large plantations changed how capitalists thought about organising and controlling workers and demanded the vast expansion of the transatlantic traffic of captive African people who would be worked to death in the name of profit. By the end of the eighteenth century, thousands of slave-traders and investors had put their capital into more than ten thousand slave-trading voyages between Britain, Africa and the Americas: half a million captive people died during these voyages, and more than two million more survived to reach lives of slavery in colonies overseas. This vast enterprise directly employed hundreds of thousands of British captains, sailors and other workers, as well as huge subsidiary industries that developed to support the trade. People active in the colonies often took care to maintain their relationships with people in Britain, whether through work, family or common interests. This helped ensure that the circuits of capital and information that were so vital for Britain's industrial development took on a transatlantic dimension, and personal relationships helped ensure that profits from one side of the ocean could be applied successfully on the other. In Britain, goods made by enslaved people were found in homes and businesses across the country and were consumed by people in all walks of life. According to recent analysis, by the final decade of the eighteenth century, as much as 11 per cent of the entire British economy depended on slavery and the slave-trade. Profits and goods from the exploitation of enslaved labour were endemic, not peripheral, and were at the heart of British economic expansion.[14]

Chapter Four investigates the development of this extractive colonial system in the second half of the seventeenth century, as capitalists experimented with brutal new approaches to controlling and exploiting enslaved people labouring on plantations in the Caribbean. The profits obtained directly from the traffic in enslaved people or from their labour were only part of their impact on Britain's economy, and wider systems of exchange and supply place these in a connected context that reached deep into Britain, where the opportunities of colonial trade shaped everything from investment in infrastructure to new types of manufacturing. Building on these foundations, Chapter Nine examines the vast expansion of the transatlantic slave-trade and the impact of colonial markets and goods on the highest-growth regions of Britain in the second half of the eighteenth century: namely around Bristol, Glasgow, London and, especially, Liverpool.

For many capitalists, profits came not only through the production of goods, but from their trade overseas. British overseas trade grew dramatically, with both imports and exports growing over five times during the eighteenth century. Much of this growth came from the vast expansion of transatlantic trade to the Caribbean and North America, which received more than half of Britain's exports by the end of the eighteenth century. A huge volume of goods was imported from Asia too, often bearing profits that were the envy of traders elsewhere. However, Europe remained a vital trading destination, absorbing, especially, the majority of colonial and Asian goods that were brought to Britain. Furthermore, global exchange and domestic innovation were often reciprocal processes, in areas ranging from the expansion of Britain's docks to the earliest advancement of copper manufacturing in Cornwall – both fuelled by the need to meet colonial demand. The emerging cotton economy around Manchester experienced this first-hand, and was tied to the wider trading networks that were transforming both Britain's and the global economy.[15]

Britain's growing economy depended on its deep embeddedness within the commercial flows of the globalising world around it, and trade appears across the book's chapters. However, the final chapters of each part focus explicitly on how these commercial dynamics shaped industries in Britain. Chapter Five examines how these linkages were established and maintained, sometimes through violence, by exposing the relationship between Britain's warmaking overseas and the expansion of dependent industries at home: shipbuilding, gunmaking and gunpowder manufacture. Chapter Ten draws all of the book's themes together by focusing on a new industry that was at the heart of Britain's industrial revolution: the manufacture of cotton thread and cloth. Cotton exemplified, above all others, a commodity that demanded global integration for it to serve maximum value to British manufacturers. It was obtained in its raw form from America through the exploitation of enslaved labour from Africa, inspired by Indian styles and techniques, and then sold everywhere. Empire and global trade were key parts of the economic system that Britain inhabited: sources of inspiration and competition, extraction and exploitation. Indeed, some historians convincingly argue that without Britain's access to trade, industrial and economic growth could not possibly have been sustained. Technology alone could not create a world of markets and customers. This combination of forces, the exploitation of land and labour, at home and abroad, was deeply intertwined with the development of Britain's new factories. Innovative machinery couldn't function without vast supply chains that provided raw materials, especially cotton wool grown and picked and packaged by enslaved workers in British and American plantations across the Atlantic. Likewise, British manufactured cotton thread and cloth was sold into the same global marketplaces, whether directly to Africa where it was exchanged for more enslaved workers, to capitalists in the Caribbean who profited from their labour, or simply to consumers in Britain and Europe who wore it to emulate the Indian cotton cloth that it was helping to replace.

The back and forth between international trade and domestic manufacture provided the vital backdrop for Britain's rise to wealth and power. Britain's capitalists depended on the connections and simultaneous exploitation of these different areas to dramatically increase the profitability and volume of goods they now produced. Networked capital provided the essential exchange of ideas, expertise and commodities that were needed to feed into a growing commercial, industrial and imperial machine. Britain's rise to wealth and power was not caused by a single trigger, but rather by the ruthless pursuit of profit across its industries and empire that made it possible for multiple triggers to be pulled together.[16]

# Part One

# INNOVATION AND EXPLOITATION, 1660–1750

CHAPTER 1

# THE SPIRIT OF ENTERPRISE

## Innovation, Investment and the State

Britain's rise to wealth and power had no single cause. By the middle of the seventeenth century, long before clattering steam-powered machines and imposing factories dotted the landscape, the ruthless pursuit of profit was already transforming how the nation's capitalists went about extracting wealth from the environment, workers and technology. Whether close to home or far away in colonies overseas, people found and exploited opportunities across a dizzying array of economic activities. Kings and queens, lords and ladies, merchants, manufacturers, ministers and more all piled into ventures that they hoped would prove worthy investments for their time and money. As they did so, they forged relationships with their profit-hungry compatriots that led to mutually reinforcing cycles of development as networks of financial, natural, human and intellectual capital were brought together in enterprises that crossed and connected economic activities throughout Britain and its empire. No sector was left untouched, and the lives of millions would be impacted by the world-altering transformations that Britain's capitalists left in their wake.

Capitalists were not starting from scratch. By the middle of the seventeenth century, some commercial, agricultural and manufacturing advances were already under way, providing an enviable foundation for further growth. In the previous century, Britain's economy had benefited from new ways of organising business that continued to make an impact. The expansion of urban and craft corporations helped spread common forms of business organisation, accounting and communication across the country. By imposing strict regulations on their members about how business was conducted, they helped standardise and ensure the quality of products. More importantly, their enforcement of accepted codes of conduct, that applied to everything from how partnerships were organised, customer credit assessed and apprentices trained, encouraged the spread of sophisticated institutions across Britain's businesses.

These same institutions underpinned the rapid expansion of Britain's economic interests far beyond its borders. New trade routes were developed that carried British merchants, ships and goods to destinations across Europe and then the wider world. The Levant Company flourished as commercial exchange with the rich markets of the Mediterranean became more accessible, while the Muscovy Company and East India Company demonstrated the efficacy of using joint-stock financing to support activities that required huge upfront costs. As profits from commerce grew, monopolistic corporations like these faced increasingly severe criticism from wealthy landowners and manufacturers who were often excluded from participating, and soon many restrictions were lifted or competing partnerships and firms were set up that combined the capital and expertise of people from across Britain. Yet, even as more people were able to take part in activities that had once been restricted, many of the business practices that they had established remained in place.

At the same time, imperial projects were also growing, and British colonists had violently seized territory in Ireland and Virginia, where joint-stock finance helped provide the financial muscle to secure their position overseas. Soon, enterprising colonisers took more territory in North America and the Caribbean, building new settlements and business ventures as they went. Thousands of settlers from Britain began travelling across the Atlantic to take advantage of the opportunities arrayed before them. Thousands more enslaved African people were trafficked to join them in British slaving vessels, and would be worked to death on new plantations producing sugar and other tropical goods that would be sent back to Britain for sale, consumption or re-export. Across these ventures, Britain's capitalists were backed by muscular state support, whether in the form of protective tariffs or bans that kept out competitors or military power that protected shipping and colonies alike.

As trade and empire began to re-shape Britain's economy, the efficacy of large-scale investment by a wider community that included landowners and manufacturers became more common in international trade than before, even as merchants themselves stepped up their participation in industrial ventures and purchasing land at home. Industry, trade and empire were all part of an interconnected economic system that was increasingly envisaged as a whole, with economic plans made by statesmen and businessmen alike designed to bring benefits to British capitalists at home and abroad. In turn, wider access to economic opportunities led to the growth of business and social relationships between people from different backgrounds that helped create the networks of exchange that in turn offered mutually reinforcing benefits across different parts of British economic activity. Britain's economic development was not overseen by the state, a single corporation, or a narrow wealthy elite, but rather grew from a vast array of enterprises that ranged from mighty joint-stock companies to small partnerships and even lone traders who struck out on their own. These were connected through personnel, investors, customers or common markets, and the widely accepted informal institutions that shaped business relationships.

By 1660, then, Britain's economy already had strong foundations for growth that built on and extended its increasingly networked capital. Textile workers were already producing woollen cloths that could be transported across the world. Traders were already taking part in exchanges that took them to every continent. Enslavers were already transporting captive African people to toil on plantations in the Americas. Across these ventures, private and public interest together fuelled economic engagement. Expanding and accelerating profits from these enterprises, though, did depend on efforts to find new ways of conducting business, whether by seeking out new markets, adopting new technology or finding ways to improve the productivity of workers. Economic development depended on innovation. In the second half of the seventeenth century, changing ways of thinking about the world led to opportunities across myriad businesses and sectors, and capitalists took advantage of webs of exchange that applied useful knowledge and novel ideas to all manner of economic activities. Even as they built on the commercial or manufacturing expertise of their forebears, broadening and deepening networks between people from all walks of life helped generate the conditions for further and accelerating economic growth. Many of the paths to profit that Britain's capitalists would pursue with ruthless ambition over the following century and a half were not taking them to unimagined worlds. Rather, incremental changes to activities that were already taking place accelerated, with innovation and exploitation together pushing the economy to heights not seen before.

## INNOVATION EVERYWHERE

When Charles II was restored as King of England, Scotland and Ireland in 1660, he returned to a nation that was reeling from the chaos, devastation and uncertainty that the English civil war had left in its wake. Yet, despite the war's discordant political legacy, some commentators and investors were enthusiastic for what might come next. The perceived stability of the new monarchy, coupled with the willingness of the new king to use his powers to promote business interests with the liberal distribution of patents and protective duties, contributed to a flurry of projects and schemes intended to profit from opportunities at home and abroad. At the same time, changing ideas about how economic assets of all sorts could be exploited for profit were encouraging enterprising capitalists to embrace innovative technologies and techniques in every sector of the economy.

With all the pomp and grandiosity that an anonymous author could muster, the writer of the *Europæ Modernæ Speculum* (1666) summed up the era's enthusiasm and expectations with aplomb. Having described all the empires, kingdoms and states of Europe, they concluded their book by turning finally to 'that fortunate island' where Charles II now ruled, and lauded the strong foundations that underpinned the nation's wealth and power: 'our kingdom is populous, our ground fertile, our gentry expert, our yeomen trained, our scholars learned, our noblemen active, our magazines ready, our court unanimous' and 'our genius warlike'. Already, they boasted, Britain's commercial expansion had opened routes to obtain commodities ranging from 'the wines and sugars of Spain, to the treasure of the Indies, to the manufactures of Turkey and China, to the cordage and naval materials of Muscovy, Sweden, and Denmark; to the delicacies of Italy, to the kerseys [textiles] of Flanders, to the wines of Bordeaux'. Success now rested on Britain's capitalists dedicating themselves to 'improving' the island's 'native commodities with the greatest art at home and exporting them with the highest freedom abroad'.[1]

The idea that Britain's people could use their inventiveness, labour and skill to bend nature to their will and increase how much or what could be extracted from the earth was a common feature in the intellectual and economic milieu of the later seventeenth century. Indeed, language encouraging investment in 'improvement' was a common feature in British writing about the economy – much as language encouraging investment in 'innovation' is today. Despite originating in the fifteenth and sixteenth centuries as a term primarily used to describe profiting from the land (even if this was achieved by a landlord simply choosing to raise rents), the term 'improvement' increasingly became a catch-all term that could be applied to every aspect of human endeavour. In 1605, Francis Bacon had used the term specifically to explain how bad agricultural practice might be 'improved and converted by the industry of man' and later expressed in his essays and letters the potential for 'improvements of things invented' and reform across myriad economic sectors. With wide applications, definitions of improvement were often imprecise: one dictionary in 1658 described it as 'a thriving, a benefiting in any kind of profession', while another sixty years later went simply for 'bettering, progress'.[2]

Recognising that human intellect and intervention could be used to increase the abundance of nature or the outputs of human industry had a wide-ranging impact. Numerous authors expressed a cornucopian view of the world, in which they imagined that the economy might be infinitely expanded through ingenuity and invention – one that became increasingly influential. In the sixteenth and seventeenth centuries, Britain had benefited from an influx of printed and often translated material from Europe that had shaped how people understood the world and the economy, and British capitalists continued to read and learn from these foreign publications even as they seized and developed foreign technologies for their own profit. In the 1650s, Samuel Hartlib, a Polish-born intellectual and avid promoter of knowledge, claimed Britain had 'in its bowels an (even almost) infinite and inexhaustible treasure' that 'ingenuity and industry well encouraged' and with the help of 'God's blessing' would deliver. Other contemporary thinkers compared the pursuit of knowledge that might enable the exploitation of the world's dormant wealth to unlocking a natural storehouse of riches. By the end of the seventeenth century, the notion of improvement as a means for achieving economic advancement was commonplace and was employed by people working across an array of sectors.[3]

Not everyone involved in Britain's economic development would have read or engaged with these sorts of texts or intellectual conversations, but their proliferation was indicative of a society that was both appreciative of and receptive to innovative ideas. Even when it happened only slowly, texts dedicated to improvement and invention were a useful vector for the transmission of knowledge between and across groups that might otherwise not have been able to benefit from improvements that were taking place elsewhere. The combination of ideas linking science, economy and the exploitation of the natural world together had considerable influence on government policy, the ongoing work of the scientific community, and people who looked to invest in the sort of inventive practices that could tap into nature's seemingly boundless wealth. Prominently, soon after his restoration to the throne, Charles II sought to formalise state support 'for the improving of natural knowledge' with the establishment of the Royal Society in 1660. This was a watershed moment in Britain's scientific history, and the new organisation provided a stable structure through which scientists, innovators and entrepreneurs could come together, share ideas, present prototypes and sometimes even raise capital.[4]

Among the society's earliest fellows were men (women were not admitted until the twentieth century) who were deeply engaged in intellectual and scientific exchange even as they applied connected ideas of improvement to business ventures of all varieties. Among them was Sir Robert Boyle, an Irish author who joined the society at its foundation following his intensive engagement in experimental science in the 1650s. Interested in how the study of the natural world could be applied usefully, Boyle's keen engagement with the scientific community continued even as he took on roles shaping colonial commerce. Likewise, the Coventry-based botanist and physician Nehemiah Grew was one of the few fellows who obtained a patent for their research, for a desalinating scheme that he sought to commercialise (with little success) with Boyle's nephew, Robert Fitzgerald. Similarly, the Paris-born merchant Sir John Chardin brought wide-ranging interests to the society when he was elected fellow in 1682. Famous for his long stay at the Safavid court in Persia, his knowledge of the world underpinned geographical interests, and he spent the following thirty years as a persuasive advocate for the expansion of British imperial interests in Asia while investing in new financial stocks and the South Sea Company. Other fellows invested in all the major investment opportunities that emerged in the following decades, with the East India Company, Royal African Company, New England Company and Bank of England proving particularly popular for the society's members. Given these links, it should come as no surprise that the encouragement of science and business often went hand in hand.[5]

In addition to providing a venue for exchanging ideas and validating or challenging new theories, intellectual societies and networks contributed to a growing appreciation for inventions that practically applied new discoveries. In the 1650s and 1660s, Robert Hooke (a fellow of the Royal Society from 1662) had pioneered the application of balanced springs in watches, alongside the Dutch scientist Christiaan Huygens, while simultaneously working in partnership with Boyle to develop a superior air pump, building on the work of the German scientist Otto von Guericke. In the following decades, other Royal Society fellows were recognised for their technological inventions: Sir Robert Gordon worked on improving pumping machines, the engineer John Hadley employed his skills on waterwheels, and the landowner Oliver Hill patented a technique for smelting ore 'in the Hungarian manner'. Of course, not every idea that emerged from the society's fellowship had useful applications. Sir William Petty, after noting 'the frequent mention of chariots in the battles of the ancients', proposed that 'chariots might also be of use in the present way of fire arms' and developed an extensive and costed analysis of how giant wagons bearing cannons, muskets, blunderbuss, grenades and pikes might trundle about the continent and revolutionise warfare. There is little to suggest the plan got further than the pages of his notebook. However, Hooke, Hadley and Petty were all driven by a similar intellectual motivation: they identified limitations in the world around them and set out to find solutions.[6]

Royal Society fellows were by no means the only people who came up with valuable new ideas and inventions, nor was this the only organisation that contributed to the social construction of scientific knowledge in the seventeenth century. Indeed, Hooke's work with Boyle, as well as with Seth Ward with whom he helped improve clockwork, took place not through the Royal Society but at Oxford University. In London, Gresham College provided a venue for the public dissemination of knowledge across a range of topics, while universities throughout England and Scotland were centres for learning and debate. The transmission of useful knowledge, whether it was codified and disseminated in scientific texts or shared by word of mouth from a craftsman to their apprentice, took place in informal settings as much as it did in the exchanges between the small and selective membership of organised societies and in the country's established universities. Many people who spent their lives working with machines and materials were at most only nebulously part of the networks of scientific exchange taking place in learned societies, but still more than capable of developing novel uses for existing tools or improving them. Innovations in areas ranging from farming to instrument making were as often a result of serendipity and trial-and-error experimentation than part of efforts to more deeply understand the natural world. Distinct types of knowledge were useful to different groups. Merchants travelling to distant lands were more likely to take advantage of new geographical material than landowners, who paid more attention to texts on husbandry as they set out to improve the yields of their fields. Combining knowledge from mathematics with engineering expertise was particularly fruitful and contributed to innovations in fields ranging from civil engineering and optics to navigation, hydraulic systems and ballistics. Whichever form it took, the exchange of scientific and useful knowledge contributed to the incremental improvement of techniques and technologies across many different parts within the British economy.[7]

The challenge, of course, lay in finding ways to apply this array of inventive potential to the profitable transformation of economic activities. As well as supporting organisations like the Royal Society, Charles II and his heirs enthusiastically embraced patents as a tool intended to encourage innovation, and while these had been used by earlier monarchs, they were issued in far greater numbers in the final decades of the seventeenth century than previously. The intention was to give surety to inventors that they would have time to profit from inventions that sometimes had taken years of effort and substantial investment to develop. Consequently, patents granted inventors (or the investors who had supported their work) a temporary monopoly for their new technologies or techniques, usually lasting fourteen years, giving them the sole right to use them within the confines of England and Wales. Similar patents were issued in Scotland. Not all inventions received patents, nor did all inventors apply for them. Obtaining a patent was expensive, often costing around £60 in fees and duties; it took a long time for patents to be granted after application; and they were often only weakly enforced. However, they did signal to other inventors that there was state backing for patentees' ventures.[8]

For many contemporaries, granting monopolies to people who developed new techniques or machinery was seen as vital for incentivising inventors. For example, the clothier William Carter picked out the Netherlands 'giving great encouragement and immunities to the inventors of new manufactures, and the discoverers of any new mysteries in trade' as an important reason for its economic success. The reality was more complex, and patents were something of a double-edged sword for promoting innovation. On the one hand, they helped encourage the development of innovative techniques that represented a competitive advantage and could boost productivity. On the other hand, they could decrease the diffusion of new techniques and make it difficult for people to develop further incremental improvements to existing technology.[9]

Either way, the patents that were issued do reveal the scale and scope of inventiveness that was taking place in Britain during the seventeenth century, and the sort of improvements that people were pitching across so many different sectors during this period. In the decades after 1660, the state granted hundreds of patents that had the potential to touch almost every part of the nation's economy. Although they represent only a fraction of the inventive activities, they are indicative of the diverse sectors where improvement was taking place and the people who were involved. The recipients were an eclectic group that included landowners, merchants, clothiers, watchmakers, ship captains, engineers, miners, chemists, surgeons, the odd clergyman and more. Although women were not precluded from obtaining patents, they were almost all granted to men, most of whom would have held at least a middling social status to access the networks necessary for the slow and expensive process of petitioning for their patent. Being part of a scientific organisation was not a prerequisite, nor was expertise in a related industry. John Tyzacke, a glassmaker from Wapping, received a patent that had nothing to do with glass, but rather for inventing an 'engine' to perform tasks including 'oiling leather, raising water, washing cloths, milling sugar canes' and 'pounding minerals.' That said, when training or expertise was noted, it was far more likely to relate to the patentee's day job. For example, the watchmakers Peter and Jacob Debaufre were awarded a patent for 'working stones, glass and crystal for watchmaking', the mariner John Cumberland for an 'invention for making planking', clothier Joshua Gaskins for a new technique to press cloth, and dyer John Wilks for a mill for grinding wooden dyes. Little is known about many patentees beyond what was specified in their applications, but we can presume from the cost of applying that many were relatively successful and that their patented techniques went on to have some impact, at least within their own businesses, or were otherwise independently wealthy.[10]

The inventions were as diverse as their patentees and related to myriad sectors. Inventors were most active in the textiles sector, and dozens of patents sought to improve what was both Britain's largest manufacturing sector and the bedrock of its international trading success. This was closely followed by inventions patented for Britain's vital shipping industry. Inventions intended to improve heavy industry were also popular, covering metallurgy, mining and machinery with more general applications. Patents relating to new chemicals, agricultural techniques, weaponry, transportation, pottery, utilities and building materials made up the rest. While all claimed to offer something inventive, some made bolder claims than others. John Dwight's pottery business in Fulham, his patent proclaimed, was home to techniques 'never before made in England or elsewhere', with the enterprising potter claiming he could replicate 'China and Persia wares' having 'discovered the mystery of transparent porcelain and opaque red dark coloured porcelain'. Others simply highlighted why they were competitive, in Britain and abroad. Silk weavers that might employ a new engine designed by the merchant John Barkstead could expect, he claimed, to produce wrought silk 'as cheap and as well as in any part beyond the seas'. John Bellingham, likewise, made clear that his 'invention for making square window glass' produced panes that excelled those from 'Normandy for strength and clearness'.[11]

The expectation, of course, was that by issuing patents like these, the state would encourage the development of innovative technologies or techniques that would make a positive impact on the national economy. In some cases, these hoped-for impacts were clearly stated in the patents themselves. Edward Mayo and Francis Fandell du Fresue improved processes for making salt, and, in expectation that it would help boost the nation's trade with Sweden, obtained support from the Committee for Trade for their patent application. The promise that inventions would substitute expensive imports with domestic produce was similarly valued. Thomas Neale aimed to produce 'Corinthian steel' that was 'never yet made in England' and used 'materials of the native growth'. Likewise, John Briscoe promised to make paper 'as good and white as any French or Dutch', Edmund Hemming made 'iron plates tinned over' that were 'as good as those brought from and made in Germany', and Gabriel Waine offered a way to make pitch as good as any from Sweden. When import substitution wasn't enough, some patents were even issued not for British inventions so much as the theft of technology from abroad. John Englebert Teshmaker and Ralph Marshall's patent for making spinnall (spindle) yarns was granted because they had 'brought several workmen out of Germany' who were skilled in the technique.[12]

A new technique was no guarantee of profit. Even when patents were issued and inventors lined up supporters from among the richest and most well-connected people in Britain, plans could easily go awry. Thomas Hale bitterly experienced how the tide could turn on an entrepreneur when his plans to use 'milled lead' to sheath English ships faced extreme criticism that ultimately forced him to focus on supplying lead for roof construction instead. Plans had begun well, and the founding of the Milled Lead Company by Sir Philip Howard and Francis Watson in 1670, of which Hale was a director, had quickly led to the production of milled lead. After early tests using the lead as sheathing on the ship *Phoenix*, a process that was designed to protect the ship's hull from decay, Charles II had ordered the same for a further twenty vessels. Quickly, though, accusations that the lead was ineffective or even damaged the ships meant that orders ceased, and the company spent much of the 1680s trying to obtain support from navy commissioners and shipwrights alike to persuade potential customers of the validity of the invention.[13]

By 1691, though, after Hale had taken control of the business, none of their attempts had worked and he was left railing against what he saw as an unfair system. In Britain, he complained 'men generally depraved by a selfish inhospitable temper' responded to innovators like him 'like the hedgehog . . . and show forth nothing but bristles'. With absolute confidence, he condemned his detractors as the sort of men who 'cry out εὑρηκα [Eureka]!' not when they had an idea of their own but 'when they have found a stone to throw at an inventor of anything beneficial to mankind'. Hale was sure 'the invention of the sea compass was maligned by the old dull coasters, and that of printing by the hackney writers, and the excellent notion of the circulation of the blood by the old Mumpsimus doctors' who 'knew how to stuff their hollow teeth with their patient's bread, without studying anatomy'. Like these earlier innovators, it was opposition to progress that had turned the market against him. Despite his best efforts, there was nothing Hale could do to persuade investors to back to his scheme (insulting them didn't work) and his dream of protecting English ships disintegrated. Much like lead does when it is fastened with iron nails and exposed to saltwater.[14]

Despite setbacks like this, neither inventors nor investors were put off from backing improvement projects of all sorts. Failure and risk were inherent to innovation and were part of the learning process. Hale's plans for sheathing the hulls of ships failed, but they added to a growing wealth of knowledge that would, in time, see many British ships receive copper plating in the following century. Patents continued to be issued in large numbers even after it became clear that not all of them were achieving the technical advances that had been promised. The application of innovative technology and techniques, whether they were patented or not, depended on an intellectual environment that encouraged their development but also their potential to boost profits, such as by reducing labour costs or producing new types of products. Irrespective of the promises that inventors made as they sought patents or investment, there was no guarantee of commercial success. Some technologies simply failed, others were too expensive, and others lacked a market that was interested in what was being offered, but they contributed to a vibrant environment even when they failed. Moreover, while patent protection offered some incentive for innovators, it certainly was not the only one and the possibility of increasing their profits encouraged people working across the British economy to seek out other means of improving their businesses. Many incremental improvements that took place were developed on the job and spread more organically by word-of-mouth instruction or as neighbours replicated techniques they could see working next door. Likewise, just as interest from an enthusiastic array of investors and inventors helped diffuse new ideas, high demand for improvements that were successful helped incentivise people to risk their time and money on all sorts of inventive pursuits. When successful, each augmentation increased the possibilities for employing or developing technology in profitable new directions. As a relatively information-rich society, efforts to calculate and measure the shape and structure of different activities provided a means by which the efficacy of new ideas could be calculated and measured in turn, further encouraging their diffusion.[15]

The consistent drive to develop existing technologies and techniques further was an important feature of Britain's economic development. Even when patents were issued for major technological breakthroughs, they benefited from further incremental improvements. The metallurgist Abraham Darby obtained a patent in 1707 for his 'invention of casting iron pots', but it would take an ongoing wider transformation of how metals were sourced, smelted and manufactured that went far beyond the scope of his patent before his industrial complex at Coalbrookdale took off. Likewise, in 1699, 'a certain new invention' by Thomas Savery 'for raising water and occasioning motion to all sorts of mill work by the impellent force of fire' had its patent extended from fourteen to twenty-one years given 'the said invention, which is likely to be of great use and advantage' was not yet commercially viable, and would require more time and 'much greater expense ... to bring the same to full perfection'. Savery's invention was the basis for the first commercially viable steam engine and underpinned later developments in this transformative technology by people like Thomas Newcomen and James Watt. However, Savery's good luck was indicative of the double-edged impact of patents. The potential for a monopoly may have encouraged Savery's inventiveness, but that same monopoly curtailed Newcomen's ongoing work and possibly slowed further improvements in the machinery.[16]

Patented or not, inventions did not always work as advertised, nor did every plan for improvement lead to economic progress. However, enough did to encourage the adoption, diffusion and ongoing improvement of technology and techniques that were pivotal for boosting profits and productivity. Despite their many missteps, British capitalists successfully employed innovative practices across a range of industries, whether through new ideas from the scientific community, the application of patented technology or from finding better ways of working on the job. No one patented the field rotation system that helped boost agricultural yields in Norfolk, nor the clever combination of coal mining and ore smelting that drove metallurgical industrial development in south Wales, nor the brutal discipline imposed on plantations across the Caribbean that made sugar production so profitable, yet all of these contributed to Britain's pursuit of power and profit. At the same time, farming, metallurgy and the exploitation of enslaved labour did take advantage of patented innovations, like new improvements to ploughs, furnaces or shipping. Britain's economic development depended on the back-and-forth exchange of ideas that carried new practices far and wide across the nation and its empire. No matter where it came from, by the beginning of the eighteenth century, the idea of improvement had become a common feature of British discussions related to economic progress and fuelled activities designed to encourage innovative, industrious and, above all, profitable activities.[17]

## CAPITAL IDEAS

Support for Britain's enterprising scientists and inventors helped generate and disseminate some of the bold new ideas that would shape the nation's developing economy. Private individuals and networks, as well as the state, took part in exchanges that saw innovative technology and techniques make an impact across everything from forging steel to desalinating water. Encouragement for improvement alone, though, could only do so much to transform a business: even the best idea needed investment, workers and resources to become reality. Working out how to pay for and to profit from new ideas was, therefore, just as important as coming up with them in the first place. In the final decades of the seventeenth century, interest in improvement as a means of unleashing the potential of the nation's natural resources and workers was matched by the embrace of financial tools that helped capitalists achieve this goal.

Whether through bankers, brokers or acting in a personal capacity, the decades before the South Sea Bubble in 1720 (a major financial crash that ruined hundreds of investors) and the subsequent Bubble Act (which banned the formation of new joint-stock companies without explicit permission from the state) saw thousands of people put their capital on the line by investing in joint-stock initiatives. In the seventeenth century, granting corporate charters that often provided companies with monopolies over particular sectors or markets was a popular tool for the state and had a similar intent to patents: the encouragement of specific economic activities. Rather than supporting the invention of an innovative technology or the development of a new technique, supporting joint-stock investment was intended to develop entire industries and trades that were believed to require protection from competitors to justify high upfront costs. The East India Company, founded in 1600, had shown the potential value of this policy. In this case, joint-stock financing had enabled hundreds of people to invest together and raise the unprecedented amount of capital deemed essential for breaking into the competitive transoceanic trade between Europe and Asia. Its ongoing monopoly was justified in part because of the enduring expense of arming fleets, fortifying outposts and offering gifts and bribes to foreign officials. Despite serious troubles during the seventeenth century, including a disastrous and expensive war with the Mughal Empire in the 1680s, the company continued to receive support from the state and investors alike. The merging of the company's old and new stock and confirmation of its monopoly in 1709 solidified its position as a leading force in Britain's imperial and commercial ambition. By this point, more than 1,500 people held stock in the company, which was now transporting goods worth almost half a million pounds between Britain and Asia each year.[18]

The final decades of the century saw royal backing for numerous joint-stock companies. Only a few months after he had set up the Royal Society to encourage scientific discovery, Charles II signed the charter to establish the Company of Royal Adventurers Trading into Africa, intended to expand Britain's commercial activities in West Africa. After initially struggling to attract investment from the merchant community, the company was quickly re-chartered in 1663, now with a specific goal of purchasing enslaved African people and transporting them to colonies in the Caribbean and North America. Over the following decades, the corporation and its successors would replace and expand existing British interests on the African coast, where the new company explicitly set out to traffic captive people from Africa to colonies in America, as well as trade for gold, ivory and dyes. This meant competing with Dutch and other European rivals on the African coast, sometimes with military force, which required capital investment in fortifications and large, heavily armed ships, which made the joint-stock model attractive. Spending heavily during the Second Anglo-Dutch War forced the company deeply into debt before it was folded into the larger and even more ambitious Royal African Company, which was chartered in 1672. With expanded privileges to maintain a military presence on the African coast, the company oversaw the rapid increase in the number of enslaved African people that were transported in British ships to colonies in the Caribbean and North America. Thousands of British people invested in the company, incentivised by the rich prospect of selling people for profit.[19]

It was not only overseas that joint-stock corporations were seen as viable tools for financing and exploiting new economic frontiers. In the final decades of the seventeenth century, a veritable flood of companies was founded with the intention of using similar corporate and financial structures to radically develop entire new industries in Britain. In 1690, Nicholas Dupin and Henry Million, following their 'continued pains and industry in foreign parts and at home' to discover 'several profitable arts and mysteries not heretofore used or practiced in England', were granted a charter to establish a Corporation for the Linen Manufacture in England. Initially selling only 340 shares for £10, the company's valuation quickly shot up, with new shares issued for £50 the following year. Although the company made some small steps towards establishing linen manufacturing and publicly sold ten thousand pieces of high-quality linen in 1692, their success was short-lived, and the stock price sank further and further, losing half its original value by 1697. Similar ventures were granted charters to exploit techniques for making sword blades, making tapestry and weaving silk, among others, or for improving the extraction of natural resources like those found in Welsh mines or Greenland's fisheries. Like the Corporation for the Linen Manufacture, several were unsuccessful, and some became vehicles for speculative investment known as stock jobbing and saw little capital expended on industrial activities, leading to growing condemnation of untrustworthy projects in the 1690s. However, even when companies failed to provide returns for investors, they sometimes did establish or increase interest in nascent industries that served as foundations for further investment and improvement in the following century.[20]

Despite having a mixed impact on industry, other domestically focused joint-stock companies were much more successful, especially in the financial sector. Most prominently, the Bank of England combined government and private interests, providing a good rate of return for investors even as it strengthened the government's capacity to protect Britain's economic interests across the world. After Charles II threw the financial system into chaos in 1672 by repudiating the crown's debts, the state's creditability with private bankers had been severely hit. While court cases to recoup their losses continued for decades, creditors moved towards setting up a more reliable means for extending credit to the state. In 1694, the Bank of England was founded to fulfil this role and raised £1.2 million to loan to the government in only twelve days, encouraged by the promise of 8 per cent interest. This was quickly spent rebuilding the Royal Navy, finding its way into the pockets of manufacturers and suppliers whose industries were suddenly buoyed by massive and well-capitalised demand. Other financial ventures such as the Land Bank and Million Bank were likewise set up to find novel solutions to fund wartime expenditure. By 1720, financial stocks were more popular than those in trading or industrial companies, and the steady flow of returns from annuities and government debt became increasingly common as a stable source of income for Britain's wealthy elite. They also helped finance the development of the fiscal-military state that would so prominently and violently support Britain's imperial ambitions in the following century.[21]

Not everyone was convinced by the efficacy of these new investment opportunities, and speculative investment and lotteries raised particular ire. In 1700, the satirist and publican Edward Ward complained that the lure of lotteries consumed the interest of too many people to 'the neglect of business', while one MP lamented that 'our trading is now dead' because speculative investing offered a better rate of return than a merchant 'makes by running a hazard to the Indies'. The Board of Trade, too, concluded that 'the ill effects of that pernicious practice of stock-jobbing' had 'drawn men's minds from honest industry in fair trade, and engaged them in tricks and artifices to ensnare others and delude the nation with an appearance of imaginary riches'. In his *Essay Upon Projects* (1697), Daniel Defoe took a more nuanced view, describing how Britain's economy had been shaped by what he called the 'Projecting Age', during which laudable investment, poor management and dubious practices all took place. Even as he lamented the failings of some corporations, Defoe believed that most investors would not risk their reputation by promoting projects that they knew were fraudulent. Most investors, he suggested, acted both for 'their own advantage' and to support projects that were 'doubtless general of public advantage' which 'tend to improvement and employment of the poor, and the circulation and increase of public stock of the kingdom'.[22]

Despite concerns about projecting schemes that added limited value or even detracted from the nation's wealth, joint-stock corporations still attracted thousands of investors in the decades either side of 1700. Although opportunities were heavily concentrated in London, investors from across Britain took part, and they did so across the full range of stocks available. The largest companies, like the Bank of England, Royal African Company and East India Company, each had over a thousand investors at any given moment, while smaller stocks were divided between hundreds or sometimes only dozens of shares. Most investors owned shares in only a single venture, perhaps taking the risky plunge after encouragement from a family member or friend, a particularly persuasive advertisement or by a trusted banker. Despite limited experience, one-time investors provided capital for all sorts of ventures and were about as likely to invest in any of the major stocks available. These investors came from all sorts of backgrounds, although they were all, of course, well off enough to have capital to invest. Whether it was the Southampton linendraper Edward Grace and sugar refiner Newcomb Dawson who helped fund the Bank of England, or Edward Fowler, the Bishop of Gloucester, who sank his money into the Mine Adventurers, the opportunity to profit from doing nothing more than investing capital was too good to pass up. Without leaving their main employment behind, investors like these were able to take part in sectors and geographies that would otherwise have been far beyond their reach. Corporate investment and private business activities often combined interests, and networks connecting people across them were important for distributing information as well as financial capital.[23]

Slightly more than one in ten investors were women. Like their male counterparts, women invested in the larger trading companies and the Bank of England, but they also made a notably outsized investment in the Million Bank, which offered multi-generational annuities, and in mining ventures. Prominent female investors included Mary Hobby, who held stock in the East India Company, Bank of England and Mine Adventurers, and Dame Dorothy Bedingfield, who was involved in the Million Bank and Amicable Society (which offered insurance). Margaret Massingberd had one of the most diversified portfolios in the country, having invested in financial, trading, mining and manufacturing ventures. However, despite their investments, women's formal participation in these organisations was more limited than for men, and there was not a single female director or governor of any joint-stock company in Britain throughout the seventeenth and eighteenth centuries. It started, and remained, a heavily patriarchal society. Informally, though, women were able to wield more influence and took part in the exchange of ideas that shaped these organisations and the wider economy.[24]

As well as a deep pool of investors who dipped their toes into the financial opportunities on offer with a lone investment, about a quarter of investors invested in multiple organisations, and the most profligate held shares in almost every venture available. A trader like Joseph Martin, who had made his money trading in the Mediterranean and Baltic, was able and willing to diversify into investments including the Hollow Sword Blade Company, East India Company, Royal Assurance Company, South Sea Company and Royal African Company. Likewise, Sir John Morden built on investments in New

England's colony and the East India Company with shares in the Bank of England and companies set up to extract lead and coal from mines in south Wales. Investors who held shares in multiple companies were very likely to invest at some point in trading companies, and more than half held financial stocks, too, while mining or manufacturing ventures remained a fairly niche investment that was more popular with landowners and the nobility. Putting their money into ventures like these helped investors connect different sectors and contributed to the rapid spread of ideas and business practices across enterprises that might have, previously, been disconnected from social and financial networks that were so important for facilitating improvement across so many different parts of the economy at the same time.[25]

Professional merchants were particularly prominent as investors across financial and trading companies, often with complex and interrelated interests that helped tie together different parts of the economy. This was also the most common professional background for the directors and governors who were appointed to lead these enterprises. The merchant Robert Hackshaw, for instance, invested in the East India Company and the Land Bank, was a founding director of the Royal Lustring Company that was chartered to encourage English silk production, and funded the New Jersey colony. Another, John Ward, invested in the Bank of England, East India Company, South Sea Company and Royal African Company, as well as serving as a founding director of the Amicable Society. Samuel Clark, likewise, invested in the South Sea Company while simultaneously funding and overseeing a project to improve the river transportation in Norfolk. Joseph Herne held stock in the East India Company alongside that for the Company for Digging and Working Mines, in which he was also a director. Remarkably, even as they held these investments, Hackshaw, Ward, Clark and Herne were also involved in independent trading ventures to Portugal, the Netherlands, North America, and the Mediterranean. Although these four men oversaw financial interests that were particularly diverse, they are indicative of the broad scope for merchants and others to take part in multiple ventures simultaneously and to carry knowledge expertise from one sector to another.[26]

Irrespective of their background or scale of investment, involvement in joint-stock firms brought more and more people into the networks that financed and oversaw economic activities across a breadth of sectors. However, despite their impressive scale and reach, corporate stocks were not the main way that capitalists, who set their sights on improving their profits with inventive technologies and techniques, invested their money. Although the East India Company continued to dominate Britain's trade to Asia and the Bank of England funded government debt with little competition, most of the joint-stock corporations that proliferated around the turn of the eighteenth century did not become dominant firms in the nation's industrialising and imperial economy. Even as these joint-stock firms proliferated, thousands more entrepreneurs, acting independently or taking part in small partnerships, were investing their time, money and knowledge into ventures far from the speculative ones that caught the eye of authors like Defoe. In the same way that the Royal Society was one contributing factor behind growing interest in improvement and useful knowledge, or that patents represented only a fraction of inventive activity, the stock market similarly covered only a small fraction of business investment that underpinned Britain's economic development.

Even the East India Company, overseeing half a million pounds of trade in 1709, paled in significance next to the scale of trade that was achieved by small partnerships and individual merchants carrying goods between Britain and Europe or across the Atlantic. That same year, trading routes to Germany, Portugal, Ireland and the Mediterranean were all more valuable than the trade with Asia, while exchange with the Netherlands alone was worth five times as much. The relative difference in value was particularly pronounced outside London: in other English ports, joint-stock companies undertook less than 1 per cent of trade. Likewise, after the weakening of the Royal African Company's monopoly in 1697, British involvement in the transatlantic slave-trade grew more quickly as hundreds of independent traders piled in. In no time at all, the corporation had been supplanted as the main source of enslaved people in the Caribbean and North America, and before long independent traders from

Bristol and Liverpool had surpassed those from London in the scale of their involvement.[27]

Although many small businesses would have been largely removed from the activities of major joint-stock corporations, they benefited at a systemic level from better funding for the navy to protect trade routes or increased financial stability that was made possible by the Bank of England. Firms producing goods for export might also take advantage of the opportunity for them to be sold to markets in Asia or Africa after the East India Company had secured the routes. For anyone involved in transatlantic commerce, the Royal African Company's role in increasing British participation in the slave-trade benefited them by supplying enslaved labour to plantations that produced the most sought-after goods. Other capitalists found ways to take advantage of investment opportunities that directly complemented their other interests.

Rather than leaning on the investing public for funds, capitalists that worked alone, or in partnerships of two or more people, depended on personal networks for credit. They were also able to draw on a growing range of banking firms that provided the financial tools needed to run more complex businesses or raise larger funds. No matter how small a business, credit was an essential feature of Britain's economic activity. Throughout the seventeenth and eighteenth centuries, it was common for people to use what were essentially face-to-face exchanges of credit to obtain their daily necessities. From this scale upwards, credit was offered in the form of loans large and small, typically requiring written contracts known as bills of exchange that were vital for business activity, especially as cash was in short supply, unwieldy and inflexible. The creditability of customers was usually assessed based on social status and reputation, further strengthening commercial networks between participants, even as it excluded others. Britain's financial services were not just offered by the precursors to modern banks, and the small local creditor continued to provide financial access to communities that were not otherwise served.[28]

Samuel Leake, a merchant in Rye in South Essex, who made his money trading with France, was one example of this vital figure that kept Britain's economy ticking in the final decades of the seventeenth century. Many of his financial interactions were quite small, but he also regularly loaned amounts in the low hundreds of pounds to neighbours and other merchants on the south coast who could offer land as surety. As a merchant, banker and minor landowner, he was an exemplar of the sort of mixed economic interests that entwined various parts of the British economy. Already personally carrying manufactured goods to France for sale, extending credit to neighbours, and looking after his property, he was also quite willing to undertake the seven-hour horse ride from the south coast to London to buy government debt and lottery tickets. In turn, he would have been a conduit between the capital and his local community. He was not alone, and by the early eighteenth century, credit lenders and brokers were familiar figures who provided credit and other financial services to local communities across the country.[29]

Taking advantage of increasing demand for financial services was one area where British capitalists were particularly effective and long-lasting. Small, local creditors like Leake were vital, but they often operated with relatively limited capital and lacked the facility to make larger loans. Merchant bankers continued to offer these services, and they were joined by new entrants that found their niche competitive advantage, especially goldsmith bankers. After the financial chaos of 1672, when King Charles II had effectively defaulted on the crown's debts, had left a number of prominent bankers penniless, surviving businesses and a flurry of new entrants set out to fill the gap. These were often just as innovative and entrepreneurial as manufacturers or merchants, offering new products and searching for customers to grow their businesses. Their rapidly expanding businesses helped underpin economic activity at home and abroad by increasing credit circulation and encouraging trade. In time, they would help shift Britain towards a financial system that was recognised for its sophisticated financial practices, growing private banking sector, and creditable public debt.[30]

One successful firm that set out to provide financial services to a widening array of customers was the partnership of Robert Clayton and John Morris, founded in 1658, who set their sights on the country's rural elite as a key market that had previously been less engaged in the commercial opportunities available in London. Their partnership rested on the two men's expertise of writing legal documents, obtained during their training as scriveners with Clayton's uncle Robert Abbott in London. This gave the partnership a useful leg-up as they helped wealthy clientele transfer assets and provided a deeper insight into the evolving legal environment that underpinned how land could be used as a surety for credit. The company initially focused on overseeing simple exchanges of funds, such as the £100 delivered to Edward Heath on behalf of his brother John Heath in 1661. This sort of transaction represented the bread and butter of the firm's early business and played a role in overcoming the challenges in money supply faced in seventeenth-century England. The partnership also supported clients to move more significant assets. For example, the landowner John South contacted the bankers in 1677 for help in meeting Sir John Maynard's demands that he pay his debts, which had become 'so insupportable both to the disadvantage of my estate and the quiet of my life'. South owned property at Kelston and Coates Grange and hoped Morris and Clayton would be able to assist in its sale, to anyone 'that would give me £10,000 for it'. The two scriveners were quite happy to do so, and acting as brokers for transactions like these made the pair a tidy profit. As their operations grew, the bankers came to oversee an operation that radically expanded their original function as money-brokers, scribes and lawyers to include services like land valuations, rent collection and estate management for absentee landlords.[31]

However, for Clayton and Morris the real money lay in the growing market for credit. By the 1670s, their firm had developed into a fully fledged banking operation, and they profited from their role as depositaries, receiving funds from clients and using these as a source of lending capital. Sometimes they offered credit in the form of simple, short-term loans, like the £100 required by Lord Rivers in advance of rental income due two months later to buy a chariot and horses (some purchases were just too vital to wait).[32] Often, they offered longer-term and much larger loans, many of which were secured against their client's landholdings or by more complex chains of mortgages and debt. Rents from estates represented a largely dependable form of income, when assessed accurately, and the bankers could be confident they would receive repayments as and when agreed. If the worst happened, the bankers could seize entire properties to recoup any losses. Following this basic structure, the scale of their credit business increased dramatically: starting out loaning only around £3,000 in their first year of operation, by the end of the 1660s this had increased to annual loans of almost £40,000, and grew further to over £200,000 during the peak of their operations in the later 1670s.[33]

Banking firms like that of Clayton and Morris were important cogs in an increasingly sophisticated financial system that helped British capitalists overcome the weak circulation of credit and lack of hard currency that otherwise threatened their ability to conduct business. No matter their background, capitalists benefited from this expanded access to larger regional or national markets for their goods, which would have encouraged improvement projects across a range of sectors. At the same time, increasing numbers of people in Britain were able to access opportunities for investment that were taking place around them. Part of the role of bankers was to facilitate transactions. Just as importantly, though, they were expected to undertake similar assessments regarding the creditability and value of different stocks, using the same networks and insight that underpinned assessments of the reputation of creditors but at a much larger scale. The same process helped establish a more connected national market and facilitated the diffusion of standardised business practices.[34]

Neither societies for the advancement of knowledge nor the granting of patents to incentivise inventors could, alone, have an impact on the British economy. Even the most important machines needed to be paid for, just as they needed workers to work them, raw materials to be shaped by them, and fuels to power them. Likewise, capital alone did not create new inventions or lead to projects for improvement. Ideas, demand and capital needed to be combined to make an impact. In the final decades of the seventeenth century, more and more people, including wealthy landowners, manufacturers and merchants alike, were drawn together through common business interests. By expanding access to opportunities, joint-stock corporations and private banks made it easier for capitalists from a range of professional, geographical and social backgrounds to work together. The networks that remained helped match interest in improvement and innovative ideas with the financial power and market knowledge that could make them a reality.

## MANUFACTURING ADVANTAGE

Britain's rise to wealth and power did not take place overnight, nor was it launched by a single invention that transformed the economy from top to bottom. Rather, it depended on improvement that was incremental, piecemeal and cumulatively contributed to enduring advances in economic activity. In the seventeenth century, the concept of improvement was applied to topics from the smallest scale – one individual's intellectual or material circumstance – to the grandest scale – a firm's, community's or even a nation's resources. The ways that improvements might be achieved were just as broad and projects intended to offer improvement covered everything from changing the way that manure was spread on fields to the establishment of learned societies to the financing of corporations that might re-make the map of Britain's trade and empire.

Charters for joint-stock companies and patents for new inventions were two ways that the British state sought to encourage profitable new business ventures. At the same time, over the course of the seventeenth and eighteenth centuries, the British state imposed a remarkably consistent industrial policy aimed at boosting manufacturing in England as a means of outcompeting its competitors, both to support existing industries and promote new ones. Tariffs and bans fluctuated in their severity and the competitors changed as war and economic development altered the dynamics of commercial and military conflict in Europe but key underlying goals of the state remained unchanged throughout: first, increasing the profits from commerce and industry that stayed in British hands, and second, moving British manufacturing higher and higher up the productivity chain. Wherever possible, British goods (and those from its colonies) would ideally be transported by British shipping, and commodities that could be made in Britain would be made in Britain, even if the raw materials had to be imported from elsewhere.[35]

The aim was not to create a British autarky that was self-sufficient and cut off from the world. Trade was understood as a vital foundation for the nation's wealth. Contemporary ideas about economic exchange encouraged this understanding, resting as they did on the premise that surplus goods from Britain could be profitably exchanged for items that could not be made locally. As Francis Lodwick, a Flemish-born merchant who moved to London and would join the Royal Society in 1681 observed: 'no tradesman can accommodate himself with all things necessary to a comfortable subsistence by his industry' without 'transmitting the surplus of his endeavours to others and receiving from them instead thereof a proportional return of their labours and commodities.' The challenge was finding the right balance, and making sure that Britain was not expending its gold and silver reserves to purchase unnecessary luxuries that were believed to have a detrimental impact on the national economy.[36]

By the second half of the seventeenth century, the British state had begun to lean on standing committees of merchants and other businessmen to advise on matters related to commerce and colonisation. In 1697, when the Board of Trade advised William III on the relative value of different commercial markets, this perspective was clear. Trade 'from Spain, Portugal, Italy, Turkey, Barbary [North Africa] and Guinea [West Africa],' they explained, 'deserve all encouragement' because 'there come from those parts many goods that are improvable by a further manufacture here.' A similar dynamic highlighted the value of colonies in the Caribbean and North America, which sent 'great quantities of sugar, tobacco, and other goods' to Britain. Some sugar was then refined in Britain, but more important than this manufacturing gain was the re-export of 'the better half of such goods' for sale in Europe – after they had paid considerable duties to the British state whilst passing through, of course. Vitally, the same colonies were also a growing market for British manufactured goods. In every case, the goal was to ensure that, wherever possible, raw materials or half-finished goods were imported into Britain, and that these were purchased through the export of manufactured products in the other direction. It was a simple formula and, when it worked, it helped increase profits, provided employment to highly skilled workers, and ensured Britain remained at the top of the production chain.[37]

Unfortunately for Britain's capitalists, they were not alone in having this bright idea, and their competitors overseas were typically unwilling to give up their own manufacturing leads. This left three options: one, Britain's traders could give up and accept purchasing finished goods at high prices; two, Britain's manufacturers could try to outcompete their rivals with innovative techniques and other improvements; or three, the British state could try to tip the scales in their favour. Competition certainly fuelled innovation in Britain, but the nation's capitalists were helped by muscular state protection, too. It did not take long after Charles II was restored to the throne for him to begin imposing bans and other restrictions on the trade in certain foreign goods. These were often wide-ranging, like a 1661 ban 'prohibiting the importation of diverse foreign wares', including 'any laces, ribbons, fringes, embroidery, laces of silver or of gold, hats, knives, scissors' or painted pottery that were manufactured overseas. The intention was clear, and the ban stated that its purpose was to protect domestic artisans and avoid a situation where young people were 'not trained up in the said sciences' whereby 'the requisite knowledge thereof' would be lost. Without support for Britain's skilled workers, free trade and competition would lead the 'realm to decay' and leave 'the whole realm greatly endangered'.[38]

The irony, of course, was that British inventors saw nothing wrong with stealing technology or adopting methods that were already in use overseas, as various patents issued during these decades made quite clear. English copies of foreign products, even when they were of lower quality or more expensive, could reliably be marketed to the domestic consumer. Sometimes, this required a novel combination of techniques to bring together British and imported raw materials (such as combinations of wool with other textiles like silk or cotton), but this was often not the case. As this strategy helped launch new industries in Britain, these too were favoured with protective policies designed to keep them there. Brought to England around the beginning of the seventeenth century from France, William Lee's 'engine for knitting and making of silk stockings' was a significant advance in the mechanisation of silk production and launched a nascent silk industry in Nottingham. Six decades later, in 1661, the machine had been 'brought to a greater perfection' by skilled knitters, who boasted that the city's silk industry was 'exceeding any place of Europe' and was already employing thousands of people. It was a major success story, and the application of this technology had catapulted Britain to the more profitable end of the production chain: it was now importing raw silk and exporting silk stockings. Yet, the very success of the silk knitters put them at risk. Nottingham's knitters were now hypocritically concerned by 'evil designs to carry beyond the seas the said art and mystery'. 'Worst of all,' they argued, limited protection from the state would result in 'the loss of an English invention, which hitherto has proved so much to the advantage, honour and benefit of this nation.' To help ensure Britain's silk industry stayed competitive, the silk knitters were granted corporate status, with instructions to impose 'some strict rules and orders' on the manufacture of silk stockings in England and to ensure that their technology was not taken overseas.[39]

London's sugar refiners, who were similarly well established by the 1660s, likewise sought support from the state to protect their interests. However, rather than concerns about the loss of British technical expertise overseas, they were instead worried about foreign manufacturers outcompeting them on their home turf. They complained that 'diverse aliens', especially the Dutch, had 'contemptuously intruded into the exercise of several trades' in the capital and had erected their own businesses. Without forcing out these competitors, the city's refiners warned that sugar refining would 'cease to be a manufacture in this kingdom' and would 'greatly nip the growing condition of the plantations of the English colonies'. The state already required that sugar from Britain's Caribbean colonies was transported to Britain for processing, and making sure that this was done by British manufacturers would further keep profits in British hands. Naturally, London's refiners didn't need to be more sophisticated or technologically advanced than their competitors if the state ensured they had a trapped market. By banning the export of precious colonial commodities like sugar to destinations other than Britain, state action helped keep domestic manufacturers in business, and in time domestic competition could still incentivise the adoption of new techniques and business practices.[40]

Industries that were considered vital for Britain's economic security, as well as having commercial value, obtained especially strong support, and the state restricted access to markets for goods like iron or timber in an effort to ensure supply. It was this context that framed the state's response when the 'King of Sweden did about the year 1680 lay a duty of above 50 per cent upon our woollen goods imported there'. The problem was not so much that this was a major market for English goods, but that Sweden was home to the most advanced mining and metallurgical industry in Europe. Its rapid territorial expansion in the Baltic during the seventeenth century had given it control over a large proportion of the region's trade, which historically had been an important source for naval supplies and other goods to Britain. The solution was twofold. First, Britain would lean more on its trading partners and overseas colonies to find substitutions for Swedish goods: pitch, tar and copper were sought in New England, and iron from Bilbao. Second, William III was encouraged to weaponise state support to hit back at Sweden's tariff regime and control of Britain's metals supply. To undercut the Swedish empire's linen-producing territories in the Baltic, £10,000 was invested into a new linen industry in Ireland, where flax could be grown, which proponents argued 'within a short time may be improved and increased to be as good and as cheap as what comes from those places that Sweden controlled'. Likewise, Britain's own extractive and metallurgical industries were incentivised. The prohibitive cost of Swedish metals made opening new mines a much more attractive proposition, and a flurry of new techniques for smelting metals with coal opened up an array of opportunities for enterprising industrialists.[41]

The state, too, sought to employ whatever pressure it could to limit the emergence of competing woollen industries beyond the borders of the British empire. In the final decade of the seventeenth century, concerns that competitors in Europe were seeking to establish their own woollen industries led to diplomats being dispatched to Spain, the Netherlands and Sweden. They were ordered to try and put a stop to 'a woollen manufacture … set up at Lada' in Galicia that had received 'encouragement of the court of Spain' and 'the like attempt in Sweden'. In Flanders, an offer was made to lift the ban on importing bone lace to England if only the government would curtail woollen manufacture, but this met with little success. Accepting increased competition was too much of a risk, and without agreements from other nations to protect British clothiers, the state doubled down on the prohibition of raw wool exports instead. Ships and officers were appointed to try and stamp out smuggling from Kent and Sussex, while stricter penalties to dissuade smugglers were imposed in the hope that cutting off this illicit supply would inhibit the efforts of Swede and Spaniard alike. Despite these initiatives, three years later, another report detailed how 'in France, Holland, Spain, Portugal, Sweden, Silesia, Lunenburg, and other parts of Germany, new woollen manufactures had been set up'. Although not always as successful as they might have liked, clothiers in Britain benefited from the strong state support that helped shield them from competitors overseas. Requests for ongoing protection were made by manufacturers across a range of industries and the state was often willing to oblige.[42]

Whether silk knitters, sugar refiners or other industries, the state's interest in promoting business in the later seventeenth century largely adhered to two key principles. On the one hand, it supported domestic monopolies with the intention of improving the quality of produce and encouraging inventiveness and, on the other, it set out to stop British innovations benefiting industries overseas. Simply, the aim was to increase the range and volume of goods manufactured in Britain and move the nation to the top of the production chain. From the middle of the seventeenth century, it was typical for the state to employ tariffs and other controls to promote British exports and reduce imports. By the early eighteenth century, many imports faced high tariffs or were banned entirely, as was the case with Indian cottons and French alamode silks. Within the connected British colonial system, this was particularly effective, and the extraction of raw materials from the Caribbean fed Britain's domestic consumption even as growing populations in North America became important destinations for British manufactured goods.[43]

State protection for industry had combined with the emerging practice of 'political arithmetic' (as it was called by William Petty), to carefully measure national resources and how they changed over time, leading to detailed assessments of commercial exchanges that were or were not beneficial to the country. Whereas in 1600 the state had depended on rough estimates for the national population or income, by the end of the century these were measured with a good degree of accuracy and the information was disseminated broadly to inform decisions by state and private actors alike. In 1700, Abraham Hill, a successful merchant and Fellow of the Royal Society, used information like this to compile a detailed report outlining the conclusions of a royally appointed Commission for Trade, which had been established as an advisory body and was manned by leading merchants, about the best ways to secure and enlarge the nation's wealth and power. Having been set up only four years earlier, the commissioners had been tasked with finding solutions to the most challenging issues that beset Britain's economy. The scope of their investigation was very broad, and they were expected to show which trades were most beneficial, consider 'by what means profitable manufactures already settled may be further improved', identify which 'new and profitable manufactures may be introduced', and assess how Britain's 'colonies may be rendered most beneficial to this kingdom'. Through the course of their investigations, the commissioners were expected to make recommendations that would achieve not only the general goal of boosting Britain's economy but also protect it from foreign competition in times of peace and war.[44]

The scale of the task certainly kept the commissioners busy, and the array of proposals offered to grow and protect Britain's economy attested to both the scale of the state's ambitions and the positivity in Britain about the opportunities that existed for further 'improvement' of the nation's assets. As a snapshot of the state's evolving economic policy, Hill's report reflected on myriad activities undertaken in the final years of the seventeenth century: the Royal Navy's deployment to suppress raw wool smuggling; diplomatic efforts in Spain, the Netherlands and Sweden to complain about efforts to establish competing woollen manufacturing industries; and support for a French entrepreneur to launch a linen industry in Ireland. Further plans were just as bold: woollen manufacturing in Ireland and in Britain's North American colonies was curtailed; the Tzar of Muscovy was petitioned to ease the passage of tobacco from Britain into Russia; French assaults on Newfoundland, Hudson's Bay and the Royal African Company were pushed back; a new treaty with Sweden was drafted to help break down barriers to the northern country's precious iron exports; armed convoys were helping British fishermen dominate the North Atlantic; and negotiations with the Jewish trading community in Livorno were taking place that would protect English trading interests from Egypt to Mexico.

Throughout these plans, the goal of using the power of the state to protect the interests of British manufacturers and merchants was a common theme. The expansion of Britain's imperial and commercial interests overseas meant that the range of natural materials that were coming into Britain was growing all the time, as were the techniques and technologies that could be employed to exploit them. Consequently, the state's interest crossed industries, was increasingly global in scope, and combined diplomacy, protectionist tariffs and bans, all of which supported Britain's steady climb up the productivity chain and its emergence as a global manufacturing powerhouse.

CHAPTER 2

# A GREEN AND PLEASANT LAND

## The Environment, Agriculture and Natural Fibres

In the febrile atmosphere of invention and investment that shaped the final decades of the seventeenth century, Britain's capitalists embraced an alluring collection of novel technologies, financial schemes and colonial enterprises in their search for profit. Across their island home, diverse and plentiful environments that were well suited for growing crops and rearing flocks presented rich prospects to enterprising landowners and farmers alike. Whether producing food to sustain Britain's growing urban populations, rearing sheep to provide wool for Britain's huge textile industry or cashing in on domestic markets to raise capital that could be invested in enterprises elsewhere, exploiting the nation's environmental bounty was a vital backbone for the nation's blooming economy.

Unfortunately for anyone looking for a get-rich-quick scheme, agricultural improvement was rarely an easy task. Specialist knowledge, hard labour and lasting patience were needed to alter soil fertility, even for the most resolute landowners in the best of circumstances. Their options were fundamentally constrained by the natural resources available. Britain's geological history has produced a hugely varied landscape, and farmers in the seventeenth century had to make do with whatever topography, climate and soil type this long history had left them with. Farmers in north-west Scotland were forced to eke out what they could on rocks half as old as the earth itself, while in south-east England their compatriots could till rich loamy soils deposited only tens of thousands of years earlier during the last Ice Age. Sometimes, the natural landscape could be reshaped to a farmer's will, as lands were drained or cleared to make place for more crops or livestock, but more often than not agriculture needed to be adapted to local conditions.

Weather, too, informed which crops and livestock could flourish in Britain, and this was beyond the power of even the most innovative landowner to alter. Faced with interminable drizzle and summer months that were far from tropical, farmers in Britain were never going to be able to grow olives, grapes, sugar or cotton, no matter how sought after these were by the island's consumers. But Britain's climate helped these windswept islands of the North Atlantic hit a different economic jackpot: food security. The island's botanic abundance was shaped by a temperate climate that rarely fell too low or rose too high, and consistent precipitation diminished the risk of drought. This was a balance that saved England and Wales from the traumatic and devastating experience of major environmental catastrophe. Even during the period of global cooling known as the Little Ice Age, which caused temperatures to drop in Britain by around two degrees in the seventeenth century, southern Britain did not face widespread dearth or famine on the scale seen elsewhere in Europe during this period. In Scotland, though, tens of thousands of people died in the 1690s after plummeting temperatures led to failed harvests. Scottish migrants fled to England, colonies in America, and especially to Ireland to escape the famine. Warming weather and agricultural improvements in the following century helped Scotland avoid such devastation again, but farmers in the northern Highlands would always suffer colder, more difficult winters than their counterparts some 500 miles to the south in England's agricultural heartland.

Adapting to local conditions in this way meant that the impact of changes in agricultural practices was not homogenous, and geography and climate together shaped the practices of British farmers even as they looked to apply new techniques. Landowners faced conditions that they often had little control over, and agricultural specialisation was mostly informed by circumstance. Trying to grow crops that were valuable commodities but unsuitable for the local environment would be a sure way to ruin the harvest. Consequently, strategies for improvement were targeted at extracting as much as they could from the land available. In the lowlands of southern and eastern England, fertile soils combined with warmer weather and relatively lower rainfall were well suited for cereals like oats and barley as well as market gardens producing vegetables and fruit. Likewise, rough, hilly landscapes were well suited for rearing sheep, whose precious wool was so important for Britain's textile industry, just as surging streams pouring down the same landscape powered water-wheels in mills to help workers maximise their labour. The coldest and wettest regions of Britain in the Scottish Highlands were exploited as rough grazing land, sometimes owned by the same landowners who embraced arable farming in the fertile Lowlands to the south of Edinburgh. Elsewhere, the mixed clay and lighter sandy soils of the Midlands encouraged mixed farming that combined herds of cattle and fields of corn, while the cooler temperatures and rugged terrain of northern England meant hardier breeds of livestock grazed in its hills. In Wales, wetter but mild weather in the fertile lowland valleys helped dairy farmers even as their compatriots in the uplands of Eryri or the Bannau Brycheiniog reared robust sheep for wool and meat.

The value of Britain's environmental circumstances did not lie, therefore, in growing luxurious, intoxicating crops that could be sold to covetous consumers across the world, but rather in making it easier for the consistent supply of abundant food and useful organic materials needed to make goods like cloth. Root vegetables and old mutton were never going to entice a trader from half the world away to Britain's shores, but they were well suited for feeding its workers. Wool lacked the sumptuous luxury of silk or cotton, but in the hands of skilled workers it could still be transformed into products sought after near and far. On the whole, Britain managed to feed its population throughout the eighteenth century, even as it continued to grow, which meant its landowners, manufacturers and merchants were able to focus on opportunities elsewhere. Many of these opportunities still had their roots in agricultural produce, such as the sale of surplus crops in urban markets or the trade in natural fibres for the textile-manufacturing sector. Britain's rural and industrial economies were tightly intertwined, and the interchange of goods, ideas, people and capital between them provided an essential foundation for the nation's economy. Extracting the natural riches of its green and pleasant land for profit, either by improving output on estates or increasing the rents paid by tenants, was an enduring source of wealth for Britain's landowning capitalists.[1]

## THE GREEN ROOTS OF INDUSTRY

Britain's wealthiest people were landowners. This was true in the seventeenth century, and it would remain the case by the end of the eighteenth. Successful manufacturers and merchants bought property that often brought with it political influence, social prestige and, of course, a chance to extract income from tenants and the land. Most of Britain's land, though, was owned by people who had simply inherited property – the surest way of securing intergenerational wealth. Sometimes, landowners lived off the rents they collected without much incentive or interest to improve their lands, but their more enterprising compatriots set out to expand and develop their properties or encouraged their tenant farmers to make their own improvements. Rent was a relatively predictable source of income, and when tenants adopted new practices to increase their own income then it was no hard thing for landowners to raise rents and exploit the ingenuity of others for their own profit. For some absentee landowners, this meant that they could extract wealth from property they rarely visited. For others, their estates represented an opportunity for more profit; they actively sought out ways to improve them, whether by overseeing the management of land directly or employing skilled experts who could do so on their behalf.

Irrespective of whether they worked on the land of an absentee or resident landowner, Britain's farmers were not assured of easy profits even when they worked in the warmer climes of southern England. Profiting from the land took hard work and careful management of resources. Depleted soil could take years to be restored, decimated woodland could take even longer to regenerate if it was lost, and the colder weather of the Little Ice Age meant even the best fields were less fertile than they had been in the past. Increasing agricultural output in these conditions was harder still. Already by the sixteenth century, there was very little usable land in Britain that was not worked by farmers. Unlike in territories seized overseas, if ground became depleted, the loss could not be overcome by simply taking land elsewhere.

Similarly, new machinery made only a minimal impact on farming productivity in the seventeenth century, although incremental improvements were made. The widespread adoption of the lightweight Dutch plough was already well under way by around 1600, and the main improvement to this essential tool was replacing wood for iron in the parts of the plough that took the most wear. Likewise, mills powered by horse, wind or water were in use across the country, but these important labour-saving enterprises changed little until interest in exploiting waterpower boomed in the following century (once it was applied by miners and manufacturers). The most dramatic technological changes would only come in the 1730s, when the Rotherham plough patented by Disney Stanyforth and Joseph Foljambe offered a lightweight, cheap and easy-to-produce alternative to the Dutch model that was suitable for general-purpose use on many farms. Importantly, the new plough made turning the soil a task that could be completed by a single worker and single horse, and advertisements for the new technology claimed it could reduce ploughing times by a third. Further mechanisation would only take place in the second half of the eighteenth century. Seed drills, including that developed by Jethro Tull in 1731, presented another technological advance, but were not widely used until much later in the eighteenth century.[2]

Consequently, workers on Britain's farms would have seen little in the way of changes when it came to the tools they used, and there was little that could be done to diminish the time it took to complete the arduous work of clearing land or harvesting crops. Throughout this period, hoeing a single acre of land would take over three days for a worker using a simple hand hoe, harvesting a single acre of wheat with a sickle could take almost five days, and threshing a single ton of wheat with a flail would take just as long again. Oxen and horses supplemented this labour, with the latter growing in popularity during this period, and British farms had notably more animals than their counterparts in France. Animal power helped workers haul ploughs and pull carts, but also to grind corn where windmills or watermills were unavailable. Likewise, landlords were also able to find efficiencies and productivity gains from changing how land was used and how their workers were employed. The enclosure of common land made it possible to subdivide their property in new ways that created larger fields, divided with walls or fences, which were easier to manage and typically needed few workers. Likewise, individual farms were also getting bigger as smaller enterprises were forced out. As they grew, labour productivity increased further still.[3]

As this suggests, instead of expanding the frontiers of farms to absorb unused land or employing new technologies, the growth of Britain's agricultural sector instead depended on farmers changing how land was organised and controlled, which crops were grown, and their adoption of techniques that boosted the long-term fertility of the soil. Agricultural skills were typically passed from one person to the next by word of mouth, and personal instruction was vital for the transmission of knowledge from one generation to the next. Although more authors were seeking to codify and disseminate agricultural knowledge, the customary practices that informed the pattern and structure of farm life were generally learned through labour. These changes were gradual and the diffusion of innovative ways of working could take decades to make an impact even within the same county, let alone across Britain. Many improvements emerged from the bottom up, as tenants and workers on the land adapted to changing circumstances to survive.[4]

Raging civil war in the middle of the seventeenth century represented a bleak backdrop of disruption and hardship, but the absence of landlords and rural dislocation did present opportunities for those that remained. Tenants could plough meadows or arable pasture that had previously been reserved for livestock and did what they could to take advantage of waste land, whether by draining swamps or using floodwaters to enrich fields. Arable farming consequently increased as a cornerstone of farming practice, and growing crops became a useful supplement to the sheep rearing that had come to dominate so much of Britain's agriculture earlier in the century when high demand for the natural fibre had seen flocks given free rein to graze even the most fertile of pastures. Yet, as the rapid spread of wheat fields led to oversupply and declining grain prices, farmers were again incentivised to increase the number of livestock they reared for meat, hides and dairy products. However, rather than returning the most fertile soils to pasture, farmers often adopted systems whereby they rotated animals between fields, and this in turn helped restore and increase the fertility of crop fields that remained.[5]

As Joshua Childrey, an author who had close ties to networks around the Royal Society, explained in 1660, thanks to sheep manure 'the heaths are made mighty rich for corn, and when they are laid again from bearing of corn, they yield a sweeter and more plentiful feed for sheep'. The value of the practice was hard to ignore. Rotating fields like this was made possible by greatly increased control that landlords ruthlessly imposed on their properties after common lands were 'enclosed': a process where landowners fenced off or otherwise restricted access to areas that previously had been freely accessible. In Norfolk, sheep farming was left almost entirely in the hands of manorial landlords or their lessees, and tenant farmers rarely owned or profited from sheep even though they paid rent for land that formed part of the county's foldcourses. The Norfolk foldcourse – or sheepwalk – was a patchwork of arable land that spread across an estate where flocks would be herded for grazing when they were not sown with corn, typically after harvest or when the ground lay fallow. The sheep would then be herded onto heathland, especially in the summer months. In this way, landowners could maximise the productivity of arable land for cereal, with sheep dung acting as a free fertiliser, while maintaining large flocks that took sustenance from even the more difficult terrain that a landlord might find on their estate. As the seventeenth century progressed, improved methods in arable farming encouraged farmers to reduce the number of sheep they owned as pasture became less profitable to maintain, but flocks numbering in the thousands stayed a common feature of the agricultural landscape.[6]

Mixed farming was certainly beneficial for improving the soil and boosting output, but it also helped farmers respond to market conditions more effectively. The most successful farmers were able to raise both animals and crops. With careful management they could adjust how they used their land to meet market expectations even if this was not an easy task. When prices for grain fell, fortunately there were not similar drops in the price of other agricultural products like meat, dairy, vegetables, fruits, wool or flax which farmers could turn their fields to, and some prices even went up in response to growing demand. Cereals like barley and oats, too, became integral agricultural commodities that were attractive due to their flexibility: in harsh times beer production could be reduced to help absorb the shock, while in times of plenty greater volumes of alcohol could flow to waiting customers across Britain. In turn, it became possible for farmers to dynamically respond to market conditions, such as profiting from soaring prices for cheese and meat during periods of peak demand by fattening cattle on land otherwise reserved for crops like cereals. Elsewhere, farmers who looked to improve the output of land with light soils planted swedes, beets and turnips in increasingly complex rotations, increasing their land-use intensity and protecting against weather risks while simultaneously expanding the range of marketable products that they had available. Farmers were unlikely to get astronomical profits by growing products like these, but the conditions that pushed them towards producing essential supplies were ideally suited for meeting the needs of a growing and industrialising economy.

Diversifying land use, crops and livestock also helped farmers counter the impact of a series of extremely cold winters in the second half of the seventeenth century. The length of the growing season was shortened by as much as four weeks, while some grains struggled to withstand colder temperatures. Just as significantly, lower temperatures diminished bacterial activity in the soil, slowing the release of nitrogen into cultivated soils, and so limiting the yields of crops. In England and Wales, more varied crops helped farmers endure unpredictable weather, alleviating the risk of even a single poor harvest that devastated economies in some parts of Europe where the entire food system depended on the success or failure of a single annual crop. While there was no single solution or technology that could be applied to boost agricultural productivity across Britain's regions, opportunities to adapt and adopt techniques that worked in one location offered something of a blueprint that enterprising farmers could follow. Whether shared by word of mouth or found in printed books by leading agricultural thinkers, knowledge about improvement spread quickly and guidance was available to anyone who wanted it about the best ways to manure a field, employ a Dutch plough or clear waste land for cultivation.[7]

In John Worlidge's *Systema Agriculturæ, The Mystery of Husbandry Discovered*, first published in 1668 and reprinted multiple times by the end of the century, the Hampshire-based landowner set out key principles for improving agricultural productivity. The combination of different crops and livestock was recommended prominently. Indeed, the detailed drawing of an idealised English farm on the book's title page presented what he considered were the most important features of a successful agricultural venture. 'Built strong and plain, yet well contrived and neat', the whole edifice lauded industriousness and order. The idealised farm, Worlidge explained, was 'situated on a healthy soil' that would yield 'much wealth with little cost or toil' to a farmer in return for his 'industry and pains'. At the foot of the drawing, to the left of the country house, were barns for 'stores of hay, pulse, corn and grain', near which oxen, cows, swine and poultry could be fed. On the right, an 'apiary for the industrious bee' would produce honey and the buzzing workers who could pollinate the 'pleasant garden' beyond. Here, protected by high walls and a row of trees, 'flowers and fruits, and nature's choicest sorts of plants and roots' could be grown. Beyond the wall, rich fields and orchards spread across the middle of his perfect property, where crops of beans, peas and corn were planted close to cherry, apple, pear and plum trees. Elsewhere, hops, clover, saffron and liquorish all made an appearance. To support such rich crops, a 'water engine, which the wind commands' reared above the fields while a 'Persian wheel' could be seen alongside the river, both helping to irrigate the estate. Finally, throughout the busy farm, workers can be seen productively turning the soil with ploughs, planting crops and herding a flock of sheep. 'Peruse the book', Worlidge encouraged his readers if they wanted to

1. *An idealised English farm combining the best practices of seventeenth-century husbandry, used on a title page for John Worlidge's* Systema Agriculturæ.

achieve the same, for what they saw on his title page was the art of husbandry presented 'in epitome'.[8]

The perfect farm that Worlidge's artwork presented was highly idealised, but it did highlight some of the ways in which British farmers were transforming the agricultural landscape in the final decades of the seventeenth century. Rather than establishing monocultures, farmers that made the effort to rotate the use of different fields from one year to the next learned an important lesson about the benefit of having both livestock and crops growing on their estates. It helped them respond to market conditions more easily even as it improved the quality of the soil. In Norfolk, farms that adopted the practice ensured that if a field grew grain one year, the next it would lie fallow and be fertilised by flocks herded onto the empty land before crops would be planted again. Intermittent planting took fewer nutrients from the soil, defecating sheep helped top them up, and the following grain crop would reap the benefits of both. In places like the Midlands, where mixed farming was particularly common, the careful management of cattle herds on farmland presumably provided an abundance of manure. Similarly, widespread efforts to protect livestock by confining them to barnyards would also have resulted in plentiful and well-composted manure that was ready to be carted to fields by some lucky workers the following spring.[9]

Manure was a hot topic for writers encouraging landowners and farmers to embrace techniques intended to improve British agriculture. Writing at the very end of the seventeenth century, Leonard Meagre explained that transforming barren ground into soil that would 'bear tolerable corn' was possible but required careful preparation. The first step was burning straw on the surface 'to kill the weeds and roots', before the resulting ashes were ploughed to manure the soil. Later, when the same soil was prepared for planting, a second ploughing would leave soil suited for growing 'very good wheat', especially if sheep or poultry had been rotated onto the field to leave 'excellent manure'. Faced with even worse conditions, the Scottish author James Donaldson suggested, during the peak of the Scottish famine in the 1690s, that farmers must 'heat the earth' with manure to boost productivity, 'seeing that nature has cast our lot in this cold climate'. According to Worlidge, too, one of the easiest ways to distinguish farms 'of the ingenious from the slothful' was to note whether they were 'well manured'. In his book's fifth chapter, a dedicated section on the 'manuring, dunging and soiling of land' detailed how everything from animal dung to ashes, hair and bones could be usefully applied to farmland. Whether distributed by farm workers or wandering animals, Worlidge noted that dung was most effective when mixed with the soil by ploughing, which was notably a process that required additional labour or the most up-to-date technology for maximum benefit.[10]

Wandering flocks and the careful distribution of manure helped boost harvests, but more novel techniques were employed too. Farmers led a wave of planting that carried clover, legumes and turnips across the fields of Britain. Planting crops like these had a fourfold impact on farm productivity. First, unproductive fallow was replaced with a growing crop. Second, the loss of grazing fodder from fallow land was more than compensated for by the new crops and could feed more animals, which in turn produced more manure. Third, clover and legumes converted atmospheric nitrogen into nitrates in the soil, fertilising land for cereal crops that needed to absorb the vital chemical through their roots. Fourth, growing turnips helped smother weeds during the fallow months and provided a new source of winter fodder for livestock as they remained in the ground during the first half of winter. If they were planted in rows, they also eased the labour of hoeing soil, improving productivity further.

Together, crop rotation and the careful planting of new crops could lead the way to a virtuous cycle of soil improvement and increasing yields. The diffusion of these practices took time even after they were understood well and widely advertised by agricultural texts or word of mouth. For example, planting clover to rejuvenate the soil had been enthusiastically encouraged by Samuel Hartlib and others after its efficacy had been observed in Dutch farming as early as the middle of the seventeenth century. Despite this encouragement, this practice took decades to spread. In Norfolk and Suffolk, the proportion of farmers that planted turnips increased from almost none in the middle of the seventeenth century to around one in five in the 1680s, two in five by the 1700s, and more than half by the 1720s. Planting clover increased over a similar time-frame, but only around 20 per cent of farms in these counties were planting the soil-enriching crop by the 1740s.[11]

Innovative techniques like these helped Britain's farmers feed the nation, release workers for industry, and connect rural and urban markets. However, food was not the only natural resource taken from the nation's diverse landscapes. Sheep reared for their wool were big business in seventeenth-century Britain and large flocks were easily worth as much as industrial sites like forges and mills. Indeed, Worlidge recommended that, after cattle, 'sheep deserved the chiefest place' in an enterprising landowner's plans, in recognition of 'the great profit and advantage they bring to mankind, both for food and apparel'. Greater control of land also meant that careful crop and livestock rotation was easier to manage, and even as sheep helped manure fields, the same mixed land use helped increase the profitability of a farm's sheep. Henry Best, a landowner in the East Riding of Yorkshire, left a detailed account of how he looked after his flocks in the 1640s that clearly highlighted this relationship. After feeding his ewes hay and pea stalks in winter, Best moved his flock to warm 'enclosed grounds' in mid-February for lambing, where they were given extra feed for two more months before they were moved onto poorer common pastures nearby, leaving fat lambs ready to be sold at the highest prices in early May.[12]

Best understood that the most significant influences on the weight and quality of fleece was diet. However, the value of a flock to landowners was also found in their ability to graze sheep on parts of a property that were less suited to growing crops, an opportunity to profit from otherwise unused land. Different conditions were suited for different breeds of sheep, and farmers adopted practices that maximised the yields of land that could be profitably given over for grazing sheep. In the Midlands, the conversion of arable land to pasture had helped improve the feed available for flocks and made a notable impact on the weight of fleeces. Heavier but coarser wool from Midlands farms became popular for wool manufacturers in northern and eastern England, who produced new varieties of cloth that did not require the finest fibres that were sought after by broadcloth manufacturers. In Norfolk, on the other hand, the local sheep breed was characterised by a lighter fleece weighing less that one kilogram. Their value, instead, was found in their ability to thrive on the extensive but poor-quality pasture available. While they were wasted on rich pasture, some farmers in places like the Midlands acquired the breed for flocks that could be reared on estates with heathland that otherwise served no productive purpose.[13]

Not all wool was equally valued, and the link between environmental conditions and breed characteristics was well established. Wool shorn from Lincoln Longwool sheep, as they became known, produced finer and more expensive fibres than those taken from breeds that were commonly reared in farms across the lowlands of eastern and southern England. Joshua Childrey, in his 1662 book *Britannia Baconica*, explained how Cornish sheep produced coarser wool than those reared in the hills of Gloucestershire where 'small sheep which are long necked and square of bulk' produced fine wool or sheep from the vales of Buckinghamshire that 'have most excellent fine and soft fleeces'. His observations were sometimes inaccurate, like his presumption that it was red clay in the soil that dyed the wool of sheep in Rutland 'into a reddish' colour, but they were indicative of a general recognition that different breeds carried unique qualities. In recognition of these differences, Worlidge recommended that landlords carefully consider which breeds were most suited to their properties. 'There are divers sorts,' he explained, 'some bearing much finer wool than others', noting that Herefordshire and Leicestershire breeds had 'the fairest fleeces of any in England', while also lauding the size of Dutch sheep and the richness of Spanish fleeces. It was not just livestock breeds that received this sort of attention, and by the second half of the seventeenth century, farmers were aware of the benefits of selecting their seeds precisely, too. The understanding that different varieties were more or less suited to different environmental conditions was widely established. John Houghton, an apothecary and fellow of the Royal Society, dedicated multiple issues of his edited periodical, *A Collection of Letters for the Improvement of Husbandry & Trade* (1681–3), to describing the benefits of different types of wheat. Among them was a detailed account by Robert Plot, who described thirteen varieties grown in Oxford. Agricultural knowledge was, over the course of the seventeenth century, changing how people understood the environment and how it shaped the agricultural economy.[14]

Ideas about agricultural improvement shifted away from landowners simply increasing the rents of their tenants or seizing land that had previously been shared, although these practices continued. In their place, the goal of sustaining yields in the face of challenging climatic conditions and rural economic dislocation led to practices designed to increase productivity that in time gained widespread use. This meant that the same acre of farmland would produce more than it had before. In the century after the 1650s, the national output of crops, meat and dairy products increased, which coincided with an increasing proportion of land being dedicated for sowed crops and the growing productivity of cultivated land. Wheat production in Norfolk and Suffolk, which had already increased from twelve to fourteen and a half bushels per acre between 1600 and 1650, continued on this upward trend, with yields of sixteen bushels per acre in 1700 and twenty in 1750. In Lincolnshire, a similar, but slower, increase in wheat yields was topped up with more substantial increases from fields planted with rye, barley and oats. From the 1730s onwards, Britain's population began to grow at an unprecedented rate, buoyed by an agricultural sector that was producing substantially more than it had even half a century earlier.[15] Achieving these gains in the face of climatic crisis caused by the Little Ice Age was an astonishing result, and they were not caused by any single revolutionary factor.

Although poor harvests certainly continued to cause hardship when they occurred, Britain's agricultural economy was able to survive and in places flourish during the prolonged period of colder weather that stretched from the seventeenth and into the eighteenth century. Shocks led to temporary surges in grain prices, even to the point where riots took place to oppose the inflated cost of food, but these were not common. In general, the later seventeenth century witnessed a decreasing trend in the price of grain. When the price fell too far and landowners complained that they were suffering unduly, the state stepped in. In 1663, public subsidies were used to promote cereal exports while imports were hit with heavy duties. This bounty was only removed once before the end of the century, in 1699, when domestic grain prices temporarily rose, before it was quickly re-established. In a similar vein, upper price limits for cereal were removed in 1670 to help farmers increase their profits from the important crop when selling it overseas.[16]

Much closer to home, most farmers served the urban markets that lay nearest to their properties, and the biggest market for agricultural goods was found in London. When farms were close enough to the capital, market gardens could provide an array of perishable crops to be quickly carried to market. Elsewhere, landowners profited from leasing pasture to passing shepherds who fattened their herds of Irish and Welsh cattle on the long journey to London. The centrality of London in Britain's domestic and agricultural economy was clear when a group of Royal Society fellows began collecting and disseminating geographical material in the 1670s with the intention of compiling information on the trades and agricultural practices across the country. In the only published book that came out of the project, John Ogilby's *Britannia*, the cartographer's road maps displayed all roads leading outward from the 'prime and great metropolis' of London. Most were precisely measured, carefully detailed the routes that could be traversed to carry agricultural and other goods to the capital's markets, and the volume was produced in response to the huge growth in Britain's internal trade that was already well under way. Taking advantage of London's market, or indeed transporting goods to any town or city across Britain, encouraged improvement to roads, bridges and the wagons and coaches that travelled upon them. The coasting trade in bulk goods increased by two thirds in the final decades of the seventeenth century, but this was dramatically outstripped by the growing capacity of carrying services by road in and out of London. After 1689, Parliament passed numerous Turnpike Acts to support the improvement of roads across the country, and in 1697 legislated for the adoption of a novel new technology to help people find their way: signposts.[17]

Ogilby's volume had been published 'to improve our commerce and correspondency', and the exchanges that took place along Britain's roadways were not just limited to the transport of agricultural commodities. The movement of ideas, people and capital were just as important as London's huge markets for British agricultural development. Farmers might have been cash-poor in times of crisis, but the land represented the most enduring form of productive wealth available, despite the vicissitudes of weather and markets. People who owned land were more likely to be able to take advantage of the capital's quickly growing banking sector, and wealth from rural landowners was essential for the development of private banking in the capital, which in turn contributed to the growing connectivity between landowners and wealthy urban craftsmen and merchants. Successful landowners used their relationships to obtain a deeper understanding of the wider national and even international market. Merchants and bankers in London could tap into the city's gossip to advise business partners or clients in the country, and by the 1670s the most sophisticated information networks could give their members a considerable advantage. Bankers like Robert Clayton and John Morris found opportunities serving clients who profited from their agricultural landholdings. They also ruthlessly exploited the impact of rural depressions which left landowners desperately searching for funds to make up for their loss of income, Clayton and Morris were more than willing to offer mortgages that were secured against the value of estates. When landowners defaulted, their properties could pass to other landowners who sought to increase their holdings, or to manufacturers and merchants who sought to boost their wealth and prestige with agricultural assets. In time, the sale and resale of land increased and Britain's manufacturing, agricultural and trading sectors became ever more deeply entwined.[18]

Remarkably, then, despite the challenges left by the devastation of civil war and the enduring impact of colder weather during the Little Ice Age, the adoption of new agricultural practices led to notable increases in Britain's agricultural productivity. By the early decades of the eighteenth century, Britain's farmers were benefiting from changes that had seen yields grow substantially, especially as the climate warmed and approaches that had just kept heads above water during colder years were gifted with a sudden boost in the form of longer seasons and higher temperatures. Through their efforts, and those of the workers that cleared, tilled or fertilised the land, Britain's capitalists oversaw the beginnings of a dramatic increase in agricultural diversification and productivity. This vital sector was not only able to sustain the nation's population, but increasing productivity per worker was so great that demand for farm labour declined. This contributed to growing numbers of rural people moving towards manufacturing enterprises to find their own fortunes or taking whatever work they could in urban areas to make ends meet. At the same time, it was not uncommon for agricultural workers to spend some of their time completing work that could easily be classified as manufacturing, such as spinning woollen threads. While a growing agricultural workforce had boosted outputs in the previous century, the later seventeenth and first half of the eighteenth centuries were defined instead by the fastest rate of growth in agricultural productivity per worker compared to any other period in British history – it would not be until the advent of chemical and other industrial fertilisers in the nineteenth century that such a rapid expansion would be seen again.[19]

## THE GOLDEN FLEECE

Rich soils and favourable weather presented an abundance of riches for some lucky landowners while others struggled to make a profit from less fertile properties. In addition to feeding Britain's growing urban population, farmers produced the essential natural fibres for the country's most important industry: the manufacture of woollen cloth. While an immense variety of fabrics was made across Europe, frequently from plant fibres including flax, hemp and silk, most important in Britain were textiles made from animal fibres shorn from sheep that could be reared by landowners across the country. By the seventeenth century, Britain's sheep farmers had been producing the raw material for cloth makers for centuries and wool remained an important marketable produce for anyone who sought to extract wealth from the land. Profit for farmers was just the start, though, and natural produce from Britain's farms, in the form of wool, was an essential requirement for a large part of the island's manufacturing output in turn. The exploitation of this natural resource was a fundamental part of ongoing industrial innovation and expansion.

Woollens were made for customers across all levels of society, and everything from humble and coarse burel cloth to sumptuous weaves so fine they were almost like silk could turn a profit. Selling raw wool to spinners and weavers created and maintained connections between sheep-rearing landowners, traders specialising in transporting raw wool, urban manufacturers who produced the finished product, and merchants who would sell it at home or abroad. By the sixteenth century, the manufacture of fine broadcloths, dyed and finished, had become concentrated in the southern Cotswolds, the Stroud Valley and along the River Avon and its tributaries. Further north, the rocky slopes that tumbled down from the Pennine moorlands nourished a hardy breed of mountain sheep whose wool sustained a thriving industry on the upper reaches of the Aire and Calder rivers producing lighter-weight but coarser cloths known as kerseys. Here, in almost every village, hamlet or homestead, people could be found supplementing their meagre agricultural income with profits from manufacturing work. In time, technological advances gave clothiers in the west of England a productive advantage, as hills and rivers provided the power needed to mechanise parts of cloth production after the development of the fulling mill, but innovative techniques ensured that specialised cloth manufacture in all parts of the country remained profitable. In Norfolk, the long-standing manufacture of lightweight, high-quality textiles made of combed rather than carded wool, that were known as serge or worsted cloth, received a considerable boost following the arrival of Protestant refugees from Europe, who brought with them new skills that fed into Britain's rapidly developing textile industry.

Part of the importance of woollen manufacture, from the perspective of the state and supporters of the industry, lay in the huge number of workers that it employed across England. The route from farm to fibre to fabric was long and complicated. Obtaining the wool fibres for cloth production required many hours of labour in the field. After the wool was shorn, it needed more workers to sort and clean it before being sent onwards to be prepared for spinning. Downland breeds produced wool with a short staple that needed to go through a process called carding, while wool from sheep producing longer fibres could be combed and used for fabric known as worsted cloth. Often undertaken by women, carding and combing were tasks where workers used wooden tools, bearing either short metal hooks or with long metal teeth, respectively, that untangled and aligned the woollen fibres. Only then could raw wool be spun into yarn by twisting fibres against each other so that their microscopic hooks would tightly interlink and combine into a single, continuous length of thread. Spinning was another task that primarily fell to female workers, and often took place in homes using a spinning wheel, which was notably the first part of the textile-manufacturing process that had been mechanised. Although each worker used their own energy to power their own machine, the spinning wheel greatly improved their efficiency, and the vital apparatus had become widespread across Britain long before the seventeenth century.

Once raw wool had been transformed into usable woollen thread, it was passed either to dyers or weavers, depending on whether the yarn or a finished fabric was intended for dyeing. Colouring yarn or cloth demanded considerable skill to achieve the best outcomes. Dyers needed a deep understanding of the various materials involved and how they could be combined for different outcomes. The process of dyeing was done in large circular vats where the woollen thread or fabric could be constantly turned with long poles to achieve a consistent finish. This was hard, physical labour and was typically undertaken by men.

Weaving too, required very high levels of skill, especially to produce the finest textiles. Woven fabric was made by using looms that held the strongest woollen threads (known as the warp) taut and in place, while a weaver drew a second thread (known as the weft) over and under each warp in turn to create a tightly interlaced mesh. This was no simple task, and a typical broadcloth, Britain's main export commodity at the start of this period, would contain more than two thousand warp threads held in place on a two-yard-wide frame, large enough so that two weavers would sit side by side as they worked on the same cloth. Narrow cloth, which became increasingly popular, used a smaller loom that only required a single weaver to work, which probably contributed to their widespread use by weavers in places like the north-east of England where independent weavers often worked in their homes.

After it left the loom, a woollen cloth would be passed to fullers whose labour helped produce smooth, tightly finished fabrics that were more water-resistant and warmer. First scouring the cloth to remove impurities, often using fuller's earth (a type of clay used for bleaching wool fibres), the cloth was then cleansed and put through a process known as milling that pounded wool fibres into an even tighter mesh under the percussive force of feet or mallets. This was a task that was well suited to mechanisation, and water-powered hammers could be used to process huge quantities of cloth without the need for exhausting human labour. Finally, cloth was stretched on tenterhooks to ensure consistent shape and size, which was undertaken on large frames and required yet more labourers to move the heavy cloth. Further tasks prepared fabric for market, and it could be shorn, brushed, pressed and folded before it was sold.

These processes meant that the woollen industry employed a lot of workers and required people with specialist knowledge to undertake complex procedures that, if not completed properly, led to poor-quality fabric. This often meant that textile workers could demand higher wages than their compatriots working on farms. At the same time, the sale of woollen cloths could achieve much higher profits than was possible for Britain's main agricultural products. In the seventeenth century, changing labour patterns contributed to a rise in the number of workers who took part in the textile industry, often alongside agricultural labour or otherwise closely connected with the rural economy. In northern Britain, especially, taking part in processing, spinning and weaving woollen cloth could be a lucrative opportunity for rural workers to supplement their incomes. Where rural life and urban manufacturing were in close proximity, it was common for children who might previously have expected to remain tied to the field to find opportunities to train in the emerging manufacturing sector that was growing around them. For enterprising capitalists, the opportunity to employ rural workers more cheaply than their urban counterparts incentivised the establishment of larger enterprises in these areas. Likewise, in areas such as northern or south-west England, where the control or protection that urban and craft corporations offered workers in many urban areas was weakest, it could be easier to exploit them further and turn them towards producing types of cloth that might otherwise be restricted by monopolistic regulations.[20]

As Britain's woollen manufacturers changed their business practices, so did its merchants seize a much greater degree of control over the export of cloth to Europe. Italian, Flemish and Hanse merchants had been prominent features in British commercial centres for centuries, but by the beginning of the seventeenth century British merchants had come to control an increased proportion of Britain's export trade. Ever-increasing quantities of woollen cloth found their way to Britain's ports by cart, packhorse, river barge and coasting boats in advance of being shipped overseas. As production increased across Britain, manufacturers sold their cloth to merchants who operated in ports like Bristol, who carried them onwards to markets across the Atlantic seaboard including Ireland, Spain and Portugal; or Hull, whose ships traversed the cold northern seas to sell woollen fabrics to consumers in Scandinavia and the Baltic. It was through London, though, that most woollens were taken, and the capital's merchants came to dominate their export to the Netherlands, Germany and places further afield like the Mediterranean and India.[21]

The increasing participation of British merchants in overseas trade contributed to the expansion of the nation's domestic textile industry in another vital way. While the nation's woollen industry sourced its raw wool primarily from British sheep, and fuller's earth was produced locally, it imported many of the other materials to produce finished and dyed cloth. Madder and woad, the most common dyes, used for various shades of red, blue and even black, were cultivated in increasingly limited quantities in Britain as farmers specialised in rearing sheep, and had to be supplemented with supplies from France and elsewhere in Europe. A rich deep shade of blue known as perse, dyed with woad, produced among the most sought-after cloths on the market, while less intense, lighter blues were among the cheapest of coloured cloths. By carefully combining these dyes, various shades of purple could be manufactured, while woad was mixed with another dye called weld to stain green cloths. Weld alone, producing yellow dye, was in little demand. Potash was needed to bind dyes like woad to bleached woollen fibres and was primarily sourced from Baltic forests. Other materials were carried to

British ports from the Mediterranean, which provided the most prized and brightly coloured red kermes and much of the alum needed to fix dyes, or from further afield still, such as African redwood, South American brasil wood or indigo from Asia. In the seventeenth century, British merchants were transporting woollen textiles and other commodities to these destinations, and returning with the very dyes needed to produce the goods sought after by these traders with whom they intended to do business.[22]

These foundations laid the groundwork for expansion and continued innovation in different regions that contributed to the flourishing of Britain's woollen industry through the sixteenth and into the seventeenth and eighteenth centuries. By 1660, woollen cloth manufacture was a well-known, deeply understood and hugely important part of Britain's economy. William Carter, in his boosterish tract *England's Interest Asserted*, made clear that he thought wool represented 'the richest treasure' that the kingdom's natural abundance had to offer. It was the 'strength and sinews of this nation', 'the milk and honey to the grazier and country farmer', 'the gold and spices of the East and West Indies to the merchant' and 'bread for the poor'. The precious fibres shorn from the nation's sheep were, 'in a word, the exchequer of wealth'.[23]

Carter's enthusiasm for keeping wool for British industry should come as no surprise. He was a clothier and made his money from transforming woollen fibres into finished cloth that was sold in Britain and internationally. In the final decades of the seventeenth century, his zeal for all things woolly had put him in a position of prominence in debates about how Britain could best take advantage of this great source of riches. He spoke before Parliament, published pamphlets, and personally spent hundreds of pounds travelling to Kent and Suffolk to police these counties' coastal badlands where smugglers sought to traffic their fluffy contraband overseas. His objective was simple: 'England's Glory', he confidently asserted, rested on 'the benefit of wool manufactured therein' and was therefore at considerable risk 'by the evil consequences of its exportation unmanufactured'. Without export controls in place, he worried that clothiers in Europe would outperform English producers. On the one hand, they were threatened by the French, who 'being very populous and living harder than we can in England' could exploit labour more cheaply, while on the other, they risked losing out to Dutch and Flemish manufacturers who 'by care and industry' did 'endeavour to excel our English'. Whether due to cheap labour or superior innovation overseas, Carter worried that English manufacturers would struggle to compete on an equal playing field. Stopping international competitors in their tracks by monopolising raw wool seemed like a sound strategy for England's textile industrialists.[24]

Persuaded that the manufacture of woollen cloth was 'the great staple-trade of this Kingdom', Charles II immediately set out, after being restored to the throne, to enforce a clear ban on the export of raw wool that undermined domestic manufacturing. The fear was not so much that British manufacturers would be threatened by diminishing access to wool at home, but rather that the export of raw wool gave clothiers in other countries the opportunity to make woollen cloths themselves, often at prices that could undercut British industry. Officers across England's ports were appointed to ensure that ships were not carrying the prohibited commodity, and everybody was encouraged to alert the authorities to any breaches of the ban, incentivised with rewards worth half the value of any goods seized as a consequence of their information.[25]

National statutes to support woollen manufacture in England came thick and fast. Five were enacted by Charles II in the 1660s alone, and ten more would be passed before the end of the century. Most focused on enforcing the ban on exporting raw wool, which became part of a coherent strategy across this period. Others made provisions for changing how wool was processed, manufactured and consumed. One banned the import of foreign wool cards (used by workers who prepared raw wool for spinning) which were considered to process wool at a lower quality. A linked benefit was to protect British iron manufacturers whose iron wire was deemed the best material for high quality cards. Another statute appointed wardens under the auspices of a Corporation of the Free Clothiers to oversee the West Yorkshire woollen industry, and a handful were passed 'For Burying in Woollen Only' that imposed heavy fines on people who buried their loved ones in clothes or caskets made of linen or silk rather than the nation's own textiles. The most consistent focus, though, was on establishing an economic system that pushed England further up the production chain while denying competitors overseas the chance of doing the same.[26]

As the language of statutes like these attested, as well that used in contemporary petitions by clothiers or tracts by interested commentators, policy was developed that looked to clearly prioritise the enrichment of clothiers and merchants in England. Plans were put in place that ruthlessly segregated manufacturing regions from a periphery of raw-material-producing territories – beyond England – that were left underdeveloped, sometimes intentionally, to boost the profits of the core. Even as the export of raw wool from England was banned to benefit local manufacturers, the state encouraged the transfer of Irish raw wool to English manufacturers, and ports including Whitehaven, Bristol and Liverpool were designated to receive the precious fibres and funnel them onwards to the growing English woollen industries in England. The Royal Navy was appointed to patrol the British coastline 'with orders to seize all ships, vessels and boats which shall export any wool with intent to carry it into foreign parts'.[27]

Bans on the export of woollen cloth from Ireland were explained quite openly by the Board of Trade as an opportunity to diminish the growth of Irish industry in favour of manufacturers elsewhere in Britain. The goal, they explained in 1697, was to 'divert the people of Ireland from applying themselves to the trade of woollen manufacture', and to do so 'by giving them such encouragement in the manufacture of linen as might engage them heartily in it'. There was no major linen industry in England, although one was developing in Scotland, and Ireland would make for a better source for the material than those in Europe without any risk of the new industry damaging English manufacturers. It was a decision that aligned colonial policy in Ireland closely with that employed in North America, where British colonists had also 'applied themselves to the improvement of woollen manufacturers . . . to the hinderance of the exportation of our English manufactures'. These manufacturers, too, were undermined by the state as a means of protecting the metropole's key industry. Ireland and North America were both understood as key markets for English woollen goods, and the economic interests of the state would be hurt if they began producing their own.[28]

By the beginning of the eighteenth century, support for Britain's textile industries and fibre-focused agriculturalists had started to bear dividends. Britain's textile manufacturers were experimenting with and employing innovative techniques to boost their productivity long before technological advances dramatically altered how woollen cloth, linen, silk and cotton fabrics were produced in the following decades. The Committee for Trade calculated that 'there had been of late years a considerable increase in the exports of our woollen manufacture, and that the value thereof in the year 1701 exceeded that of the year 1662 more than a million' pounds. Three causes were offered: increasing supplies of raw wool from Ireland; growing domestic production 'occasioned by the improvement of land in England'; and the development of products more suited to international markets like 'stuffs, says, serges' and 'super fine cloths made of Spanish wool'.[29] Woollen manufacturing in general had 'very much increased' over the previous decades and 'our weavers and makers are improved in making several useful sorts with great variety'. At the same time, advances in silk production, too, meant that 'our English weavers do make several sorts as good as any made in foreign parts'.[30]

Across Britain, industrious clothiers were adopting new methods to produce a wide array of styles that made the most of available natural and human capital. The small-scale clothier in West Yorkshire oversaw a quite different enterprise than the largest manufacturers in places like Norfolk or around Bristol, but both were able and willing to adopt innovative techniques when they were available. Clothiers in rural industry were often weavers themselves, with one or two looms in their own home representing the extent of the investment required to establish themselves in business. Often employing members of their own family alongside a small number of other workers, the production of wool from combing and carding to spinning and weaving was undertaken under the same roof. The opportunity for profit was reasonably limited, and with little capital behind them such a weaver could lead a precarious existence, but by taking part in manufacturing they could supplement the income of their smallholding or agricultural labour. Sometimes, weaving would be combined not only with farm work but also other trades such as milling corn or working as a butcher. Cloth manufacturing was typically undertaken not by large enterprises or major joint-stock companies, but by dozens of small partnerships and independent producers who could take advantage of changing market conditions and the diffusion of innovative manufacturing processes. As the woollen industry in West Yorkshire grew, the combination of fuel, cheap labour and running water all attracted capitalists to expand their businesses further, employing methods to boost productivity that put the region at the forefront of industrial innovation throughout the remainder of the eighteenth century.[31]

Changes in the sorts of cloth that were manufactured in Britain were influenced by a range of factors, including consumer demand and the availability of different materials. Traditional woollen broadcloths were warm and heavy, but often monotonous in design, and needed to be made entirely of short, carded wool. These were popular in northern and central Europe and would remain so. However, they were unsuited to many of the warmer climes to which British merchants increasingly travelled, nor were they made with the longer staple and coarser wool that was being produced in larger volumes on British farms. Instead, this coarser wool was better suited for use, wholly, or more often partly, in fabric made of combed, long-staple fibres. This could create a lighter-weight cloth, made in a range of patterns and new styles that were suited for markets in Portugal, Spain and the Mediterranean. As Britain's farming industry changed, its manufacturing industry changed with it, creating virtuous cycles that boosted both. Some manufacturers also experimented with new techniques that generated further variations of cloth, and it became increasingly common for manufacturers to combine British wool with fibres including linen, silk, cotton and Spanish merino wool.[32]

Making these new types of blended cloth required much more than just purchasing the right raw materials: the skills required needed to be carefully acquired too. In south-west England, imported Spanish wool had become a mainstay in cloth produced in the region over the early decades of the seventeenth century, producing fabric that was notably lighter than other varieties available. The success of the south-western industry had only been possible because of a general neglect in the regulation of woollen manufacturers in the region which otherwise would very likely have banned the practice. However, it was also the result of constant innovation as clothiers strove to keep up with competitors in international markets. Competition from Dutch *lakens*, which were similarly produced with a medley of merino and other woollen threads, were a particular threat, with merchants and political commentators alike reporting on the risk of Dutch superiority in the textiles. English manufacturers like John Ashe reported unhappily that the foreign fabric had fewer faults and brighter colours than English-made, Spanish-wool cloth.[33]

Rather than turning to regulation to try and enforce higher standards, however, the south-western clothiers sought to replicate the Dutch model instead. In the final years of the 1650s, clothiers like Paul Methuen (John Ashe's son-in-law) encouraged Dutch workers to move to England to work for them, and they introduced the techniques needed to produce the very lightest Spanish-wool cloth in England. Among them was a 'Dutch spinner' named Derick Jonson who was recruited to teach local workers the sort of techniques that had recently been developed in Leiden. Quickly, traders like Edward and Jonathan Ashe (two brothers of John Ashe who worked in partnership) were selling cloth that was identified as 'Holland made' or 'fine Dutch black' but had been produced by the clothier Mr Waymans. In the following decades, other capitalists built on the advances made by Methuen and Waymans. Christopher Brewer recruited another twenty-four Dutch migrants in Bradford-on-Avon in 1674, while more still adopted Dutch methods. These included the adoption of technology like 'Dutch cards' for preparing wool and new techniques for spinning thread. By the 1680s, the Ashe family was reported as boasting that the region's cloth was now made 'so thin' that it was half the weight it had been a few decades before.[34]

The arrival of migrant workers also contributed to the emergence of a more urban-based production process in south-west Britain.

This, too, replicated the Dutch model, which had seen an urban and male workforce increasingly replace the largely female and rural labourers who had previously undertaken tasks like spinning and carding wool. Much like the concentration of cloth workers that Brewer oversaw in Bradford-on-Avon, his fellow clothiers Richard Yerbury and Sarah Whitechurch had built a housing complex for their carders, dyers, spinners and weavers in nearby Frome. In time, more and more workers came to be housed in urban environments in cloth towns, rather than living and working in semi-rural conditions on their outskirts. The combined living- and workspaces in Bradford-on-Avon and Frome were not – yet – taking the shape of factories that would appear in the following century, but they certainly contributed to the more intensive concentration of cloth making in urban environments and gave clothiers greater control over their workers' lives.[35]

South-west England was not the only place where innovative textile production was taking place, although woollen production in many parts of southern England was forced to innovate to keep up with the highly sought-after fabrics produced in the region. Many of their changing practices were built on methods that had been developed by manufacturers like the Ashe family and Brewer, but most important was their widespread adoption of Spanish wool as a core material for their cloth. In the Stroudwater district north of the River Severn, cloths made primarily of Spanish wool appeared after 1677, while clothiers in nearby Worcester likewise switched to making fine-quality fabric using the same material after 1682. In the following two decades, the use of Spanish wool would spread to Norfolk, Salisbury and Kidderminster. Each region developed its own variety of the cloth and by the eighteenth century Spanish Stroudwaters, Spanish Worcesters, Spanish Salisburys and others were available. English wool was still used in some of the blended fabrics, and some farmers began rearing Spanish merino sheep to cater to the fast-growing market for those fibres, but the produce of many flocks had to find other uses. Indeed, in these same areas, coarser English wool underpinned the emergence of another new industry making hard-wearing rugs, carpets and upholstery.[36]

Elsewhere, manufacturers developed a huge array of other cloth variations to meeting changing customer demand. In Norwich, the town's long-standing skill making worsted cloth led to widespread experimentation as local manufacturers substituted popular European cloths with cheaper alternatives. Weaving in Norfolk expanded enormously in the seventeenth century and new techniques were diffused to towns across the region. Likewise, manufacturers across south-east England, often developing skills that had been introduced through Norwich by Flemish clothiers in the sixteenth century, experimented with combinations of wool, silk and linen threads. In Canterbury, another group of resident cloth workers with roots in the Low Countries had become well established by the 1670s, producing fabric that replicated styles that had been popularised in France as well as novel varieties that wove gold and silver into woollen, cotton and linen fabrics. By the early eighteenth century, skills like these had diffused across much of Britain, influencing further experimentation and popularising European methods and materials in the nation's textile industry.[37]

Likewise, mixing wool with imported linen and cotton thread to make fustians also drew on a prolonged period of innovation in advance of the rapid expansion of production towards the end of the seventeenth century. Spreading from Maidstone across the west of England in towns like Gloucester, Stow-on-the-Wold and as far north as Carlisle, as well as in south-eastern towns like Ipswich and Bury St Edmunds, where the industry had taken hold by the 1660s and remained until the middle of the following century. However, it was further north that the fustian industry gravitated, and manufacturers in Bolton, Blackburn, Oldham, Manchester and Preston were making fustians in the fashion of Genoa, Milan and Piedmont as early as the 1650s. A finishing touch to these cloths was made around the same time as English manufacturers began to make imitation Indian cloth called chintz. Unable to produce cotton cloth of the same quality as Indian imports, but keen to imitate the popular styles that were being carried on East India Company ships to Europe, they set out to mimic designs even as they remained dependent on fabric that could be made in Britain. Using printing blocks, workers pressed dyed outlines onto fustian cloth before colour was painted in. The popular new fabric sought to substitute the popular cotton cloths that were arriving from India, but modified to fit Britain's environmental conditions.[38]

The advance of textile production that combined woollen fibres from Britain's vast flocks of sheep with materials that were imported from overseas led to an industry that depended on international exchange for key materials as much as it looked to sell cloth overseas. As the Board of Trade explained in 1703, the exchange of woollen cloth in Italy and Turkey for raw silk had provided the impetus for the nascent silk industry in Britain. This was an ideal situation 'because the vent of our [woollen] goods in those parts' could increase; 'a great number of her Majesty's subjects are supported by manufacturing those silks here'; and British consumers were 'supplied with wrought silks at the cheapest rates'.[39] By exchanging British manufacturers overseas for raw materials that then supported yet more British manufacturing, commercial exchanges like this furthered the consistent aim to move the nation higher up the production chain. Tens of thousands of pounds of silk fabric were being exported from Britain for sale overseas, often in exchange for raw materials that could not be grown, reared or extracted at home, and the cycle continued.[40]

Patents for new techniques were indicative of the kinds of cloth that was especially sought after, and even a handful of examples from the final decades of the seventeenth century attest to the scope of innovative practices that were taking place. Joshua Gaskins, a merchant tailor from London, secured the privilege of 'beautifying cloth' by 'pressing thereon certain indented lines or creases, resembling the wale [vertical ridges] of tabby or mohair'. Ralph Lane received a patent for a new technique that improved how woollen and silk cloth was dyed, not only in colours, but also with 'figures, flowers, forestry, and landscapes'. William Bayly invented 'a new sort of glazed printed hangings' that could be made of cotton or wool and designed with 'all sorts of curious figures and landscapes'. The new product was, he claimed, 'hard to be distinguished from the finest silk tapestry hangings brought from foreign parts'. Similarly, interest in alternative fibres to wool had persuaded John Englebert Teshmaker and Ralph Marshall to hire workmen from Germany, who helped them set up a flax yarn business. Echoing what was to come the following century, John Barkstead obtained a patent in 1691 for making calicos and muslins 'out of the cotton wool of the growth and product of their Majesty's plantations in the West Indies'. Whether seeking to improve the texture of the fabric, the colour and beauty of designs, or the materials used, British clothiers moved quickly to keep up with consumer demand.[41]

Changes in Britain's textile industry, then, were mostly a consequence not of power-saving technological change, although water-powered mills were growing in popularity where conditions allowed, but rather due to numerous incremental improvements in manufacturing processes and the adoption of new techniques that increased the value of goods produced. All the while, clothiers benefited from strong state support for domestic manufacturers. Even as the types of textile goods changed, danger persisted 'by the growth of the like manufactures made in other countries'. Engaging with a wider world of trade provided British manufacturers with a vast range of new markets for their goods, but it also exposed them to increasing competition. Consequently, 'the manufactured goods of India, Persia or China' made of silk and cotton were, like European or colonial woollens, seen as a major threat to English industry, and plans advanced in the final decades of the seventeenth century to prohibit their consumption.[42]

While combinations of blended fabrics and experimental styles supported the production of new types of products in manufacturing centres across England, more traditional styles did remain. For these, it was vital that new methods were employed to increase their competitiveness, including, in parts of northern England around the turn of the eighteenth century, the use of water-powered machinery to radically boost productivity. In the West Riding of Yorkshire, local clothiers were still producing 26,671 broadcloths annually in the 1720s, and that number doubled by the middle of the century. More remarkable still was the exceptional growth in the production of narrow cloths. These were made with techniques that had been popularised elsewhere in Britain the previous century but had previously had a negligible impact on the Yorkshire industry. As market demand shifted, so did the region's manufacturers, and the production of the narrow variety quickly surpassed the output of broadcloth. By 1750, the West Riding was producing 78,115 narrow cloths. In only twenty-five years, the total woollen cloth production of the region had increased almost five times.[43]

As this enduring and growing production suggests, by the early decades of the eighteenth century British woollen cloth manufacturers were willing and able to produce a wide variety and a huge volume of fabrics. In some parts of the country, cloths were being made that would have been unrecognisable to clothiers a century before, while in others, new techniques and materials altered and improved how cloths that would have been very familiar were made. Demand for woollens of many varieties remained strong and they were able to produce cloth that stood out from their competitors, clothiers were in an enviable position. The best-quality fabric was so sought after that even disagreements might be set aside by merchants in order to obtain it. In 1729, when the woollen manufacturer George Stansfield reached out to John Doville, a woollen merchant from near Halifax, in 'hopes of a reconciliation' following 'your former uneasiness', he pointedly encouraged Doville to consider that he could offer 'such goods . . . as you cannot procure elsewhere'. Stansfield had taken advantage of the 'great advance both in wool and making' that had taken place over the previous decades, and even though competition was fierce he was confident that he was ahead of the curve and in a position of considerable advantage.[44]

Doville seems to have taken the hint: for a well-made cloth, even enmity might be traded away. Unfortunately, Stansfield's command of the market meant that before long he was no longer seeking out the Halifax trader's business but rather turning it away. Only a year after their reconciliation, Stansfield was in a position that he had no cloth to spare in any case. As he explained, he was selling out of his finest 'Stansfield Bowood Kerseys' and 'Bowood Best Fieldhouse' cloths quicker than he could make them and boasted that 'I think if I had 1000 store of them, I could have sold them all'. The booming market put negotiations strongly in Stansfield's favour, and when Doville tried to pressure him to lower his prices, he was simply told that, in Leeds, 'I can sell them when I please' at the high prices he was now demanding. The following year, Stansfield's stocks remained in high demand, and he was well positioned to bluntly tell Doville that he had better hurry if they wanted his kerseys at market price and 'it is your own fault if you have them not'. With his cloths so sought after, especially by merchants carrying them onwards for sale in Amsterdam and elsewhere in northern Europe, Stansfield was able to increase production and prices with ease. By 1732, his business with Doville, despite the trader's earlier uneasiness, had increased to £2,374 in sales each year and accounted for approximately half of Stansfield's stock. By now, Stansfield was making four different types of cloth, with Doville purchasing most of the lower-quality variety, while the enterprising clothier supplemented these bulk sales to the Halifax merchant with smaller but highly profitable sales to other businesses that presumably catered to the demands of wealthier customers.[45]

A few thousand miles away from Halifax on the shores of the Red Sea, British merchants were also feeding back the demands of local consumers to their bosses at the East India Company headquarters. On this occasion, though, British manufacturers were struggling to meet their needs. Here, in Mocha, the main entry point for the world's only major coffee producer, the corporation's factors were desperate for a ready supply of colourful and well-priced textiles to sell into an increasingly competitive market. With demand for coffee growing in Europe, and supply becoming more scarce, British traders needed to maintain a cutting edge above their French and Dutch competitors, but too often they were sent English woollens in styles that local people just did not find appealing. Consequently, the East India Company factor Edward Day wrote to London in 1719 begging for cloth 'as thin as the French cloth' and dyed crimson, scarlet, blue or green, as 'it would suit this people better'. He was keen to emphasise that local traders sought 'not the finest' quality but rather vibrant, lightweight textiles that were sought after across the wider Red Sea region. When this first letter was ignored, and the company sent more cloth that was 'coarse and thick, which is altogether improper', the traders in Mocha complained once more, this time sending examples of the patterns and styles that would sell most easily. When the company's factors wrote to London in 1721, they informed the company's management that 'ten moor's ships' had recently arrived from Surat, Gogo, Cambay and the Malabar Coast, where they joined not only the English traders but also ships under the Dutch, Hanoverian, French and Ostend flags.[46] Their frustrations were clear: if the company did not take the demands of local consumers more seriously, it was highly unlikely that they could sell the woollen cloths and their ability to obtain ludicrously profitable coffee would suffer.

In time, the quality of cloth sent to Mocha did improve. They were still deemed too thick to be highly prized but by 1725 the factors were at least making the sales necessary to keep their coffee trade going.[47] However, their experience in Mocha was representative of a common complaint by British traders across much of Asia, who were not only selling woollens in markets full of other European fabrics of similar styles but directly competing with Indian and other Asian producers. Crisp, lightweight taffeta from Bengal, and brightly printed *bastas* from Gujarat, among dozens of other designs and styles, were all sharing space on market stalls alongside English woollens.[48] More success was expected when English textiles at the higher end of the market were shipped to Asia, such as one thousand pieces of colourful 'Long Ells' and 'three bales of broad cloth . . . of the finest sort made in England' sent to China in 1712, but only when quantities were kept relatively small, and even then sales remained slow.[49] The company kept experimenting, though, and new styles and types of fabric were sent across Asia in the hope of improving sales.[50] When customers overseas made clear demands, clothiers were often willing and able to specialise their business to match. Woollen cloth might have been a hard sell on the edges of the Arabian desert, but high-quality cloths or blended fabrics with linen, silk or cotton all offered possibilities for diversification.

The changes that manufacturers and merchants made were not always so dramatic as when catering to consumers as distant as those in Mocha. Simply focusing on different types of cloth for nearby markets in Europe was well worth the effort when there was consistent demand. This certainly worked out for John Firth, a worsted manufacturer in Halifax, who told the merchants Mr Whilton and Mr Harrop that he was 'well pleased to hear you intend to deal more largely in the shalloon trade' and focus on only three types of cloth for export. Shalloons were a type of thin twill cloth that were sold for 25 shillings per piece in the 1730s. Although Firth could not supply all three types required immediately, 'as you propose being constant in the three sorts' he was happy to adjust his own operations 'to fix myself with such makers as will please you'. Given that the Halifax clothier had suffered from a shrinking market for long ells, another staple of the Yorkshire industry, a good market for him to target with alternative goods was a desirable opportunity.[51]

Likewise, when the clothier Walter Stanhope, who ran a successful woollen cloth manufacturing business from Leeds, set out to obtain silk thread from Messina, he was given clear instructions that 'none of the woollen manufacturers are so proper for this market as blue northern cloth' or 'fine scarlet shalloons', with two or three bales the most the market could handle. Along with the advice, he was sent 'a sample to imitate both in colour and quality' to make sure that he met the expectations of his potential Sicilian customers. Without doing so, there was little hope of obtaining silk thread: to meet one set of customer's demands for silk-wool blends, he needed to meet those of another for rich, colourful fabrics. The Yorkshire clothier met the challenge head on, and two decades later was not just still active in the Italian market but had increased his sales beyond all expectations, to as many as eighteen bales of woollen cloth a year.[52]

To say the least, wool's hard-wearing nature and the warmth of broadcloth were not always the easiest selling points for traders to pitch in subtropical climates but British manufacturers had found ways to overcome this challenge. In the eighteenth century, British fabrics were sold around the world. In 1700, textiles dominated the commodities that made up England's overseas trade: almost £3 million of woollen cloths were sold overseas by British merchants that year alone. More than eight varieties were exported at values worth over £100,000 each, including the Spanish woollens that had shaken up south-west England's industry and the coarser styles that were reshaping the industry further north. These were joined by the export of over £120,000 worth of non-woollen or mixed-fibre textiles, including £26,702 worth of fustians, £12,610 of English linen and £67,118 of English wrought silk. By the middle of the eighteenth century, these volumes had spectacularly increased. Well over £5 million worth of woollen cloth was being shipped overseas, now with eleven varieties surpassing £100,000 in exports. Part of this increase was met by demand from customers far from the markets of northern Europe that had long represented the textile industry's most important vent. Over £130,000 of woollens were carried to Asian markets on East India Company ships, as much again to British colonies in North America and the Caribbean, and almost half a million pounds of British woollen cloth was sold in Spain, some to be carried onwards for sale across the Spanish empire. These woollens were joined by £355,044 of non-woollen fabrics, a dramatic increase mostly explained by the huge growth of linen exports, which had now reached over £200,000 a year: sixteen times more than at the beginning of the century.[53]

These were huge volumes. Woollen cloth was far and away Britain's most important export and much of this was made from wool shorn from British sheep. At the start of the eighteenth century, it accounted for around three-quarters of all British goods sold overseas, a proportion that was matched in the middle of the century even as the types of fabric changed. Indeed, woollens were Britain's largest export every single year, until cotton cloth took over in the final years of the eighteenth century. The enduring value of woollen cloth was important for providing profitable employment for the nation's clothiers and merchants, and wool served as a connecting thread through so many activities across the country. Britain's textile industry depended on raw materials and provisions supplied from the fields and pastures of landowners across the country; it also stimulated the import of dyes and other materials from across Europe, the Mediterranean, and a wider world of trade that tied woollen manufacturers to the exploitation of land in Africa, America and Asia. In turn, ongoing demand for raw wool boosted Britain's farms and encouraged the rotation of livestock and crops that avoided environmental degradation and boosted agricultural yields. As farms became more productive, more workers could leave the rural world behind and live in urban areas that were increasingly the site of the most sophisticated manufacturing ventures. The cloth that was eventually produced might be sold in markets overseas, with everything from luxury goods to essential materials returning to Britain to be sold to British consumers.

The woollen industry was Britain's golden fleece, the source of so much wealth and work for manufacturers across the country even as the sale of raw wool benefited the nation's landowners. Efforts to produce goods for a global clientele revolutionised how these goods were produced, how they were designed and where they were sold. The industry tied together landowners, manufacturers and merchants from across Britain, fostering innovation in Yorkshire and Norfolk as much as in London or Bristol. Much of this process was made possible by Britain's environment. Inventiveness and improvement were necessary for economic progress, and even in poor conditions these could help people grow a little bit more even in the most inhospitable soils and to make the most of whatever materials they had available. Exchange, too, could make up for some missing ingredients, and British capitalists would certainly find ways to profit from importing agricultural products that they were unable to grow at home. However, for building an industrial economy, it certainly helped that many of the materials needed could be obtained easily nearby. According to the ever-keen clothier Carter, Britain's wealth and power lay in profitably exploiting the natural abundance of its islands. No other country, he lovingly told his readers, had 'such variety of staple commodities within itself, and in such abundance' as the 'hundred native commodities, which produce a thousand sorts of manufactures' available in Britain. 'If those advantages were duly improved', then the future was bright indeed, and Britain would become a market for 'the whole world'.[54]

CHAPTER 3

# DESCENT INTO DARKNESS

## Mining and Metallurgy

Britain's capitalists by no means limited themselves to extracting wealth from the fertile soils of their homeland, and for those who looked quite literally beneath the surface there were plentiful opportunities to be taken. Britain was endowed with extraordinarily varied and abundant mineral resources and the conquest of this underground treasure was vital for the development of its industrial economy. Mining and selling coal, tin, iron, copper or other minerals could turn a tidy profit, and the importance of these commodities went far beyond their first sale. They fuelled Britain's furnaces and supplied its metallurgical industries where they were transformed into hoes and ploughs for planting new crops, into bolts and gears for turning the nation's new machinery, and into guns and shot for protecting its trade and seizing new territories.

Britain's capitalists certainly played a key part in extracting, processing and transporting this subterranean wealth across the country. However, its foundations were laid in the bedrock millions of years before the first humans laid hands on them. Born in the crushing chaos of colliding continents, Britain's islands carried the legacies of an eventful geological past that had raised and flattened mountains, swamped coastlines only to see them re-emerge as stark white cliffs, and eventually dragged the island from near the equator to the temperate climes of the North Atlantic. Repeated and violent tectonic events transformed what had once been rich river deltas and tropical jungles into vast coal deposits across Britain, while layer upon layer of rock formations butted against each other to give shape to hills, valleys, rivers and plains, leaving generous deposits of copper, tin and other minerals in their wake. By the time humans arrived around 400,000 years ago, the planet had begun to settle down, but what was left was a remarkably diverse geological environment seemingly tailor-made to underpin a complex industrial economy. To take advantage of it, though, Britain's miners and makers of metal needed to change how they approached their businesses, using technology and hard labour to tear these precious materials from the ground and to turn them into valued goods ready for market.

Many commentators who set out visions for improving Britain's wealth and power were well aware of the natural cornucopia that lay beneath their feet. Among them was Edward Chamberlayne, one of the founding fellows of the Royal Society who had travelled extensively in Europe. In his popular book *The Present State of England*, reprinted multiple times in the final decades of the seventeenth century, he lauded Britain's fertility, power, good governance and glory. 'Though we have no mines of gold', Chamberlayne noted, 'the many mines we have of other metals' were a source of pride. Cornish tin mines had been 'famous from all antiquity', Chamberlayne claimed, and 'long before the Romans' arrival' Britons had traded tin 'with the Greeks and Phoenicians'. It was 'no less wonderful to observe what abundant supplies of fuel are yearly sent up from the coal mines of Newcastle' to London, a resource so vital that it was 'hard to conjecture how this city could subsist before the discovery of this great mine'. In 'other parts of the north of this country' there was 'pit coal of a bituminous nature', well suited for industrial work. Iron extraction in Kent and Yorkshire was only surpassed by that in the Forest of Dean which, by the seventeenth century, was so extensive and had consumed so much fuel it made 'those woods very thin, in respect of what they have been formerly'. Elsewhere, copper mines in Cumberland, Shropshire and Richmondshire prospered, just as lead mining enriched Staffordshire, Denbighshire and Derbyshire. Taken together, Chamberlayne concluded 'there is surely no nation better stored'. In the search for wealth, British capitalists quickly learned to embrace the baser things in life.[1]

## BASE FOUNDATIONS

Despite plentiful reserves of useful minerals, enterprising industrialists could not simply head to these regions, stoop down and pick up the earth's bounty to take for sale at the local market. Nature did not give up its mineral abundance so easily and mining was a brutal business. Throughout the seventeenth and eighteenth centuries, a range of methods were deployed, some more complex than others. Where close to the surface, it was possible for workmen to clear the earth 'and dig the coal under their feet and carry it out in wheel-barrows', but this was not typical. Where seams outcropped on or near the slopes of a hill or valley, they could be worked by digging into the slope as much as possible before the hillside collapsed. Once this happened, or when the seam was further from the surface, miners would drive a tunnel – known as 'in-gaun-e'en' (ingoing eyes) in Scotland, and in Cumberland as bear-mouths – into the hillside. If seams were only slightly deeper, some twenty feet beneath the surface, miners dug out what were known as beehive or bell-pits. In these, miners would descend by rope down narrow shafts to rip coal from around the seam, with coal or ore hauled back to the surface in baskets. To save money, the crudest pits of this sort were not built with supporting pillars, and miners simply had to judge how far they could go before the roof collapsed on them. Simple pits like these were common across Britain and were used by small-scale and the largest collieries alike. Even as mining technology advanced in the eighteenth century, they remained a cheap and miserable option, especially when new industrial activities like copper or iron smelting made untouched seams suddenly much more profitable in areas like south Wales that had previously been too far from major markets.[2]

In sites that had already been dug, or where minerals were buried even deeper, mines were larger and more complex. Tunnels dug horizontally into hillsides grew into major enterprises when the cost of supports and facilities were worth the effort. At the largest scale, such as in Llanelli in Wales, tunnels so large that three or four horsemen could ride into them together were excavated by the eighteenth century. Where this was the case, the mines became sophisticated undertakings, with extensive supports, drainage systems and ventilation shafts needed to make them viable. Elsewhere, miners turned to deeper vertical shafts that reached far beyond those of the shallower bell-pits, sometimes descending hundreds of feet. In part, this was to reach seams further from the surface, but they also helped increase efficiency. Looking back in 1705, John Spedding, the steward of coal mines in Cumberland, lamented that his forebears had been 'very ignorant in the manner of working their coals and only got some small quantities' which 'were easy to come by', rather than employing more effective shaft and tunnel systems. In the eighteenth century, the most advanced collieries in north-east England used horse-powered engines to draw baskets up shafts 600 feet deep after they had been filled with coal by the men toiling below. Later still, these engines would be improved further with steam-powered systems.[3]

No matter the technologies employed, extracting coal and ore required hazardous, hard labour in dank and claustrophobic conditions. Digging shafts became easier with the introduction of boring, which used rotating iron rods on a beam to cut downward, but excavating pits and tunnels always depended on the muscle of labourers wielding pick and shovel. When they met harder rocks, digging became even more treacherous, and workers often suffered serious injuries from flying fragments of stone. Using gunpowder for blasting, which had been introduced to England by German miners, helped overcome this challenge and grew in popularity around the turn of the eighteenth century. Once shafts had reached their target, hewers descended on makeshift ladders or simple winches into the narrow confines below, working their way through precarious tunnels that extended steadily deeper as mine owners drove them on for profit and to keep pace with demand. So tight that miners had to stoop or crawl, hewers worked hunched or even lying down, wearing little clothing due to the oppressive heat. In dusty coal pits, a skilled hewer toiled alone, relying on their skill, athleticism and stamina to cut the largest blocks of coal that they could. Others then loaded the precious cargo into baskets, which were dragged and carried to the surface, up steep inclines or makeshift ladders, often by children. Once above ground, metal ores needed washing, breaking and crushing, tasks

*2. Miners at work. Note the hewers working on their knees by candlelight in the highest tunnels and the use of the hand-pulley to raise coal from one level to another.*

that likewise typically relied on brute force alone. Only after this had been done were these vital rocks and minerals loaded onto wagons or waiting boats to carry them onwards to market.[4]

Working deep underground, miners faced danger every day. Cave-ins were a constant threat. Deeper pits and tunnels were typically lined with timber that could be treated to try and make the tunnel watertight, either by using techniques similar to those for making barrels or by using clay or hemp caulking. However, the cost of buying timber and installing supports ate into the profitability of any mine and, invariably, owners concluded that a balance had to be struck between the costs of protecting workers and the decision to abandon a tunnel for a more favourable location. Pillars of coal could be left to support roofs, but this could mean leaving large amounts of the valuable commodity behind. To boost profits, smaller pillars could be left and more coal removed, but the risk of roof falls then increased considerably. While there were, of course, ruthless owners who undermined the safety measures in their mines, workers whose earnings were tied to their output were also known to risk cave-ins. Another risk was the build-up of methane gas, known as firedamp, which could lead to deadly explosions, while blackdamp, a dangerous mix of carbon dioxide and nitrogen, made it difficult to breathe. Ventilation was rudimentary at best, with simple shafts to the surface or hand-pulled bellows offering only some small level of improvement.[5]

While skilled hewers, borers and viewers could demand higher salaries than some of their peers in other sectors, life working in the pits for even the most talented labourer remained a dangerous and merciless profession even as new technologies were adopted. Technology did not remove the threat of pit collapses or explosions so much as mean that when they happened, they did so deeper underground with more workers present. J. C., author of the *Compleat Collier* (1708), who witnessed an explosion in Gateshead in north-east England that killed thirty people in 1705, noted dispassionately that 'there was one strange thing in it . . . that a youth of 15 or 16 years was blown up the pit and shaft and carried by the blast about 40 yards'. The victims were mostly adult men but also included the children of workmen present. Only three years later, disaster struck the Fatfield colliery near Durham, when 'a sudden eruption of violent fire came from the mouths of the three pits with a noise like the firing of a cannon. Sixty-nine people lost their lives.' The shaft was 342 feet deep, but still two men and a woman were hurled from it by the power of the explosion. Daniel Defoe, travelling to the region shortly afterwards, 'had an account of a melancholy accident' which described how the blast had been 'like 1000 barrels of gunpowder going off' and 'made the very earth tremble for some miles around'. It is impossible to count all the injuries and deaths that consumed Britain's mining workforce, let alone the long-term health implications of their work, but accounts like these expose the violent and sudden end that all miners risked. In the decades that followed, more explosions and more deaths occurred in mines across Britain, taking a terrible toll on miners and their communities.[6]

Even if they avoided injuries from collapses or explosions, these working conditions left a painful and lasting legacy on miners' bodies. Arthritis and musculoskeletal trauma from years working in contorted positions was common, and damage to hands was so widespread it became a well-known sign of the miner's trade. More insidious still was the impact of inhaling coal and other mineral dusts. Impossible to avoid, miniscule particles would settle in a miner's lungs where it could neither be removed nor destroyed, which could lead to pneumoconiosis, a condition that made it difficult to breathe. In extreme cases, so much coal dust was inhaled it would stain a miner's lungs black. Miners were disparaged for this ill health, the dirtiness of their work, and the perceived impact it had on their character, despite their key role in Britain's economic prosperity. One customs officer, seeking men to press into the navy in the final decades of the seventeenth century, sought out coal workers in Newcastle only to conclude that it 'would do more harm than good . . . to have such nasty creatures on board' the King's warships. Technologies like the steam engine became widespread later in the century, marking a major further advancement in Britain's mining history, but this by no means diminished the need for hard and difficult labour.[7]

Pushing workers already at their physical limits would not extract more coal or ore. Instead, building a bigger and more profitable mining industry depended on finding ways to dig in increasingly difficult locations. This introduced technical problems that earlier generations had never seriously faced, and three challenges were particularly notable. First, coal pits filled with water that required constant draining or pumping out so that workers could reach the richest seams. This only got harder as pits got deeper. Second, ores and coal were heavy, cumbersome loads, and the more that was dug the more difficult and expensive it was to transport. Hauling wagons stuffed to bursting over soggy ground was no mean feat, and if the distance to the nearest port or city was too far, the logistics quickly became untenable. Finally, separating metals from ore was a difficult and wasteful process that often led to wildly varying degrees of quality. British industry's seemingly insatiable demand for coal and metals (and for coal to fuel the furnaces that produced metals) meant that there was a considerable incentive to overcome these challenges, but doing so required new ways of doing business, new technologies, and the widening exploitation of the environment into places previously untouched by pick and shovel.[8]

By the sixteenth century, English mines had already reached depths of around 150 feet, but these had nothing on the cinnabar mines in Almadén in Spain or Idria in Slovenia that descended some 400 feet, nor the most extensive mines working argentiferous copper ores in Saxony, Bohemia and Hungary that depended on workers struggling 600 feet or more under the earth. At such depths, powerful pumps turned by waterwheel or horsepower were essential for pumping out water. Even in the seventeenth century, though, such devices were hardly ubiquitous and, more commonly, mining in Britain, Europe and the wider world remained an affair undertaken closer to the surface, with increasing production dependent on the discovery of previously unmined seams. Britain's mining and metallurgical industries expanded rapidly in the century after 1660 by adopting and adapting existing technologies and ways of working that were already used in the more sophisticated mines. Knowledge at home and abroad about mining had been honed over the previous decades and centuries, and in some parts of Britain mines were already using the most advanced techniques to extract large volumes. Improving techniques for draining water made it possible to delve deeper underground, while more sophisticated ventilation somewhat diminished the risk of noxious and volatile gases.[9]

The industry benefited from the widespread use of business practices that helped groups of investors work together for common profit – usually through partnerships that included two or more people. As some of the very largest industrial activities in the early modern world, mining and metallurgical works were among the first businesses in Europe to embrace joint-stock financing that helped pool capital. As early as the thirteenth century, parts of Europe had seen companies of miners that worked and owned mines together replaced with absentee shareholders. By the sixteenth century, the ownership of mines in Saxony, Bohemia and other technologically sophisticated and capital-intensive regions was divided among hundreds of shareholders.

Mercantile families in Leipzig, Nuremberg, Augsburg and other German towns – most famously the Fuggers – capitalised on ventures across Europe, owning mining interests stretching from Spain to Sweden. Separated from the management of their mines, which was left to supervisors appointed for the task, investors like these were able to sit back and receive dividends in cash or ore, sometimes without even stepping foot in a general meeting of the enterprise, let alone the pits themselves. In many parts of Europe, rulers supported this arrangement, granting monopolistic privileges to investors and experts to exploit certain metals, seams or techniques. In this way, they could call on private investment and innovation to open and expand mines that were of significant benefit both in terms of direct taxation on their production as well as their extraction of vital commodities for the wider economy.[10]

In Britain, though, the royal family had historically taken a minimal interest in the 'Mines Royal', probably because the precious metals that particularly attracted the interest of their continental counterparts were not a common feature of the island's geological bounty. While this may have held back the adoption of advanced mining methods in England and Wales in the sixteenth century, by the eighteenth it left space for Britain's capitalists to profit spectacularly from copper, iron and coal. Rather than anything like a national mining administration, mines in Scotland, England and Wales were left to private enterprise to exploit. Earlier efforts by Queen Elizabeth I to launch companies to expand mining had not been particularly successful, although they did help speed the diffusion of continental mining practices into Britain. Consequent proponents of royally backed mining operations struggled to set their plans in motion. Some royals did try to get in on the act, such as plans by Prince Rupert in 1670 to raise £4,000 for leasing the Mines Royal in Wales alongside 'certain smelting and refining mills', but these achieved little. Gold and silver mines were controlled on behalf the crown, as were mines on royal estates, but these were few and far between, and in 1688, the Mines Royal Act lifted the crown monopoly on many base metals, greatly incentivising landowners to exploit previously untapped mineral resources. The relative lack of interest from British royals to control mining for more common metals and coal meant that there were plenty of opportunities for landlords, mine proprietors and investors to take advantage of whatever ores and coal they could. By the time these commodities became more profitable, the balance of political power had swung considerably from the royal family to the landowners that occupied Parliament, and they had little incentive to change things.[11]

The potential for profit was considerable and the allure of Britain's mineral wealth aroused the curiosity of investors and natural philosophers alike. Various authors in the earlier seventeenth century imbued the earth with living qualities, or with a religious or philosophical aura. Others entertained the idea that coal and ores could be grown by 'manuring' the surface with water or sulphur. However, knowledge was improving all the time, and the founding of the Royal Society in 1660 had raised the profile of natural scientists interested in mining. Within a few years, publications about underground gases and explosions had brought attention to these mining challenges, and books like Dr Robert Plot's *Natural History of Staffordshire* (1686) detailed the geological environment in the area and provided descriptions and drawings of minerals. Plot's conclusions that a dinosaur fossil belonged to a giant deceased human, or that the source of springs were underground channels carrying water inland from the sea, are a helpful reminder of the limits of contemporary academic study.[12]

The practical knowledge of experienced workers was more important for the success of extractive enterprises. Miners who cut through layers of earth in search of the earth's treasures had an intimate acquaintance with its features. Skilled 'viewers' who could help landowners identify and exploit riches that might lie unknown beneath their feet were highly sought after. The more unscrupulous were able to take eager landowners for a ride, searching in places where no coal was likely to be found and charging by the yard for boring shafts that served no purpose. In general, though, the earning power of professional prospectors depended on their success rate; a reputation for under-delivery would spread quickly. As was the case with agricultural improvements, workers' rules of thumb and practical knowledge were often more effective than the formal training or theoretical frameworks of natural philosophers. Some of the biggest leaps forward were made only when these two forms of knowledge – theoretical and practical – were brought together. Unlocking the secrets of the earth required a deeper understanding of what was going on beneath the surface, and mining firms brought together people from different social and professional backgrounds who had the right combination of skills to successfully improve the industry.[13]

It was in this context that new ventures seeking to take advantage of Britain's mineral wealth were launched around the turn of the eighteenth century. Many easily accessible mines in areas with existing mining industries had already been exploited, and simply hoping that new veins of precious commodities would reveal themselves was hardly a strategy for success. One option was to process metals in locations where multiple resources were available together – such as the combination of coal and iron ore in Coalbrookdale, where Abraham Darby built the first profitable coke-fired blast furnace in 1709. But this perfect combination of extraction and consumption was unusual: mines could not be moved nor grown and had the unfortunate habit of being found far from the ultimate markets in which their proceeds would be sold. These only became tenable once proprietors were confident that their integration into wider regional or even international economic systems was worth the effort. This took time, it took money, and it took a clear understanding of how to transport and sell coal and metals across Britain and further afield.

## COAL, COPPER AND BURNING CASH

In the final years of the seventeenth century, one of the most ambitious plans for extracting more wealth from Britain's rich foundations came from Sir Humphrey Mackworth. He helped found, manage and bankrupt a joint-stock company called the Mine Adventurers, and employed novel approaches to radically expand the industrial output of his own estates. Like many mining proprietors, Mackworth was never a miner. He grew up in Shropshire before studying law at Oxford. Yet, he came to manage extensive mining interests through his wife Mary Evans, who inherited estates worth approximately £12,000 in Gnoll that included leases over almost all the coal mines of Neath. This area of south Wales was ideally suited for a new combination of mining and metallurgical industries that brought ores and coal together for smelting. Good-quality coal could be reached with relative ease by using simple mines dug into the hillside or vertical shafts, which did not improve the working conditions for miners, but did reduce the need for more complex and expensive machinery that ate into profits. Refining metal ores required a lot of coal, and this was only needed to be carried short distances to the banks of the rivers Tawe and Neath, where small boats could deliver copper from Cornwall and Devon almost to the doorstep of the smelters. In Cornwall, the opening of new mines occasioned the migration of whole communities of miners, moving to where work could be found until a pit was exhausted before moving onto another. Often, the ore they extracted wasn't processed locally but was transported further afield: the weight of coal needed for the smelting process was much higher, and it made economic sense to carry ore to where this vital energy source could be obtained. Following this simple rule, copper works in Neath were notably cheaper than competing smelters like the Redbrook works in Gloucestershire: in Wales it cost £850 to smelt ten tons of copper, while the English alternative cost £914. Plus, when the smelting process was complete, it was only a short coastal voyage to nearby manufacturers in Cardiff and Bristol, or along the River Severn and into the growing industrial towns of the Midlands.[14]

Mackworth's newly inherited estates were well positioned to seize these opportunities. In 1695, he built his first copper-smelting furnaces, which he quickly expanded by reopening the dilapidated Melincryddan copper works nearby. These sites were ideal for linking coal extraction with copper ore deliveries, and observers noted that 'his men may run the coal, with wheelbarrows, into the very furnaces, and bring the ore by water within a stone's cast of the work'. To boost productivity, Mackworth adopted some unusual techniques. First, he used cofferdams (dams built around the mine works to stop water entering) to alleviate the demands for drainage, 'thereby preventing the charges of water engines' to pump water from the shafts. Second, he strapped sails to the top of wagons to carry coal from the mines, creating 'sailing-wagons' that, according to one incredibly supportive commentator, were ten or twenty times as efficient than those that relied on horses or men to haul them to the nearby river. These 'sailing-engines on land, driven by wind' had been constructed 'not for any curiosity, or vain applause, but for real profit', and were widely advertised as evidence of Mackworth's innovative brilliance. 'The poor miners and labourers' employed at his works were also 'punctually paid', which may have helped incentivise his workforce to push harder and deeper to slightly improve their incomes. As Mackworth noted in his diary, 'several persons observed' that he was 'too fond of these new designs', but his enthusiasm paid off. Quickly, the works were churning out copper and generating profits of £600 per year. This 'great profit made of copper' added to Mackworth's 'great vent secured for his own coal' at his own works and 'abroad in the West of England', where he traded coal directly for copper ore. By 1700, through these acquisitions and improvements, Mackworth had a well-established mining and smelting operation under way. While sailing coal down Welsh hillsides caught the imagination of visitors, the most valuable feature of Mackworth's approach was the efficient interconnectedness of extractive and industrial processes.[15]

Unlike many of his rival smelters, Mackworth did not initially invest in Cornish copper mines as a means of further interlinking his investment. This was certainly not due to a lack of ambition. Instead, in 1698, he took control of a scheme aimed at creating nothing less than a 'Welsh Potosí' – invoking the famous silver mine in Bolivia that had flooded the Spanish empire with silver over a century before. To achieve this goal, Mackworth spectacularly overextended himself by acquiring Sir Carbery Pryse's Gogerddan estates in Cardiganshire for £16,400, where rich mineral deposits had been found only a few years earlier at Esgair Hir. Forced to turn to a wider investing public to fund the a new mine, Mackworth established the Mine Adventurers company, opening offices at Lincoln's Inn in London where he set out to entice financial heavy hitters and speculative stockholders alike.[16]

To drum up interest, the new company flooded London with printed accounts describing the remarkable riches that would flow from Wales, if only investors would back its vision. In *An Essay on the Value of the Mines* (1698), William Waller (an investor in Mackworth's new company who had stewarded Pryse's efforts to establish the mine) expressed how he had been 'much concerned to see so great a treasure lie dead and unwrought'. Happily, though, Waller had the 'fortune to travel to Neath' where he met with Mackworth and observed his copper works and coal mine. Here, novel management 'not seen before in any part of this Kingdom', coupled with Mackworth's 'judgement in matters of law' and 'generous disposition for the public good', convinced Waller that this was the man for whom he had been searching. 'The several improvements I observed at his works', including the coffer-dams and sail-wagons as well as others 'kept as secrets', convinced Waller 'what his genius is capable of in matters of that nature'. He was confident that supporting Mackworth would finally realise profits for himself and unlock the value of a mine that would be 'as famous in foreign countries, as most other mines in the world'.[17]

*The Mine-Adventure* (1698) set out Mackworth's own vision for the new enterprise. With 'eight large veins of silver, lead and copper ore lying near together in one mountain', the opportunity 'it is presumed, cannot be paralleled in any part of the Christian world'. Taking advantage of this bounty required 'raising a large stock of £20,000' which he claimed was necessary for 'the working and carrying on of the said mineral works, to the great advantage of the King and Kingdom'. Mackworth argued that the proposed £20,000 would go a long way and lead to astronomical profits. First, he suggested that while it often cost up to £7,000 to reach a single vein in other circumstances, the close proximity of multiple veins together would considerably reduce the overall charge, representing a 'conveniency' that would 'be valued at a very high rate by all persons experienced in the art of mining'. Similarly, the closeness and richness of the veins would easily absorb the employment of more workmen. With each miner pushed individually to their limit, the number that could work at any one time was often the key limiting factor in the productivity of mines, and Mackworth believed that if a mining company 'can raise and employ five times the stock, they will have and receive five times the profit; for their gains are greater or less in proportion to the number of hands they employ'. Citing Waller's text as evidence, Mackworth suggested that a stock of £4,000 would employ 120 men who could extract 3,000 tons of ore each year, which 'will yield a clear profit' of £14,100. The proposed stock, at £20,000, would therefore be enough to employ 600 men and would catapult the company's profits to £75,500 per year – a ridiculously high rate of return to promise even in the heady days of investment schemes in the 1690s. Elsewhere in the text, he suggested profits would be even higher. This scale of operation, he assured his readers, was not overly ambitious, and he described that the Keswick mine in Cumberland had employed four thousand workers, while the mine at Potosí 'has lasted one hundred and fifty years with twenty thousand men'. Once rich seams of ore were found, exploiting labour was the surest way to maximise extraction. To sum up the offer, he concluded that 'this adventure will be profitable to the fortunate, advantageous to the public good, charitable to the poor, and cannot be unprofitable to any person whatsoever'.[18]

Building on these bold claims and with staunch support from a well-connected group of investors, the Mine Adventurers was incorporated in 1704, six years after initially raising funds as an unincorporated company. Its charter named forty-two participants, with Mackworth as the company's deputy governor and de facto leader. Among their number were the Duke of Leeds Thomas Osborne, MP, and former Lord Mayor of London Sir William Ashurst, banker Sir Richard Hoare, merchant and fellow of the Royal Society Robert Nelson, and the court painter Sir Godfrey Kneller. It was, as these few examples suggest, an organisation that drew on networks of interest, as well as financial and political capital, which reached the very highest tiers of English society. Their connection was not only economic and some partners were long-standing Mackworth allies with common political agendas, while others worked together in the Society for Promoting Christian Knowledge and the Society for the Propagation of the Gospel, organisations that were part of Britain's empire-building project in North America and 'desirous that Christian Knowledge be propagated in the plantations'. Most of the men listed in the charter were landowners like Mackworth but also held wider commercial interests. At least eight of the members had existing interests in Welsh lead mining, more than half held financial stocks in the Bank of England and other banks, and between them they had invested in trade with Europe, North America, the Mediterranean, Asia and in transatlantic slavery. Among this group, at least, the company's composition represented an enviable mix of people who could contribute not only capital but also an understanding of the wider economic landscape – often an important factor for success.[19]

However, in the frenetic investing environment of the early 1700s, interest in the Mine Adventurers exploded. In addition to promises of astronomical profits, the proposition had been made even more attractive by the sale of shares through an elaborate lottery system, in which holders of winning tickets would obtain shares, while losing tickets would still receive 6% interest from the mine's profits. Despite warning from commentators like Thomas Bateman that the proposals 'have fiction for their foundation', hundreds of mostly speculative investors piled in. The new investors encompassed a broad slice of wealthy British society, but far fewer participants now brought commercial or industrial experience with them. While the stock did attract some of the biggest names in London's financial elite, who owned large and diversified portfolios, it was avoided by many others. A handful more investors were merchants or craftsmen, but people with metallurgical or mining skills, like smiths or refiners, were notably absent among the company's owners. It did attract a surprisingly high number of religious scholars or people who held positions in the Church of England, but these were no more likely to have other business pursuits. Most of the company's investors were landowners who had not invested in other stocks or trading ventures. Almost a third of investors were women (the second highest proportion in any stock during this period, after the Million Bank) who represented a great well of capital but were refused any position of power in the company. Growing stock ownership in the previous decade had led to more people owning the occasional share in a company, but the Mine Adventurers included an unusually high number of people who were inexperienced with shareholding. It is unclear whether this was because mining was deemed a less attractive investment than banking and trade or due to scepticism about Mackworth's plans, but it did not bode well for the company.[20]

Having raised more money than he had ever expected, Mackworth should have been able to set in motion his plans for the most brilliant mining operation that Britain had ever seen. This was not to be. The company did begin to excavate the mines in Wales, but these were neither as rich nor as easy pickings as had been hoped. Costs quickly spiralled as draining water from the pits proved harder than expected and the company burned through its cash reserves at breakneck speed. The works did introduce new mining practices to Wales: Mackworth brought skilled miners and smelters from Shropshire, his workmen cut a river and installed flood gates to allow larger ships to reach the mines, and 'an artificial waggon-way of wooden-rails' was constructed. Despite these efforts, when ore extraction did get under way, annual profits from Esgair Hir amounted to less than £1,900, rather than the tens of thousands of pounds that Mackworth had hoped. Even turning to practices like using indentured convict labour could not boost returns quickly enough.[21]

It soon became clear that the company could not possibly extract and refine enough ore to cover even the interest owed to holders of losing tickets from the lottery, let alone turn a significant profit for its shareholders. To cover the difference, the company began borrowing money and issued new shares to raise funds. An effort to set up a bank and issue its bills as semi-legal tender only led to more debts. To make matters worse, Mackworth had taken powers allowing him to dispose of the company's assets 'without account' (words which had been missed out in the published descriptions of its governance) and sunk much of this new capital into buying more mines and expanding refining capacity in the hope of profits, but these never lived up to his expectations. With little oversight from other partners or the company's investors, some of the cash raised flowed directly to Mackworth as the company leased the works he owned in Neath for refining ore and bought coal from his mines to fuel them. More mismanagement followed, and directors were accused of spreading false news to boost the share price in advance of selling their own shares. By 1707, the company had cash reserves of only £927 and owed over £33,000 to creditors. The company quickly unravelled. As a vehicle for raising capital, the Mine Adventurers was hugely effective, but the dubious lottery system, ludicrous valuation and poor governance all carried with them the seeds of its eventual demise. Only a few years after obtaining its charter, Mackworth was removed from the company in 1710, leaving behind him vast debts and mines producing far less ore than had been dreamed.[22]

Despite his expulsion from the Mine Adventurers, and the House of Commons finding him 'guilty of many notorious and scandalous frauds', Mackworth emerged relatively unscathed from the affair. He also remained committed to mining and metallurgy, but his next effort, the Company of Mineral Manufacturers, was no more able to achieve his lofty goals and ceased operations in 1719, after only six years. Ventures further afield also enticed his interest, including the slave-trading South Sea Company, which he told his brother had 'very probable expectations of real profit', and a scheme for a national fishery. He also finally invested in Cornish copper mines. Mackworth was still very wealthy, and his estates in the Neath Valley most likely benefited from the experimentation he had been able to take with the Mine Adventurers' cash, as did the wider Welsh mining industry. A wooden tramway built in Neath was the first railway in Wales, gunpowder for blasting was used there for the first time, and the company built the first coal-fired reverberatory furnace in Britain.[23]

Even before the Mine Adventurers, Mackworth's innovative streak had borne fruit. In the 1690s, he had hired Robert Lydell as chief refiner, who brought experience working in north Wales and Newcastle and had gained some level of fame by patenting a process for separating silver from lead. Soon after in Neath and following Lydell's lead, smelting copper ore mined in Cornwall was supplemented by working with lead acquired from mines in nearby Cardiganshire. Nor was Lydell the only expert brought to Wales. In 1713, Mackworth described how he was 'surrounded by Germans' who were 'preparing diverse mills, ponds, dams, and all sorts of iron engines for the works'. Further metallurgical outputs followed, and by

1720 the works were producing small amounts of silver as well as lead oxide that was sold to glassmakers and apothecaries. At the same time, the reduction of zinc ore on site for the first time allowed the production of brass, and Mackworth took advantage of the valley's surging water supply to power waterwheels in new rolling mills that could produce metal ingots as well as products like brass kettles and wire. Through these efforts, Mackworth built an industrial project that found added value in bringing together the diverse minerals that hard labour by other men brought up from his mines. It was a model that would be replicated across many types of enterprise in Britain's quickly changing economy, with the exploitation of natural resources, workers and technology tightly bound together through efforts to maximise profits.[24]

When Mackworth died in 1727, his estates passed to his son Herbert and then to his grandson, also Herbert. The two descendants were MPs for Cardiganshire continuously from 1739 to 1790, with the seat changing hands only once, in 1766, when Herbert senior died, and his son was elected in his place, holding the seat until 1790, a year before he died. After selling some assets to pay off Humphrey Mackworth's debts, the two men built on their inheritance and continued to expand and profit from their coal mines, with further diversification into providing banking services for the wider business community in south Wales. They even returned to copper smelting as the Gnoll Copper Company, producing salt boilers, pitch kettles, copper nails, and copper for brass ordnance, becoming important suppliers for the East India Company during the final decades of the century. Inheriting profitable estates was a considerable advantage for men seeking wealth and power. It was certainly easier than building a business from scratch.[25]

Humphrey Mackworth's various schemes had pushed the boundaries of what was possible in Welsh mining, driven by the hope that novel technologies like sailing-wagons or methods for separating silver from lead would increase the productivity of his operations. This was never enough to make up for the financial chaos that undermined the Mine Adventurers, but it did contribute to the eventual emergence of a phenomenally successful copper industry built on the extraction of Welsh coal. By the 1720s, Mackworth's works were among several industrial sites that had been set up in south Wales that sought to take advantage of the same confluence of coal, metals and trading links. Sometimes these works included expensive technology like waterwheels for raising water or railways for transporting coal. But just as important was the extraction of minerals from previously untouched environments, integrating different parts of the industrial system, or reducing costs at any point in the process. Rather than a giant public joint stock, Britain's booming mining and metallurgical industries came to depend on a multitude of smaller firms and partnerships. This limited the amount of capital available to any single firm, but it also meant that new entrants could more nimbly take advantage of opportunities and that partners could work more closely together and give people with technical skills a greater say in operations. In a competitive environment, efficient and effective operations were essential for survival. Partnerships enabled capitalists to draw on links across industries and regions and facilitated the impact of networked capital in ways that would have been increasingly familiar in every part of Britain.

Other ventures in south Wales and the rest of Britain were indicative of the importance of this type of business structure. In 1718, one group drew together investors from across England and Wales to found a 'company for making and manufacturing copper, brass, lead and iron with pit coal'. They had designs to lease mines from Mackworth and take advantage of his earlier efforts prospecting productive seams, even as his own plans to exploit them came apart. Dividing their undertaking into equal shares among the partners, the firm was able to raise £20,000 to fund the venture. Much of this capital was invested by sixteen landowners from Gloucestershire, Shropshire, Glamorgan and Cornwall, but the final four shareholders brought with them a deeper knowledge of the industry, as well as financial capital. These were blacksmith Thomas Forest from County Durham, carpenter Mr Watkins from Cornwall, foundry owner William Morgan from Carmarthen, and a smelter from Cumberland. Working together across social boundaries, the group were well prepared to take advantage of the opportunities left in Mackworth's wake.[26]

Nearby, in Swansea, another partnership between Dr John Lane and John Pollard built the town's first copper works in 1717. Living in Bristol, Lane had trained in Oxford and Leiden and ran a successful business as a medical doctor. He also had a keen interest in experimental metallurgy. This combined fruitfully with Pollard's experience operating copper mines in Cornwall, which provided the partnership with practical knowledge of shipping copper ore for smelting nearer the sources of Welsh coal. Lane had attempted to establish a copper smelter in nearby Ty-llwyd a few years earlier, with little success, but the new partnership was much more effective and was a first step in the rapid expansion of Swansea's copper industry and a booming maritime trade that carried Welsh copper across the British empire. Extractive industries needed to do more than raise capital, obtain mines and hire workers to undertake the brutal work of tearing coal and ores from under the earth if they were to be successful. They needed to understand how to connect multiple stages of the industrial process, whether controlling wider supply chains, smelting ore themselves, or taking part in the manufacturing process of finished goods. The coal mines of Wales were ideally placed to fuel the flames of its nascent metallurgical industries, and their profitability was not dependent on just improving the efficiency of the mines but connecting them with Britain's growing industrial system.[27]

## MOVING MOUNTAINS

For owners of the vast coalfields in north-east England, linking to metallurgical industry was not their main goal. Their main market was London, where coal was the main fuel consumed by the city's huge urban population. Increasing profits required improvements to existing mining enterprises. By the early seventeenth century the area's mining industry was already among the most technologically sophisticated in the world: competition and the agglomeration of mining expertise had led to numerous advances. In 1708, a guide to mining called *The Compleat Collier* by J. C. set out in intricate detail how the great collieries in north-east England functioned. Many of the technological improvements that had boosted their productivity related to fairly simple labour-saving devices, such as using sleds for hauling coal through tunnels, or having horses available to quickly carry coal away from the entrance of the pits. Around the same time, wheeled carts and trolleys became more common for hauling coal underground, and rails were laid in tunnels to further improve the efficiency of transportation, though this was only economical in the largest pits once it was clear the tracks would stay in use.[28]

The most advanced techniques related to drainage. Where leaks could not be plugged and drainage trenches were incapable of carrying water away, miners would dig another shaft next to the flooded one and to a slightly greater depth, into which excess water could be drained by 'horses or water wheels, as there is a conveniency for it, that so the water may not follow' the miners as they continued their work. For J. C. this was a far more effective method of dealing with a substantial flow of water than attempting to staunch it by timber lining or tubbing. But it was expensive. These practices led to the construction of some impressive machinery in north-east England. At the Fatfield colliery in Lumley Park, reportedly the largest in England in the 1660s, the pits were drained by two engines powered by waterwheels that were constructed two and three storeys high to provide enough power. When water was too scarce, horses were harnessed to the machines. By around 1750, in nearby Ravensworth colliery, drainage was provided by a complex system that drew up water in buckets. Here, 'Sir Thomas Liddell, a most ingenious gentleman', had erected three waterwheels to power the system. The first was erected 'upon pillars like a windmill, pretty high above the ground, from which the falling water makes the second go close above the ground. And to make the water fall to the third'. Complicated systems like these were expensive though and required considerable expertise to design, install and operate.[29]

By the eighteenth century, coal miners in other parts of Britain were sending experts to Newcastle to learn about these advanced techniques for extracting coal. Viewers of the Tyneside works were a prominent feature in the development of Scotland's coal mining industry and there was significant dependence on English experience in the most advanced Scottish mines. In 1709, the Earl of Mar sent his colliery manager to Newcastle to obtain drainage plans. In 1724, Sir John Clerk of Penecuik travelled from Edinburgh to see how mining was carried out, and during the trip he met with Martin Triewald, a steam engine engineer, whose knowledge was then carried back north. Likewise, in 1754, William Brown supervised the installation of an underground railway at Bo'ness colliery on the Duke of Hamilton's estates, having established himself as an expert in the field through his work in the Tyneside collieries. These exchanges, much like the partnerships in south Wales that helped launch a new copper industry during this period, facilitated the movement of technological knowledge and practical expertise from region to region and from industry to industry.[30]

Extracting coal was only one step in the chain that linked Newcastle's mines to their ultimate consumers. Other stages in the process started as soon as coal reached the surface and included its transport to waiting keels (small boats used to carry coal), its ongoing transport to major shipping ports, and its eventual sale on the nationally integrated market. Local landowners certainly took care to improve their own estates by employing techniques and machinery like those described above. However, they also maintained institutional structures that intentionally cut them off from engaging in deeper levels of partnership with people from elsewhere in Britain, with the intention of monopolising production. In Newcastle, the local Incorporated Company of Hostmen dominated and governed the coal trade in the seventeenth century, imposing strict prescriptions that could make it incredibly difficult for investors or experts from outside the region to take part on an equal footing. They did not operate as a single joint stock or partnership, but they did insist on their members abiding by common rules and regulations. In 1688, when King James II sought to encourage Newcastle's company to accept new members, they refused, arguing that 'the persons of quality and gentry of these northern counties put their sons apprentices to serve and abide ten years' before they were allowed to join. Letting in people who had not would diminish the value of the training. They also feared they would lose the wealth that they obtained through their monopoly. Local governance like this had its benefits, but it also limited new investment coming into the region's coal mines and infrastructure. By 1700, the Hostmen's monopoly over the coal trade from Newcastle was beginning to fracture. Their privileges meant that non-members could not trade coal from Newcastle but there was nothing – beyond the practical difficulties of carrying coal across the rugged land of north-east England – to stop collieries transporting coal directly to other ports. The Hostmen did not own every mine in the region but, so long as they ensured most of the coal was carried to Newcastle, then their monopoly would remain intact.[31]

It was in this context that William Cotesworth entered the scene, who aggressively pursued his agenda to profit from the wider Northumberland and Durham coalfield. In particular, he focused on sites where coal could be carried to the River Wear or elsewhere for export, avoiding Newcastle and the monopolistic organisation that would never allow him to become a member. In doing so, he contributed to the decline of traditional guild and local corporate control that had previously regulated much of Britain's economy. As these structures began to crack, capital began to circulate more freely across different sectors, and people like Cotesworth were able to take advantage. The son of a yeoman, born in 1668 in nearby Gateshead, the port town just over the river from Newcastle, Cotesworth had not inherited the large estates and mines that the richest members of the region's elite were able to call their own. Nor was he part of the Newcastle mercantile elite who leased mines and dominated the coal trade between the city and London. Instead, he was and remained something of an outsider, eventually coming to use this to his advantage.[32]

During his youth, Cotesworth apprenticed as a tallow candle maker before making his fortune as a merchant. Having started out trading goods like flax, tallow, hops and soap with markets in north Germany and the Baltic, Cotesworth rapidly expanded his business interests. By 1705, he was selling sugar grown by enslaved labour on British plantations, purchasing indigo from the East India Company or from Spanish ships recently returned from the Caribbean, and shipping redwood (another dye) to Newcastle from London. A few years later he was selling tobacco in Newcastle, which was almost certainly sourced from Virginia, which joined an array of global goods that he had added to his core business in more typical staples. As well as making considerable profits, Cotesworth's trading experience left him with a deep understanding of how Newcastle's and London's commercial interests intersected. After initially being excluded from the trading benefits of the local monopolies, he would have been well aware that the most technologically advanced mines were not, necessarily, the ones that produced the most profit for their owners. Controlling more of the market and keeping prices high were just as important.[33]

In the north-east, Cotesworth had used this knowledge when selecting investments. He acquired both a salt works, from which he delivered salt to the Navy Victualling Office, and a colliery. He also married well, and he persuaded his wealthy brother-in-law William Ramsay (a member of the Hostmen) to purchase collieries in Gateshead and Wickham in 1712, which passed to Cotesworth only four years later when Ramsay died. In 1719, he bought the Stella and Winlaton collieries in partnership with the Lincolnshire MP Joseph Banks, after they had been forfeited by previous owners during the Jacobite rebellion. By 1722, rents from his properties provided an income that exceeded £4,500. Not all of Cotesworth's accounts have survived, but they reveal a quickly growing business and throughout the 1710s he was selling around £1,800 of coal each year. New pits and repairs to existing facilities kept production high, and the profits absorbed the costs of excavating in new areas, such as the £409 3s 9d spent in 1725 on sinking and working the Barlofield pit, as well as the cost of pumping out water and laying a new branch of a wagonway. Cotesworth was not always present during these developments and spent much of his time in London. However, as an absentee mine owner he was able to maintain a high level of communication with his agents in the north, much as he would with factors serving his mercantile interests overseas. Thomas Sisson, who was employed by Cotesworth as his steward at the Gateshead Park estate, played a key role in coordinating his business activities. These related not just to coal but to Cotesworth's wider interests in the north-east, including salt, transport infrastructure, rents and fines from tenants, land acquisition, hiring contractors, disposing of waste, and farming.[34]

This was all achieved despite what seem to have been considerable efforts on the part of some local landowners to forcefully resist the expansion of Cotesworth's business: he was beaten up by his rivals and had his life threatened on several occasions. Among the most audacious attempts of this sort came in 1720, when one Albert Silvertop sent men to steal a coal mine that the Gateshead merchant had sunk in Winlaton. James Weatherby, who had been appointed to oversee the work, had extracted 130 tons from one pit and was excavating another when 'Silvertop and his overmen' came at night and 'took off our ropes' and threatened Cotesworth's employees when they tried to stop him. After this sabotage, Silvertop went a step further, opening a new shaft to the same seam that Weatherby was working on, 'notwithstanding the great charge we had been at in winning the same', and took away all the coals that were available. At another pit, Silvertop was more aggressive still and 'sent his workmen at an unseasonable time of night and took possession of our workings', throwing away Cotesworth's workers' gear in the process. This ran counter to the customary norms of business in the north-eastern coalfields, where the first person to dig a pit traditionally had the right to extract coal from the site, but Cotesworth was not part of this community and was forced to 'quiet them by due course of law' to re-establish his control over the sites. Other efforts to stop Cotesworth were more dramatic and criminal still. In 1725, his gardener and butler colluded to dose his morning cup of chocolate with arsenic, an attempted murder that left him seriously ill. It was never proven, but suspicions were raised that their murderous endeavour had been at the behest of their former employer, Cotesworth's rival Richard Ridley, a former Mayor of Newcastle and prominent member of the city's traditional coal-trading elite.[35]

Despite these challenges, Cotesworth was successful in expanding his extractive business. Clearly, one aspect of his success was the productivity of his mines. However, his plans for controlling the region's mining industry did not rest solely on improving the volumes extracted by his miners. He also focused on controlling the essential infrastructure on which colliers depended to carry coal from the region's mines to market. This was an essential part of the process, and carrying thousands of tons of coal was not easy. Cotesworth's solution was wagonways – wooden rails that were laid to efficiently carry enormous carts from mine to river. Constructing and maintaining these routes was a huge undertaking and in one year alone Cotesworth purchased 24,335 wooden rails, 664 wheels, 2,912 sleepers and hundreds of other items for their construction. Over the course of the 1710s, Cotesworth was involved in almost constant negotiations with landowners regarding access to the land which the rails would run through. Not all mine owners were convinced, and the connected system would not benefit all collieries equally. Some, too, sought to control the wagonway in their own lands rather than allow Cotesworth to connect otherwise disparate parts of the system under his own control. However, reducing costs by even a few shillings per ton of coal would lead to considerable savings in time, and eventually the network that Cotesworth envisaged started to come together.[36]

With each landowner that Cotesworth persuaded, he was closer to setting up the most sophisticated industrial infrastructure in the country. In 1712, when one such step was made, he celebrated that 'I have conquered Mr Alderman Ramsey by forcing a way through his liberty', an agreement that allowed the rails to access the River Derwent. Around the same time, Cotesworth reached a deal with a group of local landowners – Lady Clavering, George Pitt, Robert Wright and Gilbert Spearman – to ensure the wagonways would be kept in a state of good repair. As each branch of the wagonway was maintained by the owner of the land it ran over, poor maintenance could cut off entire sections of the network. Whether out of spite or strategy, some landowners were willing to let this happen. When asked to repair his section of the wagonway, Silvertop (who earlier had stolen Cotesworth's coal) responded with an antagonistic letter that informed Cotesworth that 'I received your angry letter', but that he would wait to see him 'when I am sure to find you in a better temper. I am resolved to avoid scolding as much as possible.' Silvertop's anger came, in part, from Cotesworth's status as an absentee owner, and he challenged him to prove that the wagonway was actually damaged when 'you see not these things yourself' and suggested that his agents did not know the business as well as they should. A year later, reports confirmed that the wagonway across Silvertop's land was 'so much out of repair that scarce one sleeper in the whole length of Silvertop's way is whole and nothing to hold the rails together'. Repairs cost just over £50 but resisting the impositions of Cotesworth and his associates who profited in the wagonway was seemingly more important for this curmudgeonly colliery owner.[37]

While the wagonway improved efficiency, it also gave Cotesworth unprecedented levels of control over who could access vital transportation links. During this same period, Cotesworth had come to establish a close working relationship with the Liddell, Montagu and Bowes families, who were all major colliery owners, and all sent family members to London as MPs. Like Cotesworth, they also had ties to the capital's wider commercial and political circles: George Liddell had invested in the Bank of England and Edward Wortley Montagu was part of the Levant Company and served as ambassador to the Ottoman empire. Together, the group began to take more control of essential infrastructure around Newcastle and grew their coal extraction businesses. In addition to Cotesworth's work on the wagonway, boosted further by plans for a new and improved route that were set in motion in 1723, the group had also moved closer to monopolising the loading spaces on the riverside where boats could be filled with coal for onward transportation to Newcastle. Silvertop's river access halved just as Cotesworth's doubled. Like the Hostmen, they used their growing control as the basis for agreeing what was known as a 'Regulation' to keep prices high by restricting output. Unlike the Hostmen, they maintained their control not through regulatory enforcement, but by ruthlessly pursuing investments that brought every part of the coal industry under their control. Cotesworth was part of the first 'Regulation' that ended in 1715 and served as secretary for the group, an experience that motivated the establishment of deeper partnerships as their new self-regulating cartel surpassed the previous century's corporate monopoly in scale and wealth.[38]

In the following years, this group of Liddell, Montagu and Bowes, with Cotesworth as an active partner before he died, set out to ruthlessly establish control over the coal market. In 1726, alongside another collier Thomas Ord, they all signed an agreement to form a partnership and pooled their investment to purchase mining leases and branches of the wagonway. The new partnership used its increased spending power to further dominate the infrastructure that carried coal from mines to the market and to work together to keep coal prices high. In the following fifteen years the group, who became known as the Grand Allies, invested as much as £120,000 in mines and mining infrastructure. This was a sum that no individual mine owner could hope to compete with. While this probably did boost efficiency in their collieries and for transportation by making it possible to buy new engines and keep the wagonway in top-notch repair, this spending also gave them such control over coal production that they were able to manipulate prices on the market by limiting outputs from their mines. For British capitalists like these, efficiency and innovation were only part of the story of success: financial power and control were another. Innovative mechanisms for sharing financial risk and extending credit enabled investors in London and elsewhere to mobilise unprecedentedly large sums that could be channelled into activities including mining. In the case of Mackworth's Mine Adventurers this had ultimately proven unsuccessful; in the case of the Grand Allies it was a major success. The former had a more dramatic vision for change but the latter manipulated the market system much more effectively.[39]

When Cotesworth died in 1726, only a year after surviving arsenic poisoning, he left a radically transformed north-eastern coal industry behind him. The ways in which coal was extracted was relatively unchanged, but the way the business was organised and regulated had little in common with the Newcastle-dominated Hostmen who had effectively used regulation to monopolise the trade only three decades before. Improvements in transportation between mines and waiting transports on nearby rivers gave Cotesworth and his partners an edge, and served to sever the control that Newcastle's traders had previously imposed. As well as familial links and inheritances that provided them with a solid foundation in the practicalities of coal mining, this group was more successful than the inward-looking Hostmen at drawing on the skills and capital obtained through their strong interests in other industries, international commerce and national politics. Moving mountains of coal profitably was a hugely complex enterprise and having support at every stage of the process from extraction to sale to regulation was a considerable advantage. Using the wealth and power that their association provided, the Grand Allies invested in further improvements to the region's collieries and infrastructure and would go on to dominate the north-east coal trade for the rest of the century.

For the mine owners and industrialists who invested wisely, booming businesses that provided huge profits year after year were common. Britain was particularly well-endowed in its geological foundations, which left valuable and accessible deposits of numerous minerals to be used both as commodities themselves and as vital supplies for the metallurgical industries that were central to Britain's industrialisation. To extract and process ever-growing volumes of coal and metal ores, mining and metallurgical enterprises depended on capitalists who began to take new risks by experimenting with novel technologies, financial innovations, infrastructure development, complex supply chains and, eventually, expanding domestic and global markets. Not every effort was a success, certainly, but even financial failures like Mackworth's giant joint stock served to link different industries, conceptually and materially, in ways that contributed to the diffusion of new technologies and techniques across Britain. In the north-east, the historic monopoly of Newcastle's coal-trading corporation was stripped back by Cotesworth and his partners who ruthlessly pursued new collieries for their portfolios and the infrastructure that provided the vital link between pit and market. Whether in south Wales or north-east England there was no single factor that generated the conditions for the more profitable extraction of the earth's bounty: Britain's industrial development required networked capital that facilitated the intersection of people with different types of expertise and from different social backgrounds.

On the backs of the working men, women and children in mines and metal works, combined with changing ways of doing business and investment in more productive techniques, Britain's industrial output grew at a pace unlike anything seen before. In 1690, the global output of smelted copper was only around 2,400 tons, and none of this was produced in Wales. By 1712, the region around Swansea alone was producing 1,000 tons a year. By 1800, south Wales was producing around 7,000 tons: most of Britain's and two-fifths of global supply. Inevitably, this rising output depended on growth in the extraction of copper ore, and Cornish mines likewise increased extraction from around 5,000 tons in 1726 to ten times that volume by the end of the century. Coal production, already an established industry, grew more slowly, but still almost doubled in the first half of the eighteenth century, and doubled again by 1800 to some ten million tons a year. The extraction and production of metals including lead, tin and iron also grew dramatically, as more labour and more mines were exploited. These early rates of growth were only possible as new mines were opened: they were sustained in the second half of the century as mines became key sites of steam-powered industrialisation.[40]

Domestic extraction of metal ores meant that expensive imports, notably from Sweden, were increasingly insignificant. But it was not primarily by competing with European producers on their home turf that Britain's metal-minded capitalists profited. Instead, booming production found a ready market in Britain, as makers of metal goods developed techniques that allowed them to churn out ever larger quantities of finished goods. Many of these found their way into British homes or were used for building infrastructure or by other businesses as part of their own production processes. Britain was soon extracting more than enough minerals to cater to its own demands and selling to customers overseas, in Europe and beyond, promising enviable profits. In the first half of the eighteenth century, coal exports more than doubled, and they tripled again by the end of the century. Exports were even more important for Britain's metallurgical industries. While the export of lead grew only negligibly over the course of the century, the sale of tin overseas doubled in volume, and expansion of iron, brass and copper were astronomically successful, growing sixteen times, fifty-two times and fifty-four times, respectively. Together, the value of exports rooted in extractive industries increased from £392,796 to over £3 million. Domestic sales alone did not supply the huge amount of demand needed to expand the mining and metallurgical industries profitably: international commerce made up the difference. Even as Britain's capitalists ruthlessly extracted the natural resources that were so richly distributed across their island, their compatriots were busy overseas finding whole new worlds and markets to exploit.[41]

CHAPTER 4

# BETWEEN HEAVEN AND HELL

## Conquest, Colonisation and Slavery

In Britain, the land and the bedrock beneath provided abundant sources of wealth for those able to extract it. Some landowners that exploited resources on their properties invested in technologies that could wring a little bit more from the environment, while others found new ways to structure their businesses that gave them an edge over competitors. Manufacturers and merchants alike embraced opportunities to make connections across different markets and supply chains to profit further still, often drawing together the expertise and capital of people who had already profited from different parts of the economic system. For Britain's capitalists, extracting all they could from their homeland represented a great opportunity for making money. But it was not their only opportunity.

The use of force to take land was a well-established and profitable activity. In the sixteenth century, the practice and experience of violently enforcing English and Scottish rule over territories in Wales and the Highlands had been carried overseas. First King Henry VIII and then Elizabeth I sent troops to Ireland to suppress resistance and seize the lands of anyone who did not bow to the throne: by 1603, the whole island had been brought under English rule. Some of the Irish land seized by the state was granted to the City of London to manage, with the city's corporations left to find ways to extract profit from territories in what became the Londonderry plantation, named in their honour. Violent conquest and colonisation also saw territories thousands of miles further west fall under British control. In 1606, King James I had supported the colonisation of Virginia by granting the right to seize and settle land to a private corporation, the Virginia Company. King Charles I had taken that land back under royal control, but still supported further private colonisation in North America and the Caribbean. In the 1650s, a design supported by Oliver Cromwell and the Commonwealth expanded Britain's colonies in America and occupied yet more land. After the Restoration, Britain's colonies continued to expand, taking more land that was settled as hundreds of thousands of Britons migrated overseas in search of religious freedom, power and profit.[1]

These territories were taken and secured by force. In North America, land was often seized directly from people whose ancestors had lived in the region for generations, while in the Caribbean it was more usually taken from other European colonists who had already decimated the region's earlier inhabitants. Occasionally, it was taken from lands newly deserted. In Barbados, for example, disease and raiding had annihilated the island's Arawak and Carib people in the sixteenth century, leaving British colonists able to settle on an uninhabited island, but this was an atypical experience. In the Chesapeake, the seventeenth century saw numerous conflicts between colonists and local people, with more and more of the latter being forced from their land as colonists encroached further and further inland. Before the end of the century, indigenous people who had lived in what had become Virginia had been almost entirely wiped out. In St Kitts, English and French settlers together attacked the island's resident Carib population, killing as much as half of the population in only a few days in 1626: by the middle of the century the survivors had been enslaved or forcibly removed to Dominica. In New England, in 1636, colonists in Massachusetts and Connecticut went to war with the nearby Pequot, offering bounties for the heads or scalps of people killed. Hundreds more indigenous prisoners were enslaved and trafficked to the Caribbean to work on British plantations. A consequent treaty prohibited the Pequot people from returning to their lands. Violence like this was a common feature of colonial settlement in the seventeenth century, and continued throughout the eighteenth as British colonists expanded their territories and took yet more land.[2]

Conflict with indigenous people did not disappear with, or even shortly after, conquest, especially in North America where colonial expansion continued in the following centuries. But this was also the case in some islands in the Caribbean. Around 1660, almost three decades after the conquest of Antigua, a proposal by the island's merchants and landowners set out the benefits of colonising the island, describing how its rich soils 'not inferior to any of the other' nearby islands was attracting enterprising capitalists, who were enticed by the promise of land that would 'produce provisions, tobacco, sugar, ginger, indigo and . . . cotton'. However, they warned that too few settlers were arriving from Britain, which had left the island at risk from 'merciless Indians' – the indigenous Arawak or Carib peoples whose lands were being taken for profit and power. The island's colonists and merchants needed support to fully establish their control, and they petitioned King Charles II to send hundreds of flintlock muskets and dozens of cannons to protect their new acquisitions. Additionally, the same group encouraged absentee landowners to proactively settle territory they had acquired to ensure no 'inlet to the common enemy the Indians' remained. The island's 'merchants, planters and traders' brooked no compromise: they thought that annihilation was the only way to ensure their assets were safe. More violence was ordered, and yet more land was secured for Britain's capitalists to exploit.[3]

Elsewhere, Britain's colonists were willing to work with indigenous peoples, but only when it suited them. Often, this was when peaceful relations offered trading opportunities or defence against other European settlers. In 1664 300 British soldiers led by Colonel Richard Nicholls take 'from the Dutch their chief town then called New Amsterdam, now New York', as well as forts at Albany and Delaware, 'without the loss of a single man'. Nathanial Crouch, who in 1685 wrote a detailed account of the conquest and colonies' consequent development, described the new territories as 'blessed with the richest soil in all New England', and that, when it had been seized, the town had already been home to 500 houses worth £50,000 and a harbour that was 'very commodious for shipping'. Having been forced from these lands already, indigenous people still living nearby were seen not as an immediate threat but rather as a source of income: the new colonists undertook a busy trade for furs and foodstuffs. Likewise, in 1700, the Board of Trade recommended 'the necessity of preserving the friendship' of indigenous people in North America who were 'a barrier between His Majesty's plantations and Canada', which was occupied by French colonists. Despite these relationships, in both New York and in Canada, Britain's colonies grew during the following century, forcing former friends and allies from their land.[4]

Taking and holding land was just the start. To profit from it, Britain needed workers to toil in difficult conditions. This, too, was often achieved through violence that shaped every stage of a booming transatlantic trade that saw millions of captive African people trafficked to the Americas to work in Britain's ever-expanding territories. Whether dependent on enslaved labour or worked by European settlers who migrated to Britain's colonies, the territories that Britain acquired were exploited with a similarly ruthless dedication to 'improvement' that had seen capitalists extract more from the environment in Britain. Land across the Atlantic could produce crops that simply could not be grown at home, both because of the climate and because almost all of Britain's arable land was already under cultivation. In the eighteenth century, territories overseas provided the equivalent of millions of acres worth of produce that was shipped to Britain where it was consumed, fed into the nation's industries, or re-exported for additional profit. Capitalists seized land in America to exploit, they traded enslaved people for profit, and they took advantage of myriad opportunities to work with commodities coming from colonies or to manufacture goods that would be shipped to them. Britain's rise to wealth and power was built on slavery and empire.

## SWEET RETURNS

In December 1654, Robert Venables and William Penn had sailed from England in command of seventeen warships and three thousand men to attack Spanish colonies in the Caribbean. Stopping first at Barbados and St Kitts early the following year, they were joined by thousands of volunteers who sought to profit from the conquest, including 'women and children that went with a design to plant'. Landing first at Santo Domingo (now in the Dominican Republic), disease and Spanish attacks blunted the assault: '600 men killed, 200 lost in the woods, 300 wounded'. The fleet moved on to Jamaica where the smaller population 'being not above 500 men besides negro slaves' provided less resistance and quickly surrendered. The Spanish population were given two weeks to leave the island or otherwise be killed, and some previously enslaved people fled the invading forces into Jamaica's mountainous interior where they continued to resist the British occupation of the island. Victorious British soldiers and volunteers who stayed received 'parcels of land equally apportioned' among them, becoming the first British landowners on the island. The invasion was quick and overwhelming. It would establish British rule over the island for more than 300 years.[5]

Published three decades later, in 1685, Nathanial Crouch's account of *The English Empire in America* described Jamaica as an island that was rich with opportunity. 'The soil of Jamaica is very fruitful,' he reported, and produced 'many excellent commodities as sugar very good, cacao, indigo, cotton, tobacco, hides, tortoise shells, curious wood, salt, saltpetre, ginger, pepper, drugs of several sorts, and cochineal, with many others.' Likewise, Francis Hanson's *The Laws of Jamaica* from 1683 reflected on how the island's unique geography made it so suitable for colonial exploitation. He described how the Blue Mountains dominating the centre of the island, some 'so high that they are not habitable, scarce accessible', were responsible for the island's unique climate. On their slopes, 'large timber-trees of diverse sorts of wood' grew freely that could be used for building work, and provided habitat for fruits, fowl and hogs that would help feed the island's settlers. In the shadow of the mountains, lowlands provided 'meadows (full of grass) called *savannas*', that previous Spanish colonists had used to breed cattle, horses and sheep, as well as wooded slopes that were cleared to make way for planting sugar. 'If well improved,' Crouch concluded, 'this isle will be the best and richest plantation that ever the English were masters of.'[6]

Despite these later accounts of Jamaica's wondrous natural environment, the island's earliest British colonists had not been able to easily take advantage of the island's abundance. Malnutrition and disease decimated the original occupying force of around seven thousand, and only a third survived the first year. After the Restoration, Charles II, 'being well satisfied that our island of Jamaica, being a pleasant and most fertile soil', sought to quickly grow the island's population and agricultural output by promising that 'thirty acres of improvable lands' would be 'allotted to every such person, male, or female, being twelve years old or upwards' that settled on the island. Vitally, 'all children of our natural born subjects of England to be born in Jamaica' would have the 'same privileges to all intents and purposes as our free-born subjects of England'. It was an offer that later commentators would credit as the foundation of the island's wealth, which they explained 'depends wholly on His Majesty' for support and encouragement. But no matter what support the state offered, few were prepared for the challenges they faced once they reached the Caribbean. The islands they reached were populated with strange plants and animals, the food and drinks were unfamiliar, and colonists' conclusion that overcoming the challenge of their tropical climate and diseases demanded the exploitation of enslaved workers had no parallel in Britain.[7]

Settlement in Jamaica pushed forward despite these challenges primarily because of its suitability for growing sugar. By the 1660s, brutal, innovative practices already used in plantations in Barbados were being replicated in colonies across North America and the Caribbean, including in Jamaica. While sugar was not the first commodity produced on plantations, the demands of harvesting and processing sugar cane intensified the exploitation of enslaved labour and the natural environment in ways that had never been undertaken before. These practices were carried to Jamaica by plantation owners and merchants who had invested in Barbados's booming sugar economy over the previous two decades; were described in detail by books for planters; and were shared through informal networks across land and sea. They rested on two connected 'improvements': violent slave codes that imposed harsh discipline on enslaved workers, and integrated plantations that concentrated the complete process of sugar production in each landowner's estate. Such experimental new methods for organising enslaved labour had boosted productivity, and planters from Barbados had acquired a reputation as the most capable landowners in the British Caribbean.[8]

On the face of it, Jamaica's tropical climate and rich soils presented British colonists with the same opportunity for profitable plantations as they had 1,300 miles to the east in Barbados. However, the newly seized territory was not a simple replica. For starters, at more than 4,400 square miles, Jamaica was about twenty-five times larger than Barbados. Jamaica also had a much more diverse geography, with a rugged mountain range running down the centre of the island representing the most obvious challenge. The climate, too, was more varied: the 900 millimetres of water that fell annually around Kingston was far too little to support sugar production, while the 5,000 millimetres that fell in the island's north-eastern mountains made cutting and grinding grain incredibly demanding work.[9]

Overcoming these challenges and extracting profit from the larger island depended on networks that enabled the mutually reinforcing exploitation of social and human capital and took advantage of the island's natural resources. Agriculture was not the only source of profit for the island's early capitalists, who used its westerly location to trade or privateer in the Caribbean, where long-established Spanish colonies represented a good target for either vocation. It did not take long, though, before more people with the skills, capital and motivation needed to establish plantations came to the island, including, prominently, many people with strong links to extractive agriculture in Barbados. Numerous merchants with investments in Barbados moved to Jamaica, acquiring land for themselves and tying the larger island into networks that carried essential supplies to the burgeoning colony. They were joined by plantation owners and, in 1664, over 700 colonists from Barbados led by Sir Thomas Modyford, Jamaica's new governor. In the following two decades, as many as ten thousand more people migrated from Barbados to other colonies including Jamaica, disseminating capital, ideas and institutions as they went. Another injection of wealth and expertise from plantation owners fleeing from Suriname, which was ceded to the Netherlands following the Treaty of Breda in 1667, further boosted investment in sugar production in Jamaica. Building on these links, colonists in Jamaica went about accumulating land and overseeing the demanding work needed to clear the island's difficult landscape for sugar planting. Capital generated locally through piracy, trade and plantation production was invested in building sugar mills and purchasing huge numbers of enslaved African people. Despite noting with some concern that the island was 'underpeopled', an anonymous official report from 1675 described seventy sugar works already in operation and forty more under construction, and by the 1680s, the development of a large-scale plantation and commercial sugar industry was well under way. Before long it had become the dominant economic activity on the island.[10]

As well as financial capital, plantation owners needed skills that went beyond the methods of estate management that were common in England. Two features of sugar production made it a particularly challenging proposition: one, sugar cane could take up to eighteen months to mature; and two, when ripe canes were cut, they had to be processed within three days. Growing and harvesting cane was labour-intensive. To clear a field and fertilise the soil, enslaved workers cut down trees and burned the stumps, hoed the soil, planted pea crops for at least a year, and then planted yams or potatoes. Only in the third year would it be ready for planting canes. This use of peas and root crops to fertilise the soil may have been passed from the Caribbean to Britain, where similar practices became more popular over the following decades to improve wheat yields. In time, sugar cultivation leached the soil of essential nutrients and manure was required to help fertilise the soil and maintain productivity. After preparing a field, enslaved workers placed old canes in holes or trenches, where they sprouted. Not long after, they weeded and fertilised the field, adding new plants anywhere that the old canes had not sprouted. A year or so later, they would be ready to harvest, and enslaved workers would return to the field to cut canes more than two metres tall to be sent for processing. Despite the long wait for crops to develop, the rush to process the cane demanded that sugar plantations take on the trappings of industrial production. Each plantation needed its own sugar mill, boiling mill and curing house, as well as more enslaved workers to operate them. Making sure that these processes occurred at the right time, in the right place, with sufficient enslaved labour and without spoiling any of the crop all required complex agricultural and managerial know-how.[11]

When it came to clearing land or planting and harvesting crops, there was little that existing technology could do to increase productivity, and so plantation owners exploited people and the land instead to boost output. Conversely, sugar processing depended on complex machinery, which led to the establishment of closely linked agricultural and industrial processes. The basic design of the Caribbean sugar mill had diffused across the Caribbean following the transportation of two-roll mills from the Canary Islands by Spanish colonists in the sixteenth century. Further advances led to the adoption of three-roll mills in Brazil, which, in turn, were brought to British colonies in the Caribbean in the first half of the seventeenth century. This underlying design, which remained in use until the nineteenth century, required that enslaved workers pass sugar cane between turning rollers, crushing it and releasing juice that could be collected for boiling. Where natural resources allowed, the mills used wind- or waterpower, but cattle, horses, mules, donkeys and occasionally enslaved people were employed to turn the rollers. Mills depended on equipment that was procured from Britain and contributed to growing demand for certain goods that presented a positive boost for emerging metallurgical industries in south Wales and the Midlands. Plantations in the Caribbean incentivised capitalists to invest in industrial enterprises in Britain.[12]

Networked capital made this possible and connected agricultural industry in Britain's colonies with the same exchanges of knowledge, expertise and skill that proved so important for stimulating economic development on the other side of the Atlantic. Efforts to increase productivity in the Caribbean were tied into networks that sought to disseminate useful knowledge and encourage improvement in Britain. The unknown environments of Jamaica and other colonies were intriguing to Britain's scientific community, and the Royal Society posed a series of questions to Jamaica's governor Sir Thomas Lynch in 1672 in the hope that empirical data might be obtained about topics ranging from the rock formations in the harbour to whether eating tortoise fat turned urine 'yellowish green and oily'. In the following years, the Royal Society maintained close links with Jamaica: two of the colony's governors were fellows, one of whom later became the society's president. Links like these helped ensure that letters were sent regularly from American colonies to the society, tackling topics of value for plantation owners and natural scientist alike. For example, Nehemiah Grew sent a letter with a thorough description of Jamaican potatoes and their usefulness for feeding pigs, Lynch reported on the challenges of growing cacao in Jamaica, and many more letters commented on the skin colour of African people, reflecting the rise of racist attitudes amongst colonial settlers who had begun to associate enslaved status with a person's melanin.[13]

British inventors, too, were also well aware of the opportunities that Caribbean production offered. In 1693, Thomas Winter and Mathew Elliston received a patent for 'a new sort of mill' that could be worked 'by the strength of men only'. Such a man-powered mill, they noted, would be 'very useful where other mills are not' and especially 'in the West Indies' where enslaved workers could be forced to undertake the arduous labour required. Likewise, a few years later in 1709, Jeremiah Weisehamer developed a plan to improve the 'easy grinding or pressing of sugar canes with a less number of oxen, horses, or cattle than by those mills formerly used throughout our dominions in America'. Whether using these designs or others, landowners in the Caribbean used whatever power source was most readily available. By the eighteenth century, windmills had come to dominate the landscape in Barbados and Montserrat, while waterwheels were more popular in Martinique, Guadeloupe and St Lucia. Jamaica, with its more diverse landscape, had both, but animal-powered mills remained the most popular. The application of all of these tools was already well under way in the seventeenth century; as one enslaved worker in Barbados purportedly declared, 'the Devil was in the Englishman' who 'makes everything work; he makes the negro work, the horse work, the wood work, the water work, and the wind work'. When it came to exploiting workers or nature for profit,

British capitalists were quick to implement whatever techniques they could.[14]

The sugar that flowed from Britain's Caribbean colonies and the wealth its sale brought to plantation owners and merchants came at an enormous human cost. The island's early promoters and later plantation owners expected that enslaved African labourers would undertake the hardest labour on the island, irrespective of advances in managerial techniques or machinery. The cost of paid British labour, even if workers could be found willing to work in conditions that reduced their life expectancy to a few years, would have radically increased the capital required by planters and made sugar prohibitively expensive for consumers in Europe. As early as 1660, one commentator noted that 'the advantage arising by blacks in planting compared to that of white servants is very considerable'. It was a ruthless conclusion. Sir Balthazar Gerbier's *Summary Description*, published the same year chillingly set out the added value that he thought exploiting enslaved workers offered plantation owners: first, unfree workers were much cheaper than free British workers; second, they would 'do more work (at their ease) than two Christians can perform', especially in tropical climates. It was considered accepted fact that plantation work was 'best carried on by the labour of negroes', and that the expansion of colonial production was most easily achieved simply by sending more and more enslaved people to work until they died under the sweltering heat of the Caribbean sun. The death of an enslaved labourer did relatively little to impact the profits of a plantation, and colonial landowners saw minimal incentive to limit the loss of life. As plantations in the Caribbean expanded and became more profitable, ships transporting enslaved people to Britain's colonies increased in line with growing sugar production on the islands.[15]

In the 1680s, the plantation owner John Taylor wrote a detailed account of the work and treatment of enslaved workers. When African people first arrived in Jamaica, he reported, they seemed 'to grieve and lament their loss of their country freedom', and they took whatever opportunities they could to maintain relationships and culture that was separate and independent to their work. When possible, their time after dark was filled with music and dancing, but their waking lives were otherwise spent toiling on behalf of plantation owners. Rising at four in the morning, enslaved people worked for seven hours before breaking during the hottest part of the day. Returning to work at two in the afternoon, they continued until dark. Rest was permitted on Saturday afternoons and Sundays. Additionally, many Jamaican plantations demanded their enslaved workers maintain small plots for growing crops, which saved them some of the expense of providing food. Taylor concluded that planters 'spend their time in ease and pleasure', while their 'slaves, which not only wait on them, but also do their work both in their houses and plantations' brought 'great profit to the planters'.

Plantation work was back-breaking, unremitting and unrewarding labour, punctuated by the routine application of extreme violence and with little hope of reprieve. Despite suggestions that enslaved workers would 'willingly submit' after being set to work, Taylor was convinced rather that enslaved people 'would sooner cut your throat than obey you', a conclusion he used to justify appalling psychological and physical abuse in the name of discipline. If an enslaved person struck a white colonist they could be 'severely whipped'; a second offence would see their 'nose slit and be burned in some part of the face'. If there was a third offence, 'greater corporal punishment as [owners] shall think meet to inflict' was permitted. To deter enslaved people from the potential release offered by suicide, some plantation owners tried to convince them their souls would not return to Africa if they did so. Despite these conditions, some planters simply disavowed any suffering. Observing that some enslaved women were 'at work the same or next day' after giving birth, one anonymous author claimed that their diligence was down to the remarkable impact of the island's climate on their health, disregarding the cruel punishment these women would face if they did not immediately return to work.[16]

Enslaved people who fought for their freedom, or were caught planning their escape, faced the most savage response from Britain's enslavers. This was exemplified in the anonymously authored *Great Newes from the Barbadoes* (1676), which recounted a plan by enslaved people to break their shackles. It promised its readers in England 'a true and faithful account of the grand conspiracy' and 'the happy discovery of the same', which had recently been suppressed on the island. The colonists' response had been vicious, and the author included details of 'the number of those that were burned alive, beheaded, and otherwise executed for their horrid crimes', to convince his readers that the threat to British wealth had passed. Later, an enslaved person, known only as Tony, was dragged before a judge and told to identify co-conspirators involved in another plot. He refused, and a member of the crowd that had gathered to watch his interrogation crowed 'we shall see you fry bravely'. Tony reportedly spat back contemptuously, 'if you roast me today, you cannot roast me tomorrow'. Extreme and horrific violence was a common feature of British society in its colonies, imposed by judges and plantation owners, and celebrated by the British crowd. Despite horrific punishments meted out, and the coercive, violent conditions in which they were forced to live, resistance was endemic among enslaved people and would remain so until slavery was finally abolished more than a century later.[17]

The increasing population of enslaved workers led to colonists' concerns that 'the proportion of blacks might in short time be such that in rebellion' they might overwhelm the island's British settlers. In the seventeenth and eighteenth century, revolts and resistance to slavery were common, although they were brutally suppressed. This in turn led to colonial policies designed to stop any such resistance that, like violent and coercive practices employed on plantations to control workers, became common features of British rule. In the 1660s, Jamaica's governing Assembly had 'enacted that for every eight' black people each plantation owner would 'be obliged to keep one white man', although this was not enforced consistently. Two decades later, the Assembly passed another Act that sought to increase the free, white population further, insisting that 'all and every master or masters of slaves, for the first five working slaves, shall be obliged to keep one white man servant'. Jamaica's plantations came to rely on violent reprisals and increased security on its plantations, limiting opportunities for enslaved people to flee. Jamaica's 'mountains of difficult access, and great rivers not passable by boats' were seen as a useful natural barrier. Unable to easily travel into the highlands, those seeking to escape from slavery were restricted to moving across plantations that by the 1680s were, according to Hanson, a contiguous block across the island from 'one end to the other'. According to the island's laws, 'if any slave be found wandering outside of his master's plantation, any person may seize and carry him to his owner'. Despite the ongoing risk of escape or rebellion, the Assembly never considered stopping the arrival of enslaved people or imposing regulations that would demand colonists improve conditions. They relied instead on new arrivals to keep growing their plantations and to replace those who had already been worked to death.[18]

As a result, investment in the traffic of enslaved people significantly increased in the second half of the seventeenth century, growing to match the expansion of plantation economies in Jamaica, Barbados and elsewhere in the Caribbean and North America. One author boasted in 1683 that Jamaica's sugar production 'increases so much every year' that 'trade and shipping will both increase' in kind. For many capitalists involved in the exchange, their profits increased with them. A cycle of productive gains was radically reshaping the island's economy. More workers meant more land could be cleared and more sugar produced, which led to more sugar being sold for profits that could be reinvested back into the colonies or into other industries in Britain. By the 1690s, well over 100,000 enslaved people were being exploited across Britain's American colonies, toiling in awful conditions to extract products for British landowners to sell onward for transport to eager consumers in Britain.[19]

Profits from their plantations had an enormous impact on Britain's wealthy landowning elite in the Caribbean. Bridgetown in Barbados became a bustling commercial hub, and in 1676 one author described the small island as 'the most flourishing colony the English have in the world'. Not to be outdone, by the 1680s, British commentators were claiming that Jamaica's sugar 'excels any that is made in any other of His Majesty's plantations' and that the island's capital Port Royal was filled not only with profits from sugar, but also gold and silver from trading with Spanish colonies in America. For Jamaica's plantation owners and merchants, 'the manner of living there for gallantry, good housekeeping, and recreations sufficiently demonstrate the flourishing condition of the island', and bowling, dancing, music, 'plays at the public theatre', and horse races were all available. Taylor, too, noted that 'the merchants and gentry' of Port Royal lived in 'the height of splendour', and that wealth had brought 'vile strumpets and common prostitutes' to the town who filled it 'with all manner of debauchery'. Many colonists indulged in living to excess.[20]

Barbados and Jamaica became important hubs within the British transatlantic economy. They operated as markets where enslaved people were traded onwards to colonies that were too small to make for attractive ports for slave-traders to visit directly; destinations for farmers in Britain or North America to export crops; sites of trade with Spanish America; and sources of hundreds of thousands of pounds of goods that were exported to Britain, often for re-export to further destinations across Europe and beyond. The exchange of goods across the Atlantic fuelled the wealth in these ports, even as trade grew to Asia, Africa and across Europe, too. By the end of the seventeenth century, Britain's Caribbean colonies were sending over £800,000 worth of goods to Britain. Jamaica alone produced £239,759 of this, with only Barbados shipping more. This was not a poor return from an island that had been a Spanish domain only fifty years before. Sugar exports were only the start of the island's value, though. Jamaica also imported £101,934 worth of goods from Britain, everything from beer and books to soap and shovels. It's plantation owners also purchased thousands of pounds of wrought copper, iron and brass goods from Britain's metallurgical workshops alongside similar amounts of woollen fabric, worked leather and wrought silk. Myriad industries across Britain produced these goods and benefited from their eventual sale into colonial markets.[21]

Considering that none of these colonies had yet been seized at the start of the seventeenth century, their significance within Britain's commercial landscape by the start of the eighteenth century was extraordinary. Together, the territories that dotted the American coastline from Barbados and Jamaica in the south to Hudson's Bay in the north were now the source of more than a fifth of British imports. They were also growing in importance as markets for British manufacturers, receiving more than a tenth of goods that were shipped from British ports overseas. Yet, this was just the beginning. As the transatlantic economy boomed in the following decades, and the number of enslaved people trafficked to the Caribbean vastly increased, the impact of empire on Britain's wealth and power would only grow further.

## ENTERPRISE AND EMPIRE

Across the Caribbean, plantation owners expected enslaved workers to survive only around seven years upon their arrival; about a quarter died within the first three. This shocking mortality, coupled with the expansion of plantations across newly acquired islands, meant that demand for enslaved workers was consistently high. To ensure Britain's colonies would receive the huge number of captive African people that plantation owners demanded, Charles II chartered the Company of Royal Adventurers Trading into Africa in 1660 and the Royal African Company in 1672. Support from the state continued over the following decades, and royal participation in the transatlantic slave-trade, as governors and investors in the two companies, helped ensure that their activities on the African coast were backed with the might of the Royal Navy during times of war. Likewise, governors in North America and the Caribbean were encouraged to support the corporation's monopoly and 'to give all due encouragement to merchants . . . especially to the Royal African Company'.[22]

Thousands of investors took part in hope of enrichment. Landowners, merchants and manufacturers all invested capital with its roots in Britain's soil to support the provision of enslaved labour to extract yet more wealth from lands overseas. Buoyed by this support, and exclusive rights to purchase enslaved people in Africa and to sell them in British colonies, these two companies quickly increased the number of people transported across the Atlantic. Almost 30,000 enslaved people were transported in British ships in the 1660s, which grew to almost 50,000 in the 1670s, and to almost 100,000 in the 1680s. At the peak of the corporate slave-trade in the 1680s, it was exporting as much as £70,000 of British goods each year to Africa, most of which were exchanged for captive people to be taken to the Americas. Most of the company's voyages ended in Barbados or

Jamaica, the two most important sugar-producing islands, but some enslaved people were also trafficked onwards to other colonies in the Caribbean or North America.[23]

By the 1690s, though, the quid pro quo that saw the Royal African Company receive its monopoly in return for providing 'a constant and sufficient supply of merchantable negroes, at moderate prices' was starting to unravel. Complaints from plantation owners and private traders about the company's monopoly became increasingly common. This was partly because of the corporation's failure to provide the number of enslaved workers that Britain's growing colonies needed, but also because of the limits that it placed on the freedom of Britain's merchants to trade where they wished. Before long, support for the company started to crumble, as increasing the number of captive African people transported to Britain's colonies as cheaply as possible became a priority for the state, merchants and planters alike. In 1697, the Board of Trade recommended that 'all encouragement should be given that the said colonies be supplied plentifully with negroes and at the cheapest rates'.[24]

The 'Trade with Africa Act' of 1697 transformed the system. It removed the monopolistic privileges that the Royal African Company had held since its inception and opened the trade to anyone who could find a ship and send it to Africa. Critics argued that 'many inconsiderate persons, who knew little or nothing of the nature and circumstances of that trade' were tempted to take part, with some simply taking the opportunity 'to be rid of damaged India goods' (cotton textiles from South Asia) that could be sold in Africa for a little profit before they returned to their usual business. The corporation found itself competing not only with well-capitalised merchant partnerships, including figures who had petitioned for Parliament to pass the Act in the first place, but also with a larger number of speculative traders who sought a quick and easy profit. Many of these, though, either due to initial failure or the promise of richer opportunities elsewhere, did not become regular participants in the trade after this early bubble burst. The most successful independent traders had links with the company's trade or with the Caribbean, and a number of partnerships were set up that together quickly surpassed the company.[25]

Faced with competition like this, proponents of the company shifted tack in the following decade, arguing that the slave-trade was so important for Britain that it was too great a risk to leave it in the hands of private traders who had no collective responsibility for maintaining Britain's forts and settlements on the African coast. It was through the corporation's great efforts, they argued, that Britain now had 'a more certain and enlarged trade that any other European nation whatever'. The company had built forts at great cost to protect British interests, and by bringing the 'whole trade to them' had allowed for the establishment of warehouses and markets where British goods could be sold. It had also profitably overseen the transportation of thousands of 'young and healthy' African people for 'large returns in gold', all while improving Britain's economic security. Without the financing that only a joint-stock fund could deliver, they concluded, 'the trade will be totally lost to this nation, and end in destruction of the plantations'.[26]

They were mistaken. By drawing on their networked capital, ruthlessly pursuing efficiencies and targeting different markets, the new traders dramatically increased the number of voyages taking place between Britain, Africa and the Caribbean, and consequently the number of captive African people who were trafficked across the Atlantic. In the first years of the newly open trade, people took part from all manner of backgrounds: some were merchants who had lobbied against the Royal African Company, others had invested or worked in the corporation, and others were skilled at running estates and businesses. Robert Heysham, a leading proponent of opening the African trade and successful sugar merchant, invested in numerous ships that trafficked thousands of enslaved people to plantations in the Caribbean. One of his partners was Edward Searle, who had been the Royal African Company's chief agent in Anomabo on the African coast in the 1690s before returning to London and lending his knowledge of the African trade to numerous partnerships sending ships to the region. Searle worked closely with Abraham Houlditch, whose father had commanded troops that had helped impose corporate authority in Cape Coast Castle. Unlike his father, the younger Houlditch opposed the company's monopoly, but did support imposing duties on independent traders for the maintenance of the British military presence on the African coast. Other partners of Heysham, Searle and Houlditch included James Waite, who brought experience of trading tobacco in Virginia; the ironmonger Anthony Tourney; and the linen-draper Robert Brooke. Networks like these drew on financial capital from a wider investing public as well as stimulating growing connectivity between different parts of the economy.[27]

Ship captains were likewise able to share useful knowledge with partners who invested together in the trade. The captain Edmund Saunders commanded some of the first ships that were sent from Bristol to Africa before returning and reinvesting his profits as a ship owner, happy to send others in his place as he took a cut. Before his death in 1747, ships owned by Saunders had trafficked more than 10,000 enslaved people. Other captains and mariners also stepped from lives aboard ships into roles as merchants and investors, putting their capital back into the slave-trade but also other commercial and manufacturing enterprises, and purchasing land.[28]

Together, independent traders like these quickly changed how the slave-trade was practised. They increased their profits by using smaller ships that spent less time on the African coast before travelling onward across the Atlantic. The number of captive Africans transported on each ship stabilised at between 200 and 300 people, considerably lower than the 500 people transported by the larger ships popular in the seventeenth century. The added flexibility provided by employing a greater number of smaller ships meant that, rather than trying to control market conditions in Africa like the Royal African Company had attempted, independent traders were more likely to stop wherever they were able to do business. At the same time, smaller, swifter vessels took less time to fill to capacity with enslaved people on the African coast, helping reduce costs incurred during the voyage and further boosting profits.[29]

Similarly, once they crossed the Atlantic, independent traders were more willing to trade beyond the company's most prized markets. Jamaica was their most popular destination, where they fiercely competed with the corporate trade and quickly gained the ascendancy, and the colony's rapidly expanding plantations were more than capable of taking in the increasing numbers of enslaved workers. However, many traders also tried their luck in colonies in North America, sometimes in places where they had already been active in colonial businesses before their entry into the slave-trade. The effectiveness of independent traders in connecting the trade with new markets, their greater flexibility vis-à-vis the Royal African Company, and the willingness of new entrants to operate beyond the traditional geographies that the increasingly defunct company had targeted, allowed them to quickly surpass the scale and range of the corporation's seventeenth-century activities. Increasing competition between British traders led to the prices demanded by African traders for an enslaved person increasing from around £3 to £10, and the sale price of enslaved people in the Caribbean had consequently risen from £14 to £23. Merchants complained about the rising prices, but the demand for enslaved labour in the Caribbean was undiminished. The price slave-traders put on an African life was still far less than the cost needed to tempt free workers from Britain to undertake such dangerous work as the plantations demanded.[30]

Even as independent traders from London had quickly found ways to outcompete the Royal African Company, in the following decades waves of new entrants, first from Bristol and then Liverpool, found ways to undercut their predecessors. By the later 1720s, Bristol had overtaken London as the busiest slave-trading port in Britain, and Liverpool surpassed Bristol twenty years later. Liverpool offered slightly quicker access to American markets than Britain's southern ports, and to important markets in Scandinavia and the Baltic that were essential for supplies of iron, timber and everything else needed for shipbuilding. Ships leaving the port also had some protection from the privateering that plagued shipping in the English Channel during war time.

Whether by snipping a few days off the length of the voyage, having access to specialised facilities in their home ports, or tying their businesses into existing colonial trading networks, the same search for improvement that benefited other sectors of Britain's economy was ruthlessly employed to find efficiencies in the transatlantic traffic of enslaved people. Not all independent traders taking part in the transatlantic trade were successful, and some were bankrupted as ships were lost or captured, or they were outcompeted. Most traders took part as they would in any other commercial opportunity, happy to take home a decent profit that helped them live a comfortable life, even as others made much more substantial sums. According to the merciless criteria of the Royal African Company, to provide 'a constant and sufficient supply' of enslaved people, eighteenth-century slave-traders would have considered their businesses a resounding success. In the first half of the eighteenth century, approximately 850,000 captive African people were forced to board British ships for America: almost four times as many as during the entire seventeenth century. The scale of the slave-trade conducted by independent traders over the eighteenth century was vastly larger than that launched by the slave-trading corporations that preceded it, even as many traders continued to depend on the same fortifications in Africa, slave-trading networks, and forceful support from the British state that these earlier ventures had established.[31]

The direct profits acquired from selling enslaved people were not the main economic impact that the trade had on the British economy, though. Rather, forced labour enabled the exploitation of more land, the production of more commodities, and the growth of colonial societies whose wealth depended on the purchase of enslaved workers. Whether they owned plantations, transported and sold the goods produced by plantations, provided services for the new markets opening in colonies overseas, or simply invested in others' ventures, the opportunities for British capitalists were wide-ranging. In the first half of the eighteenth century, the exploitation of enslaved people and consequent growth of Britain's colonial trade, linked to the simultaneous expansion of businesses of all sorts that underpinned and profited from the transatlantic economy, led to mutually reinforcing outcomes for capitalists across multiple sectors.[32]

Thousands of British entrepreneurs seized the chance to build businesses that rested on the dependable and growing supply of goods from colonies in the Caribbean and North America. Sometimes, this saw the reinvestment of profits from the transatlantic trade into British business directly. For example, the Cornish merchant Peter

Day trained as a merchant in Bristol before taking advantage of the port's slave-trading boom in the early eighteenth century. Investing in more than thirty slaving voyages, Day's business profited from the sale of almost 8,000 African people. He used capital from these ventures to build up a 'considerable interest in the new sugar house' in Bristol and encouraged his executors to increase his family's stake in the business. Their capital, he explained, 'cannot be better employed or produce a greater interest' than in preparing and reselling colonial produce. Sugar refining in Britain was certainly highly profitable. Muscovado sugar bought in Jamaica could be sold to consumers for about twice as much in the middle of the century, but if it was refined in Britain before sale, profits could double. Another merchant in Bristol, Isaac Hobshouse, had profited from an even larger stake in the slave-trade, owning ships that transported 20,000 people from Africa to British colonies, and taking advantage of the chance to trade directly with markets in the Caribbean and North America. Like Day, Hobshouse used proceeds to invest in the local economy, including a sugar refinery that processed goods coming to the port across the Atlantic and a metal works that produced goods for export in the opposite direction.[33]

Other capitalists used proceeds from the sale of colonial goods to invest in a wide variety business ventures, including the slave-trade. Among them was Henry Richards, a London merchant whose business depended on imports from plantations in the Caribbean and North America, particularly Virginian tobacco. This profitable enterprise underpinned, among other things, direct investment in the slave-trade through the Royal African Company and, when he died in 1764, large donations to three of the city's hospitals. A similar path was followed a few decades later by the tobacconist Sir Richard Brocas, whose wealth supported his rise to Alderman and Lord Mayor of the City of London. His investment of thousands of pounds in the Royal African Company in the 1720s mutually reinforced links between British business growth and investment in the slave-trade. On a smaller scale, John Gilpin, a sugar refiner from Whitehaven, used profits from a business dependent on colonial goods to invest directly in the traffic of enslaved people. Purchasing a share in the ship *Princess* alongside its captain Thomas Rumball in 1718, this Whitehaven manufacturer funded a single voyage to Antigua that saw more than 100 people sold into slavery, many of whom would have worked to plant and harvest the very sugar on which Gilpin's business depended.[34]

Colonial goods presented entrepreneurs with opportunities that otherwise would not have been available to them. It certainly helped transform the prospects of the London-based entrepreneur John Fleet, who had moved to the city from Buckinghamshire where his father had owned an inn. After training as a cooper, the enterprising capitalist set up as a sugar baker with enormous success. By the later 1680s, Fleet had risen to prominence among the city's social and political elite: he was elected Alderman and Sheriff before the end of the decade and sat on the governing board of the East India Company, rigorously promoting the corporation's interest in the following decade. Around the same time, Fleet doubled down on his interest in the exploitation of enslaved people by buying thousands of pounds' worth of stock in the Royal African Company, quickly taking on management positions in this corporation too. By the end of the century, his wealth and power had grown further. His stock in the East India Company had reached highs of £18,000, and now a Member of Parliament, Fleet helped build the city's social infrastructure, making donations to St Bartholomew's Hospital and a school for boys in Battersea. Colonial commerce was not the main source of Fleet's wealth but it had provided a leg-up into a business world where diversification and reinvestment across different sectors could be richly rewarded. In a similar vein, the Liverpool mariner Bryan Blundell, who had served on ships travelling to America from the age of twelve, grew to command business interests that transported more than 15,000 captive African people to America, built ships in Virginia to take part in colonial trade, and carried goods between customers in Ireland, Britain and the Caribbean. Like Fleet, he too used his wealth to improve his local area's social infrastructure, founding Liverpool's Blue Coat School in 1708 and expanding the same with a prominent new building in the heart of Liverpool that was finished nine years later.[35]

Profitable possibilities for serving customers in the Caribbean and North America also incentivised Britain's entrepreneurs to diversify into an array of industrial activities that could profit from colonial demand. Abraham Elton was one particularly successful example of how a British capitalist could exploit these opportunities to rise to a position of political and economic power. The son of a market gardener, Elton worked as an apprentice in Bristol in the 1670s before establishing himself as a merchant and manufacturer. By the early decades of the following century, he had established himself in industries including textiles, brass and iron manufacturing, glass making, salt mining, potteries and gunpowder milling, and maintained trading links with the Americas. Despite choosing not to invest heavily in the slave-trade, his interests were still intimately linked with the transatlantic economy, with goods made for African and Caribbean markets among his most important ventures. In time, this profitable web of interests made Elton among the wealthiest members of Bristol's mercantile elite, and he established himself as a major landowner and political figure in south-west England, becoming a baronet in 1717 and Member of Parliament for Bristol between 1722 and 1727. When he died the following year, his £100,000 fortune was left to his sons Abraham and Jacob, and his grandson Issac, which underpinned their own investment in the rich commercial opportunities that tied Britain's markets to its rapidly growing colonies.[36]

Although colonial trade had a greater impact on economic development in ports like Bristol or Liverpool, capitalists across the country took up opportunities where they could. For example, in the West Yorkshire market town of Halifax, migration and business interests tied local trader Samuel Lister to colonial markets thousands of miles away. His brothers Thomas and Jeremy, who lived in Virginia, were part of a business that took place at a transatlantic scale despite having its roots in northern Britain's rural and wool-manufacturing economy. Thomas and Jeremy thought Virginia was too hot in summer and too cold in winter for their liking, but that, 'where there is money to be got the unpleasantness of the country must not be taken notice of'. One letter from the American-based brothers noted that they planned to use a small sloop, newly named the *Yorkshire Defiance*, to take advantage of opportunities that crossed over continents, oceans and empires. This was not so unusual that it required much explanation, and they simply told their brother that their purchase of 'two thirds of this vessel for £200 which is very cheap' gave them the means to carry thousands of bushels of wheat from the American colony. It would first travel from Virginia to Portugal, where it would sell its foodstuffs and take on board commodities that could be sourced from across Portugal's empire, and continue 'from thence to London' and 'into Yorkshire' before returning to the North American colony. Another business concern of the two brothers rested on their access to 'pork to pickle and pack' in Virginia which they could exchange for 'rum and sugar' in Barbados.[37]

Further north, in Cumberland, the exploitation of enslaved people and the extraction of colonial goods was similarly woven through the wider economic interests of John Lowther. Lowther had inherited a large estate in Cumberland and Westmorland, which he expanded by acquiring more and more land in the region. This estate had rich coal mines, and Lowther supported a range of other industrial enterprises including copper smelting and salt panning. He also played a vital role in the establishment of a new port at Whitehaven, through which he initially exported coal to Ireland. Whitehaven quickly expanded as a centre for importing tobacco from plantations in North America, and Lowther made a hefty profit, while some local traders took the opportunity to send ships from the port to directly take part in the slave-trade. To cater to his colonial customers, the enterprising landowner attempted to stimulate the county's textile industry, with woollen and linen fabrics both in growing demand in North America. Largely an absentee landlord, Lowther saw the improvement of his property in Cumberland as something that would be to 'the general benefit of the whole country', building industries, connecting markets, and adding to the flow of wealth from colonies overseas into domestic assets.[38]

Colonial produce and markets were important for manufacturers in Britain across a range of sectors who sought to profit from the transatlantic economy, even as they grew to support other parts of Britain's economy, too. Clothiers across the country produced fabric for sale in Africa or in colonies in America, with certain styles produced explicitly to clothe enslaved people as they worked in plantations. The Caribbean's tropical climate made linen and cotton particularly attractive, and these quickly surpassed woollens as the main textiles shipped to these colonies in the early decades of the eighteenth century. Metallurgists working with iron or copper, too, benefited both from growing domestic consumption and selling goods to colonies in the Caribbean and North America, to slave-traders in Africa, and to the East India Company. More unusually, Samuel Jacob, a major slave-trader in Bristol, used his knowledge of these networks to shape his investment in manufacturing: in this case helping develop a workshop in Burfield that produced clay pots for Bristol's sugar refiners.[39]

A rare account book, possibly belonging to the Yorkshire cloth merchant George Stansfield, detailed how a single ship, the *Bonadventure*, depended on connections across multiple markets to turn a profit. The surviving accounts only cover business activities from 24 June 1725 through to 17 February 1726, but over the course of the period, the ship's enterprising owner made £390 from his trading activities on this ship, in addition to profits from a one-eighth share in the frigate *James* which earned him £86 that same year. Part of this income came from directly trading with international markets, and French sherry, Virginian tobacco, Italian black cloth, Indian cotton cloth and English woollen textiles were all traded on the ship owner's own account. For the Caribbean trade, sugar and tobacco were purchased 'in company' with Steven Dawner and James Dissell, who each invested £350 in the ship's outgoing voyage to Marseilles that carried the colonial produce onwards alongside a large quantity of lead and serge cloth obtained from producers in England. Finally, a commission at 2½ per cent was received for work undertaken for the merchant Emerson van Tromp, overseeing the sale of 40 pieces of Holland cloth and 560 yards of lace, valued at £1,498.

With a single ship travelling between England, France and Barbados, the owner of the *Bonadventure* was certainly part of the Atlantic slave-economy that produced sugar and tobacco for consumers in Europe, but this was only a small part of their interest. Selling colonial goods in France provided the bumper profits needed to purchase goods like sherry or brandy that could be sold for similarly high margins back in Britain. For the owner of the *Bonadventure*, the colonial market was an opportunity for diversification and profit that any enterprising eighteenth-century merchant would have been keen to take part in.[40] As the re-export of colonial produce like tobacco or sugar became increasingly common for merchants trading from Britain into Europe, the interconnectedness of Britain's transatlantic commercial interests only deepened. Profits and commodities with their roots in slavery were endemic, even when merchants did not take part in trading enslaved people themselves.

The Glaswegian firm of Alexander Shairp & Company likewise took advantage of links like these to obtain sugar, rum, cotton and mahogany from plantations in the Caribbean. Sending ships either to Jamaica directly or via Philadelphia, where they could exchange British goods for provisions desperately sought after further south, Shairp oversaw the sale of fabric that he had purchased from the British Linen Company, pricey Scottish linens, fine furniture for his 'friends in the North', herring from the North Atlantic, and even 'a little bay mare'.[41] In the range of goods sent by Shairp's firm alone, it is clear that the transatlantic economy cannot be understood as one simple triangular trading circuit but rather formed a complex network that tied multiple sectors and the widest array of British commercial interests together. By the middle of the eighteenth century, Britain's colonies in North America and the Caribbean had become key features in the commercial webs that merchants and manufacturers alike took advantage of in the search of profit.

The shipping industry of course benefited from increasing trade of all sorts, and ports like Liverpool and Bristol, where transatlantic commerce was particularly important, were boosted by a growing demand for ships that could traverse the long route to Africa, the Caribbean and North America. The variety of goods needed to keep Britain's shipping industry going included everything from the materials needed to build and maintain ships, like ropes, sails, masts and nails, to the provisions needed to feed sailors during their long time at sea. In Liverpool, the development of sawmills, docks, roperies and other related industries fundamentally shaped how the port developed. Here, prominent shipbuilders like John Okill, Richard Golightly and Richard Gildart were all closely linked to the slave-trade, and Gildart especially profited from direct investment in it. Around the same time, the Royal Navy began to commission ships from Liverpool, further boosting the industry. As well as increasing the demand for ships, colonial trade changed how they were built. Colonies in North America helped supply timber for planks and masts, supplementing the import of similar materials from Scandinavia. Shipping, irrespective of the goods the vessels would later carry, supported a plethora of connected skilled trades, including gunsmiths, braziers, coopers, ironmongers and carpenters, as well as connected businesses from naval store suppliers to lodging houses and public houses for sailors, all of which stimulated further economic activity.[42]

Carpenters were among those whose work depended on this demand. An accounting book used by William Rathbone gives a rare insight into the day-to-day employment that sustained this sort of business. Rathbone worked as a sawyer in Liverpool before establishing a timber business in the 1740s. His work included hundreds of small jobs, usually for less than one pound, including working on ships for slave-traders including William Williamson, John Hardman, Richard Trafford, Peter Pemberton, David Agnew and the Gildart family. He also cut wood for cabinet makers, who sometimes were able to obtain prestige woods like mahogany from colonies in the Caribbean that would end up under Rathbone's saw. The slave-trade was among the activities that funded his work at the Gildarts' properties on Strand Street, Phenwick Alley and Cundliffe House, and his work on the Presbyterian Chapel for the Liverpool Corporation. Businesses like Smithson's Brewery and Thomas Lewes's bakery, whose customers lived and worked in the bustling port town, also hired Rathbone for small jobs. These jobs all depended on demand generated by the growing port industries, whether shipping or construction. Rathbone was just one worker in a city of thousands, whose livelihoods frequently depended on serving Liverpool's colonial traders in one way or another.[43]

The astronomical growth of Liverpool's trade was part of a virtuous cycle of economic and structural development in the prosperous port. In the seventeenth century, Liverpool had not been a prominent port nor a shipbuilding hub, but it was transformed in the first half of the eighteenth century as coastal shipping, trade with Ireland, and the exploitation of transatlantic commercial activities boosted the number of merchants based in the northern town. Around 1700, Liverpool had been home to fewer ships than Bristol, Exeter, Yarmouth or Hull, let alone London, which was far larger still, and the northern port's ships were capable of carrying little more than 5,000 tons of goods in 1709. This quickly increased. Liverpool's shipping capacity had doubled by 1737, and doubled again by 1771, by which point the port had surpassed Bristol to the south and was twice the size of Hull's shipping capacity on England's eastern coast. By the end of the century, Liverpool's shipping could carry 140,632 tons of goods. This was a remarkable rate of growth.[44]

Private shipbuilders did not achieve this alone. Rather, it was a concerted effort on the part of the port's wider commercial community to invest in the essential infrastructure needed to transport their home into one of the leading destinations for colonial goods. A prominent feature of their efforts was the construction and ongoing improvement of Liverpool's docks along the River Mersey. Although it would be the first commercial dry dock in the world, the technology employed in Liverpool was not especially innovative (although they did employ a paramount engineer of the day, Thomas Steers, to oversee the work). However, its backers envisioned a commercial benefit that was quietly revolutionary. The new dock quickly made the port more attractive than nearby competitors like Lancaster or Whitehaven which, despite their considerable trading heritage, lacked the facilities and ease of access that modern, long-distance trading vessels required.

To achieve this goal, in 1710, an Act of Parliament was granted that allowed the port to raise funds for constructing 'a convenient dock . . . for the security of all ships, trading to and from the said port of Liverpool'. Later that year, workers in Liverpool began building the new facility. Rather than seeking external investment, the dock was funded by local lenders, most of whom were the very people who would be using the docks: Liverpool's merchants. They were willing to pay for this large, expensive infrastructure because they recognised that they would benefit in time from it, and because the port

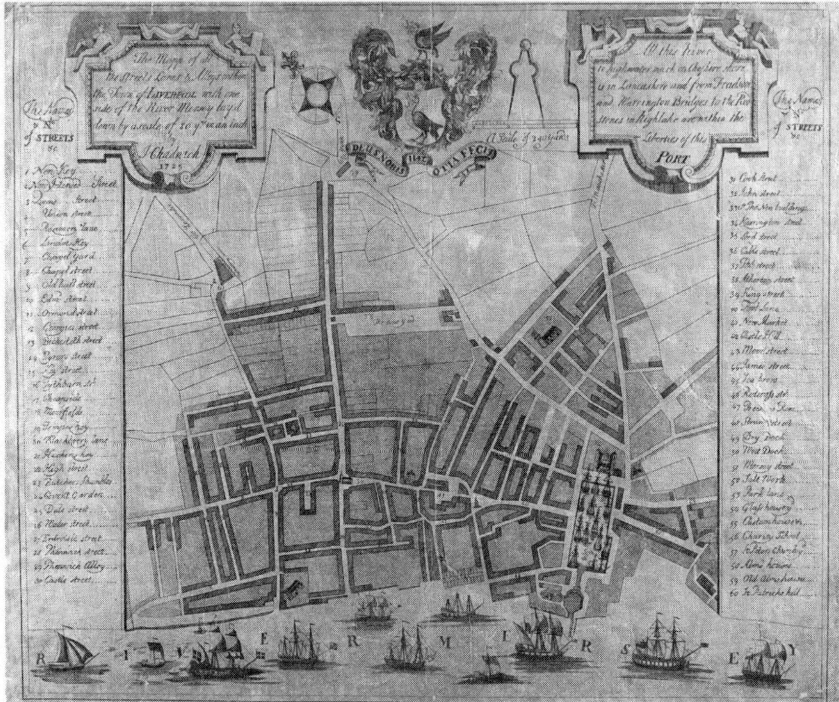

*3. Map of Liverpool from 1725. As Liverpool grew along the River Mersey, specially built facilities, including Britain's first commercial dry dock seen here, supported the extraordinarily rapid growth of the port's trade with colonies in North America and the Caribbean.*

was deemed creditable. After an initial loan of £11,000, further loans were taken out for £14,000 in 1734, £25,000 in 1761 and £70,000 in 1784 – all for further expansion of docks and the development of more advanced facilities. These were paid back through port fees. Essentially, those paying for the dock were the ones using the port, and they paid themselves back for the cost of building their own infrastructure. The governance structure was also designed to ensure that the port met the demands of this same group, and was made up of representatives elected by them. The dock's trustees were unpaid but it was the sort of commitment that was expected from members of a community that depended on trust and personal relationships to sustain everyday business activities. Most importantly,

*4. Map of Liverpool from 1824. Liverpool's remarkable growth can be seen in this map, from a hundred years later, which starkly shows the port's greatly expanded urban area and plethora of docks that by now had spread across the River Mersey's shoreline.*

the returns from the dock for the merchants and ship owners of Liverpool were not expected to be immediate or short-term: it was a multi-generational investment for multi-generational beneficiaries. Liverpool's dock improvement required long-term thinking and a model for investment and governance that placed the burden on people who would profit most from its construction. The impact of the changes to Liverpool's docks was a microcosm of systems that were taking place across Britain's economy: improvement in one area often had positive impacts on others.[45]

By the middle of the eighteenth century, British imports from its Caribbean colonies had surpassed £1.5 million each year, with a further £1 million coming from colonies in North America. Jamaica's exports had more than tripled in volume since the start of the century, now accounting for almost half of the Caribbean's total, while Virginia was similarly dominant in North America, with plantation-grown tobacco representing by far its most valuable commodity. Across Britain's colonies, the impact of population increases was also notable, and almost £2 million of British goods and re-exports were leaving Britain's ports to be sold to colonists living on seized and stolen land overseas. Whereas transatlantic commerce had accounted for 16 per cent of goods carried to and from the nation's ports at the start of the century, this had grown to almost 21 per cent by 1750. Although the import of commodities from plantations remained the richest part of colonial trade, markets in Africa and America had grown in importance for British manufacturers, and these now received 16 per cent of all British manufactured goods that were shipped overseas. This benefited certain industries more than others and their market spread varied depending on local demand. While colonies in North America had grown into markets for diverse goods, including different types of woollen textiles, the same was not the case in the Caribbean. There, Jamaica's wealth, for instance, brought a huge increase in the value of British wrought copper, brass and iron goods that were needed in its burgeoning sugar industry, but also provided a growing market for the metropole's linen manufacturers. Manufacturers serving African ports, on the other hand, found a booming market for gunpowder, wrought copper and brass, linen, and checked cotton cloths. While its impact was not even, transatlantic commerce was a significant part of Britain's overall trade; for many of the nation's fastest-growing and most innovative sectors, it was essential.[46]

Contemporaries understood the value of colonies for Britain's wider economy very well. In 1733, promoters of a new colonial project in Georgia had confidently asserted the benefits of colonial expansion for Britain's growing economy. 'Portugal', they noted 'owes her riches chiefly to her plantations', and Spain's colonies made up for its lack of domestic industry. 'Sweden, Denmark, and Germany', on the other hand, 'find themselves poor, because they have none at present' even 'though they abound with laborious men'. British people were 'manifestly the gainers' from their colonies as their economy simultaneously exploited colonies abroad and industry at home to generate a compounding cycle of economic growth. Britain took 'the benefit' not only from 'manufacturing the products which they raise', which employed the poor and made for profitable exports of goods like refined sugar, but also from re-exporting colonial goods for more profit. As the colonies grew, their free and enslaved populations consumed an ever greater share of British goods. These links pushed private and state actors alike to find new ways to extract more wealth from Britain's colonies overseas, just as it drove support for the textile or metallurgical industries at home. After all, 'the attention of almost all the powers in Europe is turned towards the improvement of [their] settlements abroad' and effort and investment were needed to keep up.[47]

The most successful of Britain's slave-traders, plantation owners and colonial traders made huge profits. Their ties to transatlantic slavery were clear-cut and direct. However, this was just the start of the impact that the colonies and trade in enslaved African people had on Britain's economy. Capitalists profited in a multitude of ways: some sold British goods in the growing markets of Africa and the Caribbean while trafficking enslaved people; some exploited land in colonies that depended on enslaved workers; some transported, sold and re-exported commodities produced by enslaved workers to Britain and around the world; some built ships that were used to transport enslaved people or goods; some provided financial or legal services to slave-traders or colonial merchants; and so on. The list is endless: Britain's economy was highly connected and interdependent, and slavery was an endemic feature. Colonies in the Caribbean and North America were a vital part of an economic system that placed Britain at the centre of a web of exchanges that criss-crossed the Atlantic and stretched around the world. Taken and held with violence, the extraction of wealth from land and enslaved labour far beyond the shores of Britain led to plentiful opportunities for capitalists to enrich themselves and contribute to the nation's growing wealth and power.

CHAPTER 5

# WAR PROFITEERING

## Violence, the State and Economic Development

After the peaceful restoration of Charles II to the British crown in 1660, mainland Britain was largely spared the horrors of war that decimated the lands of its European rivals time and again over the coming century. When William of Orange arrived with Dutch troops to take the throne 1688, he was welcomed by Parliament and met little resistance before his coronation alongside Queen Mary II. Rebellions, sometimes backed by foreign states, were not unheard of, but even the most prominent Jacobite uprisings in 1715, 1719 and 1745 caused minimal damage outside Scotland despite the latter reaching as far south as Derby before withdrawing. While hundreds of thousands died on the battlefields of Europe, conflict on Britain's shores involved thousands of soldiers at most, and did little to disrupt its economic development.[1]

British capitalists would in fact profit greatly from eighteenth-century warfare, which changed the shape of the nation's trade and empire across the world. Whether to protect the crown's interest in Hanover or to stop the balance of power shifting against Britain's favour, the involvement of British troops in conflict overseas was common. Many of these conflicts took place at a global scale, with Britain's hugely expensive fleets patrolling the seas and its armies deploying on land to protect and expand its economic and political interests. In America and Asia, especially, military force often went hand in hand with commercial expansion: new lands were forcibly taken for colonial settlement and British rule imposed violently over growing populations of non-British people. Even as the island of Britain itself was largely spared the horrors of war, the use of military power overseas was a key part of state formation in Britain, with the need to finance and supply armed forces across the world having an impact on everything from the national debt to tax collection and the shape and structure of the armed forces. Private actors took part, too, from privateering merchants to the East India Company and its army of thousands. The spectre of conflict never darkened the doors of Britain's capitalists at home, but that did not stop them seizing opportunities to profit from a world at war.[2]

In 1661, Britain's limited military capacity had forced the state to make difficult choices about where to deploy its naval resources. It did this through the Council of Trade, which assessed the relative importance of different trade routes, which concluded that trade to the Netherlands, Britain's largest trading partner, would be protected by convoys 'constantly going to and from' the two nations' ports, as would merchants travelling across the narrow English Channel to Le Havre. Likewise, the coal trade from Newcastle to London was so important that naval ships would be assigned 'all along the North Sea coast of England', and the fleets of fishing vessels heading to the North Atlantic would have constant protection between June and October. However, only three convoys to the Baltic would take place each year, traders to Hamburg, Bordeaux and Spain would have to make do with two, and those for Greenland or the Canary Islands just one. The East India and Levant trading corporations, who oversaw trade to Asia and the Mediterranean, could make do on their own with larger and more powerfully armed ships at their disposal.[3]

Forty years later, at the beginning of the eighteenth century, when the 'prospect of the War against France and Spain' forced the Commissioners of Trade and Plantations to take stock of the state's capability of protecting Britain's trade, they were dramatically more confident in their ability to impose British military power across the world. 'Ships of war, soldiers, guns and ammunitions' were all available for colonial governments, and orders came thick and fast for supplies. The Governor of Virginia, Colonel Nicholson, requested and received 11,500 firearms and five 5,000 swords to resupply his militia, as well as gunpowder, shot and other supplies to match, at a cost of £3,388. Likewise, a dozen cannon, 500 muskets, and 200 barrels of gunpowder worth £5,568 were sent to New York to help repair the province's outdated and poorly maintained fortifications. Further north, 'the fort at Pemaquid (a place of great importance to the security of the eastern frontiers of New England)' was rebuilt at a cost upwards of £7,000, and the commissioners told that securing the site would cost £5,000 a year, as well as more cannons, mortars, muskets and pikes, and 'two master gunners' to oversee the artillery. More than a hundred cannons, thousands of muskets and hundreds of swords were ordered for Barbados, Antigua and Nevis. The cost of all this would be repaid over time through levies on colonial land and goods. Manufacturers back in Britain would fulfil the orders. Further funds, personnel and supplies followed to protect British interests from the frozen forests of Canada to the humid plantations of the Caribbean.

The growing wealth of colonies in North America and the Caribbean also meant that protecting transatlantic shipping took on a much greater significance even as naval protection for shipping in European waters remained a priority. The commissioners identified 'the great importance of the tobacco trade from Virginia and Maryland' as a source of concern, with 150 ships employed to carry the valuable intoxicant to ports in Britain. A convoy supported by four Royal Navy warships was immediately appointed to accompany them. At the same time, another fleet was sent to protect British colonial interests in the Caribbean. Such protection was considered to be for the good of Britain. If it did not ensure the 'safety of their trade', colonists might be forced 'to turn their industry from the planting of tobacco (so beneficial to England) to producing European manufactures' instead. If paying for armed warships to patrol the world's oceans was the cost of protecting British industry, then it was, the state reckoned, a price worth paying.[4]

This confidence in, and the scale of, the state's military capacity only grew further in the following decades. King George II oversaw a foreign policy shaped by complex commitments that linked his Hanoverian interests in Europe with Britain's colonial and commercial ones, especially competition with France and Spain abroad. By the middle of the eighteenth century, Britain's expanded armed forces and ability to commit forces across the world had reshaped its imperial ambitions. In the 1740s, across a series of conflicts connected to the War of the Austrian Succession in continental Europe, Britain flexed its financial and global military muscles. Despite Britain's Austrian and Dutch allies struggling to push back Prussian and French power in Europe, by deploying tens of thousands of troops and providing funds that enabled its allies to employ tens of thousands more, Britain altered the balance of the conflict. Just as significantly, British armed forces took part in conflicts in Canada, the Caribbean and India, increasing its military presence in each region and demonstrating the power and reach of Britain's navy. By the end of the eighteenth century, the Royal Navy could easily deploy more warships than its French and Spanish competitors combined. This fleet had a double benefit for the nation's capitalists and the British state: it stopped them from suffering the horrors of war on their own soil, while offering plentiful opportunities to inflict those same horrors on other people.

The people who profited from the bloody march of trade and empire included the traders who secured access to markets, the landowners who expanded or obtained new estates overseas, the settlers who moved to newly acquired territories to make their fortunes, and many more. For Britain's military suppliers, especially, this era of seemingly constant conflict was a bonanza, and their workshops and dockyards churned out ever-growing volumes of weapons and warships to meet the demands of the warmongering state. Of course, war did not benefit everyone. Hundreds of thousands of mostly poorer people died, serving in their nation's armed forces in return for the paltry wages available. Nor did every capitalist profit, as merchants might suffer attacks on their ships or manufacturers could lose their access to markets overseas. The state, too, spent a huge amount of money. Losses like these were apparently considered a worthwhile exchange. It would only be a few more years before Britain went to war again, sending thousands more to their deaths in service of taking a little more land and keeping trade flowing.[5]

## FINDING WOOD FOR WOODEN WALLS

For a nation in a state of more or less perpetual war across far-flung territories overseas, financing conflict was only part of the challenge. Supplying the armed forces also depended on the ever increasing production of the machinery of war by Britain's manufacturers, with the state purchasing everything from massive warships to firearms, munitions and uniforms. For an island nation with colonial and commercial interests that were increasingly global in scope, establishing naval supremacy was a primary objective for the state – first to protect the island from invasion, and then to impose its will across the world. Warships were hugely expensive to build, requiring specialised skills and facilities, and there were only a handful of ports in Britain capable of building the very largest vessels for the Royal Navy. They also needed massive amounts of wood: a single large warship required timber from 3,000 trees. Smaller ships, including those for trade and fishing, were built in many ports, and these too needed skilled labour and ready access to supplies. Dramatic increases in the size of Britain's shipbuilding industry took place in the seventeenth century, and the volume of the nation's ships increased around three times, to 323,000 tons in 1702. By 1788, this had increased to over a million tons. Building more ships required everything from hundreds of thousands of tiny iron nails for securing planks to the immense timbers needed for masts. Supplying these supported a range of subsidiary industries in Britain, many of which made improvements in their organisation or facilities to achieve the rapid growth needed to meet the demands of military and commercial shipbuilders.[6]

Sourcing so much timber for planks and masts, though, was one problem that no amount of innovation in Britain could overcome. Much of the island's climate and soil was unsuited to growing the incredibly tall pine trees needed for masts. At the same time, fears of deforestation restricted the number of deciduous trees that could be cut for planking and other uses. For a long time, this was offset by importing wood and other naval supplies from Scandinavia, but in the eighteenth century exploiting territories seized in America became an increasingly popular option. Britain's colonies in North

America had long been recognised as an important fixture in its warmaking capabilities. During the earliest years of settlement, before the expansive forests of North America had been seized or exploited, William Bradford had encouraged support for colonisation on the basis that 'there is much good timber, both oak, walnut-tree, fir, beech, and exceeding great chestnut trees' that could be exported to Britain. Around the same time, the New England Company's leadership published a pamphlet emphasising the availability of timber for 'spars, masts, for ships of all burdens' and 'commodities to make pitch, resin, tar'. Before long, colonists were building ships with local supplies. Another early colonial promoter, Christopher Levett, declared that 'I dare be so bold to say also, there may be ships as conveniently built there as in any place in the world'. To say the least, in the seventeenth century the possibility of using produce extracted from territories recently seized in North America was already understood as a means to boosting Britain's shipbuilding capacity.[7]

By the end of the seventeenth century, supplying the Royal Navy was increasingly centralised, and a specialist administrative unit called the Navy Board had been set up to oversee the purchase of essential materials. Stronger state finances enabled the Navy Board to administer contracts more effectively with suppliers, increasing competition between merchants and resulting in a fall in prices for many important types of naval stores. Increasing demands were also placed on merchants to import vast amounts of naval stores – especially from the Baltic. However, access to this market was far from guaranteed, and conflict breaking this link and reducing supply were common concerns among contemporary commentators. Extracting the vital raw materials needed to sustain Britain's military force and commercial shipping industry from forested territories seized by colonists in North America was one solution. Commissioners were sent to New England in 1700 specifically, as they reported, 'for the viewing and inspecting [of] the woods lying upon that coast, for providing His Majesty's navy with masts and other necessary materials for building of ships'. The expedition was a success, and they returned to London with specimens of the region's timber, pitch, tar and resin for assessment. Securing naval supplies also shaped how the state used its military force, and the cost of defending New Hampshire 'which is a small province' was justified on consideration that it was 'very considerable on the account of naval stores' supplied from its forests.[8]

Proposals to supply the navy with key commodities from North American colonies were met with a favourable response. Much like demands for ordnance and gunpowder would change how industries producing these key goods were structured, the Board of Trade encouraged production in the American colonies with the specific intention of increasing imports of vital supplies to England. In 1705, the Naval Stores Act incentivised merchants to provide American timber, pitch, tar, hemp, rosin and turpentine for the navy. This was designed to boost production within Britain's empire and create an internal market for naval supplies. Just as the Royal African Company had lost out to private traders, the Board of Trade concluded that 'private persons' would 'better open this trade than corporations, who must bring a load upon that trade by salaries to managers, officers and other out goings, which select numbers may excuse'. Naval suppliers were largely left to their own devices in finding the most profitable and productive ways of connecting Britain's shipyards with the output of vast forests an ocean away.[9]

By the 1720s, though, Acts of Parliament were issued in response to ongoing failures to secure 'sufficient quantities of naval stores' that were blamed on 'frauds and abuses' on the part of the navy's contractors: most prominently, the payment of excessive premiums for goods. At the same time, concerns that illegal logging was diminishing available supplies led to the passage of an act for 'the better preservation of His Majesty's woods in America', which was designed to secure masts made from the best 'white pine trees' for the navy. This required colonists to have a royal licence to cut down trees and reinforced prohibitions on tree felling that had been imposed two decades earlier without the intended effect. While many settlers almost certainly continued to ignore the restrictions, the effort alone reveals the importance of these key goods. The state also enacted legislation to minimise abuses within the contracting system, publishing precise, guaranteed rates for different goods. In theory, this also incentivised enterprising suppliers of masts, tar, pitch or turpentine that met the navy's requirements to find efficiencies or otherwise reduce their costs, as they were reassured that increasing supply would not drive prices down and so every penny saved was a penny of profit made.[10]

Hopes that the vast forested expanses of north-eastern America would provide Britain with vital naval stores remained a popular theme for concerned authors. There was certainly plenty of evidence that colonial timber was well suited for shipbuilding needs, and dockyards in North America would build hundreds of ships from local supplies, large and small, to support trading and fishing activities across the region. Writing in the 1720s, Daniel Defoe enthusiastically supported plans 'for turning the whole trade for naval stores' away from Scandinavia and the Baltic, and towards 'our own colonies' in America. The North American territories were replete with hemp, flax, tar, turpentine and timber, 'and perhaps, in time, with iron also', and 'with proper encouragements' would produce them 'all as cheap' as their northern European competitors. If the right solution was found, the 'boundless extent of woods' that were 'unexhausted, and indeed, inexhaustible' would easily meet Britain's demands.[11]

By the mid-eighteenth century, New England was the second largest supplier of large masts in Britain's dockyards. While the Baltic and Scandinavia remained the most common markets for many naval supplies, the largest ships of the Royal Navy required masts that were difficult to obtain from anywhere but America. By the breakout of the Seven Years War in the 1750s, large masts from the region dominated the supplies of the Royal Navy. In the first year of the war, 243 large masts were delivered from New England, compared to only two from Riga and Norway. The following year saw 205 brought from North American colonies and sixteen from the Baltic. This trend continued, with New England supplying up to five times as many large masts as the Baltic trade in the following years. The development of the Royal Navy as a well-organised and creditable institution had significantly improved the competitiveness of suppliers who set out to secure naval stores from North America rather than traditional sources in the Baltic. In time, the effects of naval supply on local ecology were considerable, with demands from Britain's shipbuilders contributing to massive deforestation across much of the New England coast.[12]

Even as supplies increased, the infrastructure needed to build ships in Britain was undergoing continuous improvements as docks and yards were built to cater to mercantile and state demand for ships. The Liverpool docks expanded rapidly across the eighteenth century as their merchants took a growing share of the transatlantic trade, a trajectory that also saw Bristol's docks expand to build ships for the colonial trades. Similar impetus encouraged shipbuilding in Scotland, and Greenock and New Port Glasgow, both on the River Clyde, saw new yards and dock works built and expanded throughout the eighteenth century. Likewise, in Hull on Britain's north-eastern coast, ten yards were in operation by the middle of the century, supplying both the navy and commercial clients with ships. Even private landowners were getting in on the act, and the Montagu family built yards on their estate near Southampton that made ships for the navy in the 1740s. The largest concentration of shipbuilders, though, remained in the south of England, serving state and private clients, especially in docks built on the banks of the River Thames.[13]

As this suggests, the knock-on impact of increasing timber supplies could be felt across different sectors of the British economy. Ports and shipbuilding across the country benefited from increasing military orders just as they benefited from increasing supplies brought from places that were secured with the very warships that they built using them. Better supplies and a larger navy benefited British merchants undertaking long-distance trade, providing vital protection for English merchants across the world. Yet, in doing so, the British state became increasingly reliant on the very colonies whose exploitation had been encouraged to limit the metropole's dependence on any single region for its most important goods. In the face of conflict with France in Canada and growing support for independence in Britain's North American colonies, one commentator simply asked: 'if we should lose the northern colonies, where shall we get pitch and tar, masts and naval stores for our navy?' Violence had secured the goods that were needed for Britain to make war, and further conflict would be justified, in part, by the need to keep control of them.[14]

## ARMING AN EMPIRE

Securing supply chains for essential materials that could be obtained from Britain's colonies was one way that the state encouraged domestic industry. The state was also the biggest purchaser of essential military hardware that could be made in British workshops and factories. Among the most important were firearms. By the eighteenth-century, firearms were popular and widespread in European armies and had come a long way from the simple 'hand cannons' in use three centuries earlier, which were little more than tubes mounted on a pole. Arms like muskets, rifles and pistols followed, with added parts such as locks and springs boosting the weapons' mechanical power. While firearms remained unreliable, slow and unwieldy, they dramatically changed how warfare was conducted, and no state could ignore them if it intended to compete on the modern battlefield. This presented challenges for the state and opportunities for capitalists. Even the best-made firearms were perishable and regularly broke down, which drove a relentless demand from the state, even as the size of armed forces increased. However, at the beginning of the century, matching this demand was far beyond the capacity of existing gunmakers. The cannons, muskets and swords sent to colonies in America described above were only a fraction of the volume that colonial governors requested, and officers of the Ordnance Office complained that they simply didn't have enough supply to spare more weapons. However, within a few decades, state support and private innovation in gun manufacture had radically altered this dynamic, and Britain's manufacturers were churning out more guns than ever before. This was both an opportunity for profitable enterprise and an essential part of the state's ability to execute its will across the world.[15]

The state's role in the expansion of the gun manufacturing industry was clear in its adoption of protectionist policies. Much like woollen manufacturers had benefited from prohibitions on the export of raw wool, domestic gun manufacturers and other metallurgists received support in the seventeenth century with bans on the export of key metals. In the 1690s, a petition from braziers and founders from across Britain was published in support of 'diverse statutes prohibiting the exportation of iron, copper and bell metal', which they understood was vital for their livelihoods. They warned 'the French King will be supplied . . . with guns' if metal was exported, and that European competitors would quickly surpass them. Likewise, when the Royal African Company sought to buy cheaper guns from Dutch gunmakers in the 1680s, the exchange had been prohibited: the state did what it could to support British manufacturers at the expense of their overseas rivals.[16]

However, the government's interest in gun manufacturing was also much more direct. The Ordnance Office was the industry's largest customer and placed massive orders for firearms, artillery, gunpowder and other supplies. It also used its power to shape how arms were procured in ways that had major repercussions for the structure of Britain's militarily focused manufacturing sectors. In the seventeenth century, almost 200 London gunsmiths had supplied the Ordnance Office with arms, with the production of weapons regulated by the Company of Gunmakers. Most of these gunmakers had workshops in the vicinity of the Tower of London but, with strict regulation and little room to expand or alter their methods, they were at risk from more nimble competitors. After concerns were raised in the 1690s that the kingdom was becoming too reliant on imported Dutch arms, which had become popular after the Glorious Revolution, the Midlands-based Member of Parliament Sir Richard Newdigate suggested that Birmingham had everything needed to set up a competing centre of gun manufacture. Not only had the Midlands been home to metal workers for centuries, but it was already home to gunmakers who repaired London-made firearms and armourers that produced swords and other goods. Promising that 'the men of Birmingham can do whatever skill and metal can do', Newdigate obtained permission to send a Dutch gun to the town's smiths for a trial: could they replicate the popular model and offer a viable alternative to London's gunmaking dominance? They could.

The London Company of Gunmakers complained at once that the Birmingham manufacture would be a violation of their monopoly, but to little effect. Further trials from the Ordnance Office followed, and in 1693 it issued a contract to 'The Company of Gunmakers in Birmingham' to manufacture 2,400 muskets in the next twelve months. Newdigate, confident of their success and the benefits it would bring the town, extended credit to local gunmakers for the necessary supplies. His gamble paid off, and Birmingham manufacturers contributed to the widespread rearming of British forces during the 1690s that saw pikes and matchlock muskets replaced with the modern flintlock muskets and bayonets that the Ordnance Office had ordered. These changes were all part of the state's concerted efforts to multiply the number of gunmakers, initially as a response to political concerns that an overconcentrated arms industry might give too much influence to individual producers or, much worse, fall into the hands of rebels. At the same time, the promise of profit encouraged gun manufacturers to produce more weapons for private traders for export, most prominently the East India Company and corporate and independent slave-traders. The benefits were twofold: a more competitive and diffuse gun-manufacturing industry helped increase productive capacity, securing supplies for the state while simultaneously lowering prices.

Before long, gun manufacturers was established in Birmingham and nearby villages including Harborne, Bilston, Darlaston and Wednesbury. Despite ongoing complaints about the infringement of their monopoly, the new workshops even received orders from London gunsmiths when they needed to fulfil a contract for 30,000 locks that the capital's workshops had not met. Having immediately specialised in the newer flintlock models, the Midlands-based manufacturers were well positioned to take advantage of the Ordnance Office's growing demand for the weapons in the first decades of the eighteenth century, as old matchlocks were replaced and London's gunmakers were incapable of matching the state's demands. By 1707, the integration of Birmingham into the state's system of obtaining firearms was well under way, and in the following decades parts from the Midlands would increasingly find their way into firearms that were assembled in London.[17]

It was in this environment that the ironmonger Joseph Farmer moved to Birmingham from Bristol, drawn by the opportunities of the booming gun trade, who set up alongside 'many hundreds of workmen' who were already making guns. Farmer's firm would become, over the course of the century, one of the largest suppliers of weapons to the British state and a major player in Birmingham's development as an industrial city. Farmer's early efforts benefited from a change in how the Ordnance Office ordered stock: rather than ordering finished weapons, it began to give contracts to people who carried out a particular stage in the production of firearms. One manufacturer would carve the walnut stocks for the guns, another would make their locks, another the barrels, and so on. By keeping larger stores of parts, the Ordnance Office hoped to keep bottlenecks in the market to a minimum. Birmingham's growing specialism making specific parts, like locks, worked in its gunmakers' favour, and they would ship millions of precise metal fixtures to London over the coming decades. An early contract for another gunmaker, Jacob Austin, in November 1707 required 2,000 locks to be made and sent south, while Farmer's first order in 1708 saw 200 carbine barrels manufactured and shipped to London for assembly. At the same time, the Midlands gunmakers began selling more goods to merchants trading in North America and Africa, where firearms were demanded in 'greater quantities, than was ever known before'. By the end of the 1710s, the Birmingham manufacturers had become integral parts of a system that saw the Ordnance Office order growing numbers of parts from the town's workshops, while a profitable surplus was exported overseas.[18]

For such a system to work effectively, standardisation was essential, and the Ordnance Office began to send more exacting guidance to manufacturers about the precise design of different parts of weapons, followed by agents who could instruct workmen and measure products to ensure they matched expectations. This was a critical step towards achieving mass production, and the state's organisation of supply and assembly of guns had begun to resemble a dispersed assembly line. These changes led to the first standard-pattern British firearm, known as the Brown Bess. A heavy, large-calibre, smoothbore flintlock musket with a 46-inch-long barrel, it remained the standard weapon of British infantry for the remainder of the century, with minimal changes to barrel length and the replacement of iron fixtures with brass the only alterations to the accepted design. A skilled soldier could fire it three times a minute, and the damage caused by the large lead balls it fired on the human body was tremendous. Although seen as slightly worse than the Dutch model, the agreed pattern could be produced in large volumes at prices that kept the Ordnance Office and manufacturers alike relatively happy. There were limited technological changes to how guns were produced in British workshops that accounted for the industry's growing productivity. Instead, the expansion of the gun trade depended on dramatic changes in industrial organisation and the combination of small-scale workshops within larger contracting systems that could respond quickly to changing demands from the state in times of war and from other commercial customers during peacetime. It also depended on manufacturers being willing and able to shift production from one type of good to another, a process that benefited from subcontracting orders to numerous small workshops that could respond more flexibly to changing demand.[19]

The workshops in Birmingham that had grown to supply weapons to the state continued to expand and interact with other parts of the metallurgical industry, and workshops capable of producing locks for guns could often swap to producing other goods when the need demanded. Fuelled by the Midlands' easy access to coal and plentiful amounts of iron, Birmingham's workshops were involved in metallurgical innovations that sometimes had nothing to do with the gun trade, but still contributed to the growth of expertise and specialised facilities that benefited people across metallurgical industries. Farmer's firm was involved in many of these changes. Starting out with a small smith's shop in Birmingham's Old Square, the enterprising ironmonger rapidly expanded his business over the coming decades: he was part of a partnership in 1717 that leased an iron furnace at Rushall, in 1718 he travelled to America to experiment with alternative sources of iron ore, in 1720 he joined in partnerships with a group of Birmingham and London businessmen to set up an ironworks near Baltimore, and by the late 1720s he had outgrown the workspace in Old Square and moved to a larger site on the edge of Birmingham. By 1735, wealth from his success in gun manufacturing, ironworking and property had led to another expansion, this time to Steelhouse Lane, which would be the beating heart of his firm's activities even as it passed to future generations of the family.[20]

When Joseph Farmer died in 1741, his son James Farmer took over. He quickly went into business with another gunmaker, Edward Jordan, and the two men set out to produce complete arms as well as locks and barrels before another partner (and James Farmer's brother-in-law), Samuel Galton, joined the firm in 1746. By now, the firm depended on a national network of skilled workers that they employed to complete distinct parts of the manufacturing process, all of whom shipped goods to their warehouse in Steelhouse Lane. Its suppliers connected the business to an even wider web, with walnut imported from Italy and Germany and iron from North America, Sweden and Russia both making their way into finished firearms. Unfortunately for them, peace had begun to dampen sales. While they continued to produce parts for guns, the firm tried to find ways to adapt their expertise towards the manufacture of alternative products. There was certainly opportunities for other well-made, complicated metal goods, and in 1748 Farmer wrote to Galton from Dunkirk to let the metallurgist know that there was great demand for 'all sorts of toys of Birmingham' (small metal items like buckles, buttons or snuff boxes that were produced by the town's metalworkers). However, they lacked the long-term and regular orders needed to make it viable as a major part of the business. Only a year later, in 1749, and now writing from Rouen, Farmer's assessment of the arms trade had grown even more dire. Reports from Bristol and Liverpool that sales of 'English arms are bad' were compounded by complaints from his brother Joseph about 'the hardness of trade at Liverpool', where his commercial activities were delivering little more than 3 per cent returns. Farmer hoped that Galton had 'taken some steps to put in execution what I wrote about, lessening our manufacture of guns', because it looked like 'returns will never answer for the stock employed': it currently cost more to make a gun than the firm could make selling it.[21]

In light of the awful peacetime trading conditions, Joseph was tempted to follow the advice of John Hardman, a merchant who exchanged metal goods in Africa for enslaved people that he trafficked to Britain's colonies, and simply withdraw his capital from overseas commerce to reinvest it in setting up as an ironmonger. If Galton came 'upon any scheme that's feasible' to support such a radical shift in the northern trader's interests, James made sure that his partner was aware that his brother would very much like to hear about it. Finally, demand for Birmingham 'toys' was increasing quickly at home and abroad, but manufacturers had to adapt their styles and processes to meet the expectations of their customers. In 1750, Galton received more letters from James, now writing from London, who had secured orders for specific goods and had sent the Birmingham manufacturer 'the patterns' that he needed to follow. These included designs for 'black steel buckles', comb handles, buttons and 'little round bells to put round the necks of sheep, dogs [and] cats'. For a firm that had been built producing instruments of violence, this was quite a change of pace. However, the firm's ability to rise to the challenge attests to possibilities available for entrepreneurial capitalists to quickly shift between sectors and markets as conditions demanded. At the same time, Farmer and Galton further diversified their business interests by taking stakes in a new business producing iron and steel, erecting furnaces at Belbroughton, in the hope of supplying better-quality metal for their workshops.[22]

Despite the troubling impact that peace had on his core business, Farmer found increasing opportunities to sell firearms improved in the 1750s, and the firm sold 4,000 guns of various styles to slave-traders in the first half of the decade. By now, the firm was producing thousands of both wooden and metal parts, which could all be fed into the supply chain. It was also producing guns that followed Danish and Dutch designs to meet the requirements of private customers, and making swords, pistols, knives and birding guns. It benefited, especially, from a change by the Ordnance Office that made it possible for the company to gain accreditation for the quality of their finished guns, rather than selling parts for assembly elsewhere. Gun manufacturers like the Farmer & Galton firm catered to a strong customer base across Britain's commercial and colonial interests in North America, West Africa, and Asia. West Africa was a particularly prominent market for British guns during peacetime when the state's purchase of arms decreased. Commercial and colonial conflicts also encouraged the shift towards the mass production of standardised firearms. In Jamaica, resistance by free, formerly enslaved African people had seen the interior of the island fall increasingly beyond the control of British colonists. In India, too, conflict with coastal Maratha forts saw more guns purchased by the East India Company for the corporation's own warmaking or to be sold to allies. Whether supplying the private companies with arms for their own use or for sale, gunmakers found a ready market for their goods.[23]

After the punishing conditions that had seen the Farmer & Galton firm's value fall from £10,000 in 1746 to £8,670 only five years later, the uptick in demand in the 1750s saw it quickly recover its value. By 1754, the firm was making more than 25,000 guns for the African trade, mostly sold to traders in Liverpool and Bristol, and they were struggling to keep up with orders. Despite the increase in sales, the firm was almost bankrupted when Farmer mortgaged it to gain capital to invest in Portuguese trade, which quickly collapsed, leaving Galton in a position where he was forced to beg agents in Liverpool and Lancaster to secure payments to save them from ruin. Fortuitously for Britain's gunmakers, war was never far away, and demand for firearms was quickly back on track in the following years as Britain went to war again. The outbreak of conflict with France and the prospect of massive profits from state contracts helped keep the firm's creditors at bay. Sales to traders with interests in America picked up too, as guns for militia in Britain's colonies became a priority. One of the firm's customers, John Hanbury, who controlled a vast 200,000 acres in the Ohio River Valley and made huge profits from trading tobacco, advocated not only arming British colonists but also their indigenous allies. Another contract was made with colonists in Montserrat to provide arms for the island's militia. Soon, the orders from the state followed. War and profit went hand in hand.[24]

## EXPLOSIVE GROWTH

The expansion of gun manufacturing was part of a wider boom in Britain's metallurgical industries. Improvements in business organisation and techniques, and the combination of different parts of Britain's economy – coal mining, ore extraction, smelting – made this expansion possible. The fate of other industries relied on similar interlinkages. Gunpowder production for example was intricately connected to arms manufacturing, and the state was a primary purchaser of the explosive powder much as it was for guns, ammunition and other equipment necessary for making war. Like guns, gunpowder was also sold to private customers, whether as a good for export or for use in the nation's growing mining sector, where it became increasingly common as a means to blow up rocks. The precise combination of charcoal, sulphur and saltpetre that were ground together to produce the explosive powder was altered depending on the target market, as was the fineness of the grains produced. The best-quality gunpowder, for hunting weapons or military use, was ground into the finest consistency to produce a sustained charge. However, this absorbed moisture easily, and 'Guinea' or 'African' powder was more desirable in the tropics. Helpfully, this coarser powder also combined better with the low-quality 'trade guns' that were exported to Africa in enormous numbers, whose barrels could burst if fired using the more explosive fine powder.[25]

Gunpowder manufacture depended on imports and was historically concentrated close to London. Trade with India, the global centre of saltpetre production, was particularly important, and the East India Company benefited from a massive contract to supply the state with hundreds of tons of saltpetre every year. Bought by its agents in India, huge volumes of the precious chemical were collected and then shipped to Britain for delivery to the government's warehouses. Sulphur was imported primarily from Sicily, where child labourers were forced to mine the volcanic element. Much like advances in iron and coal mining combining with gun manufacturing in cycles of increasing production, the gunpowder industry benefited from, and contributed to, the growth of trade. These were not the most expensive products coming to Britain from India or Italy by any stretch, but they were among the most vital for Britain's growing war machine.[26]

Already in 1700, there were around twenty gunpowder works in operation in south-east England that had been able to keep up with the army and navy's growing demand and continued to profit from their close links to the British state. These works sold their product to businesses including the Royal African Company and other merchants, as well as hunters in Britain, which provided a useful counterbalance to declining demand from the state during peacetime. Producing gunpowder was not labour-intensive, and a small team of workers refined saltpetre and sulphur to remove impurities before they were combined with charcoal to produce what was known as a 'green charge'. This would then be moved to the incorporating mill, where waterpower provided the energy to grind the materials together into a 'mill cake', which in turn would be forced through a series of sieves until the required fineness of grain was achieved. This was capital-intensive and skilled work. In London, the mills that had served the state at the start of the century expanded and worked together to produce more powder and keep prices high.[27]

Even as growing demand from the state incentivised the expansion of the gunpowder mills that surrounded London, British capitalists were selling guns and powder to customers in West Africa, primarily to buy enslaved people. With ever more ships involved in this trade departing Bristol and Liverpool, local investors were incentivised to establish their own manufacturing firms to ensure they were well supplied. In 1722, a consortium of four Bristol merchants erected a new powder works at nearby Woolley, which was expanded in the 1730s to double its capacity. A competing works was built at Littleton in 1749, six miles from the port, which was similarly expanded in the 1760s to keep up with demand with the construction of two new mills in nearby Chew Stoke and Chew Magna. In northern England, a group of Liverpool merchants built a powder works at Thelwall in 1757, which rapidly expanded in the following two decades with four extensions added to the original works. Another major gunpowder firm was set up at Sedgwick by a consortium of businessmen from Kendall in 1764, and here, too, further investment saw an additional mill built at Basingill in the 1790s. Much like the development of Birmingham gun manufacturing, these were among the first efforts to establish gunpowder-producing facilities outside London and were part of the industrial development of Liverpool and Bristol.[28]

Gunpowder making was a multi-stage and energy-intensive process, and the establishment and expansion of gunpowder mills like these required significant expenditure as well as expertise and understanding of interlinked international markets. The large works at Sedgwick were housed in as many as twenty separate buildings across an extensive industrial site that included multiple mills and storerooms and a blacksmith, cooper and sawmill. Waterwheels were needed to power the mills, with weirs and waterways cut to ensure a steady supply of energy would reliably flow into the site. Ensuring water supply required similarly extensive work at the Woolley works, which, according to one visitor, were 'situated in a deep picturesque spot, and almost environed with wood', where two corn mills had been converted to serve a new role grinding powder. By the 1740s, the site had four mills running, with water running first over one wheel and then a second to maximise productivity, a process that a memorandum about the site described as water being used 'twice over'. To increase production, the new owners invested in cutting a channel almost a mile long to a nearby dam that had been built to keep a ready supply of water available for the mill's vital waterwheels. Work like this required skilled engineers and numerous labourers who needed paying long in advance of the sales of gunpowder that followed. Consequently, business owners needed considerable upfront capital, often around £10,000 or more. This was comparable to the charges of setting up other large and complex industrial enterprises during this period, whether sugar plantations in Jamaica, coke-fired ironworks in Birmingham, or textile factories in Lancashire.[29]

To meet these costs, gunpowder works were typically founded by partnerships with both capital and know-how. More than half the partners involved operated as slave-traders, using their profits from the sale of enslaved people to invest in the production of gunpowder that would feed into the same trade. The Woolley works was founded by two slave-traders from Bristol, Abraham Hooke and Edmund Baugh, and their principal agents in Liverpool were another pair of slave-traders, Benjamin Heywood and Arthur Heywood. The founders of the Thelwall mill included Ellis and Robert Cunliffe, who owned ships that trafficked 8,000 captive people from Africa before they established the gunpowder works. Other partners included the brewer and textile manufacturer John Wakefield, who profited from trading with the Caribbean, and Christopher Wilson, a banker and hosier. Inevitably, this group were also tied into wider commercial networks producing and transporting goods to West Africa and other overseas markets, with interests in iron, linen and sugar all feeding into the gunpowder mills' partnerships. Investment in gunpowder manufacturing also came from local landowners: another route by which rural and urban wealth were combined to fund Britain's industrial development. No matter the background, all were linked through their production of the explosive powder to the exploitation of enslaved people and the extraction of wealth from territories seized and secured through war. While the profit of manufacturing gunpowder could fluctuate from year to year, in the long term it was a very good investment. Within four years of its founding, the partners of the Thelwall works had doubled their money, and other works were similarly highly profitable.[30]

Mills like these had dramatically increased the capacity of the industry to fuel the state's demands and those of overseas traders. In total, Britain's mills produced over 220,000 tons of gunpowder during the eighteenth century, the majority of which was bought by the state. However, commercial expansion also drove the manufacturing boom. Whereas in 1698, British traders in Africa were selling around twenty-five tons of gunpowder each year to customers on the Atlantic coast, this had grown six times by 1750 and would only grow further in the following decades. Manufacturers in London, likewise, profited from the sale of their powder to customers around the world. Almost half of the capital's exports were sold to customers in colonies across the Americas, and large volumes also found their way to European markets and into the hands of the East India Company. Of course, it was the return of saltpetre from India that made much of this increase possible, and the growth of British military interests in South Asia went hand in hand with its production. Huge demands on the part of the warmongering British state for explosives were a driving factor for the industry's development, but investment in gunpowder manufacturing depended on circuits that brought together commodities, capital and expertise from across Britain's economy, contributing to ongoing gains in multiple industries simultaneously.[31]

Warfare was an important factor in Britain's rise to wealth and power, linking networks of capital across business, empire and the state. As the scale of conflict continued to grow, the state's capacity to finance conflict grew with it. The bulk demand for instruments of war stimulated innovations in business organisation that continued to drive productivity gains in the following decades. By setting minimum standards at a level that incentivised producers to innovate, whether in how they made guns or ground gunpowder, the state encouraged wider participation and booming productivity. Between 1680 and 1780, the army and navy tripled in size, and spending by the state multiplied in kind. Millions of pounds were spent, providing suppliers of everything from uniforms to ships, powder, arms, shot, foodstuffs and more with the opportunity to profit from wars across the world. The state was the largest borrower, spender and employer in the country. By the end of the century, workshops in London and Birmingham would produce and sell millions of guns and the requisite powder to fire them that ended up in the hands of buyers in Britain, Africa, India, the Caribbean, North America, and Europe.[32]

## THE COST OF TRADE

Ships, guns and gunpowder were all products that Britain's capitalists enthusiastically set out to provide. They benefited from being able to sell their goods to, and buy supplies from, actors operating across Britain's trading and imperial interests while also profiting from state demand. This, though, was just part of the nexus of colonial supply, warmaking and domestic manufacturing that contributed to Britain's economic development. The use of military force, too, was an important means by which traders and colonists secured their economic interests across the world. Sometimes they were supported by the British state directly, with ships from the Royal Navy or soldiers from the growing army supporting them, but private actors were often heavily armed enough on their own. By the middle of the eighteenth century, the capacity for private actors to make war had grown dramatically in line with the state's growing expenditure and support for military production. In Asia, Africa and America, capitalists used violence to secure and expand Britain's economic interests, sometimes by taking new territories that could be exploited for profit, and sometimes by enforcing demands on local people for more favourable trading conditions.

The East India Company did both of these things in Bengal, where, supported by the Royal Navy, it took advantage of ongoing conflicts with local rulers and European competitors to rapidly expand its authority far beyond the trading sites that it controlled on the Indian coast. That is not to suggest that these were insignificant, and the British presence in Kolkata had coincided with the growth of the port city into a major commercial metropolis in the first decades of the eighteenth century. Despite having a high mortality rate, it had flourished as a centre of trade. Between 1704 and 1756, the city's population exploded from only a few thousand people to around 400,000: easily larger than any town in Britain's American colonies. Incomers were attracted by the East India Company's policies and promises of protection, and the possibility of profit, and the city had grown to become a bustling hub of Bengali enterprise and culture. Threatened by the growth of the city and loss of control over wealthy migrants who moved there, the Nawab of Bengal Siraj-ud-Daulah responded to the fortification of the East India Company's Fort William in Kolkata in 1756 by launching a brutal surprise attack. Overrun and captured, the fort's residents were imprisoned in what would become known as the 'Black Hole', a tiny dungeon too small to hold them, where many died of suffocation and heat exhaustion in only a few hours. Survivors shared graphic tales of their suffering, which were distributed to the British public in print among explanations of the conflict that followed. The corporation quickly retaliated, and a force under the command of Robert Clive and Charles Watson was sent to recapture the fort and demand access to the region's trade on agreeable terms. Clive, who had made his name during the conflict on the Indian coast with France and other local rulers in the previous decade, led a force of around 900 European and 1,500 Indian soldiers and seized Kolkata in January 1757.[33]

British factors in India began to write home celebrating that the 'cruel situation' had ended with the recapture of Fort William. Soon, the merchant James Killpatrick hoped, there was a good chance of 'seeing everything resettled'.[34] The change in fortune had given them the confidence to initially refuse an offer of neutrality from the French that would have kept trade open for both nations on the Bengal coast. Instead, the sudden windfall in military assets available on the coast even led to some traders proposing an aggressive attack 'against the French openly by sea and land and using our whole force to exterminate them totally out of these provinces'. For the moment, though, it was agreed that this could wait and that a temporary peace with the French granted 'liberty to prosecute the war against the Nabob [Nawab] with more vigour'. The goal, of course, was profit, and military power increasingly favoured the British position. It was expected that the East India Company would 'compel the Nabob to make restitution and reparation for the private and public losses sustained by the Europeans', and that this would just be the start. The ultimate aim was 'to obtain such an increase of our revenues and such immunities for our commerce as to render this settlement more beneficial to the company'.[35]

After expressing concerns that he lacked the troops to engage the Nawab's forces any further, Clive soon bought into the spirit of his belligerent English compatriots and launched a successful surprise attack on the Bengal ruler's army as it camped near Kolkata.[36] The Nawab quickly came to terms (likely swayed by the Afghan invasion of the Mughal empire that threatened his western border), and Clive agreed to terms that were 'both honourable and advantageous for the company'. Reconfirming and expanding on an agreement made thirty years earlier, the new treaty included British control of a regional mint for producing coin, the return of villages that had been under corporate control, and 'the free transportation of goods without customs of any kind' into the Nawab's domains. Not long after, Clive agreed a renewed French proposal for neutrality between the competing European companies. To a casual observer, it might have looked like the British trading company had secured peaceful commerce through force of arms, but it was not to last. In the very same letter that he informed the East India Company of his victory, Clive left no illusions about where he thought their priority should lie: 'the importance of this colony is such that I cannot conclude better than by recommending to your honours in the strongest manner to send out as large a military force as you can'. He was not to be disappointed.

Over the next six years, the company would use its military strength to seize more territory and impose its own political control. The conflict with the Nawab, however, was not the only cause of the company's increasing military presence. Shortly after the attack on Kolkata, on 17 May 1756, Britain had declared war on France. Consequently, even before news that the company's troops in India had retaken control of Kolkata, the East India Company had decided to boost its massive investment in securing its Bengal trade and territories with the dispatch of a powerful fleet of nineteen heavily armed ships in March 1757. More than capable of protecting themselves on the journey east, the fleet represented the company's willingness to use military force to protect its interests and exploit any opportunity it could find to expand them further. In case their own armed forces were insufficient, the British state lent a hand, and five Royal Navy warships joined with the private corporation's armada as it left England. After reaching Asia, parts of the fleet would disperse to different ports in Persia, Sumatra and China, but India was the most important destination, with thirteen ships ordered to the company's positions in Bombay, Madras and Bengal.[37]

Ensuring that their goods reached these trading destinations safely was only one reason the East India Company sent such a powerful fleet following the outbreak of war with France. The corporation's instructions to the fleet's commanders gave considerable leeway for them to take the initiative in the name of the corporation's interests. Cautious about the risks of the conflict expanding further, they warned their commanders to avoid 'embroiling us with the country governments of India' and instructed them only to use force if they were attacked first. 'The war with France justly alarms us', and the company feared 'your settlement may be justly liable to an attack' from its European rivals. However, the fleet was carrying 'as many recruits on these ships as we can raise', and the company's commanders in India were encouraged to hire 'as many Europeans in Bengal to strengthen' their possessions 'as can possibly be procured'. With considerable naval power and a growing military presence on the Indian coast, the corporation's leadership were careful to make sure that their defensive focus was 'not by any means meant to invalidate' the option 'to employ the ship as well in a warlike manner as in affairs of commerce' if local conditions called for it. Indeed, even as they cautioned against conflict with powerful Indian states, the company acknowledged local rulers were 'subjecting the English flag to contempt', and there was nothing in their orders to suggest that the attack on Kolkata had been forgiven. The decision to send such a large and well-armed fleet to India was taken with a clear awareness of how a muscular display of military power might help reinforce the British position against their adversaries.[38]

When it arrived off the coast of India, the fleet was met not by a cautious English presence still reeling from the loss of Kolkata but by an enthusiastic and empowered British establishment revelling in the rich rewards of their own conquests. In the months that the fleet had been at sea, Clive had continued to wield the limited military assets he had at his command with ruthless effect. Despite having only just ended hostilities with the Nawab and agreeing neutrality with the French, the corporation threw its troops into another campaign against the town of Chandannagar which was controlled by the French. With assistance again from a naval squadron commanded by Watson, the fort was quickly captured and plundered by the East India Company's troops. The attack restarted the corporation's war with the Nawab, who began to seek closer ties with the remaining French forces in Bengal. At the same time, British efforts to find support in Bengal were increasingly successful, and major Bengali merchants and local administrators agreed to break from the Nawab in hope of improving their own conditions. Renewed warfare quickly followed, leading to further victories for the corporation's troops and their allies. After a battle at Plassey in June 1757, the Nawab was overthrown in favour of one of the East India Company's allies, Mir Jafar. A new treaty granted the British corporation further territory, reaffirmed its trading privileges in Bengal, and even promised a reparative payment from the new ruler to compensate for losses incurred during the conflict.[39]

In the following years, as war with France continued, further assaults on French positions extended Britain's domination of European trade to and from India. Further conflict also saw Mir Jafar deposed and replaced with Mir Qasim, an arrangement that saw yet more territory fall under the East India Company's control in Bengal, before he too was deposed by the corporation's forces following the battle of Buxar, after which the corporation's dominance of much of Bengal was expanded further. Despite remaining nominally part of the Mughal empire, the East India Company was granted 'full powers' to 'act in a civil, military, and judicial capacity, without control'. Opportunities for profit were quickly found and some British participants, like Clive, became fabulously wealthy through their exploits. No longer just a site of commercial profits for the corporation, control of territory in Bengal made them direct recipients of taxes from local people who lived under its dominion, giving them increasing control over the local economy. Peasants were taxed and the income used to purchase cloth for export to Britain. Political authority made it possible to enforce contracts, sometimes using force to coerce weavers into accepting deals that were preferential for the corporations. Most simply, the Bengal treasury was plundered. By focusing on how they could extract wealth, incompetent administration contributed to the catastrophic Bengal famine of 1770, during which as many as ten million people died. Within only a few years, conflict had transformed the British presence in India from one of primarily traders to that of imperial rulers.[40]

It wasn't only in India that the massive expansion of British arms manufacturing and the use of state and privately funded armed forces changed how Britain engaged in global conflict. During the same period, military power was employed to improve and expand British interests across the world. Raids on French positions in West Africa, the Caribbean and North America saw new territories fall under British control that would become mainstays of the colonial economy in the following decades. The Liverpool merchant Robert Nicholson summed up the celebratory mood when he shared news of the victories in the Caribbean: 'the acquisition of the island of Guadeloupe has been of very great service to our trade, and hope of further one of Martinique will make it flourish still more.' Elsewhere, armed forces were employed to suppress rebellions by enslaved people in the Caribbean, to massacre African traders in Calabar who refused to meet the demands of British slave-traders, and to conduct privateering raids on enemy shipping across the Atlantic.[41]

Britain was certainly not alone in using warfare to pursue its commercial goals, nor was the eighteenth century the first time that the British state wielded its fiscal and military power to protect and benefit its merchants overseas. Conquest and violent colonisation had seen hundreds of thousands of acres of new territories seized and occupied by British settlers in the seventeenth century. At the same time, naval power had protected commercial shipping and been used to disrupt and damage opposing economies during wartime. These trends continued into the eighteenth century, but what changed was the scale at which Britain's military power could be applied across the world: whether deploying its navy to dominate the seas, sending its troops to distant continents, or using its huge financial advantage to fund massive military campaigns in Europe. During the Seven Years War, expenditure on the army peaked at over £9 million a year, an astronomical sum of money. No small amount ended up in the pockets of contractors and suppliers. Supporting warfare and violence was big business and underpinned some of Britain's most valuable industries. State and commercial demand for warmaking materials stimulated innovation across a range of different sectors as capitalists sought opportunities to profit from the state's growing capacity for violence and coercion. As investment in government debt had become more attractive, the state had taken full advantage of the possibilities and massively increased its expenditure. Preparing for and making war were major features in the development of the state's administrative and financial capabilities throughout the eighteenth century.[42]

Profits that stemmed directly from warfare were also common and commented on in the second half of the eighteenth century. Likening war-profiteering capitalists to a gang of robbers bent on plundering society, the radical politician John Wilkes condemned the close relationships between suppliers, financiers, merchants and the government that worked together in networks that crossed sectors, geographies and social hierarchies to ready the state for war. Likewise, in 1771, Samuel Johnson denounced the 'paymasters and agents, contractors and commissars' who 'without virtue, labour, or hazard' were growing rich through conflict that had cost Britain 'the death of multitudes, and the expense of millions'. If the soldiers and sailors who 'bled in battle grew rich by the victory', the nation could take pride in their gains, but this was not the case. Instead, Johnson complained, profits accrued to men who 'rejoice when obstinacy or ambition adds another year to slaughter and devastation' as they hoped 'for a new contract from a new armament and computed the profits of a siege or tempest'.[43]

For the capitalists who had invested in guns, gunpowder and ships, the value of war was clear, but they were not the only ones to profit from warfare. While war was costly and damaged trade in the short term, violent conquest and colonisation established economic systems that increased economic opportunities over the longer term. In 1763, the Welsh economic thinker Josiah Tucker argued that 'it is but too manifest, that both the conquering, and conquered countries, are prodigious losers by them' and argued that free trade between different places was more beneficial than conflict. He used the example of Norwich and Manchester to make his point, arguing that if the towns had 'been the capitals of two neighbouring kingdoms, instead of love and union, we should have heard of nothing but jealousies and wars', to the detriment of both. He ignored that peaceful trade within Britain had not been an eternal feature of the islands, and Manchester and Norwich had only been brought into the same kingdom through wars of conquest hundreds of years earlier. Only a few decades before Tucker's defence of peace, armed force had been used to violently suppress rebellions in Britain, and it would be used again to ensure a peaceful trade could exist across its colonies. Likewise, trade with colonies in America was only possible because warfare had seized and secured the territories that were now trading with Europe at ever growing volumes. Peaceful commerce had been secured with the roaring fire of guns.[44]

At the height of the War of the First Coalition in 1795, the government's most prominent gun supplier, Samuel Galton junior, defended his business from critics within the Quaker church who lambasted the profits he made from supplying tools of violence. Defending himself, Galton made two claims. First, that everyone in the Midlands contributed to the state's warmaking powers, whether they were making guns themselves, paying taxes that were spent on the conflict or were simply among the thousands of skilled workers transforming metal into everything from buttons or pistol springs that soldiers required. Second, he argued, guns were instruments of civilisation that protected the private property of his fellow Quakers in Britain, and everyone else living on the island nation for that matter. War and violence were simply part of the society in which they lived, and it was hypocritical to pretend otherwise. By the end of the eighteenth century, metal workers in Birmingham and London had churned out millions of guns for sale to the state and private arms traders. The impact on metallurgical industries was enormous. The organisational structure needed to produce thousands of guns at the start of the century was not capable of producing the hundreds of thousands that were in demand at the end, and businesses had experimented and adapted to keep up. Much of the Midlands' metallurgical world had become invested in mass production of arms.[45]

Peaceful trade was, of course, essential for Britain's economic development, but violence was used to break into markets, protect traders from competitors, and to impose Britain's economic requirements on people who might have preferred to follow different paths. As a rule, the larger the market that manufacturers can serve, the more opportunities they can access. Warfare created larger markets and violence helped keep them in place. By the end of the eighteenth century, Britain's ruthless application of force had created a globally connected market that increasingly followed its rules, gave its merchants the best treatment, and prioritised the needs of British consumers and manufacturers over any others. Britain's rise to wealth and power had been forged not in the doldrums of peace but the crucible of war.

# Part Two

# INDUSTRY AND EMPIRE, 1750–1800

## CHAPTER 6

# A SCIENTIFIC PEOPLE

## Inventing, Stealing and Commercialising Technology

A search for empirical facts and certain knowledge, building on European traditions developed in the sixteenth century and popularised through the work of promoters like Francis Bacon and Samuel Hartlib had flourished in Britain in the seventeenth century. Efforts to exploit innovative technologies and ideas by capitalists in Britain and its empire had led to unprecedented increases in productivity, the rapid expansion of new industries like copper smelting in Wales or gunmaking in Birmingham, and the extraction of wealth from colonies overseas through the exploitation of enslaved labour. By the start of the eighteenth century, networked capital had already made an impact on how enterprising and ruthless businesspeople approached the opportunities around them, and this continued in the following decades. For useful knowledge to be economically valuable it had to be transmitted and shared, and this was shaped by the institutions, attitudes and means of communication that made it possible. In Britain, this often took place without involvement of the state, and through social networks and exchanges of knowledge between inventors, philosophers and entrepreneurs coming together that took place informally as well as within a plethora of new organisations that emerged to cater to their interests.[1]

Reflecting on the changing world around him, the author and editor Thomas Snow published his *Apopiroscopy* in 1702, which shared with readers the 'experiments and observations' that he believed reflected the range of important discoveries of his era. Entries ranged from descriptions of improvements in iron making and agricultural tools to new ballistics theorems and designs for perpetual motion engines. Like many of his contemporaries, Snow wanted his survey to have practical value, and he set out to show how the 'transplanting of arts and manufactures' was creating new jobs. He offered four clear cases: the amalgamation of mercury with gold creating the gilding industry; the invention of metal coils or springs enabling the clockmaking trade; trials with 'aquafortis' (nitric acid) improving the refining industry; and experiments with potash on plantations making it possible to mass-produce sugar in the Caribbean. These showed the value derived from experimentation and innovation. Industry and empire alike benefited from the advancement of science, and opportunities to take advantage of new discoveries continued to inspire investment.[2]

Consequently, efforts to combine scientific exploitation, experimental methods and economic activity continued and accelerated in the eighteenth century. Even as publications like Snow's sought to show the viability of innovative practices across a range of different fields, inventors attempted to do the same, pitching goods for multiple industries and drawing on multiple scientific fields – sometimes at the same time. An exemplar of this approach was the Huguenot engineer Isaac de la Chaumette, who obtained a patent in 1721 for a bizarre range of inventions that had emerged through his 'study, industry and expense'. Rather than creating a single process or machine, de la Chaumette wanted recognition for having 'brought to perfection the making of diverse engines, machines and instruments of several kinds which were never before invented and will be of very great use to the public'. This included breech-loading firearms, ring bayonets, powder flasks, chimney covers to reduce smoke, snuff boxes, penknives, pocket knives, buckles, long-lasting mattresses for armies and hospitals, unflippable coaches, devices to prevent shipwrecks, discreet grenades, lightweight breastplates, adjustable candlesticks, safety scissors, a foldable bed disguised as an ornament and a cypher machine. A few years later, in 1734, he presented another bundle of inventions to the Royal Society that included military paraphernalia, a new type of stirrup for preventing falls from horseback, two types of lock, and an iron rod with rotating numbers for gambling. De la Chaumette made most of his money making military equipment (the inventor of the Ferguson rifle later adapted one of his designs) but his other inventions did not have the same impact. Perhaps, rather than stemming from commercial ambitions, his non-military inventions were just experimental ideas that happened to tickle his fancy. His enthusiasm for innovation was not restrained to any single field.[3]

Snow and de la Chaumette were not alone in blending their interests across multiple areas of interest, nor were they alone in their hope and expectation that innovation might benefit multiple industries. Although the Royal Society's interest in commercial projects had declined towards the end of the seventeenth century, numerous learned societies and public venues for exchanging knowledge emerged to take up the slack. Their members engaged enthusiastically with ideas that crossed the full spectrum of scientific pursuits and often took great interest in their practical applications. In Northampton, local scholars interested in antiquarian and scientific topics formed a group that was known as 'a Royal Society in miniature', while members of the London-based Royal Society would happily adjourn to the Grecian Coffee House down the road to debate advances of the day with a wider interested public. Interest and ability combined and crossed between different areas of study. The exhibition of new inventions and discoveries served a commercial purpose for some participants, but they also had a wider and systemic impact that included the promotion of inquiry, education, polite discourse, and also serving as a means of entertainment.[4]

Efforts to establish a national organisation dedicated to economic improvement in England had begun as early as 1721, when Henry Sully, a watchmaker, proposed a society to devote itself to 'preserving and improving inventions, arts, and manufactures'. Quite explicitly, the aim was to encourage the practical application of scientific advances rather than promote scientific communication and discovery for its own sake. The society Sully envisioned would compile a register of best practices and inventions, arrange trials for new ideas, and pay innovators to share their techniques rather than keep them secret. In time, he was confident, the proposed society would create the conditions by which Britain would become the 'retreat and succour of every peculiar genius for arts and inventions'. Unfortunately, his reputation was tarnished by close association with the collapsed Mississippi Company in France, and there were few takers. In Scotland, an organisation with similar goals but dedicated to agricultural improvement was successfully established in 1723, and another to improve manufacturing and fishing industries in 1727. The latter, especially, acted as a political lobby promoting the interests of Scotland's textile manufacturers, and funded efforts to obtain useful knowledge from overseas by encouraging skilled migrants to move to Scotland or sending spies to steal technology. A similar organisation was founded in Dublin a few years later.[5]

Despite critiques that curiosity was 'the first and the simplest emotion', associated with a childish and superficial yearning for novelty, authors like David Hume and Adam Smith were at the forefront of efforts to view it as a positive feature of a modern, commercial society. Curiosity, they believed, inspired the search for general laws. Rules that could be identified and explained through experimentation, observation and reason had become the guiding principles for investigating the natural world. The discovery and dissemination of universal rules would, it was presumed, accelerate the march of progress across myriad fields, leading to further curious pursuits and innovations. Many consumers, too, yearned for novel, curious and luxurious items, whether these were carried from distant producers half a world away or re-imagined in the workshops of inventive craftsmen much closer to home. It was in this landscape that Britain's industrialising economy continued to flourish.[6]

By 1750, organisations like these, alongside the wider distribution of scientific ideas in publicly printed texts and the informal exchange of ideas through social and business networks, contributed to the rapid diffusion of useful knowledge. Regular interactions with similar organisations in France, Italy and elsewhere in Europe generated a ready flow of ideas across borders too, as did the theft of technology. Capitalists in Britain were able to draw on these exchanges as they set out to improve the productivity of their business or establish new ones. Key targets for innovation included finding ways to substitute high-end manufactured goods that were imported from overseas, and intellectual espionage and the adaptation of foreign methods were popular techniques for some of Britain's most innovative businesses. Elsewhere, regular incremental improvements to tried and trusted technology, especially when combined with new methods or machinery, presented opportunities for profit that quickly saw outdated techniques replaced. Britain's growing economy continued to benefit from mutually reinforcing networks that exploited natural, human and intellectual capital across different sectors, leading to widespread and cumulative gains. By the end of the eighteenth century, the impact of these changes would be felt across Britain, its empire and the world.

## A KNOWLEDGE ECONOMY

In 1754, a group of leading lights from Scotland's political, university and business circles, including historian and philosopher David Hume, artist Allan Ramsay and physician Francis Home, founded the Select Society. The goal was 'to improve themselves in reasoning and eloquence', and 'by the freedom of debate, to discover the most effectual methods of promoting the good of the country'. When the society began distributing written essays by members the following year, the range of themes reflected its members' interests: natural history, chemistry, mathematics, letters, criticism, history and politics. For live debates, any topic was fair game, so long as it did not cross into challenging religion or encouraging Jacobitism, and the society's members, which numbered over a hundred by the end of the first year, certainly took advantage of that range. Glasgow University's Professor Adam Smith proposed opening debate topics that would consider: 'whether a general naturalisation of foreign protestants would be advantageous to Britain'; and 'whether bounties on the exportation of corn be advantageous to trade and manufacture as well as to agriculture'. Wide-ranging, complicated and grounded in the empirical analysis of historical and contemporary understanding, the debates were intended to shed light on pressing issues of the day as well as expand the intellectual horizons of participants.[7]

The range of the debates attests to a febrile atmosphere of intellectual exploration that granted time and opportunity for participants to cross disciplinary boundaries and experiment with new ways for thinking about the world – including, at times, how these might be employed for enriching themselves and the nation. Ramsay's proposal for debating 'whether luxury can be advantageous to any state?' was indicative of this balance between abstract and personal interest: the theme had serious implications for economic ideas about the balance of trade and particular relevance for a portraitist to the country's elite. Members politely argued about whether Brutus was right to kill Julius Caesar, if 'nunneries without the vows' would be beneficial in Britain, the impact of climate on the formation of 'natural characters', whether John Milton was 'a better poet than Virgil', and if 'ridicule is a proper test of truth'. The group even discussed 'whether an university in a metropole or in a remote town be most proper for the place of education?', or, to put it another way, whether Scotland's city-based universities in Glasgow and Edinburgh were empirically superior to their southern neighbour in Cambridge.

Economic topics were certainly among the interests of groups like the Select Society, but they were not their primary concern. Even when raised as a debate theme, economic questions tended to bring in the impact of business on themes like social wellbeing or morality. For example, they debated if an 'increase of trade and manufacturing' would 'naturally tend to promote the happiness of a nation', and whether 'a nation once sunk in luxury and pleasure can be retrieved and brought back to any degree of worth and excellence'. Likewise, the 'modern method of improvement by making large farms' and 'modern improvements in mechanics' were both discussed as potentially 'ruinous to the country', rather than simply accepted as positive generators of wealth. In linking social and political structures to economic expansion, the group challenged whether prevalent inequalities limited progress, asking 'whether it would be of advantage to society' if 'women held places of trust and profit in the state?' – though they also later debated whether rich men like themselves should be encouraged to have multiple wives to address Britain's declining population. Challenging preconceptions and drawing on multiple disciplines to approach topics were key features of the Select Society's debates.[8]

The Select Society was not alone in trying to bring different fields of study together under the same roof and, during the eighteenth century, a multitude of similar organisations were established. Some had similarly wide-ranging interests, while others were more clearly focused on seeking to apply knowledge from history, philosophy and natural science to the business world. In 1759, Edinburgh became the home of a competing group, the Commercial Society, which set itself up explicitly for members to lecture on topics related to the city's business. Early lectures were delivered by John Christie (under the pseudonym Portius) who presented an overview of 'the establishment and method of carrying on the commerce of the general trading companies, chambers, and banks of Great Britain'. This was followed by talks by James Cockburn (Decius) on whale fishing, Elias Martin (Cassius) on tobacco, and David Herd (Flavius) on the history of the East India Company's trade with Asia. Topics like these helped share knowledge across the city's business community, as well as giving members a chance to show off. These lectures were not intended to improve wider public knowledge of trade, but for members to privately exchange ideas, best practices and take a step back to assess the wider structures that underpinned the booming and globally connected economy that was taking shape around them.

The Commercial Society was also a social organisation, and other lectures gave people a chance to hypothesise on a much wider range of topics. William Anderson (Mecanus) presented an 'account of the Chinese Empire with the manners and customs of the people', probably a popular topic given the deference shown to the Qing state in European intellectual circles in the eighteenth century, while John Phinn (Mettellus) spoke about 'the nature of friendship and secrecy'. Later in the year, there were four speeches simply on happiness, hope, fear and ambition. Over the following decade, regular meetings kept the group in regular contact, the same breadth of topics attesting to their enduring interest in both commercial and more esoteric debate. In 1765, the topics still included staples like the 'bad effects of commerce' and the 'usefulness of trade', but also 'the cause of thunder', 'friendship', and what must have been a riveting discourse on the meaning of 'nothing'. The following year, lectures on the qualities and experience of merchants were heard alongside ones on 'bowls of nectar', 'justice', and perhaps with a little humorous self-reflection, the purpose of societies.[9]

In the second half of the eighteenth century, the passionate and extensive exchange of knowledge in organisations like these led members to enthuse that Britain had passed some sort of tipping point in terms of scientific advancement. The Select Society boldly debated whether 'we excel the ancients, or the ancients us, in knowledge and arts?'. Concerted efforts to ensure this scientific advancement led to the application of knowledge also gained in popularity. In 1755, the Select Society agreed to use its 'funds for improvement' to set up a new organisation, known as the 'Edinburgh Society for Encouraging Arts, Sciences, Manufactures and Agriculture in Scotland'. That same year, Francis Home won the society's inaugural essay prize and lauded the achievement of experimental science 'during these two last ages' even as he complained that the same methods had not been applied to better understand agriculture. Medicine and chemistry drew his particular praise, the former because 'its present perfection' had been obtained 'from this history of diseases and causes delivered down' and the latter 'by the means of experiments made either by chance or design' that had seen it 'reduced to a regular system'.[10]

Home's essay on *The Principles of Agriculture and Vegetation* set out what was understood as best practice at the time as well as a 'plan for the further improvement of agriculture'. In the first sections, Home presented what he could about different soils, methods of fertilising vegetables, and the impact of different external factors like rain, weeds or disease on farming in Britain, but admitted that his knowledge was held back by a lack of general scientific interest. Arguing that 'agriculture is not so uncertain and unscientific an art as is commonly thought' but rather 'reduceable like other arts to fixed unalterable principles', he called on the new Edinburgh Society to lead the way in supporting a new approach that would allow for scientific methods to be applied to the study of growing crops and raising animals. His focus, then, was not so much on the methods that might be employed by farmers, but rather on the intellectual infrastructure needed to improve knowledge about agriculture and disseminate this to landowners and others who might be able to apply it in the field. Finding a way to bring practical experience into the remit of scientific inquiry was essential, he believed, for improving the industry. After all, he reminded his readers, 'agriculture does not take its rise, originally, from reason, but from fail and experience' and could 'only be improved from the knowledge of facts as they happen in nature'. The problem, as he saw it, was an unwillingness to experiment in agriculture and a failure to collect the necessary information to make effective, empirically grounded conclusions.

'Mankind,' he lamented, 'are shy in attempting anything, or at least rendering it public unless they make it complete', and this seriously limited the exchange of knowledge about farming approaches that failed. This was especially challenging in agriculture because it was a slow business: crops took time to grow, selective breeding took time to take effect, and it could take years for poor stewardship to reveal itself in environmental decline. Consequently, when it came to experiments, 'one person can make but very few during their life' and they would have to be undertaken by 'the hands of the many' to provide the evidence required. What was needed was a 'proper and easy channel through which they might be conveyed to the world'. The proposed remedy was simple (and handily quite flattering to the people who awarded Home his prize): the Edinburgh Society could set up a committee to collect farming experiments, 'put them in a proper dress if they stand in need of it, and publish them to the world at stated times like a public paper'. Offering 'lucrative premiums' for 'the most ingenious and useful experiment in agriculture' would further incentivise experimentation. Home's plan certainly won its plaudits, but in their effort to promote the advancement of knowledge and business together, the Scottish society was certainly not alone.[11]

While the Scottish societies did not struggle to combine the interests of university doyens, aristocratic scholars, innovative businessmen and creative artists, the Royal Society in England did. This led William Shipley, the son of a minor landowner who had become obsessed with the need for a national society to promote useful knowledge and the public good, to set up a new organisation. Appealing to a broad audience, Shipley asked members not to support this society for private profit but for the public good, even as the outcomes of the society's work were intended to promote both. After sharing his plan with what he hoped were like-minded compatriots in rural Northamptonshire and London, Shipley launched a subscription for the society in March 1754 at Rawthmell's Coffee House in London. Only ten people turned up. This was not the immediate success for which Shipley would have hoped, but the small gathering did have one strength: the diverse scientific and business interests of its members. An innovative jeweller-turned-porcelain maker called Nicholas Crisp had shown up, as had a wax chandler, an instrument maker, a merchant, a draper and four Fellows of the Royal Society. Without further ado, the gathering declared themselves the Society for the Encouragement of Arts, Manufactures and Commerce.[12]

The name changed a few times in the following years, but the organisation, most usually known as the Society of Arts (and, since 1908, as the Royal Society of Arts), kept going. Early meetings took place in coffee houses, a library or at Shipley's residence, often with only two or three members in attendance. Shipley remained confident and wrote to the American entrepreneur Benjamin Franklin in 1755 that he expected to 'soon be incorporated and perhaps may have grants from Parliament sufficient to promote by premiums things of the utmost public utility'. His confidence was well founded and, despite its slow start, the society became a resounding success. Within two years it had over 200 members, which grew to more than 700 before the end of the 1750s. Within a decade of its foundation, the society had 2,000 subscribers. As well as artisans, merchants and scholars, the society was now home to the wealthiest members of the aristocracy, politicians at the very peak of government, and bureaucrats of all stripes. With members like these, the popular society helped distribute information far more widely than the Royal Society could achieve at its meetings. It was an exemplary demonstration of the networks between different parts of British society that connected and advanced so many different economic interests. As a founding member Henry Baker boasted to a friend, 'all rank and distance are laid aside' so that 'the greatest and the meanest are equally industrious in the same design'.[13]

The ways in which the Society of Arts set out to boost Britain's innovative business activities were wide-ranging and often wildly ambitious. It funded inventions that otherwise might not have been profitable, it encouraged new trades with colonies overseas, and it identified priority industries that might substitute overseas goods with British manufactures. A central method for achieving these goals was offering 'premiums' – prizes ranging from less than £100 to much more – to anyone who successfully completed one of their set tasks. One early programme, designed to push stylish, luxurious French textile imports off the market, was indicative of these efforts. The society set out to promote novel designs, obtain the skills and materials needed to execute them, and to develop the technology that manufacturers needed to produce them at competitive prices. Their plan even sought to cultivate consumer tastes that were distinctly British, rather than following the fashions of the continent. One area targeted by the society to achieve these goals was the identification of viable domestic alternatives to the madder and cobalt ore used for dyeing cloth red or blue, and so reduce imports. With the society's encouragement, a cobalt mine was quickly discovered, mined and exhausted in Cornwall. More significantly, though, one member, Nicholas Crisp, took the opportunity to work with cobalt ore to uncover the method needed for extracting pigment from the ore: a process that previously had been completed by manufacturers overseas before the pigment was shipped to Britain. Soon, imports of cobalt ore picked up in place of imported pigments, and British manufacturers benefited.[14]

Not all the society's efforts were as successful but offering prizes across a range of fields certainly promoted innovation. By 1758, subscriptions in the Society of Arts had grown so large that it could offer more than a hundred prizes to encourage invention. Within ten years of its founding, more than £8,000 had been spent on awards. Simply offering cash in return for inventive activities was not a new idea, and the Dublin improvement society had offered prizes to promote agricultural innovation since 1741. Likewise, the Edinburgh

*5. As well as prizes, the Society of Arts offered gold medals in recognition of people who had promoted arts and commerce. The design depicted Minerva (the Roman deity of arts and crafts) and Mercury (the deity of financial gain, merchants and trickery) offering their bounties to a seated personification of Britannia.*

Society awarded prizes for best dissertations presented on 'the rise and progress of commerce, arts and manufactures in North Britain, and the causes which promoted or retarded them'. Prizes were not always part of formal competitions, either, and Liverpool's Board of Trade simply reached out to the inventor Moses Parke to reward him twelve shillings 'for his ingenuity in inventing his curious machine' that made it possible for 'the more correct keeping of a ship's way at sea'.[15]

However, the Society of Art's efforts surpassed these in scale and ambition and were offered across every sector. The society's efforts also connected networks and diffused innovative ideas across Britain and, indeed, sometimes overseas, too. In 1766, it received drawings and descriptions purporting to show an improved waterwheel that had been invented by Andrew Wirtz and employed in Zurich and Berlin almost two decades before. The material was sent by John Henry Ziegler, another German inventor, whose own waterwheel improvements had likewise entered British design practices. A year later, a similar letter was received from Philadelphia which detailed a 'machine for maintaining a uniformity of heat', which in time would be combined with Ziegler's design in British smelting mills. By supporting continuous incremental improvements like these, the society encouraged a different sort of innovation than the patent system: here, new practices had value precisely because they were shared and could be improved upon by a larger community of like-minded individuals. As Baker put it in 1758, 'the attendance and care of all its members is almost incredible', and 'in a few years they will gain and save millions to this nation and its colonies'. This was a little too optimistic, but the society certainly contributed to the promotion of improvement and the practical application of science. Like similar organisations in Scotland and Ireland, these innovations were visible demonstrations of the changes that were reshaping the relationship between scientific, business and political interests in Britain and were part of the many interlinkages that made networked capital possible.[16]

Formal societies like these were nonetheless only part of the ongoing and widespread diffusion of scientific ideas and other forms of knowledge that were changing how people envisioned the world. Some of the networks that formed to exchange material and ideas lasted for years and took on semi-formal structures that eased regular communication. The Midlands-based 'Lunar Circle', an amorphous group of inventors, scientists and entrepreneurs, were as much a group of friends and acquaintances who regularly met for dinners and debates as they were a formal organisation. In the 1750s, Erasmus Darwin and Matthew Boulton developed a close friendship, built on shared interests and a complementary combination of the former's more theoretical education and the latter's practical experience. As visits between the two men became more common, other acquaintances began to join, sharing ideas and conducting experiments together. Before long, common commercial interests and social links brought more people together, and by the 1760s regular, informal interactions between a wider group were taking place. Correspondents including metal manufacturer Boulton, potter Josiah Wedgwood and physician Darwin had all grown up in the Midlands, while gunmaker Samuel Galton and engineer James Watt had been drawn to the burgeoning industrial town of Birmingham from Bristol and

Scotland, respectively. Others were drawn to the group following the remarkable success of its member's businesses, and their networks extended far beyond the Midlands to correspondents across Britain and its colonies. These blended social and business relationships, and members of the group regularly worked together or helped each other in the business world, too. By the 1770s, regular dinners and meetings added a formal quality to the group's activities. This network saw some of the leading entrepreneurs and scientists of their generation regularly interact.[17]

Groups like these could provide some structure, but scientific interest and exchange were just as often sustained by correspondence and communication between interested and amateur participants. As the Midlands-based William Reynolds put it in a series of letters to his cousin William Rathbone in Liverpool in the 1770s, it was 'as positive to be a chemist in a study as in a laboratory'. After all, he noted, 'Dr Priestley, the greatest man of this age in the aerial branch of that science', and another member of the 'Lunar Circle' network, had demonstrated this quite clearly when he had 'performed in a parlour' the experiments that had brought him such esteem. Both men had taken this lesson to heart, and their letters reveal broad scientific interests, as well as sharing information about their business interests and family lives. Reynolds commented on an array of topics that ranged from his pleasure at spending time in the British countryside to his expectation that soon 'I expect to get my pocket full of tropics – either sand from America, or clay from Africa'. He also explained how innovative technology could be employed for scientific pursuits. Rathbone, seemingly following his encouragement, was attempting to install 'receptacles of electric fire' in his northern home that had been designed by an artisan in Bristol. When Reynolds became frustrated with 'the inconvenience of sending to London for every instrument that I want', he informed his cousin that 'I am resolved to turn carpenter myself' and asked for advice about where he could obtain good-quality mahogany for the task. As these few interactions suggest, the two men engaged widely and enthusiastically with Britain's scientific developments, and the networks that blended the exchange of knowledge were often blurred with social and business ties.[18]

Exchanges like these reflected wider contexts of training and education that shaped Britain's industrialising economy. Scientists and engineers were typically not graduates from university – and had almost always attended Scottish universities, if they were. They also often blended interests in multiple fields of inquiry, rather than specialising in a single narrow area. The Birmingham manufacturer Boulton, for instance, combined interests in steam power (that pre-dated his partnership with Watt), electricity and balloons, among others, with his pursuit of techniques that could produce stylish metal products at the forefront of contemporary taste. As Priestley put it, Boulton was 'a friend of science as well as a great promoter of the arts'. More critically, Jabez Fisher, a Quaker from Philadelphia who toured Britain in the 1770s, remarked that Boulton was 'a sensible, ingenious, and enterprising man' who was obsessing 'over some new matter on the anvil' that was as likely 'to draw his attention from the steady pursuit of some grand object' as it was to lead to a breakthrough. Indeed, the Birmingham manufacturer was 'always inventing, and by the time he has brought his scheme to perfection, some new affair offers itself'. It was, Fisher warned, 'this volatility' that 'prevents him from becoming very rich'. Boulton, though, was not alone in having such eclectic interests, and in sites of industrial expansion like Birmingham, Manchester or Leeds, as well as older hubs of the knowledge economy in London and Edinburgh, there were plentiful opportunities for people with technological, scientific and business interests to come together in societies, social networks and partnerships as they set out to apply their growing understanding of the world around them to all manner of new business enterprises.[19]

The social exchange of scientific knowledge outside the hallowed halls of universities or formal societies helped disseminate innovative ideas across Britain. Landowners, merchants and manufacturers alike were increasingly inclined to promote the benefits that engagement in the nation's booming knowledge economy could offer them. Scientific advances gave them a competitive edge. Indeed, as well as societies and networks to help share information among themselves, contemporaries began to call for educational changes to ensure that the next generation was well trained in the practical application of empirical and observational methods. Reynolds lamented that 'children are too often taught to construe a Latin book and write a good hand without ever being made acquainted with the truths of natural philosophy'. Sadly, he thought, 'the knowledge of things is too much disregarded while that of words is too much attended to'. Apprenticeships continued to offer some opportunities to develop these skills. As one parent explained to their son's new master, the ironmonger Christopher Rawson, they expected that their child would 'be instructed in the useful branches of a mercantile and improving education' during their time together. A successful apprenticeship, they suggested, should leave 'him thoroughly grounded and perfected in the French language as well in reading as in writing it with propriety, also to be instructed in writing and cyphering, and the nature of exchanges, in geography, history, religion' – alongside the skills he would learn from operating the forge. Improvement demanded a deeper understanding of the world than simply technical skills or theoretical knowledge might offer. Practical, technical skills were an important part of Britain's industrialising economy and combined fruitfully with other forms of knowledge across the dense networks of eighteenth-century intellectual exchange. When it came to promoting innovation, liberal arts and practical science were two sides of the same coin.[20]

James Keir, a factory owner and chemist in the West Midlands, noted towards the end of the eighteenth century that 'the diffusion of general knowledge, and of a taste for science, over all classes of men, in every nation of Europe, or of European origin, seems to be the characteristic feature of the present age'. Although hyperbolic, Keir's observation was indicative of the widespread and relatively accessible scientific literature and communities that were becoming more readily available in Britain and elsewhere. The inclusion of interested gentlemen, skilled craftsmen and engineers in common networks eased the diffusion of useful knowledge in ways that crossed economic, geographic and social boundaries.[21]

Through links like these, changing ideas about how the economy operated – like those of Hume and Smith, honed during debates at the Edinburgh Select Society – could be discussed informally along-

1. Coal powered, wreathed in smoke and lit by the furious flames of furnaces, this dramatic painting of Coalbrookdale expressively portrays a classic conception of British industrialisation. This exploitation of natural resources, labour and technology was replicated by capitalists across numerous industries, in different parts of the country, and throughout Britain's empire. Connections across all these activities fuelled Britain's rise to wealth and power.

2, 3. The rapidly changing world around them proved an attractive theme for artists. Both of these paintings celebrated the advancement of knowledge that was understood to sit at the core of Britain's economic and political power. The first vibrantly depicted an excited public engaging with a device that exemplified advances in scientific knowledge and mechanical engineering (top), while the second captured the spirit of improvement behind selective breeding schemes that led to exceptionally large and woolly sheep (bottom).

4. Painted to encourage support for the abolition of slavery, this depiction of the slave-trade on the African coast sought to juxtapose the brutality of British capitalists with the dignity and humanity of captive African people.

5. This painting of a coal mine drew attention to the jarring clash between new machinery and the natural landscape. It presented the transformative but often destructive impact of economic change on the environment and traditional ways of working.

6, 7. Enthusiasm for luxurious Asian products inspired widespread efforts by British capitalists to substitute imports with domestic copies that replicated general styles or techniques or were made using already-familiar materials and methods. This dynamic is at play in this soft-paste porcelain plate produced at the Bow Manufactory in London around 1755 (bottom), which was a clear copy of this Chinese hard-paste porcelain plate that had been imported two or three decades earlier (top).

8, 9, 10. Britain's expansive colonial empire contributed to the expansion of its metallurgical industries. Muskets (middle) helped colonists seize territory overseas and were sold in Africa, where they were traded for enslaved people. Other metal goods were likewise essential for this traffic, including hundreds of thousands of shackles (bottom) that restrained captive African people on board slave-trading vessels. New consumable goods, such as sugar from Caribbean plantations or tea transported from China, stimulated demand for attractive metalware like these boxes (top), used to house colonial goods once they entered British homes.

11. This idyllic portrayal of Richard Arkwright's cotton mill in Derbyshire gives only a hint of the dramatic changes that new textile factories would instigate. First powered by precisely built water wheels and later by steam engines, mills brought new ways of working to the textile industry and saw hundreds of workers labour under the same roof. Sourcing raw cotton from American plantations, imitating Indian producers, and shipping goods to customers across the world, the impact of Britain's early mills was felt far beyond the valleys that they called home.

12. This richly embroidered bedcover from Gujarat is indicative of the high-quality cloth and vibrant colours that British manufacturers sought to replicate. Surprisingly, some of the animals depicted were copied from English embroidered textiles sent to India as models to help Gujarati artisans cater to the tastes of their British customers.

13. With the help of innovative technology, British manufacturers began to catch up with their Indian competitors by the end of the eighteenth century. This sample book was made to show off the goods that Samuel Greg's firm was producing in 1784, with dozens of patterns, colours and thread-counts available.

14, 15. It was no secret that Britain's wealth and power rested on its trade and empire. This was publicly celebrated in the new urban landscapes of Britain's towns and cities. In London, the East India Company commissioned this huge painting (bottom) to hang in the corporation's headquarters. Persian silk, Chinese porcelain, American cotton and Indian jewels were all depicted, all enriching Britain. In Liverpool, the Town Hall was decorated with a frieze depicting animals and people from Africa, acknowledging the importance of the slave-trade and colonial commerce for the port's explosive growth (top).

side experimental demonstrations in the parlours of Birmingham's capitalists or over a drink in London's coffee houses before the capital's politicians, manufacturers and artists adjourned to the Society of Arts to divvy out prizes to innovators seeking ways to put Britain at the forefront of style. These exchanges helped spread the ideas and relationships that were necessary for advances in sectors ranging from medicine to metallurgy to take place. With ideas related to improvement increasingly able to draw on practical demonstrations of new techniques and empirical assessment of their efficacy, it became easier for capitalists to assess their value and commercialise through practical applications in many different sectors. Additionally, by disseminating information more widely and deeply than might otherwise have been possible, formal societies and correspondence networks alike brought about deeper connections between Britain's key economic regions: London, the Midlands and northern Britain grew together, with regional specialisation and economic integration both benefiting from more open communication between them. No society or group alone created one big idea that transformed the British economy, but the dynamic discussion that they facilitated helped ensure that a multitude of ideas for incremental improvements accelerated Britain's scientific and economic progress.

## THE SINCEREST FORM OF FLATTERY

Britain's economy benefited in many ways from the exchange of ideas and the spread of useful knowledge across different businesses and sectors, and this by no means stopped at Britain's shores. Efforts to outcompete competitors overseas was a significant incentive for Britain's innovative manufacturers. Throughout the seventeenth and eighteenth centuries, numerous enterprising businesspeople built their wealth on techniques, styles or technology that had their roots in places far away. As one observer put it in 1730: 'it is at all times our interest to naturalise as much as we can the products of other countries.' Achieving this transfer wasn't always easy, and advanced manufacturers in other parts of the world were typically unwilling to share the secrets of their craft and lose their competitive advantage. For ruthless capitalists in Britain who set out to launch and expand manufacturing of products that replicated or mimicked global goods, there were really only two options available: they could discover the techniques they needed to make such goods themselves, or they could steal them.[22]

Of course, substituting imports with domestic products was not always possible, especially when it came to raw materials that were unique to other natural environments. There was nothing that could be done to increase the production of intoxicating new commodities like sugar, tea and tobacco on British soil. Instead, colonial expansion in the Caribbean and muscular support for corporate power in Asia had to be relied upon to supply the ever-growing quantities needed to sate Britain's new habits. Empire and commerce meant that, over the course of the eighteenth century, the clinking of porcelain cups and the floral scent of stewing tea leaves would become a staple of wealthy homes in Britain and its colonies, often with a little sugar on the side for sweetness. While the tropical organic consumables that Britain's luxury consumer society demanded were beyond the scope of domestic producers to replicate, irrespective of scientific advances that were changing how goods were produced in Britain, an accompanying range of goods presented much more viable opportunities for new techniques to be applied. Substituting manufactured imports from overseas was a major incentive for many inventors, whether they claimed to replicate methods precisely or, increasingly in the second half of the eighteenth century, to offer improvements on existing techniques that made them more competitive at the higher-quality end of the market. Britain's manufacturers continued to seek ways to move up the productivity chain.[23]

Efforts to launch a British silk industry represented among the most dramatic examples of how the theft of technology had a significant impact on the development of British industry. Raw silk could only be acquired through imports. Britain was unsuited to growing mulberry trees or raising the silkworms that fed on them and numerous attempts to produce raw silk in colonies in America were unsuccessful. Many of Britain's silk-manufacturing competitors were in a similar boat, and there was a strong export market for these raw fibres in the Mediterranean and Asia. By the time raw silk reached Britain, it had already passed through one process, the boiling of silkworm cocoons to loosen their natural sericin, that allowed workers to unravel their silken structures into long, continuous lengths. Known as reeling, this produced skeins of raw silk that could be transported and sold. After arriving in Britain and being transported onward to the hands of silk workers, raw silk skeins were wound onto bobbins and typically twisted into stronger yarns by a method called throwing, sometimes twisting multiple threads together when intended for the very finest-quality silk cloth.

As early as 1629, a corporation for the silk industry had been established in the hope of expanding production. By the 1660s, an Act of Parliament designed to encourage the industry optimistically suggested that 40,000 families were already employed producing silk thread, and by the end of the century there were numerous Huguenot silk workers active in Britain who had brought with them French production methods, as well as the new Royal Lustring Company. Heavy duties on imported silk goods boosted the efficacy of these businesses by making British products more competitive, although large volumes of smuggled silk continued to arrive in Britain. By the start of the eighteenth century, Britain had people that were used to working with silk, a strong supply chain that could provide the raw material needed for their work, and a state willing to give them an advantage over foreign competitors where it could. The challenge came from matching the technical sophistication of silk weavers, especially in Italy, who had carefully guarded their secrets for generations. Their engines for winding, spinning and twisting raw silk into *organza*, a plain, sheer fabric that had caught the envious eyes of silk weavers across Europe, were well known but seemingly impossible to replicate.[24]

In the 1710s, an enterprising pair of brothers, Thomas and John Lombe, found a solution. The latter travelled to Piedmont and worked as a mechanic, learning the secrets of the trade before returning to England. Later accounts described how he bribed workmen to gain access to the machine's designs and fled in haste when it became known that an Englishman was prying into its secrets. In either case, he returned to Derby with the long-protected knowledge of the

Sardinian silk industry. The following year, he and his brother began to build a mill on the River Derwent near Derby at the huge cost of £30,000. The mill and its three engines were constructed with the help of two Italian artificers who had been lured from Turin and the English engineer George Sorocold, who together adapted the design to meet the Lombe brothers' requirements. While work was ongoing, Thomas petitioned Parliament for a patent, which was granted in 1718. His presentation of 'three sorts of engines never before made or used in Great Britain: one to wind the finest raw silk, another to spin, and the other to twist the finest Italian raw silk ... which was never before done in this country' offered substantial improvements for the nation's industry. By 1721, the mill had been constructed, and machine-made textiles powered by waterwheel rather than hand could be produced for the first time. The silk mill at Derby was among the first examples of a fundamental shift in how work was organised in Britain: with machinery and a central power source at its heart. Five storeys high and concentrating the work of hundreds of workers in the same location, drawing on the power of the same waterwheel, was a radical departure from existing practices.[25]

John's rewards were short-lived, and in 1722 he died: rumour had it, killed by an Italian assassin intent on avenging the theft of trade secrets. Thomas, though, continued to build the business and, despite the King of Sardinia prohibiting the export of raw silk on pain of death, was producing enough *organza* to force down prices in Britain by around 20 per cent. Profits were slim, though, and difficulties with the machinery and workers unfamiliar with the technique meant efficiency savings were initially limited. The innovative mill also distressed Derby's wool manufacturers and London silk throwers alike: the mechanisation on display threatened both businesses. Many plaudits were still forthcoming. In 1732, when the state agreed not to renew Lombe's patent, he was awarded £14,000 in recompense. The following year, an account of the new works reported that 'since Sir Thomas Lombe has erected, and brought to perfection, his engines at Derby for working fine raw silk', the 'price of that commodity is greatly reduced abroad, and several of our manufacturers have been thereby much improved at home.' It was becoming quite the success story. By the end of the 1730s, the king's 'master of mechanics' Robert Smith had been called upon to produce models of the three machines that could be distributed to other manufacturers in the hope that the competitive advantage seen in Lombe's mill could be replicated across the country. After Thomas's death in 1739, the mill was sold to Samuel Lloyd and William Wilson, and it would continue to spin silk for more than a century.[26]

The expiration of Lombe's patent and diffusion of the essential technology that sat at the heart of his mill led to the rapid growth of silk mills elsewhere. Situated where the jagged hills and moors of the Pennines meet the Cheshire Plain in northern England, Macclesfield and Congleton were perhaps unlikely candidates to host the next stage in the industrialisation of Britain's domestic silk manufacturing industry. They were not major trading hubs inundated with richly finished silk goods from Italy or Bengal, nor were they coastal ports receiving raw silk from East India Company or Levant Company ships, and they certainly were not key markets for the finished product that was forever popular among Britain's wealthiest consumers. Yet, in 1744 Congleton was chosen the site of its first mechanised silk mill, and by the 1780s these two towns in East Cheshire were home to a dense concentration of over seventy silk mills. The towns were well connected, benefiting from the rivers Bollin and Dane that that ran through their boundaries, as well as sitting on the principal routes between Stockport, Manchester and the north-west, and Leek, Derby and the Midlands to the south. Such links helped maintain long-standing textile production across this wider region, including the lace, ribbon and hosiery industries in towns like Coventry, Leicester and Nottingham to the south that had been established since at least the sixteenth century. To the north, Manchester was already hub and home for manufacturing, finishing and trading mixed cotton, a role that would only grow in influence throughout the eighteenth century.[27]

As silk mills blossomed along the towns' rivers and wealth flowed, these linkages only increased, with profits invested in transportation improvements including newly turnpiked roads to Buxton in 1758 and to Stockport and Derby in 1762. These carried goods, capital and expertise that were well suited to exploiting the region's suddenly enviable assets. Unsuited for stimulating a rich agricultural economy, the cold and damp climate was ideal for working with raw silk and cotton, while the steep slopes and plunging streams of the gritstone Pennine moors were far more suited to powering waterwheels than farming. Meanwhile, the soft acidic water proved ideal for processing yarns and rich coal beds nearby fed into steam-powered mills towards the very end of the century. There was also a ready workforce who had long supplemented their poor agricultural prospects with income from processing an eclectic array of yarns, flax, silk and wool. The prospect of steady work in the region's new factories would have been appealing, and drawing on this pool of labour presented capitalists with the chance to employ a workforce already familiar with the challenges of handling silk. Not all the work could be mechanised, however, and for the simplest and most poorly paid preparatory work, women and children were often employed outside the main factory.[28]

British manufacturers never wrested supremacy of European silk manufacturing from France, which had its own advantages in the form of cheaper labour and cheaper raw materials despite lacking the mechanised production that was achieved in Britain. French designs remained fashionable and efforts to encourage a more patriotic spirit among the nation's wealthy consumers had limited effect. Absurdly, smuggled silk developed a cachet of its own, and some British manufacturers even tried to pass off their goods as contraband French fabrics at markets in London and Manchester. However, despite this continued competition, the British silk industry was still a success for mechanisation. By the 1760s, over 320,000 kilograms of silk was thrown annually in England, growing to almost 400,000 by the 1780s. Macclesfield had become a manufacturing hub at the end of a new 'Silk Road' running to London's ports, numbering almost 10,000 people, and was now renowned for its ribbons and buttons. More than half of Congleton's population, around 2,000 people, were employed in its silk mills. Coventry ribbons had become world-famous, thousands of silk weavers worked in Manchester despite the advance of the town's cotton industry, and further centres with their own niche specialisms of silk production had grown in Middleton, Glossop, Derby, Chesterfield and Barnstaple.[29]

The mechanisation of silk production following John Lombe's undercover work in Piedmont was probably the most blatant example of technology theft that underpinned Britain's industrial development, but it was not the only one. There was a long history of adapting or adopting foreign methods for the improvement of British manufacture and what we would now call intellectual property theft played an important role in many industries, as many patents attested. This was supported by the state's efforts to impose tariffs on foreign competitors and to make sure that no technological advances in Britain were lost overseas, which came with mixed success. In the eighteenth century, the state and private actors alike encouraged the adoption of methods that had proven popular and viable in Europe, and makers of everything from copper to cotton cloth replicated or surpassed the methods of their competitors overseas when they could. Even the working habits of fishermen were fair game, and in 1750 the 'Society Appointed to Manage the British White Herring Fishery' sent agents into the Netherlands to steal a sophisticated Dutch fishing boat and tempt the seamen who knew how to use it to relocate to Britain.[30]

Efforts to mimic techniques from overseas had a significant impact across British industry. For instance, copying Indian or French styles of cloth led to British printing patterns being modelled on foreign goods and to projects to find domestic alternatives for imported dyes. Import substitution certainly inspired the British production of porcelain. Initially, the delicate cups used to serve tea in Britain's wealthier homes might well have travelled from China alongside the dried leaves that were needed to make the drink. Chinese porcelain was an expensive and highly sought after commodity. In the 1741 edition of Jean-Baptiste Du Halde's *History of China*, which had been translated from French and was now into its third English edition, readers in Britain were presented with a detailed 'description of the most potent and flourishing nation of the east'. China's immense wealth rested on its 'multitude of inhabitants', its 'great commerce', and land 'so fertile that it commonly yields two crops in a year'. After a lengthy review by the French author of the empire's government, the book quickly presented readers with an overview of the key commodities produced. Within the wide-ranging account of China's regions, readers could pick out details regarding the 'beauty and goodness' of the empire's porcelain, especially one type that was 'white as snow, does not shine, nor is it stained with any kind of colour'. Du Halde could not explain how this was achieved as the potters used the same materials as elsewhere in China. Likewise, he was unable to describe how popular white and blue porcelain was coloured. It wasn't just the techniques that were beyond him: the scale of the industry was beyond anything in Europe, and Du Halde reported 500 stoves were in operation to produce the highly sought-after pottery.[31]

Tea and porcelain, much like silk, were commodities that found a ready market in Britain. While the former could not hope to be produced, and silk manufacture was increased with technology taken from abroad, porcelain required a different tack. In the 1740s, Edward Heylin and Thomas Frye, a Middlesex merchant and a painter from Essex, claimed to have cracked the challenge with a patent that set out an ambiguous recipe that they maintained could produce porcelain, and a factory was set up in Bow. A second patent, issued alone to Frye in 1749, covered 'his new invented method of making a certain ware' that promised a product 'not inferior in beauty and fineness' than the 'earthenware that is brought from the East Indies, and is commonly known by the name of china, japan, or porcelain ware'. To achieve the feat, a process for preparing the clay and a separate process for the glaze were presented, both of which required various ingredients in 'certain proportions' that were left unspecified. Enough information was shared to suggest that innovation had taken place, and enough was kept back so as not to make it too easy for competitors to infringe on his new monopoly. In this case, though, there is little to suggest they actually achieved their goal, and later experiments suggested that no combination of materials they suggested could lead to the production of anything resembling porcelain.[32]

Despite these failings, potters in Britain were already selling goods that were intended to mimic some of the attractiveness of porcelain, even though it would be some time yet before it could be substituted with domestic equivalents. Chinese porcelain, now known as hard-paste porcelain, was fired at extremely high temperatures in ovens and was less likely to break than the soft-paste and bone China alternatives that were produced in England only around the middle of the eighteenth century. After intensive experimentation, the production of hard-paste porcelain began in 1710 in Europe at Meissen, near Dresden, while a century earlier tin-glazed earthenware had been made and popularised in Delft which used similar blue and white glazes in the Chinese style. By the 1740s, a porcelain manufactory in Chelsea was producing soft-paste porcelain in imitation of the Meissen styles as much as the underlying Asian techniques, and it was soon joined by the factory in Bow and another in Derby, the latter founded by a partnership between the porcelain painter William Duesbury and jeweller Andrew Planche. By the end the century, Duesbury and the Derby firm had overtaken and bought out both of its southern rivals, with the best equipment stripped out and taken to the Midlands firm, which by 1773 had become Crown Derby, following royal endorsement of their product.[33]

Elsewhere, especially in the potteries of Staffordshire, potters followed the Delft model, ignoring the challenge of replicating porcelain and instead focusing on improving the glazes and designs of earthenware and stoneware. Potters including William Cockworthy, Richard Champion and Josiah Wedgwood all held patents that promised imitation wares that evoked Asian, Delft or antique Etruscan styles. In their effort to imitate, producers developed products that sought to look exactly like the sources of their inspiration even if they could not match them in every respect. The Worcester factory, for instance, produced affordable wares for a much larger market of British consumers – including many people that could not possibly hope to purchase authentic Chinese porcelain. It was a business model that worked very well. Creamware, a heavier stoneware that was glazed to look like the popular porcelain styles that British consumers so desired, was developed through the collective and incremental innovation of numerous potters in Staffordshire. Wedgwood, who claimed it as his own, further helped popularise the product with innovative sales and marketing campaigns that carried his products into houses across the country and even into the royal household. By the second half of the eighteenth century, the region's pottery was sold nationally and overseas, often through sophisticated commercial networks that had developed selling imported porcelain.[34]

Wedgwood's success, becoming a household name and selling his products across Britain, Europe and America, depended on a combination of factors rather than a single inventive design or mechanised process. Having worked first as an apprentice and then in a firm with Thomas Whieldon, Wedgwood remained a skilled potter throughout his career, and he immersed himself in experimentation with dyes, clays, equipment and glazes, pushing constantly to overcome problems or propel his designs in new directions. Setting out on his own in 1759, Wedgwood specialised in creamware, and eagerly embraced the possibilities that clay offered an enterprising manufacturer for catering to the whims of public demand. In the 1760s, writing to his new business associate Thomas Bentley, Wedgwood enthused about 'the great variety of colours in our raw materials, the infinite ductility of clay, and that we have universal beauty to copy after'. There were endless possibilities for innovation. Clay flowerpots, vases, elegant tea-sets, toilet furniture, snuff boxes, animals in 'various attitudes' and 'the thousand other substantial forms, that neither you, nor I nor anybody else know anything of at present' were all possible with the right touch. Wedgwood's artistic vision blended with his commercial nous, and this range of products made him confident that 'we have certainly the fairest prospect of enlarging this branch of manufacture to our wishes' and that their 'profits will be in proportion to our application'. By this stage, Wedgwood was a correspondent with Priestley and other members of the Lunar Circle and combined his practical knowledge with more theoretical scientific interests. Continuous incremental improvements followed across his business, from product quality and style to the ways in which workers and facilities were organised to save costs. Finally, Wedgwood was highly innovative in his approach to marketing and salesmanship, whether by using sales catalogues with printed images of his wares to drum up business or presenting his products to the royal family to win their acclaim. Transforming an industry required all of these skills. By the time he expanded his business with a new factory at Etruria in Staffordshire, Wedgwood was the nation's pre-eminent potter. Further innovation in design and production would bring all the profit he'd predicted in the following decades.[35]

Wedgwood, although a pioneer of certain techniques, was just one among many potters who worked and invented in Staffordshire. Within a narrow region only a few miles long, with pot shops and ovens crowded together, intense competition inevitably butted up against the quick transmission and techniques across different firms. Pottery was a knowledge-intensive, craft-based process and most workers in the potteries relied on apprenticeship and experience to develop their skills. Skilled workers were central to the businesses, no matter how many were brought together in the growing factory organisation that was becoming more common for so many types of manufacturing. Despite Wedgwood's claim that he wanted to make his men 'machines as would not err', he lavished resources on training potters in practices such as turning, mould making and figure making that were far beyond the reach of mechanisation. Their collective efforts shaped the simplest of materials into fabulous products that were highly sought after in Britain and across the world. Some innovations, such as double firing or transfer printing, came incrementally, as small improvements were made, shared and improved again, an ongoing series of advances that could rapidly spread across the industry. The buzz of creative innovation and the possibilities of rapid interaction between workers, designers and owners in the region encouraged firms to embrace improvements. This boosted the competitive advantage of leading firms, even as those that fell behind were ruthlessly forced out of business. By the end of the eighteenth century, the Staffordshire potteries, with Wedgwood at its pinnacle, were producing goods that built on all these improvements in design and production to become globally competitive. In Britain, they were boosted by growing imports of tea and sugar, which combined with sparkling ceramic products to create a new form of social interaction and luxurious consumption.[36]

## OUT WITH THE OLD

Britain's industrial development in the eighteenth century depended on the launch of industries that were either new to the island or that had the capacity to grow massively in scale. One option, clearly, was to try and uncover techniques that skilled manufacturers in other countries had already mastered. No one in Britain was troubled when finding innovative ways to substitute sought-after foreign products encouraged capitalists to do everything from stealing technology to mimicking designs. The mechanised silk production of the Lombe brothers depended on the theft of machinery and skills from Italy, and potters like Wedgwood lent on the styles and skills of Chinese and German potters to inspire the development of their own techniques. However, in both cases, precise replication was impossible: machinery was updated, production methods changed, and the organisation of workers altered to fit the materials and skills available in Britain. Continuous efforts were made to improve how these goods were manufactured. In the case of new designs or techniques carried to Britain from overseas, this adaption left industries like potteries and silk mills, or later cotton factories, looking very different at the end of the eighteenth century than they had during their inception. Whether building on existing businesses or developing brand new ones, capitalists needed to take advantage of existing technology and find ways to improve it, apply it in novel ways, or to combine it with new discoveries to add further value.

This mentality was clearly at work when, in 1730, the cartographer Richard Budgen set out to survey the damage caused by a Sussex hurricane for the Royal Society. He also took this environmental disaster as an opportunity to share a description of a new type of windmill. Following 'a long time, a close and intent application of thoughts, and a large expense in making and altering of models' this 'new engine to work by the wind' was a notable improvement on older models. Budgen judged the windmill would be secure against even the strongest of winds and more capable of drawing energy from weaker breezes. It would be more durable, too, due to the fewer parts required and having a steadier construction that differentiated it from older designs. With these benefits, Budgen argued, it could be used 'for most mechanic uses where any considerable force is required' such as 'working capstans, cranes, cornmills, powder-mills, draining of fens and marshes, spinning and making of ropes, bolting-mills, slitting-mills for iron, timber' and so on. As technology like this was incrementally improved, knock-on effects could be felt across multiple sectors. These, too, could incrementally improve their productivity further with the application of more durable and efficient technologies. Old was replaced with new and the loop continued.[37]

The windmill would not, despite improvements, become the great source of power for Britain's industries that Budgen imagined. However, his understanding of the potential for improving an old and familiar piece of technology like the windmill was indicative of the enterprising approach to innovation that was reshaping numerous types of business across the nation. While some of Britain's innovation aimed to replicate or replace techniques that were used to make the most sought-after goods from manufacturers overseas, people also innovated to improve the techniques and technology employed in existing industries. Some of these innovations were exploited to produce new types of goods that were in direct competition with imports, while some of the most successful advances were important because they could be used widely by capitalists working in all manner of different sectors.

In Britain's vital textile sector, technological change was making a transformative impact long before steam-powered factories appeared in the final years of the eighteenth century. Machinery was invented, improved and diffused across Britain's woollen, linen, silk and cotton industries, allowing workers to work faster and more consistently. This did not always create products of higher quality, but it did allow them to be produced at greater volumes that increased profits for the machine owners even as prices for many products dropped for consumers. No single technology was responsible for this shift and, indeed, the benefits were accrued across different stages of the cloth-manufacturing process, including, when agricultural improvements are noted, in the fields where sheep were reared or where flax was grown. Advances in textiles built on existing skills and technologies and saw the application of older technology transformed to support new business ventures. Some were driven by scientific advancements but many more were developed by workers with their hands on the fibres and threads that new techniques were intended to shape.

The textile-production process was well suited for increasing efficiency through mechanisation: spinning wheels were already used to spin woollen or other threads, and looms used to weave cloth. In the eighteenth century, a number of inventions were made that cumulatively had a transformative impact. In 1733, the Lancashire-born John Kay patented the flying shuttle. This simple device removed the need for two weavers to work at the same loom, with a single worker now able to do the task of two. Around the same time, the Huguenot inventor Lewis Paul was collaborating with John Wyatt, a carpenter working in Birmingham's gun industry, who together developed a machine for spinning cotton yarn that was patented in 1738. Soon, Edward Cave, a publisher, set up a cotton mill in Northampton using waterpower to turn the machine's rollers, rebuilding an existing cereal mill. For the first time, neither hand nor animal power was needed to produce yarn. Paul patented another machine in 1748, this time for carding fibres before spinning, which was immediately in competition with a different device intended to do the same that had been developed by Daniel Bourn, who owned a cotton mill in Leominster that employed the Paul–Wyatt spinning machinery. Although only marginally profitable, the new machines were part of a shift that was simultaneously taking place in silk production following Lombe's theft of the Sardinian technology. The possibility of using machines powered by water, wind and later steam was becoming more practical.[38]

The big leap forward, though, came in the following decades, as further technical improvements were made to these existing designs. James Hargreaves, a weaver and carpenter from Lancashire, invented the spinning jenny in 1764, which allowed a single wheel to turn multiple spindles at the same time, allowing several threads to be spun at once. The device was a success, albeit producing fairly low-quality yarn. Around the same time, another John Kay, a clockmaker from Leigh near Manchester, worked with his neighbour Thomas Highs, who made parts for textile weavers, on improving the Paul–Wyatt design, before Kay was employed by Richard Arkwright. Bitter disputes followed, and it was unclear whether Kay, Highs, Arkwright or Hargreaves made the technological breakthrough, but between them, a viable machine known as the spinning frame was developed. This increased the quality of yarn produced. By 1771, Arkwright had installed one of the machines at a new mill on the River Derwent at Cromford, running on waterpower and now known as a water frame. In the following three decades, the widespread use of the machine would transform Britain's cotton industry and leave Arkwright ludicrously wealthy. By 1779, Samuel Crompton combined aspects of the spinning jenny and water frame in his new spinning mule, which had multiple spindles to allow multiple yarns to be spun at the same time but ran these through rollers to improve the quality of the thread. Crompton did not patent his device, but rather sold it to the Scottish manufacturer David Dale, who used it as the basis for a water-powered factory at New Lanark. Further improvements followed, but it was these devices formed the bedrock of the dramatic expansion of Britain's cotton production in the final decades of the century.[39]

A central feature in many of these advances was the addition of external power sources to move machines: human power was insufficient to spin dozens or hundreds of threads simultaneously. To do so, mill owners turned towards technology that had been used in Britain for centuries but reimagined it for the new businesses that they were setting up. This depended on changing patterns in how work in Britain was powered. As early as the thirteenth century, waterpower had been used in fulling mills to alleviate the arduous task of beating woollen cloth, a crucial step for producing smooth and water-resistant material. In the centuries that followed, environmental conditions had already presented Britain's manufacturers with a distinct advantage over European rivals who continued to depend on less reliable windmills for power. In the hilly regions of England, Scotland and Wales, reliable rainfall and natural gradient combined to support the early and widespread adoption of mills for a number of tasks, including milling cloth but also grinding cereal crops for flour, sawing wood and forging metal. Numerous improvements in waterwheels continued in the following centuries, and capitalists who embraced them saw the power from such machinery dramatically increase. When they did not, they risked losing out to more enterprising competitors. Visting Crofton Mill in December 1793, the engineer John Rennie lamented that 'the mill is very ill constructed', so much so that its water supply was so limited, the wheel could not run for more than twelve hours each day and they could grind only five loads of wheat. The nearby Oakhill Mill, he noted, could draw on six times as much water for its wheels. Improvements in design meant that the environment could be exploited much more efficiently – so long as the latest technologies were applied effectively.[40]

By the eighteenth century, the value of some corn mills had started to deteriorate, and repurposing these for textile production was common, although new mills were built from scratch, too. On the border between Lancashire and Yorkshire, the plunging waterways of the Calder Valley had long provided mill owners with the power they needed to grind corn, and by the seventeenth century dozens had been built to serve local communities. Surviving property documents for what was known in 1677 as 'Langfield Corn Mill' reveal how the site changed hands multiple times as different tenants put it to different uses. Already a century old, it was leased by John Uttley of Warland to two millers for the final decades of the seventeenth century before it passed to Joseph Fisher in 1729 when he, too, leased the mill, also to grind corn. His son George then bought it outright for a final sum of £450 in 1741. However, despite still being operational, the site quickly depreciated in value. By 1775, Fisher was forced to accept only £185 'in full for the absolute purchase' of 'that water corn mill, called or known by the name of Lumbutts Mill, and one drying kiln thereunto belonging' as well as the 'stream and streams of water thereunto belonging and enjoyed'. Unfortunately for Fisher, his vision for the mill was stuck in a different era.[41]

When the mill was sold to its new owners John Bottomley and John Sutcliffe, it was transformed, in their mind's eye at least, from an outdated corn mill into a visionary factory at the cutting edge of a new era of water-powered textile production. The new partnership seemed well suited to take advantage of the mill's superb position next to the swift-flowing waters of the Black Clough that surged through the site. Bottomley was a practised miller and would have understood the underlying technology at the site, while Sutcliffe worked making woollen 'stuffs' for sale at home and abroad. Lumbutts, as well as the nearby villages of Todmorden, Walsden and Mankinholes, had a long tradition of supplying woollen cloth to the nearby market in Halifax, but their plans to employ the mill for textile production was a novel idea. Sadly for Bottomley and Sutcliffe, their efforts were not successful, and there is little to suggest that they made any progress in using waterpower effectively for woollen production, although they did upgrade the site's dams, water supply and waterwheel. Only five years after their purchase, they were forced to sell the mill again to pay off debts, now for only £80. Of the machinery installed, the only significant asset was 'a great water wheel', worth £30 5s 4d, but this could achieve little without being connected with compatible technology for spinning thread. Like previous owners, Bottomley and Sutcliffe had not moved quickly enough to take advantage of the benefits that the technology offered: the future lay not in improving the productivity of West Yorkshire's ancient woollen industry but in spinning the fibres of cotton plants that grew thousands of miles away.[42]

The new owner of Lumbutts Mill was John Crossley, a landowner from near Rochdale, who had most likely made the savvy purchase on the advice of his close relation Abraham Crossley, a cotton spinner. Abraham leased the mill in 1783 for twenty-one years as part of a new partnership with fellow cotton manufacturer Thomas Hughes and two local investors from Todmorden, the clog maker Samuel Law and mason Robert Law. The four men paid £9 9s in rent each year for the site. Their lease from John came with strings attached but, unlike Bottomley and Sutcliffe, the new group had clear plans for what was required to transform the site practically into a profitable cotton-spinning business. Not only were the leaseholders responsible 'at their own proper costs' for 'repairing and maintaining the mill', but they were required 'in nine months' time' to have finished 'converting, to the best advantage, the said water corn mill into a cotton mill'.

The new partnership invested £350 in the site, and the experienced cotton workers, Hughes and Crossley, were appointed to oversee 'the making and preparing or providing engines, machines and other materials for working cotton upon'. Rather than further improving the waterpower that the mill had long provided, they concentrated instead on the water frames that could be connected with it. Taking salaries of 12s and 8s per week, respectively, the two men promised to end 'their other employments' and focus on the new cotton enterprise.[43]

Their efforts saw some immediate gains, and just over a year later, in 1784, they had 'converted the said water corn mill into a cotton factory, and made other improvements upon the said denuded premises', including 'making framer machines and engines in and for the said branch of business'. Reflecting their accomplishment, Hughes was offered and took another position in York, and with Robert Law sold his shares to the Todmorden-based woollen manufacturer Samuel Fielden and one of the mill's workers John Tattersall. In a few years, the mills partners had each established themselves as part of the region's new cotton industry. By 1791 Tattersall and Crossley were employed as cotton carders elsewhere, while Samuel Law had swapped clog making for cotton weaving. As they moved on, they sold their lease in Lumbutts Mill to William Uttley and George Feather, a salter and a woollen manufacturer, who ran 'a new carding engine' and 'an old carding engine' at the site until 1794, when the Fielden family reclaimed the lease, now as 'Joshua Fielden and sons', paying Uttley £20 a year for the privilege. By now, the site's machinery was valued at £136 7d, and the 'Lumbutts factory' was ready to be enlarged two years later as the pace of cotton production continued. In 1796, the new Todmorden family firm re-leased the mill directly from Crossley, before buying it outright for £460 in 1803.[44]

The transition to new technology was rarely a linear process, as the conversion of Lumbutts Mill attests, and it was not the only means by which British producers obtained a competitive advantage. This could be seen already by the 1780s, when the possibility of a commercial treaty with France generated a need for the government to understand the impact of new industrial practices. Keen to hear directly from manufacturers and merchants alike, the Board of Trade invited businessmen from across Britain to offer their perspective on the ensuing negotiations. Among them was Alexander Anderson, a trader in Scottish linens who had interests in trade with Russia and Germany. Questioned about the quality of linens produced in France, and whether they 'might in any respect become rivals' to producers in Britain, Anderson explained that 'there is a manufacture of cambric at Glasgow; also at Paisley and Edinburgh' that were producing more and more each year. Seven hundred looms were already in operation, concentrated around new factories, and he expected 200 more would be added that year. Manufacturing linen fabric known as lawns had been even more successful, notably because they were 'a more natural manufacture for Scotland, than cambric; the lawns are made of flax, grown in Scotland, the cambric can only be made of foreign yarn'.

Consequently, 'a very great manufacture of lawns at Paisley' was producing enough to supply the entire domestic demand and were so good that 'there have not been any French lawns smuggled into this country for some time'. The legal import of foreign linens, usually made in Germany and then bleached in the Netherlands before transport to Britain, had already declined following the success of the Paisley factories. The cambric manufacturers were not so lucky and, despite prohibitions on the import of French cambric cloths, they were struggling to outcompete their Gallic competitors. The Scottish cloths were 'not so fine for the same money' when 'compared with the French smuggled cambric' and Anderson believed that banning French cloth had only served to increase the profits for those who took the risk to smuggle it. He concluded, 'a certain moderate duty' on cambric imports would keep Scottish manufacturers competitive and make smuggling unattractive, and the market in France for Scottish lawns was too good an opportunity to pass up. Over the following weeks, the Board of Trade met with further linen specialists, including linendraper Edward Payne and merchants Mr Gataker and Godfrey Thornton, who agreed with Anderson's assessment. Production was booming, and they needed help to find new customers overseas to absorb the growing volume of linen cloth.[45]

The Board of Trade also heard from the Norwich woollen cloth manufacturers George Maltby and Robert Harvey, who were likewise confident about their ability to compete for the biggest share of the international market. 'Wool is much cheaper here than in France,' they explained, 'which gives us great advantage in the coarser' sorts of cloths, while 'in the fine articles' English manufacturers benefited from 'the natural brightness of our wool.' Britain's vast sheep farms gave them a distinct advantage on both counts. When it came to quality of production, though, they were less sure of themselves, and much like Scottish concerns about cambric cloth, worried that in terms of colours and style they would struggle when compared with the best products coming out of France. In the finest articles, when wool was mixed with silk especially, they could not hope to match the quality of cloth found across the Channel. However, their dominant position in producing coarser cloth would cater to a much larger market than the fine silken luxury cloth, and overall Maltby and Harvey agreed that an open trade would work in their favour. Clothiers and merchants from West Yorkshire who appeared before the board presented a similar story. They, too, were confident that 'a trade so opened would be highly beneficial to the woollen and worsted manufactures'. After all, the 'population, fertility, and great resources of France present the prospect of a very extensive' market, and 'in the lower qualities of cloth such as suit the bulk of the people, they cannot stand in competition with us'. In finer cloths, they admitted, 'the French can furnish a cloth which may take the eye in preference to ours'. However, they did not see this as much of a risk, 'particularly as the machines for shortening manual labour are still improving'. Competition would further incentivise the benefits of innovating for the luxury market even as further mechanisation would help them produce coarser cloth even more cheaply.[46]

British manufacturers understood that command of the mass market was essential. The Norwich clothiers were much more concerned about losing the lower end of the market than they were about matching foreign clothiers at the top. Cheap wool was a major factor in keeping their advantage, and Maltby and Harvey cautioned that 'the French are acquiring an advantage over us by importing yarn from Ireland' while the clothiers from Leeds and Halifax warned that any exports of raw wool from England would threaten their industry. However, while this strict protectionism was essential, the clothiers were in agreement that high tariffs and prohibitions imposed by other states were maladies that needed to be immediately rectified. Duties on English cloth in Spain and Portugal, which had been their largest markets for much of the eighteenth century, had severely impacted the trade, causing exports of Norfolk cloth to fall almost a third in the previous decade. The Yorkshire trade had been less affected, as trade with northern European markets had remained more open, but it also encouraged the committee to give 'as much attention as possible ... to our existing trade with Portugal'. As 'a commercial nation', they argued, it was 'sound policy' for the state 'to provide many different markets for its manufacturers by which means its capital in trade is more dispersed'. When summing up their meeting with the Norfolk clothiers, the Board of Trade were thinking along the same lines, asking 'do you think it of importance to endeavour to open new markets?'. The answer was simple: 'certainly'.[47] Rather than support at home from foreign competitors, Britain's cloth manufacturers more opportunities to sell their goods. Mass production, especially in mechanically sophisticated West Yorkshire, gave the nation's manufacturers confidence that they could swamp any market with cheaper goods and still turn a profit. Technology alone didn't create the conditions for Britain's manufacturing and commercial success, but it was starting to give textile manufacturers a considerable competitive advantage.[48]

CHAPTER 7

# MASTERS OF REALITY

## Applied Science and Remaking the Natural World

> In the natural world, our bountiful creation has formed different soils, and appointed different climates; whereby the inhabitants of different countries may supply each other with their respective fruits and products; so that by exciting a reciprocal industry, they may carry on an intercourse mutually beneficial, and universally benevolent.

Welsh economic writer Josiah Tucker believed that all peoples of the world would be enriched by the peaceful exchange of nature's bounties. Yet, of course, the environment didn't simply provide the goods that people sought ready to use and easily accessible. This required human action to rip minerals from the earth or plant and harvest crops that grew upon it. People, too, shaped raw materials into finished products, and 'even where there is no remarkable difference of soil, or of climates', Tucker maintained, 'we find a great difference of talents; and, if I may be allowed the expression, a wonderful variety of strata in the human mind'. The environmental contrasts that made trade so beneficial and necessary also created the conditions whereby goods could be produced and traded for the comparative advantage of one side over the other.[1]

The mutually beneficial and benevolent exchange of goods that Tucker described was a fiction. British capitalists, both domestically and globally, operated in and profited from a fundamentally unequal system. People, the planet and scientific discoveries were all exploited to gain an advantage over competitors during Britain's rapid economic development. While trading to carry the 'superabundance of the production of one country or climate to another', British capitalists also sought to turn nature on its head and make in Britain goods that they had previously exchanged reciprocally. Science, technology and empire all presented very real opportunities to overcome the limits that nature had previously imposed. 'A full tide of wealth and opulence' had 'flowed into Europe' thanks to the exchange of goods, but more still could be extracted. Sharing nature's cornucopia was not the motivating factor for Britain's capitalists as they set out to reshape it. Profit was.[2]

Confident in their powers to shape nature to their will and buoyed by advances in everything from natural science to heavy engineering, plans for boosting productivity became grander in their scope and scale. Agricultural methods expanded and improved on those employed earlier in the century, but these were increasingly combined with techniques developed in plantations in the Caribbean and North America as much as in farms in Britain. At the same time, plans and willingness to transform the landscape grew dramatically, and the transformation of waste land into rich fields for planting or the transplant of crops from one continent to another became more common. If this wasn't enough, capitalists saw opportunities in reshaping the very landscape to match the needs of their business interests, and in the eighteenth century vast networks of canals and roads were constructed to connect agriculture, extractive industries, manufacturing centres, markets and ports. This often depended on feats of engineering that required huge capital expenditure that could only be supplied by wider networks of capitalists who together set out to reshape the world around them.[3]

## BOTANIC BOUNTIES

In the 1730s, the 'Common-Council for Establishing the Colony of Georgia' came up with a plan for extracting value from newly seized territories in America that would ensure the colony functioned as a vital part of Britain's colonial economic system. While the colony's proponents accepted as 'undoubtedly a self-evident maxim' that the 'wealth of a nation consists in the number of her people', they cautioned that this was only the case so long as they were working: unemployed people 'must lie a dead weight upon the public'. They found their inspiration in apiculture. After all, they argued, 'every wise government, like the bees, should not suffer any drones in the state'. Best for everyone to follow their example and to see a policy put in place for 'transplanting such as are necessitous and starving here' to 'promote and enlarge our settlements abroad with unusual industry'. Bees and their well-structured hives were already a well-established rhetorical tool for describing how an industrial and hierarchical society should run, and they would remain so throughout Britain's economic development in the eighteenth century.[4]

Georgia's climate was also an attractive quality for the council, as they thought it could allow it to add a new strand to Britain's economic bow: its own source of raw silk. The plan was simple. Thomas Lombe's recent theft of Italian silk-making technology had led to 'the King of Sardinia prohibiting the exportation of any raw silk out of his dominion', and Georgia would make up for the loss. With the right support, the colony would 'raise raw silk of equal goodness' and save Britain 'not only the large sum paid annually to the Italians' but also 'a large sum going every year to France for her wrought' silk fabrics. Lombe was on board and wrote to support the plan's connected goals of alleviating the 'burden' of employment in Britain and simultaneous support for the British silk industry (that he happened to dominate, thanks to his patent). The new colony offered a chance to develop specialised sericulture that Lombe believed had 'a very great probability of succeeding' and would produce silk well suited for production using his patented machines. Indeed, Lombe had already experimented with silk produced in nearby Carolina, which 'has as much natural strength and beauty as the silk of Italy' and had been used to produce samples of 'a fine, clean and even thread'.[5]

The colony's managers took this advice on board, buying silkworm eggs from Italy and hiring experts from Piedmont to 'go and settle in Georgia and instruct the people'. They hoped that an easy transition would lead to Georgia becoming a silk-producing powerhouse that would 'soon be raised to supply all Europe'. After all, they believed, 'the work of making raw silk is easy, the silk worms will multiply prodigiously' and nature's bounty would be there for the taking. The only limiting factor was whether 'there were hands enough properly instructed to carry on the work'. Ten acres of land were set aside for the sericultural experiment, mulberry trees were planted successfully, and young English women were trained to look after silkworms while male colonists learned how to look after the trees. By 1739, packages of raw silk samples had been taken to England and presented to silk merchant John Zachary and silk weaver Mr Booth, where it was 'declared it to be as fine as any Italian silk, and worth at least twenty shillings a pound'. By the mid-1740s, hundreds more trees had been planted and machinery installed in Georgia to support ongoing production. Unfortunately, the process of silk cultivation was slow, and the productivity of the nascent industry was so poor that it earned workers only half the income they could obtain elsewhere in the colonial economy. Bounties were offered to encourage further silk production and the colony's government sent people to France to learn the newest techniques, but neither approach succeeded in boosting interest. Silk production peaked by the 1760s, before declining in the final decades of the eighteenth century.[6]

While ultimately a failure, the silk experiment in Georgia was illustrative of how British capitalists understood the role of colonies in supplying Britain with raw materials for its industries. If sought-after plants and minerals occurred naturally then great, and if not, then ingenuity and scientific knowledge would find the way. Although less radical than launching silk in Georgia, plans for improving agricultural output changed how colonists exploited land across the Caribbean and North America, where plantations that depended on enslaved labour were ideally suited for experimentation because so much of the productive process could be controlled and monitored.

The oldest of Britain's sugar-producing colonies, Barbados, was often treated as a guide for plantation management on other islands in the Caribbean. Almost a hundred miles west of the Windward Island chain, the small island was well situated to support budding investors. The climate was a little cooler than other islands in the

Caribbean and it was relatively secure from invasion by other European powers. With the risk of disease or conflict reduced, the island was home to many resident planters, some of whom remained on the island for generations, learning and developing techniques for maximising the productivity of their plantations. Fortuitously for those planters who seized or purchased land early, Barbados provided ideal conditions for growing sugar. Requiring around 1,600 millimetres of rain each year, the tropical plant could be grown on much of the relatively flat island, and the existing forest cover was quickly obliterated to make way. Sugar cultivation dominated the Barbadian environment, with virtually all of its 166 square miles covered by sugar crops and plantations. Across the Caribbean, where geographic and environmental factors allowed, Britain's island colonies were likewise transformed by enslaved people whose labour cleared, planted, harvested and processed sugar cane before it was shipped to Britain.[7]

Environmental conditions in different islands also meant that British capitalists needed to employ different techniques to maximise their exploitation of these tropical landscapes. In Jamaica, rough terrain made the cultivation of sugar even more demanding for the enslaved people forced to toil in the island's steeper plantations. By the end of the eighteenth century, overcoming the limitations of Jamaica's more diverse environment had led plantation owners to embrace alternatives, whether rearing cattle in the island's lowlands or growing coffee in the mountains. Conversely, in Barbados, plantation owners faced challenges that were a consequence of the very ease by which earlier efforts to maximise production on the island had ravaged its environment. Deforestation and sugar monocultures had a deleterious effect on soil quality and by the second half of the eighteenth century the island's plantations were struggling to match the productivity of those in places like Antigua. Innovation was essential and techniques like cane holing were employed to prevent erosion, agricultural waste was used to fuel machinery that processed the crop, and extensive manuring took place to revitalise the island's soils.[8]

British colonists elsewhere in the Caribbean often lent on the Barbadian experience, whether they were on other small islands in the nearby Windward and Leeward islands or much larger territories like Jamaica. The primary focus had long been maximising the production of sugar. Written in 1755, the *Treatise upon Husbandry or Planting* by William Belgrove set out to explain how the newest techniques in exploiting land and labour could be employed profitably by people who owned plantations on the island. 'It is an obvious remark,' he began, 'that the profits arising from husbandry are always proportionate to the care and attention we give it.' Setting up a plantation was a substantial undertaking. Including the cost of acquiring land (£10,000 for 500 acres), equipment and buildings (£7,500) and 300 enslaved workers (£12,000), the upfront capital needed was over £30,000. This was a huge charge that attested to the complexity and scale of plantations. Extracting profits from plantations required the delicate management of labour, machinery and the land together. Belgrove's book offered a careful overview of the best practices for planting canes, manuring with dung, penning cattle, and so on, with a month-by-month account of tasks that needed to be completed. Sugar processing had its own instructions and required more sophisticated apparatus, including numerous copper objects that were obtained from manufacturers in Britain. A significant part of his book focused on ensuring that captive workers were pushed to work as hard as they could, and harshly disciplined if not. Establishing fairly common practices across the island, and indeed in sugar plantations across the Caribbean, had boosted productivity, and the conformity of climate and conditions in Barbados made the ideal site for experimentation. With each agricultural improvement or failure, planters could easily share knowledge about what worked and what did not. In the final decades of the eighteenth century, widespread innovation further maximised the exploitation of land and enslaved labour in the Caribbean and helped boost the volume of tropical goods that were flowing across the Atlantic.[9]

Enslaved people were responsible for the vast majority of the work needed to achieve these economic gains. Across the Caribbean, enslaved people worked long, arduous hours, typically from sunrise to sometime after sunset. Day after day, year after year, the most of their waking hours were spent labouring in fields or in other parts of the productive process. In much the same way as mining or farming in Britain, the basic work undertaken on Britain's sugar plantations changed little over the course of the eighteenth century, with simple hand tools used to clear land and harvest sugar, with mills powered by wind, water or cattle to process it. However, the cumulative effect of incremental improvements across a range of different parts of plantation management meant that their output and productivity increased substantially over the course of the eighteenth century. The profits for plantation owners could be immense. Indeed, islands like Jamaica, Barbados and Antigua, where sugar planting had become a predominant source of profit for enslavers who owned property on the islands, were among the most dynamic growth points of the British economy. Land and labour were exploited with ruthless intensity.[10]

In the second half of the eighteenth century, landowners in the Caribbean adopted a range of measures to exploit their enslaved workforces further still and took advantage of new agricultural and technological techniques. The island's largest plantations exploited the labour of as many as a thousand enslaved people at any given time, and even those of a middling size were dependent on the labour of 400 or 500 captive workers. In 1760, after the successful merchant Thomas Hibbert purchased a 3,000-acre estate in Jamaica, he turned quickly to improvement projects to increase his profits from the site. After expanding the site's cattle rearing, in 1771 Hibbert turned to sugar cultivation, exploiting enslaved workers to clear the land and prepare it for planting. In the following years, the Hibbert family acquired more land on the island, and more enslaved workers who toiled on it. Across their estates, sugar cultivation, other crops and animal husbandry were combined to boost productivity. At the same time, some agricultural changes were becoming widespread across the Caribbean: planting Guinea and Scotch grass was beneficial for livestock and reduced the cost of food on the islands, using manure to fertilise fields helped improve yields, and new agricultural methods to intersperse other crops alongside sugar helped maintain soils and reduce weeding. In Antigua in the 1790s, one overseer was picked out for praise by a local attorney, Michael Keane, who recognised that he was 'very considerably improving and meliorating the property by planting plantain', a crop that was not intended for sale but rather as 'a material source for feeding slaves'. Similarly, the extensive adoption of more efficient techniques for producing refined sugars and rum added value to plantation goods. The application of practices such as these was lauded in printed guides for plantation management and in letters between plantation owners, overseers and others. In 1776, one Jamaican planter praised the 'prodigious practical improvements' that had been made on the island, while twenty years later Sampson Wood, an overseer in Barbados, drew attention to the 'modern improvements' in sugar cultivation 'that have been made of late years'.[11]

As factories in the field, plantations were at the forefront of efforts to maximise the exploitation of land, labour and technology. Overseeing such large business enterprises required specialist skills and methods that combined agricultural expertise with modern management know-how. Whether by imposing work patterns regulated by clocks, cycling crops to minimise off-seasons, increasing manuring, upgrading sugar boilers or using new planting techniques, plantation owners exhibited the same ruthless dedication to exploiting incremental gains in productivity as their compatriots did in Britain. After over a century of extracting wealth from islands in the Caribbean, the widespread adoption of innovative practices had a remarkable impact, and productivity gains were particularly pronounced in the 1770s and 1780s.[12]

In North America, developing agricultural methods focused less on maximising the cultivation of a single crop and more on the establishment of more diverse agricultural practices. In the seventeenth century, newly seized territories in Virginia had initially focused on cultivating another highly sought-after commodity in Britain and Europe: tobacco. However, with more land available for exploitation, as well as the crop's damaging impact on the environment, intensive agricultural practices that became common in the Caribbean were not replicated. Instead, the territory's long development from the seventeenth century onward had led to the establishment of numerous small plantations spread across the flat lands extending from the coastal tidewater and towards Ohio. Expanding inland from the

Atlantic coast, by the end of the eighteenth century the Virginia colony was more than fifteen times larger than Jamaica and 400 times the size of Barbados. Although not as densely populated or intensively cultivated as the Caribbean islands, the scale of its agricultural footprint made it more than capable of sending huge volumes of the profitable intoxicant back to Britain, much of it for re-export to markets across Europe and beyond.[13]

Virginia owed its increasing productivity partly to the simple expansion of the colony's cultivated land. However, tobacco rapidly depleted soil in only six or seven years, leaving land 'used up' far more quickly than plantation owners would have liked and requiring twenty-five years to naturally regenerate. Rather than enduring and monocultural plantations, like those in the Caribbean, this left a much more varied agricultural economy as colonists experimented and rotated crops to maximise their yields. Unlike sugar, tobacco cultivation did not require processing with expensive machinery, and landowners could easily send their workers to cultivate new land when productivity dropped, clearing an ever-growing share of the back country. Employing techniques that had been popularised in British farming towards the end of the previous century, by the 1730s, many landowners had diversified their production, planting wheat and corn as well as tobacco, and investing in animal husbandry.

In the second half of the eighteenth century, these agricultural patterns intensified and left Virginia's largest plantations making more than half their revenue from grains. It was here, especially, that different types of investment and know-how were required to increase productivity. Grain mills and modern ploughs transformed the landscape as cereal crops took the place of more labour-intensive tobacco cultivation. Combined with growing diversification and Virginia's seasonal climate, it was possible for farmers to cycle between work on wheat, corn, tobacco and livestock at different times of the year, further increasing the profitability of land and boosting the productivity of labourers who no longer had down-time during off-seasons. Changing patterns of planting, coupled with the improvement of agricultural land, contributed to substantial increases in productivity, and from 1740 larger plantations on the Chesapeake achieved consistent increases to their crop yields that continued throughout the eighteenth century.[14]

George Washington's estate at Mount Vernon in Northern Virginia was among those that took advantage of changing agricultural practices in North America. Already a large estate of 2,500 acres when he acquired it, his landholdings had expanded to an enormous 8,000 acres by 1799. Despite occupying relatively flat lands that posed less demanding work conditions, Washington still exploited enslaved workers, whose numbers more than doubled in the last quarter of the eighteenth century to over 300. During this period, which included the American War of Independence and Washington's leadership of the nascent United States, the estate completed its shift away from tobacco planting towards other crops. Struggling to raise the former in the poor soils, Washington had stopped planting the cash crop in 1766 in favour of corn, wheat, rye, oats and barley. These were less profitable but were essential provisions that supported economic activity across North America and the Caribbean. Efforts to diversify further into more skilled tasks were stymied by the region's dependence on enslaved workers, who were deemed unsuitable for occupations beyond working in the fields (Washington complained, 'I have more' enslaved people 'than can be employed to any advantage in the farming system'). Further south, vast estates in Carolina and Georgia were turned towards the production of raw cotton for Britain's booming textile sector that was growing too quickly to be met by traditional sources of the precious threads from the eastern Mediterranean and India.[15]

Many transformative changes were a result of continuous improvement that rendered processes more dependable or simply cheaper, and which could be applied to a broader range of economic settings. Advances in watch and clock making were indicative of this. Improving the accuracy and accessibility of timepieces made it more viable for capitalists to employ new ideas about controlling and measuring the productivity of their workers. New systems of work and time discipline were applied in rural and urban contexts, across Britain and in its colonies overseas. With an emphasis on extracting every last possible second of labour from enslaved people to maximise productivity, it was this brutal time discipline as much as processing machinery that made sugar plantations resemble factories in the field. Increasing the productivity of enslaved workers was achieved not through efficiency savings, but by forcing them to work more hours and more days throughout the year. In the 1780s, the representative of the absentee owners of the Newton and Seawell estate in Barbados was impressed to find that their new manager, Sampson Wood, was keeping meticulous logs to manage the enslaved workforce. Likewise, overseers in Jamaica in the 1790s were carefully recording the precise number of hours that the boiling house operated, as well as the times that different cohorts of enslaved workers began and ended their shifts. At his estate at Mount Vernon in Virginia, George Washington used a simple yet precise pocket watch in the 1760s to undertake time-motion studies of his enslaved labourers, calculate hourly rates of production, and impose strict time management. The aim, as he noted in his diary twenty years later, was to compel and measure the maximum effort that could be extracted from his workers. After all, 'lost labour can never be regained' and only with careful management was it possible to ensure that 'every labourer' should 'do as much in the 24 hours as their strength, without endangering their health, or constitution, will allow'. Increasingly rigorous and precise, labour-management techniques that kept track of workers every hour of the day became ever more common in plantations over the course of the eighteenth century. Whether for enslaved people in the Caribbean or factory workers in Lancashire, keeping time changed how labour was envisaged by British enslavers and employers alike.[16]

The application of new techniques across Britain's colonial territories produced some mixed results but was part of an interconnected economic system that saw capitalists in different parts of the world seeking ways to take advantage of their particular environments and the profit that transplanting industries from one continent to another might accrue. Towards the very end of the eighteenth century, the Scottish traveller Alexander Walker left a remarkable account of one farm in southern India, owned by an Englishman called Mr Webb, where a number of industrial experiments were under way with the goal of taking advantage of global exchanges that were likewise transforming the nearby port and colonial capital at Madras (now Chennai). The farm, Walker noted, 'consists of a cotton plantation of about 400 acres' and its owner had the 'character . . . of an extravagant and unprincipled adventurer but coloured with ingenious visions'. Rather than producing cotton for the local market, which had been centre of a cotton cloth industry for hundreds of years, Webb decided to serve the British market, where mechanisation was causing demand for raw cotton to grow dramatically. 'For this purpose, he gathers the cotton clean and processes it', which was mechanised as much as possible using machines built to European designs. One, 'A machine for freeing cotton of its seeds', was considered particularly novel, and Walker took the time to draft a sketch of the device. By increasing production and focusing on ensuring the cotton was well prepared before shipment, Webb estimated that each bale would 'yield a profit each of £25 in England, thus 1,000 bales would be worth £25,000', and a hundred had already been prepared. Walker was unsure if Webb would succeed, but 'the probability of success', he thought, was improved 'by confining the operation to the [provision] of the raw material alone'. Establishing monocultures on plantations in America or farms in Britain had been successful in maximising productivity, and he had every reason to think the same would apply in India.[17]

Cotton was Webb's primary interest but not his only endeavour. He also had plans for 'making rope from the leaves of the American aloe' and had successfully transplanted the long-lived plant from Central America to his Indian farm. Making rope from the plants required 'steeping the leaves in water' before separating the fibres and drying them in the sun. Walker reported that a 'large rope works' had been built and he already 'employed a considerable number of people' who were producing aloe-rope from fine twine to large cables. These were designed for use by ships at the nearby port. Despite difficulties in producing rope that stemmed from a lack of expertise among his workers about using the fibres, Webb was confident that it was 'lighter, more pliant, stronger and as durable as hemp'. The limitation to his grand designs lay not in the manufacturing, but in the natural supply. American aloes grew slowly and took 'several years to arrive at maturity'

6. *Artists produced careful images of fauna they found in Britain and across the world, including, here, an American aloe like that transplanted by Webb to India in the hope of making rope.*

and Walker expressed concerns that they were unlikely to grow quickly enough for manufacturing rope at any great scale.[18]

However, the biggest challenge that Walker identified was not the efficacy of these schemes linking Webb's farm with commercial networks that crossed the world, but how he would compete locally for workers. Cotton picking and processing 'labours under this disadvantage, that as it is in a constant state of production the crop must be gathered daily, which requires a perpetual attendance'. Unlike in the Caribbean, Webb could not exploit enslaved workers. Instead, he had to compete with other local landowners and any effort he made to raise wages to attract more workers would force up the price of his goods.

By using technology to change processes and by transplanting crops, Webb believed he could transform the output of his farm and cater to the British market: whether cotton manufacturers in Lancashire or ship owners needing to replace ropes after their long voyage to India. In the end, neither Webb's plan to send Indian raw cotton to Britain nor his plan to produce ropes from American aloe were as transformative as he might have liked. They were, though, indicative of efforts by landowners across the British empire to maximise the productivity and profits from the land.[19]

Webb's efforts paled in scale next to simultaneous plans in the 1790s to transform the global market for sweet tropical fauna by challenging the Caribbean's domination of sugar production. This would be achieved, it was hoped, by a new entrant on the British marketplace: Bengali sugar. This was not to be brought about through a mutually beneficial exchange with local producers any more than the import of transatlantic sugar had been, but through the continuing expansion of Britain's colonially extractive system. Newly seized territories in India opened up the possibility of producing sugar at scales that were unimaginable in the smaller territories that had brought so much profit in the Caribbean.

The East India Company, which had violently expanded its territories in Bengal after the 1750s, had 'very sanguine expectations' about 'the extent of this projected novelty'. The company's directors and shareholders were reportedly convinced that 'they have sprung a mine of wealth, that shall be as productive as the Parys mountain' (a huge copper mine in Anglesey that had made its proprietor Thomas Williams fabulously wealthy). This was quite the threat to plantation owners in the Caribbean who were 'alarmed and imagine they will be ruined by an immense importation from the East'. Not everyone was convinced, and concerns that it would take years to increase sugar production, coupled with worries about the deleterious impact it would have on 'the British Empire at large', were both aired publicly. Already, the East India Company's monopolistic privileges were under attack from multiple directions, and their demands for reduced duties on their imported sugar exacerbated tensions. Critics pointed out that they already had 'a very handsome advantage' with profits of over 25 per cent: if their plans to increase production and decrease costs came to pass this might increase 'above 100 per cent'.[20]

To obtain such incredible profits required a shift in practice and the adoption of the same plantation methods that had so remarkably increased sugar production in the Caribbean, with Indian labourers to work on them. In *A Short Review of the East India Trade* (1793), one anonymous author argued that 'there are in Bengal large tracts of uncultivated lands, and people in sufficient numbers accustomed to the cultivation of sugar, for enabling that country to answer the demand for the whole of Europe'. However, the scale of investment required to exploit this new frontier would be considerable. One estimate suggested that Caribbean sugar cultivation required around 400,000 acres of high-quality land and the labour of over one million enslaved African workers: a vast scale of exploitation that had taken over a hundred years to construct. They predicted that, by contrast, over a million acres 'of the richest land in India must be appropriated to this speculation' for any hope of success – an area roughly ten times the size of Barbados. It was perhaps unsurprising, then, that this scale, coupled with poor management and inadequate adaption of technology for the Indian environment (notably too little irrigation), meant that the corporation's efforts struggled to compete with their Caribbean counterparts. In fact, British efforts to expand sugar production were so disastrous that in the nineteenth century India's sugar industry collapsed, and it began importing the product from Java. British agricultural interest in India refocused on the production of silk and tea, and extracting revenue through taxes on India's huge working population.[21]

Such failed efforts stemmed in part from a growing belief that extracting value from land could be shaped through careful management, sometimes without appreciation of local conditions. Agricultural exploitation in Britain's colonies was not taking place in an intellectual vacuum, and landowners who were resident on their plantations or living in Britain alike shared useful experiences that contributed to the spread of profitable practices. Agriculture in Britain was transformed during the same period as the widespread enclosure of common land, the adoption of the plough, the application of manure, improvements in animal husbandry and new systems of crop rotation increased yields across the country. These were not too different from the methods being used to reshape the increasingly unnatural environment of the monocultural plantations in the Caribbean or the vast estates of colonists in North America. After 1750, there was a rapid increase in the number of agricultural books published to share best practices on both sides of the Atlantic. The insights of resident planters appeared alongside those of English farmers in collections like Arthur Young's *Annals of Agriculture* and were distributed to a wider audience in Britain. Young, in his 1770 book *Rural Oeconomy*, explained that 'it is the business of the nobility and gentry who practice agriculture, and of authors, who practice and write on it, to help forward the age' by embracing improvements. Echoing the complaint that Francis Hone had made twenty years earlier in his prize-winning essay for the Edinburgh Society, one Jamaican plantation owner in 1776 argued that 'husbandry ought to be more generally understood as a science' and encouraged fellow landowners to experiment with new methods to render the earth 'more and more profitable'. Practical and demonstrable knowledge had its own cachet, and a review of Gordon Turnbull's *Letters to a Young Planter* in 1786 compared the new English text favourably to a competing French manual that had been written more for 'the study of the philosopher than the planter'. Books, personal networks and scientific societies were all important to the distribution of knowledge and changes in agricultural practice that took place across Britain's imperial territories.[22]

Much of this work rested on changing ideas about the role of landowners and the importance of controlling knowledge to maximise authority over land and labour (similar processes were taking place in Britain's developing factories). Young's call for improvement needed landowners 'to endeavour to quicken the motions of the vast but unwieldy body, the common farmers', who for too long had controlled how agriculture was undertaken. Knowledge of working people who 'love to grope in the dark' for solutions, was unable to meet the demands of the age, and instead 'it is the business of superior minds' to 'shine forth and dissipate the night' – that is to say, to enlighten them. Indeed, the goal of much of this literature was not to inform farm workers but the landowners who commanded them, so that they could 'check the negligence, correct the ignorance, or detect the imposition, of servants'. At the end of the day, another author Thomas Robertson explained, a successful agricultural capitalist 'does not perform manual labour'. Farming was 'a liberal art, and consists in appointing and superintending labour': the same could be applied to capitalists running mines and factories. It was a shift in perspective that saw the intellectual task of management and organisation fundamentally separated from manual work. As Robertson concluded, if someone managing a farm performed 'menial tasks, he could not have time to make observations, to think, to read, to go to markets, to meet with his neighbours, to ride through the Parish and County'.[23]

Ideas like these facilitated the diffusion of agricultural techniques across Britain and its empire. They were also part of business thinking across many other sectors, too. Workers who could be controlled in systems that extracted more for land- or business-owners were to be valued, while those that could not were to be disciplined or ruthlessly dismissed. A similar logic was applied to the land, too, and efforts were made during this period to ensure that as much land as possible was productively used to maximise the profit of landowners. In Scotland, the Lowland and Highland clearances saw huge amounts of land taken into closed, large-scale pastoral farms at the expense of former tenants who had worked the land for their own profit. Rents increased, landlords benefited, and the use of techniques to increase output became widespread, but the clearances also displaced thousands of people from their homes. Some landowners tore down entire villages to make way for changing land use, sometimes building alternative housing on the edge of estates or on Scotland's coasts from which displaced people could seek employment as wage labourers on the new, larger farms. Others emigrated to Glasgow, Edinburgh or other growing industrial cities in northern England. Likewise, in England, the Enclosure Act in 1773 saw huge amounts of land taken away from common usage so that landowners could exploit it privately. More people were forced from their homes, and more workers were funnelled towards industrial sites in search of work.

The manufacturer Matthew Boulton was one landowner who took advantage by enclosing common land that he believed was wasted through the 'idle' and 'beggarly' condition of the people who had used it. From the perspective of Britain's eighteenth-century improvers, the land, like its workers, needed to be managed and exploited effectively to achieve its potential.[24]

As well as taking greater control over the use of land through enclosures, enterprising landowners also sought to use new technology to make previously unprofitable land yield more. Drainage, notably, combined technological developments in pumping water and reshaping the landscape to create huge new expanses of rich farmland. In the Fens, workers dug, drained and pumped water from the land to transform the map of England between the Bedford River and the Great Ouse. An economy that depended on the shallow channels and peat bogs for fishing and fowling had, by the second half of the eighteenth century, become rolling fields of some of the most fertile land in the country. Engineers like John Smeaton and John Rennie turned their talents to keeping the water at bay, building first windmills and then steam engines to pump out the rising waters and unlock the bounty of the rich dark soils that drainage left behind. Windmills powered pumps that carried water away from the new farmland and vast drainage networks were dug to ensure that a perfect balance between poor irrigation and overflooding was maintained. This new land was used to grow food crops but also exploited intensively for industrial crops like flax and hemp. By the end of the eighteenth century, drainage efforts had increased Britain's total arable farmland by as much as 10 per cent. The people who had made their living from the fens lost their livelihoods, but the landowners who extended their profitable holdings benefited greatly, as did the manufacturers who were supplied or the workers in growing cities who consumed the crops.[25]

Some landowners cashed in on the technologically driven changes offered by new industries by simply leasing previously unprofitable land to manufacturers. In the 1790s, booming demand for access to water to power cotton mills led to numerous exchanges of property in suitable locations, whether through the transformation of existing corn mills into modern factories or the construction of new facilities from scratch. The innkeeper and landowner William Patchett took advantage by leasing non-productive land in the Calder Valley to the Lancaster merchant Thomas Edmondson, who paid £124 a year for rent to build a mill at Laith Holme near Mytholmroyd. This was only viable after Patchett also secured an agreement from his neighbour William Greenwood to divert water from his Hawksclough estate. After paying £176 for 'damages' caused by the construction of the dams and weirs needed to channel water towards the new mill, Patchett paid only 5 shillings for the continuous supply of the precious liquid that would power the site. More dramatically still, Patchett constructed 'several tunnels or covered aqueducts' to carry water across his estate. In the following months, further grants to dam and divert water were obtained from other landowners along the same stretch of river, with more and more water diverted towards the wheels that powered the new factory's machinery. With a little imagination and the ability to bend the natural landscape to his will, the enterprising landowner had dramatically increased the rents from his property and opened up another site for industrial development.[26]

Elsewhere, landowners who had made their money in manufacturing sometimes set out to use their entrepreneurial skills to improve their properties, with mixed success. Some took more interest in the land than others. In 1749, for instance, the gun manufacturer and arms trader James Farmer, who owned a farm near Birmingham, asked his friend Samuel Galton to lease the property for him while he was in Paris. Little advice was given beyond noting that 'now is the most proper time to do it before any ploughing or sowing is done', and that Galton should pick whatever choice 'will bring the most money'. He had little interest in improving the estate, although he was certainly happy to take rent from it. Conversely, other new landowners were much more proactive. At his farm in Cheshire, the Irish-born cotton manufacturer Samuel Greg took great care in developing his agricultural assets even as his mills expanded. The village he built at Styal provided housing for workers even as its shops sold produce from his farms. By the 1790s, he had taken advantage of opportunities to plant new types of crops, too, including fields of potatoes, receiving £44 for an acre's yield. He also inherited the Hillsborough plantation in Dominica, where enslaved workers toiled on his land.[27]

For manufacturers and merchants, buying property had many benefits that were social and political as much as they might have been economic, and many successful capitalists did likewise. After making tens of thousands of pounds from manufacturing cotton cloth in Lancashire, the textile entrepreneur Samuel Oldknow set out to establish an agricultural enterprise to sit alongside his industrial interests. He had been brought up in a farming community and could draw on the support and advice of farming family members, such as his stepfather John Clayton, to do so. For example, when Oldknow wanted to buy bullocks, Clayton informed him that purchasing them at suitable prices in the current market wasn't possible. The more experienced farmer promised to look out for heifers and 'young baron cows' at the fairs, which could be sold again in the spring. A few years later, Clayton warned Oldknow against purchasing cattle too eagerly, noting that 'you had better let the grass rot upon the ground than run hazard for nothing'. Oldknow's efforts to sell on the national market struggled, too, as 'fat and lean stock' were abundant and had lowered prices considerably. A letter from another associate, Robert Needham in Ashford, recommended that he might have more luck 'selling them to better advantage in your own neighbourhood'. In each case, the landowner, famed for his impact on the cotton industry, could draw on social networks for advice about how to better manage his land.[28]

Similar links between manufacturing, trade and empire underpinned the development of the estate of David Gavin, a Scottish merchant who was part of the scientific networks in Edinburgh that were promoting agricultural improvement and might have benefited from the ideas in Home's prize-winning essay. Gavin was just one among many landowners who used their capital to invest in various improvement projects, and efforts to transform the landscape using new methods of farming and organisation were buoyed by the simultaneous growth of the wider economy. Already established as a wealthy trader by this point, Gavin oversaw a business enterprise that benefited from connections across Britain's manufacturing and commercial sectors and sent ships to European ports including

Rotterdam, Dunkirk, Königsberg and Copenhagen. His trade depended on the export of fine Scottish lawn and cambric cloth and the import of commodities including wine, spirits, and even tea transported from China by the Dutch East India Company. Building on these foundations, Gavin had profited from the transatlantic slave-trade in partnership with another merchant Richard Oswald, invested in the Leith Sugar House to process Caribbean produce, and purchased thousands of pounds of government bonds. He was, as this brief survey suggests, a capitalist keen to take advantage of opportunities in every direction that Britain's deeply interconnected economic development allowed.[29]

In addition to his various international interests, Gavin also applied his wealth towards his establishment as a member of Scotland's landed elite. First buying an estate at Langton, which, as he put it in a letter to a business partner in Newcastle, Ralph Carr, had '900 acres good old grass', the merchant then married Lady Christine, the daughter of the Earl of Lauderdale. Thereafter, Gavin got to work tearing down existing homes and replacing them with a carefully planned village that he rather immodestly named Gavinton, with new houses constructed around the crossroads that ran through his estate. The new property was rented to dozens of separate tenants, mostly farmers who raised crops, sheep and cattle, as well as at least one weaver. Each tenant paid rent to Gavin that provided a consistent source of income alongside his ongoing commercial interests in Britain and abroad. For capitalists like Gavin, land at home and abroad was a commodity that could be seized, bought and traded, and if exploited effectively, was a source of wealth and plenty as vital for Britain's economy as any factory or furnace. Vitally, the interests of landowners, manufacturers and merchants intersected, and the eighteenth century saw more and more links established between agriculture and other parts of the economy that contributed to ongoing cycles of development.[30]

## REMAKING BRITAIN

By the second half of the eighteenth century, new industries were blossoming across the country and their goods were turning a tidy profit when sold to consumers at home, in colonies across the Atlantic, and with trading partners around the world. Connecting different economic activities had already been a key feature in the development of many sectors, making it possible for them to combine materials extracted from different parts of the country or carried to Britain's ports from overseas. In metallurgy, the Bristol Channel and River Severn had provided the necessary infrastructure for carrying copper ore from Cornwall to Swansea for smelting before the metal was carried onwards to Bristol or the Midlands for final manufacture. But when it came to bringing commodities to market, nature was not always this cooperative. Extractive industries like mines, quarries or farms had no choice but to set up wherever Britain's geology demanded. Factories had to be built wherever their access to surging streams or seams of coal could be guaranteed to power their machines. Products needed transporting to markets and ports for sale, but rivers flowed where gravity dictated with no interest at all in the needs of Britain's industrialising economy. For Britain's capitalists, who were reshaping the environment at home and abroad in the pursuit of profit, this simply wouldn't do. Innovative methods had been found to extract more and more natural resources; now it was time for the natural world to be reshaped to suit their needs too.[31]

Physically carrying goods from one place to another was often expensive, took lots of time, and followed the path of least resistance to whichever port or market was reached most easily. This served the economy well up to a point but, as productivity increased, the road and riverine networks that had long been used to connect Britain became strained. This existing infrastructure also did not go where it was now needed, and new industries often required access to goods that were not easily brought to their door. Places like Manchester could draw on deep wells of textile expertise locally, but without finding a way to efficiently carry thousands of cartloads of coal and cotton to its mills it hardly made sense as a site for steam-powered cloth manufacturing. Ineffective infrastructure was a constraint for where and how new industries could develop. More fundamentally, it constrained the deeper integration of Britain's economy, limiting access to customers, goods, labour and skills for businesses everywhere. In the final decades of the eighteenth century, it was a challenge that Britain's capitalists set out to solve with gusto. If nature would not provide, then they would find a way to remake the world to fit the demands of industrial Britain.

Over the previous century, numerous projects across the country had been set up to 'improve river navigation', by widening or easing access to existing waterways. The Aire and Calder Navigation was completed in 1704 and was credited with connecting the salt works of Cheshire and mills of Manchester, which in time 'contributed to the present flourishing of the port of Liverpool'. Both merchants and landowners were understood to benefit, as each could use 'this artificial navigation' to carry corn, timber, iron, coals and stone 'to a profitable market' whereas, before, the heaviest goods had been so expensive to transport that it was not worth the effort of extracting them. Reshaping and opening existing rivers for improved navigation had already changed the shape and structure of the British lead industry, among others. In north-east England, investment to improve navigation on the River Derwent after 1719 and later the River Trent made it possible to cheaply carry thousands of tons of the metal from mines and workshops in Derbyshire to the coast. The rivers Ure and Ouse likewise carried Yorkshire lead to the same destination at Hull, which came to dominate this market for much of the eighteenth century. The north-eastern port was exporting as much as 8,000 tons each year by the middle of the century, while other rivers carried lead from northern mines to smaller markets like Stockton and Newcastle. Likewise, the River Dee carried lead from mines in north Wales to Chester, a route that more than doubled in capacity after a project to deepen the river's channel was completed. Access to these ports helped miners and manufacturers ship their goods to overseas markets, and between 1706 and 1769, exports had increased from 15,782 to 28,040 tons. The scale of the industry increased and so too did the type of work undertaken, and over the course of the century the proportion of lead that was manufactured before it was sent overseas almost tripled: it was yet another industry where British manufacturers captured further stages of the productivity chain.[32]

More navigable rivers were part of a puzzle that helped connect sites of mining and metallurgical production with consumers at home and abroad. As many commentators recognised, improved rivers, canals, ports or roads made the economic system work more efficiently. However, as combinations of technical knowledge, financial capital and market incentives were brought together to connect different sites of extraction with sites of production and with customers, Britain's capitalists became even more ambitious in planning and executing the construction of entirely new waterways. In 1766, the *History of Inland Navigations* presented an enthusiastic introduction for budding canal investors, in honour of the Duke of Bridgewater's construction of a canal between his coal mines in Worsley and the growing city of Manchester. The entrepreneurial nobleman was given 'hearty thanks for the great good done the Kingdom', and readers were told that planning for further canal construction 'certainly merits the public attention and applause'. The author also lauded the many contributions that this expensive infrastructure made to Britain's economy. Of course, the 'greatest benefits arise to trade and commerce', with canals reducing transportation costs and connecting different markets, but canals were also expected to transform the natural environment by carrying water to 'dry, withered' spots that lacked natural water supplies, helping to raise cattle that 'are fatter, more delicious in taste' and horses 'fitter for labour' by sustaining greener pastures. Likewise, new towns might be founded as canals brought manufacturing and industry to regions 'of little value and bare of inhabitants' by adding 'riches and fertility in every part through which they are extended'. Canal building offered a competitive advantage. After all, the author claimed, 'distant counties already see the mercantile profits' and would be rushing to imitate the Bridgewater Canal's design. Indeed, the Bridgewater Canal was the first of dozens of new waterways that carried more commodities across Britain, contributing to industrial, urban and commercial development.[33]

Britain was not the first place to invest in canals, and promoters were keen to point out the impact they had had elsewhere, even as they hoped to quickly surpass foreign competitors. Inspiration came from as far away as China, 'whose policy in many particulars is well worth attending to', and where British commentators believed 'the greater part of its riches and fertility' stemmed from canals that connected the vast country. The Grand Canal, especially, 'which is three hundred leagues in length, is without comparison; which, at infinite expense, and with amazing industry, is carried on through many provinces'. Similarly, the Canal Royal in Languedoc was described as the 'noblest work of the kind, that ever has been executed' and connected the 'Gulf of Lyons and the Bay of Biscay', running across hundreds of miles of French countryside. However, while it had overcome huge technical challenges, this project was understood to have cost over £600,000 and was seen as a financial failure. Instead, even as they recognised the technical achievements of giant canal projects like these, British observers reflected that the joined-up industrial vision of Britain's canals had more in common with that of their Dutch competitors. The Dutch, 'out of a small tract of marshland, by this means, particularly, have raised a populous and powerful state', and the canals 'receive those waters which otherwise would drown their country'. In addition to staving off environmental disaster, canal waters brought 'goods of every kind' to market and were used to power 'mills, weave tape, split iron, and perform [an] abundance of other profitable labour'. Britain's capitalists hoped their own artificial waterways would similarly improve the land, connect markets and fuel industry and help them stay ahead of the competition. Consequently, canals were often encouraged by the very people who would benefit from the proposed infrastructure.[34]

Building rivers from scratch was not a skill that most capitalists could call their own, and throughout Britain investors leaned on engineering experts to oversee these works that were both hugely expensive and confoundingly complicated. John Smeaton was among a new cadre of engineers who used their expertise to advise on and oversee canal construction. Born in Leeds in 1724, Smeaton studied at the town's grammar school before he started working for his father, an attorney, at the age of sixteen. In 1744, he gave up the law and focused on making mechanical instruments, possibly following guidance from his close friend, the clockmaker Henry Hindley of York. Now living in London, Smeaton employed three craftsmen to help his work while also taking a deep interest in the local scientific scene. Since at least 1752, he had been investigating wind- and waterpower, visiting sites across the country and taking copious notes of the most effective machinery in action. Seven years later, he was awarded the Royal Society's Copley Medal, before he was elected a fellow and published numerous papers on his favourite topics. During this period, he had begun working as a consulting engineer at sites across England, and his designs were employed to improve old mills and construct new ones. He also advised on improvements to the navigation on the River Clyde and the draining of peat bogs near Dumfries, designed bridges, and built a new lighthouse at Eddystone on a small windswept rock off the south English coast. He also had a look at steam engines and quickly produced improvements that dramatically upgraded the efficiency of Newcomen's design.[35]

Having earned both a scientific and entrepreneurial reputation, Smeaton was appointed to design a project for making the upper Calder River navigable. This was a devilishly complicated project given the river's steep gradient and his plans required twenty-six locks, twelve new weirs, miles of new channels dug, floodgates and bridges. He completed them by 1764, and the new navigation added to the growing web of new waterways that were drawing the industrialising towns of Yorkshire, Lancashire and Cheshire together. If the Calder navigation was not hard enough, in the later 1760s, Smeaton was approached to lead an audacious plan to construct a canal that would bisect Scotland. Tasked with identifying the 'practicability and expense of joining the rivers Forth and Clyde by a navigable canal', the project was intended to do nothing less than 'join the east sea and the west'. The 'great utility' provided by such a link was heightened by its avoidance of the 'long and dangerous' sea journey around the north of Scotland that otherwise was the only current option for transporting goods. This compared favourably to canals like the French Canal Royal in Languedoc, which offered an alternative to a seaborne route that was 'open at all times, though long', and had been hugely expensive to build due to its extreme height and length. Consequently, Smeaton concluded, 'the same tolls that will hardly keep the French canal in repair, will make this a very beneficial undertaking to British adventurers'. The business case was clear: a canal across Scotland would benefit the economy, was technically feasible, and would profit its investors.[36]

Smeaton was aware of plans to connect 'the Thames and Severn; the Trent and Severn; the Trent and Weaver; the Calder and Mersey', as well as the Forth and Clyde. However, the technical challenges that the northernmost project faced were considerable. Not only was it likely to be the longest canal yet attempted in Britain, it had to rise and fall the most, requiring more locks for barges to pass through from one side to the other. Two routes had been proposed, but both had to deal with Scotland's rugged landscape. Either the canal could wind its way through the Trossachs and across Loch Lomond or it could intersect with the River Carron further south. The first option had the benefit of requiring a shorter 'artificial part' to the system, but Smeaton quickly dismissed it anyway because it was 'equally embarrassed with difficulties' and the final canal route would take much longer to pass through. To maximise the benefits of the canal over the existing sea routes, transportation from one side of Scotland to the other had to be as quick as possible.[37]

The Carron route also helped the engineer overcome serious practical concerns. Canals constantly lost water and, not having natural sources of their own, needed to be designed in places where they could take water from elsewhere to top up. For the Forth and Clyde Canal, this meant connecting the canal to streams that criss-crossed the region. However, this had 'to be done without injury to the mills' on the rivers Carron and Kelvin that used the same water sources for powering their waterwheels. The solution, Smeaton suggested, was to divert water from the River Enrick and Blain where there were 'no mills of any consequence' to disrupt. Other options included taking advantage of industrial sites where wastewater was available. At Wineford, he noted, a 'coal-pit drain discharges itself, which affords a constant supply of water' for the canal. When Smeaton submitted his report in 1766, he estimated that the total cost of the Forth and Clyde Canal would be £78,970.[38]

This was a huge sum and required investment from a much larger group of entrepreneurs than were involved in most domestic business enterprises. In 1767, Smeaton's survey and estimate were presented to the Merchants House in Glasgow, whose members, 'unanimously of opinion that it will be of the greatest advantage to the trade, commerce, and manufactures of Britain', wrote in support of the Act of Parliament needed to start work on the massive project. Support like this was essential for the project and attests to the value that was placed in the world-altering powers of eighteenth-century engineers. A year later, when Parliament approved the canal, the project raised funds from major noble landowners, including £10,000 from Sir Lawrence Dundas whose lands it would run through, and hundreds of other shareholders from various walks of life. Smeaton was appointed Chief Engineer, earning £500 a year, and Robert McKell his assistant, earning £375. Soon, thousands of labourers were employed to dig the channels and tunnels through which it could flow, earning as little as one shilling per day, while skilled woodworkers, masons and others were employed to undertake complex tasks like lock construction. By the time the canal was completed, warehouses, tile works, timber yards and coal stores had multiplied along its banks. From the iron manufacturing hub at Falkirk in the east to the Port of Glasgow in the west, the canal offered access to markets and manufacturers that, linked together, underpinned ongoing economic development across northern Britain.[39]

Smeaton was not alone in applying technical expertise and engineering knowledge to various projects, and many of the surveyors and overseers of canals across the country acted as trusted advisors for investors and landowners who wanted to profit from their construction. James Brindley, for instance, trained as a millwright from the age of seventeen, which included working on silk mills and paper mills. He continued to work with machinery until 1742, when, now twenty-six, he settled in Staffordshire. By the 1750s, Brindley owned two workshops, one leased from members of the Wedgwood family, and began to work with Newcomen steam engines as well as traditional waterwheels. His work with a local colliery, where he installed a complex drainage system, drew the attention of proponents of a canal to link Liverpool and the Mersey with the potteries and the Trent. While that work was under way, Brindley was hired by the Duke of Bridgewater to work on his canal, including the addition of an aqueduct across the Irwell River that would carry the canal on to Manchester. In the following two decades, Brindley would use this self-taught insight and experience to advise and oversee many of the canals that reshaped the British landscape. James Watt, better known for his steam engine design, also lent his engineering expertise to the canal craze when he surveyed land between Inverness and Fort William for a canal. Unlike some other engineers, though, he warned that his estimated cost of the scheme would 'be a bar to its execution'. This proved to be the case, and it would be the nineteenth century when the Caledonian Canal was finally built along this route.[40]

Where they were built, the impact of new transport links could be dramatic for growing industries. In the Midlands, turnpiked roads connecting Birmingham and Stafford were early beneficiaries of enthusiastic investment in infrastructure among the region's capitalists. Soon, these were surpassed by canals, and the Birmingham Canal linking the town's forges with vital supplies from Black Country collieries was opened in 1762 and expanded in the 1790s. Further canal building from 1772 onwards carried finished goods from the Midlands manufactories to major ports, with links to the Trent and Mersey Canal and the River Severn improving access to Liverpool and Bristol: the gateways to Britain's colonial economy. Among the participants in these works was the ironmaster William Reynolds, who was employed to survey and oversee the construction of the Ketley Canal that ran from Oakengates to the Ketley works in Shropshire and transported coal and iron ore for the region's furnaces. A short, privately funded canal, the one-and-a-half-mile-long route employed '300 men at work upon it' and was quickly completed by the end of 1788. However, there were some technical challenges that required novel solutions, and an inclined plane to move barges on rails between the canal's different levels was built using cast iron with great effect. Indeed, in doing so, the canal demonstrated yet another useful application for local manufacturers' products even as it eased the supply of vital resources to their mills. Another ironmaster with links to Coalbrookdale, Richard Reynolds, was similarly involved in the Severn Navigation in 1789. In the West Midlands alone, new canals

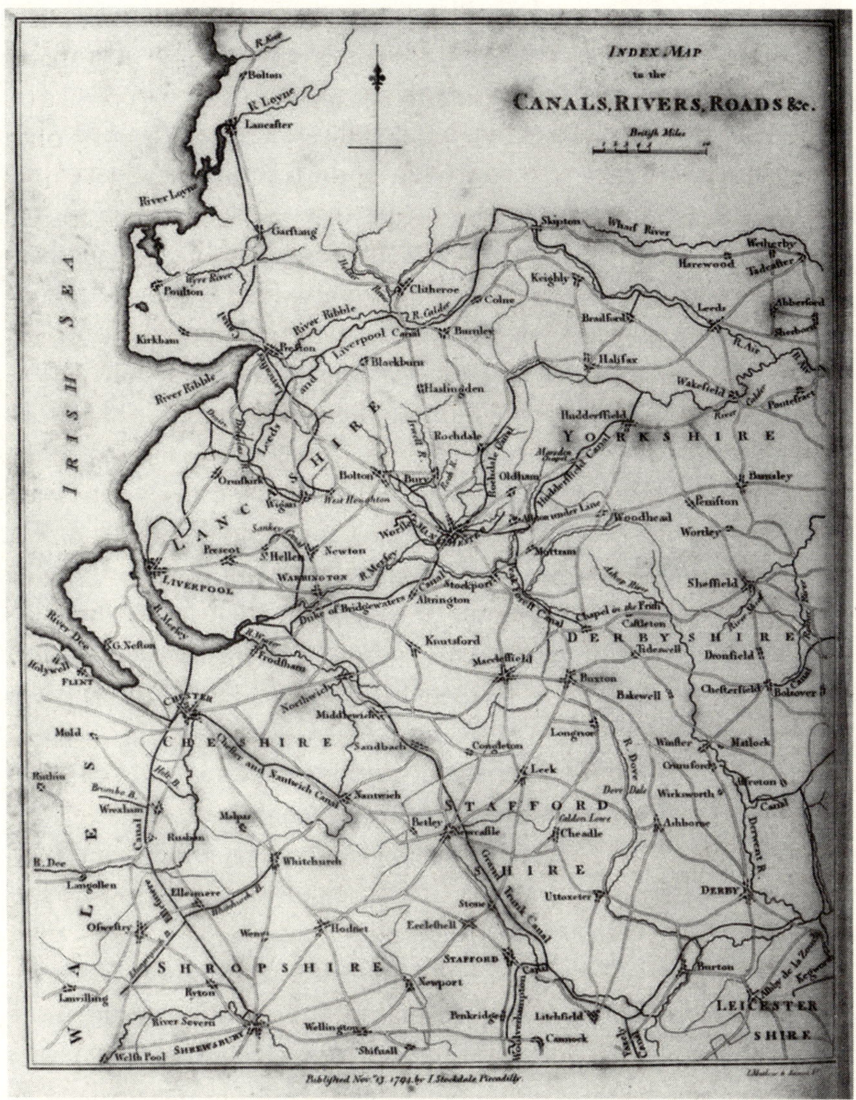


7. *As this map of north-west England from 1794 shows, new roads and canals together created a dense web of transportation options that tied together the region's growing industrial towns.*

were central to a new industrial landscape that had begun to form. By the end of the century, around 1,500 collieries and ironworks would be built alongside the region's rapidly expanding canal network.[41]

Skilled overseers, sometimes but not always formally trained engineers, were needed to overcome many of the technical challenges that canal construction demanded. Cutting through the land and using locks to lift water needed careful calculations (and huge amounts of labour and capital) to be achieved. Canals also consumed vast quantities of water which, in some parts of the country, quickly diminished supplies that were needed for Britain's water-powered manufacturing. When the Scottish engineer John Rennie was employed in the 1790s by the Rochdale Canal committee (which was set up to oversee the establishment of a company that would build the canal) to measure the impact of mill usage on the water available from the Sladen Brook, he described that 'when the mills were set to work they lowered the head 2 inches', due to the volume of water taken that served the mill's wheel. Taking water for a canal instead could easily leave a mill short of water to the chagrin of its owners. Elsewhere, hot weather could cause the levels of canals to drop, leaving them impassable. In Scotland, Smeaton had dismissed this risk, suggesting that water could be taken from rivers nearby or from water pumped from mines. Rennie, likewise, intended to use a torrent of otherwise useless mine water to fill canal reservoirs. With powerful steam engines now able to extract more and more water from Britain's ever deepening mines, canals near the largest collieries could be kept in abundant supply. However, scarcity was harder to resolve in places where water remained the most important source of power for industry, which were often places where coal was also scarce and pumping from mines was unviable.[42]

The experience of the Rochdale Canal committee, seeking to establish a navigation through the Calder Valley that would connect the West Riding of Yorkshire with Manchester and Liverpool, was dramatically shaped by demands regarding water supply. All canal building in the eighteenth century required an Act of Parliament, passed by a majority in the House of Commons, and the Rochdale Canal was no different. In 1791, proprietors of the canal appointed a committee to oversee the planning and regulatory process, and

£350,000 was committed by investors. However, their plans were immediately challenged by local mill owners who argued that the proposed canal would consume the region's limited water supply, which they depended on for power. Consequently, applications for regulatory approval failed in 1792 and in 1793, largely because of local pressure groups demanding revisions to the canal's design to minimise impact on water scarcity. Success would come in 1794, when an Act of Parliament finally passed that included environmental protections designed to ensure water supply.[43]

Numerous complaints, negotiations and resolutions were detailed in the canal committee's records. Not all nearby mill owners and landowners were interested in the implications of the canal on water scarcity, and even some who were quickly accepted compensation for any damages. However, there was a wealthy and politically significant constituency of mill owners whose business interests depended on water, and it was their interests that most shaped the regulatory process. Water scarcity was their common and recurring concern. Edward Gregg Hopwood argued that 'taking the brook' into the canal 'would necessarily destroy his corn mill' and refused any offer of compensation. Likewise, Mr Sutcliff of Stansfield Mill assessed 'that he should probably sustain some damage by the water being taken from his mill to supply the intended canal', while Mr Rawdon and Mr Patchett, owners of Lob Mill, Callis Mill and Bank Foot Mill, were concerned the canal would drain water from a reservoir they had already built to ensure their own supply. In a similar vein, the trustees of the Free Grammar School at Manchester maintained that the 'water which now flows down the [River] Irk is insufficient for the regular supply of the mills thereon and the School Mills being the lowest upon the River are peculiarly straightened for want of water'. The threat of scarcity here was acute because 'in common seasons they have not a regular supply and in dry seasons are unable to work for hours in a day', meaning even 'a small diminution of water may render them insufficient'. As these examples suggest, for mill owners, the canal's impact on water supply represented an existential crisis for their business.[44]

Protests from these local businesses about the canal's impact were the primary cause for its failure to secure Acts of Parliament in 1792 and 1793. Consequently, the canal company made considerable efforts to engage with this community and to persuade it that solutions would be found to ensure water supply. The main way in which the canal company set out to obtain support was by inserting clauses into future submissions to Parliament that guaranteed how water supply would be monitored and managed. Following pressure from, and regular engagement with, stakeholders across the Calder Valley, the canal was repeatedly redesigned over a four-year period in advance of its securing regulatory approval. The canal company outlined its proposed solutions for the water scarcity challenge in regular communications with Parliament, local and national press, and directly to Members of Parliament. It also obtained letters and petitions of support from across England, including 'from the owners and holders of mills in that valley [the Calder] in the county of Lancaster' that had been persuaded to support the proposal, distributing them widely.[45]

The expectation that the canal company should find solutions to these challenges led to an array of clauses inserted into the Act of Parliament that enabled the canal's construction. This was an important part of the planning process, and the Rochdale Canal Company 'resolved that a clause similar to one contained in the Act of Parliament for the Leeds and Liverpool Canal respecting the preservation of the water' would be inserted. To prove it could meet these obligations, the company turned to experienced canal engineers William Crosley and John Longbotham, who were responsible for designing and measuring the intended canal, completing assessments of its impact on water supply, and developing novel solutions to water scarcity. Their plans were highly detailed, including 'each brook, stream and feeder upon the line'. Furthermore, by measuring existing flows in the system, the canal company could demonstrate that new reservoirs would take water from existing supply only 'in times of flood, and when the water of that river runs to waste three inches in perpendicular depth at the least'. Where water was interrupted, this too was measured. For example, on the River Irk, engineers identified 'that a quantity of water equal to a gauge of four inches long by two inches and three-eighths deep' would be diverted, 'equal to one hundred and seventy eight thousand two hundred cubic feet of the down fall water or showers in each year' – an undersupply that required a reservoir to be built by the canal company to supply the same amount of water to the mills. As well as mapping and measuring existing systems, the engineers took care 'to take gauge' of specific streams and to compare them with others across river systems.[46]

Whereas measurement and mapping made it possible for the canal company to understand the impact of its proposed construction, the clauses intended to protect water supply required novel techniques and the application of unexpected technologies to be effective. The regulatory expectation that the canal proprietors resolve the issue of water use meant that the company's committee were keen to use the most effective techniques for either supplying water or using it more efficiently. For instance, it was proposed that the canal might consider 'raising the water from collieries' using coal-powered pumps, and the canal's engineers were ordered 'to attend Mr Green's trial of raising vessels in canals without locks' – a technique that would save water. Predominantly, though, the company relied on the innovative application of existing techniques to ensure water supply. Gauges, too, were expected to be built to stringent criteria to be 'made of cast iron an inch and one quarter of an inch in thickness and fixed in good and substantial stonework'. Throughout the process, the canal company's design sought to reassure mill owners that their plans would not create water scarcity, noting that 'the surplus water *only* passing over such side-weirs in times of excess, and which would otherwise turn to waste, [would] be applied to the use of their said intended canal'. The company's engineers also proposed to 'make large reservoirs, with proper drains thereto' designed 'to collect and retain the rainwater only', as well as reservoirs near rivers 'to take the overplus water only, in time of floods'. Although there was no national body to oversee these works, regulation did set out how these features would be built by engineers appointed by the canal company and by the mill owners. Following the passing of the Act, the co-appointed engineers oversaw the construction of weirs, gauges and reservoirs across the Calder Valley, intended to ensure that mill and canal alike were able to operate in an environment of growing water scarcity.

These proposals did not require new technology, but they did require it to be applied in novel and unexpected ways, with mastery of nature central to their purposes.[47]

The Rochdale Canal was one of dozens of projects that saw engineers, investors and other stakeholders take advantage of improving scientific and engineering knowledge to reshape nature. Their purpose was to connect different parts of Britain's developing industrial sectors more efficiently together, especially those that depended on the movement of heavy goods like coal that could be so much more easily carried by water than overland. In places where canals connected with each other and existing waterways, like the north-west of England, the impact could be dramatic, and Manchester, Liverpool and Leeds all benefited from the new connections that were built between them in the second half of the eighteenth century. In Liverpool alone, the Sankey and Leeds and Liverpool canals had made it possible for the city to connect with coalfields across the region that played an important role in the port's explosive growth. Industries that worked with copper, iron, salt, sugar, pottery and grain all benefited from the easier movement of coal, even as they benefited from capital and commodities coming into the port from its transatlantic trading network. A similar trajectory could be seen for other growing industries in the region. Canals, much like innovations in shipbuilding, the development of roads, or other improvements that made it easier, cheaper and quicker to move goods from one place to the next, were not the most dramatic technologies, but they all offered incremental benefits that reduced the costs of transactions across Britain's economy. The belief that human ingenuity could reshape nature was a driving force behind plans for silk cultivation in Georgia, growing sugar in Bengal or overcoming the scarcity of water in the Calder Valley. Across Britain and its empire, finding ways to maximise the exploitation of land by changing what it could do was a key feature of the nation's rise to wealth and power.[48]

CHAPTER 8

# FIRE AND IRON

## Power, Metal and Engineering

In the eighteenth century, demand for iron grew dramatically as its strength, durability and malleability made it the basic material for the manufacture of everything from armaments to agricultural tools and domestic hardware. It was a key feature of Britain's emerging industrial economy, and finding new and better ways of making iron, steel and other metals, and transforming these into sought-after products, was a challenge that enterprising capitalists enthusiastically set out to meet.

Producing decent-quality and usable metal was no easy task and needed intensive labour, burning-hot flames and a sophisticated knowledge of metallurgical processes. The infrastructure of traditional smelting had been relatively simple and was cheap to build, equip and operate. Smelters used various combinations of hearths, trenches, pots, ovens and furnaces depending on the type of ore. For softer metals like lead, smelting could sometimes occur in open-air hearths where the wind fanned the fires, but for harder metals like iron, tiny forges were equipped with hand- or foot-driven bellows. When a mine was exhausted, smelting facilities could be abandoned with little regret and any movable items transported to another, more promising location. Relying on charcoal, they were often situated near woods that were cut down and consumed before a smith moved on. Simple works still made complex, sophisticated products but, as firms, they were artisanal in scale and structure. By the end of the eighteenth century, many sites like these were replaced by vast industrial undertakings where new forges burned hot enough to produce cascades of liquid metal that could be poured into casts. These depended on coke (a type of fuel made by baking coal without air), which was no less novel than the production of massive quantities of metal, and the expansion of Britain's heavy industry depended on the simultaneous development of both mining and metallurgy.

A vital breakthrough had been the rediscovery and diffusion of the charcoal-fuelled blast furnace from France and Italy in the fifteenth century. Much more complex than traditional forges, blast furnaces required more investment in land, buildings and machinery, and a degree of permanence that meant ongoing expenditure on larger bellows, hammers and other devices. They were an essential step in the production of abundant and higher-quality iron. Larger fires kept the iron ore in contact with carbon for longer periods at higher temperatures, allowing carbon to be absorbed into the reduced iron and forming that key industrial alloy: cast iron. Molten metal was funnelled into moulds where it solidified into pieces called 'sows': as larger amounts were cast at once, branching moulds were added, called 'pigs'. The new process was more efficient and was particularly suited for the production of simple products including cannon and shot. To be used for making more complicated 'wrought' products, like gears, machine parts or locks, the pig iron was reheated under oxidising conditions to produce bar iron. Despite the extra stage of processing, producing bar iron was essential for making the wrought-iron products that made up the vast majority of iron goods sold before the eighteenth century. Further innovation quickly followed for manipulating bar iron. Mills for flattening metal or drawing it into wire were established where surging streams were harnessed or otherwise artificially created with dams to turn waterwheels or to drive larger and more powerful overshot wheels that turned and turned and hammered and hammered.

Already by the sixteenth century, ironworks had expanded in scale across Europe to sustain more complex industrial economies, and it was not long before enterprising capitalists introduced the same technological phenomena to Britain. Sir Ambrose Crowley's ironworks in

County Durham, established by the start of the eighteenth century, was one of the earliest large-scale industrial sites in the country: two slitting mills (which used waterpower to cut metal bars into rods) employed 500 workers, and a factory producing wrought-iron goods set another 300 to work. These works were atypical in their size, but other large-scale metallurgical enterprises quickly became more common. The dramatic expansion of extractive and metallurgical industries across Britain contributed to the diffusion of modern technologies, even as inventive manufacturers pushed them further with incremental improvements in many areas of the production process. By the 1730s, the Mine Adventurers – which had been relaunched following Sir Humphry Mackworth's calamitous efforts to use it as a massive public joint-stock fund – had set up numerous facilities across the country. In Yorkshire, one of its smelting mills had installed a waterwheel standing three metres tall to improve the quality of its product. Using water to consistently power four bellows, the facility maintained the temperature in each of the two iron hearths much more effectively, and smelted lead ran into two large 'sumpter pots' from which the metal could be extracted. Complaints that massive new forges and workshops had transformed quiet villages into noisy bedlams spoke to their scale even as these complaints were ignored, and they grew even further. Across Britain, the stench of smoke from new ironworks troubled travellers and locals alike, their waste products polluted streams and annihilated fishing stock, and the blows of massive power-driven hammers echoed through the hills. It was on these foundations that the dramatic expansion of Britain's metallurgical industry was built. By the final decades of the eighteenth century, metal goods ranging from muskets and cannons to shackles and hoes, cogs and machine parts, or decorative household goods were all produced by Britain's metal workers at volumes that had never been possible before.[1]

## BRITISH IRON

Some of the most transformative advances in making metal took place in the West Midlands, where the rich Black Country coal seam was conveniently located near large iron ore deposits. The towns of Birmingham and Wolverhampton, especially, would become hubs of metallurgical activity producing goods for consumers across Britain and the world. Ironmongers had been a presence in the region for a long time and had become renowned as armourers during the civil war. However, advances in business organisation and the scale and sophistication of metallurgical sites radically transformed the region in the following century. Whereas Birmingham had been a town of a few thousand people in 1700, a hundred years later it would be lauded as a workshop that served the whole world, with more than ten times as many people living and working under a canopy of smoke from its furnaces and factories. Hundreds of workshops, tens of thousands of workers and technical innovation were needed to achieve these advances, and small independent ironmongers that undertook work for larger firms provided for a vibrant local economy, even as much larger factories also became more common. This combination of many small and large firms together, and the competition it engendered, contributed to the region's collective innovation much like it would in south-west England's woollen industry or in Staffordshire's potteries.

A principal difficulty for ironworkers at the turn of the eighteenth century was obtaining iron itself, much of which was imported to Britain from abroad. An ambitious attempt by William Wood to meet this challenge head on attested to the scope and aspiration of the growing industry. Like earlier proponents of major extractive and metallurgical projects, Wood drew attention to the natural bounty that Britain's geology offered: 'the dominions of Great Britain abound in as great [a] variety of minerals, perhaps, as any country whatever'. Wood argued that iron manufacturing was the second largest industry in Britain, surpassed only by woollen textile production, but that the nation still lost some £200,000 every year by importing 20,000 tons of pig iron from Sweden – approximately two-thirds of the total demand. As well as being costly, this had the 'ill consequence of having the iron trade and manufacture in some measure in the power of our neighbours', and it might 'be kept from us, either by design or accident', with little recourse for relief. Inspiration was close to home, however, and he highlighted that in Cornwall 'copper mines that have been discovered' only thirty years before, even though they were still 'capable of improvement', had already had a transformative impact on Britain's economy. 'Whereas formerly we had all our copper and brass from Sweden and Germany ... now we are, in a great measure, supplied from our own mines.' Discovery, improvement and connecting different parts of the manufacturing process were key for success. Wood believed that the same could and should be achieved for iron.[2]

The scheme that Wood developed to overcome this challenge was hugely ambitious and rested on little in the way of personal experience. Born in 1671, Wood was the son of a silk weaver and would have understood how imported raw silk could be transformed in the hands of a skilled artisan and resold as much more valuable finished products. However, in 1690 he left the textile world behind when he married Margaret Molineux and entered a partnership with her ironmonger father Richard, joining a family of well-established metallurgists and merchants based in Wolverhampton. Building on these links, in 1714, he established a partnership with three fellow ironmongers, Thomas Harvey, Thomas Maynard and the aptly named Robert Spark, and they were initially joined by John Hayes and William Marsland who provided links to rural capital and mercantile networks, respectively. The group's first mill, in Shropshire, made brass and iron, and the business quickly expanded. First, they bought the nearby Sutton Forge and the Bursham Forge in north Wales, and then a site in Rushall in the West Midlands, where they intended to use coke as fuel rather than charcoal. If a business opportunity involved metal, the partners wanted the chance to profit from it, and they covered all sorts of work undertaken in the 'business of running of pig metal, making of iron, and converting of steel; drawing of iron wire, and in all sorts of manufacturing of iron, and making of nails, and other iron goods; and also in making of copper, brass, iron, tin and lead, and extracting silver from lead, and in using, selling, converting, disposing and manufacturing the said metals'. They had no plan to specialise and simply wanted to set up larger furnaces and workshops. To this end, the men 'raised a joint stock' and together 'purchased diverse freehold and leasehold houses, mills, lands, forges

[and] furnaces'. When one-tenth of the company's shares were sold to Dr Charles Driver in 1720, the company committed to paying £5 dividends every year for every £50 invested: a reasonable rate of return.[3]

To take their plan further, and to deliver what Wood described as 'that vast advantage' which 'may accrue to this nation, by encouraging improvements in mineral affairs', the overconfident capitalists set out to obtain a huge public investment from 'a body of persons with large sums of money, to be employed and managed by persons, well skilled in all sorts of minerals and metals, and their several manufacturers'. By now, around 1720, the existing partnership had obtained 'a freehold estate, rich in iron-mines and pit-coal, with which their furnaces are supplied', located near 'some of the best iron works in the kingdom, conveniently situated near the navigable River Severn'. The location was ideal, bringing together the heavy loads of iron ore and coal together cheaply and efficiently, while the river could power waterwheels for the site's mills as well as serve as an effective conduit for carrying goods to market. This was a mine-to-market industrial vision. Forges were burning to refine ore, a slitting mill was ready to 'roll, slit and prepare' this iron for manufacture, and 'houses, shops, and all other conveniences for lock-smiths, nailers [nail makers], hinge-makers' were prepared to transform the metal into useful wrought iron goods. The partnership also had you covered if cast iron was more your thing, and the site housed 'furnaces for making pig iron, pots, rails and bannisters, backs and hearths for chimneys' that used charcoal and pit coal 'to great advantage'. Copper and lead mines were also sending ore to the site, which boasted 'also the best conveniences for making brass' of all sorts. Once finished, goods could be quickly ferried down the river to Bristol for sale, carried to London or sent to 'the inland and northern parts of the nation ... better and cheaper (and yet with greater profit to the company) than can be done by others'. A joint-stock corporation led by people like Wood and his ironmongering partners was the only option, they argued, to exploit the rich array of mineral resources available across the country by bringing all of the nation's metal-working enterprises under the command of a single, well-financed entity.[4]

Unfortunately for Wood, there was limited interest in a national project of this sort, and the South Sea Bubble ended any hope of this sort of attempt. However, Wood's vision of a connected metal industry was well founded in some respects. The efficiencies he identified from smelting more ore, connecting metallurgical workshops with important ports, and combining different processes were all features of the industry in the West Midlands over the coming decades. Indeed, Wood's various forges were relatively successful in their own right – even if they did not revolutionise the industry. In the 1720s, he added another forge to his business portfolio, this time in London. He also began minting copper coins for Ireland, although these turned out to be loathed on the island and unprofitable for Wood. A few years later, his son Francis was granted a patent for a method of using coal to make iron, leading to the erection of a giant site near Whitehaven, but the technique did not produce metal of the necessary quality. Two other sons, Charles and John, followed more successfully in their father's footsteps and were involved in the discovery of platinum, the conversion of pig iron to bar iron, and the construction of the Cyfarthfa iron foundry in Glamorgan.[5]

Wood's plans for boosting Britain's iron production did not have the impact he had hoped. Yet, the first half of the eighteenth century did see significant development in parts of Britain's iron-smelting and iron-working industries, even though the dominant technique of using charcoal to fuel furnaces was the same that it always had been. Increased production came with the further exploitation of iron ore resources in Britain and taking advantage of land seized in North America that was rich with ore. Furnaces in places including south Wales and Shropshire each grew as closely linked landowners, ironmongers and merchants invested in expanding output and meeting the needs of their respective customers. In south Wales, buoyed by the networks that supported the simultaneous expansion of copper smelting and coal mining that were transforming Swansea into a hub for copper production, there was a rapid expansion in iron output as furnaces took advantage of easy access to nearby mines. Fewer than ten Welsh furnaces were responsible for around 10 per cent of the pig iron produced in Britain, which was often refined into bar iron nearby for shipping to the coast, where it was carried onward to manufacturers in Bristol and the Midlands. Conversely, efforts to increase production at ironworks in Yorkshire focused less on smelting and more on the manufacturing of iron goods. Capitalists like local ironworker John Cockshutt and merchant Joseph Broadbent established partnerships to combine their capital that was needed to improve the facilities used to make iron wares. Broadbent and Cockshutt's enterprise included a furnace, forge and two mills, and depended on pig iron sourced not from Britain but furnaces in Virginia and Maryland, which was shipped via London to Scarborough and carried overland to their forges.[6]

As Cockshutt's and Broadbent's experience suggests, imports of colonial iron were proving a useful alternative to Swedish iron by the early decades of the eighteenth century. The first imports reached Britain in 1717, when two tons of bar iron were shipped from Nevis and St Kitts, and similarly small amounts were obtained from the Caribbean over the following decades. However, in North America, a surge in productive capacity made a much bigger impact. Beginning with just over 15 tons of pig iron arriving from Virginia and Maryland in 1723, this colony exported over 200 tons the following year and by 1730 was exporting a considerable 1,526 tons. These exports were boosted by a growing pig iron industry in nearby Pennsylvania that contributed a further hundred tons or more each year. By the 1740s, American metallurgical industries, driven particularly by Virginia and Maryland, were producing around 2,000 tons most years for export to Britain, peaking at 3,459 tons in 1741. Further production would have supplied the demand for iron in these colonies in addition to the volumes sent to Britain.[7]

Even as America's forges began to take off, they were caught in the web of protectionism that defined much of Britain's economic policy as manufacturers and politicians alike sought to secure the highest end of the production chain. As the Yorkshire ironmonger John Watts explained to his neighbour and forge owner William Spencer in 1736, 'all the ironmasters in these parts have met and consulted' about American iron and were supporting plans to let pig iron be imported duty-free. However, if bar iron received the same treatment, 'it will ruin all the ironworks' in the country as well as leaving 'the spring woods and other woods of little value' with the wood no longer needed for charcoal. Manufacturer and landowner alike would miss out if the American market was not curtailed and shaped to meet the needs of manufacturers in Britain. The imperial economic system was structured to try and ensure that ores and other commodities were returned to Britain to manufacturing.[8]

While increases in traditional iron extraction and smelting were ongoing, innovative attempts to radically transform how iron was produced in Britain were taking place at a soon-to-be famous industrial site situated in a dale, next to a brook, and not far from plentiful deposits of coal: Coalbrookdale. Here, the aim was not just to use coal for later stages of iron making, but to use it (or more precisely the coke that could be made from it) to make pig iron too. With plentiful supplies of coal, if a way could be found to productively use this abundant resource to make high-quality metal that could be used in Britain's forges and factories, then the sky was the limit. Here, Abraham Darby, and then his son and grandson, both Abrahams, set about developing and improving facilities needed for smelting iron with coke. This was not a new discovery, but the Darby firm was the first to find ways to make it commercially viable. Coal was much cheaper than wood, which meant using coke rather than charcoal would immediately save money. However, this only mattered if the iron it produced was of equal quality, and unfortunately, when coke was used to make pig iron, it introduced too many impurities for it to be suitable for many uses. Overcoming this challenge would lead the cost of iron production to plummet.[9]

Darby had probably learned about coke smelting from another ironmonger, Shadrach Fox, who supplied cast iron shot for the British government in the 1690s and owned the Coalbrookdale furnace that Darby would go on to lease. Fox was part of a wider network of metallurgists with firms in London, the Midlands, Newcastle and south Wales who had been experimenting with similar techniques for smelting other metals, especially lead and copper. Skilled workers and investors crossed between multiple ventures across the country, facilitating the diffusion of new practices. By the time Darby took over

Coalbrookdale in 1708, work to improve cast iron was already being undertaken, and many of the workers involved in this (like the founder John Tyler) stayed on. Darby had also already begun experimenting with casting methods, which were used to make brass objects that could be cast with metal directly from the furnace (unlike metal needed to make wrought-iron goods which required an extra stage of refining). In 1702, he was part of a group that established the Baptist Mills Brass Works near Bristol and, the following year, he tried to cast iron pots using the same brass-casting methods. He failed, so in 1704, he travelled to the Netherlands to study their sand-casting techniques for bronze and bring some workers back to try them out on iron. This, too, was unsuccessful and so he eventually turned to a Welsh apprentice, John Thomas, who was confident he could overcome the challenge. He paid the young metallurgist until 1707, when he finally succeeded in making the process work.[10]

The following year, Darby received a patent for the new cast iron-making process. The goods he produced were not particularly exciting, but the productivity gains were immense: an iron pot that had previously required six kilograms of iron now only needed three. The successful commercialisation of a reverberatory furnace, a design that separated fuel from ore during smelting, helped improve the quality of the iron further. Already, Darby's innovative approach to ironwork had borrowed from practices learned from a wider network that incorporated Bristol's bronze works and Dutch sand casting, and it had taken more borrowing and adaptation before he was able to successfully use coke to smelt iron. Even his preparation of coke required techniques that he had learned elsewhere, in this case during his apprenticeship in a malt mill in Birmingham, where coke was burned to warm sprouting barley. In addition to drawing on knowledge from his wider network, Darby depended on it for financial capital, and the business was divided into numerous shares to fund his research and the construction of the ironworks. By the time Darby finally started producing iron with coke, networked capital had already played a major role in the development of his business.[11]

The coke furnace could achieve a higher internal temperature than a charcoal furnace, and produced iron that was more fluid and allowed for lighter, thinner-walled castings. As employees came and went, this knowledge was diffused across Britain. One of the firm's managers, Thomas Baylies, left to build a coke furnace in Lancashire, in the 1720s a partnership between investors from Stourbridge and Newcastle probably built another near Whitehaven, and another was built near Neath in Wales. Other imitators tried to employ Darby's process for making cast iron, with firms set up in Bristol and Stourbridge, with some success. However, there were limitations to the technique, which meant it was not immediately picked up by iron manufacturers elsewhere. The coke furnace could not produce as much iron as a charcoal furnace, and the process still added impurities that made the resulting pig iron more expensive to refine into wrought iron, although it was now a viable source of metal for making cast iron products. As Darby and his successors learned to control the smelting process and further reduce impurities, these costs declined, but the majority of iron Coalbrookdale's furnaces produced ended up being used to produce cast iron products on site. For the moment, coke-smelted iron was an innovation that transformed mainly only how the Coalbrookdale firm produced metal.[12]

Essentially, this was because when Abraham Darby died in 1717, the cost of coke pig iron was still higher than charcoal pig iron, and it was never going to find a wider market unless it beat that price. The poorer quality of the pig iron produced, likewise, put off some ironmongers. Efforts to produce bar iron from the pig iron produced with coke were successful in the 1730s, but the cost was prohibitive, and the company lost money. In the next three decades, costs were cut and quality raised by incremental improvements to existing practice, typically learned through doing. There were three major improvements. First, the reliance on inconsistent waterpower for the blast furnace was overcome with a horse gig in the 1730s and then a Newcomen steam engine in 1742. The impact was dramatic. Now the furnaces could be operated continually at top speed, and output rose from 4.5 to 7.5 tons per week. Unexpectedly, the amount of ore needed fell too, as the smelting process became more efficient. The cost of other materials dropped in kind and coke smelting could now produce pig iron at the same price as charcoal. Coincidentally, it was also during this period that the firm started casting iron parts to be used in steam engines. Second, new blast furnaces were brought online in 1755 that were wider and held more ore. These were designed specifically to employ wooden bellows powered by a water-wheel that was kept running continuously with water pumped by steam engine. Production doubled again, to 15.4 tons per week. Coke iron was now notably cheaper than charcoal iron, and after this date not a single new charcoal furnace was built in Britain. Third, after a series of experiments using different mixes of iron ore in the 1730s and 1740s (ore from different mines had different phosphorous content), a mixture was finally found that made coke iron ideally suited for refining into bar iron. Together, these improvements meant that, by 1755, Britain had a process for making iron with the country's abundant supplies of coal that could leave its rivals in the dust.[13]

With demand for iron continuing to grow, the success of the Coalbrookdale coke-smelting process in 1755 quickly led to imitators elsewhere, and further incremental improvements to the process. Coke-fired furnaces were built at Lightmoor and Ketley in Shropshire, to supply the forges of Edward Knight & Company in the Stour Valley. Ironworks at Carron in Scotland were built by a partnership including the merchant Samuel Garbett and the chemist Dr John Roebuck from Birmingham, who had already worked together in a laboratory, and the iron trader Willam Cadell from Scotland, who had made his money importing Swedish and Russian iron. Wolverhampton's iron forges were increasingly supplied by coke-smelted iron produced by furnaces at Bilston, three miles to the east of the town. This site was developed by John Wilkinson, who was also partner in firms that erected a furnace at Willey in Shropshire and at Bersham in north Wales. Links like this were common between different firms: the Madeley Wood furnaces along the River Severn shared partners with Mathrafal Forge in Montgomeryshire, while the Dowlais furnace at Merthyr Tydfil had partners in common with Pentyrch and Cardiff forges. Many of the partners involved were ironworkers but others were landowners, merchants and manufacturers with other business interests.[14]

Beyond the use of coke for smelting, these furnaces benefited from further technological advances that boosted their productivity and the quality of their iron. John Wilkinson's father, Isaac, rose to prominence in the 1750s following his move to the Bersham ironworks and his 1757 patent for a new method of blowing that involved using crank-operated water-sealed chests to compress the air and blow it into the furnace. These water bellows became a central feature of the new Dowlais furnace that was completed in 1759, and meant it could operate without needing a waterwheel to power bellows. His son John, in contravention of his father's patent, employed the same design at the works in Bersham and Willey, but complained they were ineffective. He devised his own improved system in 1766, now using pistons to compress the air, which was soon employed at the Carron ironworks. Recommendations from Samuel Walker, who ran an ironworks in Rotherham using the new method, encouraged the managers at Cyfarthfa furnace in Merthyr Tydfil to do the same. Before long, whether by imitating competitors or taking advice diffused through social networks, the use of cylinders became the norm. Concurrent improvements in steam-engine technology boosted the effectiveness of the innovation further still, and more efficiencies followed.[15]

Britain's iron industry depended on numerous instances of incremental improvements like these and their rapid diffusion across different enterprises. In 1763, for instance, John Cockshull junior sent a copy of his father's design for metal bellows to the secretary of the Society of Arts, Dr William Lewis, with an attached letter explaining their efficacy. His father's invention had 'some advantages over the common leather ones, one great one is that they may be made strong enough to blow with twice the force that would burst any leather'. While they cost 'rather more money at their first erection than common leather bellows', Cockshull claimed, by lasting much longer and requiring less repair than their leather competitors, 'on the whole they are much cheaper'. He had even come up with an improvement on his father's design, a second smaller cistern attached to the main device to keep the water lukewarm and prevent freezing. Information like this, about useful innovative practices, spread quickly across the networks that surrounded Britain's industrialising economy. Managers of new ventures were well aware of the developments that had contributed to the technological advances on which their industry depended. A contemporary description of a new lead-smelting mill left no doubt about the importance of incremental gains that had benefited the industry over the previous decades. Employing the so-called 'perpetual oven' design, the facility was modelled on a similar mill in Norwich and incorporated the benefits of 'Wilkinson's water bellows', 'Cockshull water bellows', 'Ziegler's water wheel' and 'Wilkinson's improvement in water blowing machine' to regulate the heat of the furnace. The final improvement came from 'Watt's steam engine'.[16]

At Coalbrookdale, keeping up with these technological improvements was an important part of the firm's ongoing progress. After the death of Abraham Darby II, management of the site passed to his son-in-law Richard Reynolds, and he oversaw the expansion of the business and the implementation of numerous technical advances. This continued into the following decade, and by the later 1770s, his son, William Reynolds, who was an avid participant in scientific exchange, was working with James Watt to set up a steam engine at the site. Despite some initial problems finding suitable timber for the machine – oak was in short supply and they had to use imported fir from North America instead – it was quickly up and running. Once in place, Reynolds invited his Liverpool-based cousin William Rathbone to travel south to visit 'this improved engine which is well worth looking at'. It was certainly a novel addition to the site's machinery, and Reynolds's installation of a steam engine was among the earliest at any of Britain's furnaces, alongside Isaac Wilkinson's use of the same at Willey and Bradley. Technological advances like this were advertised and shared through the scientific and business networks that criss-crossed different sectors in Britain's deeply interconnected economy. Like many other advances in iron production, it did not take long for others to follow suit.[17]

By the final decades of the eighteenth century Britain was on its way to becoming a pre-eminent producer of iron wares, but there was still a long way to go before the quantity and quality of Britain's iron would dominate international markets. In the mid-1780s, the Lord Chancellor Edward Thurlow sought advice from leading ironmasters about how to bring 'a monopoly to this country' in iron production, and what support the state could offer to help make this a reality. One of the respondents, William Gibbons, was a Bristol merchant whose family owned collieries in Sedgley and ironworks in the Stour Valley, which sustained a profitable business exporting finished metal wares. Gibbons was not confident that a monopoly could be achieved in the current climate. In Germany, 'a lower price of iron and labour' had 'nearly driven us out of several European markets', including Portugal and Spain 'which we were used to supply'. Relief on export duties might help British manufacturers be more competitive, but would be insufficient to dominate the continental market. Despite huge increases in the productivity of Britain's iron manufacturers, it was not alone in producing the important metal for the international market, and European competitors were able to outcompete their British counterparts in certain markets. This was especially the case when it came to the production of the highest-quality bar iron that was still produced using charcoal or poorer-quality but very cheap products.[18]

Gibbons was joined by other ironmasters who were concerned about competition, including from within Britain's own imperial system. Richard Reynolds, of Coalbrookdale, complained to the Member of Parliament Isaac Hawkins Brown that the Reilly family had 'taken 500 acres of land near Lough Allen [in Connaught] abounding with coal and ironstone whereon they are erecting furnaces'. With the short Irish Sea route carrying iron ore from Lancashire or Cumberland to the Irish site more cheaply than to ironworks in Monmouthshire, Gloucestershire or at Carron, he saw this as a substantial escalation in the island's metallurgical competitiveness. In a letter to Earl Gower, Reynolds therefore begged for support against 'a reduction of the duties on the importation of foreign iron into England, to decrease our revenue' as well as supporting the duty on Irish iron. Without imposing a duty to ensure that Irish iron was as expensive to sell overseas as its Welsh, Scottish and English counterparts, Reynolds warned that it would not be long before other iron manufacturers began 'removing themselves and their capital to Ireland, to the great loss of this nation and the ruin of many ironworks in it'. His worries were overdone, and the

Irish ironworks struggled to take off in the face of competition from England, Scotland and Wales whose existing works were already shipping good quantities of relatively cheap iron to Dublin. However, Reynolds's concern was indicative of the position of many manufacturers: any sign of competition was a threat.[19]

By the 1780s, Samuel Garbett estimated that about 10,000 tons of 'iron wares' were exported from Britain, worth up to £400,000 each year. This was an impressive expansion and was around five times larger than it had been at the beginning of the century, but, from Garbett's perspective, there was still work to be done. Despite increasing the production of manufactured iron goods, the 'quantity of bar iron imported into Britain [was] about 60,000 tons annually' while only 'about 30,000 tons annually' was mined and smelted at home. It was vital, Garbett believed, to reverse this pattern. Encouraging iron smelting in Britain 'would render us more independent of foreigners, for this essential article' as well as improving the wider domestic economy, even if it cost more in the short term. Boosting domestic mining and processing of this vital raw material represented a 'clear gain or saving to the kingdom' that could only be achieved by extracting 'the product of land by human labour'. If all of Britain's supplies of bar iron were met at home, Garbett believed international competitors would lose £1 million of revenue, with the cash filling the pockets of British mine owners and smelters instead. Garbett recognised that in terms of quality, 'the inferior sorts of English iron and that made with pit coal' were comparable to the Russian offering, while 'the superior sorts of English iron, made with charcoal, are used for some of the same purposes as Swedish iron'. Meeting the huge demand of new metallurgical industries meant that simply producing high volumes was important too. Russia, especially, had stepped up in this respect, modernising and expanding its own iron industry over the previous decades to outpace its competitors. Despite starting out with only an exceedingly small iron industry at the beginning of the century, Russia had surpassed Britain's bar iron output by 1750 and Sweden's by the 1770s.[20]

The Russian industry's growth was fuelled by the effective application of existing methods, the wide availability of all-important ore (including huge iron deposits in the Urals), and the prodigious use of waterpower to achieve economies of scale. A single ironworks in Yekaterinburg was served by as many as fifty waterwheels that powered twenty-two hammers, 107 bellows, ten rolling mills, twelve fining hearths and other equipment: a sophisticated system that surpassed the size of anything seen in Britain. When they had the opportunity, Russian manufacturers innovated, too. In the 1780s, according to Garbett, Russia 'erected a powerful mill for rolling and slitting of iron' and had stolen tools and machinery from Britain to copy themselves. In one year alone, '135 manufacturers (including some wives and children) were induced to go from Scotland to St Petersburg in one ship, and 30 afterwards in another ship' to 'work at their trades in Russia'. Waterpower remained the preferred choice for Russian manufacturers, and a lack of continuous improvement through experimentation stymied the development of Russian steam power despite it being introduced as early as 1763 by the inventor Ivan Polzunov. Nonetheless, almost half of Russia's total iron production was destined for export to Britain where it would be fed into the island's manufacturing machine.[21]

Britain could not contend with the scale of the Ural operations, but as demand rose and the Empress of Russia imposed increasingly heavy duties on exports, the incentive to further develop British production rose in kind. As Garbett put it, 'a great increase in the English works' producing bar iron might reduce the price 'and it is not probably that any other event will produce that effect'. He warned that attempting to lower the duties in Russia would be a mistake anyway, as cheaper imports 'would certainly have a tendency to depress our iron works, and discourage that spirit of enterprise which is now prevailing to extend them – and ultimately prove a great public injury'. Competition with Russia was forcing British manufacturers to innovate and invest in novel technology, and for an ironmaster like Garbett at the peak of the industry, this was a battle he believed he could win. The most important concern was making sure that British manufacturers stayed at the highest end of the productivity chain. Reducing tariffs to help sell finished iron wares overseas was preferable for ironmakers like Garbett to bolster any support further down the chain that might make British bar iron more competitive domestically.[22]

Gibbons, too, was confident that 'spirit of industry and competition which pervades all the manufacturers of this island' would likewise drive the nation's ironmasters to new heights. Rather than international competitors, though, it was domestic competition that underpinned his expectations of further technological progress. After all, he explained, the 'iron trade of Great Britain is in the hands of hundreds scattered over the face of England and Scotland' and it was here that competition would drive advances and 'secure the proper exertion of our manufacturers both as to good quality and low price'. It was a sentiment that was matched by Richard Crawshay and Alexander Raby. When they presented their own evidence to the 'Lords of Trade' around the same time, they were adamant that on an equal footing they could match 'iron and steel wares' in foreign markets. This was a call to arms that found support among metallurgist and landowner alike. As the ironmaster Reynolds pointed out to Earl Gower in 1785, the value of land depended on its productive value. Gower was the Lord of the Privy Seal and, with property in Staffordshire, would have been well aware of the impact that booming metallurgical industries were making in Britain. These productive ventures, Reynolds reminded him, were valuable to the manufacturers themselves, to investors 'who have adventured their fortunes' to fund such projects, and 'to the landed estates of many noblemen and gentlemen' whose 'rents depend on the success of their engagement in the ironworks and mines which they rent or occupy'. Gower was among the lucky group who had inherited land from which coal and ore could be extracted. Coalbrookdale was built on estates he owned, and Gower happily reported that 'many hundreds of poor people' extracted so much coal that a large surplus was sold even after 'sixteen fire engines, eight blast furnaces, and nine forges' that had been built by Darby and Reynolds had been supplied. Reynolds estimated that the site 'employs a capital of upwards of one hundred thousand pounds'. By the end of the century, at least sixteen steam engines had been erected at Coalbrookdale, alongside blast furnaces, forges and mills, which were supported by infrastructure including 'more than twenty miles of iron railways' to carry coal, ore and metal around the site.[23]

To really make British iron dominant, though, more development was needed to improve the quality of iron that coke furnaces could produce. Important steps in this direction were taken following experiments by Charles Wood in the 1750s, who patented a process for 'potting and stamping' in 1761 and 1763, the latter with his brothers. The technique involved running molten pig iron into water where it hardened. The resulting solid was then crushed with wooden rollers and pounded with stampers, before the resulting granules were washed with potash lye and then mixed with rich slag and limestone. The mixture was then held in clay pots and put back into the furnace to be forged in the usual way. Unfortunately, the ironworks where Wood worked was in desperate financial straits due to its owner's concurrent interest in the Virginia tobacco trade (where they lost a lot of money), and the site was sold and sold again, eventually being converted into a paper mill. However, Wood was recruited by a partnership between his brother-in-law Dr William Brownrigg and Anthony Bacon, a London-based merchant who had made his money trading with America, and the pair's new ironworks at Cyfarthfa used Wood's potting and stamping method. However, it was a competing variation of the technique, patented by Wright & Jesson of West Bromwich in 1773, that won out. In this process, the iron that was cooled in water was melted with 'desulphurised' coal rather than being crushed, and then hammered and broken up and put into pots for forging. This technique was adopted at ironworks in Shropshire, the Midlands and even at the Cyfarthfa works where it replaced Wood's process in the early 1780s.[24]

One final step was needed before the domestic production of bar iron could substitute imports from Russia or Sweden: puddling. This process, too, had a long trajectory of development littered with failure. It had been attempted at least as early as the 1730s by Thomas Tomkyns, but his process proved uneconomical due to an influx of cheap Russian imports. Dr Roebuck, a partner at the Carron ironworks in Scotland, patented a technique to use two hearths to produce iron, but this was also unsuccessful in producing better iron. Thomas

Cranage, who had worked at Coalbrookdale and then Carron before returning to England, undertook further experiments with the process and obtained a patent in 1766, but this too was unviable commercially. When it came to refining higher-quality pig iron to bar iron, a major advance had come in Leeds at Hunslet foundry with the development of the cupola furnace, but this was unsuitable for use with coke-fired iron. The breakthrough came in the 1780s, when Henry Cort patented a new process for fining pig into bar iron. Cort was an agent for the Royal Navy, responsible for purchasing iron supplies for the navy's use from suppliers across the country. After he began recycling scrap iron by melting together old iron hoops from barrels and putting them through a rolling mill, in 1784 Cort patented a method for melting pig iron in a reverberatory furnace. This involved stirring the molten metal, consolidating the resultant puddled ball with a hammer, and then rolling it into a bar, using grooved rolls. With contacts in the Midlands from his time ordering iron goods, he may well have been attempting to reproduce the potting and stamping techniques or Cranage's method. Indeed, some commentators, including William Reynolds and Charles Wood, argued that Cort's new method was essentially the same as existing techniques. However, Cort gained a supporter in the respected Scottish scientist Joseph Black, a mentor of James Watt, and licences were soon taken up. Including, most prominently, by the iron merchant-turned-manufacturer Richard Crawshay.[25]

Crawshay, an importer of Russian and Swedish iron, had taken over the running of the Cyfarthfa Ironworks in Merthyr Tydfil following the death of Bacon in 1787. Licensing the Cort method in 1790, it quickly became clear that it was still not immediately suitable for making bar iron from pig iron produced in a coke-fired furnace. Crawshay reached out to owners of nearby ironworks, and ideas and personnel were shared in search of a solution. The breakthrough came in 1791 from Samuel Homfray, a partner at Penydarren (the most recent of the four Merthyr ironworks), who suggested that the pig iron should be melted before it was puddled, to remove some of its impurities. This essentially meant using the first stage of the Wright & Jesson method to produce metal for puddling. It removed the additional silicon that coke firing added to pig iron and enabled a higher-quality bar iron to be produced. It was the final part of an answer that had been troubling Britain's ironworkers ever since Darby had demonstrated the viability of using coke furnaces to produce pig iron decades earlier. The new puddling process replaced all others and would dominate iron production for much of the following century.[26]

## A NEW TYPE OF POWER

To keep up with the massive increase in metal production that had taken root across the country, Britain's mining industry similarly upped its game. Even the most sophisticated metal-making enterprise still depended on miners to tear ores and coal from the ground to feed their furnaces. Across the eighteenth century, advances in metallurgy and mining went hand in hand. Mining was the first industry to adapt the widespread use of steam engines, mainly for pumping water out of pits so that miners could travel deeper and deeper underground. A breakthrough had come in the very final years of the seventeenth century, when Thomas Savery patented an invention, in 1698, for a commercially viable steam vacuum pump, which used condensed steam to create a vacuum, which sucked up water. Over the following fourteen years, Thomas Newcomen conducted numerous experiments to build on the basic premise of the Savery device in a cylinder with pistons to move a pump up and down. When Newcomen installed his first working engine at a mine in Dudley in 1712, the machine was still highly inefficient and only employed steam at low pressures: but it worked. It was only viable at coal mines, where abundant fuel could be funnelled in at essentially no cost, and the uneven motion that was produced could raise and lower pumps, its main function. By 1733, about 100 engines had been installed across England, burning coal to pump out water that made it possible for miners to dig more coal.[27]

For some mines, the steam engine might as well have been a fantasy. It required high upfront costs, technical expertise and the willingness to sink capital over decades into a site. Where coal could be accessed closer to the surface, miners were happy to continue relying on brute force and the labour of skilled hewers to turn a profit. At the Gladsmuir colliery in East Lothian, where a new pit was opened in the 1750s, coal was still simply extracted until one seam was exhausted and the miners sent onto another location. The relatively small scale of the colliery, which employed just thirteen miners, did not mean that either its value or contribution was insubstantial: 300 tons of coal were carried to the surface every month. The costs of operating this simple mine was relatively consistent, although from time to time there were extra charges for unusually difficult tasks, like the extra 3 shillings paid to William Chalmers for 'working through a piece of foul coal' or for hiring 'sinkmen' who received £3 7s 6d for digging a shaft almost ten fathoms deep. For the mine's owners, profit from the colliery amounted to around £500 each year after workers were paid and its simple supplies were purchased. They were seemingly content with this and made no move to invest in the expensive engines for pumping water or raising coal that were required to delve more deeply underground. When workers' lives and health were understood by Britain's capitalists to be relatively cheap and expendable, the conditions of work made little impact on decisions to invest in new machinery. The Cornish surgeon William Pryce, who was an investor in two copper mines in Dolcoath and Pednandrea, left a graphic account of workers draining a pit with a simple chain pump. Here, a three-foot wheel was turned on the surface by five or six workers, working in six-hour shifts, that continuously raised a looped metal chain bearing leather-stiffened knobs of cloth up the twenty-foot-deep shaft. Carrying a steady stream of cold water, the pump drained the mine, but inefficiently. Working naked to the waist, the men turning the wheel, Pryce reported, 'suffer much in their health and strength from the violence of the labour, which is so great that I have been witness to the loss of many lives by it'. Hand pumps or horse-powered pumps continued to be used to keep mines clear of water, despite advances in steam-engine technology.[28]

Detailed surviving inventories from the collieries of Thomas Botfield illuminate the choices facing larger mine owners. A colliery required hundreds of tools that ranged from simple shovels to complex coal-fuelled engines. At Botfield's smallest and simplest coal works, Sandycroft, the inventory was valued at £382, and the most advanced equipment included two water pumps (one horse- and one hand-powered), worth £31 and £25, respectively, as well as larger, more sophisticated iron pulleys that Botfield had recently installed to improve efficiency at the site. However, at Botfield's Mancott site, the inventory was worth £3,277 and Old Park had equipment worth £4,828. Some of this stemmed from these sites' larger size and workforces (they required twice as many simple tools, for instance), but the vast majority of this extra value came from the industry's newest technologies. At Mancott, £40 was expended on a 'new machine to weigh coals', £168 on '12 railway wagons (new)', £850 on laying railway. Most significantly, Botfield had spent £1,896 on acquiring steam engines at Old Park. This was a huge cost, almost five times more than the entire inventory required to run the Sandycroft site, and would have needed careful consideration and serious capital. As this suggests, even by the end of the century, not all mines were employing steam engines, even though the long-term benefit of the machines had become widely accepted. By 1800, around 2,500 steam engines were in operation in Britain, and around 60 to 70 per cent of these were Newcomen engines probably used in mining. Where profit was in the offing, capitalists were able to take advantage of the capital-intensive technology.[29]

At many larger pits, then, older technology like a hand-powered pump was quickly surpassed. Improvements in design also made steam power more and more attractive to mine owners. Quickly, changes were found that rapidly decreased the amount of fuel required to pump water. Much of this was the result of local knowledge finding better ways of working and collective innovation in the application of the engines, rather than any fundamental changes in design. William Brown, an engineer at Throckley colliery, installed multiple machines across the country between 1750 and 1772, with some notable additions. In 1758, he installed a pump that used parts made at Coalbrookdale foundry. In 1760, he built an engine at Harley colliery in Country Durham that was used to drive a pump and to draw up coal. This was further improved by Joseph Oxley and

Thomas Delaval before 1765 and was such a novelty that Watt visited the colliery while developing his own engine. However, major improvements in efficiency only came in 1769, when John Smeaton demonstrated that fine-tuning each part of the machine could improve efficiency. Machines in Northumberland and Cornwall were built as exemplars of best practice. A few years later, a more significant change was made following Watt's recognition, while working at the University of Glasgow repairing a Newcomen engine, that too much energy was lost in the existing design due to the rapid cooling of the cylinder. The young engineer concluded that the steam could be led into a second chamber for cooling. This became known as the separate condenser. Further experiments followed before a prototype was made in 1769 and a patent obtained. Financial issues meant that commercial production was delayed until 1776, when a partnership with Matthew Boulton commenced.[30]

As early as 1766 Boulton had been corresponding with Watt, but it was only after the Scottish engineer's first partner, Dr Roebuck, fell into financial difficulties that Boulton could snatch up a share of Watt's patent. Through Boulton and Watt's partnership, workshops in Soho were adapted and expanded to accommodate the precision engineering required to make parts for the machines. Highly skilled workers were employed to make the most intricate components, and dedicated foundry areas were set up to make cylinders, pistons and valves. All these had to fit together perfectly. In the 1770s, a further link across Britain's engineering and metal-working networks added a further boon to the production process. John Wilkinson had invented a method of boring to make very accurate and smooth cannons, which he immediately benefited from by obtaining larger government contracts (the state was about to go to war again). Boulton and Watt became aware of the technology in 1775 and recognised that it could be adapted to produce strong, durable and precisely made cylinders. The addition was a hit and the Midlands firm continued to order cylinders bored by Wilkinson. Later, Boulton and Watt's firm would make larger cast-iron parts for complete engines themselves, but in the meantime these pieces, including cylinders, were purchased from new forges like Wilkinson's that were at the forefront of Britain's iron industry. The addition of precisely bored cylinders was an immediate success and Watt's new machine doubled the efficiency of steam engines overnight. Further gains from improving designs meant that engineers and industrialists were well incentivised to keep up with the newest technologies. In 1776, when 'a new fire engine on Mr Watt's principle' was favoured at Bloomfield colliery in Staffordshire over machinery 'on the old construction', the site engineer Mr Perrins had an easy decision to make. The older model required two boilers, built at twice the expense and using twice the fuel of Watt's single-boiler design. Also, 'more blast is obtained than the furnace requires' from the newer model. The Birmingham Canal Company was another early adopter of Watt's improved steam engine, which was installed to replenish the supply of water to the locks in 1776. With a design that was cheaper and more powerful than its competitors, it is unsurprising that Watt's engine was quickly established as the market leader, and further improvements by the Scottish engineer helped ensure that it maintained this dominant position.[31]

Improvements to the steam engine continued, and advances were made in finding innovative ways to employ the new technology for tasks that went far beyond pumping water. Initially, as described above, engines were added to furnaces at sites like Coalbrookdale to pump water on industrial sites onto waterwheels that were then used to power bellows. Wilkinson, whose boring technology was used to make the machine, took advantage of the increased efficiency of the Boulton and Watt engine, installing one at his Bradley furnaces that doubled his output from twenty tons to forty tons of iron per week. Towards the very end of the 1770s, adjustments to the machine, namely, to ensure that it ran at a consistent speed, also made it viable for factory work, turning machines that had for so long depended on waterwheels as their main source of power. Demand was booming, and left Watt in the enviable position of complaining that his business with Boulton 'requires an uncommon share of our personal attention'. While it continued 'going on successfully', he admitted they could 'look for no better and probably will never find another equally good'. Indeed, when an offer came in 1784 asking if he would be willing to take up the 'engineership of the Grand Canal', he felt forced to turn it down. The lucrative opportunity was not enough to distract him from 'the contriving of engines and the other necessary attentions' that his business with Boulton demanded. Focusing on anything else was simply impossible, he explained, while 'my mind' was 'almost wholly turned towards the steam engines'.[32]

Obsession like this bore dividends. Already, in 1782, a steam engine had been installed at the Soho Manufactory, and more followed at other sites. Another of Boulton's ventures, the Albion flour mill in London, also used steam-engine technology, and around the same time it was employed in a cotton factory for the first time. To cater to growing demand, Boulton and Watt's firm built the Soho Foundry in the 1790s. This was set up as a separate ironworks that specialised in heavy engineering, and a purpose-built steam-engine workshop was carefully standardised and systematised to improve production. By the end of the century, the site included a cylinder casting pit, a boring mill, a blast furnace, and ten distinct engineering workshops. By 1800, over 300 steam engines for running machinery would be installed across the country. This was still only a small proportion of the total number of steam engines operating in Britain, mostly in mines, but was already having a transformative impact on where manufacturers could build their factories. Waterwheels were still much more common, providing as much as three times as much power, but the steam engine began to change the calculation of where factory work could be based: no longer was a surging supply of water the main factor, but rather a cheap supply of coal.[33]

## WORKSHOPS OF THE WORLD

Simply extracting iron, copper, coal and other materials was only part of the process that saw metallurgical industries take such a prominent role in Britain's economic development. The production of finished metal goods was just as important, although these were, of course, dependent on the rapid expansion of supplies of the raw materials they needed. During the long decades of innovation that so dramatically expanded metal production, many manufacturers had been getting on with their businesses using whatever supplies were available, whether iron made from charcoal in Britain or imported material from Britain's colonies, Sweden and elsewhere.

By the first decades of the eighteenth century, opportunities to sell finished metal goods to customers at home and overseas had already seen a rapid expansion in the output of Britain's metal workshops. Indeed, even as Wood's schemes were falling apart in the 1720s, his Molineux brothers-in-law had been slowly getting on with the business of manufacturing finished metal goods and they oversaw successful businesses spanning from the supply of raw materials to manufacturers in the Midlands to the sale of finished brass and iron goods in Ireland and elsewhere overseas. For the Molineux company and many others, the colonial market was vital for keeping demand for metal goods high, and as early as the 1730s, when war with France and Spain disrupted supplies of iron to the Caribbean, poor law payments in Wolverhampton increased fourfold as demand for workers plummeted: a pattern that was repeated during wars later in the century. Despite temporary setbacks, the Molineux family were just some of the ironmongers who profited from the explosive growth of the metallurgical industry in the Midlands. Already in 1726, the road between Birmingham and Wolverhampton had been described as 'dangerous and almost impassable by reason of the great number of carriages constantly employed in carrying of iron, and iron goods, and coal'. These levels of productivity were achieved not by the adoption of steam power or large factory complexes, but rather the expansion of smaller workshops that vastly increased production.[34]

Generous natural resource endowment was essential for the growth of Britain's metallurgical industries, but it was only one factor. Businesses in places like Wolverhampton and Birmingham also depended on a highly integrated regional economy that helped drive specialisation and process efficiencies, whereby firms were ever on the lookout for cost savings found in the division of labour. By the first decades of the eighteenth century, more workers were being drawn towards metal work as their main source of income, rather than mixing agricultural and industrial labour as had been more common in the previous century. The putting-out system did remain in place, and as late as the 1760s visitors to Wolverhampton described how, in the villages around the town 'every farm has one forge, or more, so that the farmers carry on two very different businesses, working at their forges as smiths, when they are not employed in the fields as farmers'. That said, in workshops in the town itself, the work undertaken changed as the industry became more sophisticated, with goods that required higher levels of expertise, such as lock making, favoured over low-skill work like nail making. New skills were applied in an array of connected industries. In Wolverhampton, new businesses were set up in the 1720s for producing decorative 'japanned' lacquerware, while the 1740s saw a rapid expansion of enamelling enterprises. Creative work like this added a new dimension to traditional metal trades, reached new customers, and contributed to the growth of the West Midlands metal industry. The Molineuxes' interests would spread more deeply into the colonial economy by the second half of the century, once the Caribbean became a major market for Midlands-made hardware. Benjamin Molineux became a major importer of Jamaican rum, feeding his profits from these businesses into interests in banking and infrastructure, including investment in the first canals that linked the region's factories directly to the Cannock coalfields.[35]

As the Wolverhampton example suggests, the British metalworking industry was undergoing a handicraft- and workshop-led industrial transformation. Birmingham was now leading the world in the production of new, desirable consumer goods: while many were not high value, they were produced in volumes that would have seemed impossible only a few decades before. Metal works grew from foundries set up by ironmongers, by millwrights who desired to make their own castings, or by blacksmiths who chose to produce cast-iron as well as wrought-iron goods. Growth was incremental rather than explosive. Even by the end of the eighteenth century, it was common for ironworking to be undertaken in small workshops rather than large factories. The metal goods produced in small workshops like these could include agricultural tools or cater to the specific requirements of a nearby market: manufacturers with links to textile centres might specialise in bobbins, or those with links to the Ordnance

Office in locks for firearms. As iron manufacturers found in Yorkshire, the rapid expansion of the region's woollen industry incentivised shifts in production towards products sought after in growing textile towns. New managers at Kirstall forge shifted to selling finished goods to wealthier clientele in nearby Leeds, while the Walker brothers ironworks in Masbrough continuously reinvested profits in improving their facilities as they came to dominate the regional market for large iron castings. This was just the start and, as markets became more closely integrated, even smaller manufacturers could produce goods for national and colonial markets. In Sheffield, where metal work was the most common source of employment, the production of agricultural tools and parts for industrial machinery found a ready market in merchants transporting them to colonies overseas.[36]

The metal industry's dependence on mostly smaller workshops began to change with the advent of larger, well-planned works that were capable of producing metal goods at higher volumes and lower prices. These manufacturers were overseeing the labour-intensive production of consumer goods, including nails, locks, hinges, horseshoes and cutlery. Even larger sites, like the Farmer & Galton warehouse in the Steelyard, were often part of wider 'putting out' systems, where much like in the textile industry, they contracted work to numerous independent ironworkers. Larger enterprises found efficiencies in scale even when they remained tied to wider networks of suppliers. After some of the earliest and largest sites, like William Kempson's manufactory in the middle of Birmingham that operated throughout the 1740s and 1750s, produced enormous numbers of buttons, snuffboxes, brass furniture fittings and lamps: other capitalists quickly followed his lead. However, as these industries grew, space in cities for such sites became increasingly scarce, and for more ambitious and more generously capitalised founders, establishing larger premises on the edge of built-up urban areas, preferably with access to the transport links, was an attractive proposition. Rivers and canals could supply power or offer a way to ship goods cheaply which made watercourses sites of dense industrial activity stretching out from urban centres like Wolverhampton or Birmingham. Before long, factory owners were encouraged to build alongside the canal which served as vital conduit for both the coals and water that their steam engines required to operate, stretching industrial sites along artificial waterways that often depended on iron equipment to operate their locks. Once large forges and workshops were up and running, iron-workers toiled amidst a dizzying cacophony as clattering machinery, hissing steam and bubbling ore created what one visitor described as 'a dismal concert that strikes the ears' while 'a continuous eruption of flames, ascending from the mouth of their artificial volcanoes, dazzles their eyes with a horrible glare'.[37]

The growth of larger metal workshops and firms accelerated in the second half of the eighteenth century as well as a shift in focus on the part of the most innovative manufacturers away from utilitarian hardware and towards the production of metal goods known as 'toys', often in the form of luxurious trinkets that combined new ways of working with metal with popular designs. Some toys were functional, such as those used to store foodstuffs or cosmetic products, while others were simply designed as decorations to delight their owners and, quite possibly, display their wealth and taste. Products like these could be made of precious metals, like silver, and sold at the highest prices, but many more were made with relatively inexpensive materials like copper, brass or steel for a much wider market. Advances in rolling and stamping metal, especially in Sheffield in the first half of the eighteenth century, had helped manufacturers break into a market traditionally dominated by traditional silversmiths in London, using machinery to produce cheaper imitations of products such as tea services or candlesticks that were widely sought after. Before long, these had been brought to Birmingham, notably by Boulton, who gathered the requisite machinery, design expertise and skilled work-force under the same roof to enable rapid product development and turnover. The silver plate or enamelling that lent Birmingham toys an attractive veneer were necessary for their popularity, but this was at least matched in importance by the innovative working of the brass, copper and steel that sat beneath.[38]

To meet demand for goods like these, major enterprises were established in the second half of the eighteenth century that specialised in producing large numbers of goods catering to consumers who sought items emulating the most luxurious fashions of their day. Capitalists like Henry Clay, a japanner, established a workshop that employed 300 people, while John Taylor grew his business from making buttons to become a major firm producing enamelled snuff boxes. These were just two firms among many that specialised in the production of metal toys. By the time Boulton and Watt entered into their partnership and began working together on steam engines, the former had already established one of the most prominent sites in Birmingham's metal-making development: the Soho Manufactory. This was completed in 1765 and was essentially a vast warehouse with multiple loading bays for bringing in and carrying out all sorts of goods produced by workmen in nearby Birmingham. The site also contained its own workshops, stocked with the most advanced metal-working equipment of its day, and employed hundreds of workers to make desirable Birmingham toys for sale. It cost at least £10,000 to build. When Jabez Fisher visited the Soho Manufactory, he wrote that it looked like 'the stately palace of some Duke' but was 'divided into hundreds of little apartments, all of which like bee hives are crowded with the sons of industry. The whole scene is a theatre of business, all conducted like one mechanism, men, women, and children full of employment according to their strength and docility.' At the site, the firm worked with all sorts of metals, including sterling silver for the most prestigious customers and cheaper metals to cater to the less wealthy end of the market. Despite benefiting from the innovation and skill of Birmingham's ironworkers, the site made lots of products with brass, silver and steel, which could be shaped, stamped and assembled into all manner of consumer goods. Boulton had a keen eye for design and the demands of the retail market, and corresponded with other local industrialists like Josiah Wedgwood to share design tips and keep up with the trends of the national and international market. To achieve this, the Soho complex was notable for its use of machines to stamp precise metal parts and designs, and for its organisation of workers that focused on mass-producing standardised goods. To keep the machines running, waterwheels powered by the Hockley Brook drove mechanical processes across

*8. Matthew Boulton advertised the new designs of goods produced at the Soho Manufactory, and carefully produced drawings, like these of a milk ewer and tea pot, for inclusion in his sales catalogue.*

the site, which, coupled with the specialisation of labour, helped boost productivity. By 1774, even before he started producing steam engines, Boulton summed up the business in very simple terms: 'I sell here . . . what all the world desires to have – power.'[39]

As early as 1759, Taylor claimed that the metal toy trade employed 20,000 people around Birmingham and made wares worth £600,000. Most of these, he believed, were destined for export overseas. Indeed, reflecting on a specific product – steel buckles – Boulton explained why Britain's producers could outcompete their Iberian rivals: they lacked the necessary technology, having 'no slitting or rolling mills'; they lacked the natural resources required; and they lacked 'workmen' expert in their production. In Britain, the opportunity to exploit inventive technology, skilled workers and abundant natural resources together gave it an edge in international markets. Additionally, Birmingham's success depended on the speed in which new fashions could be emulated and cheaply produced. One ironmonger, Samuel Garbett, summed up the region's entrepreneurial vision in 1787 when he simply noted that 'our object is to excel in pretty appearances for little money – and in that respect we are wonderfully eminent'.[40]

This spectacular expansion of metal production in places like Wolverhampton and Birmingham in the second half of the eighteenth century grew from multiple roots. First, the Midlands was helped by the absence of a powerful local aristocracy or even particularly wealthy gentry, which, coupled with relatively limited interest on the part of the state to regulate trade, meant that local urban manufacturers were given plenty of space to construct their own politics, culture and tradition. Second, like so many industries, changing how labour was organised and connecting sites of production helped firms draw on the skilled work being conducted across the region in ways that increasingly centralised how particular products were ordered, collected and sold. Third, the region could extract the natural bounty that a remarkable ten-yard-thick coal seam running through it provided. Initially used to fuel forges to work with bar iron that had been refined, once coal became widely used for smelting too, the impact of the local seam was even more significant. Finally, the region was well connected to markets for the goods produced, with relatively straightforward routes to Liverpool, Bristol and London, especially as waterways were improved. The capital and these booming port towns were important markets in their own right and offered gateways to a wider world of customers. Gun manufacturers, for example, benefited both from selling their arms to slave-traders who exported them to Africa, and to the state. Likewise, Wolverhampton metal workers took advantage of markets in the Caribbean and North America to grow their businesses. Feedback loops between the British state, colonial demand, the transatlantic traffic of enslaved people, and the development of manufacturing skills in Britain could be felt even in the heart of the Midlands. Birmingham and Wolverhampton were on their way to becoming workshops of the world.[41]

Catering to consumer demand at home and overseas was no easy task, but it bore dividends. The example of burgeoning British exports to Asia was indicative of the opportunities available for enterprising producers. In 1721, for instance, English merchants working for the East India Company in Mocha found a strong market for a variety of metal goods including iron and steel sword blades. Their customers were discerning about what they wanted but well satisfied with the outputs of Britain's industries. They promised that as many as 5,000 steel blades could be sold each year, provided they 'be straight, double edged', and very specifically, 'have the mark of a fox stamped on the blade', either as a recognised mark of quality or to cater to local preferences in design. In a similar vein, other metal industries were expected to change what they produced to meet the demand of customers like this. Tin that was shipped to the Indian Ocean needed to be kept softer than some customers in Britain preferred, while the East India Company's exports of copper, probably extracted from Cornish mines and smelted in south Wales, were made explicitly 'in small bars in imitation of Japan copper' for the Asian market. The manufacture of iron, steel, tin and copper were all developing at pace, and manufacturers needed to keep up with the expectations not only of customers at home but also those half a world away.[42]

Increasing production in Britain and the adaption of products to meet consumer demand helped fuel dramatic growth in metal exports. From only £78 worth of steel heading eastward in 1700, over £8,000 was shipped by the middle of the century and more than £48,000 by 1780. In the second half of the century, copper exports grew even more dramatically, with little more than £500 sent from England to Asia in 1750 ballooning in value to over £82,000 only thirty years later. Wrought iron, likewise, grew in popularity, with exports increasing in value by over £100,000 between the turn of the century and 1780. By this latter date, metal goods made up more than a quarter of all goods heading from England to destinations in Asia: quite the change from less than 2 per cent eighty years before. British manufacturers, merchants and the state quickly noticed the potential offered by the Asian market. Already by the 1720s, when the Board of Trade complained that the East India Company was not exporting enough woollen cloth, the corporation was able to argue that its exports of British manufactured metals more than made up the difference. By

1780, manufactured metal goods had surpassed woollen cloth as the main product sold by British merchants in Asia.[43]

Steam engines like those made by Newcomen, Smeaton and Watt were all part of the explosive growth of Britain's economy during the eighteenth century, but they were only small cogs in a much larger system. The impact of steam engines was, for a long time, restricted to helping increase the depths at which British workers could extract essential materials from the earth. Ores and coal were fed into furnaces, forges and workshops, to produce metals that were turned into all manner of goods for sale in Britain and across the world. Efforts by Darby and then others to use coal to produce goods-quality iron were, eventually, a huge success, but the final stages of puddling metal came after productivity had already increased dramatically in the metal industry. The biggest impact of changes in how iron was smelted instead came at the expense of Britain's competitors in Sweden and Russia, who were eventually squeezed out of the market. By 1800, Britain was producing more than five times as much iron as it had a hundred years before.

The concentration of skilled workers in places like Wolverhampton and Birmingham had already made it possible for more finished goods to be produced even before these technological advances had taken place. As metal work became a primary source of income for more workers, rather than an activity undertaken alongside agriculture, the concentration of skill and competition in the main centres of metal manufacturing created ideal conditions for rapid, incremental gains in the productive process. Even towards the end of the century, the metallurgical industry combined huge manufacturers like Crowley's nail factory or Boulton's Soho factory with 'putting out' systems by which subcontractors in smaller workshops produced goods to order. Much like simultaneous advances in industries such as pottery or textiles, older techniques and practices combined and improved alongside, and symbiotically with, rapid developments in machinery and the use of power. Where possible, many capitalists sought to shift their production towards higher-end items that required more skilled labourers and sometimes specialised machinery or materials. Across the century, inventive metallurgists who were part of wider scientific networks had swapped ideas, competed, and found improvements across many different parts of the metal-making process. Collective innovation among the workers in hotbeds of metal work like Wolverhampton would have seen changes in how metal goods were made. The most successful producers of metal goods combined this human capital with investment in machinery, processes and purpose-built manufactories to produce huge numbers of specialised but increasingly standardised products.

By the end of the eighteenth century, the owners of the largest metallurgical firms had become part of the nation's social elite, rubbing shoulders with wealthy bankers and merchants and buying huge estates, leaving the deafening cacophony of forges behind. However, while capitalists like Darby, Molineux or Boulton were a driving force behind the diffusion and application of innovative technology across Britain's metallurgical industry, they were not the only beneficiaries. In places like Birmingham or Wolverhampton, hundreds of small forges and workshops continued to make iron goods to be fed into the wider industrial machine. Some of their goods were fed into ongoing industrial expansion in other sectors, while other precise, small metal items were essential for many sorts of work. Elsewhere, even simple goods such as nails were needed to support massive industries like shipbuilding or construction, while items like buttons and buckles were used all over the place. The increased sale of iron goods depended on the wider expansion of agriculture, manufacturing and trade across the economy, whether to enrich potential customers for metal goods in Britain or to grow the businesses – including colonial and imperial enterprises – that ordered metal parts. Although ironworking and engineering were key skills in many metal-working enterprises, partnerships often included landowners and merchants, too, whose wealth and knowledge of markets fed into the development of the industrial sector.[44]

Technological advances, outlay on expensive furnaces and forges, and the labour of hundreds of skilled workers clustered in large new factories together contributed to the development of a metal industry that made goods to be sold to customers in Britain and overseas. In the 1780s, Richard Reynolds estimated that Britain's colonies and the United States together took as much as two-thirds of Britain's manufactured iron exports. Land seized by force of arms (often made by the nation's ironworkers) was now home to populations that were among the most important markets for its metal goods. Invention and manufacturing skills in Britain transformed the industry, but the profits that flowed into the hands of the men of metal were rooted in arming the British state and selling goods to enslavers as much as they were in the exploitation of mines at home and the labour of their workers. In the final decade of the century, even though the take-off of cotton textile production (using machines with iron parts, of course) quickly surpassed iron exports in value, metal sales continued to grow. By 1800, the value of iron goods sold overseas had increased to more than £1.4 million, almost twenty times more than a century earlier.[45]

CHAPTER 9

# MADE BY SLAVES

## Colonial Goods, Capital and Networks

When George Whatley penned his 1774 essay *Principles of Trade*, he was well aware of the interconnections upon which the economy rested. Indeed, Whatley's foundational idea was that 'the all-wise creator has ordained that a mutual dependence shall run through all his works' and that trade was part of a divine plan to make humans more reliant on each other. Unfortunately, he acknowledged, 'our limited capacities will not admit us fully to comprehend the nature and end of this connected chain of things'. This self-awareness, of course, was not going to stop him from attempting to do so over the following forty-eight pages. Whatley argued that 'the spring, or movement' of exchange 'is, and ever must be, gain, or the hopes of gain; as neither the public, nor the individual, would intentionally pursue, any unprofitable intercourse of commerce'. For fruitful commercial exchange to work, he explained, 'the gain to each may be equal' between the people involved. 'An incentive to labour' was 'and ever will be' the only cause for poverty and want in such a system.[1]

Yet, despite growing interest in economic ideas that promoted the value of free and well-incentivised labour by authors like Whatley, the immense productivity achieved in Britain's colonies was not realised through high wages to attract workers to the Caribbean plantations. Rather, even as Whatley wrote so passionately about the importance of equal gains, the British colonial economy and that of some of its largest trading partners depended on the exploitation of enslaved people who were certainly not incentivised by hopes of gain, but through dependence, violence and cruelty. Exploiting agricultural frontiers in the Caribbean required extremely difficult labour to clear forest and construct the key infrastructure that sugar cultivation required. Even after plantations were established, planting, harvesting and processing sugar all required a workforce that was pushed to its physical limits in tropical conditions. Mortality rates were extremely high.

Despite the murderous toll that Britain's colonies took on their workers, the scale of plantation agriculture only expanded during the eighteenth century in older colonies, and the seizure of further territory during wars with France and Spain added yet more land that could be transformed and exploited to produce tropical goods. As Britain's colonies grew, the demand for enslaved labour grew with it. Colonial expansion was a boon for Britain's enslavers, and demand for enslaved labourers reached higher and higher peaks throughout the eighteenth century. Pushing workers beyond their limits was a key feature of plantation economies, where maximising production and profits took precedence over protecting the lives of their workers. Enslaved men, women and children did not receive a salary and after they were purchased from enslavers and trafficked from Africa to ports across the Caribbean, minimal sustenance and shelter represented the only ongoing cost for plantation owners. With no need to attract workers with higher pay or better working conditions, British slave-owners focused on extracting as much labour from enslaved people as they could before they were killed by their work. So long as the price of enslaved lives remained cheap, and British merchants continued to benefit from transporting captive people across the Atlantic, plantation owners saw little reason to employ measures that might limit the mortality on their estates.[2]

British landowners and estate managers were fully aware that the merciless treatment of enslaved people was resulting in hundreds of thousands of deaths. After all, the high mortality of workers on plantations was considered an important justification for exploiting enslaved labour in the first place, as fear of death reduced the number of free workers willing to move to colonies for work. Plantation owners also chose not to adopt practices that would have saved enslaved people's lives. In Jamaica, where land was often unsuitable for sugar production, it was common for landowners to use part of their estates to raise livestock. Enslaved people newly arrived from Africa would sometimes be sent to work in these farms for 'seasoning', which was meant to acclimatise them to their unfamiliar environment before being sent to the harder labour of planting, harvesting or processing sugar. This was a deliberate effort to maximise return on investment: landowners hoped that giving enslaved people lighter duties to begin with would decrease their mortality. Of course, they could have chosen not to force people to undertake the heavier, more deadly duties entirely, but that would have destroyed the economic model on which they depended.

Despite 605,000 African men, women and children disembarking from British slaving voyages in Jamaica during the second half of the eighteenth century, this ruthless exploitation of workers meant the island's enslaved population grew only by 151,000 during the same period. Even after accounting for the onward sale of people to plantations elsewhere in the Caribbean, the loss of life for those that remained on the island must have been catastrophically high. Conversely, in Virginia, where the eighteenth century had seen a shift towards agricultural production that was more akin to that in England, enslaved workers lived longer and healthier lives, although harsh discipline and brutal conditions were still typical. Indeed, the enslaved population of Virginia grew more rapidly than in Jamaica despite a steep decline in African captives that were sold in the colony. Despite knowing that their enslaved workers would survive longer if they improved working conditions, many British capitalists decided that on plantations it was simply more profitable to let them die.[3]

## UNFREE TRADE

To meet this horrific demand for labour, hundreds of ships criss-crossed the Atlantic carrying people and produce between Britain, Africa and colonies in the Caribbean and North America, adding to thousands more that ferried goods back and forth between Britain and Europe. The scale of the British slave-trade was immense. Across the eighteenth century, 2.85 million African people were forced to board British ships to be trafficked to America. Five hundred thousand would die during their voyages across the Atlantic. The vast majority of those who survived would be forced to work, without pay or any chance to change their lot, until they died. Communities were ripped apart and families and friends separated forever. The vast system that achieved this forced migration was not overseen by any one state or company, but rather networks of capitalists whose focus on increasing profits from the sale of enslaved people saw the trade get bigger and bigger over the eighteenth century. Merchants in British cities arranged to finance and supply ships for dispatch to the African coast. African brokers marched captives to markets across 3,000 miles of coastline to await the arrival of European traders. Middlemen in Britain's colonies waited for ships packed with captive people to funnel onward into the plantation complex. Overseers and landowners forced new arrivals to work to produce sugar and other commodities. More traders purchased these goods and shipped them back to Britain. A greedy public happily consumed the proceeds of enslaved workers across the ocean. At every stage of that process, there were opportunistic capitalists ready to take a slice of the huge economic pie that colonial trade represented.[4]

The complex networks that tied all of this activity together had been growing since the seventeenth century, when islands seized by British colonists in the Caribbean and expanding territories they commanded in North America turned to enslaved people as the main source of labour on plantations. First by royally supported corporations, and then by hundreds of private traders, the British slave-trade had grown and grown in its scale and significance. Already by 1750, traders from Bristol had surpassed those from London as the most active participants in the trade, before they too were taken over by slave-traders from Liverpool, although merchants in all three ports continued to take part in and profit from the exchanges. At the same time, Liverpool and Bristol grew into bustling commercial metropolises and growing industrial centres, buoyed by the wealth that flowed from the slave-trade and the exploitation of enslaved labour alike.

The role of Liverpool in the transatlantic slave-trade is difficult to overstate. Between 1700 and 1807, slaving ships departing from Liverpool forcibly displaced an estimated 1.5 million captive Africans to the Americas, the majority of whom would work and die in horrific conditions on the Caribbean's plantations. By the second half of the eighteenth century, Liverpool had become the world's largest slave-trading port, eclipsing both London and Bristol, and by 1790, 80 per cent of Britain's transatlantic slave-trade was being orchestrated from Liverpool.[5]

A snapshot of Liverpool's trade from October 1752 offers some insight into just how important colonial trade was for the growing port, but also how deeply intertwined this was with the wider economic activities taking place around it. That year, the port saw twenty-one ships depart to destinations in Europe, carrying English manufacturers or re-exporting colonial goods to customers in the Netherlands, Germany and the Baltic. More than twice as many were heading to Africa to buy enslaved people and sell products sourced from Britain's metallurgical and textile industries. Sixty more headed directly to the Caribbean or North America, carrying British goods of all sorts to exchange for luxury cash crops, especially sugar, or essential commodities like timber. The rest were trading with Ireland, extracting raw wool, linens and copper ore in return for items including coal, corn, iron, woollen cloth and refined sugar. Liverpool served as an intersection for many parts of Britain's economy. A similar set of connections could be seen in Glasgow, though rather than investing directly in the slave-trade, Scottish merchants were more likely to profit from trading directly with colonies in the Caribbean and North America, and links were common between the city's financial and manufacturing elite, plantation owners and factors overseas, and the merchants moving goods in between. In other words, the slave-trade was not the only activity that merchants who profited from the traffic of enslaved people undertook. The colonial goods and capital that flowed into Britain because of the transatlantic slavery economy contributed significantly to the country's astronomical growth in the eighteenth century.[6]

The speed and scale of the expansion of trade taking place through the port of Liverpool was remarkable, and it was recognised as such by contemporaries. In the 1769 edition of the *Tour through Great Britain*, the port town's 'prodigious increase of trade and buildings, within the compass of a very few years' was recognised, and it was now 'rivalling Bristol in the trade to Virginia, and the English colonies in America'. Goods coming through Liverpool supplied not only the town itself, but also 'a large consumption of goods in Cheshire and Staffordshire' too. The cause, the editors made clear, was because the town's inhabitants had become 'like the Londoners, universal merchants'. A willingness to trade far and wide and embrace all the skills of the capital's older mercantile establishment was just the start. Liverpool's merchants were lauded 'for frugality in management, which enables them to do everything upon the cheapest terms, and to sell at the lowest prices'. Participation in trade was not limited to a narrow elite, but rather 'all degree of people' and 'even their own servants' were able and willing 'to employ the smallest stock in trade, by which they become interested in the event'. Finally, Liverpool's merchants had 'shown surprising spirit in works of large expense, for the improvement of the town and port; and, in a word, whatever may contribute to the public interest'. A ruthless focus on efficiency, a willingness to work with the broadest network of partners possible, and a common commitment to improving shared facilities had left the port as nothing short of 'one of the wonders of Britain'.[7]

Even the experience of a relatively minor merchant like Robert Nicholson was indicative of how the slave-trade and colonial trade intersected different parts of the economy in Liverpool. While never as heavily involved in the transportation of enslaved people as some of his peers, Nicholson was still among the thousands of capitalists in Liverpool whose livelihoods depended on slavery in Britain's colonies. Nicholson set up as a merchant after completing his training under Matthew Nicholson, a linen merchant who had been the first member of his family to settle in Liverpool. Although he maintained a keen interest in textiles in particular, his surviving letter book reveals that he was sharing news about business opportunities and overseeing commercial interests that stretched across Britain's overseas territories from Gibraltar to Jamaica. In the 1750s, Robert Nicholson was recorded as one of eight owners of the *Alice Galley*, a ship used to traffic captive African people from the Gold Coast to colonies in the Caribbean. He withdrew from the slave-trade after its second voyage and focused instead on direct Liverpool-to-Caribbean trade, sending goods including cloth and cheese and returning with sugar and cotton harvested by enslaved workers.

For traders like Nicholson, the value invested in each voyage to colonies in North America and the Caribbean was not necessarily large. The goods he sent to Jamaica on another ship called the *Tiger* were worth only £38. Nevertheless, his trade depended on understanding consumer demand in the Caribbean and the products available from manufacturers that were flourishing across northern Britain. They included 'wide stripe and check' linens, 'fine and wide Irish linen', twelve surtout overcoats and seven bottles of the 'best Scotch' available. Efforts to sell a wig in Virginia came to nothing when it 'was sent back unsold' to Liverpool. The same year, he sent twelve cheeses on the *Elizabeth* that were worth little more than £1, but they were exchanged for coffee and chocolate from nearby plantations that achieved returns of 35 per cent. Slavery was not his core business, but profiting from the wealth generated by enslaved labour certainly was. Quickly, Nicholson had made so much money that he could drop £600 on building a new town house in Liverpool on Paradise Street: a sum that might have bought him a share in a coal mine or a new ship, but that he used to establish himself as a well-to-do member of Liverpool society. The following year, Nicholson informed a friend that he 'was married to Miss Arabella Cropper, a young lady in this town possessed of every qualification that I think likely to make the marriage state happy and agreeable'. Soon, the family's business expanded into selling timber and chemicals, as well as an array of general merchandise. Networked capital drew numerous industries together through investment in the transatlantic colonial trade, even as returning profits from slave-made goods were reinvested into Liverpool's economy and beyond.[8]

In places like Liverpool, where transatlantic trade formed such a significant part of the local economy, profits from slavery and goods made by enslaved people were endemic. It is unsurprising, then, that the capitalists who invested in voyages to purchase captive people in

Africa and sell them in the Americas for profit were drawn from myriad backgrounds: the port's burgeoning trade provided opportunities for merchants, mariners and craftsmen to invest even small sums. Partnerships were a key element of business development, just as they were in other industries, and many ships used to transport enslaved people had two or more owners, with shares divided and subdivided between different investors to spread risk and provide a broader section of the population the chance to benefit. Even when they were not deeply involved in the Caribbean trade as part of their everyday working lives, many still took the opportunity to profit from it when they had a chance. The trade attracted investment from people like the shipbuilder Edward Lyon, ironmonger John Cope, sailmaker John Richardson and linendraper John Kaye: the four men invested in five, six, eleven and twenty-two slave-trading voyages, respectively. Many mariners, too, took advantage of the chance to invest in ships involved in the trade, and although the shares were often quite small, they gave them a chance to profit from an activity that already provided them with employment. Ship captains, especially, were able to use their profits and expertise to invest in the trade, such as John Maddock who earned enough to set up as a property owner and gentleman in Liverpool. None was more committed than the mariner William Boats, who by popular legend was found as a waif aboard ship before being raised at the Blue Coat School (founded by another enslaver) and then rising to prominence as a ship captain. After this rags to riches rise, Boats invested in more than 150 voyages that trafficked over 50,000 enslaved people. When considering the most active slave-trading dynasties in Liverpool's history, including the Earles, Davenports and Gregsons, many had first come to the trade from families with relatively humble origins as craftsmen or farmers.[9]

Other investors drew on landowning wealth to invest in Liverpool's colonial economy, often blurring the lines between property ownership and commercial interests. Richard Kendall, for instance, owned land in Cumbria and in Liverpool while investing in twenty-two voyages that carried almost 6,000 African people to British colonies. Henry Ellis, a major landowner in Ireland, invested in only a single

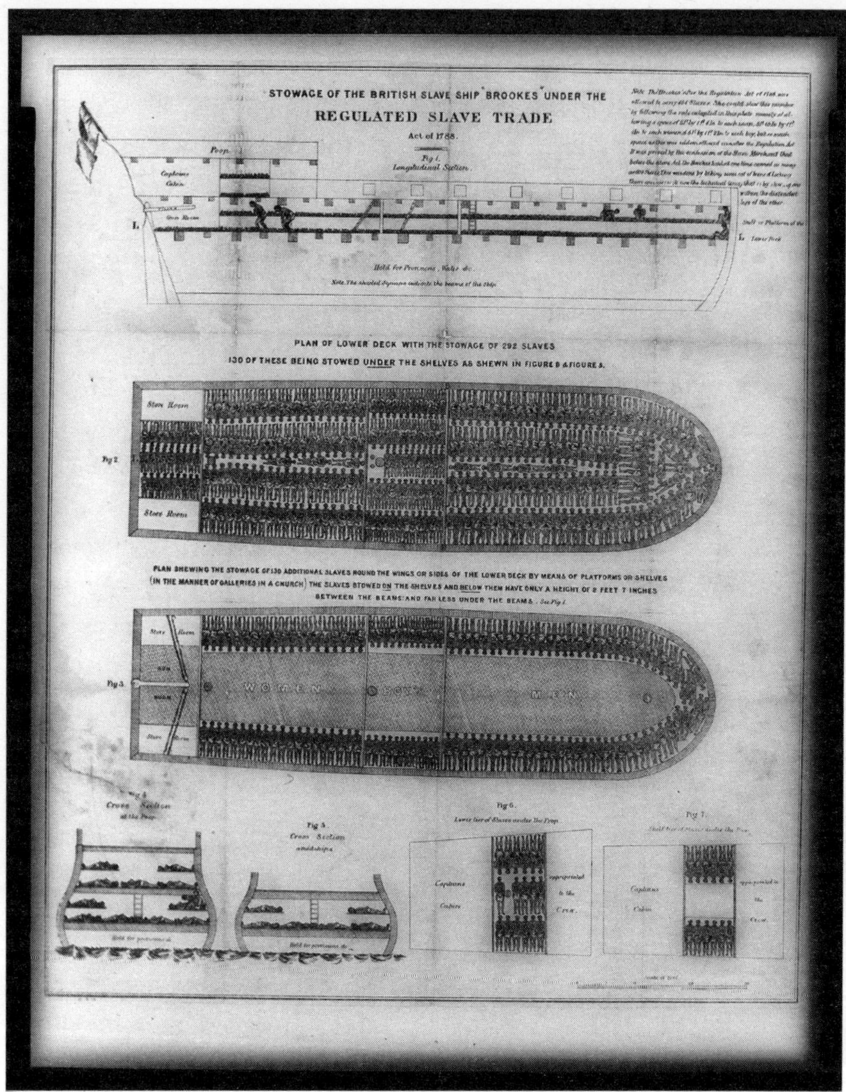


*9. The merciless treatment of people in the name of profit was exemplified in this plan of the ship* Brookes *that was produced to garner support for the abolition of the slave trade.*

voyage that departed from Liverpool. This was just the start of his long involvement in wider colonial interests, though, and he eventually became governor of the Georgia and then Nova Scotia colonies, before returning to London and advising the British government on colonial affairs. Conversely, Thomas Staniforth was the son of a prominent landowner in Sheffield but moved to Liverpool in his twenties to launch himself into business. Here, he married Elizabeth Goore, and it was through his father-in-law, Charles – a prominent slave-trader, merchant and Mayor of Liverpool himself – that Staniforth might have been introduced to the possibilities that the slave-economy offered an enterprising Englishman. Staniforth sent ships that he owned (in partnership with numerous other slave-traders including William Davenport and Bryan Blundell) on fifty-seven slave-trading voyages between 1763 and 1793, returning year after year and increasing the size and profitability of the ships he used as time went on. In the 1760s, his ships normally trafficked between 100 and 200 enslaved people, with the largest, the *King of Prussia*, carrying 336 African captives. By the 1780s, this would have been considered a disappointing voyage. His new ships like the *Brooks* and the *Rumbold* had been designed to maximise the numbers of people that could be cruelly shackled beneath their decks and could carry as many as 640 men, women and children to plantations in the Caribbean. Across his lifetime, Staniforth's ships took almost 25,000 people from Africa.[10]

Investments like these connected Liverpool's slave-traders to people who were drawing on capital and expertise from a wide range of backgrounds. To enter the business, many trained as merchants during apprenticeships or followed family members into the trade. For example, Thomas Seel, a tobacco trader, invested in only a single voyage in 1714, but it was a step into the trade that his son and grandson, also both called Thomas, took up to a much greater degree, investing in thirty more voyages. By the end of the eighteenth century, Seel's grandson had used this foundation to become a considerable landowner and financier, with a personal estate worth £15,000. Blundell, who had worked as a mariner from the age of twelve, went on to own numerous ships and established himself as a prominent slave-trader: his vessels carried more than 15,000 captive people from the African coast. He saw the next generation of his family enter business as members of the city's mercantile elite before they, in turn, established themselves as financiers and industrialists. Likewise, the descendants of major slave-traders like Richard Gildart took only a minimal role in the trade while expanding other interests that their forebear had set up. Gildart had overseen a business enterprise that included shipbuilding, rock-salt manufacture and trade in tobacco and sugar on his way to becoming Mayor and Member of Parliament, even while his ships undertook regular voyages to Africa that led to the traffic of over 6,000 enslaved people. More unusually, the trader Thomas Leyland, who had a business trading food goods with Ireland, won £20,000 in a lottery in 1774 (which he shared with his business partner), and used the proceeds to invest in an array of commercial activities, especially transatlantic slavery. Before the abolition of the slave-trade, almost 25,000 captive people were trafficked on his ships. Wealth from these ventures propelled Leyland up the Liverpool social ladder, and he became Mayor of Liverpool on three occasions before he died as one of the richest men in Britain.[11]

The range of different routes that people took into the transatlantic trade in enslaved people attests to its scale and spread. Opportunities to invest even relatively small amounts in the possibility of extremely high profits made the slave-trade an attractive proposition that many people were willing to take up. Indeed, while typical returns for investment in slave-trading voyages were around a healthy but by no means extraordinary 10 per cent, voyages that made 100 per cent profits were not that uncommon. As one Liverpool captain described it, trading in enslaved people was something of a 'lottery' and the potential for huge gains meant many participants 'hoped to gain a prize'.[12]

Once investment had been secured, Liverpool's traders were just as dedicated to finding ways to increase their profits as their compatriots working in any other part of the British economy. This meant constantly seeking new markets on the African coast and making efforts to establish strong relationships with African brokers who brought enslaved people to the coast for sale. The result was the massive expansion of the British slave-trade in the eighteenth century. Whereas the Royal African Company and independent traders from London had focused on a stretch of coastline near to Cape Coast Castle, Liverpool's merchants quickly expanded the scope of their operations. By the 1730s, ships from Liverpool were carrying people from Sierra Leone and the Windward Coast. Twenty years later, Liverpool merchants opened the trade at the Cameroon River before, only a decade later, building forts hundreds of miles inland along the Gambia River. By the 1780s and 1790s, previously unexploited sites along lagoons in the Bight of Benin were attracting Liverpool traders, even as their ships traversed the Congo River to buy enslaved people. For the slave-traders who reached these markets first, the profits could be extraordinary. Davenport, for instance, having already financed numerous voyages to busy slaving ports on the Gambia River and Old Calabar, sent a small ship to the Cameroon River in 1756 in the hope of finding low-priced captives and ivory. Asking that his captain take note of the specific goods that the local Duala people most valued, Davenport not only identified a new geographical market to exploit but also gained valuable commercial intelligence. The benefits for the ruthless trader were considerable, and between 1758 and 1785 he worked with various partners to finance forty-one voyages to Cameroon, which carried off almost 10,000 people from the port. With regular profits of 28 per cent, Davenport and his fellow investors outdid many of their compatriots.[13]

Liverpool's slave-traders were keen to exploit opportunities to increase their profits when they could, and peacefully trading into new markets in Africa was not the only means by which they achieved them. Important examples concern incidents like the Old Calabar massacre, where Liverpool slave-traders benefited from the violent action their captains and crews took in order to preserve and protect their employer's profits. Old Calabar was the principal port of the Cross River estuary in the Bight of Biafra, which had been largely dominated by British slave-traders from Bristol. However, in 1767, with 'seven large vessels' waiting at anchor, 'each of which expects to purchase 500 slaves', British traders struggled to purchase the captive people they wanted due to a dispute between African traders in Old Town and those from New Town, a competing market only a few miles away. Ambrose Lace, the captain of a slaving ship from Liverpool called the *Edgar*, believed that the situation 'will never be ended before the destruction of all the people at Old Town'. With his fellow captains, he arranged a supposed mediation between the traders

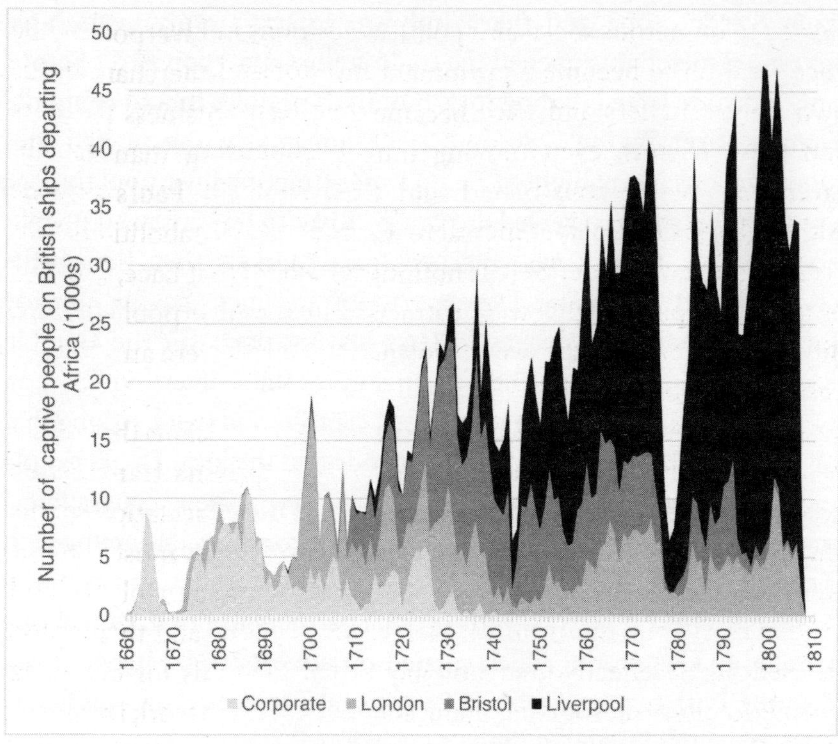


*Figure 3. Number of captive people trafficked from Africa in ships owned by British slave-trading corporations and independent slave-trades from London, Bristol and Liverpool, 1660–1810 (data from TASTD).*

from the two towns. It was a trap. The British ships began firing on the canoes of Old Town traders in the river, killing dozens, even as their allies from New Town, who were in on the conspiracy, joined with British sailors to slaughter Old Town's residents. By the end of the night, nearly 400 people had been killed. In the aftermath, the owners of the *Edgar* made enormous profits and rewrote the commercial landscape of Calabar, with Liverpool traders and Lace's New Town allies now dominating the slave-trade. One of Lace's captives, Otto Ephraim Robin John, was forcibly carried to Liverpool where Lace paid for his education and upkeep, before the young African man was returned to Calabar where he became an important slave-trader. The massacre also helped launched the career of Edward Chaffers, one of the owners of the *Edgar*, and soon after he was elected to numerous social and political positions in Liverpool, while Lace went on to become a prominent investor and merchant in his own right. Chaffers and Lace became long-term business partners and close friends, even moving into neighbouring mansions in Liverpool's newly constructed and fashionable St Paul's Square. Although the Old Calabar massacre was later used by abolitionists to critique the slave-trade, there is nothing to suggest that Lace, Chaffers or any other participants were ostracised by the Liverpool community for their parts in the event: violence and death were an accepted cost of doing business.[14]

Trusting captains, agents and partners to take decisions that would benefit all parties was a necessary aspect of Britain's transatlantic economy. While Lace went above and beyond the expectations of his ship's owners at the time, by the later eighteenth century most captains were expected to be willing and able to use extreme violence and cruelty in the pursuit of profit. Merchants, captains and their crews devised highly effective but horribly brutal methods for enslaving people, forcibly transporting them, and making them work in plantations. Once at sea, captains locked their unwilling passengers below decks on their floating dungeons and maintained heavily armed crews to stop any attempt at insurrection. When enslaved people were brought on deck, for meals or for humiliating forced exercise, they were shackled to long chains to restrict their movements. Ships were built with guns aimed towards their own decks as a countermeasure to any revolt, and had features more familiar in warships including barricades that were as capable of stopping captives from attacking the crew as they were of repelling enemy boarders. These design features were continuously improved by shipbuilders and captains as best practices were established. Rebellions by enslaved people were still common, but enslavers were increasingly able to suppress them. This meant increased profitability for British capitalists, with fewer rebellions and more time spent on deck helping to decrease overall mortality, even though one in six enslaved people still died during eighteenth-century voyages. While ships continued to operate as independent ventures rather than being managed by an overarching corporation, the standardisation of these kinds of methods meant Britain's traders were able to vastly increase the volume of their trade. It was the same closely knit competition and diffusion of ideas that generated improvements in textiles, potteries or ironworks, but applied to human beings whom slave-traders systematically dehumanised and viewed as commodities.[15]

Ship owners incentivised captains to maximise the profits from each and every voyage: avoiding risks where they could, and using every inch of available space to transport as many people as possible. A set of detailed instructions given to William Young, the captain of his ship *Spitfire*, by Leyland in 1795 is indicative of how British businesspeople understood and described their trade. Loading a large quantity of guns and Manchester-made cotton goods alongside a cargo of Indian textiles, the £4,905 12s 2d of goods shipped on the *Spitfire* represented the proceeds of British mechanical innovation and global trading interests. A small amount of tobacco, probably from plantations in North America, was re-exported, which was to be used to buy 'about six tons of rice' on the Windward Coast to feed the ship's enslaved passengers as cheaply as possible during the voyage to the Caribbean. After buying these grains, Young was expected to continue to the River Congo, attacking any Dutch or French shipping along the way if it looked like a profitable endeavour, but otherwise seeking to make good time and avoid any unnecessary risks.

Once he had reached the African coast, Young was expected to 'barter the cargo for slaves and ivory', and was encouraged to 'push your purchase in males only' as these 'will make the highest average' profit in the Caribbean. Due to recent regulation of the trade, the 'ship is intended to carry 253 full grown' adults 'and 169 small' – that is, children. The inclusion of children was intended to increase profitability: 'additional room small slaves will give in the ship' might increase the 'chance of their escaping any mortality' during the middle passage. Once this was done, Young was instructed to proceed to Grenada where 'I hope that island will afford an agreeable sale'. The *Spitfire*'s crew were well incentivised to follow Leyland's instructions and to force as many people as possible into the tight confines of their ship: on successful completion, Young would receive a share of the sale, his first mate a gratuity, and the ship's surgeon Mr Scott would receive an extra shilling for every enslaved person that was sold in the Caribbean. Reaching Barbados in January 1796, the captain, crew and Leyland alike would have been delighted with their good fortune. Four hundred and twenty-one people survived the voyage and were sold at auction for £24,453.[16]

The organisation of Britain's trade with the Caribbean and North America depended on thousands of individual investors like these. No matter their incentive or background, taking part in the transatlantic trade brought capitalists seeking to profit from colonial trade or the traffic in enslaved people into the same skein of overlapping and entangled networks that were needed to keep the immense enterprise going. Britain's economy depended on these networks being flexible, accepting of investors with different backgrounds operating together, and having accepted codes of conduct that helped strengthen trust between them. This, in turn, deepened ties across different parts of Liverpool's regional economy and made it easier for people with interests in one part of the economy to work with people from another. It was common for merchants to be members of enduring commercial partnerships that conducted one type of business, like John Hodgson's involvement with Henry Hutton & Company or Peter Hunt's in his father-in-law's firm Roger Fisher & Sons, even as they took part in dozens of transatlantic voyages on their own account or in other partnerships.[17]

The constant back and forth of ships between Britain's ports, Africa and colonies in America was so commonplace that when writing to John Paterson in Jamaica, the Glasgow trader Alexander Houston simply noted that provisions for the plantation had shipped already from Cork, that they had received and sold forty hogshead of sugar that had come in on their ship *Ulysses*, and that in ten days they would send another letter on the next ship outward to the Caribbean. Provisions moved one way, sugar the other, and the complex exploitation of labour, materials and capital that underpinned the entire system simply did not need to be explained. To keep this system moving smoothly, though, did require careful management and the constant exchange of information between partners, suppliers and customers. On every ship that traversed the seas, packs of letters carried information back and forth between merchants, their factors, family members and others, and with them went bills of exchange, legal documents and all manner of other essential commercial paraphernalia. Much like business in Britain that relied on social networks and common cultural practices that made it easier for people to work together, the same applied across the British commercial world in the Atlantic. Indeed, generations of merchants had shaped the practices that kept the colonial economy ticking, and these continued to underpin business practices.[18]

The Scottish ship owner Houston was among the thousands of British capitalists who depended on these standardised practices for his business. A remarkable surviving package of his letters, sent onboard the *Caledonia* to Grenada in 1776, reveals how different relationships and networks came together to support these ventures. The ship's cargo was representative of the sort of trade that dominated British exchange with the Caribbean, and large volumes of herring, flour, bricks and coal were shipped to the tropical island alongside various manufactured goods. By shipping 'plantation stores' that the island desperately needed to fuel its agro-industrial economy, the Glasgow merchant was well placed to profit from the return of 'West India produce'. He did not grow wealthy through direct involvement in the slave-trade but rather through the transportation of goods needed within the slave-economy. However, there were risks in the transatlantic enterprise and Houston was aware of the 'great dependence' he owed to his agents for 'bringing this about in an agreeable manner'. In his instructions he was clear that 'we beg you will do nothing rashly, for it is better to have little business than a great deal with much risk of bad debts, which is too frequently the ruin of the West India trade'. Sending ships back and forth across the Atlantic was difficult enough, but running a business where partners and customers were weeks or months away meant that being able to rely on people to work on your behalf was vital.

Houston's letters attest to these challenges. Some of his letters were strictly business, and people who had contracted Houston to ship goods received polite updates about their orders, while those who owed him money received somewhat less friendly reminders to pay their debts. The firm of Bartlett, Campbell & Bartlett were simply provided with the demand that they repay debts of over £500. A similar message was sent to John Graham who owed over £750 and the partnership of Turner & Paul who owed almost £6,000. For Alexander Wilson, who had borrowed £5,000 by using his island properties as surety, Houston asked his associate Robert Bogle to step in and help recover them by insisting fifty hogsheads of sugar were sent immediately to Glasgow. If not, the ship owner could always look to recoup his losses by forcing his claim to Wilson's Mount Alexander Estate, a plantation on Grenada.

In addition to reassuring clients or calling in debts, Houston's letters often included wider-ranging updates alongside the basic business information that had to be transmitted. This could be about markets, such as an update that sugar and rum prices had gone up in Glasgow 'so what you may ship this year has a chance to coming to a good market', or about family, like the messages informing his agents that 'your friends here are all in good health' and to Duncan Campbell that his 'brothers are in good health' back home. Houston also shared news about the ongoing War of American Independence, which 'seems to be still in a deplorable state', and his hope that a major offensive the following year would prove 'decisive in favour of Britain'. This was not to be, and the 'Eagle Privateer of Rhode Island' would capture Houston's *Caledonia* on its return voyage later that year.

By keeping relationships that blurred the lines between business and personal news, Houston was able to lean a little more on his trusted partners when it was needed. In Grenada, associates like Patrick Maxwell were told Alexander would be 'obliged to you for any freight you can throw her [the ship's] way' to boost business. Another letter conveyed Houston's hopes that Robert Hamilton's herrings 'will arrive sage and good' and that this might 'encourage your further orders in future years'. To increase the prospect of a return order, Maxwell was reassured that, if he 'made a small trial' of his products for the Glasgow market, Houston was confident he 'might turn it out equal to any other in Britain'. Houston's reputation also depended on his assurances that he would look after his customer's business interests. Another contact, Ashton Warner Byam, was given assurance that Houston was looking into the case of his missing sugar. Interactions like these all sat behind a business that continued to expand despite the American Revolutionary War, with new ships (now heavily armed), new trade routes (to Honduras for buying mahogany) and even more sugar heading back to Glasgow in the following years.[19]

Bundles of letters like those sent on the *Caledonia* were carried on every ship that traversed the Atlantic. They carried not only information about business dealings but also notes between friends, colleagues and family that sustained relationships across the oceanic expanse. Throughout his own correspondence, Nicholson, too, maintained relationships with his partners and friends, and just like any eighteenth-century merchant, ties with people at home and overseas were essential for him to operate his business effectively. Seeing people that you cared about depart overseas could be an emotional experience, even when they did so voluntarily, and letters sometimes served simply to keep relationships going. When one friend, Harry Hutton, left Liverpool to settle in Hamburg, Nicholson was reduced to tears through the 'great loss of your company since you went abroad' and wrote mournfully how he missed 'my friend to whom I used to unfold the secrets of my breast, to whom I used to lay open all my thoughts, my projects and schemes for my earthly and future happiness'. If only, he mused, 'the power of an Invisible Agent' were able to transport him to Europe so that he might 'find my friend sitting round the Tea Table … smoking with sage dons of Germany'. Perhaps, fortune would truly favour him, and he would 'find my friend employed in writing to myself expressing himself in that epistolary eloquence which flows with such easy elegance from his pen'. It was hard to be separated, but at least the continuous circulation of letters sustained a sense of community for Britain's capitalists, no matter where they were. Often, letters covered both personal and commercial topics. Even in his emotional letter to Hutton, Nicholson still took the time to tell him that Tom Hodgson's 'capacity for business is very good', although gossip about this young trader's feud with Adam Lightbody over their shared romantic interest in Molly Bent appears to have been the main reason to mention him at all.[20]

Personal relationships were vital for Nicholson's business interests, and friendly gossip and emotional exchanges certainly didn't diminish the importance of keeping on top of complex trading arrangements and business relationships, even when the value of goods was fairly small. Nicholson was happy to tell William Tylston in Jamaica that he would 'leave it entirely in your judgement' to select whether cotton or sugar was most suitable for the return voyage to Liverpool, only asking the agent to 'please take care what you send be of the good kind' so that it could be sold 'to advantage at home'. If Tylston chose poorly, the chances of a good return on investment were slim. Fortunately, on this occasion the system worked for Nicholson and when the goods from Jamaica's plantations were sold in Liverpool, he made a profit of over 40 per cent. Likewise, another contact in Kingston, James France, was trusted to provide 'a list of articles you think the likeliest to find a profitable market on the island', after which Nicholson would adjust his business accordingly. Nicholson's letters to his agent Tylston ended on a friendly note, wishing him 'a safe, pleasant and prosperous voyage and a happy return home', but in the brutal world of colonial trade nothing should be taken for granted. 'In case of your mortality (but which God forbid)', the Liverpool merchant expected his agent to have planned ahead and arranged for his goods to be passed into 'the care of Mr Chetham'.[21] Death, after all, was not the sort of thing to stand in the way of business. Relationships like these blurred the lines between business, family and friendship, and Nicholson had no qualms asking France to help 'Robert Wilson, a boy who is a relation of mine on board the *Elizabeth*'. Wilson had been given '9 cheeses to dispose of on his own account'. With his training wheels of cheese and the support of a family friend in Jamaica in place, Wilson would have been expected to take his first steps into the trading world. No mention was made of the fact the boy's first profit would stem from the work of enslaved labourers toiling on the island's plantations not far from Kingston.[22]

Long-distance relationships overseas were important, and networks bringing together capitalists from across Britain were similarly vital for ensuring Liverpool's trade connected to suppliers and customers across the country. In Staniforth's notebook, details of the trader's business activities were interspersed with the everyday appointments and activities that crossed between business and personal affairs. Regular trips to Yorkshire with his wife Elizabeth were not taken for business but most likely helped him keep in touch with suppliers and customers across northern England. The merchant, slave-trader and banker Benjamin Heywood was likewise in regular correspondence with the Farmer & Galton gun manufacturing firm in Birmingham who supplied him with firearms for the African trade. The ironmaster William Reynolds was in regular contact with his cousin William Rathbone in Liverpool, a prominent cotton trader, about everything from scientific experiments to changing productive methods in metallurgy. And so on. Maintaining open channels of communication and relationships like these across Britain was essential for doing business. Some firms were even structured specifically to ensure they had partners living in both Liverpool and London to ensure that good, trusted contact between the two cities was maintained.[23]

Networks that underpinned the work of so many British capitalists were also strengthened by engagement in the same societies, clubs and political organisations. Efforts by some traders to establish lobbies in support of their commercial interests led to organisations like the African Company of Merchants, which was set up in 1750, to bring together the representatives of enslavers from Bristol, London and Liverpool. Its members were tasked with 'extending and improving the trade to Africa'. While the company was expected to govern and support the cost of maintaining Britain's fortifications on the African coast, the most prominent being Cape Coast Castle, it was not a joint-stock corporation, and its members continued to trade privately. However, they saw the value of paying small fees to keep the forts on the African coast supplied and well fortified, and they knew that in doing so they earned the support of the British state and Royal Navy during times of conflict. Among the company's first decisions was to insist that 'the castles and forts on the coast of Africa' would be open to all members if they chose, but that they would not be required to trade through them. There would be no return to the smaller, monopolised trade that had characterised that of the Royal African Company a century earlier. This decision was taken because it was considered 'more proper to have a number of markets to go to than one', and captive African people were sold to British traders at sites along the coast stretching from Senegal to

Angola. The company also thought that African slave-traders should be unrestricted in where they traded with British merchants. Instructions were sent to the governor on the African coast to make it clear that employees were strictly prohibited from using their influential positions to try and control or profit from the trade.[24]

The African Company of Merchants was not the only organisation that brought together traders, although others were not so explicitly focused on promoting the slave-trade. A local Chamber of Commerce and Board of Trade were both established in Liverpool to bring together slave-traders and other capitalists to discuss and shape the town's economic policy. Less formally, the establishment of various clubs, libraries, intellectual societies and churches also provided further spaces in which Liverpool's capitalists could interact. Sites were set up to enable meeting spaces for different groups, with the Tontine Hotel serving as an informal newsroom for the port and a forum for knowledge exchange while the Liverpool Library was the first public library in England designed 'to promote the Advancement of Knowledge'. The operating costs of organisations like these were typically met with subscriptions or membership fees, a form of investment by participants in the networked capital on which their wider business interests depended. Except for churches, many of these were effectively, if not legally, denied to women, who consequently struggled to participate in many of the partnerships and schemes that developed within such networks. But male capitalists could utilise them to great success. Following the Old Calabar massacre, Chaffers took part in many organisations like these, and was a member of the Chamber of Commerce, Tontine Hotel and the Liverpool Library, and subscriber to Liverpool's Music Hall, Female School of Industry, Infirmary, Ladies Charity, School for the Blind and Dispensary. Social infrastructure like this grew with the port, its slave-trade, and the wealth of Liverpool's merchants. Together, they provided opportunities for men like Chaffers to generate forms of cultural capital and expand their networks across a wider community.[25]

Profit from transatlantic slavery drew on the social, financial and human capital that thousands of British investors, tens of thousands of British workers, and hundreds of thousands of enslaved African people collectively contributed. The gains, of course, were not shared equally. Thomas Paine, the radical British author, condemned the people that he called 'traders in men', and lamented that they were quite 'willing to steal and enslave men by violence and murder for gain', sacrificing their integrity 'at the golden idol' of profit. Yet, many of the slave-traders he described as 'desperate wretches' were part of the British commercial and political elite. They were Liverpool's Members of Parliament, leaders of its town council, presidents of its charities, financers of its infrastructure, and partners in every sort of business the town had to offer. In port towns like Glasgow, Liverpool or Bristol, with major commercial links with Britain's colonies, people whose wealth had roots in slavery were simply part of the civil and social environment. At the same time, the deep entanglement of social and business lives that provided institutional structures for the vast traffic of enslaved people was a central feature of businesses of all sorts across Britain. Towns and cities across the nation had their own versions of the societies, clubs and organisations that cropped up in Liverpool, and these were all part of creating the polite, civil society that proved so important for the functioning of the economy. Wealth, business success and trustworthiness went hand in hand, and people involved in enslavement and colonial trade were part of the same networks as people who owned mines, furnaces, factories or farms. The ruthless pursuit of profit pushed Britain's capitalists to do whatever was needed to maximise their returns in every sector: the enslavement and exploitation of their fellow man was no different.[26]

## HIGH-GROWTH HUBS

The capitalists who took part in the colonial economy, whether from Liverpool, Glasgow, Bristol or elsewhere, saw to it that the millions of enslaved people that were deemed necessary for the exploitation of colonial land were cruelly trafficked across the Atlantic. Once in America, they worked on plantations producing commodities that had become vital to Britain's growing economy. By 1770, Britain's trade with Africa, the Caribbean and North America accounted for more than a third of all imports, and the same destinations took British exports in huge quantities, too, with almost a third of manufactured goods destined to the same regions. Jamaica alone sent more goods to Britain than anywhere else in the world, with customs records showing more than £1.2 million coming from the island. The colonial exploitation of Ireland continued, too, and was the second largest trading destination for British merchants, outdone only by the trade to Asia. Trade with other colonial empires also accounted for millions of pounds' worth of goods coming into Britain. Spain had become Britain's single largest export market in Europe, after Ireland, and Portugal wasn't far behind, and traders in both would carry British goods onwards to be sold in markets in Spanish and Portuguese colonies. Goods including Manchester textiles, Birmingham firearms, Staffordshire pottery, Macclesfield silks and Halifax woollens were all circulating through Britain's Atlantic trade. They were carried alongside Chinese tea, Indian cloth, Arabian coffee, Virginian tobacco, Caribbean sugar and Mexican chocolate that British merchants had obtained from across the world. Huge numbers of less spectacular commodities moved with them, from coal and soap to cheese and flour: a whole world of trade could be found in a ship's hold as it traversed the wide ocean to meet the demands of customers on both sides of the Atlantic. For businesses operating in almost every sector of the economy, the opportunities of profit from selling colonial produce in Britain or making goods in Britain that could be sold in colonies were enormous.[27]

Britain's colonial trade had a significant impact on the nation's wider economy, and many of the most rapidly growing hubs of innovation were in close proximity to the nation's major ports. Colonial goods, international trade and merchant capital promoted the growth of ports and their hinterlands, contributing to positive cycles of expansion in local commerce, consumption and manufacturing. London was the premier port and economic region in Britain and was home to almost one million people by 1800, an increase from around 600,000 in the previous century. The capital had been transformed, as a huge expansion of overseas trade led to the accumulation and improvement of its port facilities and transport networks, the diversification of manufacturing in its hinterlands, and inventive activities that helped establish the country as a technological pioneer. During the same period, Liverpool's population grew sixteen times to almost 80,000 people, while Bristol's tripled to 64,000. By 1789, the Liverpool slaving merchant Robert Norris described how his home town's 'emergence from obscurity' had seen it grow from a town of only a thousand houses to 'above 10,000 houses' and docks that 'excel everything of the kind in Europe': growth that he believed was 'owing principally' to transatlantic trade. Liverpool's phenomenal growth was impossible to ignore, and even the schoolboy Thomas Boardman was able to write enthusiastically to his cousin in 1799 that 'people are building very fast in Liverpool' and imagined within forty years his village home would be subsumed into the town's urban sprawl. The regions next to the ports saw their populations grow more quickly than the British average, too, and the expansion of villages and towns in adjacent counties boosted the population density of whole regions in addition to the explosive growth of ports themselves. Taking part directly in colonial trade as a trader or mariner was an opportunity that attracted some people towards the coast, but accessing goods from, and markets in, America that came through the port provided a clear incentive for many more enterprising capitalists to move, too. Overall, the direct and indirect economic activities connected with slavery accounted for as much as 11 per cent of Britain's total productive output: the proportion would have been even greater in high-growth regions like the one around Liverpool.[28]

In ports like these, the commercial elite and local government (which often closely overlapped) were well aware of how these links benefited the city and that a connected vision for the city's prosperity was needed to oversee them effectively. This could be seen clearly in Scotland's premier commercial hub: Glasgow. Much like the major colonial ports in England, Glasgow had also grown dramatically as opportunities in the Caribbean and North America suited its position on Britain's north-western coast, through which flowed Scottish products in one direction and colonial goods produced by enslaved labour in the other. Some Scottish merchants did invest in the slave-trade directly through partnerships with people in other ports, and Scottish traders like Richard Oswald and John Tailyour accumulated fortunes as they trafficked captive people on a huge scale even as they invested in improving Scottish agriculture. However, wealth obtained by sending ships directly to colonies in North America and the Caribbean was much more common and significant for the development of the city. By the middle of the eighteenth century, more tobacco was imported into Glasgow than all other British ports together.[29]

Merchants needed facilities like docks, warehouses, shipbuilders and transport links to undertake their trade at any scale, and to support Glasgow's commercial expansion new and improved infrastructure on the River Clyde had been built in the late seventeenth century to facilitate transatlantic shipping. Over the following century, these were improved and expanded to meet the growing needs of the city. Indicative of the wide-ranging support for these projects, the members of the Merchants House in Glasgow – an organisation that had been founded in 1605 to represent the city's traders – selected a committee to promote their collective interests. Twelve men were chosen to stand for the 'Sea Traders', twelve for the 'Home Traders' and a final twelve from among the city's craft guilds: people making their money at home and abroad benefit from increasing trade, after all. Their goal was not to regulate the commercial or manufacturing firms that operated in the city, but rather to use their combined wealth to promote projects that would benefit them all. Following in the best British tradition of reshaping nature for economic benefit, a key focus was to increase navigation to and from the city by improving its access to the sea. In 1755, concerned that the route into the port was 'dangerous for shipping to approach in the nighttime', they proposed that a lighthouse 'properly erected and maintained' on the island of Little Cumbra 'will be of great public use'. Of course, a grateful public would pay for the privilege with higher fees due in Glasgow for use of the city's more accessible docks.[30]

A decade later, another lighthouse was proposed for the 'North and Fourth rocks, very dangerous places where many ships have been wrecked', that lay to the north of Ireland. Again, the Merchants House supported the proposal on the basis that 'much of the shipping of Glasgow' passed nearby. The lighthouses were just the start. Further suggestions that 'removing some shoals and flats' from the river fed the group's ambitions. In 1757, John McCaull, a merchant and representative of the city's guilds, raised concerns again that 'the many inconveniences attending the trade of this place arising from obstructions and sometimes the absolute impossibility of transporting goods' along the Clyde were becoming prohibitive. His motion to make 'the navigation in the said river more certain, easy and commodious' was met with unanimous approval and a petition was dispatched to Westminster seeking an Act of Parliament to support the scheme. Once again, 'defraying the charges which must attend this undertaking' would be met by tolls or duties paid by the people who would use the new infrastructure. In the 1760s, plans to deepen the river were joined by plans to repair and expand the harbour at Port Glasgow, with a huge new basin excavated to welcome the largest ocean-going ships. Not long after, Lang Dyke was built to deepen the Clyde, allowing ships to reach almost the very gates of the city.[31]

Bringing engineering ingenuity to bear on the natural challenges that faced Britain's colonial merchants was not limited to Scotland. In London, too, dock development had reshaped the metropolis over the eighteenth century. By the 1790s, the slave-economy permeated London's commercial landscape, even as the city's diversified economy simultaneously benefited from many other economic activities, including the domination of British trade with Asia and the Mediterranean. Two-thirds of the nation's sugar imports arrived through London's docks, and the capital's financiers were central to organising banking services for much of the Caribbean and the system for purchasing enslaved people in Jamaica. To keep up with this scale of activity, London's shipping facilities had, at great expense, developed alongside its commercial growth. Notably, the West India Dock Company built a dedicated facility to handle sugar, rum and other Caribbean imports on the Isle of Dogs, while the London Dock Company built a complimentary dock in Wapping for receiving wine, brandy, tobacco and rice. Both were built with investment from people involved in colonial trades, but many more investors in both schemes were happy to profit from the improvement of facilities that would receive the fruits of enslaved labour overseas. Networks entangled the commercial lives of people across the city, and developments like the docks and other economic improvements drew on capital with roots in every type of business that London's capitalists took part in. Profits from slavery were a constant feature in its growth.[32]

The importance of slavery to Liverpool's docks, and the port's wider economic development, were more substantial still, and widely recognised by contemporaries. After the construction of the world's oldest commercial wet dock in Liverpool earlier in the eighteenth century, ongoing investment had seen a vast expansion of facilities. The town's Committee for Trade regularly promoted further investment. In the 1770s, almost immediately after it had been founded, the group judged that the harbour at Liverpool was overflowing with shipping and threatened to go to court to force the port's customs officers to let ships unload directly onto the docks to improve efficiency. At the same time, they recommended lengthening the existing dry docks to admit more ships at one time. The same docks were extended again less than a decade later. The King's Dock and Queen's Dock, as they became known, named in honour of George III and his consort Charlotte, were designed by the engineer Henry Barry who also worked on canals connecting the port to Leeds and the Lancashire coalfields. Despite these efforts, by the 1790s increasing trade and constant use meant some of the facilities were deemed to be in 'very bad condition' and the docks' surveyor was instructed to rebuild them once again, 'taking care to introduce proper cranes for hoisting timber and cisterns for water'.[33]

Once completed, in 1794 the docks were praised by the Corporation of Liverpool for the ongoing impact they made not only to the local but also the national economy. The vast dockyard complex on the Mersey was now taking in more than thirty times as much shipping as it had a century before, and the city's luminaries were keen to highlight how they had put their own money at risk 'for affecting these laudable purposes'. Consequently, thanks to the 'superior conveniences of the docks and other local advantages', and of course 'the enterprising spirit of the people', the port had become the hub for 'the trade of Liverpool, and particularly the African trade, which forms the most extensive branch thereof'. Liverpool's trade had grown so large, and so deeply interwoven with the wider national economy, that it 'in effect gives strength and energy to the whole' and had 'arrived at such a pitch of consequence' that it was now 'materially and inseparably connected with the wealth and prosperity of the Kingdom at large'. Development like this underscored how important investing in improvement works could be, and how they needed to take place over multiple generations to promote continuous economic development. As well as supporting the merchants whose goods passed through them, infrastructure like ports supported numerous connected industries, from shipbuilding to timber works to iron manufacture, and increasing trade benefited an even wider array of manufacturers whose products could now be sent to customers overseas.[34]

Using income from transatlantic trade to improve vital infrastructure was just one way in which the wealth obtained by exploiting enslaved African workers found its way into Britain's wider economy. Some industries emerged that directly depended on processing goods that were sourced from colonies in the Caribbean and North America. Sugar arriving in Britain needed to be refined, tobacco had to be processed and retailed to eager customers, and cotton had to be spun and transformed into cloth. Once unloaded in Britain, unrefined muscovado sugar was sold to sugar factories for refining into consumer-ready products: white sugar, powdered sugar, canary sugar and so on. In 1751, the opportunity to take part in this productive and profitable activity led a group of enterprising merchants, manufacturers and landowners to invest £10,000 in a 'Sugar Copartnery' in Edinburgh. Recognising the growing trade 'between the Port of Leith and the sugar-colonies in the British American plantation', and that consumption of sugar was 'much increased', the established 'Edinburgh Sugar House Company' drew capital from merchants like William Alexander and Robert Baillie, but also partners as diverse as the saddler Malcolm Brown, plumber John Graham, jeweller James Ker, surgeon George Cunningham, the senators of the College of Justice Andrew Fletcher and Henry Home, and the Lady Strathnaver. This group provided financial capital and connected the new firm with social networks and a deep pool of expertise across Scotland. Quickly purchasing 'houses with an area of ground in the Canongate', the company 'did invite from London, Hans Christian-Knack, sugar-boiler' to advise on the construction of the sugar house and the purchase of all the necessary equipment they'd need. Overseen by a skilled manager, the sugar house would operate with limited oversight from the company and an elected representative of the investors would visit just once a week to check things were running smoothly. All the partners had to do was sit back, let the technical experts and wage labourers take over, and wait for their dividend. While many of the investors weren't active in transatlantic trade themselves, the refined sugar the company sold certainly had its roots in Caribbean plantations, and they were quite happy to profit from the enslaved people whose labour underpinned the transport of this tropical crop to Scotland's cold shores. In the end, the Edinburgh company lasted only a few years – there was too much competition from capitalists setting up similar projects elsewhere in Britain. In nearby Leith, another attempt, the Leith Sugar House, operated only from 1757 to 1762, while a New Edinburgh Sugar Company founded in 1771 also struggled.[35]

Irrespective of the difficulties of sugar refiners in the Scottish capital, the skills and investment exhibited by the group that founded the sugar partnership were replicated in cities across Britain, and many other sugar houses were set up with greater success as competition drove innovation. Sugar refining had already become an important industry in London by the end of the seventeenth century, and production only increased during the eighteenth. Like many British industries, foreign expertise and technical skill contributed to its development: as an article in the *London Tradesman* lamented in 1747, 'the Dutch are better [sugar] boilers than we, and we have a great number of working boilers from thence and Hamburg' living in the British capital. Around this time, London was home to around eighty sugar refineries, with the largest employing up to a hundred workers. As the industry developed further, it continued to draw on labour and skill from European migrants, especially from Germany, who became workers and managers in British firms. The much smaller town of Bristol had proportionally more refineries in operation, with twenty established in the port, part of the huge investment from colonial merchants in industry and land that reshaped the port and its hinterland during the eighteenth century. The town's refiners were often prominent citizens, merchants and financiers, with social and economic networks across the port and beyond. Indeed, this was often necessary for establishing refineries, which required substantial upfront costs of £8,000 or more, and across Britain they were typically founded by partnerships, drawing on wealth that in part had its origins in transatlantic trade. By the end of the eighteenth century, so much refined sugar was produced in Britain that it not only served the growing demands of the nation's sweet-toothed consumers but had also become a major manufactured product for export: only metal and textile exports were more valuable. Each refinery, of course, added further value to the economy through their payment of wages to workers, consumption of fuel, purchase of copper equipment and so on.[36]

As well as benefiting from the import of colonial goods, British firms also profited from manufacturing products moving in the opposite direction. Plantations' stores and provisions filled the holds of British ships travelling westward over the Atlantic, as well as those that traversed between British colonies carrying foodstuffs from North America to the Caribbean. The Glasgow trader Houston, for instance, obtained goods from suppliers across northern Britain but also as far away as Bristol, where a brick works had been set up to supply the south-western port's own Caribbean trade but was happy to sell stock to the Scottish ship owner, too. Other manufacturers that benefited from overseas trade included firms like the gunpowder mills of Bristol, gunmakers in Birmingham, linen manufactories of Scotland, and the cotton spinners of Manchester. Shipbuilders in every port, of course, benefited, too, as did the various subsidiary manufacturers that supported them.

Britain's metallurgical industries were particularly strongly linked with markets in the Atlantic. Exports of brass and copper to Africa alone, an important market given the high demand for these goods for the purchase of enslaved people, tripled in the first three decades of the eighteenth century, and by the 1780s had tripled again, joining the even larger sale of iron products as the main goods British slave-traders sold on the African coast. The growth of shipping to Africa boosted copper industries in Britain as well, and the up-and-coming Liverpudlian slave-trader Boats was one of the first slave-traders to spend money on copper sheathing to protect his vessels from wood-boring parasites. Many others followed. The importance of Atlantic slave-economies for the British metal industry didn't end with the purchase of enslaved people. In the Caribbean, where enslaved labour made up the vast majority of workers in plantations across all of Britain's colonies, the production of sugar and rum were heavily dependent on copper goods from the metropole. Operating at an industrial scale, huge copper vessels called clarifiers were needed to collect the sap from sugar cane, the largest of which reached 1,000 gallons' capacity. More usually, average-sized plantations producing around twenty hogshead of sugar a week required three clarifiers of up to 400 gallons each. Rum, too, needed copper utensils for the distillation process, and stills capable of holding between 600 and 1,100 gallons were typical, while the largest estates invested in receptacles two or three times larger than this. All depended on enslaved workers to work in the fields where sugar cane was grown in the first place but also throughout its processing.[37]

Not surprisingly, the scale of these industrial processes meant that the Caribbean generated a massive demand for copper products and the rapid expansion of sugar production depended on the simultaneous growth of copper extraction and manufacturing in Britain, as well as a corresponding increase in enslaved people working in the plantations. In the four decades after the establishment of an intensive British smelting industry in the 1720s, the export of copper products to Jamaica increased almost four times, while sugar production on the island more than doubled during the same period. The impact of linking industry and empire could hardly be clearer. For every seven tons of copper goods shipped overseas in 1770, one was destined for plantations in Jamaica, while other sugar plantations across Britain's Caribbean colonies accounted for another two. The demands of sugar production made the Caribbean by far the largest overseas market for British copper, followed by the East India Company's trade to Asia, the trapped market of Ireland, and slave-traders in Africa. Little more than a tenth of Britain's copper exports reached markets in Europe and the Mediterranean. For many copper miners, smelters, refiners and manufacturers in Britain, the ruthless exploitation of enslaved workers in the Caribbean generated a major market for their goods.[38]

Copper mining could barely keep pace with the demand for the metal in Atlantic markets, which absorbed the majority of all copper mined in Britain in the 1770s. By this point, innovation and expansion of Britain's copper industry had already increased production from virtually nothing at the start of the century to almost 25,000 tons, almost all of which was dug from Cornish mines. In south Wales, copper smelting, too, had grown at remarkable rates since the first decades of the eighteenth century, and between Cornish extraction and Welsh production, imports of Swedish copper into Britain by the 1780s had been completely substituted, despite the increase in demand from copper manufacturers. The growth in production had also been buoyed by technological breakthroughs, including the reverberatory furnace that substituted coal for charcoal in smelting and the addition of steam-powered pumps for draining deeper mines, which had a major impact on copper mining and manufacturing as well as other metallurgical industries. Indeed, as their biggest single market, Cornwall had proved especially important for Boulton and Watt's sale of steam engines, with the county and its copper playing a critical role in the machine's commercial success: by 1780, Cornish mine owners had ordered forty of the machines.[39]

In the final decades of the eighteenth century, a further boost was given by the exploitation of new mines in Anglesey at Mynydd Parys, where the Welsh lawyer Thomas Williams was appointed manager in 1785. In the following fifteen years, an enormous amount of copper was extracted, processed and shipped from facilities that included huge buildings at Ravenhead and Stanley, smelting furnaces at Amlwch, a cluster of mills in Holywell, and a veritable fleet of coasters sailing out of a newly developed port. Indeed, the copper mine made such remarkable wealth so quickly that it came to overshadow the Peruvian Potosí mine in the British imagination of inconceivable extractive riches. From sites across Cornwall and Wales, then, copper was shipped onwards to further factories and workshops in places like Bristol and London where it would be fashioned into the products that customers overseas desperately sought. The demand for copper boilers, coolers and rum stills and other equipment in slave-economies made it among the most dynamic industries in Britain, connecting thousands of workers across Britain to enslaved labour in sugar producing colonies throughout the Caribbean, while creating vast fortunes for capitalists who exploited them on both sides of the Atlantic. The dynamic industrial hubs of Cornwall and south Wales were intricately and deeply entwined with colonial exploitation, even though the goods they produced passed through a number of different manufacturing stages before they were eventually shipped from Glasgow, Bristol, London or Liverpool to their ultimate destinations overseas.[40]

The importance of colonial goods and markets to industries in Britain as different as sugar refining and copper mining attests to the impact of this connected system on various sectors within Britain's economy. In ports like Liverpool, these links were deep and widespread, and all sorts of businesses in the bustling port profited and grew thanks to wealth and goods flowing from colonies overseas. Over multiple generations, colonial trade transformed the port as well as those who lived in it. The work of the carpenter William Rathbone was indicative of how networks connecting colonial capital to business enterprise could change the town. Not only had he been fixing ships for slave-traders like Thomas Gildart and Richard Trafford in the 1740s but he was also offering his services to bakers and brewers, who in turn supplied merchants and workers of all stripes. At the same time, Rathbone's work shaped the grand new buildings of Liverpool's churches and its corporation, even if his contribution was small and very likely went unseen. Even through the small workshop of a craftsman like Rathbone, networks passed that tied together business, social and political life in the port. Rathbone's imprint on the built environment of Liverpool was not his only legacy: the profits from his labour and skill were enough so that his son, also William, could enter the business world as a ship owner and merchant himself, with business interests connecting Liverpool with Ireland and London, as well as ports further afield. His son, another William, grew the family business further still, and established the Rathbone firm as a major force in Liverpool's transatlantic trading community. As well as keeping their interest in selling tropical woods, the Rathbones were also beneficiaries of enslaved labour through the sale of sugar and especially cotton. With close ties to the Reynolds family who helped develop the iron industry in Coalbrookdale, among many other relationships with people beyond Liverpool, the Rathbone family were deeply integrated within the wider social networks and exchanges that were so vital for Britain's development. Within a few decades, the Rathbone family had seized the opportunities that a booming port like Liverpool provided and had moved from migrant craftsmen to the highest levels of the city's business elite.[41]

Not every capitalist in Liverpool was as successful as the Rathbones, but stories like this were not uncommon. Liverpool was growing incredibly quickly, and opportunities for profit across a broad sweep of economic activities grew alongside the town's participation in the slave-trade. The knock-on effect of new wealth could be felt everywhere, and beneficiaries even included people like musicians from London hired to perform 'several concerts of music every month', or the ministers employed to serve the port's dissenting community at a newly built Octagon Chapel, a church whose founding benefactors included slave-traders like John Hogson and John Dobson and the Manchester warehouse owner Thomas Bentley, who would soon found a long-time partnership with the potter Josiah Wedgwood. Shipping and port facilities, as noted already, were more obvious beneficiaries of investment, and the impact of their development was considerable. Infrastructure like this only tied Liverpool more deeply into an expanding transport system, including better roads and canals, which in turn supported the expansion of new industries in the port itself as well as facilitating business and personal connections with people in the manufacturing hinterlands of Manchester and elsewhere in northern Britain. At nearby Lachford, paper mills, gunpowder mills and slitting mills butted up against each other along the River Mersey while, next door in Warrington, manufacturers making copper, refined sugar and glass likewise benefited from the same close links to the booming markets of Liverpool and Manchester. Around Warrington, thousands of workers were employed making linen sails for the Royal Navy alone, in contracts valued at £70,000 a year by the 1760s.[42]

Slave-traders were found taking part in all manner of businesses alongside their investment in vessels that carried captive people across the Atlantic. Property was a particularly common and attractive investment. Richardson owned property in Liverpool, Lancaster and Hawcoat while Kaye owned property in Fazakerley and Walton-on-the-Hill. These were two men whose investment in shipping and property overlapped with core business interests in sailmaking and linen manufacture, respectively. The merchant Hunt invested in Liverpool property, renting out dwelling houses to people who found work in the growing town. Slave-traders also invested in larger manufacturing enterprises. The firm Roger Fisher & Sons, of which Hunt was a partner, invested in industrial sites including a timber yard, while John and Thomas Hodgson invested in a cotton mill in Caton. Business networks that facilitated investment across industries and welcomed partnerships between people from varied backgrounds made it possible for capitalists like these to establish interests across different sectors, strengthening each in turn through the transmission of social, financial and human capital.[43]

Many of Liverpool's largest slave-traders took advantage of similar opportunities. Staniforth, who had travelled from Sheffield to the port to make his fortune, used his access to vessels and maritime labour in Liverpool to take advantage of numerous opportunities in addition to profiting from the enslavement of African people. After 1771, he also started buying ivory, which could be highly profitable, with his largest single haul valued at £7,006 and carried home on a single voyage in 1781. Occasionally, too, his ships carried back African gold, although this was a rarity. The Liverpool ship owner also used his ships to extract wealth from the Atlantic Ocean itself, sending at first one and then two ships each year to the rich fishing grounds around Greenland, where they obtained whales, seals and even the occasional 'unicorn' (narwhal). Staniforth also took advantage of Britain's far-flung trading opportunities. His ships were dispatched to destinations including Bordeaux, Gothenburg, Hamburg and Bremen in Europe, as well as carrying goods directly from Liverpool to North American destinations like New York and Virginia. Iron was the main British export he noted in his ledgers for these voyages. Finally, in times of war, Staniforth was more than willing to arm his ships and send them on 'privateering' voyages to capture foreign merchant vessels and bring the rich prizes home. All this he did, of course, while profiting from the transport of almost 25,000 captives to colonies in the Americas. By the 1780s, Staniforth had earned enough from these activities to launch a bank in Liverpool alongside partners that included his father-in-law Goore and Francis Ingram, the latter one of the most active slave-traders in British history. In 1797, the Sheffield-born Staniforth was elected Mayor of Liverpool. His son Samuel followed in his father's footsteps and continued to profit from the same tangled web of interests in slavery, shipping, trade and finance.[44]

Whereas the Staniforths invested mostly in other maritime ventures alongside the slave-trade, other prominent slave-traders took advantage of a much wider range of opportunities. This was the pattern pursued by Chaffers and Lace, whose violent ambition had so dramatically expanded Liverpool slave-traders' access to markets in Old Calabar in 1767. Chaffers had invested in voyages to Africa alongside not only Lace but also major slave-traders such as William Earle, Davenport and Jonathan Blundell. Links with each would all continue to shape Chaffers's business and long after he had stopped investing in the slave-trade: social networks and business opportunities blended throughout his life. While he was still involved in the slave-trade, Chaffers began to invest in opportunities that were emerging in the port of Liverpool's hinterland. One of the largest investors in the Leeds and Liverpool Canal, Chaffers was at the leading edge of a boom in canal building that was reshaping the dynamics of trade between northern Britain's growing manufacturing towns and his home port. Chaffers's investment in Britain's industry and infrastructure didn't end there, and alongside his long-term partners in the slave-trade, Earle and Blundell, he invested in establishing a major coal-mining enterprise not far from Liverpool. This coal concern was not a small undertaking. It involved purchasing flats, barges and vessels, to the tune of £480, to transport coal from mines in Aspul, Ince and Wigan along the Douglas Navigation and Leeds and Liverpool Canal. A further £1,600 was then expended on purchasing plots of land in Liverpool where the partnership's coal yard was built, close to the banks of the River Mersey in Oldhall Street. Significantly, part of this land was soon granted to the Leeds and Liverpool Canal, which happened to have Blundell and Chaffers as prominent investors, who used it to build their basin terminus. This was of mutual benefit and the coal partnership subsequently erected 'a weighing engine, countinghouse and other conveniences' and cut a channel to directly access the canal basin.[45]

While this was the extent of Chaffers's interest, Blundell continued to expand his property holdings across Lancashire, including land near Chorley that Samuel Oldknow had leased to build his nerve centre of a rapidly growing cotton-spinning and -weaving enterprise. Much of Blundell's investment focused on coal, though, and in time he bought out his partners in the Liverpool coal yard and purchased collieries in Lancashire which he ruthlessly improved to maximise production. By 1793, if not earlier, Blundell had installed a powerful steam engine at, at least, one of his collieries, that was capable of pumping 53,640 cubic feet of water, which John Rennie, the Scottish canal engineer, hoped could be used to fill the locks in the nearby canal. The Blundell coal business continued to grow, and by the nineteenth century was among the largest mining companies in the country.[46]

Around the same time, another family member, Henry Blundell, had likewise used his wealth and experience of Liverpool's colonial economy as a launchpad for expansion into other business interests: in this case, government contracting and finance. During his earlier career he had worked in London as a merchant, linking his experience of Liverpool's transatlantic trades with the capital's even broader commercial opportunities. These underpinned projects like a partnership with Henry William Mason and Nicholas Masterson to provide supplies for the Royal Navy. This was a massive contract with the state. The partners invested £12,000 together in the hope that the three men's experience of trade, shipping and agricultural markets would overcome any challenges. Around the same time, Henry set up another partnership with George Dallas 'in the business and employ of insurance brokers', paying £500 for the privilege of inserting himself into the existing business. Dallas would provide the experience and the younger Blundell the capital. Two generations earlier, Henry's grandfather, Bryan Blundell, had been among the first of Liverpool's merchants to exploit the opportunities that trafficking enslaved people and transporting goods from colonial markets could offer. By the end of the century, the family had transformed this wealth into a business and industrial empire that brought them even more profit exploiting land, labour and technology across the widest expanse of Britain's industrialising economy.[47]

These were only some of the many slave-traders who invested their wealth into developing Britain's burgeoning industrial infrastructure. The nearby Bolton and Bury Canal was likewise built in part with capital from Liverpool. Costing £127,000, the canal's investors included the Earl of Derby, a landowner with property across Liverpool, numerous traders, landowners and manufacturers, and members of the slave-trading and banking Heywood family. Further links to the port could be seen in the participation of cotton manufacturer Robert Peel, who owned a mill alongside the proposed route of the canal, who depended on raw cotton arriving in the port for his business, natural fibres that often originated in plantations that exploited enslaved labour. Canals like these would carry goods from a deep hinterland to the docks at Liverpool, and vice versa.[48]

As these varied experiences of business enterprise suggest, there was no single way by which capitalists sought to take advantage of the colonial trade. Sometimes, the slave-trade was a small, speculative investment made to supplement income from other work; sometimes, it was a central part of businesses over many years, with investment in other ventures making up a speculative, additional source of income. In either case, the slave-trade was part of an economic system that saw profits from this exploitation reinvested into other commercial opportunities, just as profits from Britain's agriculture, trade and industry were invested in the slave-trade. It was a cyclical and symbiotic relationship.

In the 1790s, British capitalists who profited from the transatlantic economy faced what they saw as existential threats to their businesses:

*10. Hope that 'East India Sugar' from Bengal might replace that of the Caribbean was used as an opportunity by the abolitionist movement to show that alternative sources of the precious commodity could be found, an idea encapsulated by the production of vessels like this in the following decades.*

growing support for the abolition of the slave-trade, and sugar planting in Bengal creating competition with the crop they carried from the Caribbean. Although neither threat was realised immediately, with the abolition of the slave-trade not taking place until 1807 and efforts to grow sugar in India failing spectacularly, proponents of the slave-trade were incentivised to set out the importance of colonial commerce, as they saw it, for private profit and the British nation as a whole. The risk of revolt by enslaved people, likewise, was a threat to the very fabric of the British empire, and fear that something like the

Haitian Revolution, that had seen the French colonial state thrown out of Saint-Domingue by a rebellion led by Toussaint Louverture, was reason enough to strengthen the imperial hold over British positions rather than restrict it. In addition to political risks like these, the wider concerns of the abolitionist movement were roundly dismissed by slave-traders as nothing more than 'the zeal of certain speculative writers' and 'associations' with 'the avowed purpose of annihilating the commerce in slaves': a position that, in the mind of these pro-slavery capitalists, was anti-business and antithetical to the very British freedoms on which the nation's wealth depended.[49]

The importance and value of colonial commerce was well known and used by proponents of slavery, who of course sought to present their trade in the most positive light, to resist the abolitionist movement. Indicative of this trend was a 1792 tract called 'The Case of the Sugar Colonies', whose author was keen to remind his readers that the quick riches and bloodshed that had defined Spanish conquest in the Caribbean was far removed from the 'more slow, but certain means of acquiring wealth by agriculture' that defined British colonisation in the region. This had been no easy process, readers were told, and early colonists had lacked the discipline for 'the monotonous occupations of husbandry', severely limiting the exploitation of the region's great capacity for sugar production. The breakthrough came only following the transportation of enslaved African labourers, whose back-breaking work on plantations increased sugar production 5,000 per cent between 1660 and 1790. The author understood that this trajectory would be recognised and accepted by his readers, noting that 'there are few who stand in need of being told', and there was no further need to persuade them of the impact of slavery on Britain's colonial wealth. For the people profiting from the vast expansion of sugar production in the Caribbean, exploiting enslaved labour had become as natural as exploiting the fertile soils and tropical conditions that the islands offered.[50]

Another tract written in 1792, 'founded on plain facts and incontrovertible arguments', and confidently entitled by its author 'An Appeal to the Candour and Justice of the People of England', condemned 'the unfair arts' of the abolition movement. Concerned that the abolition position spent more time worrying about nebulous concepts of 'humanity' than it did offering a 'candid and dispassionate' view of how slavery profited Britain, the author hoped that their text would fill that void. What was needed, they were sure, was 'an investigation very different from which it [the slave-trade] has received' that recognised abolition 'involves in its consequences the marine, the manufactures, the trade, and the finances of England'. Indeed, 'with respect to the value of the African and West India trade to this country, examined either separately or connectively, no person has yet presumed to doubt the benefits derived from them'. Indeed, it was clear that 'the manufacturers and merchants of this country find their interest materially allied to the existence of the former'. If the slave-trade were abolished, they believed the disaster would be immense: 'several hundred ships, several thousand sailors, and some millions of industrious mechanics would lose their employment'. The impact would be so catastrophic that, they warned, it might even lead to social unrest and revolution.[51]

The growth of Liverpool in particular was highlighted as a positive outcome from the trade, and was used as an argument against its abolition. Promoting the slave-trade was taken on by the Board of Trade in Liverpool, who set aside funds for printing and publishing texts on the 'African Slave Trade' that would 'promote the interest of the freemen and merchants of this port in a very important article of commerce'. Likewise, money was set aside to support a delegate who would travel to London 'to oppose the abolition of the African slave trade'. A petition from the port explained that, in the view of 'the Mayor, Aldermen, Bailiffs and Common Council of the Town of Liverpool', the risk of abolition was enormous. They urged the House of Lords to remember that the slave-trade was deeply and inextricably linked with the wider British economy. Abolition, they argued, would 'so materially and essentially affect not only the revenues and estates of this corporation and the general welfare and prosperity of the town and port of Liverpool but also the public revenue of the landed interest, the manufactories and the maritime strength of the Kingdom in general'. Landowners, industrialists and merchants alike profited from the slave-economy, and the civic leadership of Liverpool were keen to remind the landowning doyens in Parliament of that fact.[52]

Over the following decade, pressure to end the transatlantic slave-trade increased, even as the number of captive African people being transported to lives of slavery also increased; plantation owners rushed to market to ensure the end of the trade wouldn't leave them without the workers they believed they needed. After 1807, when the slave-trade was finally abolished, over 750,000 enslaved people continued to live and work in British colonies, and a further four million lived in the United States. Their labour continued to extract vital materials for Britain's booming industrial economy long after the trade in enslaved people was declared illegal. Abolitionists who went on to promote the sale of pots bearing ethical branding encouraging consumers to buy sugar that was 'Not Made By Slaves' were aspiring towards British consumption that no longer depended on enslaved labour. In the eighteenth century, though, this was little more than a dream of a better tomorrow. No small part of Britain's economy was tied to the labour of enslaved people working in plantations thousands of miles away. The impact of slavery and colonial goods on Britain was deep and wide-ranging, shaping intense regional development, the expansion of major ports, the growth of industry and the wealth of thousands of British people whose livelihoods were linked in some way to the transatlantic economy. This was all built on the suffering of enslaved African people whose labour made it possible. During Britain's rise to wealth and power in the eighteenth century, the lives of millions of people were spent in the name of profit.

CHAPTER 10

# THE EMPIRE'S NEW CLOTHES

## Cotton and the Transformation of British Industry

In 1785, the Marquis of Lansdowne quipped that if 'you were to ask a manufacturer of Halifax ... what was the greatest crime upon earth, was it felony, was it murder, was it patricide? he would answer, no, none of these; it was the exporting of wool'! Fifteen years later, they might have given a different answer. In just a few short years, Britain's most important product for more than a century was supplanted by the manufacture of a fabric that had barely been made in Britain even a hundred years before: cotton cloth.

Sumptuous high-quality cotton fabrics had started to reach Britain in large numbers in the previous century, after the East India Company began importing them in growing quantities directly from India. The highest-quality cottons known as muslins quickly drew admirers; at the very highest end of the market, they were so light that they would become known as 'woven wind'. Somewhat cheaper cloths known as calicos, still made entirely of cotton but with thicker threads and weaves, were also highly prized as light, durable cloths ideally suited for dyeing and printing. Indian cloth was made in an enormous range of styles, patterns and colours that dazzled and inspired customers across Britain, Europe, Africa and Asia. They quickly became a staple of cargoes carried by British merchants, re-exported alongside the woollens on which so much of the country's trade depended.

However, even as they drew delighted customers to the stalls of British merchants, cottons presented a challenge for the British state:

how could they support British woollen manufacturers in the face of such competition? Complaints about the threat of imports of manufactured textiles from 'India, Persia or China' built in the early eighteenth century, as 'the decay of trade' for clothiers, weavers and textile merchants was blamed 'principally by reason of the wearing printed, painted and stained calicos and linens'. This led to legislation known as the Calico Acts, which sought to protect British textile industries by banning the sale of all cotton goods in Britain, with the exception of raw cotton or British-made fustians. The East India Company could continue to carry the cloths back to Britain so long as they were re-exported, keeping the magnificent Indian cloth in the public eye but protecting British manufacturers from competition.

The allure of cotton, though, never went away. Consumer demand was already pushing British manufacturers to make lighter, thinner and more colourful fabrics, and those trends continued over the course of the eighteenth century. The addition of natural fibres from flax, silkworms and cotton plants had pushed innovative designs and processes further, with linen and silk especially seeing a rapid increase in production after the necessary technology was acquired and mills built to accommodate new type of production. By the middle of the eighteenth century, linen and silk products were made in considerable volumes, with specialised industries in places like Edinburgh or Macclesfield supporting numerous incremental improvements in production and design. Cotton, though, despite some success in spinning thread and mixing it with wool or linen, did not establish itself as a major industry during the same period. Indeed, producing more cotton cloth in Britain would not have been a priority for the state or merchants. The East India Company might struggle to sell traditional British woollens in places like Bengal, where it remained 'so heavy an article' that many Indian consumers were uninterested, but across Europe and North America there were plenty of customers who were very happy to buy them. In time, even the trade of woollens to Asia doubled in size, as new, lighter varieties moved into production. British wool was a huge incumbent industry, and protecting it was much more important to the state than competing with Indian textiles on international markets. Indeed, the latter might have seemed like a fool's errand. Indian artisans were producing huge volumes of magnificent cotton fabrics that Britain simply could not hope to match with the tools it had.

What Britain's cotton industry needed was a catalyst for explosive growth, which it found as new ways to exploit land, labour and technology transformed how Britain's cotton industry was powered, supplied and mechanised. It was not going to be easy: the raw material could not be grown in Britain and the nation's textile workers had little expertise in its production. However, a trapped market of millions for fustians – cloths that mixed cotton and other fibres – was certainly an incentive to try. Although designed to protect existing woollen, silk and linen manufacture, as time passed, the Calico Acts helped sustain the possibility that a domestic cotton industry might be competitive. The nascent industries taking shape by the turn of the eighteenth century, which sought to make lighter fabrics and combine several types of fibre, were the first step towards establishing a cotton industry in Britain that was protected by state policies. In time, they developed a whole new way of working that transformed how cotton cloth could be produced. By the 1770s, British manufacturers were lobbying for the Calico Acts to be repealed: they were now ready to sell pure cotton cloths of all sorts to an eager consuming public in Britain and were willing to risk the competition from an influx of Indian cottons.

By the end of the eighteenth century, British capitalists had successfully exploited their networked capital to build, from scratch, an industry that was a driving force for the nation's ongoing industrial transformation and made them hugely wealthy in the process. Made from a plant that grew nowhere in the land, the British cotton industry depended on supply chains that crossed oceans and shaped the lives of millions long before the precious fibres were fed into bustling, clattering factories that were transforming how people lived and worked in Britain. As exports boomed, British cotton goods began to make an impact on markets worldwide. In 1803, for the first time, woollens lost their place as Britain's most valuable export. A truly global product had taken its place.[1]

## RISE OF THE MACHINE

In the sixteenth century, the north-west of England had been dismissed by the London-based John Leake, who was responsible for searching cloth sold in the capital to weed out poor-quality products, as a region 'where no true cloths [of pure wool] are made', and it certainly was far from Britain's wool manufacturing heartlands in the rich and highly regulated cloth-producing towns in the south of the country. Yet, the north-west was already the home of myriad manufacturers, but ones that focused on producing fabrics that were produced without the oversight and regulation of southern guilds. Rather than sticking with wool alone, textile workers in the region had turned to other fibres to produce novel varieties of cloth. This included flax that was locally grown or imported from Ireland and used to produce linen, an industry that had employed as much as a third of the Lancashire labouring population as early as the sixteenth century. The region was also quick to adopt imported raw cotton as a useful fibre, mixing it with linen to make fustian, which was first produced around Manchester in the first decades of the seventeenth century. These innovations set Manchester and the wider Lancashire region apart, and already by 1641, the successful merchant Lewes Roberts, who had traded extensively across Europe and the Mediterranean, commended how 'they buy cotton wool in London, that comes from Cyprus and Smyrna, and at home work the same and persist it into fustians, vermilions, dimity, and other such stuffs, and then return it to London where the same is vented and sold'. 'It may be wished,' he added, 'that all other parts of our country could be so industrious.'[2]

Initially limited in scale, much of the wider region's early textile work focused on buttons, lace, ribbons and other narrow ware. Still, this array of textile work helped to create the conditions for textile industrialisation in the eighteenth century. Much like the concurrent growth of silk production in Macclesfield and Congleton or the founding of new metallurgical industries in Swansea, Carron and Birmingham, the growth of northern Britain's cotton manufacturing was driven by a confluence of factors that included a skilled workforce, suitable environmental conditions, and a base of investors and traders familiar with the trade. Britain's existing textile industry provided foundations on which cotton production depended, and workers, inventors and traders who were already familiar with textiles would find it easier to adapt existing practices than people with no relevant skills at all. However, turning Britain into a leading producer of cotton cloth by the end of the eighteenth century would be a long and winding road. No single technological leap or productive process could make that happen. Large-scale cotton manufacturing in Britain required interlinking benefits from many different parts of the economy to bring it about: innovation in textile technology, advances in using water to power mills, agricultural improvements that left workers in need of employment, the expansion of territory in North America, the exploitation of enslaved people to pick cotton, and the constant inspiration provided by the beautiful fabrics of skilled Indian manufacturers. British capitalists also depended on strict controls on the import of Indian cotton thread and cloth, which was produced more cheaply and at qualities far higher than workers in Britain could hope to match. On an equal footing, the new industry stood no chance.[3]

In 1720, in an effort to outdo producers in India, a group describing themselves as 'eminent merchants, linen drapers and other considerable traders and manufacturers of this Kingdom' sought government support to launch a cotton manufacturing industry in Britain. Part of their demand, that the sale of Indian cotton cloth should be banned, was met by the 1721 Calico Act, but the group's wider ambitions reflected the changing global perspective that made even the notion of a British cotton industry possible. Their scheme depended on obtaining over 600 tons of raw cotton every year, and they saw the exploitation of land in Britain's American colonies as the most likely source for such a huge increase. Increasing demand for raw cotton in Britain would 'cause large tracts of land, now uncultivated and waste, to be annually tilled, to the great advantage of our plantations', and increase the profits of landowners in the colonies. Likewise, 'the number of slaves, which must necessarily be employed in raising cotton' would increase, and these would be purchased in Africa with 'our commodities of all kinds, and thereby employ many of our manufacturers and artificers' in Britain. The group believed implementing their new venture would employ '4,006 weavers, 32,051 spinners, 2,003 winders and 100 warpers': the equivalent of the population of Manchester four times over. Once up and running, a British cotton industry, they predicted, would 'transplant a very considerable branch of the treasures of the Indies into Great Britain'. It was a ludicrously ambitious project for a world-dominating British cotton industry and did not attract serious investment. However, the general structure of the international market they imagined was not far off. Over the following decades, government protection against Indian competition, the extraction of raw cotton from American territories, and the exploitation of enslaved African workers would all contribute to the transformation of Britain's textile industry. This global system remained the same, even as a technological revolution that would fundamentally alter how raw cotton was processed in Britain took place.[4]

There was no hope of growing cotton in Britain, and early cotton entrepreneurs accepted that they needed to import the raw fibres. Replicating the work of Indian producers required not only using the same material, cotton, but also finding ways to match the skills of craftsmen who had been continuously improving their techniques for hundreds of years. Matching the market-approved Indian product demanded a steep learning curve, but having a pattern to replicate also presented manufacturers with a clear target, as well as presenting some opportunity to gain knowledge about how to accomplish it through observation and experimentation. The innovation that underpinned Britain's cotton-led industrialisation was driven by the attempt to match the quality of Indian cottons, a competitive stimulus that offered benchmarks for every stage of the manufacturing process that could be recognised by consumers in Britain and abroad.[5]

The first major hurdle for British cotton manufacturers stemmed from the need to dramatically improve the methods available for spinning thread. Primarily, this was a question of improving quality, and advances in spinning technology needed to increase the fineness and strength of thread if there was any chance of competing with Indian cotton fabric, but increasing productivity mattered, too. In the early eighteenth century, efforts to produce cotton yarn had succeeded only in producing coarser threads, which would never produce fine cotton cloth, no matter how talented the weaver using it. Spinning mechanisation was already under way in Britain by the 1720s, following the acquisition of Italian technology by John and Thomas Lombe and the establishment of their silk mill in Derby, and this served as an inspiration for later cotton manufacturers. Around the same time, Elias Barnes attempted to spin fine cotton yarn, specifically to rival Indian muslins in the global market, but his invention was little more than a modification of existing spinning wheels, and neither extra spindles nor a source of power were added that might have simultaneously increased productivity. While the wheel did successfully produce more uniform yarn, there was little enthusiasm for the design in Britain, forcing Barnes to leave for France where the new wheel was adopted in numerous provinces. Unfortunately, making small improvements without increasing the volume of yarn produced had limited commercial value. In the following decades, efforts by Lewis Paul and John Wyatt led to some watermills having machinery installed for spinning cotton, but these too struggled competitively.

Two breakthroughs came in the 1760s, with James Hargreaves's spinning jenny and Richard Arkwright's water frame both offering mechanical solutions for the key challenge facing cotton spinners in Britain. Together, the two devices helped increase the strength and volume of cotton yarn produced by any single worker. They also began a process of transferring the responsibility for quality from the spinner to the machine: an important step in shifting the role of workers from that of skilled craftsmen whose feel, control and dexterity shaped their product, to a uniformity of production that depended instead on the quality of the machine being used. The operators of Arkwright's water frame were mainly responsible for refilling the rovings that fed cotton onto the machine, piecing together broken yarn ends, and removing the bobbins full of spun yarn. Unskilled workers, including children, could work on the new device. More yarn could be made, workers could be paid less, and product quality had improved: it was a capitalist's dream. The smooth, wiry yarn produced on the new device was usable in all sorts of cotton goods, including calicos entirely made of cotton. Production volumes could now increase, but, there was still some way to go before machines could produce yarn to compete with the finest Indian fabrics. By 1769, visitors to Manchester understood that cotton production had been 'greatly improved of late', but neither Hargreaves nor Arkwright were given the credit. Rather, according to the editors of *The Tour through Great Britain*, it was their 'imitation of the silk manufactories of Genoa' (most likely a reference to Arkwright's observation of the silk mill built by the Lombe brothers), the 'invention' of new products and designs, and new looms that had been 'improved by some inventions adopted from the Dutch'. Like so many developments in Britain's economic transformation, causes were often numerous, widespread and interconnected.[6]

The advent of improved spinning technology, especially once Arkwright's device was connected to a waterwheel at his new mill in Cromford in 1771, began to transform how cotton production was organised. Suddenly, larger mills with machinery and waterpower together contributing to worker productivity meant that more capital and more control over workers could be used to boost profits. Indeed, the water frame was responsible for dramatically changing where spinning could take place, with the larger machine unsuitable for spinners' homes, especially with the added cost and facilities needed to power them with water. Arkwright jealously protected his patented technology and dominated the development of mills using the device in the 1770s. Indeed, by the end of the decade there were only about twenty mills across Britain that had installed water frames to spin cotton, all of which were either owned by Arkwright, his partners, or proprietors who paid him for permission to use the machine.[7]

A jump in productivity only came after Arkwright's patent was successfully challenged for the first time in 1781, and in the following eight years around 190 more mills were built that used water frames to spin cotton. This was a remarkable expansion of the industry, and far quicker than what had followed the mechanisation of silk production in Derby half a century earlier. Concentrated in northern Britain, the new cotton mills were often remarkably similar, with cotton capitalists choosing to replicate the design of Arkwright's Cromford mill: three or four storeys tall and using a 10-horse-power waterwheel to drive 1,000 spindles (similar, in turn, to the nearby silk mill, which Arkwright had taken care to visit before constructing his own cotton mill). They cost around £3,000. Improvements to spinning machinery, too, had seen the cost and size of the machine become untenable for many previously independent workers. Instead, textile workers were increasingly likely to be employed as wage labourers in larger workshops, producing yarn that was then sold on to capitalists employing the putting-out system, who would then distribute the yarn to weavers. The proliferation of mills created firms with huge numbers of workers and facilities spread across the country, with the largest like Robert Peel's firm operating twenty-three mills across Blackburn, Bury, Bolton, Burton upon Trent and Tamworth. At a slightly smaller scale, William Douglas and his partners owned nine mills spread between Manchester, north Wales, and Scotland, while the Robinsons of Nottingham owned five mills in close proximity near the city. Not all cotton capitalists oversaw enterprises on this scale, and some developed slowly as partnerships combining capital and expertise set out to take advantage of opportunities by converting existing watermills to produce cotton or build a single mill in a viable location.[8]

This expansion had been helped by a further technological leap, in 1779, through the combination of parts from Arkwright's and Hargreaves's machines by Samuel Crompton, whose new spinning mule made it possible for manufacturers to increase both quality and output. These were larger and more complex devices and required both physical strength and mechanical ability, and they further removed the need for dexterity or skill with fibres from the spinning process. Britain's absence of skilled labour, like the artisans who made the highest-quality yarn in India, had begun to be overcome with technology. The mule spread rapidly across the north-west of England, and female workers using spinning jennies were quickly displaced by male spinners using the new device. Requiring strength and endurance, mule spinners were relatively well paid, but it didn't require lengthy training to use and individual spinners were increasingly interchangeable as part of a growing industrial workforce of wage labourers. After the development of Crompton's mule, fine-quality cottons and muslins could be produced in Britain for the first time, with weavers able to benefit from the fine yarn that had previously been denied them. Crompton credited his device as the 'mechanism that has produced and increased one of the first manufactories in Europe' of 'many sorts of cotton goods that were made in an inferior manner before', which were now replaced with high-quality muslins and calicos 'all of which would have been lost to us without this machine'.[9]

The inventor sold the patent of the new machine to David Dale, who had trained as a handloom weaver in Scotland before working as an agent for a firm that used a putting-out system to make linen cloth. He then worked as a clerk for a silk merchant: the enterprising capitalist understood the textile business from top to bottom. As his wealth grew, Dale became an important figure in Glasgow's mercantile community, forming strong relationships with traders who had made their fortunes in colonial trade. In the 1780s, Dale entered into a partnership with Arkwright to establish a major cotton-spinning development at New Lanark in Scotland, before taking full control of the enterprise in 1786. Before long, Dale employed more than a thousand workers at the site, which combined a complex water-management system with powerful waterwheels and the newest spinning technology to rapidly grow into the major Scottish supplier of cotton yarn. With raw cotton readily available in the nearby port of Glasgow, where it had been transported primarily from plantations in America, Dale had an ideal set-up to take advantage of new technology and colonial supply. At the nearby Paisley works, too, English investors and Scottish manufacturers worked together to set up mills that could take advantage of the region's ideal landscape and close location to the Glasgow and Edinburgh markets. Through technology, a whole new industry had been born.[10]

Reaching this stage had been no easy process. Indeed, Arkwright had depended on networked capital to support and develop his industrial vision. Among his partners was Jedediah Strutt, a technologically sophisticated inventor in his own right. The son of a small farmer and maltster, Strutt grew up in a Presbyterian community in

Derbyshire, and received his training as an apprentice to Ralph Massey, a wheelwright in Findern. Working with his brother-in-law William Woolatt, in the 1750s the inventive wheelwright began to dedicate their work towards the development of a machine to make silk stockings. Despite its practical use, the machine was no immediate commercial success as Strutt lacked the capital to expand his business. In the two years after 1756, efforts to obtain capital from friends and members of his congregation had only limited success, before, in 1758, the inventor set out to partner with two major manufacturers in the hosiery business, John Bloodworth and Thomas Stamford of Derby. With their backing, and a business already growing with more machines and workers employed, Strutt and Woolatt successfully petitioned for a patent in 1759. This underpinned a partnership between the four men that quickly grew, so much so that Strutt was able to buy out Stamford and Bloodworth's shares in 1762, for almost £600. Immediately, a new partnership was established with a major hosier in Nottingham, Samuel Need, and the business continued to grow. By 1772, annual sales were valued at more than £11,000, mostly to customers in London, which was also the source of the raw silk that Strutt purchased and transported to his spinners in Derbyshire. A decade later, sales had increased to over £16,000 and remained that high until the end of the century.[11]

However, even as Strutt's hosiery manufacturing went from strength to strength, drawing on partnerships built and sustained through familial, religious and business interests, similar relationships also saw Strutt use his capital to move beyond the production of stockings. With his expertise using machinery to profitably run textile mills in Derbyshire, by 1769 Strutt was well established as a leading figure at the cutting edge of Britain's industrial development. The year before, Arkwright had left Lancashire to bring his spinning machine to Nottingham, the leading centre of the hosiery industry where there was strong demand for cotton yarn. Arkwright was already working with one partner, the Preston-based liquor merchant and painter John Smalley, who supported the cost of obtaining a patent, but funds quickly dried up. It's unclear how the introduction was made, but by 1771, Arkwright had presented the invention to

Need and Strutt together, and perhaps with the input of the two manufacturers, shifted the focus of his machinery away from horsepower and towards waterpower. Strutt was aware of the success of Lombe's water-powered silk mill in Derby, and Arkwright would later visit the same site while developing his plans for a cotton-spinning mill. By the end of the year, work was under way at Cromford to construct this new mill, as well as homes for workers who were enticed to move to the cotton factory for employment.[12]

In the following months, further experimentation with his machine led to improvements in its design that left Arkwright and Strutt hopeful of producing cotton thread not only for hosiery, but also for making calicos, fustians and worsted fabrics. Soon, the mill employed hundreds of workers and was operating twelve hours a day. Not long after, in 1776, Strutt began building a cotton mill of his own at Belper, which opened two years later, and a further site at Milford opened in 1782. These, too, were industrial sites where workers' homes were built alongside the mill complex to house the hundreds of workers needed at the large growing factories. Around the same time, Arkwright had reached an agreement with the landowner John Chadwick to build another factory at Birkacre in Lancashire, although this was quickly attacked by workers who saw the rising edifice and its machines as a threat to their livelihoods. In the end, the Birkacre factory was never rebuilt, but it was a shallow victory for the workers.[13]

Workers' complaints were well known, but neither attacks on machinery nor the concerns of spinners, weavers and other workers were enough to slow down Britain's new cotton capitalists. Supporters of the new technology were quick to dismiss the complaints of workers in any case. In 1780, Dorning Rasbotham, a local landowner and self-proclaimed 'friend of the poor', sought to assuage concerns that 'the large machines' set up 'for spinning cotton' would be detrimental to workers. After he proudly explained that while 'in some countries, where arbitrary power prevails' workers 'are no more considered than cattle', he continued that this was not the case in Britain (no mention was made of the hundreds of thousands of enslaved workers in Britain's colonies overseas), where 'nobler sentiments' prevailed and business owners were aware that workers needed to be looked after. However, fears among workers of new industrial practices couldn't be justified and efforts to damage or destroy the new machinery were 'madness'.

Throughout history, Rasbotham suggested, it was 'the use of machines, which chiefly distinguishes men in society from men in a savage state'. From simple tools to complex factories, human ingenuity had long set out to make work easier for workers, not harder. Looms, he noted, were 'improving continually in simplicity, usefulness, and conveniency' and 'every age has been adding some little new inventions to them'. Only 'a few years ago', the introduction of the flying shuttle had been embraced by thousands of workers and was 'a most excellent, and happy discovery'. The transformation of cotton manufacture had led to the creation of something that was 'now almost a new trade', and 'the fabric, the quality of goods we make, is amazingly changed'. The 'new kinds of cloth', he suggested, 'could not possibly have been made, at least in any quantity, or so cheap as to sell, without our machines'. While the author acknowledged that the new machinery was 'shortening labour' as it reshaped the manufacturing landscape and reduced the number of workers needed to produce thread, he expected the disruption would be short-lived. 'All improvements in trade by machines,' he argued, 'do at first, produce some difficulty to some particular persons', before people retrained or new jobs emerged to take advantage of the changes.[14]

In the end, despite fears of workers about the impact on their livelihoods, the adoption of machines in the textile industry only increased in speed and scale. The mills at Cromford and Belper were far too profitable for enterprising capitalists to be put off for long. After Arkwright and Strutt broke their partnership in 1781, the former doubled down on his northern interests, becoming fabulously wealthy as he built more and more mills in Lancashire over the following two decades. Strutt's cotton mills in Derbyshire likewise flourished, and when he died in 1797 the business passed to his three sons, who would go on to expand the firm into the largest cotton manufacturer in the country. None of it would have been possible if not for the networks and partnerships that were needed, at every stage, to turn inventive idea into commercially successful business.

None of it would have been possible without the workers, either, with their well-founded fears that the expansion of mills and factories would rapidly do away with the smaller-scale cottage industry that had provided work in the previous decades. Instead, wage labour in factories awaited them, with their tactile skill quickly surpassed by the efficiency and standardisation of machines.[15]

## WEAVING THE WIND

In 1789, Samuel Oldknow received an important document: the catalogue for the East India Company's upcoming sale at the 'Bengal-Warehouse'. Perusing the items on sale, Oldknow could learn exactly what stunning array of fabrics had arrived on the company's ships, which at this auction alone were valued at around a quarter of a million pounds. The most common type of cloth on sale was a kind of high-quality calico known as *khasa* and more than 28,000 were on sale for between 13 and 68 shillings each. Tens of thousands more calicos could be found alongside them including the cheaper *baftas* from Gujarat (15 to 25 shillings), *gurrahs* from north-east India (15 to 50 shillings) and *callipatties* from Bengal (20 shillings). The higher end of the market included delicate cotton muslin called *mulmul* (48 to 185 shillings), checked or striped cotton *doreas* (20 to 90 shillings) and soft, lightweight *nainsooks* (40 to 100 shillings). Hundreds of each were available. The most luxurious were the sixty-eight Bengali *jamdani* muslins stitched with gold thread. These were expected to sell for £4 10s each – the monthly salary of a skilled tradesman. As a manufacturer of cotton cloth in Lancashire, Oldknow needed to know what sort of cloths were available, how much they had sold for, and what gaps there might be in the market for him to fill. After all, the cloth he sold might have been made by weavers in northern Britain, but every single one copied a style that originated in India.[16]

Britain could not hope to replace the experience and skill that had been passed down by generations of weavers in India. They had a tactile knowledge of cotton and cloth that enabled them to make the most delicate and luxurious fabrics in the world. In the first two steps of the process – sourcing raw cotton and spinning it into yarn – British capitalists had found ways to undercut their Indian competitors. Plantations had spread across lands seized in tropical regions where cotton could grow, and enslaved labour was brutally exploited to plant and pick it. This was made possible by webs of exchange that carried all manner of British goods to sell to colonists in these territories, and the same networks carried back huge volumes of raw cotton: enough to supply a brand new industry in Lancashire and to keep it growing at incredible speed. Once the raw cotton arrived in Britain, innovative technology – often including machinery built with metal parts now produced from British ores and powered by surging rivers or by new engines that burned coal dug by British miners – made up for the disadvantage. Mechanisation could not make up for the limited experience that British workers had with the tropical fibre, but it did help them spin cotton yarn more cheaply, at greater volumes, and increasingly at higher quality. By the time a spool of yarn left a spinner's hands, the fibres that formed the thread had already travelled thousands of miles, tying a multitude of economic functions together in its wake. And there was still a long way to go before a finished 'British' cloth could be sold at its final destination.

Mechanised production of cotton yarn turned the raw fibres into the threads that could be woven together to make pure cotton calicos and muslins. The drive to produce the highest-quality cloths had incentivised the development of improved tools for spinning the necessary yarn, but there were not yet the same advances to help weavers. As he set out to produce cloths like those in the East India Company's catalogue, Oldknow was at the forefront of Lancashire's industrialising textile boom, embracing both the newest technology and ways of organising labour to boost productivity. Born locally in 1756, near Chorley, he had grown up on an estate that his mother had inherited and studied at the local grammar school, before apprenticing with his uncle who was a draper in Nottingham. Here, he would have seen the trials and tribulations of working in Britain's textile industry first hand, as well as the profits that could be made selling woollen goods and fabrics mixing linen, cotton and silk. The young Oldknow was entering the textile business at an opportune moment, and advances in technology were quickly changing how fabrics of all sorts were being produced. When he returned north, it did not take long before he took his first leap into the world of mechanised cotton manufacture, purchasing a number of spinning mules in 1779. A loan from Abraham Crompton, a nearby landowner and member of the same congregation as the Oldknow family, helped him expand the business further. By 1781, he had set up a partnership with his brother Thomas, who helped oversee a rapidly expanding enterprise designed to boost the efficiency of the production process by bringing it under the command of the same firm. Oldknow was unskilled as a mechanic, spinner or weaver. Rather, business depended on using his access to capital to insert himself into every stage of cotton manufacturing and finding efficiencies in the system to boost his profits.[17]

The system that he used, the putting-out system, would have been familiar to people working in many other sectors in Britain, but it represented a level of control over production that was unusual for the north-western textile industry. In addition to subcontracting to multiple producers, Oldknow sought to establish his control over every part of the system: he purchased raw cotton directly, he distributed it to spinners, he collected their yarn, he distributed it to weavers, he collected their cloth, which he checked for quality at his own warehouse before payment was made. Finally, he sold the finished products directly to merchants, with any savings from efficiencies going into his own pocket. At the core of Oldknow's early business enterprise was a warehouse he built near Anderton, costing £90, on land that he leased from the Liverpool slave-trader Jonathan Blundell, who had purchased the property after making huge profits from colonial trade. Initially, spinners and weavers that Oldknow paid would have been working in their homes but, increasingly, technological advances would make that untenable. Helped by his wealthy upbringing, education and strong links with the wider community around Chorley, Oldknow could access networks of clients, creditors, business partners and others to establish this system, and he lent on the same to grow it further. In 1784, financed by a loan from Arkwright (who would become a bigger and bigger creditor to Oldknow in the coming years), Oldknow moved to Stockport to take part in the rapid expansion of its cotton industry. Rather than contributing to the growing number of spinning mills, he bought warehouses and other facilities aimed specifically at producing finished fabric. Primarily focused on higher-quality fabrics, he obtained yarn from lots of small spinning firms, and occasionally bought thread from major producers like Arkwright, which he fed into a system employing as many as 300 weavers. By 1786, Oldknow was the foremost cotton-cloth manufacturer in Britain, with more than 500 looms dedicated to making cloth for his enterprise. His early profits were enormous, reaching £17,000 a year.[18]

Within this system, workers were pushed to work longer hours to produce more goods and were often paid with piece-rates. These were a feature of work across many industries, whereby workers earned income for each item produced rather than the number of hours worked. Excessively long hours, poor pay, deficient diet and ill health often went together. An occupation like dressmaking, which was dominated by women, could easily become a vicious cycle that they had no hope breaking out of: low rates led to long hours, long hours exacerbated eye strain, worsening sight caused lower-quality output, which triggered low rates, longer hours, and so on to eventual destitution. Adam Smith was aware of this concerning trend and noted that a carpentry worker paid by piece-rates was so overworked that they could only work with 'utmost vigour' for eight years. Workers' bodies were sacrificed to the altar of productivity and profit. Yet capitalists had little difficulty finding workers. Even as his site manager Thomas Horsfield complained about delays in the supply of machine parts, he was confidently telling Oldknow that 'a great number of weavers made application for work' with him, both those who had worked with him previously and new labourers.[19]

In the putting-out system, workers kept some degree of control. If Oldknow offered uncompetitive rates, then they could seek to sell their goods elsewhere. In 1788, complaints from spinners about low supplies of raw cotton, from weavers about delays in payment, and from 'winders' about low prices were all causes for concern. One of Oldknow's nearby competitors, Mr Swift, poached five weavers as a consequence. However, by the later 1780s, the putting-out system was becoming more standardised and Oldknow was able to oversee the different parts of the manufacturing process with an increasingly high degree of regulation: his warehouses would distribute materials on Monday, take in work from spinners on Tuesday and Friday, from weavers on Wednesday and Saturday, and send on finished goods to Stockport every Thursday. In theory, this helped to improve efficiency while reducing Oldknow's risk, as each spinner or weaver was essentially self-employed and in competition with all the others. However, the putting-out approach had its limitations, especially when it came to quality control. To improve spinners' work, Oldknow's site manager Horsfield 'charged them to use every endeavour in their power to make it [yarn] as good as possible' and altered the list of prices to try and incentivise them. These efforts were apparently ineffective, but Horsfield cautioned against any effort 'to assume too much authority over the work people' or abusing 'them with bad language' because they could take their work elsewhere. For a while, Oldknow's efforts to boost productivity by improving how different parts of the cotton-manufacturing process came together were successful. However, it also meant that every week, the firm's warehouses would receive unpredictable supplies of thread and fabric, with the result that making their own deliveries to exacting customers could be an unpredictable affair.[20]

Keeping the system going and connecting it into the changing demands of customers required streams of letters flowing back and forth across the country. As well as orders, requests for payments and other typical business correspondence, these exchanges helped people stay on top of the state of the market and what customers thought of their product. Oldknow also took part in social engagements with clients and creditors. Whether that was receiving invitations to dine with his supplier Mr Barlow as thanks for help provided to his wife, or choosing to 'take a ride over' to meet Blundell and agree a lease agreement 'at the time of the music meeting' in Liverpool, the lines between business and pleasure were often blurred. In letters from Robert Parker, a regular customer in London, Oldknow was advised about popular styles in the capital even as he was kept abreast of the southern trader's health issues. Social obligations and trust were essential and could also help to navigate disputes. In 1787, when a shipment of Oldknow's cloths was sold accidently by one Edward Bowden, who had not realised they had been reserved for a different customer, restitution was quickly forthcoming. Rachel Bowden wrote to explain that her husband was 'exceedingly sorry for what he has done' and promised that they would 'in a very short time ... either pay you the value in cash or buy and deliver' replacement goods 'of equal or better quality'. In a similar vein, in August the same year, when the Edinburgh merchant Robert Gourlay received 'some muslins that morning' that had been delivered without an invoice, he reached out to ascertain whether Oldknow had sent them and asked that any related documents be dispatched by courier as quickly as possible to make sure they were handled correctly.[21]

Oldknow's dependence on networks like this also informed which products he should have his spinners and weavers make. Orders for cotton cloth made to a particular minimum quality, 'or finer if you have any', were common. Many customers were more specific, with particular styles or patterns set out precisely. The Leicester-based trader Ellis Brewin needed 'checked muslins' only, while the Nantwich firm of Barclay & Steven requested *jandanna* muslins 'of the newest patterns and the finest that you have got' so that they could stay ahead in a competitive market. Likewise, the London trader Parker believed that new styles 'will do for a while', but warned that as a fashion 'they are whimsical and therefore I fear [they] will be short lived' in the capital. *Soossees*, yet another style of cloth, were apparently a better option, as they were 'much more lively and being mixed with silk make them cheaper'. Writing from Coventry, an order from Goodwin & Jenkinson was more precise still. Not only did they want muslins, handkerchiefs and patterned cloth 'as soon as possible', 'good in quality' and 'charged on the very lowest terms', but they even doodled a little diagram of the checked pattern they desired in the margin of their letter. The London firm of Greaves, Hodgson & Company, which ordered hundreds of calicos at a time, were less demanding about specific styles but were adamant that the quality of cloth needed to be the very best. Oldknow was told only to send cloths if 'they are as good as the last 50 pieces' as 'we cannot dispense with them if they are one jot inferior'. After all, the firm served the

Paris market and only the very best would do. Parker wrote to Oldknow again in 1784 to tell him about 'a thin muslin superior to any we have had' that he had seen overseas. This was not a direct threat to the northern manufacturer's business, as its price suffered from 'the disadvantage of so many duties', but rather a potential inspiration for Oldknow's 'future prospects'. A few years later, the same trader sent a cloth sample that 'is made of cotton of French manufactory' and was suitable for gentlemen's coats. Hoping that Oldknow might be able to 'see if it can be made and what will be the expense', he dangled the lure of a large London market for such cloth if it were counterfeited effectively.[22]

Unfortunately, predicting the changing demands of Britain's consumers was never easy. In 1787, the Newcastle trader Benjamin Gibson was disappointed to find that Oldknow's muslins did not find a ready market in the north-eastern port. However, he kept his faith in the product, which he still believed was 'superior in general to any other British or India[n]' cloth, and asked Oldknow to let him know when 'a good assortment' was available in future. Likewise, in 1793, responding to a glut of supplies, Robert Blackwell returned cravats and calicos to Oldknow, explaining that 'you have sent so many cravats in the former parcels that I am quite overstocked with them'. As well as accepting orders of small numbers of products so that customers could experiment with selling his goods in new markets, Oldknow also sent pattern books of samples in the hope of encouraging further orders. James Cazanove wrote to Oldknow to ask for patterns of the 'wide white calico which you manufacture' and suggested that the Stockport manufacturer could 'expect to receive [a] very good order from us' if the samples 'please our friends abroad'.[23]

When quality dropped or deliveries did not meet with expectations, customers were quick to complain. John Carwood, a Bristol trader, wrote to Oldknow to express how he was 'disappointed in not finding your patterns and quality of your calico handkerchiefs agreeable'. He was especially frustrated because he had 'very particularly' explained that 'none but small patterns would suit my sale' when he had made the order, but that the goods delivered were 'too large and very coarse'. To highlight his point, he drew the offending pattern into his letter, just to make sure there were no further blunders. Only two options remained: either Oldknow would have to approve a steep discount for the goods or Carwood would be obliged to return them. Even more scathing, the London firm of Bowles & Birch sent a withering letter to Oldknow about the quality of his cottons. A recent delivery of wide romals (a thin fabric with a checked pattern) had arrived safely, but they had felt forced to return them because 'they do not seem square'. They told the northern manufacturer plainly that 'if you intend to make a trade of that article you must make them square and the large check pattern', otherwise he might as well not bother. Piling on further, they criticised the inferior quality of Oldknow's spotted muslins in comparison to fabric they could buy from Scotland and mercilessly questioned: 'why can't you do them as well as the Scotch people?'[24]

The growing number of cotton-cloth producers flooded the market with goods, and increasing competition meant that manufacturers needed to stay at the top of their game. The Manchester-based Jonathon Haworth used this to his advantage when he complained that a recent calico delivery had been 'bad indeed', and encouraged Oldknow to 'take more pains in the choice of the next goods' he sent them. If not, he warned ominously, 'you will favour us to another market'. Unfortunately for Oldknow, later the same year Haworth wrote again to complain about poor-quality deliveries and suggested that he would travel to Stockport to pick out cloths himself from the warehouse to 'avoid making so many returns'. A couple of years later, a further affront brought him to the end of his tether. Oldknow had offered to sell Haworth cloths for printing before they were shipped overseas but had failed to deliver on time, and so Haworth had been forced to use inferior products that he had to hand, at no small cost to his business. As he frostily informed Oldknow, his losses were the 'disagreeable consequences of not fulfilling a promise'. It could be even worse when customers made their dissatisfaction public and risked the reputation of Oldknow's business. In 1789, John Barrill wrote to Oldknow to let him know that he had recently been at a meeting with Lancaster & Gilbert who had complained about the standard of products they had received, and he urged him to write to them and find a resolution.[25]

Customers who encouraged manufacturers to produce a wider range of goods, and those that complained about poor or unpredictable quality, both incentivised producers like Oldknow to try to develop their businesses away from the putting-out system and towards factory manufacture. For Oldknow, this led to a plethora of connected enterprises. In 1787, he purchased land near Mellor to build his first spinning mill, to ensure the quality of yarn for his weavers would be consistently made at the quality he required. It was a huge complex, six storeys high and 120 metres long, employing hundreds of spinners. The new mill used a Boulton and Watt steam engine for power. Soon after, Oldknow constructed further steam-powered mills at Mellor and in Stockport. Oldknow's spinning was now undertaken in the factory system, while weaving continued to operate by putting out work to independent weavers. However, weavers were increasingly encouraged to move their looms into a building that Oldknow constructed explicitly to house them, and eventually he began purchasing looms on his own account and paying weavers a wage to work for him directly. Oldknow's other investments included the purchase of a smaller factory near Stockport, the construction of a plant for bleaching cotton at Heaton Mersey, workshops for finishing cloth in Disley and growing warehouse complexes at Anderton and in Manchester where goods were collected and distributed.[26]

Increasing mechanisation only compounded the logistical complexity that cotton manufacturers had to manage. For his new factory in Stockport, Oldknow ordered machine parts that were shipped from Sheffield. In 1792, a single order of 'spindles and flyers' that had been 'finished to your pattern' were obtained from John Dewsnap, with 600 delivered to the factory over a period of only a few months. However, not all orders went so smoothly. Nathaniel Binns, who was contracted to supply 'fine shirt cards' for the same factory, wrote that delivery from his West Yorkshire workshop would take longer than expected. The only ones he had available 'would be too coarse for you', unless Oldknow changed his business strategy to do 'common work'. Moving to the lower-quality and less profitable end of the market was unappealing, and there was little option but to wait, as these were specialist and vital pieces of equipment; Oldknow ordered cards from Binns at least ten times over the following year. Cotton factories needed to be fed continuously with products made by other parts of Britain's emerging industrial economy.[27]

A business like Oldknow's added value to Britain's economy in ways that stretched far beyond the factory door. His extensive warehouses, mills and other facilities required upkeep and ongoing development that contributed to the expansion of the building industry. Regular orders of lime, timber, nails and other construction materials stimulated the growth of various local industries. At a facility in Marple, he employed workers directly to complete tasks like brickmaking, cutting a watercourse or levelling a kiln. Factories likewise needed to be supplied with raw materials, tools and machinery to stay in operation. In 1788, a letter from Horsfield highlighted the challenges that the firm faced as it expanded production. Raw cotton was in short supply and might have to be rationed for more valuable parts of the business. Sourcing basic equipment, too, was proving difficult. Heald frames that were installed on looms to handle warp yarns had not been delivered, and the firm was also short of reeds, tools that were needed to separate warp threads and to guide the shuttle on the loom. These were all common items needed for cotton manufacturing, but if Oldknow was unable to keep up their supply, his workers simply could not produce higher-quality merchandise. Three days later, the problems were still piling up. Horsfield's attempt to purchase raw cotton had found twenty other spinners seeking to purchase the same limited stock available, and weavers had started coming every day to demand both cotton and reeds. In time, blockages in supply like this abated, and spinners and weavers continued their labours but, with every day that supply chains were sundered, workers went without pay and Oldknow's profits declined.[28]

The rich surviving archive of Oldknow's letters reveals that matching Indian products sold by the East India Company in London, both in terms of quality and style, was a key incentive for his business. His letters likewise illustrate the significance of social networks and informal methods of exchanging information on the way that cotton was produced during the rapid, mechanically driven rise of Britain's industry. This was most important, technologically, from the perspective of spinners, who gained new machines capable of matching the threads produced by Indian artisans. However, the work of weavers was also a vital part of the production of British cotton even if it was less affected by new technology. Oldknow pioneered new forms of managing huge numbers of workers, first in the putting-out system and then in his factory complexes, and the latter became the norm for British textile production. Oldknow's experience also exemplified how networked capital shaped British business development: at every stage of his career, relationships that crossed sectors and interests were important for how he did business, and the work he conducted demanded the simultaneous exploitation of land, labour and technology.

In the end, Oldknow's ambition and use of credit to expand contained the seeds of his downfall. Not long after the construction of his innovative Mellor and Marple factories, exogenous factors crippled his business. War broke out with France, the market for high-quality muslins crashed, and Oldknow was forced to lease, sell or mortgage many of the properties he had built. Before long, he was left with little more than the Mellor factory, which continued to employ hundreds of workers, but was not profitable enough to keep up with his debts. Sadly for Oldknow, the industry had already moved on and he was surpassed by new entrants that could produce better yarn or employ weavers more successfully. Oldknow's astounding rise and even more sudden fall is indicative of the ways that the cotton industry was developing in Britain – especially efforts to control labour and technology and to respond proactively to consumer demands. While the brief decline in muslin purchases was too much for Oldknow's overstretched finances to bear, war with France did not have the same effect on the rest of the industry. Instead, the dynamics of cotton manufacture began to shift further towards urban production where thousands of workers were available to work in new steam-engine-powered spinning and weaving factories that were quickly transforming the nearby city of Manchester.[29]

*11. In towns such as Manchester, cotton factories like this one introduced a new type of industrial organisation. Steam engines belched smoke into the air as they powered machines manned by hundreds of workers who toiled together in huge, specially designed buildings in which their labour could be more easily controlled and monitored.*

## GLOBAL THREADS

Within a few decades, inventive efforts to substitute skill with machinery had transformed the productive potential of British manufacturers: rather than the coarse, linen-cotton blends that had been the pinnacle of cotton-spinning achievement in the 1740s, by the 1780s British cotton magnates were growing in confidence about going toe to toe with competitors anywhere in the world. As Rasbotham put it in 1780, 'the first effect of our machines has certainly been, to produce and continue a flourishing trade, ever since they were invented'. At no time in living memory, he claimed, had trade increased so quickly as it had in recent decades: 'and to what can we ascribe this, but, under God, to our machines?'[30]

Lauding the almighty power of the machine was a common theme in discussions about Britain's flourishing industry, both as a cause for its rapid growth and the ability for domestic manufacturers to outcompete their European rivals. In 1786, during the period of rapid expansion in the industry, the Board of Trade invited cotton manufacturers to express their views on the current strength of the industry. The group that travelled to London included calico manufacturers and printers Joseph Smith and Robert Peel, as well as the fustian manufacturers John Hilton and William Frodisham. Looking back at the development of their industry, they acknowledged that, while low-priced goods had been produced before the 1760s, it was the 'invention of Mr Arkwright's machine' that 'gave a further spring' to 'the trade of the high-priced articles'. This meant, according to Hilton and Frodisham, that 'we have great advantage at present in skill and machines' in Manchester, which 'reduce the price of labour below that which the French now pay'. Likewise, Peel and Smith were confident that they held a 'principal advantage' that 'would arise from our machines, both for spinning and printing' that made it possible for them to produce printed cotton cloth 'cheaper and better' than their French competitors. Technology had given British manufacturers a serious edge.

However, the group still had concerns about a possible trade agreement with France creating a shift in the global supply chains on which the European industry depended. Better machines would not help them counteract France's access to cotton from its Caribbean colonies, which was considered better than that produced in British territories. To compete, British manufacturers would have no option but to purchase finer raw cotton from France itself, or from the Ottoman empire, at rates that would be uncompetitive. Rather than tariffs or treaties, they only had 'hopes that some of our remaining islands will take to planting cotton and afford us some relief'. Unlike Scottish linens or Yorkshire woollens, when it came to cotton-cloth production the extra cost of raw materials meant that, while British manufacturers had a 'decided advantage in fine goods' thanks to their mechanical skill, 'the French may beat us in coarser articles'. This would only change if plantation owners in the British Caribbean or the newly independent United States began producing more suitable cotton for the British market. Just as important for the cotton manufacturers was ensuring was that any treaty with France kept them 'secure from the importation of India calicos' without paying duties. If France became a back door to the British market, then the domestic industry would struggle. In European markets, where British cotton goods had to compete with those from India, recent declines in the sale of British fustians had given the manufacturers cause for concern, and calico exports were increasing but 'not to a considerable degree'. The sale of Indian cloth, especially, usually meant that British products were uncompetitive unless interruptions to trade with Asia caused their prices to spike. British cotton cloth depended on international links for its raw materials and was competing in a global marketplace: empire and technology had not yet given British manufacturers an advantage on all counts.[31]

Despite recognition from cotton manufacturers like Peel and Smith that the water frame had contributed to a transformation in the industry, not everyone was so impressed with Arkwright's acumen, and the engineer James Watt eviscerated the spinning magnate's work, claiming that he had stymied further advances in technology that might have been possible if his patent hadn't restricted other entrepreneurs from seeking to improve on his machine. In a blistering letter to his father-in-law, the Glasgow-based merchant James MacGregor, 'Mr Arkwright', he complained, was 'one of the most ignorant men I have ever met with'. Watt seems to have doubted he had invented the water frame at all, and admitted only that Britain was 'much indebted' to him for 'performing the most difficult part, which was the making it useful'. Arkwright seems to have earned the engine maker's disdain 'some years ago' when he had 'applied to us at two different times for our advice which we took the trouble to give him' about the possible application of steam power for cotton production rather than relying on waterwheels. The Lancashire-based cotton manufacturer had ignored Watt's advice (and rudely not even responded to say thank you for it) and instead 'followed his own whims till he threw away several thousand pounds', 'exposed his ignorance to all the world' and eventually 'in disgust gave up the scheme'. Watt considered this an embarrassing failure that had held up the adoption of steam power, crowing that 'our rotation engines which we have now rendered very completed, are certainly very applicable to the driving of cotton mills'. No matter where they might be built, Watt was confident that 'in every case' the convenience of operating 'the mill in a town or ready built manufactory' would 'compensate for the expense of coals and our own premium'.[32]

By the 1790s, many manufacturers had indeed turned to Watt's steam engine as a means of powering spinning machinery, especially in places like Manchester where they removed the need to build mills near suitable water sources. However, the costs were still very high. In fact, Manchester's spinners used the 'very large sums [that] had been expended in erecting machines' to bargain with the city's cotton-cloth producers to keep prices and demand for their yarn high. Waterwheels therefore remained the most important source of power for many manufacturers, and even new mills were being designed that used bigger and more efficient waterwheels. At Quarry Bank Mill near Manchester, Samuel Greg leaned on the expertise of one of his business partners, Peter Ewart – an engineer who had previously worked with Boulton and Watt, with whom he traded goods between the northern city and customers in Italy, Russia and America. At the mill, Ewart installed a powerful waterwheel that could provide more power than even the most effective steam engines on the market. This enabled Greg to install more and more machines on the premises to increase cotton production. Whether mill owners were using waterwheels or steam engines, powering the machines that sat at the heart of Britain's new industry remained the most expensive part of setting up these businesses. Improvements here, too, changed how the industry was structured by bringing workers to sites where energy sources could power machines. Workers were expected to move to sites like Manchester where coal could be brought easily to the city by canal to fuel new steam engines, or to places like the Calder Valley where fast-flowing springs could power waterwheels. Specialised regional growth generated highly distinctive patterns of industrialisation: the relative importance of different triggers for growth were, consequently, just as distinctive.[33]

Throughout these advances, the skill involved in spinning high-quality cotton yarns had shifted away from artisan spinners and into the hands of machine builders, fitters and the producers of machine parts like ironworkers. Numerous industries fed into the production of every water frame or mule, and they depended on precision workmanship much like any other mechanised industry. Scottish machine makers James McConnel and John Kennedy were among the entrepreneurs whose technical ability was essential for the diffusion of innovative technologies like these. Early in 1795, and only a few months before they would shift into producing cotton yarn on machines of their own design, they were fulfilling orders for other cotton manufacturers in north-west England. Among their clients was Stockport-based Joseph Sykes, who acted as a broker selling raw cotton to manufacturers and ran a cotton factory himself. Requesting 'to know the price of 168 spindle mule', Sykes quickly learned that the pace of technological development meant he was already behind the curve. The Manchester-based pair wrote back that they 'would recommend a larger size as 180 is the smallest we have made these 9 months' and only cost £2 10s more than the smaller device. Three months later, two mules were ready 'on Thursday at noon', and Sykes was told to collect 'them at that time so that a man can go with them and set them up this week'. The two machines worked a treat, and Sykes returned to the company the following year to order eight more: despite radically improving quality and productivity, they only cost £42 each.[34]

As McConnel and Kennedy transitioned towards producing cotton yarn, the same focus on improvement and mechanical expertise that had driven their successful machine-making business continued to influence how they produced cotton. In an effort to reach the highest end of the market, they experimented on multiple fronts, both in terms of the sorts of goods they were producing and the raw materials that fed into their machines. In May 1795, soon after they had finished building their new mill and had installed 'our new machinery', the partners were offering customers in Liverpool and Glasgow a range of different products. These included coarser English yarn, imitation Dutch thread and their best effort at copying 'India twist', which was available at the highest quality and the highest price. Improvements in technology, probably undertaken by the two partners who had trained as machine makers, meant that they were capable of spinning more of the finer yarn than ever before and were now confident that it 'will give our friends satisfaction'. After the upfront cost of installing more sophisticated machinery, the expense of producing different threads was about the same, and if the company could find enough buyers for their best 'India twist' they stood to double their profits.[35]

Not every customer felt the same way, and the Gordon & Cairns firm in Glasgow encouraged McConnel and Kennedy to produce coarser threads which were 'most wanted in this market'. As techniques and technology improved, Britain's cotton industry flourished not only because it could challenge more at the highest end of the market, although many companies did specialise in this area, but because it could churn out vast volumes of low- and medium-quality products, too. At first, finite demand for the very best yarn meant that firms such as McConnel & Kennedy could not just focus on the highest-quality 'India' thread and often found a readier market for the middling 'Dutch' variety. Even so, a growing customer base meant that they more than made back their investment in the best machinery money and talent could supply. After only a few months in business, by the end of 1795 they were able to report that 'we now spin about 200lbs of Dutch weekly and nearly the same weight of India', generating enviable returns every week. In time, too, they found customers who had been crying out for quality thread. By 1798, they had found a ready market among the style-setting weavers of Paisley, where their 'India' thread was considered ideal for the high-quality cotton fabrics being produced in the Scottish town. By 1801, the firm's annual profit had reached £8,164.[36]

Changes in how the firm obtained raw cotton from brokers in Liverpool reveal its efforts to find a secure source of supply for this essential commodity even as they investigated which types were most suited for spinning with their new machinery. In their first two years of operation, the partners purchased raw cotton from a wide variety of sources and types. This included imports from colonies across the Caribbean, but sources in Brazil were their most popular choice and accounted for more than half of the 12,000 kilograms they bought before the end of 1797. The two men recognised that the South American fibre's length and fineness gave it an advantage over some of the Caribbean varieties that grew with shorter fibres, and was more suitable for Lancashire's cotton producers. However, it was not quite the winning formula and, by the end of this initial period of experimentation, the company settled on raw cotton from Georgia as their first choice. The North American fibres were longer still and 'undoubtedly produce[d] stronger yarns', and supply was increasingly secure. The state's sprawling plantations were exploiting ever-growing numbers of enslaved workers to rapidly expand, and so its extraction of raw cotton was booming. To make the highest-quality cotton yarn that would become their signature product, McConnel & Kennedy found a reliable supply from plantations in Georgia that worked well with their steam-powered machinery in Manchester.[37]

Unbeknownst to the earlier developers of cotton machinery in Britain, their efforts to copy the very finest of Indian muslin cloths with machine-spun cotton would have been impossible had they continued to depend on the shorter fibres obtained from the genus of cotton plants most common in India. Their machinery was much more suitable for spinning yarn using the longer fibres of the types of cotton plants more common in the Caribbean and North America, especially one genus called Sea Island cotton. This enabled plantation owners and merchants trading with the Caribbean or North America to diversify away from sugar when its price dropped. As early as the 1770s, Glaswegian merchant Alexander Houston had encouraged his agents to purchase cotton when they learned 'that prices of sugar and rum have already fallen considerably at London'. However, the shift took time, and it was only in the last two decades of the eighteenth century that raw cotton imports into Lancashire grew dramatically from British colonies, as well as from producers in the United States of America. Sources were also found across imperial boundaries in South America, with Brazil supplying around a third of Liverpool's supply. After peace was signed with the new United States of America in 1783, raw cotton from plantations in North America increased, too, and it would become the dominant supplier by the early decades of the following century. Between 1780 and 1800, raw cotton imports grew from just over two million to over twenty million kilograms, all of which was fed into northern Britain's industrial machine. As luck would have it, the Sea Island cotton was among the fibres that made up a large part of this growth.[38]

As well as increasing the amount of land exploited for cotton production in America, often through the toil of enslaved labourers, the supply of cotton for Britain's cotton-spinning industries required merchants and shipbuilding to keep up with market demand. The Liverpool firm of Waterhouse & Co. were one of many businesses that operated as brokers between colonial merchants and the British customers who would buy their goods. In 1799, during a single year of their operations, they oversaw the sale of hundreds of thousands of pounds of colonial goods – taking a £3,683 10s share for their role. Some small amount of coffee and sugar passed through their warehouse, but most of their time was spent moving raw cotton off Liverpool's docks and into the storehouses of northern Britain's mechanised cotton factories. Their biggest suppliers, with accounts of over £50,000 each, included John Bolton, James Kenyon and the partnership of Thomas & William Earle, while more than a dozen other traders also traded cotton at smaller volumes. Among these suppliers was the merchant William Rathbone, whose grandfather had moved to Liverpool decades before to repair the ships of slave-traders; now, the family was overseeing a business that fuelled the next stage of northern Britain's manufacturing development in Manchester. Dozens of manufacturers bought the cotton and distributed it for spinners to twist into yarn before it was passed on to weavers who would produce fine cotton cloth. William Evans bought forty-four bags of cotton from Suriname for £1,618, another thirty-five from Demerara for £1,520, and twenty more from North America for £470. He was among the smaller clients that Waterhouse & Co. served. John Simpson & Company obtained over £10,000 of raw cotton for their spinners, as did John Walker & Company, William Rigby and Richard Padmore. By far the largest client was Arkwright, who purchased over a thousand bags of cotton for more than £30,000. Only a few years later the Scottish writer and biographer Robert Bisset summed up the importance of supplies like these: 'all the genius of an Arkwright, and all the liberality and talents of Manchester, with the highest degree of industry and skill, can make no cotton manufacture without cotton wool.'[39] Industry depended on empire.

By the 1790s, new technology and abundant supplies had transformed Britain's textile industry, but some manufacturers feared their dominance would continue only so long as the technology and its product were both monopolised in the home market. In 1794, Manchester's cotton-cloth manufacturers were quite clear that it was 'the advantages we receive . . . from the yarn spun upon the late invention of machinery' that allowed them 'to bring the goods to market of a better quality than any other country whatever'. Without privileged access to the yarn, they worried this advantage could be undone. After all, German weavers were technically capable and were much cheaper to employ. The same challenge that had shaken woollen manufacturers a century before now faced the cotton makers: without protection from the state to monopolise access to the raw materials they needed, how could they dominate their rivals? British muslins, already, they argued, had lost their place in Berlin's markets. Before, 'the manufacturers there were incapable of making them', but now, 'in consequence of our yarn, they are now enabled to make them'. If the export of cotton yarn were not banned, they worried much of Britain's advantage would go with it. Innovation and technical ability, coupled with access to raw cotton-producing colonies in America, had put Britain ahead of its rivals in some areas, but there was no reason to believe this would last unless further improvements were found in other parts of the industrial process. If Britain was going to dominate the cloth market, then it would have to find ways to produce more, cheaper or better fabric than its rivals. Not only those in Europe, but in India too.[40]

New ways of working and investment in the most innovative machinery were the only way British manufacturers could compete with Indian manufacturers, and people like Peel and Arkwright built new factories in and around Manchester to do it. In time, steam engines supplanted the need for waterwheels, and companies like McConnel & Kennedy were quick to take advantage, building smoke-belching factories on the fringes of the rapidly growing metropolis. The city was at the centre of a web that connected it to raw cotton imports arriving in nearby Liverpool and increasingly connected with improved roads and canals to other sites of production and consumption across northern Britain. Manufactures took care to cater to markets overseas that were vital for the industry's continued growth. The market in Britain alone was not big enough and already in the 1780s Peel and Smith had complained that 'the home trade bears but a small proportion to the foreign trade'. The two fustian manufacturers from Manchester who had travelled with them to London put it even more succinctly: 'we have prospered only since we turned merchants.'[41]

By 1800, British cotton weaving was still mostly undertaken by hand, although improvements in technology that built on the flying shuttle had increased the productivity of individual weavers. Mechanisation had transformed how thread was made, but cloth production was affected more by changing ways of organising labour. Styles of cloth in Britain were made to fit the demands of customers at home and abroad. Manufacturers specialised in cloth for workers, for prisoners, for men of means and for merchants to carry overseas. Changes in printing and design were adapted quickly to suit different markets, and manufacturers in Manchester sought to design goods for the West African or the European markets, a transmission of style that went both ways. From India, especially, exciting colours and patterns inspired English manufacturers to experiment and innovate. Diversification of cotton products demanded the complementary exploitation of spinning technology to produce the various different yarns needed and the concentration of weaving and printing jobs to maximise the quality of production.[42]

One manufacturer, Greg, believed this rapid innovation had elevated British industry to new heights. In 1793, he wrote to the raw cotton supplier Rathbone to explain how he and his fellow cotton manufacturers understood the changing threat posed by the East India Company. No longer did they 'believe we should have any cause to fear from a competition' from Indian cloth and imports from Asia were not the greatest concern. Technological advances and colonial supplies had helped Britain's cotton workers catch up with their Indian competition. Indeed, the East India Company tacitly confirmed this conclusion, reporting the same year that, in the two decades after 1771, their import of cotton cloth had remained relatively unchanged, and was valued at around £1.5 million most years, and included the highest-quality fabrics available. Raw cotton imports, on the other hand, fuelling Britain's industrial machine, had risen extraordinarily quickly, from just over 1,000 tons to over 10,000. The corporation observed that 'the slow progress of an Indian manufacture, unaided by machinery, will require ten, twelve, perhaps fifteen persons to perform the same work which a single British manufacturer can execute, assisted as he is by numerous inventions and improvements'. Rather than competition from the sale of Indian cloth in Britain, then, Greg argued that it was the inability of British merchants to trade directly with Asia without interference from the corporation, that was damaging the industry. With freedom to trade themselves, 'our greatest hope is the reduction of the price of [raw] cotton, indigo and drugs' from Asia, alongside expanding the market for 'woollen goods, and thereby relieving us from the very strong competition we experience from them in the European and American markets'.[43]

Greg recognised that their businesses were international in scope and technologically competitive and that they were selling into global markets that included many more goods than only the very highest quality Indian cottons. Mechanisation in cotton spinning gave Britain the advantage in terms of competing with their European rivals but biggest profits were not found in producing thread but in selling fine cotton fabrics. Millions of Indian cotton cloths had found a ready home in Europe over the previous two centuries, and the richest, most expensive fabrics were sought after by the wealthiest consumers around. Britain's cotton manufacturers had two options. They could find ways to mass-produce cotton cloth at prices low enough to undercut Indian producers or makers of linen and woolen goods in Europe, or they could go toe to toe with them in terms of quality. In the final decades of the eighteenth century, manufacturers tried to do both. They succeeded in the first as Britain's new ways of exploiting technology and labour boosted productivity. In the second, technological improvements got them closer. However, there were limits to the mechanised approach and Britain's industrialists could never quite replace the artistry and skill that lent Indian weavers their remarkable ability to produce webs of woven wind.

# CONCLUSION

## Wealth and Power

In 1797, two Scotsmen in Manchester ordered a steam engine. It was a simple delivery, up the canal from the booming metallurgical hub of Birmingham to the outskirts of a growing northern town dominated by the clattering sounds of cotton factories working at a scale that would have been unimaginable only a few decades earlier. The engine would be used to power machines that could spin raw cotton, easily sourced from nearby Liverpool, which too had boomed in the eighteenth century thanks to its docks that housed hundreds of ships with holds that were packed with the produce of an empire. Every inch of yarn that John Kennedy and James McConnel produced relied on a web of interactions and exchanges stretching across the globe.

Indeed, the story of a British cotton cloth could start in India, where sumptuous fabrics inspired Britain's envious textile manufacturers to replicate them. Or it could start in Italy, with a young Englishman stealing technology to manufacture silk back home in a mill that will later inspire Richard Arkwright to use a similar structure to house his new spinning machine. The cloth's story could begin in a Yorkshire farm, too, where agricultural improvements meant there was less work to go around, and a desperate worker left their home in hope of finding work at a mill in a growing urban area not too far from home. It might also start in America, where an enslaved worker toiled in brutal conditions to harvest the precious fibres needed for Britain's growing industrial machine. Or it could start on the shores of the Calabar River in Africa, with British traders eagerly selling guns from Birmingham before forcing captive people onboard a ship who would be carried across the Atlantic to replace workers who had died labouring to pick cotton for the profit of a British landowner far away.

The making of a single cotton cloth was just one small turn in the vast machine of Britain's productivity. Yet, to understand it requires following the path of all these stories and more. The same could be said for every other commodity that shaped the revolutionary changes that were taking place across Britain's economy. Sugar, iron, copper, pottery, silk and everything in between depended on networks of supply, production and delivery to make a profit. The causes of economic growth were no simple matter. Rather than a sudden industrial revolution transforming Britain's economy through inventive brilliance, the century and a half before 1800 saw radical transformations take place across the wider supply chains and markets on which later technological innovations depended. A key feature of Britain's longer trajectory of economic development was that the system on which these exchanges depended became more efficient in many different parts of the economy at the same time. This depended on the combination of various types of financial, natural, human and intellectual capital through networks that connected people from across British society. Landowners, industrialists and merchants were able and willing to work together, and businesses could draw on relatively diverse pools of talent and wealth in ways that were often innovative, resourceful and single-minded in their pursuit of profit. Links like these made it easier for new ideas to develop and spread, contributing to ongoing, progressive and cumulative improvements in all manner of business activities that, together, resulted in widespread economic growth.

Changes in growing crops, rearing cattle, mining for ore and planting tropical cash crops led to booming outputs for British capitalists who made their money extracting wealth from the environment. At the same time, new techniques transformed how British workers made products for customers at home and abroad. A desire to copy, imitate and eventually substitute luxurious objects such as

Chinese porcelain or Indian cotton cloth was a common feature of British inventiveness, and received considerable support from the state, which eventually led to the production of cheaper, desirable knock-offs that could be produced in growing volumes in Britain's workshops and factories. However, economic growth was not felt evenly across Britain, and some industries benefited more than others. In parts of the country that had just the right sort of natural resources or that were well placed to tap into trading networks needed to procure materials and sell goods, the change was truly transformative. Liverpool, Manchester and Birmingham all experienced remarkable and very similar trajectories, each growing from only around 5,000 people in 1670 to around 20,000 in the middle of the eighteenth century, reaching around 70,000 to 80,000 people by the end of the eighteenth century. Where Britain had once been a peripheral actor in the global production of metals, cotton, silk or sugar, by 1800 it possessed burgeoning industries that made and sold a vast array of commodities to consumers at home even as more were shipped to customers abroad. In Britain and its empire, the ruthless pursuit of profit pushed businesses to adopt scales of business organisation, capital investment and productive output that would have been unimaginable to earlier generations.

To take advantage of these opportunities, capitalists in Britain set out to change what goods were made in the nation's workshops, how to obtain the raw materials they needed, and the ways in which workers could be organised and controlled to extract the most profit from their labour. Even as Britain's population increased from around six million in 1660 to almost eleven million by 1800, productivity increased more quickly. This was achieved in part by adopting new machines and providing better training, and in part through new ways of organising labour, controlling the working poor and situating businesses in new, densely populated urban areas. The cotton industry, especially, was notorious for employing and exploiting children for labour, with as many as half of all workers under the age of nineteen working long hours in dangerous conditions. In colonies overseas, the exploitation of enslaved people on plantations applied this same, horrific business logic to its extreme conclusion, working people to death to maximise profits. As much as steam engines or other machinery, the industrial revolution was defined by the movement towards vast factories and plantations with hundreds of people toiling under the same roof. Capitalists across the economy depended on these workers being competent, capable and cheap enough not to undermine their profit. While output per person in Britain almost tripled during this period, wages rose far less significantly or even declined. The difference, to one degree or another, ended up in the hands of capitalists: investors and owners who were often quite willing to exploit workers even as their profits increased through technological and other forms of improvement, too.

Through violent colonisation and commercial exchange, British capitalists reaped the benefits of a world of resources. The back and forth between international trade, colonial exploitation and domestic manufacture provided a vital backdrop for Britain's industrial development. Colonies produced commodities that simply could not have been produced in Britain, whether due to the climate, labour supply, or simply a lack of available land. They changed the ways in which people could work and live in Britain. For example, by 1800, Britain's 150,000 tons of imported sugar provided calories equivalent to the total needs of over half a million people for an entire year – enough to feed the population of industrial Manchester almost eight times over. This freed up an estimated 858,000 acres of prime agricultural land in Britain, an area roughly the size of Shropshire.[1] Similarly, and essentially for Britain's textile-driven industrialisation, it was only through imports of raw cotton from plantations in America and the Caribbean that the demand could be met for the nation's new machinery to pump out the vast volumes of manufactured cotton cloth that so radically transformed its own and the global economy. Indeed, while Britain surged ahead with the employment of labour-saving technologies, it lagged in various land-saving technologies: without the conquest of new overseas territories to plug the gap, it might have been forced onto a much more labour- and land-intensive path. Instead, profits torn from the land, enlarged with new tools, techniques and brutal ways of exploiting labour, filled the pockets of capitalists on both sides of the Atlantic.

Britain's capitalists invested their money, their time and their resources for profit. Some were narrowly focused on maximising a single enterprise, others invested widely in ventures ranging from colonial trade to coal mining, and most were part of business networks that crossed different sectors as ideas, goods and capital were exchanged. There was no single industry nor any single capitalist or firm which led to the changes that were part of this long industrial transformation. Rather, Britain's economic growth depended on widespread and cumulative gains across multiple vectors: its capitalists had to connect and combine exploitative practices across Britain and its empire with scientific and technological advancements. Relationships between the people involved, the materials they needed and the markets they reached added value as capitalists sought opportunities to increase their profits wherever they could find them. Doing so led to the simultaneous exploitation of financial, natural, physical, human and social capital that was enabled by mutually reinforcing networks of knowledge exchange, innovation and wealth. Industry and empire together were at the heart of Britain's ruthless rise to wealth and power.

# NOTES

## INTRODUCTION: FOR PROFIT

1. Britain is used to refer to England, Scotland and Wales throughout the book, before and after the Union of Crowns in 1707. This recognises the shared histories and connections across these geographies before and after the formalisation of the Kingdom of Great Britain, while acknowledging that differences in economic regulation and practice continued to exist between England and Scotland after this date. McConnel & Kennedy's efforts to obtain a steam engine were recorded in their surviving correspondence. JRRIL, GB133 MCK/2/2/2: McConnel & Kennedy to Boulton & Watt, 12 May 1797; McConnel & Kennedy to Boulton & Watt, 22 May 1797; McConnel & Kennedy to The Committee of the Rochdale Canal, 13 October 1797; GB133 MCK/2/1/3: Boulton & Watt to McConnel & Kennedy, 26 May 1797; Boulton & Watt to McConnel & Kennedy, 8 October 1797. For the plan of the steam engine made for McConnel & Kennedy: LOB, MS 3147/5/151, McConnel & Kennedy, 1797; and contract: LOB, MS 3147/2/10/123, Agreement for erecting a steam engine at Manchester. Contextual material related to these developments is from: Kennedy, 'Brief Notice of my Early Recollections'; Daniels, 'Early Records', pp. 175–88; Daniels, 'Valuation of Manchester Cotton Factories', p. 216; Andrew, 'The Soho Steam Engine Business'. The first study of the global origins of McConnel & Kennedy's raw cotton (using JRRIL, GB133 MCK/3/5/1/1–2) was completed by Sylvie Cunliffe in their BA dissertation at the University of Manchester.
2. Mokyr, *The Lever of Riches*, pp. 1, 81–4. The transformative role of technological skill in particular has been celebrated in numerous studies as a defining feature of Britain's economic development, see: Ashton, *The Industrial Revolution*; Landes, *The Unbound Prometheus*; Toynbee, *Lectures on the Industrial Revolution*; Jacob, *Scientific Culture*; Jacob and Stewart, *Practical Matter*; Mokyr, *Gifts of Athena*; Cookson, *Age of Machinery*.
3. Hahn, *Technology and the Industrial Revolution*, p. 19.
4. This longer trajectory for economic development has been identified across a number of factors including GDP, productivity, urbanisation rates and workforce participation in industry: Broadberry et al., *British Economic Growth*,

appendix D; Acemoglu et al., 'The Rise of Europe', pp. 546–61; Boucasse et al., 'When Did Growth Begin', pp. 1–49; Shaw-Taylor and Wrigley, 'Occupational Structure', pp. 53–88; Wallis et al., 'Structural Change', pp. 862–903. A wide array of different combinations of factors has been offered and hotly debated as explanations for Britain's economic growth: Acemoglu and Robinson, *Why Nations Fail*; Parthasarathi, *Why Europe Grew Rich*; Reinert, *How Rich Countries Got Rich*; Voigtländer and Voth, 'Why England?', pp. 319–61; Allen, 'Why the Industrial Revolution was British', pp. 357–84; Allen, 'The High Wage Economy', pp. 1–22; Hoppit, 'The Nation, The State', pp. 307–31.

5. These individuals, or sub-groups within them, have been described as entrepreneurs, innovators, investors, profiteers and businesspeople. For a wide-ranging review of how British actors were involved in 'imperialism' and 'capitalism', see Cain and Hopkins, 'Gentlemanly Capitalism', pp. 501–25. Incentives for investment were not limited to profit alone any many capitalists were also influenced by other things, including religion, politics, patriotism, family or scientific interest. See, for example: Grassby, *The Business Community*, pp. 364–94; Kadane, *The Watchful Clothier*; MacLeod, *Inventing the Industrial Revolution*, pp. 159–60; McCloskey, *Bourgeois Dignity*, p. 7; Mokyr, 'Intellectual Origins', p. 322; Mokyr, *Enlightened Economy*, pp. 37, 210; Bottomley, *British Patent System*, pp. 25, 266; Broadberry and Gupta, 'Lancashire, India and Shifting Competitive Advantage', pp. 295–7; Meisenzahl and Mokyr, 'Rate and Direction of Invention', pp. 460–73.
6. British economic output using 1700 values. Adapted from Broadberry et al., *British Economic Growth*, appendix D.
7. Adapted from Broadberry et al., *British Economic Growth*, appendix D.
8. For a consideration of alternative 'capitalisms', see: Yazdani and Menon, *Capitalisms*, pp. 1–34. The question of comparative development and how Europe exploited non-European geographies has received widespread attention, see, for example: Bayly, *Birth of the Modern World*; Frank, *ReOrient*; Goldstone, *Why Europe?*; Parthasarathi, *Why Europe Grew Rich*; Pomeranz, *Great Divergence*; Hobson, *Multicultural Origins*, pp. 353–92; Palma and Reis, 'From Convergence to Divergence', pp. 477–506; Álvarez-Nogal and De La Escosura, 'The Rise and Fall of Spain', pp. 1–37. For Japan: Richards, *Unending Frontier*, pp. 148–92. For the Netherlands: De Vries, *First Modern Economy*; Soll, 'Accounting for Government'. For Egypt: Hanna, *Ottoman Egypt*. For scientific and intellectual exchange: Findlen, *Empires of Knowledge*; Fumaroli, *Republic of Letters*; Hsia, *Sojourners in a Strange Land*; Porter, 'The Scientific Community in Early Modern China', pp. 529–44; Huff, *Rise of Early Modern Science*. For Mysore: Yazdani, *India, Modernity and the Great Divergence*, pp. 454–75.
9. Schumpeter, *A Theory of Economic Development*, p. 66; Wrigley, *Continuity, Chance and Change*, p. 3; Yazdani and Menon, *Capitalisms*, p. 2; Beckert et al., 'Commodity Frontiers', pp. 435–50.
10. Informal institutional structures have often been sidelined as a significant feature in studies of Britain's imperial and economic development, with focus instead on states, individual corporations and their formal institutions: Pomeranz, *Great Divergence*, p. 4; Acemoglu and Robinson, *Why Nations Fail*; North, *Institutions*; Harris, *Going the Distance*; Ashworth, *Industrial Revolution*. For wider studies of the impact of informal institutions on economic and commercial development, see: Smith, *Merchants*; Muldrew, *Economy of*

*Obligation*; Cowan, *Social Life of Coffee*; Trivellato, *Familiarity of Strangers*, pp. 4, 13; Mokyr, *Gifts of Athena*, pp. 284–98; Smail, 'The Culture of Credit', pp. 299–325; Hancock, *Citizens of the World*; Langford, *Polite and Commercial People*; Thomas, *In Pursuit of Civility*. Sometimes, religious, political or familial links strengthened ties within specific British commercial networks even as they remained embedded in wider economic exchanges, see Sahle, *Quakers in the British Atlantic World*; Gauci, *Politics of Trade*; Smith, 'Social Networks of Investment', pp. 912–39; Pizzoni, *British Catholic Merchants*; Barker et al., *Faith in the Town*. For mobility between business, trade and landowners, and concomitant social identities, see Grassby, *The Business Community*, pp. 384–8. For the importance of social capital in helping combine conditions for economic development: Meier, 'The Older Generation', pp. 13–50.

11. There is considerable debate about the ways invention was incentivised and commercialised, and the relationship between what might be distinguished as pure science and useful knowledge in this process. Slack, *Invention of Improvement*; Hunter, *Establishing the New Science*; Stewart, *Rise of Public Science*; Shapiro, *Culture of Fact*; Yamamoto, *Taming Capitalism*, pp. 1–8; Feingold, 'Projectors and Learned Projects', pp. 63–79; Allen, *British Industrial Revolution*; Howes, *Arts and Minds*, pp. 1–28; Mokyr, *Gifts of Athena*; Berg, 'Useful Knowledge', pp. 117–41; Jones, *Industrial Enlightenment*; Miller, 'The Usefulness of Natural Philosophy', pp. 185–201; Roberts, *Slavery and the Enlightenment*, p. 32; Cookson, *Making an Industrial Revolution*, pp. 8–29, 142–70.
12. The agricultural revolution is still a widely debated topic, and while dramatic increases in yields are generally accepted, the precise causes and chronologies of these changes are still debated. Turner et al., *Farm Production*, pp. 9–26; Overton, *Agricultural Revolution*, pp. 1–9; Fisher, *Enclosure of Knowledge*. The most critical essay regarding agricultural productivity increases in Britain and the consequent impact on industrialisation remains O'Brien and Heath, 'English and French Landowners', pp. 23–30. The classic study of urbanisation and agricultural development remains Wrigley, 'Urban Growth and Agricultural Change', pp. 683–728. For wider studies on the relationship between exploitation of natural resources and economic development, see: Beckert et al., 'Commodity Frontiers', pp. 435–50; Barbier, *Scarcity and Frontiers*, pp. 1–46; Barbier, *Natural Resources*, pp. 51–107; Richards, *The Unending Frontier*; Hansen, 'Colonial Economic Development', pp. 611–12.
13. For the development of mining and metallurgy in Britain, see Clark and Jacks, 'Coal and the Industrial Revolution', pp. 39–72; Hyde, *Technological Change and the British Iron Industry*; Cunha, 'Coppering the Industrial Revolution', pp. 40–69; Wrigley, 'Reconsidering the Industrial Revolution', pp. 9–42. This typically compares positively to coal mining in China or India, which was beset with challenges despite having extensive coal deposits, see, Pomeranz, *Great Divergence*, pp. 59–68; Hume, 'Of Commerce', pp. 93–104.
14. For the scale and significance of Britain's colonial economy, see Higman, *Slave Populations of the British Caribbean*; Hacker, 'From "20 and odd" to 10 Million', table 1; Blackburn, *The Overthrow of Colonial Slavery*, pp. 1–38, 60; Combrink and Van Rossum, 'Introduction', pp. 1–14; Best and Levitt, *Essays on the Theory of Plantation Economy*; Beckert et al., 'Commodity Frontiers', pp. 435–50; Harvey, 'Slavery, Indenture and the Development of British Industrial Capitalism', p. 67; Swingen, *Competing Visions of Empire*; Pomeranz, *Great*

*Divergence*, pp. 4, 274–8, 313–15. For origins and development of debate about the relationship between enslaved labour and industrial development, see Williams, *Capitalism and Slavery*; Inikori, *Africans*; Eltis and Engerman, 'The Importance of Slavery'; Berg and Hudson, *Slavery, Capitalism and the Industrial Revolution*; Beckert, *Empire of Cotton*; Baptist, *The Half Has Never Been Told*; Eltis, *Atlantic Cataclysm*. Data in this paragraph is from TASTD and RBS.

15. Thomas and McCloskey, 'Overseas Trade and Empire', pp. 88–9; Davis, 'English Foreign Trade', pp. 285–303; Pettigrew, *Freedom's Debt*, pp. 11–44; Pettigrew, *Global Trade*; Price, 'What did Merchants Do?', pp. 267–84; Zahedieh, *The Capital and the Colonies*, pp. 137–72; Zahedieh, 'Eric Williams and William Forbes', pp. 784–808; Cain and Hopkins, 'Gentlemanly Capitalism', pp. 501–25.
16. Findlay and O'Rourke, *Power and Plenty*, p. 344. For Indian inspiration for British industrialisation, see Parasarathi, *Why Europe Grew Rich*, pp. 89–114; Berg, 'In Pursuit of Luxury', pp. 85–142. For different approaches to understanding the impact of cotton, see: Beckert, *Empire of Cotton*; Riello, *Cotton*.

## CHAPTER ONE: THE SPIRIT OF ENTERPRISE

1. Anon., *Europæ Modernæ Speculum*.
2. Slack, *Invention of Improvement*, pp. 1–14, quoted p. 5.
3. Jonnson and Wennerlind, *Scarcity*, pp. 54–8, quoted p. 55; Slack, *Invention of Improvement*, p. 2; Mokyr, *Culture of Growth*.
4. Sprat, *History of the Royal Society*, p. 1. For the development and impact of the Royal Society, see Shapin and Schaffer, *Leviathan and the Air-Pump*; Wojcik, *Robert Boyle*; Hunter, *Establishing the New Science*; Hunter, *Science and the Shape of Orthodoxy*; Stewart, *Rise of Public Science*; Shapiro, *Culture of Fact*.
5. 'Investing in Innovation Dataset'; 'Boyle, Robert', 'Chardin, Sir John [Jean]', 'Grew, Nehemiah' in ODNB.
6. BL, Add Ms 72897, f. 134, On War Chariots, c. 1680s.
7. 'Hooke, Robert' in ODNB. For the transmission of skill and knowledge, see: Shapin and Schaffer, *Leviathan and the Air-Pump*; Wallis, *The Market for Skill*, pp. 49–66; Cookson, *Making an Industrial Revolution*, pp. 8–29; Mokyr, *Lever of Riches*, pp. 72–7; Fisher, *Enclosure of Knowledge*, pp. 1–35.
8. MacLeod, *Inventing the Industrial Revolution*, pp. 40, 69, 76; Bottomley, *British Patent System*, pp. 1–3; North, *Structure and Change*, p. 164; Mokyr, *Lever of Riches*, p. 79; Mokyr, *Enlightened Economy*, p. 409; Mokyr, 'Intellectual Property Rights', pp. 349–53; Mokyr, 'Cultural Entrepreneurs', p. 4.
9. Carter, *England's Interest Asserted*, p. 32.
10. Woodcroft, *Titles of Patents of Invention*, patents 241, 271, 371, 392.
11. Woodcroft, *Titles of Patents of Invention*, patents 234, 244, 265.
12. Woodcroft, *Titles of Patents of Invention*, patents 211, 246, 272, 282, 286, 301.
13. Hale, *An Account of Several New Inventions*.
14. The result of a chemical reaction called galvanic corrosion. Hale, *An Account of Several New Inventions*, pp. ii, vi–vii.
15. Slack, *Invention of Improvement*, pp. 2, 7–8; Allen, *British Industrial Revolution*, p. 149; Bottomley, *British Patent System*, p. 12; Harris, 'Copper and Shipping', pp. 550–68.
16. Woodcroft, *Titles of Patents of Invention*, patent 356; PA, HL/PO/JO/10/1/517/1412, Amended Draft of an Act for the encouragement of a new

Invention by Thomas Savery for raising water and occasioning motion to all sorts of mill-work by the impellent force of fire, 20 March 1699; for Newcomen's and Watt's developments see Chapters Six to Ten, for Darby's ironworks see Chapter Eight, for the ongoing development of the silk industry see Chapter Six.

17. For field rotation in Norfolk see Chapter Two; for south Wales mining and metallurgy see Chapter Three; for the violent exploitation of enslaved labour see Chapter Four.
18. 'Investing in Innovation Dataset'.
19. 'Investing in Innovation Dataset'; Carr, *Selected Charters*, pp. 172–81; TASTD; RBS.
20. Carr, *Selected Charters*, pp. 212–15; Murphy, 'Trading Options before Black-Scholes', pp. 8–30.
21. Kynaston, *Till Time's Last Stand*; Murphy, *Origins of English Financial Markets*; Milevsky, *The Day the King Defaulted*; Horsfield, 'The "Stop of the Exchequer" Revisited', pp. 511–28; Dickson, *The Financial Revolution*; North and Weingast, 'Constitutions and Commitment', pp. 815–16; Brewer, *Sinews of Power*, pp. 73–108. For contemporaneous financial development in Scotland: McDiarmid, *Credit, Currency and Capital.*
22. Quoted in Tawny, *Small Credit*, p. 44. PA, HL.PO.JP.10.6.52, Report from the Commissioners of Trade and Plantations, 16 Dec. 1703. Defoe, *An Essay Upon Projects*, pp. 1–24; Yamamoto, *Taming Capitalism*, pp. 229–6.
23. 'Investing in Innovation Dataset'. For relationship between joint-stock investment and other activities, see Bennett, 'Merchant Capital', pp. 2–5; Bennett, 'Caribbean Plantation Economies', pp. 508–39; Smith, *Merchants*; Smith, 'Social Networks of Investment', pp. 912–39; Pettigrew, *Global Trade*; Gauci, *Emporium of the World*; Grassby, *Business Community*; Carr, *Selected Charters.*
24. 'Investing in Innovation Dataset'. For female investors and business owners in the seventeenth and eighteenth centuries, see: Froide, *Silent Partners*, p. 59; Erickson, *Women and Property*; Erickson, 'Wealthy Businesswomen', pp. 29–58; Barker, *The Business of Women*; Phillips, *Women in Business.*
25. 'Investing in Innovation Dataset'.
26. 'Investing in Innovation Dataset'.
27. TNA, CUST 3/12, Ledgers of Imports and Exports, 1709. For expansion of slave-trade, see Chapters Four and Nine.
28. Muldrew, *Economy of Obligation*; Hancock, *Citizens of the World*, p. 5; Langford, *Polite and Commercial People*, pp. 59–122; Marshall, 'Polite and Commercial People in the Caribbean', pp. 173–90; Thomas, *In Pursuit of Civility.*
29. Tawny, *Small Credit*, pp. 43–53.
30. Winter, *Banking, Projecting and Politicking*, pp. 1–9; Kim, 'How Modern Banking Originated', pp. 939–59; Temin and Voth, *Prometheus Shackled*, pp. 176–86; Temin and Voth, 'Banking as an Emerging Technology', pp. 149–78; Kerridge, *Trade and Banking*; Dickson, *Financial Revolution*, pp. 6–7; Wennerlind, *Casualties of Credit*, pp. 95–108; Chapman, *Rise of Merchant Banking*; Cassis and Cottrell, *Private Banking in Europe*. The simultaneous expansion of London's insurance industry and transnational banking firms were especially important for international traders, see: Leonard, *London Marine Insurance*; Carlos and Neal, 'Amsterdam and London', pp. 21–46; Neal, 'How It All Began', pp. 117–40.

31. JRRIL, Eng MSS 986, ff. 8; 35: John Heath's Order to Robert Clayton, 17 March 1661; John South to John Morris, 12 February 1677.
32. JRRIL, Eng MSS 986, f. 21, Letter from Lord Rivers to Robert Clayton, 23 October 1673.
33. Melton, *Sir Robert Clayton*, pp. 141–2, 147, 156.
34. Smith, *Merchants*; Smith, 'Social Networks of Investment'; Pearson and Richardson, 'Business Networking in the Industrial Revolution', pp. 657–79.
35. For the role of Britain's state in shaping economic policy, see: Pincus, 'Rethinking Mercantilism', pp. 3–34; Hutchinson, *Before Adam Smith*; Stern and Wennerlind, *Mercantilism Reimagined*; Rössner, *Managing the Wealth of Nations*, pp. 164–202; Hoppit, *Britain's Political Economies*, pp. 102–38; Vries, 'Governing Growth', pp. 67–193; Ashworth, *Industrial Revolution*.
36. BL, Sloane Ms 857, f. 103, Francis Lodwick's observations on trade, n. d.
37. BL, Sloane Ms 2902, ff. 171–80, Board of Trade to William III, 23 December 1697.
38. BL, 21.h.1.(164), Proclamation Prohibiting the Importation of Divers Foreign Wares and Merchandizes into this the Realm of England, 1661.
39. BL, Add Ms 25115, ff. 141–3; 148–9: Petition of the framework knitters of silk stockings, 1661; Response of the Council of Trade to the petition of the framework knitters of silk stockings, 23 February 1661. Styles, 'Product Innovation', pp. 131–3.
40. BL, Add Ms 25115, f. 304, Reasons offered by the corporation for the refiners of sugar in support of their petition, 1661.
41. BL, Sloane Ms 2902, ff. 171–80, Board of Trade to William III, 23 December 1697. For British metallurgical industry, see Chapters Three and Seven.
42. BL, Sloane Ms 2902, ff. 171–80, Board of Trade to William III, 23 December 1697; PA, HL.PO.JP.10.6.52, Report from the Commissioners of Trade and Plantations, 16 December 1703.
43. Styles, 'Product Innovation', pp. 124–69.
44. PA, HL.PO.JP.10.6.52, Report from the Commissioners of Trade and Plantations, 16 December 1703; Slack, *Invention of Improvement*, pp. 1–14.

## CHAPTER TWO: A GREEN AND PLEASANT LAND

1. For the scale and timing of changes in agricultural productivity and the impact of environmental change, see: Broadberry et al., *British Economic Growth*, pp. 80–124; Wrigley, 'Urban Growth in Early Modern England', pp. 79–112; Hoyle, 'Why Was There No Crisis', pp. 67–98; Tello et al., 'Onset of the English Agricultural Revolution', pp. 448–9; Muldrew, *Food, Energy and the Creation of Industriousness*; De Vries, 'Economic Crisis', pp. 152–3. For the impact of the Little Ice Age on Scotland: Smout et al., 'Scottish Emigration', pp. 76–112; Cullen, *Famine in Scotland*.
2. Overton, *Agricultural Revolution*, pp. 121–2.
3. Overton, *Agricultural Revolution*, pp. 124–5.
4. Hindle, *Social Topography*, pp. 353–81; Fisher, *Enclosure of Knowledge*, pp. 60–88.
5. Melton, *Sir Robert Clayton*, p. 13.
6. Childrey, *Brittania Baconica*, p. 103; Allison, 'Sheep-Corn Husbandry', pp. 12–30; 'Childrey, Joshua' in ODNB.

7. Jones, 'Agriculture and Economic Growth in England', pp. 1–18; Overton, *Agricultural Revolution*, pp. 3, 76–80; Turner, Beckett and Afton, *Farm Production in England*, pp. 117–33; Yelling, 'Probate Inventories and the Geography of Livestock Farming', pp. 111–26; Glennie, 'Continuity and Change in Hertfordshire Agriculture', pp. 55–75; Tello et al., 'Onset of the English Agricultural Revolution', pp. 445–54; Melton, *Sir Robert Clayton*, p. 13; Merchant, *Death of Nature*; Allen, *Enclosure and the Yeoman*, pp. 69–88.
8. Worlidge, *Systema Agriculturæ*, unnumbered front matter.
9. Overton, *Agricultural Revolution*, pp. 3, 99–100; Tello et al., 'Onset of the English Agricultural Revolution', pp. 445–54.
10. Meager, *Mystery of Husbandry*, p. 23–4; Donaldson, *Husbandry Anatomized*, p. 64; Worlidge, *Systema Agriculturæ*, pp. 58–72.
11. Overton, *Agricultural Revolution*, pp. 3, 99–100, 106–10; Tello et al., 'Onset of the English Agricultural Revolution', pp. 445–54.
12. Best and Woodward, *Farming and Memorandum Books of Henry Best*.
13. Worlidge, *Systema Agriculturæ*, p. 161; Allison, 'Flock Management', pp. 104–6; Bowden, 'Wool Supply', pp. 48–9.
14. Childrey, *Brittania Baconica*, pp. 8, 71, 84; Worlidge, *Systema Agriculturæ*, p. 161; Houghton, *Collection of Letters*; Carus-Wilson, 'The Woollen Industry', pp. 614–74; Overton, *Agricultural Revolution*, pp. 106–10.
15. Overton, *Agricultural Revolution*, pp. 75–82; Broadberry et al., *British Economic Growth*, appendix D.
16. Schumpeter, *English Overseas Trade Statistics*; Tello et al., 'Onset of the English Agricultural Revolution', p. 449.
17. Melton, *Sir Robert Clayton*, p. 13; Slack, *Invention of Improvement*, pp. 20–3. For an overview of transportation and development of road system, see Hey, *Packmen, Carriers and Packhorse Roads*; Albert, *Turnpike Road System*; Bogart, 'Did Turnpike Trusts Increase Transportation Investment?', pp. 439–68.
18. Ogilby quoted in Slack, *Invention of Improvement*, p. 23; Melton, *Sir Robert Clayton*, p. 10–14, 156; Wrigley, 'Urban Growth in Early Modern England', pp. 79–112.
19. For labour structure, see: Shaw-Taylor, 'Occupational Structure of Britain'; Wallis, *Market For Skill*, pp. 75–107. For the relationship between landowners and investment, see: Yamamoto, 'Piety, Profit and Public Service', pp. 806–34; Habakkuk, 'Rise and Fall of English Landed Families', pp. 187–207; Bogart, 'Did Turnpike Trusts Increase Transportation Investment?', pp. 439–68; Aston and Philpin, *Brenner Debate*; Cain and Hopkins, *British Imperialism*, pp. 73–102.
20. For an expanded and detailed discussion of the wool production process and the workers involved at different stages: Carus-Wilson, 'The Woollen Industry', pp. 614–74.
21. For the European woollen industry at the start of this period, see: Carus-Wilson, 'The Woollen Industry', pp. 614–74; for the English woollen industry, see: Bowden, *The Wool Trade*.
22. Carus-Wilson, 'The Woollen Industry', pp. 614–74.
23. Carter, *England's Interest Asserted*, p. 2.
24. Carter, *England's Interest Asserted*, pp. 1–2, 6–7, 24.
25. BL, 21.h.1.(105), Proclamation for the Preventing of the Exportation of Wools, Wool-Fells, Wollen-Yarn, Fullers-Earth, and other scouring earths, out of this Kingdom, 1660.

26. Raithby, *Statutes of the Realm*.
27. Raithby, *Statutes of the Realm*.
28. BL, Sloane Ms 2902, ff. 171–80, Board of Trade to William III, 23 December 1697.
29. PA, HL.PO.JP.10.6.52, Report from the Commissioners of Trade and Plantations, 16 December 1703.
30. BL, Sloane Ms 2902, ff. 3–4, Answer of the Commissioners of Trade and Plantations to the Honourable the House of Commons, 22 March 1700.
31. Carus-Wilson, 'The Woollen Industry', pp. 614–74; Clapham, 'The Transference of the Worsted Industry'; Minoletti, 'The Transition to Factory Production'; Sugden et al., 'Adam Smith Revisited', pp. 163–91; Sugden, 'Clapham Revisited', pp. 203–24.
32. Bowden, 'Wool Supply', p. 53.
33. Kerridge, *Textile Manufacturers*, pp. 38–9; Chevis, 'Innovations in Cloth Manufacture', pp. 207–11.
34. Kerridge, *Textile Manufacturers*, pp. 38–9; Chevis, 'Innovations in Cloth Manufacture', pp. 207–11.
35. Chevis, 'Innovations in Cloth Manufacture', pp. 211–14.
36. Kerridge, *Textile Manufacturers*, pp. 40–1.
37. Kerridge, *Textile Manufacturers*, pp. 42–59.
38. Kerridge, *Textile Manufacturers*, pp. 121–5.
39. PA, HL.PO.JP.10.6.52, Report from the Commissioners of Trade and Plantations, 16 December 1703.
40. TNA, CUST 3/7, Ledgers of Imports and Exports, 1703.
41. Woodcroft, *Titles of Patents of Invention*, patents 276, 286, 343, 362.
42. BL, Sloane Ms 2902, ff. 3–4, Answer of the Commissioners of Trade and Plantations to the Honourable the House of Commons, 22 March 1700.
43. WYAS Bradford, SpSt/14/8;37: Woolen Broad Cloths made in the West Riding of Yorkshire, 1725–9; Woolen Broad and Narrow Cloths made in the West Riding of Yorkshire, 1730–68.
44. WYAS Calderdale, FH:396, George Stansfield to John Doville, 13 February 1729.
45. WYAS Calderdale, FH:396: George Stansfield to John and Peter Doville, 11 August 1730; 8 October 1730; 23 February 1731; Annual Account with John and Peter Doville, 23 January 1733.
46. BL, IOR/G/17/1, ff. 17–20; 52–63: Edward Day in Mocha to the East India Company in London, 17 August 1719; Factors in Mocha to the East India Company in London, 20 July 1721.
47. BL, IOR/G/17/1, ff. 269–278: Factors in Mocha to the East India Company in London, 1 April 1725.
48. For instance, in just one year, the East India Company gifted more than ten different types of cotton cloths to the Governor of Mocha alongside only two samples of English woollens. BL, IOR/G/17/1, f. 34, List of goods presented to the Governor and Officers of Mocha, August 1720.
49. BL, IOR/G/12/8, ff. 1295–6; 1298; 1321: Instructions to Supercargo of the Loyal Bliss, 1712; Instructions to Supercargo of the Hester, 1713; Instructions to Supercargo of the Marlborough, 6 January 1716.
50. BL, IOR/G/12/8, f. 1363: Instructions to Supercargoes to Canton, 16 December 1719.

51. WYAS Bradford, HAS:307(321): John Firth to Mr Lord and Mr Woollenden, 13 August 1739; John Firth to Mr Whilton and Mr Harrop, 29 April 1740.
52. WYAS Bradford, SpSt/14/6;11: Hampson and Tatem of Messina to Walter Stanhope of Leeds, 3 November 1732; Abraham Henckell and Mason to Walter Stanhope, 27 June 1757.
53. TNA, CUST 3/4 and CUST 3/50: Ledgers of Imports and Exports, 1700; Ledgers of Imports and Exports, 1750.
54. Carter, *England's Interest Asserted*, pp. 1–2.

## CHAPTER THREE: DESCENT INTO DARKNESS

1. Chamberlayne, *Present State of England*, pp. 24–30. For wider range of authors writing about Britain's abundant resources: Jonsson and Wennerlind, *Scarcity*, pp. 1–20, 46–102.
2. Plot, *Natural History of Staffordshire*, p. 129; Hatcher, *History of the British Coal Industry*, pp. 189–90.
3. Quoted in Hatcher, *History of the British Coal Industry*, p. 190; 'UK Mining Disasters, 1707–99'.
4. J. C., *The Compleat Collier*, pp. 22–3; Hatcher, *History of the British Coal Industry*, pp. 187–238.
5. Hatcher, *History of the British Coal Industry*, pp. 201–12.
6. 'UK Mining Disasters, 1707–99'.
7. Quoted in Nef, 'Mining and Metallurgy', p. 745; 'UK Mining Disasters, 1707–99'.
8. Nef, 'Mining and Metallurgy', pp. 691–761.
9. Nef, 'Mining and Metallurgy', pp. 691–761.
10. Nef, 'Mining and Metallurgy', pp. 691–761.
11. Anon., *Articles of Agreement & Subscription between His Highness Prince Rupert and Diverse Noble and Honourable Persons*, p. 1; Nef, 'Mining and Metallurgy', pp. 691–761.
12. Hatcher, *History of the British Coal Industry*, pp. 191–2; 'Plot, Robert' in ODNB.
13. Hatcher, *History of the British Coal Industry*, pp. 192–201.
14. Pounds, 'Population Movement in Cornwall', pp. 37–46; Evans and Miskell, *Swansea Copper*, pp. 40, 43.
15. NLW, 14362 E, Diary of Sir Humphrey Mackworth, 27 September 1696; Waller, *An Essay on the Value of the Mines*, unpaginated epistle dedicatory.
16. 'Mackworth, Sir Humphrey, Industrialist and Parliamentarian' in Online Dictionary of Welsh Biography.
17. Waller, *Essay on the Value of the Mines*, unpaginated epistle dedicatory.
18. Mackworth, *Mine-Adventure*, pp. 1–2, 4, 8–11.
19. Carr, *Selected Charters*, pp. 243–4; Wyeth, *An Answer to a Letter from Dr. Bray*, p. 3. For the role of religion in imperial projects and investment, see Smith, *Religion and Governance*; 'Investing in Innovation Dataset'.
20. Mackworth, *Mine-Adventure*, pp. 10–15; Anon., *An Answer to a Paper Published by One Bateman*; 'Investing in Innovation Dataset'.
21. Waller, *The Second Abstract of the State of the Mines of Bwlchyr-Eskir-Hyr*, pp. 2–3; Waller, *The Third Abstract of the State of the Mines of Bwlchyr-Eskir-Hyr*, p. 4.
22. Yamamoto, 'Piety, Profit and Public Service', pp. 806–34, quote p. 815.
23. WGA, RISW/Gn 4/552, Letter from Humphrey Mackworth to his brother, 29 May 1711; Yamamoto, 'Piety, Profit and Public Service', pp. 816–30, quote p. 816.

24. WGA, RISW/Gn 4/184, Letter from Humphrey Mackworth to Bulkley Mackworth, 25 May 1713; 'Mackworth, Sir Humphrey (1657–1727), of Gnoll Castle, Neath, Glamorganshire' in HOPO.
25. 'Mackworth, Herbert (1687–1765), of Gnoll, Glamorganshire' and 'Mackworth, Herbert (1737–91), of Gnoll, Glamorganshire' in HOPO; Bowen, *Wales and the British Overseas Empire*.
26. WGA, NAS Gn/I 1/3: Articles of Agreement of Co-partnership, 1718; Articles of Agreement to Raise a Joint-stock, 1719; Articles of Agreement between the Co-partners of the Company and Sir Humphrey Mackworth, 1720.
27. Evans and Miskell, *Swansea Copper*.
28. J. C., *Compleat Collier*; Hatcher, *History of the British Coal Industry*, pp. 210–12.
29. J. C., *Compleat Collier*, pp. 20–1, 24–8; 'UK Mining Disasters, 1707–99'.
30. Oldroyd, *Estates, Enterprise and Investment*, p. 17.
31. TWA, Journal of the Company of Merchant Adventurers of Newcastle, 4 September 1688.
32. Ellis, *Study of the Business Fortunes*.
33. TWA, Cotesworth: CM 2/28, Counterparty for the *St Peter of Arundel*, April 1703; CM 2/59, Nathaniel Remington in Hamburg to Sutton & Cotesworth, 30 March 1694; CM 2/63, John Samwaine in London to Sutton & Cotesworth, 3 April 1705; CM 2/64, Thomas Bard from London to Sutton & Cotesworth, 7 April 1705; CM 2/74, John Greatheed from London to William Cotesworth, 9 August 1705; CM 2/136, Richard Brocas from London to William Cotesworth, 7 April 1712; CM 2/66–300, Letters to William Cotesworth regarding shipping, 1705–15.
34. TWA, Cotesworth: CM 2/290, Benjamin Sleigh from London to William Cotesworth, 14 May 1715; CM 2/226, Agreement between William Cotesworth and Andrew Naylor junior, 24 March 1714; CK 11/4, James Weatherby's Report on Stella Engines, 5 July 1719; CK 11/36, Charges for establishing the Barlofield Pit, June to November 1725. Oldroyd, *Estates, Enterprise and Investment*, pp. 10, 59.
35. TWA, Cotesworth: CK 11/28, James Weatherby to William Cotesworth, 7 January 1722. Oldroyd, *Estates, Enterprise and Investment*, p. 10; Ellis, *Study of the Business Fortunes*; Bath, 'Violence and Violent Crime', p. 251.
36. TWA, Cotesworth: CK 12/5, Lady Carr to William Cotesworth, 7 July 1713; CK 12/8, Nathaniel Weatherall's note, 6 October 1713; CK 11/60, Extract of deliveries of wood for wagonway, April 1710–October 1711.
37. TWA, Cotesworth: CM 2/180, William Cotesworth to Gilbert Spearman, 25 November 1712; CK 8/3, Agreement between Dame Jane Clavering, George Pitt, William Cotesworth, Robert Wright, Gilbert Spearman and Thomas Brunell, c. 1710s; CK 11/37, Albert Silvertop to William Cotesworth, 26 October 1726; CK 11/42, A view of that part of Winlaton wagonway kept by Albert Silvertop, 10 February 1726.
38. TWA, Cotesworth: CK 11/30, Plan of the new wagonway, c. 1723; CK 11/35, Account of keel berths and staiths in Stella & Wilanton freehold, 12 May 1725; CK 11/50, Account of keel berths and staiths in Stella, September 1726. Oldroyd, *Estates, Enterprise and Investment*, p. 16.
39. Ashton and Sykes, *Coal Industry*, p. 212; Evans and Miskell, *Swansea Copper*, p. 174. For an overview of the wider colliery-owning community around Newcastle, see: Purdue, *Merchants and Gentry*.

40. Hughes, *Copperopolis*, p. 2; Evans, *Slave Wales*, pp. 39–40; Pounds, 'Population Movement in Cornwall', p. 41; Broadberry et al., *British Economic Growth*, pp. 137–44.
41. Data from Schumpeter, *English Overseas Trade Statistics*. For ongoing development in mining and for the iron industry specifically, see Chapter Eight.

## CHAPTER FOUR: BETWEEN HEAVEN AND HELL

1. Games, *Web of Empire*; Horning, *Ireland in the Virginia Sea*; Roper, *Advancing Empire*; Stern, *Empire, Incorporated*; Smith, *Merchants*, pp. 227–8; Smith, 'Reinterpreting the Virginia Plantation', pp. 884–914; Siochrú, 'Extirpation and Annihilation', pp. 163–85.
2. Hubbard, *A History of St Kitts*, pp. 17–18; Madley, 'Too Furious', pp. 215–42; Dunbar-Ortiz, *An Indigenous People's History*, p. 64; Menard, *Sweet Negotiations*, p. 1; Cave, *Lethal Encounters*; Grenier, *The First Way of War*.
3. BL, Egerton 2395, f. 288, The Most Humble Proposal of the Merchants, Planters and Traders to the Island of Antigua, c. 1660.
4. R. B., *The English Empire*, pp. 92–4; BL, Sloane Ms 2902, ff. 1–10, Answer of the Commissioners of Trade and Plantations to the Honourable the House of Commons, 22 March 1700. For the expansion of British territories in North America and relationship with indigenous peoples, see Mancke, *Fault Lines of Empire*, pp. 1–22; Slater, 'The Economy of Colonial British America'; Fogleman, 'Migrations to the Thirteen British North American Colonies', pp. 691–709; Owens, *'Indian Wars'*; Anderson, *Crucible of War*; Hämäläinen, *Indigenous Continent*.
5. BL, Egerton 2395, f. 60, Journal of the Conquest of Jamaica, 1655. See also Pestana, *English Conquest of Jamaica*. This book contains racialised language describing black enslaved people only when it is quoted directly from original sources and the inclusion of the quote helps demonstrate the ways in which race formed part of how British people understood and discussed the exploitation of enslaved people. For early modern views of race and slavery in Britain, see: Brown, *Reaper's Garden*; Jorati, *Slavery and Race*; Smith, *Nature, Human Nature, and Human Difference*.
6. Anon., *Laws of Jamaica*, p. A4; R. B., *The English Empire*, pp. 207–9.
7. BL, 21.h.1.(167), *Proclamation for the Encouraging of Planters in His Majesty's Island of Jamaica in the West-Indies* (1661); Anon., *Laws of Jamaica*, p. B3–4; Amussen, *Caribbean Exchanges*, pp. 43, 73.
8. For practices of enslavement and colonial management, see: Gragg, *'Englishmen Transplanted'*; Bennett, 'Merchant Capital', pp. 2–5; Bennett, 'Caribbean Plantation Economies', pp. 508–39; Menard, *Sweet Negotiations*, pp. 2–4, 98–121; Roberts, 'Surrendering Surinam', pp. 225–56; Greene, 'Colonial South Carolina', pp. 192–210; Zacek, *Settler Society*; Thompson, 'Henry Drax's Instructions', pp. 565–604; Burnard, *Mastery, Tyranny & Desire*.
9. Roberts, *Slavery and the Enlightenment*, pp. 9–10.
10. Quoted in Amussen, *Caribbean Exchanges*, p. 53. The networks across colonial economy, see: Bennett, 'Merchant Capital', pp. 280–2; Dunn, *Sugar and Slaves*, pp. 110–16; Roberts, 'Surrendering Surinam', pp. 248–54; Zahedieh, 'Trade, Plunder and Economic Development', pp. 210–13; Arena, 'Indian Slaves from Guiana', pp. 65–90; Murphy, 'Kalinago Colonizers', pp. 17–30.

11. Amussen, *Caribbean Exchanges*, pp. 79–80.
12. Menard, *Sweet Negotiations*, pp. 1–2, 91–104; Tann, 'Steam and Sugar', p. 65; Amussen, *Caribbean Exchanges*, p, 80. These links are examined further in chapters Three, Five, Eight, Nine and Ten.
13. Govier, 'The Royal Society, Slavery and the Island of Jamaica', pp. 203–17. See also Jorati, *Slavery and Race*.
14. Woodcroft, *Titles of Patents of Invention*, patents 326 and 385; quoted in Menard, *Sweet Negotiations*, p. 98; Tann, 'Steam and Sugar', p. 66; Rönnbäck, 'Sweet Business', p. 234.
15. BL, Egerton 2395, ff. 466–7, Some Reflections on the Royal African Company's Interest in the Plantations & the Use of a Major General in the Island of Jamaica, c. 1660. Gerbier quoted in Otremba, 'Enlightened Institutions', pp. 226–7. Zahedieh, 'Merchants of Port Royal', pp. 570–93; Eltis, *Rise of African Slavery*, pp. 205–7.
16. TNA, CO 139/1, An Act for the Better Ordering and Governing of Negro Slaves, 1664; Taylor quoted in Amussen, *Caribbean Exchanges*, pp. 64–5. Violence and other forms of coercive control were prominent features across plantations in Britain's colonies in the Caribbean and North America, see Vidal, 'Violence, Slavery and Race'; Stubbs, *Masters of Violence*; Roberts, 'The Whip and the Hoe', pp. 108–30; Burnard, *Planters, Merchants and Slaves*, pp. 53–96.
17. Anon., *Great Newes from the Barbadoes*; Tony quoted in Menard, *Sweet Negotiations*, p. 99.
18. Anon., *Laws of Jamaica*, pp. D3–D4, p. 7; BL, Egerton 2395, ff. 466–7, Some Reflections on the Royal African Company's Interest in the Plantations & the Use of a Major General in the Island of Jamaica, c. 1660. For resistance and revolt by enslaved people, and the colonial response, see Craton, *Testing the Chains*; Gaspar, *Bondmen and Rebels*; Beckles, *Black Rebellion in Barbados*; Rediker, *The Slave Ship*; Brown, *Tacky's Revolt*; Sharples, 'Discovering Slave Conspiracies', pp. 811–43; Rugemer, *Slave Law*.
19. Anon., *Laws of Jamaica*, p. B2; Zahedieh, 'Merchants of Port Royal', pp. 570–93; Menard, *Sweet Negotiations*, pp. 1–2; Otremba, 'Enlightened Institutions', p. 225.
20. Anon., *Great Newes from the Barbadoes*, p. 1; Anon., *Laws of Jamaica*, pp. B2, D4; Taylor quoted in Amussen, *Caribbean Exchanges*, p. 59.
21. TNA CUST 7/3, Ledgers of Imports and Exports, 1700.
22. BL, Egerton 2395, ff. 466–7, Some Reflections on the Royal African Company's Interest in the Plantations & the Use of a Major General in the Island of Jamaica, c. 1660; BL, Sloane Ms 2902, f. 87, Instruction to the Governor of New Hampshire, July 1696; Quoted in Govier, 'The Royal Society, Slavery and the Island of Jamaica', p. 212.
23. TASTD; ManchesterRO, GB127.Tracts/P.2881.22, A Supplement to the Royal-African Company's Memorial, 5 February 1708.
24. Quoted in Govier, 'The Royal Society, Slavery and the Island of Jamaica', p. 212; BL, Sloane Ms 2902, ff. 171–80, Board of Trade to William III, 23 December 1697.
25. ManchesterRO, GB127.Tracts/P.2881 20; 24: A Memorial Touching the Nature and Present State of the Trade to Africa, 4 January 1708; Letter to a Member of Parliament Setting forth the Trade to Africa, 12 March 1708.
26. ManchesterRO, GB127.Tracts/P.2881.16, The British Interest on the Coast of Africa Considered, 18 March 1708.

27. 'Robert Heysham', 'Edward Searle', 'Abraham Houlditch', 'James Waite', 'Anthony Tourney' and 'Robert Brooke' in RBS. For details of their voyages, see: TASTD.
28. 'Edmund Saunders' in RBS.
29. ManchesterRO, GB127.Tracts/P.2881.20, A Memorial Touching the Nature and Present State of the Trade to Africa, 4 January 1708. See also, Pettigrew, 'Free to Enslave', p. 18. Data from TASTD.
30. ManchesterRO, GB127.Tracts/P.2881.17, The Falsities of Private Traders to Africa Discovered, 25 March 1708.
31. For continued development of the slave-trade see Chapter Nine.
32. Rönnbäck, 'Governance, Value-Added and Rents', pp. 130–50. Despite often being treated separately, consumption and production in Britain and abroad both contributed to economic development, to different degrees in different times and places, see: Berg and Hudson, *Slavery, Capitalism and the Industrial Revolution*; Radburn, *Traders in Men*; Davis, *Industrial Revolution and British Overseas Trade*, p. 63; Morgan, *Slavery, Atlantic Trade*; Eltis and Engerman, 'The Importance of Slavery', pp. 123–44; Burnard, *Jamaica in the Age of Revolution*, pp. 217–25; Engerman, 'The Slave Trade and British Capital Formation', pp. 430–43.
33. 'Peter Day' and 'Isaac Hobshouse' in RBS. For value of sugar refining, Rönnbäck, 'Sweet Business', p. 229.
34. 'Henry Richards', 'Sir Richard Brocas' and 'John Gilpin' in RBS.
35. 'Fleet, Sir John (1648–1712), of Allhallows Staining, London, and Battersea, Surr' in HOPO; 'Sir John Fleete' and 'Bryan Blundell' in RBS.
36. 'Abraham Elton (Sr)' in RBS; 'Elton, Sir Abraham, 1st Bt. (1654–1728), of Clevedon Court and Whitestaunton, Somerset' in HOPO.
37. WYAS Calderdale, SH:7/LL/88, Letter from Thomas and Jeremy Lister to Samuel Lister, 25 June 1735.
38. Beckett, *Coal and Tobacco*, pp. 4–8, 14, 19–37, 132–4; 'Lowther, Sir John, 2nd Bt. I (1642–1706), of Whitehaven, Cumb.' in HOPO.
39. Schumpeter, *English Overseas Trade Statistics*; Zahedieh, 'Colonies, Copper, and the Market for Inventive Activity', pp. 805–25.
40. WYAS Calderdale, STN:328, Double entry account book dealing with trade in tobacco, sugar, cloth, sherry, etc to and from France and Barbados on the ship 'Bonadventure'.
41. SBA, UGD 019, Alexander Shairp & Company Cash Book, 1754.
42. Stewart-Brown, *Liverpool Ships*, pp. 1–7, 111; 'Richard Gildart', 'John Okill', 'Richard Golightly' and 'Robert Bogle' in RBS.
43. ULLSC, RP XXIII.4.1, William Rathbone Day Book, 1742–7.
44. Stewart-Brown, *Liverpool Ships*, pp. 17–20; Rönnbäck, 'Sweet Business', p. 229; Draper, 'The City of London and Slavery', pp. 432–66.
45. LMM, MDHB/P/1/1, Collected Acts of Parliament related to the Liverpool Docks, 1710–1804.
46. TNA, CUST 3/50, Ledgers of Imports and Exports, 1750.
47. ManchesterRO, GB127.Tracts/P.2044.4, Reasons for Establishing the Colony of Georgia (1733), pp. 4–9, 22.

## CHAPTER FIVE: WAR PROFITEERING

1. Keeble, *The Restoration*; Dillon, *The Last Revolution*; Riding, *Jacobites*; Roberts, *Jacobite Wars*.

2. For the relationships between warfare and the state, see: Simms, *Three Victories and a Defeat*; Tilly, *Coercion, Capital, and European States*; Storrs, *Fiscal-Military State*; Dickson, *Financial Revolution*; Findlay and O'Rourke, *Power and Plenty*; Brewer, *Sinews of Power*; Stone, *An Imperial State at War*; Hoppit, *Britain's Political Economies*, pp. 277–305; Dal Bó et al., 'Dissecting the Sinews of Power', pp. 1–34.
3. BL, Add Ms 25115, ff. 133–6, Meeting of the Council for Trade, 14 March 1661.
4. PA, HL.PO.JP.10.6.52, Report from the Commissioners of Trade and Plantations, 16 December 1703.
5. Anderson, *War of the Austrian Succession*; Harding, *Emergence of Britain's Global Naval Supremacy*; Bruijn, *The Dutch Navy*, p. 129; Bannerman, *Merchants and the Military*, pp. 7–22.
6. Davis, *Rise of the English Shipping Industry*, p. 26; Rosier, 'Construction Costs', pp. 161–72; Howes, *Arts and Minds*, p. 62.
7. Bradford, *A Relation or Journall*, p. 44; Council for New England, *A Brief Relation*, p. D3; Levett, *A Voyage into New England*, pp. 23–4, 29.
8. BL, Sloane Ms 2902, ff. 1–10, Answer of the Commissioners of Trade and Plantations to the Honourable the House of Commons, 22 March 1700; PA, HL.PO.JP.10.6.52, Report from the Commissioners of Trade and Plantations, 16 December 1703. Grainger, *British Navy in the Baltic*, pp. 116–35; Smith, 'Corporate Naval Supply', pp. 586–9. For overviews of the state's involvement in naval supplies, see: Wilkinson, *The British Navy and the State*; Pool, *Navy Board Contracts*.
9. Anon., *An Act for Encouraging the Importation of Naval Stores*; PA, HL.PO.JP.10.6.52, Report from the Commissioners of Trade and Plantations, 16 December 1703.
10. Anon., *An Act for Better Preservation of His Majesty's Woods in America*.
11. Defoe, *A Plan of the English Commerce*, pp. 348–60. For the impact of extractive agriculture and forestry in North America, see: Cronon, *Changes in the Land*; Pluymers, *No Wood, No Kingdom*.
12. Anon., *An Act for Encouraging the Importation of Naval Stores*; TNA, CUST 3/50–54, Ledgers of Imports and Exports, 1750–1754; TNA, ADM 95/17, 6–7, 62–3; TNA, ADM 106/3182; Hiono, 'Sustaining British Naval Power', pp. 18–29.
13. Scammell, *Seafaring, Sailors and Trade*, pp. 32–3; Rosier, 'Construction Costs', pp. 161–72; Knight, 'Devil Bolts and Deception?', pp. 34–51; Graham, *A Maritime History of Scotland*.
14. Tucker, *A Series of Answers to Certain Popular Objections*, p. 32. Hillman and Gathmann, 'Overseas Trade and the Decline of Privateering', pp. 730–61.
15. PA, HL.PO.JP.10.6.52, Report from the Commissioners of Trade and Plantations, 16 December 1703; Satia, *Empire of Guns*, pp. 8–17.
16. PA, HL/PO/JO/10/1/465/818, Petitions of the Founders and Braziers of England, 13 and 22 March 1694; Satia, *Empire of Guns*, p. 29; Black, *Britain as a Military Power*, p. 47.
17. For an expansive assessment of the emergence of the Birmingham gunmaking industry, see: Satia, *Empire of Guns*, pp. 1–7, 21, 27–31. Also, Bailey and Nie, *English Gunmakers*; Goodman, 'The Birmingham Gun Trade', pp. 408–11.
18. Satia, *Empire of Guns*, pp. 31–4, quotes p. 34.
19. Satia, *Empire of Guns*, pp. 39–40.
20. Satia, *Empire of Guns*, p. 68; Hopkins, *Birmingham*, pp. 3–22.

21. LOB, C/D/15/5/2, James Farmer to Samuel Galton, 14 October 1748; Satia, *Empire of Guns*, pp. 43–51, 67–8.
22. LOB, C/D/15/5/3; 4; 7: James Farmer to Samuel Galton, 3 January 1749; James Farmer to Samuel Galton, 15 December 1749; James Farmer to Samuel Galton, 20 January 1750. Satia, *Empire of Guns*, pp. 72–3.
23. LOB, C/D/15/5/13, James Farmer to Samuel Galton, 10 December 1753; Satia, *Empire of Guns*, pp. 3, 41–55; Inikori, *Africans*, pp. 457–67; Radburn, 'British Gunpowder Industry', p. 364; Russell, *Guns of the Early Frontiers*; Chew, *Arming the Periphery*.
24. Satia, *Empire of Guns*, pp. 53–65.
25. Radburn, 'British Gunpowder Industry', pp. 367. For the wider gunpowder industry, see: Crocker, *Gunpowder Mills*; Tyler, *Gunpowder Mills of Cumbria*; Buchanan, *Gunpowder, Explosives and the State*.
26. PA, HL/PO/JO/10/1/465/821, Petition of the Governor and Company of Merchants of London trading into the East Indies, 16 March 1694. For India's saltpetre: Frey, 'Indian Saltpeter Trade', pp. 507–54. For Italian sulphur: Cunha, 'Frontier of Hell', pp. 279–302. For impact on British manufacture, see: West, *Gunpowder, Government and War*; Radburn, 'British Gunpowder Industry', pp. 363–84.
27. Crocker, *Gunpowder Mills*, pp. 5–20, 107–72; West, *Gunpowder, Government, and War*, pp. 197–221; Radburn, 'British Gunpowder Industry', pp. 368–77; Buchanan, 'Technology of Gunpowder Making', pp. 125–59.
28. Radburn, 'British Gunpowder Industry', pp. 368–73; West, *Gunpowder, Government and War*, pp. 119–29; Tyler, *Gunpowder Mills*, pp. 27–37.
29. Buchanan, 'Bath's Forgotten Gunpowder History', pp. 82–6, quotes pp. 82 and 85; Radburn, 'British Gunpowder Industry', pp. 371–2.
30. For the most detailed analysis of the mills near Bristol, see: Buchanan, 'Bath's Forgotten Gunpowder History', pp. 78–82; For slave-traders investing in gunpowder mills, see: Radburn, 'British Gunpowder Industry', pp. 372–7.
31. Radburn, 'British Gunpowder Industry', pp. 363–7, 373–9.
32. Brewer, *Sinews of Power*, pp. xvii, 27–34; Satia, *Empire of Guns*, pp. 2–7.
33. For Kolkata and Bengal, see: Roy, *The East India Company*, pp. 164–70. For a contemporary account of the Black Hole: Holwell, *A Genuine Narrative of the Deplorable Deaths*. For historical assessments of the Black Hole and its impact, see: Gupta, *Sirajuddaullah and The East India Company*, pp. 70–80; Dirks, *Scandal of Empire*, pp. 3–4. For an overview of the East India Company's rule in India, see: Bowen, *Business of Empire*; Bowen, Lincoln and Rigby, *The Worlds of the East India Company*; Marshall, *Bengal*.
34. BL, IOR Fort William – India House Correspondence, vol. II, James Killpatrick near Fort William to East India Company in London, 25 January 1757.
35. BL, IOR Fort William – India House Correspondence, vol. II, Roger Drake junior and Richard Becher at Fort William to East India Company in London, 26 January 1757.
36. BL, IOR Fort William – India House Correspondence, vol. II, Colonel Robert Clive near Calcutta to East India Company in London, 1 February 1757.
37. BL, IOR Fort William – India House Correspondence, vol. II, East India Company to President and Council at Fort William, 25 March 1757.
38. BL, IOR Fort William – India House Correspondence, vol. II, East India Company to President and Council at Fort William, 25 March 1757.

39. Harrington, *Plassey, 1757*, pp. 23–9, 83–4.
40. Roy, *The East India Company*, pp. 160–72, quote p. 171. Harrington, *Plassey, 1757*, pp. 23–9, 83–4; Roy, *How British Rule Changed India's Economy*, pp. 88–117; Damodaran, 'The East India Company', pp. 80–101.
41. JRRIL, GB133 English Ms 1048, f. 30, Robert Nicholson to Henry Hutton, 6 August 1762; Roberts, *Slavery and the Enlightenment*, p. 2; Raudzens, 'War-Winning Weapons', pp. 403–33; Raudzens, 'Military Revolution or Maritime Evolution?', pp. 631–42; Cooper, *Anglo-Maratha Campaigns*, pp. 310–11.
42. O'Brien, 'Mercantilist Institutions', pp. 179–208. For fiscal-military relationship, see: Tilly, *Coercion, Capital and European States*; Brewer, *Sinews of Power*; Pool, *Navy Board Contracts*; van Crevald, *Supplying War*; Knight and Wilcox, *Sustaining the Fleet*; Bowen, *War and British Society*; Baker, *Government and Contractors*; Bannerman, *Merchants and the Military*.
43. Quoted in Satia, *Empire of Guns*, p. 17.
44. ManchesterRO, GB127.TractsH.137.8, Tucker's 'The Case of Going to War for the Sake of Procuring, Enlarging or Securing of Trade'.
45. Satia, *Empire of Guns*, pp. 1, 6.

## CHAPTER SIX: A SCIENTIFIC PEOPLE

1. Mokyr, *Gifts of Athena*, p. 288; Jones, *Industrial Enlightenment*, p. 139.
2. Otremba, 'Inventing Ingenios', pp. 119–47, quotes pp. 119–20. For wider scientific exchanges, see: Slack, *Invention of Improvement*; Hunter, *Establishing the New Science*; Stewart, *Rise of Public Science*; Shapiro, *Culture of Fact*; Cavazza, 'The Institute of Science of Bologna', pp. 3–25; Lux and Cook, 'Closed Circles or Open Networks', pp. 179–211. For links to commercial activity, see: Yamamoto, *Taming Capitalism*, pp. 1–8; Feingold, 'Projectors and Learned Projects', pp. 63–79; Tann, 'Borrowing Brilliance', pp. 94–114.
3. BL, Egerton Ms 7803, Warrant for inventor's patent issued to Isaac de la Chaumette, 1721; RS, CLP/3ii/35, Paper on Six Inventions by Isaac de la Chaumette, 9 May 1734; Hayward, 'Huguenot Gunmakers of London', pp. 649–63.
4. Howes, *Arts and Minds*, pp. 1–28, quote p. 2; Miller, 'The Usefulness of Natural Philosophy', pp. 185–201; Roberts, *Slavery and the Enlightenment*, p. 32; Fontes da Costa, 'Culture of Curiosity', pp. 147–66; Cookson, *Making an Industrial Revolution*, pp. 8–29, 142–170. For range of topics examined within the Royal Society: Thomson, *History of the Royal Society*.
5. Howes, *Arts and Minds*, pp. 5–7, Sully quote p. 5.
6. Fontes da Costa, 'Culture of Curiosity', pp. 147–66, Burke quote p. 147; Howes, *Arts and Minds*, pp. 1–4; Berry, *The Idea of Luxury*, pp. 126–76; Brewer, *Pleasures of the Imagination*. For impact on consumer goods, see: Brewer and Porter, *Consumption and the World of Goods*; McKendrick, 'The Consumer Revolution', pp. 9–33; Berg and Clifford, 'Selling Consumption', pp. 145–70; Kasumitsu, 'Novelty, Give us Novelty', pp. 114–38; Berg, 'Commerce and Creativity', pp. 173–204.
7. BNA, *The Scots Magazine*, 3 March 1755, pp. 14–15. For the wider context of the society's development, see: Broadie, *Cambridge Companion to the Scottish Enlightenment*; Berry, *Idea of Commercial Society*; Emerson, *An Enlightened Duke*; Smout, 'A New Look at the Scottish Improvers', pp. 125–49; Jacob, *Secular Enlightenment*, pp. 124–56.

8. NLS, Adv.MS.23.1.1, ff. 1–3, 4–10, 15, 19, 28, 31, 37, 43, 46, 49–50, 53–4, 56, 58, 60, 62, 68, 80, 84, 116, 149, 167–8, 187, 195: Minutes of the Select Society of Edinburgh, 1754–1762.
9. NLS, Acc.9097. Minute Book of the Commercial Society of Edinburgh, 1759–1770.
10. NLS, Adv.MS.23.1.1, p. 43. Minutes of the Select Society of Edinburgh, 1754–1762; NLS, MS.17833, pp. 87–90. Home, *Principles of Agriculture and Vegetation*.
11. NLS, MS.17833, pp. 87–90; NLS, Adv.MS.23.1.1, pp. 53–4, 84. Minutes of the Select Society of Edinburgh, 1754–1762; Home, *Principles of Agriculture and Vegetation*.
12. Howes, *Arts and Minds*, pp. 10–18.
13. Labaree, *Papers of Benjamin Franklin*, pp. 186–9; Howes, *Arts and Minds*, pp. 18–19, Barker quote p. 19.
14. Howes, *Arts and Minds*, pp. 34–5.
15. NLS, Adv.MS.23.1.1, pp. 53–4, 84, Minutes of the Select Society of Edinburgh, 1754–1762; LiverpoolRO, 353 MIN/COI 1/2/1, f. 12, Committee for Trade Meeting, 9 October 1775; Howes, *Arts and Minds*, p. 14, 18–19, 34–5, 68–74.
16. BL, Eg Ms 1941, ff. 17–18; 22–9, Letter from John Henry Ziegler to Dr William Lewis, 9 February and 13 March 1766; Eugenius to Dr William Lewis, 9 October 1767; Baker quoted in Allan, 'Society of Arts', p. 443.
17. Schofield, *Lunar Society of Birmingham*, pp. 146–54; Robinson, 'The Lunar Society', p. 160; Uglow, *Lunar Men*; Jones, *Industrial Enlightenment*; Mokyr, *Enlightened Economy*. For the relationship between Watt and Boulton, and the development of Birmingham's iron industry and steam power, see Chapter Eight.
18. ULLSC, RP II.1 28; 29; 30: William Reynolds to William Rathbone, 23 July 1777; 26 July 1777; 30 December 1777.
19. Priestley and Fisher quoted in Jones, *Industrial Enlightenment*, pp. 117, 123–5, 255. For relationship between training and education in relation to technical skills, see: Cookson, *Making and Industrial Revolution*, pp. 62–94; Cookson, *Age of Machinery*; Wallis, *The Market for Skill*, pp. 111–32.
20. WYAS Calderdale, WYC: 1525/6/1/2, Anonymous Letter to Christopher Rawson, 18 April 1769; ULLSC, RP II.1 29, William Reynolds to William Rathbone, 26 July 1777. For changing education and training practices, see: Sanderson, 'Literacy and Social Mobility', pp. 75–104; Money, 'Teaching in the Market-Place', pp. 335–79; Wallis, 'Between Apprenticeship and Skill', pp. 155–70; Wallis, *The Market for Skill*, pp. 49–73, 111–33; Mokyr, *Enlightened Economy*, p. 447; Justman and van der Beek, 'Market Forces', pp. 1177–202.
21. Keir quoted in Jones, *Industrial Enlightenment*, p. 1.
22. ManchesterRO, GB127.Tracts/P.2044.4, Reasons for Establishing the Colony of Georgia, 1733, pp. 3–4. For import substitution as incentive for British innovation, see: De Vries, 'Understanding Eurasian Trade', p. 22; Inikori, *Africans*, pp. 405–9; Edwards, *Growth of the British Cotton Trade*, pp. 45–6, 126–32; Lemire, *Fashion's Favourite*, pp. 30–4; Parthasarathi, *Why Europe Grew Rich*, pp. 98–109; Riello, *Cotton*, pp. 224–5; Berg, 'Useful Knowledge', pp. 117–41.
23. For consumption of global goods in Britain, see: Brewer and Porter, *Consumption and the World of Goods*; Lemire, *Global Trade*; Schäfer, 'Patterns of Design in Qing-China and Britain', pp. 107–18; Berg, 'The Merest Shadow of a Commodity', pp. 119–37; Mackillop, 'A North European World of Tea', pp. 294–308. For

changing incentives for inventors and patentees: MacLeod, *Inventing the Industrial Revolution*, pp. 159–60; O'Brien, Griffiths and Hunt, 'Technological Change', p. 164; McCloskey, *Bourgeois Dignity*, p. 7; Mokyr, 'Intellectual Origins', p. 322; Mokyr, *Enlightened Economy*, pp. 37, 210; Bottomley, *British Patent System*, pp. 25, 266; Allen, 'Why the Industrial Revolution Was British', p. 368; Allen, *British Industrial Revolution*, pp. 136, 168–72; Broadberry and Gupta, 'Lancashire, India and Shifting Competitive Advantage', pp. 295–7; Meisenzahl and Mokyr, 'Rate and Direction of Invention', pp. 460–73.

24. Rothstein, 'Canterbury and London', pp. 33–47.
25. Lombe, *A Brief State of the Case*; ManchesterRO, GB127.Tracts/P.2044.4, Reasons for Establishing the Colony of Georgia, 1733, pp. 5–9; Smiles, *Men of Invention and Industry*, pp. 107–20; Jones, 'Technology, Transaction Costs', pp. 75–7; Hertz, 'English Silk Industry', pp. 710–27; Rothstein, 'Huguenots in the English Silk Industry', pp. 125–40.
26. ManchesterRO, GB127.Tracts/P.2044.4, Reasons for Establishing the Colony of Georgia, 1733, pp. 5–9. Hertz, 'English Silk Industry', pp. 710–27; Rothstein, 'Huguenots in the English Silk Industry', pp. 125–40.
27. The most thorough survey of Cheshire's silk industry remains Calladine and Fricker, *East Cheshire Textile Mills*, pp. 4–8.
28. Calladine and Fricker, *East Cheshire Textile Mills*, pp. 4–8; Jones, 'Technology, Transaction Costs', pp. 5–7.
29. Hertz, 'English Silk Industry', pp. 720–2; Warner, *The Silk Industry*, pp. 199–201.
30. These practices went both ways, and European states tried to obtain British practices too, see: Harris, *Industrial Espionage and Technology Transfer*.
31. Du Halde, *General History of China*, pp. *dedication*, 13, 152–4.
32. Woodcroft, *Titles of Patents*, patent 649; Lane, 'Secrets for Sale', pp. 879–90.
33. Berg, 'From Imitation to Invention', pp. 24–7; Weber, 'Copying and Competition', pp. 331–73; McKendrick, 'Josiah Wedgwood', pp. 99–143; Bemrose, *Bow, Chelsea and Derby Porcelain*; Anderson, 'Derby Porcelain'.
34. Berg, 'From Imitation to Invention', pp. 24–7; Weber, 'Copying and Competition', pp. 331–73.
35. Holt and Popp, 'Josiah Wedgwood', pp. 105–10, quote pp. 9–10; Blaszczyk, *Imagining Consumers*, p. 5; Berg, *Luxury and Pleasure*; McKendrick, 'Josiah Wedgwood'; Lane, 'Secrets for Sale', pp. 861–906.
36. Holt and Popp, 'Josiah Wedgwood', pp. 99–119; Lane, 'Secrets for Sale', pp. 861–906; Weatherill, 'The Growth of the Pottery Industry', pp. 15–46. For cross-over in organisational practice between pottery and other sectors: Roll, *An Early Experiment*; Chapman, *Early Factory Masters*; Stobart, *First Industrial Region*.
37. ManchesterRO, GB127.Tracts/H.246.2, Richard Budgen, The Passage of the Hurricane, 1730, pp. 24–5.
38. Mann, *The Cotton Trade*, pp. 451–4; Paulinyi, 'John Kay's Flying Shuttle', pp. 149–66; Raman, 'From Hand to Machine', pp. 715–25.
39. Fitton and Wadsworth, *The Strutts and the Arkwrights*; Raman, 'From Hand to Machine', pp. 715–25; Cookson, *Age of Machinery*; Sugden, 'An Occupational Study', pp. 160–75.
40. NLS, MS.19848, Notebook of John Rennie, Aug–Dec 1793; Carus-Wilson, 'The Woollen Industry', pp. 614–74; Sugden et al., 'Adam Smith Revisited', pp. 163–91.
41. WYAS Calderdale, FIE 131–134: Indenture between George Fisher and John Bottomley and John Sutcliffe, 10 October 1775; Details of ownership

of Langfield Mill, 1775; Lease and Release between George Fisher and John Bottomley and John Sutcliffe, 10 October 1775; Lease and Release between Thomas Sayer and John Bottomley, 27 December 1777; Indenture between Thomas Sayer and John Bottomley and John Sutcliffe, 27 December 1777.

42. WYAS Calderdale, FIE 136, Conveyance between John Bottomley and John Walton, John Crossley and John Greenwood, 11 July 1782.
43. WYAS Calderdale, FIE 137; 138: Lease for Lumbutts Mill, 15 April 1783; Agreement between Thomas Hughes, Robert Law, Samuel Law and Abraham Crossley to enter into a co-partnership, 15 April 1783.
44. WYAS Calderdale, FIE 139–152: Bargain and Sale for Lumbutts Mill, 30 August 1784; Notes on assignment of lease and sale of machinery at Lumbutts Mill, 9 October 1787; Articles of agreement between William Uttley and George Feather, 29 January 1789; Articles dissolving co-partnership at Lumbutts Mill, 1 November 1791; Articles of agreement relating to the workings of Lumbutts Mill, 30 November 1794; Articles of agreement relating to the leasehold at Lumbutts Mill, 15 January 1796; Lease for Lumbutts Mill, 31 December 1796; Lease and Release for Lumbutts Mill, 22 April 1803.
45. BL, Add Ms 34462, ff. 1–6, Examination of Alexander Anderson at Committee for Trade and Foreign Plantations, 4 January 1786.
46. BL, Add Ms 34462, ff. 24–9; 30–6: Examination of George Maltby and Robert Harvey at Committee for Trade and Foreign Plantations, 20 January 1786; Examination of William Winne, Michael Hutchinson, John Bramley, William Rawson and Alexander Turner at Committee for Trade and Foreign Plantations, 20 January 1786.
47. BL, Add Ms 34462, ff. 24–9; 30–6: Examination of George Maltby and Robert Harvey at Committee for Trade and Foreign Plantations, 20 January 1786; Examination of William Winne, Michael Hutchinson, John Bramley, William Rawson and Alexander Turner at Committee for Trade and Foreign Plantations, 20 January 1786.
48. For the ongoing development of the West Yorkshire woollen industry and the shift to steam powered woollen manufacturing, see: Sugden et al., 'Adam Smith Revisited', pp. 163–91; Hudson, *Genesis of Industrial Capital*; Hudson, 'Landholding and the Organization of Textile Manufacturing', pp. 261–91; Wilson, 'The Supremacy of the Yorkshire Cloth Industry', pp. 225–46; Tann, 'Borrowing Brilliance', pp. 94–114.

## CHAPTER SEVEN: MASTERS OF REALITY

1. ManchesterRO, GB127.TractsH.137.8, Josiah Tucker, The Case of Going to War for the Sake of Procuring, Enlarging or Securing of Trade.
2. Brindley, *History of Inland Navigations*, p. 1.
3. For the wider intellectual landscape that encouraged capitalists to transform the environment, especially in colonial contexts, see: Mulry, *An Empire Transformed*; Jonsson and Wennerlind, *Scarcity*; Pluymers, *No Wood, No Kingdom*; Anderson, 'Nature's Currency', pp. 47–80; Winterbottom, *Hybrid Knowledge*; Drayton, *Nature's Government*.
4. ManchesterRO, GB127.Tracts/P.2044.4, Reasons for Establishing the Colony of Georgia, 1733, pp. 3–4.

5. ManchesterRO, GB127.Tracts/P.2044.4, Reasons for Establishing the Colony of Georgia, 1733, pp. 4–9. Lombe's letter of support was printed on pages 6–7.
6. ManchesterRO, GB127,Tracts/P.2044.4, Reasons for Establishing the Colony of Georgia, 1733, pp. 7, 11; McKinstry, 'Silk Culture', pp. 225–35, quote p. 229; Bonner, 'Silk Growing', pp. 143–8. For the most detailed study of the introduction of silk to North America, see Marsh, *Unravelled Dreams*.
7. Roberts, *Slavery and the Enlightenment*, pp. 9–12; Menard, *Sweet Negotiations*.
8. Roberts, *Slavery and the Enlightenment*, pp. 9–12; Menard, *Sweet Negotiations*.
9. Belgrove, *Treatise upon Husbandry or Planting*; Roberts, *Slavery and the Enlightenment*, p. 9.
10. Evans, *Slave Wales*, pp. 39–42; Roberts, *Slavery and the Enlightenment*, pp. 9–12, 30–9; Sheridan, *Sugar and Slavery*.
11. Roberts, *Slavery and the Enlightenment*, pp. 1, 30–40, quotes pp. 39–40, 43.
12. Roberts, *Slavery and the Enlightenment*, pp. 30–7.
13. For an extensive study of agricultural and colonial development in Virginia, see Walsh, *Motives of Honor, Pleasure, and Profit*. For use of innovative measurement and accounting practices in plantations, see Rosenthal, *Accounting for Slavery*, pp. 9–48.
14. Walsh, 'Plantation Management in the Chesapeake', pp. 393–406; Roberts, *Slavery and the Enlightenment*, pp. 16–17, 30.
15. Quoted in Roberts, *Slavery and the Enlightenment*, pp. 22–3; Edwards, *Growth of the British Cotton Trade*, p. 79; Bailey, 'The Other Side of Slavery', pp. 35–50.
16. Roberts, *Slavery and the Enlightenment*, pp. 1, 26–31, quote p. 26; Thompson, 'Time, Work-Discipline, and Industrial Capitalism', pp. 56–97; Voth, 'Time and Work', pp. 29–58; Roll, *An Early Experiment*, pp. 199–217.
17. NLS, MS.13628, Alexander Walker's Notebook, 1799.
18. NLS, MS.13628, Alexander Walker's Notebook, 1799.
19. NLS, MS.13628, Alexander Walker's Notebook, 1799.
20. ManchesterRO, GB127.Tracts.P.3700.3, Three Letters Addressed to a Friend in India, by a Proprietor: principally on the subject of importing Bengal sugars into England, 1793.
21. ManchesterRO, GB127.Tracts.P.3700.3. Three Letters Addressed to a Friend in India, by a Proprietor: principally on the subject of importing Bengal sugars into England, 1793; Hutková, 'West Indies Technologies', pp. 1072–98; Hutková, *East India Company's Silk Enterprise*; Aldous, 'From Traders to Planters', pp. 803–20; Bosma, *Sugar Plantation in India and Indonesia*; Chaudhary et al., 'Agriculture in Colonial India', pp. 100–16.
22. Young, *Rural Oeconomy*, pp. 20–1; Roberts, *Slavery and the Enlightenment*, quotes pp. 32 and 33; Fisher, *Enclosure of Knowledge*, pp. 122–69; Overton, *Agricultural Revolution*.
23. Young, *Rural Oeconomy*, pp. 20–1; Trusler, *Practical Husbandry*, pp. iii–v; Robertson quoted in Fisher, *Enclosure of Knowledge*, pp. 179–80.
24. Uglow, *Lunar Men*, quote p. 66; Clark and Clark, 'Common Rights to Land', pp. 1009–36; Allen, *Enclosure and the Yeoman*; Chambers, 'Enclosure and Labour Supply', pp. 319–43; Richards, *Highland Clearances*, p. 212; Aitchison and Cassell, *The Lowland Clearances*; Gibson, 'Proletarianization', pp. 357–89.
25. Overton, *Agricultural Revolution*, p. 90; Hoppit, *Britain's Political Economies*, pp. 179–215. For earlier efforts at fen drainage in Britain and North America, see Mulry, *An Empire Transformed*, pp. 74–158.

26. WYAS Calderdale, WYC:1206 17; 30; 32; 33; 37: Lease for properties in Wadsworth, 8 April 1793; Articles of agreement between William Greenwood and William Patchett, 14 April 1791; Agreement between William Patchett and Trustees of the Turnpike Road from Halifax by Todmorden to Burnley and Littleborough, 27 March 1793; Agreement between William Greenwood and William Patchett, 10 September 1793; Grant of liberties to erect dams on the River Calder, 19 December 1793 and 11 July 1794.
27. LOB, C/D/15/5/4. James Farmer to Samuel Galton, 15 December 1749; ManchesterRO, GB127.C5/1/1/1. Personal Ledger of Samuel Greg, 1794–1824; Rose, 'Gregs of Styal', pp. 239–42; Rose, *The Gregs of Quarry Bank Mill*, pp. 13–35.
28. JRRIL, SO/1/63; 65; 184: John Clayton to Samuel Oldknow, 4 November 1787; John Clayton to Samuel Oldknow, 19 September 1791; Robert Needham to Samuel Oldknow, 10 October 1798.
29. For the wider context of Scottish agricultural change, see Smout, 'A New Look at the Scottish Improvers', pp. 125–49; Cornell, Goodare and MacDonald, *Agriculture, Economy and Society*.
30. Scottish Border Archive, UGD 041: Receipt for David Gavin's Subscription to the Edinburgh Society for Improving Arts and Manufactures in Scotland, 1758; Receipt of Promissory Notes from British Linen Company, 23 January 1758; David Gavin to Richard Oswald, 1 April 1756; David Gavin to Richard Oswald, 9 April 1755; David Gavin to Coutts Brothers & Company, 25 October 1757; David Gavin to Ralph Carr, 29 April 1758. SBA, SBA 133: 123; 124; 125: Rental of Estate of Langton, 1798; Rental of the Estate of Langton, 1793; Rental from fields and quarry, [undated].
31. Crompton, 'Canals and the Industrial Revolution', pp. 93–110.
32. Brindley, *History of Inland Navigations*, p. 10; Burt, 'Lead Production', pp. 250–7.
33. Brindley, *History of Inland Navigations*, pp. A2, 1–2; Maw, *Transport and the Industrial City*, pp. 1–27. Canals and new roads together contributing to the growth of urban areas and Britain's national market, see: Wrigley, 'Urban Growth in Early Modern England', pp. 79–112; Bogart, 'Did Turnpike Trusts Increase Transportation Investment?', pp. 439–68.
34. Smeaton, *Report of John Smeaton Engineer*, pp. 29–30; Brindley, *History of Inland Navigations*, pp. 3–8.
35. 'Smeaton, John' in ODNB.
36. Smeaton, *Report of John Smeaton*, p. 1, 29–30; 'Smeaton, John' in ODNB.
37. Smeaton, *Report of John Smeaton*, p. 15.
38. Smeaton, *Report of John Smeaton*, pp. 15, 17–20.
39. Mitchell Library, T-MH/1/3, pp. 103–4, Merchants House Minute Book, 1754–1790; Bailey, *Locks, Stocks and Bodies in Barrels*, pp. 1–23.
40. 'Brindley, James' in ODNB.
41. ULLSC, RP II.1 33, William Reynolds to William Rathbone, 16 January 1788; ULLSC, RP IV.1.72, Isaac Hawkins Browne MP to Richard Reynolds, 23 October 1785; SBA, DC90/2/11/1, James Watt to James MacGregor relating to building a canal near Inverness, 1784; Morriss, *Canals of Shropshire*, pp. 14–16; Smith, 'Industry and Social Change', pp. 135–7; King, 'Innovation in the British Iron Industry', p. 13; Trinder, 'Towns and Industries', pp. 110–11; Jones, *Industrial Enlightenment*, p. 28; Albert, *The Turnpike Road System*, pp. 49–55; Wrigley, 'Urban Growth in Early Modern England', pp. 79–112; Bogart, 'Did Turnpike Trusts Increase Transportation Investment?', pp. 439–68.

42. NLS, MS.19848. Notebook of John Rennie, August to December 1793; NLS, MS.19846. Notebook of John Rennie, January 1793; Crompton, 'Canals and the Industrial Revolution', p. 96.
43. ManchesterRO, B2/1/1/1, ff. 2–4, 19, 36, Rochdale Canal Company Minutes. UMLSC, R129473, An Act for Making and Maintaining a Navigable Canal from the Calder Navigation, at or near Sowerby Bridge, in the Parish of Halifax, in the West Riding of the County of York, to join the Canal of his Grace the Duke of Bridgewater, in the Parish of Manchester, in the County Palatine of Lancaster, 1794.
44. ManchesterRO, B2/1/1/1, ff. 37–41, 43–4, Rochdale Canal Company Minutes; ManchesterRO, B2/1/1/2: Meeting of the Rochdale Canal Company, 16 December 1793; Copy of a memorial of the Trustees of the Free Grammar School at Manchester against the intended Rochdale Canal, undated [c. November 1793].
45. ManchesterRO, B2/1/1/1, ff. 27–8, Rochdale Canal Company Minutes; ManchesterRO, B2/1/1/2, Meeting of the Rochdale Canal Company: 10 May 1793; 10 August 1793; 30 September 1793; 11 October 1793; 22 November 1793.
46. ManchesterRO, B2/1/1/1, ff. 45–7, Meeting of the Rochdale Canal Company, 21 February 1792; ManchesterRO, B2/1/1/2, Meeting of the Rochdale Canal Company, 18 September 1792; 10 August 1793; 17 August 1793; 13 October 1792; 22 November 1793; Copy of Memorandum of John Sutcliffe, James Drury and William Shewatt, undated c. April 1794.
47. ManchesterRO, B2/1/1/1, Meeting of the Rochdale Canal Company: 26 September 1792; 10 October 1792; 13 October 1792; 3 November 1792; 20 December 1792. ManchesterRO, B2/1/1/2, Meeting of the Rochdale Canal Company, 10 August 1793; Copy of Agreement by Thomas Bradley and James Drury for Construction of Gauges for Rochdale Canal, undated c. April 1794.
48. Maw, *Transport and the Industrial City*, pp. 1–27; Crompton, 'Canals and the Industrial Revolution', p. 99.

## CHAPTER EIGHT: FIRE AND IRON

1. BL, Eg Ms 1941, f. 1, Design of smelting-mill used by the Company of Mine Adventurers of England and others in Yorkshire, 1735; Flinn, *Men of Iron*, pp. 75, 184; Nef, 'Mining and Metallurgy', pp. 691–761; 'Crowley, Sir Ambrose, of Greenwich, Kent' in ODNB.
2. Wood, *The Present State*.
3. BL, Add Ch 70568, Partnership for the manufacture of iron, steel and other metals, 1720; BL, Add Ch 70571, Sale of Shares from William Wood to Dr Charles Driver, 1720; Rowlands, *Masters and Men*, pp. 16–38, 110–24; King, 'Production and Consumption of Iron', pp. 1–33; Treadwell, 'William Wood', pp. 97–112.
4. Wood, *The Present State*.
5. Wood, *The Present State*; Flinn, 'William Wood', pp. 55–71; King, 'Production and Consumption of Iron', pp. 1–33; King, 'Fritzington Fraud', pp. 161–86; Rowlands, *Masters and Men*, pp. 125–46; Treadwell, 'William Wood', pp. 97–112; Treadwell, 'Swift, William Wood, and the Factual Basis of Satire'.
6. Hayes and Evans, *Letterbook of Richard Crawshay*, p. x; Satia, *Empire of Guns*, p. 7; Raistrick, 'South Yorkshire Iron Industry', pp. 51–86; Hayman, 'Shropshire

Wrought-Iron Industry', pp. 19–48; Johnson, 'Charcoal Iron Industry', pp. 167–177.

7. PA, HL/PO/JO/10/3/245/16, House of Lords Account of the Imports of Iron from America, 5 April 1750.
8. WYAS Bradford, SpSt/5/5/1/4, John Watts to William Spencer, 26 February 1736. For iron industry in Britain's North American colonies, see: Bining, *British Regulation*; Robbins, 'The Principo Company'.
9. Allen, *British Industrial Revolution*, pp. 217–21. Other metals in Britain were simultaneously undergoing rapid change in modes and scale of production. For example, see Chapter Three for expansion of copper production in Wales. For steel, see: Evans and Withey, 'An Enlightenment in Steel?', pp. 533–60; Tweedale, *Steel City*.
10. Allen, *British Industrial Revolution*, pp. 217–23; King, 'Innovation in the British Iron Industry', pp. 16–20.
11. Allen, *British Industrial Revolution*, pp. 222–3; King, 'Innovation in the British Iron Industry', pp. 20–2.
12. Allen, *British Industrial Revolution*, pp. 225–6.
13. Allen, *British Industrial Revolution*, pp. 226–7; King, 'Innovation in the British Iron Industry', pp. 22–4; Johnson, 'Midland Iron Industry', pp. 67–74.
14. King, 'Innovation in the British Iron Industry', p. 23. For the changing social lives of Midlands businessmen, see: Money, *Experience and Identity*; Uglow, *Lunar Society*; Jones, *Industrial Enlightenment*.
15. King, 'Innovation in the British Iron Industry', p. 24.
16. BL, Eg Ms 1941, ff. 6–8, Letter from John Cockshull junior to [Dr William Lewis], 2 June 1763; BL, Eg Ms 1941, ff. 2–3, Design of a lead-smelting mill, c. 1780s.
17. ULLSC, RP II.1 30, William Reynolds to William Rathbone, 30 December 1777; King, 'Innovation in the British Iron Industry', p. 27.
18. ULLSC, RP IV.1.83a, William Gibbons to the Lord Chancellor Thurlow, July 1785; 'Gibbons Family' in ODNB.
19. ULLSC, RP IV.1.86, Richard Reynolds to Earl Gower, 28 March 1785; ULLSC, RP IV.1.70, Richard Reynolds to Isaac Hawkins Brown, 17 February 1785.
20. ULLSC, RP IV.1.73–4, Observations on the Iron Trade by Samuel Garbett, 21 June 1785; King, 'Innovation in the British Iron Industry', p. 12.
21. ULLSC, RP IV.1.73–4, Observations on the Iron Trade by Samuel Garbett, 21 June 1785. For details of Russian industry, see: Hill: *Russian Iron Production*, pp. 118–67; Hill, 'Polzunov's Engine', pp. 107–39.
22. ULLSC, RP IV.1.73–4, Observations on the Iron Trade by Samuel Garbett, 21 June 1785.
23. ULLSC, RP IV.1.83a, William Gibbons to the Lord Chancellor Thurlow, July 1785; ULLSC, RP IV.1.75, Richard Crawshay to Richard Reynolds, 28 December 1785; ULLSC, RP IV.1.86, Richard Reynolds to Earl Gower, 28 March 1785.
24. King, 'Innovation in the British Iron Industry', pp. 26–7.
25. Cookson, 'Wortley Forge', pp. 52–73; King, 'Innovation in the British Iron Industry', pp. 28–30.
26. Hayes and Evans, *Letterbook of Richard Crawshay*, p. xiii–xiv; King, 'Innovation in the British Iron Industry', pp. 28–30; Ince, *South Wales Iron Industry*.
27. Allen, *British Industrial Revolution*, pp. 156–64.

28. SBA, UGD 111, Gladsmuir Colliery Account Book, 1759–1762; Pryce quoted in Rule, *Experience of Labour*, p. 75; 'Pryce, William' in ODNB. For the wider development of coal industry in the eighteenth century, see Flinn, *History of the British Coal Industry.*
29. UMLSC, BOT 2 15; 21: Inventory for Old Park Colliery; Inventory for Sandycroft and Mancott Collieries; Allen, *British Industrial Revolution*, p. 162.
30. BL, Eg Ms 1941, ff. 29–30, Section of the Steam Engine on Mr Watt's Construction lately erected at New Willey furnace near Broseley, Shropshire by Mr John Wilkinson, c. 1776; Trinder, *The Industrial Revolution in Shropshire*; Allen, *British Industrial Revolution*, pp. 165–9; 'UK Mining Disasters, 1707–99'.
31. BL, Eg Ms 1941, ff. 29–30, Section of the Steam Engine on Mr Watt's Construction lately erected at New Willey furnace near Broseley, Shropshire by Mr John Wilkinson, c. 1776; Jones, *Industrial Enlightenment*, p. 28; Allen, *British Industrial Revolution*, pp. 165–9; Uglow, *Lunar Men*, pp. 68–9, 246–8; Tann, 'Matthew Boulton', pp. 40–6; Quickenden, Baggott and Dick, *Matthew Boulton*; Andrew, 'Soho Steam Engine', pp. 63–5; Andrew, 'Boulton, Watt and Wilkinson', pp. 85–100; Derry and Williams, *A Short History*, p. 475. For a business overview of the Boulton and Watt firm, see Roll, *An Early Experiment*.
32. SBA, DC90/2/11/1, James Watt to James MacGregor relating to building a canal near Inverness, 1784. For studies on the development of machinery, see: Derry and Williams, *A Short History*, pp. 311–63; Allen, *British Industrial Revolution*, pp. 169–73; Cookson, *Age of Machinery*.
33. SBA, DC90/2/11/1, James Watt to James MacGregor relating to building a canal near Inverness, 1784; Allen, *British Industrial Revolution*, pp. 169–73; Jones, *Industrial Enlightenment*, p. 55. After 1750, access to coal was an important factor in the rapid expansion of urban areas across Europe, see: Fernihough and O'Rourke, 'Coal and the European Industrial Revolution', pp. 1135–49.
34. Smith, 'Industry and Social Change', pp. 135–7, quote p. 136; Evans, 'A Skilled Workforce', pp. 143–59.
35. Defoe and Richardson, *A Tour, Seventh Edition, Vol. 3*, pp. 410–12; Smith, 'Industry and Social Change', pp. 135–7.
36. Berg, 'From Imitation to Invention', pp. 24–7; Cookson, *Making an Industrial Revolution*, pp. 30–61; Cookson, 'Wortley Forge', pp. 52–73; Smith, 'Industry and Social Change', pp. 135–6; Trinder, 'Towns and Industries', pp. 110–11; Johnson, 'Midland Iron Industry', pp. 67–74; Tweedale, *Steel City*, pp. 41–2; Evans and Withey, 'An Enlightenment in Steel', pp. 533–60; Evans, 'The Plantation Hoe', pp. 589–92.
37. Quoted in Rule, *Experience of Labour*, p. 81; King, 'Innovation in the British Iron Industry', p. 13; Cookson, *Making an Industrial Revolution*, pp. 30–61; Berg, 'From Imitation to Invention', pp. 24–7; Smith, 'Industry and Social Change', pp. 135–6; Trinder, 'Towns and Industries', pp. 110–11; Jones, *Industrial Enlightenment*, p. 28.
38. Jones, *Industrial Enlightenment*, pp. 39–45; Berg, *Luxury and Pleasure*, pp. 164–9; Berg, 'Commerce and Creativity'.
39. Boulton quoted in Uglow, *Lunar Men*, p. xiii; Jones, *Industrial Enlightenment*, pp. 39–50, Fisher quoted p. 50; Demidowicz, 'The Origins of the Soho Manufactory', pp. 67–84.
40. Jones, *Industrial Enlightenment*, pp. 39–45, Garbett quoted p. 39; Berg, *Luxury and Pleasure*, pp. 164–9, Boulton quoted p. 168.

41. Smith, 'Industry and Social Change', pp. 135–6; Berg and Hudson, 'Slavery, Atlantic Trade and Skills', pp. 272–3; Satia, *Empire of Guns*, p. 7; Evans, 'A Skilled Workforce', pp. 143–59; Jones, *Industrial Enlightenment*, pp. 26–7.
42. BL, IOR/G/17/1, ff. 52–63, Factors in Mocha to the East India Company in London, 20 July 1721; IOR, Fort William – India House Correspondence, vol. II, East India Company to President and Council at Fort William, 25 March 1757; Schumpeter, *English Overseas Trade Statistics*, p. 21.
43. BL, IOR E/1/18, f. 66, Secretary Alured Popple to Thomas Woolley, 20 April 1727; Schumpeter, *English Overseas Trade Statistics*, p. 21; Jones, *Industrial Enlightenment*, pp. 39–45.
44. Satia, *Empire of Guns*, pp. 19–21.
45. ULLSC, RP IV.1.70, Richard Reynolds to Isaac Hawkins Brown, 17 February 1785; Berg and Hudson, 'Slavery, Atlantic Trade and Skills', pp. 272–3.

## CHAPTER NINE: MADE BY SLAVES

1. Whatley, *Principles of Trade*, pp. 1–2, 8.
2. Roberts, *Slavery and the Enlightenment*, p. 38.
3. Roberts, *Slavery and the Enlightenment*, pp. 9–17; Dunn, *A Tale of Two Plantations*, pp. 23–73; TASTD.
4. For the organisation and structure of Liverpool's transatlantic slave-trade: Radburn, *Traders in Men*; Radburn, 'Keeping "the wheel in motion"', pp. 660–89; Radburn, 'Guinea Factors, Slave Sales', pp. 243–86; Morgan, *Slavery, Atlantic Trade*, pp. 36–73; Tibbles, *Liverpool and the Slave Trade*; McDade, 'Liverpool Slave Merchant Entrepreneurial Networks', pp. 1092–109; Haggerty, 'Liverpool, the Slave Trade', pp. 17–34; Haggerty, *Merely for Money?*, pp. 66–96; Haggerty, 'A Link in the Chain', pp. 157–72. For Bristol's slave-trade: Buckles, *Crisis and Resilience*. For Glasgow's mercantile links to slave-trade: Mullen, *Glasgow Sugar Aristocracy*. For a wider, comparative perspective of the Atlantic slave-trade: Eltis, Lewis and Richardson, 'Slave Prices', pp. 673–700; Eltis, *Atlantic Cataclysm*; Araujo, *Humans in Shackles*.
5. Data from TASTD.
6. ManchesterRO, GB127.Broadsides.F1752.2, A list of all ships belonging to Liverpool, 30 October 1752. TNA, CUST 3/52, Ledger of Exports and Imports, 1752. For the relationship between slave-trade and British manufacturing innovation, see: Mullen, *Glasgow Sugar Aristocracy*; Tibbles, *Liverpool and the Slave Trade*; Berg and Hudson, *Slavery, Capitalism and the Industrial Revolution*; Inikori, *Africans*, pp. 405–9; Zahedieh, 'Eric Williams and William Forbes', pp. 784–808
7. Defoe and Richardson, *A Tour, Seventh Edition, Vol. 3*, pp. 256–8.
8. JRRIL, GB133 English Ms 1048, ff. 1; 4; 36: Invoice of goods shipped on the Tiger to Jamaica for Robert Nicholson of Liverpool, 18 January 1748; Invoice for goods sent and received by Robert Nicholson of Liverpool in the Elizabeth [c. October 1749]; Robert Nicholson to Coy Green, 6 November 1752; 'Robert Nicholson' in RBS.
9. 'Edward Lyon', 'John Cope', 'John Richardson', 'John Kaye', 'John Maddock' and 'William Boats' in RBS; Longmore, '"Cemented by the Blood of a Negro?"', p. 240; Williams, *History of the Liverpool Privateers*, pp. 484–5; Radburn, *Traders in Men*, pp. 29–32.

10. LiverpoolRO, 920 STI/1/4, Thomas Staniforth's Notebook, 1763–1793; 'Richard Kendall', 'Henry Ellis', 'Thomas Staniforth' in RBS.
11. 'Thomas Leyland' and various 'Seel', 'Gildart' and 'Blundell' family entries in RBS; Richardson et al., *Liverpool and Transatlantic Slavery*, p. 202.
12. Quoted in Radburn, *Traders in Men*, p. 29; Morgan, *Slavery, Atlantic Trade*, pp. 36–48.
13. For details of these trading sites and the development of ports and markets by African traders, see Radburn, *Traders in Men*, pp. 36–7.
14. Sweet, 'Slave Trading as a Corporate Criminal Conspiracy', pp. 1–30.
15. Radburn, *Traders in Men*, pp. 2–3, 98–104; McDade, 'Liverpool Slave Merchant Entrepreneurial Networks', pp. 1092–109; Allen, 'Collective Invention', pp. 1–24.
16. ULLSC, LUL MS 1075, Thomas Leyland's Instructions for Captain Young, 1795.
17. For the role of networks in shaping commercial and imperial economic systems, see: Smith, *Merchants*; Rothschild, *Inner Lives*; Hancock, *Citizens of the World*; Radburn, *Traders in Men*; Pearson and Richardson, 'Business Networking', pp. 657–79; McDade, 'Liverpool Slave Merchant Entrepreneurial Networks', pp. 1092–109; Haggerty, 'Structure of the Trading Community in Liverpool', pp. 98–100; Haggerty, 'Liverpool, the Slave Trade', pp. 17–34; Haggerty, *Merely for Money?*, pp. 66–96; Haggerty, 'A Link in the Chain', pp. 157–72; Glasier, 'Networking', pp. 451–76.
18. NLS, MSS.8793, f. 152, Alexander Houston & Company to John Paterson, 27 January 1777; PA, HL.PO.JP.10.6.52, Report from the Commissioners of Trade and Plantations, 16 December 1703. For the networks that criss-crossed transatlantic commerce, see: Hancock, *Citizens of the World*; Radburn, *Traders in Men*, pp. 196–216.
19. NLS, MSS.8793, ff. 1, 3, 5–9, 11, 13, 16–19, 38, 379–85, 406: Alexander Houston's Foreign Letter Book, 4 March 1776–24 April 1778; NLS, MSS.8793, ff. 233–6, Foreign Letter Book, 14 May 1778–1781; Hamilton, 'Scottish Trading in the Caribbean', pp. 94–126.
20. JRRIL, GB133 English Ms 1048, f. 39. Letter from Robert Nicholson in Liverpool to Harry Hutton, 10 October 1751.
21. JRRIL, GB133 English Ms 1048, f. 2. Letter from Robert Nicholson in Liverpool to William Tylston, 10 November 1748.
22. JRRIL, GB133 English Ms 1048, f. 2; 3; 5; 6; 15; Robert Nicholson to William Tylston, 10 November 1748; Sales of sundry merchandises received by the Tiger Frigate from Liverpool on the account of Robert Nicholson of Liverpool, May 1649–May 1650; Robert Nicholson to James France, 29 October 1749; Robert Nicholson in Liverpool to Robert Wilson, 29 October 1749; Robert Nicholson to James Nicholson, 15 April 1749.
23. LiverpoolRO, 920 STI/1/4, Thomas Staniforth's Notebook, 1763–1793.
24. LiverpoolRO, Committee Book of the African Company, ff. 11–12, 18, 21–2.
25. For British social and cultural networks: Clark, *British Clubs and Societies*; Thomas, *Pursuit of Civility*; Langford, *Polite and Commercial People*. For Liverpool's social networks: McDade, 'Liverpool Slave Merchant Entrepreneurial Networks', pp. 1092–109; Haggerty, *Merely for Money?*, pp. 161–96; Haggerty, 'Structure of the Trading Community in Liverpool', pp. 97–125; Haggerty and Haggerty, 'Networking with a Network', pp. 566–90.
26. Quoted in Radburn, *Traders in Men*, p. 1.

27. TNA, CUST 3/70 and 3/80, Ledgers of Imports and Exports, 1770 and 1780; Schumpeter, *English Overseas Trade Statistics*; Haggerty, 'Structure of the Trading Community in Liverpool', p. 98; Draper, 'Helping to Make Britain Great', pp. 79–80.
28. JRRIL, GB133 English Ms 1048, f. 51, Thomas Boardman to his Cousin, 16 December 1799; Zahedieh, *Capital and the Colonies*, p. 285; Gauci, *Emporium of the World*, pp. 204–5; Haggerty, 'Structure of the Trading Community in Liverpool', pp. 98–100; Radburn, *Traders in Men*, pp. 19–25, Norris quote pp. 19–20; Mullen, *Glasgow Sugar Aristocracy*, pp. 15–18; Inikori, *Africans*, pp. 279–361; Harley, 'Slavery, the British Atlantic Economy', pp. 161–83; Rönnbäck, 'On the Economic Importance of the Slave Plantation Complex', pp. 309–27; Berg and Hudson, *Slavery, Capitalism and the Industrial Revolution*; Scanlan, *Slave Empire*.
29. Hancock, 'Scots in the Slave Trade', pp. 63–83; Mullen, *Glasgow Sugar Aristocracy*, pp. 8–29, 293–302.
30. Mitchell Library, T-MH/1/2, Merchants House Minute Book, 1711–1754; Mitchell Library, T-MH/1/3, pp. 7, 34, 113–14, Merchants House Minute Book, 1754–1790; Monteith, *Old Port Glasgow*, pp. 3–20.
31. Mitchell Library, T-MH/1/2, Merchants House Minute Book, 1711–1754; Mitchell Library, T-MH/1/3, pp. 7, 34, 113–14, Merchants House Minute Book, 1754–1790; Monteith, *Old Port Glasgow*, pp. 3–20.
32. Draper, 'The City of London', pp. 432–66. The expansion of British banking services was closely linked with the needs of merchants and manufacturers across every part of the economy. For the development of the banking industry more broadly, see Chapman, *Rise of Merchant Banking*; Cassis and Cottrell, *Private Banking in Europe*; Kosmetatos, *The 1772–73 British Credit Crisis*; Neal, 'How It All Began', pp. 117–40.
33. LiverpoolRO, 353 MIN/COI 1/2/1, ff. 11, 72, 141, Committee for Trade Meeting, 5 June 1775; 3 April 1784; 19 May 1794; LiverpoolRO, 900 MD 3, Petition of the Corporation of Liverpool against Abolition [1796]; Radburn, *Traders in Men*, pp. 39–40; Haggerty, 'Structure of the Trading Community in Liverpool', pp. 98–100. For Anti-Abolition movement in Glasgow: Mullen, 'Proslavery Collaborations', pp. 601–43.
34. LiverpoolRO, 353 MIN/COI 1/2/1, ff. 11, 72, 141, Committee for Trade Meeting, 5 June 1775; 3 April 1784; 19 May 1794; LiverpoolRO, 900 MD 3, Petition of the Corporation of Liverpool against Abolition [1796]; Radburn, *Traders in Men*, pp. 39–40; Haggerty, 'Structure of the Trading Community in Liverpool', pp. 98–100.
35. ManchesterRO, GB127.Tracts/P.1898.7, Articles of Sugar Copartnery at Edinburgh, 1751; Rönnbäck, 'Sweet Business', pp. 223–45. The impact of cotton is the focus of Chapter Ten.
36. Rönnbäck, 'Sweet Business', pp. 223–45; Rössler, 'Germans from Hanover', pp. 49–63, quote p. 51; Jones, *Bristol's Sugar Trade*, pp. 1–22; Morgan, 'Bristol West India Merchants', pp. 186–201; Dresser, *Slavery Obscured*, pp. 96–128; Richardson, 'Slavery and Bristol's "Golden Age"', p. 49; Buckles, *Crisis and Resilience*; Buchanan, 'Capital Investment', pp. 206–322; Schumpeter, *English Overseas Trade Statistics*.
37. TNA, CUST 3/30 and 3/70, Customs Ledgers 1730 and 1770; Evans, *Slave Wales*, pp. 39–42; Longmore, '"Cemented by the Blood of a Negro?"', p. 240; Williams, *History of the Liverpool Privateers*, pp. 484–5.

38. TNA, CUST 3/30 and 3/70, Customs Ledgers 1730 and 1770; Evans, *Slave Wales*, pp. 39–42; Longmore, '"Cemented by the Blood of a Negro?"', p. 240; Williams, *History of the Liverpool Privateers*, pp. 484–5.
39. ManchesterRO, GB127.Tracts.P.3700.3, Three Letters Addressed to a Friend in India, by a Proprietor: principally on the subject of importing Bengal sugars into England, 1793; Zahedieh, 'Eric Williams and William Forbes', pp. 784–808; Evans, *Slave Wales*, pp. 39–42; Harris, *The Copper King*, pp. 69–87; 'Thomas Williams' in Online Dictionary of Welsh Biography.
40. ManchesterRO, GB127.Tracts.P.3700.3, Three Letters Addressed to a Friend in India, by a Proprietor: principally on the subject of importing Bengal sugars into England, 1793; Zahedieh, 'Eric Williams and William Forbes', pp. 784–808; Evans, *Slave Wales*, pp. 39–42; Harris, *The Copper King*, pp. 69–87; 'Thomas Williams' in Online Dictionary of Welsh Biography.
41. ULLSC, RP XXIII.4.1, William Rathbone Day Book, 1742–7; ULSSC, RP I.1.1, William Rathbone to John Elliot, 26 March 1772; ULSSC, RP II.1 161, Rathbone & Co to John Hollins, 14 August 1798.
42. JRRIL, GB133 English Ms 1048, f. 30, Robert Nicholson to Henry Hutton, 6 August 1762; Defoe and Richardson, *A Tour, Seventh Edition, Vol. 3*, pp. 263; Hyde, *Liverpool and the Mersey*, pp. 25–42; Clemens, 'Rise of Liverpool', pp. 211–25; Morgan, *Slavery, Atlantic Trade*, p. 88; Pope 'Wealth and Social Aspirations', pp. 164–226; Longmore, '"Cemented by the Blood of a Negro?"', pp. 227–51.
43. 'John Richardson', 'John Kaye' and 'Peter Hunt' in RBS. Hyde, *Liverpool and the Mersey*, pp. 25–42; Clemens, 'Rise of Liverpool', pp. 211–25; Morgan, *Slavery, Atlantic Trade*, p. 88.
44. LiverpoolRO, 920 STI/1/4, Thomas Staniforth's Notebook, 1763–1793.
45. LancashireRO, DDBB/1/1, Chaffers and Lace to Mr Jonathan Blundell, Assignment of their Shares and Interests in the Coal Concern, 8 July 1776; BradfordRO, JOW/11/a/3/3. Principal Parties in the Leeds & Liverpool Canal, c. 1769; BradfordRO, JOW/11/a/2/35. List of Subscribers in the Leeds and Liverpool Canal, c. 1780. 'Edward Chaffers' and 'Jonathan Blundell' in RBS.
46. JRILL, SO/1/185, Samuel Oldknow to Mr Gill [undated, c. 1780s]; NLS, MS.19846, Notebook of John Rennie, January 1793; 'Jonathan Blundell' in RBS.
47. LancashireRO, DDBB/1/4. Co-partnership Agreement, 1 May 1781; Lancashire Archives, DDBB/1/3. Co-partnership Agreement, 17 December 1777; 'Henry Blundell' in RBS.
48. ManchesterRO, GB124.E4/78/419, List of subscribers for Bury, Bolton and Manchester Canal, c. 1791.
49. ManchesterRO, GB127.Tracts/P.356.2, The Case of the Sugar Colonies, 1792. For the abolition movement, see: Swaminathan, *Debating the Slave Trade*; Brown, *Moral Capital*; Pinarbasi, 'Manchester Antislavery', pp. 349–76; Oldfield, *Popular Politics and British Antislavery*.
50. ManchesterRO, GB127.Tracts/P.356.2, The Case of the Sugar Colonies, 1792.
51. ManchesterRO, GB127.Tracts.P.3700.4, An Appeal to the Candour and Justice of the People of England in behalf of the West India Merchants and Planters, 1792.
52. LiverpoolRO, 353 MIN/COI 1/2/1, f. 129, Committee for Trade Meeting, 17 June 1791; LiverpoolRO, 900 MD 3, Petition of the Corporation of Liverpool against Abolition [1796].

## CHAPTER TEN: THE EMPIRE'S NEW CLOTHES

1. Quoted in Hoppit, *Britain's Political Economies*, p. 216; Quoted in Beckert, *Empire of Cotton*, p. x; BL, Sloane Ms 2902, ff. 3–4, Answer of the Commissioners of Trade and Plantations to the Honourable the House of Commons, 22 March 1700; IOR, Fort William – India House Correspondence, vol. II, East India Company to President and Council at Fort William, 25 March 1757. For impact of Indian textiles on Britain's textile industry, see: Lemire, *Fashion's Favourite*, p. 42; Raman, 'Indian Cotton Textiles', p. 455; Eacott, *Selling Empire*, pp. 1–13, 276–332.
2. Leake, 'Treatise on the Cloth Industry', p. 214; Roberts, *The Treasure of Traffike*, p. 33. For a wide-ranging overview of shape and structure of England's early modern textile industry, see Kerridge, *Textile Manufacturers*. For Leake and sixteenth-century textile manufacturing, see Ramsay, 'Distribution of the Cloth Industry', pp. 361–9.
3. Calladine and Fricker, *East Cheshire Textile Mills*, pp. 7–8.
4. ManchesterRO, GB127.TractsP.2881.14, Scheme for Effectually Employing the Manufacturers by Making of Calicos in Great Britain [1720].
5. Raman, 'Indian Cotton Textiles', p. 450; Raman, 'From Hand to Machine', p. 708; Styles, *Dress of the People*, p. 186; Berg, 'Useful Knowledge', pp. 117–41; Lemire, *Fashion's Favourite*, pp. 30–4; Parthasarathi, *Why Europe Grew Rich*, pp. 98–109; Riello, *Cotton*, pp. 224–5.
6. Defoe and Richardson, *A Tour, Seventh Edition, Vol. 3*, p. 268; Raman, 'From Hand to Machine', pp. 711–19; Chapman, *Cotton Industry*, pp. 20–1; Warner, *The Silk Industry*, pp. 199–201.
7. Chapman, *Cotton Industry*, pp. 26–9; Edwards, *Growth of the British Cotton Trade*, pp. 3–5; Styles, 'Rise and Fall of the Spinning Jenny', pp. 195–236.
8. Chapman, *Cotton Industry*, pp. 26–9; Edwards, *Growth of the British Cotton Trade*, pp. 3–5; Styles, 'Rise and Fall of the Spinning Jenny', pp. 195–236.
9. Quoted in Raman, 'Indian Cotton Textiles', p. 453; Sugden, 'An Occupational Study', pp. 160–75. For the linked technological development of spinning machinery and waterpower, see Chapter Six. For steam engine technology, see Chapter Eight.
10. Raman, 'Indian Cotton Textiles', p. 453; Hancock, 'Scots in the Slave Trade', pp. 63–83; Mullen, *Glasgow Sugar Aristocracy*, pp. 8–29, 293–302; Campbell, 'Paisley Before the Shawl', pp. 162–76; 'Dale, David' in ODNB.
11. Fitton and Wadsworth, *The Strutts and the Arkwrights*, pp. 3–49.
12. Fitton and Wadsworth, *The Strutts and the Arkwrights*, pp. 50–65.
13. Fitton and Wadsworth, *The Strutts and the Arkwrights*, pp. 66–81, 169; Cooper, *Transformation of a Valley*, p. 68; Rose, 'Early Cotton Riots in Lancashire', pp. 77–100. For wider context of industrial protest, see: Archer, *Social Unrest*; Randall, *Before the Luddites*.
14. Rasbotham, *Thoughts on the Use of Machines*, pp. 3–15.
15. Fitton and Wadsworth, *The Strutts and the Arkwrights*, pp. 66–81, 169; Cooper, *Transformation of a Valley*, p. 68; Styles, 'Rise and Fall of the Spinning Jenny', pp. 195–236. For impact of machinery on workers: Griffin, *Liberty's Dawn*, pp. 23–56; Honeyman, *Child Workers*; Honeyman, *Women, Gender and Industrialisation*; Horrell and Humphries, 'Women's Labour', pp. 89–117.
16. JRRIL, SO/11/9, Calicos and Other Goods for Sale at the East India House, March 1789.

17. For an overview of Oldknow's life and business, see: Unwin, *Samuel Oldknow*.
18. JRILL, SO/1/185, Samuel Oldknow to Mr Gill [undated, c. 1780s]; Unwin, *Samuel Oldknow*, pp. 2–71.
19. JRRIL, SO/1/150, Thomas Horsfield to Samuel Oldknow, 24 September 1788; Rule, *Experience of Labour*, pp. 74–92.
20. JRILL, SO/1/150; 153; 155: Thomas Horsfield to Samuel Oldknow, 23 September 1788; 30 October 1788; 15 December 1788.
21. JRRIL, SO/1/14; 185; 197; 44; 120: J.B. [Barnes?] to Samuel Oldknow, 2 December 1787; Samuel Oldknow to Mr Gill [undated, c. 1780s]; Robert Parker to Samuel Oldknow, 20 September 1786; Edward and Rachel Bowden to John Oldknow, 14 June 1787; Robert Gourlay to Samuel Oldknow, 13 August 1787.
22. JRRIL, SO/1/36; 11; 46; 195; 115; 126; 127; 193; 199: Robert Blackwell to Samuel Oldknow, 8 May 1790; Barclay & Steven to Samuel Oldknow, 12 May 1788; Ellis Brewin to Samuel Oldknow, 21 July 1789; Robert Parker to Samuel Oldknow, 20 May 1786; Goodwin & Jenkinson to Samuel Oldknow, 17 July 1794; Greaves, Hodgson & Co to Samuel Oldknow, 23 August 1787 and 24 November 1789; Parker, Topham & Sowden to Samuel Oldknow, 20 October 1784.
23. JRRIL, SO/1/106; 37; 61: Benjamin Gibson to Samuel Oldknow, 12 December 1787; Robert Blackwell to Samuel Oldknow, 17 November 1793; James Cazenove to Samuel Oldknow, 1 February 1792.
24. JRRIL, SO/1/138; 45: John Carwood to Samuel Oldknow, 23 November 1789; Bowles & Birch to Samuel Oldknow, 6 June 1787.
25. JRRIL, SO/1/139; 140; 143; 15: Jonathon Haworth & Sons to Samuel Oldknow, 22 February 1787; J. Smith on behalf of J. Haworth and Sons to Samuel Oldknow, 7 November 1787; J. Haworth to Samuel Oldknow, 13 March 1789; John Barrill to Samuel Oldknow, 20 November 1789.
26. Unwin, *Samuel Oldknow*, pp. 131–74.
27. JRRIL, SO/1/88; 23–32: John Dewsnap to Samuel Oldknow, 24 July 1792; Nathaniel Binns to Samuel Oldknow, 5 February 1793–26 July 1794.
28. JRRIL, SO/1/13; 91; 150; 151; 168: John Barlow to Samuel Oldknow, 12 October 1801; John Downes to Samuel Oldknow, 14 May 1793; Thomas Horsfield to Samuel Oldknow, 24 September 1788; Thomas Horsfield to Samuel Oldknow, 27 September 1788; James Lythgoe to Samuel Oldknow, 29 November 1792.
29. Unwin, *Samuel Oldknow*, p. 194.
30. Rasbotham, *Thoughts on the Use of Machines*, p. 12.
31. BL, Add Ms 34462, ff. 61–8; 69–77: Examination of John Hilton and William Frodisham at Committee for Trade and Foreign Plantations, 22 February 1786; Examination of Joseph Smith and Robert Peel at Committee for Trade and Foreign Plantations, 24 February 1786. Raman, 'From Hand to Machine', pp. 721–5; Raman, 'Indian Cotton Textiles', p. 451; Roy, *Crafts and Capitalism*, p. 16.
32. SBA, DC90/2/11/1, James Watt to James MacGregor relating to building a canal near Inverness, 1784.
33. ManchesterRO, GB127.8, ff. 53–5, Proceedings of the Society of Merchants Trading on the Continent of Europe, 1794–1796; ManchesterRO, GB127. C5/1/1/1, Personal Ledger of Samuel Greg, 1794–1824; ManchesterRO, GB127. C5/1/2/1, Partnership Book for Samuel Greg and Peter Ewart, 1805–1810.
34. JRRIL, GB133 MCK/2/2/1, ff. 25; 71: McConnel & Kennedy in Manchester to Joseph Sykes in Stockport, 24 April 1795; McConnel & Kennedy in

Manchester to Joseph Sykes in Stockport, 21 July 1795. JRRIL, GB133 MCK/3/1/1, f. 44, McConnel & Kennedy Nominal Ledger, 1795–1801; ManchesterRO, GB127.8, ff. 53–5, Proceedings of the Society of Merchants Trading on the Continent of Europe, 1794–1796; Raman, 'From Hand to Machine', p. 719.

35. 5lb of the coarsest 'Mule twist' cost £3 5d, while 5lb the finest 'India twist' sold for £6 19s 2d. JRRIL, GB133 MCK/2/2/1, ff. 40–1, McConnel & Kennedy in Manchester to Gordon & Cairns in Glasgow, 20 May 1795; JRRIL, GB133 MCK/2/1/1/1, Gordon & Cairns in Glasgow to McConnel & Kennedy in Manchester, 19 September 1795; JRRIL, GB133 MCK/2/2/1, ff. 151–2, McConnel & Kennedy in Manchester to Gordon & Cairns in Glasgow, 4 December 1795; JRRIL, GB133 MCK/2/1/1/1, Gordon & Cairns in Glasgow to McConnel & Kennedy in Manchester, 26 May 1795; JRRIL, GB133 MCK/2/1/3; 4: Robert Kennedy to McConnel & Kennedy, 20 October 1798; John Kennedy to Mr McConnel, 1 July and 5 July 1798; Lee, *Cotton Enterprise*, p. 167.
36. JRRIL, GB133 MCK/2/2/1, ff. 40–1, McConnel & Kennedy in Manchester to Gordon & Cairns in Glasgow, 20 May 1795; JRRIL, GB133 MCK/2/1/1/1, Gordon & Cairns in Glasgow to McConnel & Kennedy in Manchester, 19 September 1795; JRRIL, GB133 MCK/2/2/1, ff. 151–2, McConnel & Kennedy in Manchester to Gordon & Cairns in Glasgow, 4 December 1795; JRRIL, GB133 MCK/2/1/1/1, Gordon & Cairns in Glasgow to McConnel & Kennedy in Manchester, 26 May 1795; JRRIL, GB133 MCK/2/1/3; 4: Robert Kennedy to McConnel & Kennedy, 20 October 1798; John Kennedy to Mr McConnel, 1 July and 5 July 1798; Lee, *Cotton Enterprise*, p. 167.
37. JRRIL, GB 133 MCK/3/5/1/1; MCK/3/5/1/2; MCK/2/1/3: James Bland to McConnel & Kennedy, 7 September 1797. For the first study of these invoices, see Cunliffe, 'McConnel & Kennedy Co', pp. 24–32; Bailey, 'The Other Side of Slavery', p. 37.
38. NLS, MSS.8793, f. 38, Alexander Houston & Company to Mssrs Houston & Paterson, 6 June 1776; Deane and Cole, *British Economic Growth*, p. 52; Bailey, 'The Other Side of Slavery', pp. 35–50; Kritchal, 'Liverpool and the Raw Cotton Trade', p. 115; Raman, 'From Hand to Machine', p. 711.
39. ULLSC, LUL MS 138, Waterhouse Cotton Ledger, 1799–1803.
40. ManchesterRO, GB127.8, ff. 44–6, Proceedings of the Society of Merchants Trading on the Continent of Europe, 1794–1796.
41. BL, Add Ms 34462, ff. 61–8. Examination of Alexander Anderson at Committee for Trade and Foreign Plantations, 4 January 1786.
42. Raman, 'From Hand to Machine', p. 729.
43. ULLSC, RP II.1 61, Samuel Greg to William Rathbone, 6 March 1793; East India Company, *Report of the Select Committee*, pp. 1–7.

## CONCLUSION: WEALTH AND POWER

1. Pomeranz, *Great Divergence*, pp. 4, 274–8, 313–15.

# BIBLIOGRAPHY

## ARCHIVES

Bradford Archives (BradfordRO)
British Library (BL)
British Newspaper Archive (BNA)
John Rylands Research Institute and Library (JRRIL)
Lancashire Archives, Preston (LancashireRO)
Library of Birmingham (LOB)
Liverpool Central Library, Record Office (LiverpoolRO)
Liverpool Maritime Museum (LMM)
Manchester Central Library, Record Office (ManchesterRO)
The Mitchell Library, Glasgow
The National Archives, UK (TNA)
The National Library of Scotland (NLS)
The National Library of Wales (NLW)
Parliamentary Archives (PA)
Royal Society Archive (RS)
Scottish Border Archive
Scottish Business Archive, Glasgow (SBA)
Tyne and Wear Archives (TWA)
West Glamorgan Archives (WGA)
West Yorkshire Archive Service, Bradford (WYAS Bradford)
West Yorkshire Archive Service, Calderdale (WYAS Calderdale)
University of Liverpool Library Special Collections (ULLSC)
University of Manchester Library Special Collections (UMLSC)

## PRINTED PRIMARY MATERIAL

Anon., *Europæ Modernæ Speculum* (London, 1666)
——, *Articles of Agreement & Subscription between His Highness Prince Rupert and Diverse Noble and Honourable Persons, and others, Undertakers for Working of Mines Royal* (London, 1670)

——, *Great Newes from the Barbadoes* (London, 1676)
—— [Francis Hanson], *The Laws of Jamaica* (London, 1683)
——, *An Answer to a Paper Published by One Bateman against the Mine-Adventure by A New Adventurer* (London, 1698)
——, *An Act for Encouraging the Importation of Naval Stores from Her Majesty's Plantations in America* (London, 1704)
——, *An Act for Better Preservation of His Majesty's Woods in America* (London, 1729)
R. B. [Nathaniel Crouch], *The English Empire in America* (London, 1685)
Belgrove, William, *A Treatise upon Husbandry or Planting* (Boston, New England, 1755)
Bisset, Robert, *The History of the Negro Slave Trade, in its Connection with the Commerce and Prosperity of the West Indies, and the Wealth and Power of the British Empire* (London, 1805)
Bradford, William, *A Relation or Journall of the Beginning and Proceedings of the English Plantation Settled at Plimoth in New England* (London, 1622)
Brindley, James, *The History of Inland Navigations: Particularly Those of the Duke of Bridgewater in Lancashire and Cheshire* (London, 1766)
J. C., *The Compleat Collier: Or the Whole Art of Sinking, Getting, and Working Coal-mines* (London, 1708)
Carter, William, *England's Interest Asserted, in the Improvement of its Native Commodities* (London, 1669)
Chamberlaybe, Edward, *Angliæ Notitia, or The Present State of England* (London, 1669)
Childrey, Joshua, *Britannia Baconica, or, The Natural Rarities of England, Scotland and Wales* (London, 1660)
Council for New England, *A Brief Relation of the Discovery and Plantation of New England* (London, 1622)
Defoe, Daniel, *An Essay Upon Projects* (London, 1697)
——, *A Plan of the English Commerce* (London, 1728)
—— and Mr Richardson, *A Tour through the Whole Island of Great Britain, Seventh Edition, Vol. 3* (London, 1769)
Donaldson, James, *Husbandry Anatomized* (Edinburgh, 1697)
Du Halde, Jean-Baptiste, *The General History of China*, trans. Richard Brookes (London, 1741)
East India Company, *Report of the Select Committee of the Court of Directors of the East India Company, Upon the Subject of the Cotton Manufacture of this Country* (London, 1793)
Hale, Thomas, *An Account of Several New Inventions and Improvements Now Necessary for England* (London, 1691)
Holwell, John Zephaniah, *A Genuine Narrative of the Deplorable Deaths of the English Gentlemen, and others, who were Suffocated in the Black-Hole in Fort-William* (London, 1758)
Home, Francis, *The Principles of Agriculture and Vegetation* (Edinburgh, 1755)
Houghton, John, *A Collection of Letters for the Improvement of Husbandry & Trade* (London, 1681–3)
Kennedy, John, 'Brief Notice of my Early Recollections in a Letter to my Children', in *Miscellaneous Papers on Subjects Connected with the Manufacture of Lancashire* (Manchester, 1849)

Levett, Christopher, *A Voyage into New England Begun in 1623* (London, 1624)
Lombe, Thomas, *A Brief State of the Case Relating to the Machine Erected at Derby for Making Italian Organzine Silk* (London, 1732)
Mackworth, Humphrey, *The Mine-Adventure* (London, 1698)
McConnel, David, *Facts and Traditions Collected for a Family Record* (Edinburgh, 1861)
Meager, Leonard, *The Mystery of Husbandry* (London, 1697)
Plot, Robert, *The Natural History of Staffordshire* (Oxford, 1686)
Rasbotham, Dorning, *Thoughts on the Use of Machines, in the Cotton Manufacture: Addressed to the Working People in that Manufacture, and to the Poor in General* (Manchester, 1780)
Roberts, Lewes, *The Treasure of Traffike* (London, 1641)
Smeaton, John, *The Report of John Smeaton Engineer Concerning the Practicability and Expense of Joining the Rivers Forth and Clyde by a Navigable Canal* (Edinburgh, 1766)
Sprat, Thomas, *The History of the Royal Society for the Improving of Natural Knowledge* (London, 1667)
Thomson, Thomas, *History of the Royal Society: From its Institution to the End of the Eighteenth Century* (London, 1812)
Trusler, John, *Practical Husbandry* (London, 1799)
Tucker, Josiah, *A Series of Answers to Certain Popular Objections against Separating from the Rebellious Colonies, and Discarding hem Entirely* (Gloucester, 1776)
Waller, William, *An Essay on the Value of the Mines, Late of Sir Carbery Price* (London, 1698)
——, *The Second Abstract of the State of the Mines of Bwlchyr-Eskir-Hyr* (London, 1700)
——, *The Third Abstract of the State of the Mines of Bwlchyr-Eskir-Hyr* (London, 1700)
Whatley, George, *Principles of Trade* (London, 1774)
Wood, William, *The Present State of Mr Wood's Partnership* (London, c. 1720)
Worlidge, John, *Systema Agriculturæ, The Mystery of Husbandry Discovered* (London, 1681)
Wyeth, Joseph, *An Answer to a Letter from Dr. Bray Directed to Such as Have Contributed towards the Propagating Christian Knowledge in the Plantations* (London, 1700)
Young, Arthur, *Rural Oeconomy: Or, Essays on the Practical Parts of Husbandry* (London, 1773 [1770])

## EDITED PRIMARY MATERIAL

Best, Henry and Woodward, Donald, eds, *The Farming and Memorandum Books of Henry Best of Elmswell, 1642* (Oxford, 1984)
Carr, Cecil, *Selected Charters of Trading Companies,* A.D. *1530–1707* (London, 1913)
Crocker, A. G., ed., *Gunpowder Mills: Documents of the Seventeenth and Eighteenth Centuries* (Woking, 2000)
Fisher, Jabez and Morgan, Kenneth, eds, *An American Quaker in the British Isles: The Travel Journals of Jabez Maud Fisher, 1775–1779* (Oxford, 1992)
Hayes, G. G. L. and Evans, Chris, eds, *The Letterbook of Richard Crawshay, 1788–1797* (Swansea, 1990)

Hume, David, 'Of Commerce', in *Hume: Political Essays*, ed. Knud Haakonssen (Cambridge, 1994)

Labaree, Leonard, ed., *The Papers of Benjamin Franklin, Vol. 6: April 1, 1755, through September 30, 1756* (New Haven, CT, 1963)

Leake, John, 'Treatise on the Cloth Industry, With Proposals for the Reform of Abuses, 1577', in *Tudor Economic Documents: Volume 3*, ed. R. H. Tawney and Eileen Power (London, 1951 [1924])

Raithby, John, ed., *Statutes of the Realm: Volumes 5, 6 and 7* (British History Online)

Woodcroft, Bennet, ed., *Titles of Patents of Invention* (London, 1854)

## SECONDARY MATERIAL

Acemoglu, Daron, Johnson, Simon and Robinson, James, 'The Rise of Europe: Atlantic Trade, Institutional Change, and Economic Growth', *American Economic Review* 95 (2005), pp. 546–79

Acemoglu, Daron and Robinson, James, *Why Nations Fail: The Origins of Power, Prosperity and Poverty* (London, 2013)

Aitchison, Peter and Cassell, Andrew, *The Lowland Clearances: Scotland's Silent Revolution, 1760–1830* (Edinburgh, 2012)

Albert, William, *The Turnpike Road System in England, 1663–1840* (Cambridge, 1972)

Aldous, Michael, 'From Traders to Planters: The Evolving Importance of Trading Companies in the 19th Century Anglo-Indian Indigo Trade', *Business History* 65, 5 (2023), pp. 803–20

Allan, D. G. C., 'The Society of Arts and Government, 1754–1800: Public Encouragement of Arts, Manufactures, and Commerce in Eighteenth-Century England', *Eighteenth-Century Studies* 7, 4 (1974), pp. 434–52

Allen, Robert, 'Collective Invention', *Journal of Economic Behaviour and Organisation* 4 (1983), pp. 1–24

——, *Enclosure and the Yeoman: The Agricultural Development of the South Midlands 1450–1850* (Oxford, 1992)

——, 'Why the Industrial Revolution was British: Commerce, Induced Invention, and the Scientific Revolution', *Economic History Review* 64, 2 (2011), pp. 357–84

——, 'Technology and the Great Divergence: Global Economic Development since 1820', *Explorations in Economic History* 49, 1 (2012), pp. 1–16

——, *The British Industrial Revolution in Global Perspective* (Cambridge, 2014)

——, 'The High Wage Economy and the Industrial Revolution: A Restatement', *Economic History Review* 68, 1 (2015), pp. 1–22.

Allison, K. T., 'The Sheep-Corn Husbandry of Norfolk in the Sixteenth and Seventeenth Centuries', *Agricultural History Review* V, 1 (1957), pp. 12–30

——, 'Flock Management in the Sixteenth and Seventeenth Centuries', *Economic History Review* 11, 1 (1958), pp. 98–112

Álvarez-Nogal, Carlos and Prados De La Escosura, Leandro, 'The Rise and Fall of Spain, 1270–1850', *Economic History Review* 66, 1 (2013), pp. 1–37

Amussen, Susan Dwyer, *Caribbean Exchanges: Slavery and the Transformation of English Society, 1640–1700* (Chapel Hill, NC, 2007)

Anderson, Fred, *Crucible of War: The Seven Years' War and the Fate of Empire in British North America, 1754–1766* (New York, 2000)

Anderson, Jennifer, 'Nature's Currency: The Atlantic Mahogany Trade and the Commodification of Nature in the Eighteenth Century', *Early American Studies* 2, 1 (2004), pp. 47–80

Anderson, Judith, 'Derby Porcelain and the Early English Fine Ceramic Industry, c. 1750–1830', PhD thesis, University of Leicester (2000)

Anderson, M. S., *The War of the Austrian Succession, 1740–1748* (London, 1995)

Andrew, Jim, 'The Soho Steam Engine Business', in *Matthew Boulton: Selling What All the World Desires*, ed. Shena Mason (New Haven, CT, 2009), pp. 63–70

——, 'Boulton, Watt and Wilkinson: The Birth of the Improved Steam Engine', in *Matthew Boulton: Enterprising Industrialist of the Enlightenment*, ed. Matthew Quickenden, Sally Baggott and Malcolm Dick (Abingdon, 2013), pp. 85–110

Araujo, Ana Lucia, *Humans in Shackles: An Atlantic History of Slavery* (Chicago, IL, 2024)

Archer, John, *Social Unrest and Popular Protest in England 1780–1840* (Cambridge, 2000)

Arena, Carolyn, 'Indian Slaves from Guiana in Seventeenth-Century Barbados', *Ethnohistory* 64, 1 (2017), pp. 65–90

Ashton, T. S., *The Industrial Revolution, 1760–1830* (Oxford, 1964)

Ashton, T. S. and Sykes, Joseph, *The Coal Industry of the Eighteenth Century* (Manchester, 1929)

Ashworth, William, *The Industrial Revolution: The State, Knowledge and Global Trade* (London, 2017)

Aston, T. H. and Philpin, C. H. E., eds, *The Brenner Debate: Agrarian Class Structure and Economic Development in Pre-industrial Europe* (Cambridge, 1985)

Bailey, De Witt and Nie, Douglas, *English Gunmakers: The Birmingham and Provincial Gun Trade in the 18th and 19th Century* (New York, 1978)

Bailey, Geoff, *Locks, Stocks and Bodies in Barrels: A History of the Canals in the Falkirk Area* (Falkirk, 2000)

Bailey, Ronald, 'The Other Side of Slavery: Black Labor, Cotton, and Textile Industrialization in Great Britain and the United States', *Agricultural History* 68, 2 (1994), pp. 35–50

Baker, Norman, *Government and Contractors: British Treasury and War Supplies, 1775–83* (London, 1971)

Bannerman, Gordon, *Merchants and the Military in Eighteenth-Century Britain: British Army Contracts and Domestic Supply, 1739–1763* (London, 2008)

Baptist, Edward, *The Half Has Never Been Told: Slavery and the Making of American Capitalism* (New York, 2014)

Barbier, Edward, *Natural Resources and Economic Development* (Cambridge, 2005)

——, *Scarcity and Frontiers: How Economies Have Developed Through Natural Resource Exploitation* (Cambridge, 2011)

Barker, Hannah, *The Business of Women: Female Enterprise and Urban Development in Northern England, 1760–1830* (Oxford, 2006)

——, *Family and Business during the Industrial Revolution* (Oxford, 2017)

Barker, Hannah, Brown, Carys, Gibson, Kate and Gregory, Jeremy, *Faith in the Town: Lay Religion in Northern England, 1740–1830* (Oxford, 2025)

Bath, Joanna, 'Violence and Violent Crime in the North-East, c. 1650–1720', PhD thesis, University of Newcastle upon Tyne (2001)

Bayly, Christopher, *The Birth of the Modern World, 1780–1914: Global Connections and Comparisons* (Oxford, 2004)

Beckert, Sven, *Empire of Cotton: A New History of Global Capitalism* (London, 2015)

Beckert, Sven, Bosma, Ulbe, Schneider, Mindi and Vanhaute, Eric, 'Commodity Frontiers and the Transformation of the Global Countryside: A Research Agenda', *Journal of Global History* 16, 3 (2021), pp. 435–50

Beckett, J. V., *Coal and Tobacco: The Lowthers and the Economic Development of West Cumberland, 1660–1760* (Cambridge, 1981)

Beckles, Hilary, *Black Rebellion in Barbados: The Struggle Against Slavery, 1627–1838* (Barbados, 1984)

Bemrose, William, *Bow, Chelsea, and Derby Porcelain: Being Further Information Relating to These Factories, Obtained From Original Documents, not Hitherto Published* (London, 1898)

Bennett, Michael, 'Merchant Capital and the Origins of the Barbados Sugar Boom, 1627–1672', PhD thesis, University of Sheffield (2020)

——, 'Caribbean Plantation Economies as Colonial Models: The Case of the English East India Company and St Helena in the Late Seventeenth Century', *Atlantic Studies* 20, 4 (2023), pp. 508–39

Berg, Maxine, 'Factories, Workshops and Industrial Organisation', in *The Economic History of Britain since 1700, vol. 1: 1700–1860*, ed. Roderick Floud and Donald McCloskey (Cambridge, 1994 [second edition]), pp. 123–50

——, 'From Imitation to Invention: Creating Commodities in Eighteenth-Century Britain', *Economic History Review* 55, 1 (2002), pp. 1–30

——, 'In Pursuit of Luxury: Global History and British Consumer Goods in the Eighteenth Century', *Past & Present* 182 (2004), pp. 85–142

——, *Luxury and Pleasure in Eighteenth-Century Britain* (Oxford, 2005)

——, 'Useful Knowledge, "Industrial Enlightenment", and the Place of India', *Journal of Global History* 8, 1 (2013), pp. 117–41

——, 'Commerce and Creativity in Eighteenth-Century Birmingham', in *Markets and Manufacture in Early Industrial Europe*, ed. Maxine Berg (London, 2014), pp. 173–204

——, '"The Merest Shadow of a Commodity": Indian Muslins for European Markets, 1750–1800', in *Goods from the East, 1600–1800: Trading Eurasia*, ed. Maxine Berg, Hanna Hodacs, Felicia Gottman and Chris Nierstrasz (London, 2015), pp. 119–37

Berg, Maxine and Clifford, Helen, 'Selling Consumption in the Eighteenth Century', *Cultural and Social History* 4, 2 (2007), pp. 145–70

Berg, Maxine and Hudson, Pat, 'Slavery, Atlantic Trade and Skills: A Response to Mokyr's "Holy Land of Industrialism"', in *Journal of the British Academy* 9 (2021), pp. 259–81

——, *Slavery, Capitalism and the Industrial Revolution* (Cambridge, 2023)

Berry, Christopher, *The Idea of Luxury: A Conceptual and Historical Investigation* (Cambridge, 1994)

——, *The Idea of Commercial Society in the Scottish Enlightenment* (Edinburgh, 2013)

Best, Lloyd and Levitt, Kari, eds, *Essays on the Theory of Plantation Economy: A Historical and Institutional Approach to Caribbean Economic Development* (Kingston, 2009)

Bining, Arthur, *British Regulation of the Colonial Iron Industry* (Philadelphia, PA, 1933)

Black, Jeremy, *Britain as a Military Power, 1688–1815* (London, 1999)
Blackburn, Robin, *The Overthrow of Colonial Slavery, 1776–1848* (London, 1988)
Blaszczyk, Regina Lee, *Imagining Consumers: Design and Innovation from Wedgwood to Corning* (Baltimore, MD, 2000)
Bogart, Dan, 'Did Turnpike Trusts Increase Transportation Investment in Eighteenth-Century England?', *Journal of Economic History* 65, 2 (2005), pp. 439–68
Bonner, James, 'Silk Growing in the Georgia Colony', *Agricultural History* 43, 1 (1969), pp. 143–8
Bosma, Ulbe, *The Sugar Plantation in India and Indonesia: Industrial Production, 1770–2010* (Cambridge, 2013)
Bottomley, Sean, *The British Patent System During the Industrial Revolution, 1700–1852: From Privilege to Property* (Cambridge, 2014)
Boucasse, Paul, Nakamura, Emi and Steinsson, Jón, 'When Did Growth Begin? New Estimates of Productivity Growth in England from 1250 to 1870', *Berkley Working Papers* (2021), pp. 1–49
Bowden, Peter, 'Wool Supply and the Woollen Industry', *Economic History Review* 9, 1 (1956), pp. 44–58
——, *The Wool Trade in Tudor and Stuart England* (London, 1962)
Bowen, Huw, *War and British Society, 1688–1815* (Cambridge, 1998)
——, *The Business of Empire: The East India Company and Imperial Britain, 1756–1833* (Cambridge, 2009)
——, ed., *Wales and the British Overseas Empire: Interactions and Influences, 1650–1830* (Manchester, 2011)
Bowen, Huw, Lincoln, Margarette and Rigby, Nigel, eds, *The Worlds of the East India Company* (Woodbridge, 2006)
Brewer, John, *The Sinews of Power: War, Money and the English State, 1688–1783* (London, 1989)
——, *The Pleasures of the Imagination: English Culture in the Eighteenth Century* (Abingdon, 2013 [1997])
Brewer, John and Porter, Roy eds, *Consumption and the World of Goods* (London, 1993)
Broadberry, Stephen and Gupta, Bishnupriya, 'Lancashire, India, and Shifting Competitive Advantage in Cotton Textiles, 1700–1850: The Neglected Role of Factor Prices', *Economic History Review* 62, 2 (2009), pp. 279–305
Broadberry, Stephen, Campbell, Bruce, Klein, Alexander, Overton, Mark and van Leeuwen, Bas, *British Economic Growth, 1270–1870* (Cambridge, 2015)
Broadie, Alexander, ed., *The Cambridge Companion to the Scottish Enlightenment* (Cambridge, 2006)
Brown, Christopher, *Moral Capital: Foundations of British Abolitionism* (Chapel Hill, NC, 2006)
Brown, Vincent, *The Reaper's Garden: Death and Power in the World of Atlantic Slavery* (Cambridge, MA, 2008)
——, *Tacky's Revolt: The Story of an Atlantic Slave War* (Cambridge, MA, 2020)
Bruijn, J. R., *The Dutch Navy of the Seventeenth and Eighteenth Centuries* (Oxford, 2011)
Buchanan, Brenda, 'Capital Investment in a Regional Economy: Some Aspects of the Sources and Employment of Capital in North Somerset, 1750–1830', PhD thesis, LSE (1992)

——, 'The Technology of Gunpowder Making in the Eighteenth Century: Evidence from the Bristol Region', *Transactions of the Newcomen Society* 67, 1 (1995), pp. 125–59

——, 'Bath's Forgotten Gunpowder History: The Powder Mills at Woolley in the Eighteenth Century', *Bath History Journal* 10 (2005), pp. 72–96

——, ed., *Gunpowder, Explosives and the State: A Technological History* (London, 2006)

Buckles, Peter, *Crisis and Resilience in the Bristol-West India Sugar Trade, 1783–1802* (Liverpool, 2024)

Burnard, Trevor, *Mastery, Tyranny & Desire: Thomas Thistlewood and his Slaves in the Anglo-Jamaican World* (Chapel Hill, NC, 2004)

——, *Planters, Merchants and Slaves: Plantation Societies in British America, 1650–1820* (Chicago, IL, 2015)

——, *Jamaica in the Age of Revolution* (Philadelphia, PA, 2020)

Burt, Roger, 'Lead Production in England and Wales, 1700–1770', *Economic History Review* 22, 2 (1969), pp. 249–68

Cain, P. and Hopkins, A., 'Gentlemanly Capitalism and British Expansion Overseas, 1: The Old Colonial System', *Economic History Review* 39, 4 (1986), pp. 501–25

——, *British Imperialism, 1688–2015, Third Edition* (London, 2016)

Calladine, Anthony and Fricker, Jean, *East Cheshire Textile Mills* (London, 1993)

Campbell, Kimberley, 'Paisley Before the Shawl: The Scottish Silk Gauze Industry', *Textile History* 33, 2 (2002), pp. 162–76

Carlos, Ann and Neal, Larry, 'Amsterdam and London as Financial Centres in the Eighteenth Century', *Financial History Review* 18 (2011), pp. 21–46

Carus-Wilson, Eleanora, 'The Woollen Industry', in *The Cambridge Economic History of Europe from the Decline of the Roman Empire, Volume 2: Trade and Industry in the Middle Ages*, ed. Edward Miller, Cynthia Postan and M. M. Postan (Cambridge, 2008 [1987]), pp. 614–74

Cassis, Youssef and Cottrell, Philip, *Private Banking in Europe: Rise, Retreat, and Resurgence* (Oxford, 2015)

Cavazza, Marta, 'The Institute of Science of Bologna and the Royal Society in the Eighteenth Century', *Notes and Records of the Royal Society of London* 56, 1 (2002), pp. 3–25

Cave, Alfred, *Lethal Encounters: Englishmen and Indians in Colonial Virginia* (Santa Barbara, CA, 2011)

Chambers, J. D., 'Enclosure and Labour Supply in the Industrial Revolution', *Economic History Review* 5, 3 (1953), pp. 319–43

Chapman, Stanley, *The Early Factory Masters: The Transition to the Factory System in the Midlands Textile Industry* (New York, 1967)

——, *The Rise of Merchant Banking* (Abingdon, 1984)

——, *The Cotton Industry in the Industrial Revolution* (London, 1987)

Chaudhary, Latika, Gupta, Bishnupriya, Roy, Tirthankar and Swamy, Anand V., 'Agriculture in Colonial India', in *A New Economic History of Colonial India*, ed. Latika Chaudhary, Bishnupriya Gupta, Tirthankar Roy and Anand V. Swamy (London, 2015), pp. 100–16

Chevis, Hugh William, 'Innovations in Cloth Manufacture in Early Modern England: The Demise of English Fine Wools and Rise of Spanish Merino Wool', PhD thesis, University of Western Australia (2017)

Chew, Emrys, *Arming the Periphery: The Arms Trade in the Indian Ocean during the Age of Global Empire* (London, 2012)

Clapham, S. D., 'The Transference of the Worsted Industry from Norfolk to the West Riding', *Economic Journal* 20, 78 (1910), pp. 195–210

Clark, Gregory and Clark, Anthony, 'Common Rights to Land in England, 1475–1839', *Journal of Economic History* 61, 4 (2001), pp. 1009–36

Clark, Gregory and Jacks, David, 'Coal and the Industrial Revolution, 1700–1869', *European Review of Economic History* 11, 1 (2007), pp. 39–72

Clark, Peter, *British Clubs and Societies, 1500–1800: The Origins of an Associated World* (Oxford, 2000)

Clemens, Paul, 'The Rise of Liverpool, 1665–1750', *Economic History Review* 29, 2 (1976), pp. 211–25

Combrink, Tamara and van Rossum, Matthias, 'Introduction: The Impact of Slavery on Europe – Reopening a Debate', *Slavery & Abolition* 42, 1 (2021), pp. 1–14

Cookson, Gillian, *The Age of Machinery: Engineering the Industrial Revolution, 1770–1850* (London, 2019)

——, 'Wortley Forge: The Evolution of an Eighteenth-Century Ironworks', *Northern History* 60, 1 (2023), pp. 52–73

——, *Making an Industrial Revolution: Skill, Knowledge, Community and Innovation* (London, 2025)

Cooper, Brian, *Transformation of a Valley: The Derbyshire Derwent* (Cromford, 1991)

Cooper, Randolph, *The Anglo-Maratha Campaigns and the Contest for India: The Struggle for Control of the South Asian Military Economy* (Cambridge, 2004)

Cornell, Harriet, Goodare, Julian and MacDonald, Alan, eds, *Agriculture, Economy and Society in Early Modern Scotland* (London, 2024)

Cowan, Brian, *The Social Life of Coffee: The Emergence of the British Coffeehouse* (New Haven, CT, 2005)

Crafts, N. F. R., *British Economic Growth during the Industrial Revolution* (Oxford, 1985)

Craton, Michael, *Testing the Chains: Resistance to Slavery in the British West Indies* (New York, 1982)

Crompton, G. W., 'Canals and the Industrial Revolution', *Journal of Transport History* 14, 2 (1993), pp. 93–110

Cronon, William, *Changes in the Land: Indians, Colonists, and the Ecology of New England* (New York, 1983)

Cullen, Karen, *Famine in Scotland: The 'Ill Years' of the 1690s* (Edinburgh, 2010)

Cunha, Daniel, 'The Frontier of Hell: Sicily, Sulfur, and the Rise of the British Chemical Industry, 1750–1840', *Critical Historical Studies* 6, 2 (2019), pp. 279–302

——, 'Coppering the Industrial Revolution: History, Materiality and Culture in the Making of an Ecological Regime', *Journal of World-Systems Research* 26, 1 (2020), pp. 40–69

Cunliffe, Sylvie, 'McConnel & Kennedy Co.: Slavery, Industrialisation and the Economy', unpublished BA thesis, University of Manchester (2021)

Dal Bó, Ernesto, Hutková, Karolina, Leucht, Lukas and Yuchtman, Noam, 'Dissecting the Sinews of Power: International Trade and the Rise of Britain's Fiscal-Military State, 1689–1823', *Journal of Economic History* (2025), pp. 1–34

Damodaran, Vinita, 'The East India Company, Famine and Ecological Conditions in Eighteenth-Century Bengal', in *The East India Company and the Natural*

*World*, ed. Vinita Damodaran, Anna Winterbottom and Alan Lester (London, 2015), pp. 80–101

Daniels, G. W., 'The Early Records of a Great Manchester Cotton-Spinning Firm', *Economic Journal* 25, 98 (1915), pp. 175–88

——, 'Valuation of Manchester Cotton Factories in the Early Years of the Nineteenth Century', *Economic Journal* 25, 100 (1915), pp. 625–6

Davis, Ralph, 'English Foreign Trade, 1700–1774', *Economic History Review* 15, 2 (1962), pp. 285–303

——, *The Rise of the English Shipping Industry in the Seventeenth and Eighteenth Centuries* (Liverpool, 1962)

——, *The Industrial Revolution and British Overseas Trade* (Leicester, 1979)

Deane, Phyllis and Cole, W. A., *British Economic Growth, 1688–1959: Trends and Structure* (Cambridge, 1967)

Demidowicz, George, 'The Origins of the Soho Manufactory and its Layout', in *Matthew Boulton: Enterprising Industrialist of the Enlightenment*, ed. Matthew Quickenden, Sally Baggott and Malcolm Dick (Abingdon, 2013), pp. 67–84

Derry, T. K. and Williams, Trevor, *A Short History of Technology: From the Earliest Times to A.D. 1900* (New York, 1960)

De Vries, Jan, *The First Modern Economy: Success, Failure, and Perseverance of the Dutch Economy, 1500–1815* (Cambridge, 1997)

——, *The Industrious Revolution: Consumer Behaviour and the Household Economy, 1650 to the Present* (Cambridge, 2008)

——, 'The Economic Crisis of the Seventeenth Century after Fifty Years', *Journal of Interdisciplinary History* 40, 2 (2009), pp. 151–94

——, 'Understanding Eurasian Trade in the Era of the Trading Companies', in *Goods from the East, 1600–1800: Trading Eurasia*, ed. Maxine Berg, Hanna Hodacs, Felicia Gottman and Chris Nierstrasz (London, 2015), pp. 7–43

Dickson, P. G. M., *The Financial Revolution in England: A Study in the Development of Public Credit, 1688–1756* (London, 1967)

Dillon, Patrick, *The Last Revolution: 1688 and the Creation of the Modern World* (London, 2007)

Dirks, Nicholas, *The Scandal of Empire: India and the Creation of Imperial Britain* (Cambridge, MA, 2008)

Draper, Nicholas, 'The City of London and Slavery: Evidence from the First Dock Companies, 1795–1800', *Economic History Review* 61, 2 (2008), pp. 432–66

——, 'Helping to Make Britain Great: The Commercial Legacies of Slave-ownership in Britain', in *Legacies of British Slave-Ownership: Colonial Slavery and the Formation of Victorian Britain*, ed. Catherine Hall, Nicholas Draper, Keith McClelland, Katie Donnington and Rachel Lang (Cambridge, 2014), pp. 78–126

Drayton, Richard, *Nature's Government: Science, Imperial Britain and the 'Improvement' of the World* (New Haven, CT, 2000)

Dresser, Madge, *Slavery Obscured: The Social History of the Slave Trade in an English Provincial Port* (London, 2001)

Dunbar-Ortiz, Roxanne, *An Indigenous Peoples' History of the United States* (Boston, MA, 2014)

Dunn, Richard, *Sugar and Slaves: The Rise of the Planter Class in the English West Indies, 1624–1713* (Chapel Hill, NC, 2000)

——, *A Tale of Two Plantations: Slave Life and Labor in Jamaica and Virginia* (Cambridge, MA, 2014)

Eacott, Jonathan, *Selling Empire: India in the Making of Britain and America, 1600–1830* (Chapel Hill, NC, 2016)
Edwards, Michael, *The Growth of the British Cotton Trade, 1780–1815* (Manchester, 1967)
Ellis, Joyce, *A Study of the Business Fortunes of William Cotesworth, c. 1668–1726* (New York, 1981)Eltis, David, *The Rise of African Slavery in the Americas* (Cambridge, 1999)
——, *Atlantic Cataclysm: Rethinking the Atlantic Slave Trades* (Cambridge, 2025)
Eltis, David and Engerman, Stanley, 'The Importance of Slavery and the Slave Trade to Industrializing Britain', *Journal of Economic History* 60, 1 (2000), pp. 123–44
Eltis, David, Lewis, Frank and Richardson, David, 'Slave Prices, the African Slave Trade, and Productivity in the Caribbean, 1674–1807', *Economic History Review* 58, 4 (2005), pp. 673–700
Emerson, Roger, *An Enlightened Duke: The Life of Archibald Campbell (1692–1761), Earl of Ilay, 3rd Duke of Argyll* (Kilkerran, 2013)
Engerman, Stanley, 'The Slave Trade and British Capital Formation in the Eighteenth Century: A Comment on the Williams Thesis', *Business History Review* 46, 4 (1972), pp. 430–43
Erickson, Amy, *Women and Property in Early Modern England* (London, 1993)
——, 'Wealthy Businesswomen, Marriage and Succession in Eighteenth-Century London', *Business History* 66, 2 (2024), pp. 29–58
Evans, Chris, 'A Skilled Workforce during the Transition to Industrial Society: Forgemen in the British Iron Trade, 1500–1850', *Labour History Review* 63, 2 (1998), pp. 143–59
——, *Slave Wales: The Welsh and Atlantic Slavery, 1660–1850* (Cardiff, 2010)
——, 'The Plantation Hoe: The Rise and Fall of an Atlantic Commodity, 1650–1850', *William and Mary Quarterly* 69, 1 (2012), pp. 581–610
Evans, Chris and Miskell, Louise, *Swansea Copper: A Global History* (Baltimore, MD, 2020)
Evans, Chris and Withey, Alun, 'An Enlightenment in Steel?: Innovation in the Steel Trades of Eighteenth-Century Britain', *Technology and Culture* 53, 3 (2012), pp. 533–60
Feingold, Mordecai, 'Projectors and Learned Projects in Early Modern England', *The Seventeenth Century* 31, 1 (2017), pp. 63–79
Fernihough, Alan and O'Rourke, Kevin, 'Coal and the European Industrial Revolution', *Economic Journal* 131, 635 (2021), pp. 1135–49
Findlay, Ronald and O'Rourke, Kevin, *Power and Plenty: Trade, War, and the World Economy in the Second Millenium* (Princeton, NJ, 2009)
Findlen, Paula, ed., *Empires of Knowledge: Scientific Networks in the Early Modern World* (London, 2018)
Fisher, James, *The Enclosure of Knowledge: Books, Power and Agrarian Capitalism in Britain, 1600–1800* (Cambridge, 2022)
Fitton, R. S. and Wadsworth, A. P., *The Strutts and the Arkwrights, 1758–1830: A Study of the Early Factory System* (Manchester, 1958)
Flinn, Michael, 'William Wood and the Coke-Smelting Process', *Transactions of the Newcomen Society* 34 (1961), pp. 55–71
——, *Men of Iron: The Crowleys in the Early Iron Industry* (Edinburgh, 1962)
——, *The History of the British Coal Industry, Vol. 2, 1700–1830: The Industrial Revolution* (Oxford, 1984)

Fogleman, Aaron, 'Migrations to the Thirteen British North American Colonies, 1700–1775: New Estimates', *Journal of Interdisciplinary History* 22, 4 (1992), pp. 691–709

Fontes Da Costa, P., 'The Culture of Curiosity at The Royal Society in the First Half of the Eighteenth Century', *Notes and Records: The Royal Society Journal of the History of Science* 56, 2 (2002), pp. 147–66

Fox-Genovese, E. and Genovese, E. D., *The Fruits of Merchant Capital: Slavery and Bourgeois Property in the Rise and Expansion of Capitalism* (New York, 1983)

Frank, André Gunder, *ReOrient: Global Economy in the Asian Age* (Berkeley, CA, 1998)

Freudenberger, Herman, Mather, Francis and Nardinelli, Clark, 'A New Look at the Early Factory Labor Force', *Journal of Economic History* 44, 4 (1984), pp. 1085–90

Frey, James, 'The Indian Saltpetre Trade, the Military Revolution, and the Rise of Britain as a Global Superpower', *The Historian* 71, 3 (2009), pp. 507–54

Froide, Amy, *Silent Partners: Women as Public Investors during Britain's Financial Revolution, 1690–1750* (Oxford, 2017)

Fumaroli, Marc, *The Republic of Letters*, trans. Lara Vergnaud (New Haven, CT, 2018)

Games, Alison, *Web of Empire: English Cosmopolitans in an Age of Expansion, 1560–1660* (Oxford, 2008)

Gaspar, David Barry, *Bondmen and Rebels: A Study of Master-Slave Relations in Antigua* (Durham, NC, 1985)

Gauci, Perry, *The Politics of Trade: The Overseas Merchant in State and Society, 1660–1720* (Oxford, 2001)

——, *Emporium of the World: The Merchants of London, 1660–1800* (London, 2006)

Gibson, Alex, 'Proletarianization? The Transition to Full-time Labour on a Scottish Estate, 1723–1787', *Continuity and Change* 5, 3 (1990), pp. 357–89

Glasier, Natasha, 'Networking: Trade and Exchange in the Eighteenth-Century British Empire', *Historical Journal* 47, 2 (2004), pp. 451–76

Glennie, Paul, 'Continuity and Change in Hertfordshire Agriculture, 1550–1700: I, Patterns of Agricultural Production', *Agricultural History Review* XXXVI (1988), pp. 55–75

Goldstone, Jack, *Why Europe? The Rise of the West in World History, 1500–1800* (Boston, MA, 2008)

Goodman, John, 'The Birmingham Gun Trade', in *Birmingham and Midland Hardware District*, ed. S. Timmins (London, 1866), pp. 381–431

Govier, Mark, 'The Royal Society, Slavery and the Island of Jamaica: 1660–1700', *Notes and Records of the Royal Society of London* 53, 2 (1999), pp. 203–17

Gragg, Larry, *'Englishmen Transplanted': The English Colonization of Barbados, 1627–1660* (Oxford, 2003)

Graham, Eric, *A Maritime History of Scotland, 1650–1790* (East Linton, 2002)

Grainger, John, *The British Navy in the Baltic* (Woodbridge, 2014)

Grassby, Richard, *The Business Community of Seventeenth-Century England* (Cambridge, 1995)

Greene, Jack, 'Colonial South Carolina', in *Money, Trade, and Power: The Evolution of Colonial South Carolina's Plantation Society*, ed. Jack Greene (Columbia, SC, 2001)

Grenier, John, *The First Way of War: American War Making on the Frontier, 1607–1814* (Cambridge, 2005)

Griffin, Emma, *Liberty's Dawn: A People's History of the Industrial Revolution* (New Haven, CT, 2013)

Gupta, Brijen Kishore, *Sirajuddaullah and the East India Company, 1756–1757: Background to the Foundation of British Power in India* (Leiden, 1966)

Habakkuk, John, 'Presidential Address: The Rise and Fall of English Landed Families, 1600–1800: III. Did the Gentry Rise?', *Transactions of the Royal Historical Society* 31 (1981), pp. 195–217

Hacker, J. David, 'From "20 and odd" to 10 Million: The Growth of the Slave Population in the United States', *Slavery & Abolition* 41, 3 (2020), pp. 840–55

Haggerty, John and Haggerty, Sheryllynne, 'Networking with a Network: The Liverpool African Committee 1750–1810', *Enterprise & Society* 18, 3 (2017), pp. 566–90

Haggerty, Sheryllynne, 'A Link in the Chain: Trade and the Transhipment of Knowledge in the Late Eighteenth Century', *International Journal of Maritime History* 14, 1 (2002), pp. 157–72

——, 'The Structure of the Trading Community in Liverpool, 1760–1810', *Transactions of the Historic Society of Lancashire and Cheshire* (2002), pp. 97–125

——, *Merely for Money?: Business Culture in the British Atlantic, 1750–1815* (Liverpool, 2012)

——, 'Liverpool, the Slave Trade and the British-Atlantic Empire, c. 1750–75', in *The Empire in One City? Liverpool's Inconvenient Imperial Past*, ed. Sheryllynne Haggerty, Anthony Webster and Nicholas White (Manchester, 2017), pp. 17–34

Hahn, Barbara, *Technology and the Industrial Revolution* (Cambridge, 2020)

Hämäläinen, Pekka, *Indigenous Continent: The Epic Contest for North America* (New York, 2022)

Hamilton, Douglas, 'Scottish Trading in the Caribbean: The Rise and Fall of Houstoun & Co.', in *Nation and Province in the First British Empire: Scotland and the Americas, 1600–1800*, ed. Ned Landsman (Lewisburg, PA, 2001), pp. 94–126

Hancock, David, *Citizens of the World: London Merchants and the Integration of the British Atlantic Community, 1735–1785* (Cambridge, 1995)

——, 'Scots in the Slave Trade', in *Nation and Province in the First British Empire: Scotland and the Americas, 1600–1800*, ed. Ned Landsman (Lewisburg, PA, 2001), pp. 60–93

Hanna, Nelly, *Ottoman Egypt and the Emergence of the Modern World, 1500–1800* (Cairo, 2014)

Hansen, Bent, 'Colonial Economic Development with Unlimited Supply of Land: A Ricardian Case', *Economic Development and Cultural Change* 27, 4 (1979), pp. 611–27

Harding, Richard, *The Emergence of Britain's Global Naval Supremacy: The War of 1739–1748* (London, 2010)

Harley, Knick, 'Slavery, the British Atlantic Economy, and the Industrial Revolution', in *The Caribbean and the Atlantic World Economy: Circuits of Trade, Money, and Knowledge, 1650–1914*, ed. A. B. Leonard and David Pretel (New York, 2015), pp. 161–83

Harrington, Peter, *Plassey, 1757: Clive of India's Finest Hour* (Oxford, 1994)

Harris, J. R., *The Copper King: A Biography of Thomas Williams of Llanidan* (Liverpool, 1964)

——, 'Copper and Shipping in the Eighteenth Century', *Economic History Review* 19, 3 (1966), pp. 550–68

Harris, John, *Industrial Espionage and Technology Transfer: Britain and France in the Eighteenth Century* (London, 2017 [1998])

Harris, Ron, *Going the Distance: Eurasian Trade and the Rise of the Business Corporation, 1400–1700* (Princeton, NJ, 2020)

Harvey, Mark, 'Slavery, Indenture and the Development of British Industrial Capitalism', *History Workshop Journal* 88, 1 (2019), pp. 66–88

Hatcher, John, *The History of the British Coal Industry, Vol. 1: Before 1700: Towards the Age of Coal* (Oxford, 1993)

Hayman, Richard, 'The Shropshire Wrought-Iron Industry, c. 1600–1900: A Study of Technological Change', PhD thesis, University of Birmingham (2004)

Hayward, J. F., 'The Huguenot Gunmakers of London', *Huguenot Society Journal* 20, 6 (1964), pp. 649–63

Hertz, Gerald, 'The English Silk Industry in the Eighteenth Century', *English Historical Review* 24, 96 (1909), pp. 710–27

Hey, David, *Packmen, Carriers and Packhorse Roads: Trade and Communications in North Derbyshire and South Yorkshire* (Leicester, 1980)

——, 'The Development of the English Toolmaking Industry during the Seventeenth and Eighteenth Centuries', in *Eighteenth-century Woodworking Tools: Papers Presented at a Tool Symposium*, ed. James Gaynor (Williamsburg, VA, 1997)

Higman, B., *Slave Populations of the British Caribbean, 1807–1834* (Baltimore, MD, 1984)

Hill, Malcolm, 'Polzunov's Engine: An Example of Innovation in Eighteenth Century Russia', *ICON* 8 (2002), pp. 107–39

——, 'Russian Iron Production in the Eighteenth Century', *ICON* 12 (2006), pp. 118–67

Hillman, Henning and Gathmann, Christina, 'Overseas Trade and the Decline of Privateering', *Journal of Economic History* 71, 3 (2011), pp. 730–61

Hindle, Steve, *The Social Topography of a Rural Community: Scenes of Labouring Life in Seventeenth Century England* (Oxford, 2023)

Hiono, Yuici, 'Sustaining British Naval Power through New England Masts during the Seven Years War', *Mariner's Mirror* 106, 1 (2020), pp. 18–29

Hobson, John, *Multicultural Origins of the Global Economy: Beyond the Western-Centric Frontier* (Cambridge, 2020)

Holt, Robin and Popp, Andrew, 'Josiah Wedgwood, Manufacturing and Craft', *Journal of Design History* 29, 2 (2016), pp. 99–119

Honeyman, Katrina, *Women, Gender and Industrialisation in England, 1700–1870* (New York, 2000)

——, *Child Workers in England, 1780–1820: Parish Apprentices and the Making of the Early Industrial Labour Force* (Abingdon, 2007)

Hopkins, Eric, *Birmingham: The First Manufacturing Town in the World, 1760–1840* (London, 1989)

Hoppit, Julian, 'The Nation, the State, and the First Industrial Revolution', *Journal of British Studies* 50, 2 (2011), pp. 307–31

——, *Britain's Political Economies: Parliament and Economic Life, 1660–1800* (Cambridge, 2017)

Horning, Audrey, *Ireland in the Virginia Sea: Colonialism in the British Atlantic* (Chapel Hill, NC, 2013)

Horrell, Sara and Humphries, Jane, 'Women's Labour Force Participation and the Transition to the Male-Breadwinner Family, 1790–1865', *Economic History Review* 48 (1995), pp. 89–117

Horsfield, J. K., 'The "Stop of the Exchequer" Revisited', *Economic History Review* 35, 4 (1982), pp. 511–28

Howes, Anton, *Arts and Minds: How the Royal Society of Arts Changed a Nation* (Princeton, NJ, 2020)

Hoyle, Richard, 'Why Was There No Crisis in England in the 1690s?', in *The Farmer in England, 1650–1980*, ed. Richard Hoyle (Farnham, 2013), pp. 67–98

Hsia, Florence, *Sojourners in a Strange Land: Jesuits and their Scientific Missions in Late Imperial China* (Chicago, IL, 2009)

Hubbard, Vincent, *A History of St Kitts: The Sweet Trade* (Oxford, 2002)

Hudson, Pat, *The Genesis of Industrial Capital: A Study of West Riding Wool Textile Industry, c.1750–1850* (Cambridge, 1986)

——, 'Landholding and the Organization of Textile Manufacturing in Yorkshire Rural Townships, c. 1660–1810', in *Markets and Manufacture in Early Industrial Europe*, ed. Maxine Berg (London, 2014), pp. 261–91

Huff, Toby, *The Rise of Early Modern Science: Islam, China and the West* (Cambridge, 2017)

Hughes, Stephen, *Copperopolis: Landscapes of the Early Industrial Period in Swansea* (Aberystwyth, 2000)

Hunter, Michael, *Establishing the New Science: The Experience of the Early Royal Society* (Woodbridge, 1989)

——, *Science and the Shape of Orthodoxy: Intellectual Change in Late Seventeenth-Century Britain* (Woodbridge, 1995)

Hutchinson, Terence, *Before Adam Smith: The Emergence of Political Economy 1662–1776* (Oxford, 1988)

Hutková, Karolina, *The English East India Company's Silk Enterprise in Bengal, 1750–1850: Economy, Empire and Business* (Woodbridge, 2019)

——, 'West Indies Technologies in the East Indies: Imperial Preference and Sugar Business in Bihar, 1800–1850s', *Business History* 65, 6 (2023), pp. 1072–98

Hyde, Charles, *Technological Change and the British Iron Industry, 1700–1870* (Princeton, NJ, 1977)

Hyde, Francis, *Liverpool and the Mersey: An Economic History of a Port, 1700–1970* (Newton Abbot, 1971)

Ince, Lawrence, *The South Wales Iron Industry 1750–1885* (Chesterfield, 1993)

Inikori, Joseph, *Africans and the Industrial Revolution in England: A Study in International Trade and Economic Development* (Cambridge, 2002)

Jacob, Margaret, *Scientific Culture and the Making of the Industrial West* (Oxford, 1997)

——, *The Secular Enlightenment* (Princeton, NJ, 2019)

Jacob, Margaret and Stewart, Larry, *Practical Matter: Newton's Science in the Service of Industry and Empire, 1687–1851* (Cambridge, MA, 2006)

Johnson, B. L. C., 'The Charcoal Iron Industry in the Early Eighteenth Century', *Geographical Journal* 117, 2 (1951), pp. 167–77

——, 'The Midland Iron Industry in the Early Eighteenth Century: The Background and the First Successful Use of Coke in Iron Smelting', *Business History* 2, 2 (1960), pp. 67–74

Jones, Donald, *Bristol's Sugar Trade and Refining Industry* (Bristol, 1996)

Jones, E. L., 'Agriculture and Economic Growth in England, 1660–1750', *Journal of Economic History* 25, 1 (1965), pp. 1–18

Jones, Peter, *Industrial Enlightenment: Science, Technology and Culture in Birmingham and the West Midlands, 1760–1820* (Manchester, 2008)

Jones, S. R. H., 'Technology, Transaction Costs, and the Transition to Factory Production in the British Silk Industry, 1700–1870', *Journal of Economic History* 47, 1 (1987), pp. 71–96

Jonsson, Fredrik Albritton and Wennerlind, Carl, *Scarcity: A History from the Origins of Capitalism to the Climate Crisis* (Cambridge, MA, 2023)

Jorati, Julia, *Slavery and Race: Philosophical Debates in the Eighteenth Century* (New York, 2024)

Justman, Moshe and van der Beek, Karine, 'Market Forces Shaping Human Capital in Eighteenth-Century London', *Economic History Review* 68, 4 (2015), pp. 1177–1202

Kadane, Matthew, *The Watchful Clothier: The Life of an Eighteenth-Century Protestant Capitalist* (New Haven, CT, 2013)

Kasumitsu, Toshio, '"Novelty, Give us Novelty"; London Agents and Northern Manufacturers', in *Markets and Manufacture in Early Industrial Europe*, ed. Maxine Berg (London, 2014), pp. 114–38

Keeble, N. H., *The Restoration: England in the 1660s* (Oxford, 2002)

Kerridge, Eric, *Textile Manufacturers in Early Modern England* (Manchester, 1985)

——, *Trade and Banking in Early Modern England* (Manchester, 1988)

Kim, Jongchul, 'How Modern Banking Originated: The London Goldsmith-Bankers' Institutionalisation of Trust', *Business History* 53, 6 (2011), pp. 939–59

King, Peter, 'The Production and Consumption of Iron in Early Modern England and Wales', *Economic History Review* 58, 1 (2005), pp. 1–33

——, 'Innovation in the British Iron Industry in the 17th and 18th Centuries', *International Journal for the History of Engineering & Technology* 94, 1 (2024), pp. 12–41

Kirby, Peter, *Child Workers and Industrial Health in Britain, 1780–1850* (Woodbridge, 2013)

Knight, Roger, 'Devil Bolts and Deception? Wartime Naval Shipbuilding in Private Shipyards, 1739–1815', *Journal for Maritime Research* 5, 1 (2003), pp. 34–51

Knight, Roger and Wilcox, Martin, *Sustaining the Fleet, 1793–1815: War, the British Navy and the Contractor State* (Woodbridge, 2010)

Kosmetatos, Paul, *The 1772–73 British Credit Crisis* (London, 2018)

Kritchal, Alexey, 'Liverpool and the Raw Cotton Trade: A Study of the Port and its Merchant Community, 1770–1815', MA thesis, Victoria University of Wellington (2013)

Kynaston, David, *Till Time's Last Stand: A History of the Bank of England, 1694–2013* (London, 2017)

Landes, David, *The Unbound Prometheus: Technological Change and Industrial Development in Western Europe from 1750 to the Present* (Cambridge, 1969)

Lane, Joe, 'Secrets for Sale? Innovation and the Nature of Knowledge in an Early Industrial District: The Potteries, 1750–1851', *Enterprise & Society* 20, 4 (2019), pp. 861–906

Langford, Paul, *A Polite and Commercial People: England, 1727–1783* (Oxford, 1989)

Lee, C. H., *Cotton Enterprise, 1795–1840: History of M'Connel and Kennedy, Fine Cotton Spinners* (Manchester, 1972)

Lemire, Beverley, *Fashion's Favourite: The Cotton Trade and the Consumer in Britain, 1660–1800* (Oxford, 1991)

——, *Global Trade and the Transformation of Consumer Cultures: The Material World Remade, c. 1500–1820* (Cambridge, 2017)

Leonard, Adrian, *London Marine Insurance, 1438–1824: Risk, Trade, and the Early Modern State* (London, 2022)

Livingstone, Alistair, 'The Glenkens, Cattle, Cotton and Capitalism', *Transactions of the Dumfriesshire and Galloway Natural History and Antiquarian Society* 90 (2017), pp. 67–78

Longmore, Jane, '"Cemented by the Blood of a Negro?": The Impact of the Slave Trade on Eighteenth Century Liverpool', in *Liverpool and Transatlantic Slavery*, ed. David Richardson, Suzanne Schwarz and Anthony Tibbles (Liverpool, 2007), pp. 227–51

Lux, David and Cook, Harold, 'Closed Circles or Open Networks: Communicating at a Distance during the Scientific Revolution', *History of Science* 39 (1998), pp. 179–211

McCloskey, Deirdre, *Bourgeois Dignity: Why Economics Can't Explain the Modern World* (Chicago, IL, 2010)

McDade, Katie, 'Liverpool Slave Merchant Entrepreneurial Networks, 1725–1807', *Business History* 53, 7 (2011), pp. 1092–1109

McDiarmid, Andrew, *Credit, Currency and Capital: The Scottish Financial Revolution, 1690–1727* (New York, 2023)

McKendrick, Neil, 'The Consumer Revolution of Eighteenth-Century England' and 'Josiah Wedgwood and the Commercialisation of the Potteries', in *The Birth of a Consumer Society: The Commercialisation of Eighteenth-Century England*, ed. Neil McKendrick, John Brewer and J. H. Plumb (Bloomington, IN, 1985), pp. 9–33 and 99–143

Mackillop, Andrew, 'A North European World of Tea: Scotland and the Tea Trade, c. 1690–c. 1790', in *Goods from the East, 1600–1800: Trading Eurasia*, ed. Maxine Berg, Hanna Hodacs, Felicia Gottman and Chris Nierstrasz (London, 2015), pp. 294–308

McKinstry, Mary, 'Silk Culture in the Colony of Georgia', *Georgia Historical Quarterly* 14, 3 (1930), pp. 225–35

MacLeod, Christine, *Inventing the Industrial Revolution: The English Patent System, 1660–1800* (Cambridge, 1988)

Madley, Benjamin, '"Too Furious": The Genocide of Connecticut's Pequot Indians, 1636–1640', in *The Cambridge World History of Genocide, Vol. 2: Genocide in the Indigenous, Early Modern and Imperial Worlds, from c.1535 to World War One*, ed. Ned Blackhawk, Ben Kiernan, Benjamin Madley and Rebe Taylor (Cambridge, 2023), pp. 215–42

Mancke, Elizabeth, *The Fault Lines of Empire: Political Differentiation in Massachusetts and Nova Scotia, 1760–1830* (New York, 2005)

Mann, James, *The Cotton Trade of Great Britain: Its Rise, Progress, and Present Extent* (London and Manchester, 1860)

Marsh, Ben, *Unravelled Dreams: Silk and the Atlantic World, 1500–1840* (Oxford, 2020)

Marshall, Peter, *Bengal – The British Bridgehead: Eastern India, 1740–1828* (Cambridge, 1987)

——, 'A Polite and Commercial People in the Caribbean: The British in St Vincent', in *Revisiting the Polite and Commercial People: Essays in Georgian Politics, Society, and Culture in Honour of Professor Paul Langford*, ed. Elaine Chalus and Perry Gauci (Oxford, 2019), pp. 173–90

Maw, Peter, *Transport and the Industrial City: Manchester and the Canal Age, 1750–1850* (Manchester, 2013)

Meier, Gerald, 'The Older Generation of Development Economists and the New', in *Frontiers of Development Economics: The Future in Perspective*, ed. Gerald Meier and Joseph Stiglitz (New York, 2001)

Meisenzahl, Ralf and Mokyr, Joel, 'The Rate and Direction of Invention in the British Industrial Revolution: Incentives and Institutions', in *The Rate and Direction of Inventive Activity Revisited*, ed. Josh Lerner and Scott Stern (Chicago, IL, 2012), pp. 443–82

Melton, Frank, *Sir Robert Clayton and the Origins of English Deposit Banking, 1658–1685* (Cambridge, 1986)

Menard, Russell, *Sweet Negotiations: Sugar, Slavery, and Plantation Agriculture in Early Barbados* (Charlottesville, VA, 2006)

Merchant, Carolyn, *The Death of Nature: Women, Ecology and the Scientific Revolution* (New York, 1989)

Milevsky, Moshe, *The Day the King Defaulted: Financial Lessons from the Stop of the Exchequer in 1672* (London, 2017)

Miller, David, 'The Usefulness of Natural Philosophy: The Royal Society and the Culture of Practical Utility in the Later Eighteenth Century', *British Journal for the History of Science* 32, 2 (1999), pp. 185–201

Minoletti, Paul, 'The Transition to Factory Production in the English Wool Textile Industries: Individual and Family Desires for Labour Regulation, 1720–1850', in *Regulating the British Economy, 1660–1850*, ed. Perry Gauci (Aldershot, 2011)

Mokyr, Joel, *The Lever of Riches: Technological Creativity and Economic Progress* (Oxford, 1990)

——, 'The Intellectual Origins of Modern Economic Growth', *Journal of Economic History* 65, 2 (2005), pp. 285–351

——, *The Gifts of Athena: Historical Origins of the Knowledge Economy* (Princeton, NJ, 2006)

——, *The Enlightened Economy: An Economic History of Britain, 1700–1850* (New Haven, CT, 2009)

——, 'Intellectual Property Rights, the Industrial Revolution, and the Beginnings of Modern Economic Growth', *American Economic Review* 99, 2 (2009), pp. 349–55

——, 'Cultural Entrepreneurs and the Origins of Modern Economic Growth', *Scandinavian Economic History Review* 61, 1 (2013), pp. 1–33

——, *The Culture of Growth: The Origins of the Modern Economy* (Princeton, NJ, 2017)

Money, John, *Experience and Identity: Birmingham and the West Midlands, 1760–1800* (Montreal, 1977)

——, 'Teaching in the Market-Place, or "Caesar Adsum Jam Forte: Pompey Aderat": The Retailing of Knowledge in Provincial England during the Eighteenth Century', in *Consumption and the World of Goods*, ed. John Brewer and Roy Porter (London, 1993), pp. 335–79

Monteith, Joy, *Old Port Glasgow* (Glasgow, 2003)

Morgan, Kenneth, 'Bristol West India Merchants in the Eighteenth Century', *Transactions of the Royal Historical Society* 3 (1993), pp. 185–208

——, *Slavery, Atlantic Trade and the British Economy, 1660–1800* (Cambridge, 2012)

Morriss, Richard, *Canals of Shropshire* (Shrewsbury, 1991)

Muldrew, Craig, *The Economy of Obligation: The Culture of Credit and Social Relations in Early Modern England* (Basingstoke, 1998)

——, *Food, Energy and the Creation of Industriousness* (New York, 2011)

Mullen, Stephen, *The Glasgow Sugar Aristocracy: Scotland and Caribbean Slavery, 1775–1838* (London, 2022)

——, 'Proslavery Collaborations Between British Outport and Metropole: The Rise of the Glasgow–West India Interest, 1775–1838', *Journal of Imperial and Commonwealth History* 51, 3 (2023), pp. 601–43

Mulry, Kate, *An Empire Transformed: Remolding Bodies and Landscapes in the Restoration Atlantic* (New York, 2021)

Murphy, Anne, *The Origins of English Financial Markets: Investment and Speculation before the South Sea Bubble* (Cambridge, 2009)

——, 'Trading Options before Black-Scholes: A Study of the Market in late Seventeenth-Century London', *Economic History Review* 62, 1 (2009), pp. 8–30

Murphy, Tessa, 'Kalinago Colonizers: Indigenous People and the Settlement of the Lesser Antilles', in *The Torrid Zone: Caribbean Colonization and Cultural Interaction in the Long Seventeenth Century*, ed. L. H. Roper (Columbia, SC, 2018), pp. 17–30

Neal, Larry, 'How It All Began: The Monetary and Financial Architecture of Europe during the First Global Capital Markets, 1648–1815', *Financial History Review* 7 (2000), pp. 117–40

Nef, John, 'Mining and Metallurgy in Medieval Civilisation', in *The Cambridge Economic History of Europe from the Decline of the Roman Empire, Volume 2: Trade and Industry in the Middle Ages*, ed. Edward Miller, Cynthia Postan and M. M. Postan (Cambridge, 2008 [1987]), pp. 691–761

North, Douglas, *Structure and Change in Economic History* (London, 1983)

——, *Institutions, Institutional Change and Economic Performance* (Cambridge, 2012)

North, Douglas and Weingast, Barry, 'Constitutions and Commitment: The Evolution of Institutions Governing Public Choice in Seventeenth-Century England', *Journal of Economic History* 49, 4 (1989), pp. 803–32

O'Brien, Patrick, 'Mercantilist Institutions for the Pursuit of Power with Profit: The Management of Britain's National Debt', in *Government Debts and Financial Markets in Europe*, ed. Fausto Piola Caselli (Abingdon, 2008)

O'Brien, Patrick, Griffiths, Trevor and Hunt, Philip, 'Technological Change During the First Industrial Revolution: The Paradigm Case of Textiles, 1688–1851' in *Technological Change: Methods and Themes in the History of Technology*, ed. Robert Fox (London, 1996), pp. 155–76

O'Brien, Patrick and Heath, D., 'English and French Landowners, 1688–1789', in *Landowners, Capitalists, and Entrepreneurs: Essays for Sir John Habakkuk*, ed. F. Thompson (Oxford, 1994), pp. 23–62

Oldfield, J. R., *Popular Politics and British Antislavery: The Mobilisation of Public Opinion against the Slave Trade, 1787–1807* (Manchester, 1995)

Oldroyd, David, *Estates, Enterprise and Investment at the Dawn of the Industrial Revolution: Estate Management and Accounting in the North-East of England, c.1700–1780* (London, 2007)

Otremba, Eric, 'Enlightened Institutions: Science, Plantations and Slavery', PhD thesis, University of Minnesota (2012)

——, 'Inventing Ingenios: Experimental Philosophy and the Secret Sugar-Makers of the Seventeenth-Century Atlantic', *History and Technology* 28, 2 (2012), pp. 119–47

Overton, Mark, *Agricultural Revolution in England: The Transformation of the Agrarian Economy, 1500–1850* (Cambridge, 1996)
Owens, Robert, *'Indian Wars' and the Struggle for Eastern North America, 1763–1842* (London, 2020)
Palma, Nuno and Reis, Jaime, 'From Convergence to Divergence: Portuguese Economic Growth, 1527–1850', *Journal of Economic History* 79, 2 (2019), pp. 477–506
Parthasarathi, Prasannan, *Why Europe Grew Rich and Asia Did Not: Global Economic Divergence, 1600–1850* (Cambridge, 2011)
Paulinyi, Akos, 'John Kay's Flying Shuttle: Some Considerations on his Technical Capacity and Economic Impact', *Textile History* 17, 2 (1986), pp. 149–66
Pearson, Robin and Richardson, David, 'Business Networking in the Industrial Revolution', *Economic History Review* 54, 4 (2001), pp. 657–79
Pestana, Carla Gardina, *The English Conquest of Jamaica: Oliver Cromwell's Bid for Empire* (Cambridge, MA, 2017)
Pettigrew, William, 'Free to Enslave: Politics and the Escalation of Britain's Transatlantic Slave Trade, 1688–1714', *William and Mary Quarterly* 64, 1 (2007), pp. 3–38
——, *Freedom's Debt: The Royal African Company and the Politics of the Atlantic Slave Trade, 1672–1752* (Chapel Hill, NC, 2013)
——, *Global Trade and the Shaping of English Freedom* (Oxford, 2023)
Phillips, N., *Women in Business, 1700–1850* (London, 2006)
Pinarbasi, Sami, 'Manchester Antislavery, 1792–1807', *Slavery & Abolition* 41, 2 (2020), pp. 349–76
Pincus, Steven, 'Rethinking Mercantilism: Political Economy, the British Empire, and the Atlantic World in the Seventeenth and Eighteenth Centuries', *William and Mary Quarterly* 69, 1 (2012), pp. 3–34
Pizzoni, Giada, *British Catholic Merchants in the Commercial Age, 1670–1714* (Woodbridge, 2020)
Pluymers, Keith, *No Wood, No Kingdom: Political Ecology in the English Atlantic* (Philadelphia, PA, 2021)
Pomeranz, Kenneth, *The Great Divergence: China, Europe, and the Making of the Modern World Economy* (Princeton, NJ, 2000)
Pool, Bernard, *Navy Board Contracts, 1660–1832: Contract Administration under the Navy Board* (Hamden, CT, 1966)
Pope, David 'The Wealth and Social Aspirations of Liverpool's Slave Merchants of the Second Half of the Eighteenth Century', in *Liverpool and Transatlantic Slavery*, ed. David Richardson, Suzanne Schwarz and Anthony Tibbles (Liverpool, 2007), pp. 164–226
Porter, Jonathan, 'The Scientific Community in Early Modern China', *Isis* 73, 4 (1982), pp. 529–44
Pounds, N. J. G., 'Population Movement in Cornwall, and the Rise of Mining in the Eighteenth Century', *Georgraphy* 28, 2 (1943), pp. 37–46
Price, Jacob, 'What Did Merchants Do? Reflections on British Overseas Trade, 1660–1790', *Journal of Economic History* 49, 2 (1989), pp. 267–84
Purdue, A. W., *Merchants and Gentry in North-East England, 1650–1830: The Carrs and the Ellisons* (Sunderland, 1999)
Quickenden, Matthew, Baggott, Sally and Dick, Malcolm, eds, *Matthew Boulton: Enterprising Industrialist of the Enlightenment* (Abingdon, 2013)

Radburn, Nicholas, 'Guinea Factors, Slave Sales, and the Profits of the Transatlantic Slave Trade in Late Eighteenth-Century Jamaica: The Case of John Tailyour', *William and Mary Quarterly* 72, 2 (2015), pp. 243–86

——, 'Keeping "the wheel in motion": Trans-Atlantic Credit Terms, Slave Prices, and the Geography of Slavery in the British Americas, 1755–1807', *Journal of Economic History* 75, 3 (2015), pp. 660–89

——, 'The British Gunpowder Industry and the Transatlantic Slave Trade', *Business History Review* 97 (2023), pp. 363–84

——, *Traders in Men: Merchants and the Transformation of the Transatlantic Slave Trade* (New Haven, CT, 2023)

Raistrick, A., 'The South Yorkshire Iron Industry, 1698–1756', *Transactions of the Newcomen Society* 19, 1 (1938), pp. 51–86

Raman, Alka, 'Indian Cotton Textiles and British Industrialisation: Evidence of Comparative Learning in the British Cotton Industry in the Eighteenth and Nineteenth Centuries', *Economic History Review* 75, 2 (2022), pp. 447–74

——, 'From Hand to Machine: How Indian Cloth Quality Shaped British Cotton Spinning Technology', *Technology and Culture* 64, 3 (2023), pp. 707–36

Ramsay, G. D., 'The Distribution of the Cloth Industry in 1561–2', *English Historical Review* 57, 227 (1942), pp. 361–9

Randall, Adrian, *Before the Luddites: Custom, Community and Machinery in the English Woollen Industry, 1776–1809* (Cambridge, 1991)

Raudzens, George, 'War-Winning Weapons: The Measurement of Technological Determinism in Military History', *Journal of Military History* 54, 4 (1990), pp. 403–33

——, 'Military Revolution or Maritime Evolution? Military Superiorities or Transportation Advantages as Main Causes of European Colonial Conquests to 1788', *Journal of Military History* 63, 3 (1999), pp. 631–42

Rediker, Marcus, *The Slave Ship: A Human History* (London, 2008)

Reinert, Erik, *How Rich Countries Got Rich . . . And Why Poor Countries Stay Poor* (London, 2010)

Richards, Eric, *Patrick Sellar and the Highland Clearances: Homicide, Eviction and the Price of Progress* (Edinburgh, 1999)

——, *The Highland Clearances: People, Landlords and Rural Turmoil* (Edinburgh, 2000)

Richards, John, *The Unending Frontier: An Environmental History of the Early Modern World* (Berkeley, CA, 2003)

Richardson, David, 'Slavery and Bristol's "Golden Age"', *Slavery & Abolition* 26, 1 (2011), pp. 35–54

Richardson, David, Schwarz, Suzanne and Tibbles, Anthony, *Liverpool and Transatlantic Slavery* (Liverpool, 2007)

Riding, Jacqueline, *Jacobites: A New History of the 1745 Rebellion* (London, 2016)

Riello, Giorgio, *Cotton: The Fabric that Made the Modern World* (Cambridge, 2013)

Robbins, Michael, 'The Principo Company: Iron-Making in Colonial Maryland, 1720–1781', PhD thesis, George Washington University (1972)

Roberts, John, *The Jacobite Wars: Scotland and the Military Campaigns of 1715 and 1745* (Edinburgh, 2002)

Roberts, Justin, *Slavery and the Enlightenment in the British Atlantic, 1750–1807* (Cambridge, 2013)

——, 'Surrendering Surinam: The Barbadian Diaspora and the Expansion of the English Sugar Frontier, 1650–75', *William and Mary Quarterly* 73, 2 (2016), pp. 225–56

——, 'The Whip and the Hoe: Violence, Work and Productivity on Anglo-American Plantations', *Journal of Global Slavery* 6, 1 (2021), pp. 108–30

Robinson, Eric, 'The Lunar Society: Its Membership and Organisation', *Transactions of the Newcomen Society* 35, 1 (1962), pp. 153–77

Roll, Eric, *An Early Experiment in Industrial Organisation, Being a History of the Firm of Boulton & Watt, 1775–1805* (London, 1930)

Rönnbäck, Klas, 'Sweet Business: Quantifying the Value Added in the British Colonial Sugar Trade in the 18th Century', *Revista de Historia Económica – Journal of Iberian and Latin American Economic History* 32, 2 (2014), pp. 223–45

——, 'On the Economic Importance of the Slave Plantation Complex to the British Economy during the Eighteenth Century: A Value-added Approach', *Journal of Global History* 13, 3 (2018), pp. 309–27

——, 'Governance, Value-added and Rents in Plantation Slavery-based Value-chains', *Slavery & Abolition* 42, 1 (2021), pp. 130–50

Roper, L. H., *Advancing Empire: English Interests and Overseas Expansion, 1613–1688* (Cambridge, 2017)

Rose, Arthur, 'Early Cotton Riots in Lancashire, 1769–1779', *Transactions of the Lancashire and Cheshire Antiquarian Society* 73 (1963), pp. 60–100

Rose, Mary, 'The Gregs of Styal, 1750–1914: The Emergence and Development of a Family Business', PhD thesis, The University of Manchester (1977)

——, *The Gregs of Quarry Bank Mill: The Rise and Fall of a Family Firm, 1750–1914* (Cambridge, 1986)

Rosenthal, Caitlin, *Accounting for Slavery: Masters and Management* (Cambridge, MA, 2018)

Rosier, Barrington, 'The Construction Costs of Eighteenth-Century Warships', *The Mariner's Mirror* 96, 2 (2010), pp. 161–72

Rössler, Horst, 'Germans from Hanover in the British Sugar Industry, 1750–1900', in *Migration and Transfer from Germany to Britain 1660 to 1914: Historical Relations and Comparisons*, ed. Stefan Manz, Margit Schulte Beerbühl and John Davis (Berlin, 2007), pp. 49–63

Rössner, Philipp, *Scottish Trade in the Wake of Union (1700–1760): The Rise of a Warehouse Economy* (Stuttgart, 2008)

——, *Managing the Wealth of Nations: Political Economies of Change in Preindustrial Europe* (Bristol, 2024)

Rothschild, Emma, *Inner Lives of Empire: An Eighteenth-Century History* (Princeton, NJ, 2011)

Rothstein, Natalie, 'Huguenots in the English Silk Industry in the Eighteenth Century', in *Huguenots in Britain and France*, ed. Irene Scouloudi (London, 1987), pp. 125–40

——, 'Canterbury and London: The Silk Industry in the Late Seventeenth Century', *Textile History* 20, 1 (1989), pp. 33–47

Rowlands, Marie, *Masters and Men: In the West Midland Metalware Trade before the Industrial Revolution* (Manchester, 1975)

Roy, Tirthankar, *The East India Company: The World's Most Powerful Corporation* (London, 2016)

——, *How British Rule Changed India's Economy: The Paradox of the Raj* (London, 2019)

——, *The Crafts and Capitalism: Handloom Weaving Industry in Colonial India* (Abingdon, 2020)

Rugemer, Edward, *Slave Law and the Politics of Resistance in the Early Atlantic World* (Cambridge, MA, 2018)

Rule, John, *The Experience of Labour in Eighteenth Century Industry* (London, 1981)

Russell, Carl, *Guns of the Early Frontiers: A History of Firearms from Colonial Times through the Years of the Western Fur Trade* (Lincoln, NE, 1980)

Sahle, Esther, *Quakers in the British Atlantic World, c. 1660–1800* (London, 2021)

Sanderson, Michael, 'Literacy and Social Mobility in the Industrial Revolution in England', *Past & Present* 56 (1972), pp. 75–105

Satia, Priya, *Empire of Guns* (London, 2018)

Scammell, G. V., *Seafaring, Sailors and Trade, 1450–1750* (London, 2003)

Scanlan, Padraic, *Slave Empire: How Slavery Built Modern Britain* (London, 2020)

Schäfer, Dagmar, 'Patterns of Design in Qing-China and Britain during the Seventeenth and Eighteenth Centuries', in *Goods from the East, 1600–1800: Trading Eurasia*, ed. Maxine Berg, Hanna Hodacs, Felicia Gottman and Chris Nierstrasz (London, 2015), pp. 107–18

Schofield, Robert, *The Lunar Society of Birmingham: A Social History of Provincial Science and Industry in Eighteenth-century England* (Oxford, 1963)

Schumpeter, Elizabeth, *English Overseas Trade Statistics, 1697–1808* (Oxford, 1960)

Schumpeter, Joseph, *A Theory of Economic Development: An Inquiry into Profits, Capital, Credit, Interest, and the Business Cycle* (Oxford, 1961)

Shapin, Steven and Schaffer, Simon, *Leviathan and the Air-pump: Hobbes, Boyle, and the Experimental Life* (Princeton, NJ, 2011)

Shapiro, Barbara, *A Culture of Fact: England, 1550–1720* (New York, 1999)

Sharples, Jason, 'Discovering Slave Conspiracies: New Fears of Rebellion and Old Paradigms of Plotting in Seventeenth-Century Barbados', *American Historical Review* 120, 3 (2015), pp. 811–43

Shaw-Taylor, Leigh, 'The Occupational Structure of Britain c. 1379–1911 and the International Comparative History of Occupational Structure: An Overview of Findings and Where to Find Them', Cambridge Group for the History of Population Preliminary Findings (2025)

Shaw-Taylor, Leigh and Wrigley, E., 'Occupational Structure and Population Change', in *The Cambridge Economic History of Modern Britain, Vol. 1: 1700–1870*, ed. R. Floud, J. Humphries and P. Johnson (Cambridge, 2014), pp. 53–88

Sheridan, Richard, *Sugar and Slavery: An Economic History of the British West Indies 1623–1775* (Kingston, 1974)

Simms, Brendan, *Three Victories and a Defeat: The Rise and Fall of the First British Empire, 1714–1783* (London, 2007)

Siochrú, Micheál Ó, 'Extirpation and Annihilation in Cromwellian Ireland', in *The Cambridge World History of Genocide, Vol. 2: Genocide in the Indigenous, Early Modern and Imperial Worlds, from c.1535 to World War One*, ed. Ned Blackhawk, Ben Kiernan, Benjamin Madley and Rebe Taylor (Cambridge, 2023), pp. 163–85

Slack, Paul, *The Invention of Improvement: Information and Material Progress in Seventeenth-Century England* (Oxford, 2014)

Slater, Aaron, 'The Economy of Colonial British America', *Oxford Research Encyclopedia of American History* (Oxford, 2021)

Smail, John, 'The Culture of Credit in Eighteenth-Century Commerce: The English Textile Industry', *Enterprise & Society* 4, 2 (2003), pp. 299–325
Smiles, Samuel, *Men of Invention and Industry* (London, 1884)
Smith, Edmond, 'Corporate Naval Supply in England's Commercial Empire', *International Journal of Maritime History* 31, 3 (2019), pp. 574–89
——, *Merchants: The Community that Shaped England's Trade and Empire, 1550–1650* (London, 2021)
——, 'Social Networks of Investment in Early Modern England', *Historical Journal* 64, 4 (2021), pp. 912–39
——, 'Reinterpreting the Virginia Plantation, 1609–1618', *Journal of British Studies* 61, 4 (2022), pp. 884–914
Smith, Haig, *Religion and Governance in England's Emerging Colonial Empire, 1601–1698* (London, 2022)
Smith, John, 'Industry and Social Change: Wolverhampton Transformed, 1700–1840', in *Towns, Regions and Industries: Urban and Industrial Change in the Midlands, c. 1700–1840*, ed. Jon Stobart and Neil Raven (Manchester, 2005)
Smith, Justin, *Nature, Human Nature, and Human Difference: Race in Early Modern Philosophy* (Princeton, NJ, 2015)
Smout, T. C., 'A New Look at the Scottish Improvers', *Scottish Historical Review* 91, 231 (2012), pp. 125–49
Smout, T. C., Landsman, N. C and Devine, T. M., 'Scottish Emigration in the Seventeenth and Eighteenth Centuries', in *Europeans on the Move*, ed. Nicholas Canny (Oxford, 1994), pp. 76–112
Soll, Jacob, 'Accounting for Government: Holland and the Rise of Political Economy in Seventeenth-century Europe', *Journal of Interdisciplinary History* 40, 2 (2009), pp. 215–38
Stern, Philip, *Empire, Incorporated: The Corporations that Built British Colonialism* (Cambridge, MA, 2023)
Stern, Philip and Wennerlind, Carl, eds, *Mercantilism Reimagined: Political Economy in Early Modern Britain and its Empire* (Oxford, 2013)
Stewart, Larry, *The Rise of Public Science: Rhetoric, Technology, and Natural Philosophy in Newtonian Britain, 1660–1750* (Cambridge, 1992)
Stewart-Brown, Ronald, *Liverpool Ships in the Eighteenth Century, Including the King's Ships Built There, With Notes on Principal Shipwrights* (Liverpool, 1932)
Stobart, Jon, *The First Industrial Region: North-West England, c. 1700–60* (Manchester, 2004)
Stone, Lawrence, ed., *An Imperial State at War: Britain from 1689–1815* (London, 1994)
Storrs, Christopher, ed., *The Fiscal-Military State in Eighteenth-Century Europe: Essays in Honour of P. G. M. Dickson* (London, 2009)
Stubbs, Tristan, *Masters of Violence: The Plantation Overseers of Eighteenth-Century Virginia, South Carolina, and Georgia* (Columbia, SC, 2018)
Styles, John, 'Product Innovation in Early Modern London', *Past & Present* 168, 1 (2000), pp. 124–69
——, *The Dress of the People: Everyday Fashion in Eighteenth-Century England* (New Haven, CT, 2007)
——, 'The Rise and Fall of the Spinning Jenny: Domestic Mechanisation in Eighteenth-Century Cotton Spinning', *Textile History* 51, 2 (2020), pp. 195–236

Sugden, Keith, 'An Occupational Study to Track the Rise of Adult Male Mule Spinning in Lancashire and Cheshire, 1777–1813', *Textile History* 48, 2 (2017), pp. 160–75

——, 'Clapham Revisited: The Transference of the Worsted Industry from Norfolk to the West Riding, c. 1700–1851', *Continuity and Change* 33, 2 (2018), pp. 203–24

Sugden, Keith, Keibek, Sebastian, Wells, James and Shaw-Taylor, Leigh, 'Adam Smith Revisited: The Relationship between the English Woollen Manufacture and the Availability of Coal before the Use of Steam Power', *Continuity and Change* 38, 2 (2023), pp. 163–91

Swaminathan, Srividhya, *Debating the Slave Trade: Rhetoric of British National Identity, 1759–1815* (Farnham, 2009)

Sweet, James, 'Slave Trading as a Corporate Criminal Conspiracy, from the Calabar Massacre to BLM, 1767–2022', *American Historical Review* 128, 1 (2023), pp. 1–30

Swingen, Abigail, *Competing Visions of Empire: Labour, Slavery, and the Origins of the British Atlantic Empire* (New Haven, CT, 2015)

Tann, Jennifer, 'Steam and Sugar: The Diffusion of the Stationary Steam Engine to the Caribbean Sugar Industry 1770–1840', *History of Technology* 19 (1997), pp. 63–84

——, 'Matthew Boulton – Innovator', in *Matthew Boulton: Enterprising Industrialist of the Enlightenment*, ed. Matthew Quickenden, Sally Baggott and Malcolm Dick (Abingdon, 2013), pp. 33–50

——, 'Borrowing Brilliance: Technology Transfer across Sectors in the Early Industrial Revolution', *International Journal for the History of Engineering & Technology* 85, 1 (2015), pp. 94–114

Tawny, Paul, 'Small Credit and the Financial Revolution in England', in *Different Forms of Microcredit and Social Business*, ed. Paola Avallone and Donatella Strangio (London, 2024), pp. 43–63

Tello, Enric et al., 'The Onset of the English Agricultural Revolution: Climate Factors and Soil Nutrients', *Journal of Interdisciplinary History* 47, 4 (2017), pp. 445–74

Temin, Peter and Voth, Hans-Joachim, 'Banking as an Emerging Technology: Hoare's Bank 1702–1742', *Financial History Review* (2006), pp. 149–78

——, *Prometheus Shackled: Goldsmith Banks and England's Financial Revolution after 1700* (Oxford, 2013)

Thomas, Keith, *In Pursuit of Civility: Manners and Civilisation in Early Modern England* (New Haven, CT, 2018)

Thomas, R. and McCloskey, Donald, 'Overseas Trade and Empire, 1700–1860', in *The Economic History of Britain since 1700, vol. 1: 1700–1860*, ed. Roderick Floud and Donald McCloskey (Cambridge, 1981), pp. 87–10

Thompson, E. P., 'Time, Work-Discipline, and Industrial Capitalism', *Past & Present* 38, 1 (1967), pp. 56–97

Thompson, Peter, 'Henry Drax's Instructions on the Management of a Seventeenth-Century Barbadian Sugar Plantation', *William and Mary Quarterly* 66, 3 (2009), pp. 565–604

Tibbles, Anthony, *Liverpool and the Slave Trade* (Liverpool, 2018)

Tilly, Charles, *Coercion, Capital and European States, A.D. 990–1992* (Cambridge, MA, 1992)

Toynbee, Arnold, *Lectures on the Industrial Revolution of the Eighteenth Century in England* (Cambridge, 1925 [1884])

Treadwell, J. M., 'William Wood and the Company of Ironmasters of Great Britain', *Business History* 16, 2 (1974), pp. 97–112

——, 'Swift, William Wood, and the Factual Basis of Satire', *Journal of British Studies* 15, 2 (1976), pp. 76–91

Trinder, Barry, *The Industrial Revolution in Shropshire* (Chichester, 1973)

——, 'Towns and Industries: The Changing Character of Manufacturing Towns', in *Towns, Regions and Industries: Urban and Industrial Change in the Midlands, c. 1700–1840*, ed. Jon Stobart and Neil Raven (Manchester, 2005), pp. 102–18

Trivellato, Francesca, *The Familiarity of Strangers: The Sephardic Diaspora, Livorno, and Cross-Cultural Trade in the Early Modern Period* (New Haven, CT, 2012)

Turner, Michael, Beckett, John and Afton, Bethanie, *Farm Production in England, 1700–1914* (Oxford, 2001)

Tweedale, Geoffrey, *Steel City: Entrepreneurship, Strategy, and Technology in Sheffield, 1743–1993* (Oxford, 1995)

Tyler, Ian, *The Gunpowder Mills of Cumbria: A History of Cumbria's Gunpowder Industry* (Keswick, 2002)

Uglow, Jenny, *The Lunar Men: The Friends Who Made the Future, 1730–1810* (London, 2003)

Unwin, George, *Samuel Oldknow and the Arkwrights: The Industrial Revolution at Stockport and Marple* (Manchester, 1967 [1923])

Van Crevald, Martin, *Supplying War: Logistics from Wallenstein to Patton* (Cambridge, 2004)

Vidal, Cécile, 'Violence, Slavery and Race in Early English and French America', in *The Cambridge World History of Violence, vol. III, 1500–1800* CE, ed. Robert Antony, Stuart Carroll and Caroline Dodd Pennock (Cambridge, 2020)

Voigtländer, Nico and Voth, Hans-Joachim, 'Why England? Demographic Factors, Structural Change and Physical Capital Accumulation during the Industrial Revolution', *Journal of Economic Growth* 11, 4 (2006), pp. 319–61

Voth, Hans-Joachim, 'Time and Work in Eighteenth-Century London', *Journal of Economic History* 58, 1 (1998), pp. 29–58

Vries, Peer, 'Governing Growth: A Comparative Analysis of the Role of the State in the Rise of the West', *Journal of World History* 13 (2002), pp. 67–193

Wadsworth, Alfred and De Lacy Mann, Julia, *The Cotton Trade and Industrial Lancashire, 1600–1780* (Manchester, 1931)

Wallis, Patrick, 'Between Apprenticeship and Skill: Acquiring Knowledge outside the Academy in Early Modern England', *Science in Context* 32, 2 (2019), pp. 155–70

——, *The Market for Skill: Apprenticeship and Economic Growth in Early Modern England* (Princeton, NJ, 2025)

Wallis, Patrick, Colson, Justin and Chilosi, David, 'Structural Change and Economic Growth in the British Economy before the Industrial Revolution, 1500–1800', *Journal of Economic History* 78, 3 (2018), pp. 862–903

Walsh, Lorena, 'Plantation Management in the Chesapeake, 1620–1820', *Journal of Economic History* 49, 2 (1989), pp. 393–406

——, *Motives of Honor, Pleasure, and Profit: Plantation Management in the Colonial Chesapeake, 1607–1763* (Chapel Hill, NC, 2010)

Warner, Frank, *The Silk Industry of the United Kingdom: Its Origin and Development* (London, 1921)

Weatherill, Lorna, 'The Growth of the Pottery Industry in England, 1660–1815: Some New Evidence and Estimates', *Post-Medieval Archaeology* 17, 1 (1983), pp. 15–46

Weber, Julia, 'Copying and Competition: Meissen Porcelain and the Saxon Triumph over the Emperor of China', in *The Transformative Power of the Copy: A Transcultural and Interdisciplinary Approach*, ed. Corinna Forberg and Philipp Stockhammer (Heidelberg, 2017), pp. 331–73

Wennerlind, Carl, *Casualties of Credit: The English Financial Revolution, 1620–1720* (Cambridge, MA, 2011)

West, Jenny, *Gunpowder, Government, and War in the Mid-Eighteenth Century* (London, 1991)

Wilkinson, Clive, *The British Navy and the State in the Eighteenth Century* (London, 2004)

Williams, Eric, *Capitalism and Slavery* (Chapel Hill, NC, 1944)

Williams, Gomer, *History of the Liverpool Privateers and Letters of Marque with an Account of the Liverpool Slave Trade, 1744–1812* (London and Liverpool, 1897)

Wilson, R. G., 'The Supremacy of the Yorkshire Cloth Industry in the Eighteenth Century', in *Textile History and Economic History Essays in Honour of Miss Julia De Lacey Mann*, ed. N. B. Harte and Kenneth G. Ponting (Manchester, 1973), pp. 225–46

Winter, Mabel, *Banking, Projecting and Politicking in Early Modern England: The Rise and Fall of Thompson and Company 1671–1678* (London, 2022)

Winterbottom, Anna, *Hybrid Knowledge in the Early East India Company World* (New York, 2016)

Wojcik, Jan, *Robert Boyle and the Limits of Reason* (Cambridge, 1997)

Wrigley, E. A., 'Urban Growth and Agricultural Change: England and the Continent in the Early Modern Period', *Journal of Interdisciplinary History* 15, 4 (1985), pp. 683–728

——, *Continuity, Chance and Change: The Character of the Industrial Revolution in England* (Cambridge, 1988)

——, 'Urban Growth in Early Modern England: Food, Fuel and Transport', *Past & Present* 225, 1 (2014), pp. 79–112

——, 'Reconsidering the Industrial Revolution: England and Wales', *Journal of Interdisciplinary History* 49, 1 (2018), pp. 9–42

Yamamoto, Koji, 'Piety, Profit and Public Service in the Financial Revolution', *English Historical Review* 126, 521 (2011), pp. 806–34

——, *Taming Capitalism Before its Triumph: Public Service, Distrust, and 'Projecting' in Early Modern England* (Oxford, 2018)

Yazdani, Kaveh, *India, Modernity and the Great Divergence: Mysore and Gujarat (17th to 19th Centuries)* (Leiden, 2017)

Yazdani, Kaveh and Menon, Dilip, eds, *Capitalisms: Towards a Global History* (Oxford, 2020)

Yelling, J. A., 'Probate Inventories and the Geography of Livestock Farming: A Study of East Worcestershire, 1540–1750', *Transactions of the Institute of British Geographers* L1 (1970), pp. 111–26

Zacek, Natalie, *Settler Society in the English Leeward Islands, 1670–1776* (Cambridge, 2010)

Zahedieh, Nuala, 'The Merchants of Port Royal, Jamaica, and the Spanish Contraband Trade, 1655–1692', *William and Mary Quarterly* 43, 4 (1986), pp. 570–93

——, 'Trade, Plunder, and Economic Development in Early English Jamaica', *Economic History Review* 39, 2 (1986), pp. 205–22

——, *The Capital and the Colonies: London and the Atlantic Economy, 1660–1700* (Cambridge, 2010)

——, 'Colonies, Copper, and the Market for Inventive Activity in England and Wales, 1680–1730', *Economic History Review* 66, 3 (2013), pp. 805–25

——, 'Eric Williams and William Forbes: Copper, Colonial Markets, and Commercial Capitalism', *Economic History Review* 74, 3 (2021), pp. 784–808

## DATABASES

Coal Mining History Resource Centre, 'UK Mining Disasters, 1707–99'

History of Parliament Online (HOPO)

Investing in Innovation Dataset

Online Dictionary of Welsh Biography

Oxford Dictionary of National Biography Online (ODNB)

The Register of British Slave-Traders (RBS)

The Trans-Atlantic Slave Trade Database (TASTD)

# INDEX


absentee owners, 43, 56, 98, 115, 117, 125, 147, 236,
abundance, 4, 10, 23–4, 54–5, 127–8, 226
Africa, 34–5, 41, 46, 139–40, 146, 154, 168, 172, 174, 183, 301, 308–11
African Company of Merchants, 318–19
Agnew, David, 150
agricultural revolution, 10–11, 33
agriculture, 6, 11, 33, 53–90, 129–30, 147, 190, 196–7, 227, 323
Alexander, William, 326
Amicable Society, 38–9
Anderson, Alexander, 223
Anderson, William, 195
Antigua, 125, 145, 158, 230, 232–3
Arawak, 124–5
Arkwright, Richard, 219, 347–9, 351–4, 356, 366–7, 372
Ashe family, 80
Ashurst, William, 105
Asia, 14–15, 25, 34, 41, 74, 88–9, 106, 172, 180, 195, 206, 293, 324, 329
Austin, Jacob, 168
Austria, 159

Bacon, Anthony, 279
Bacon, Francis, 23, 189
Baillie, Robert, 326
Baker, Henry, 198–9, 201
Baltic, 38, 49, 74, 114, 142, 157, 161, 163, 302
Baltimore, 170
Bank of England, 25, 36–9, 41, 106, 118
banking, 36–44, 69, 109
Banks, Joseph, 115
Bannau Brycheiniog, 55
Barbados, 124, 127–9, 132, 134–6, 139, 147–8, 158, 229–33, 236, 313
Barkstead, John, 29, 84
Barnes, Elias, 347
Barrill, John, 361
Barry, Henry, 325
Bateman, Thomas, 106
Baugh, Edmund, 176
Baylies, Thomas, 271
Bayly, William, 83
Bedingfield, Dorothy, 38
Belgrove, William, 231
Bellingham, John, 29
Bentley, Thomas, 214, 332
Bersham, 272–3
Best, Henry, 65
Bilston, 167, 272
Binns, Nathaniel, 362
Birmingham, 1–2, 4, 166–72, 185, 201–3, 218, 244, 254, 264, 270, 272, 287–90, 293, 318, 321, 328, 344
Birmingham Canal Company, 254, 285

Bisset, Robert, 372–3
Black, Joseph, 280
Black Country, 254, 264–81
Blackburn, 82, 349
Blackwell, Robert, 360
Bloodworth, John, 351
Blundell, Bryan, 145, 307, 336
Blundell, Henry, 335–6
Blundell, Jonathan, 334–5, 356
Boats, William, 305, 328–9
Bogle, Robert, 315
Bohemia, 98
Bolton, 82, 349
Bolton, John, 372
Bo'ness colliery, 113
Botfield, Thomas, 283
Bottomley, John, 220–1
Boulton, Matthew, 2, 201, 203, 243, 284–6, 290, 330, 362
Bourn, Daniel, 218
Bowden, Edward and Rachel, 359
Bowes family, 118–19
Bow porcelain works, 212
Boyle, Robert, 25
Bradford, William, 161
Bradford-on-Avon, 80–1
brass, 109, 137, 146, 154, 166, 169, 265, 270, 287, 290, 328
Brazil, 131, 370–1
Brewer, Christopher, 80–1
Brewin, Ellis, 359
Brindley, John, 253–4
Briscoe, John, 29
Bristol, 14, 74, 77–8, 102, 111, 141–2, 144–6, 149, 164, 168, 172, 174–6, 254, 267–8, 270–1, 275, 293, 301, 320–2, 327–8, 360
British Linen Company, 149
Broadbent, Joseph, 268
Brocas, Richard, 144
Brooke, Robert, 141
Brown, Isaac Hawkins, 275
Brown, Malcolm, 326
Brown, William, 113, 283
Brownrigg, William, 279
Buckinghamshire, 66, 145
Budgen, Richard, 216
Burfield, 148
Bursham, 265
Bury St Edmunds, 82
Byam, Ashton Warner, 315

Cadell, William, 272
Calabar, 309–10
Calder Valley, 220, 251, 256, 258–60, 368
Canada, 126, 158–9
Canary Islands, 131, 157
Canterbury, 82
'capitalism', 5
Cardiff, 102, 272
Cardiganshire, 103, 108–9
Carib, 124–5
Caribbean, 14–15, 20, 33–5, 40, 46, 51, 84, 89, 114–55, 158–9, 176, 183, 190, 206, 226, 229–33, 293, 300–4, 313, 321–4, 326–7, 329, 370
Carlisle, 82
Carmarthen, 110
Carolina, 228, 235
Carr, Ralph, 246
Carron, 251–3, 272–3, 275, 279, 344
Carter, William, 27, 75, 90
Carwood, John, 360–1
Cave, Edward, 218
Cazanove, James, 360
Chaffers, Edward, 310–11, 334
Chamberlayne, Edward, 92
Champion, Richard, 213
charcoal, 173–4, 261–2, 265, 267, 269–72, 275–6, 280–95, 300
Chardin, John, 25
Charles I, king, 124
Charles II, king, 21–2, 24, 27, 30, 36, 42, 47, 76, 125, 128, 138, 156
Cheshire, 209, 244, 248, 251, 303
Childrey, Joshua, 59, 66
China, 23, 29, 84, 180, 195, 211–12, 246, 250, 321, 342
Chorley, 335, 355
Christian-Knack, Hans, 326
Christie, John, 195
civil war, 21, 57
Clark, Samuel, 39
Clavering, Lady, 117
Clay, Henry, 291
Clayton, John, 245
Clayton, Robert, 42–4, 69–70
Clerk, John, 113

Clive, Robert, 179–82
clockwork, 25–6, 28, 190, 235–6
cloth, 28–9, 47, 146, 176, 199, 211, 217–18, 302, 321, 328
 cotton, 1–4, 50, 84, 139, 148, 154, 221, 244–5, 312, 333, 336, 341–75
 linen, 35, 49, 77, 84, 147–9, 154, 176, 223, 303–4, 344
 mixed fibres, 35, 79, 82, 209, 224, 321
 silk, 29, 35, 39, 48, 50, 78, 83, 137, 206–9, 265, 347, 349, 351
 woollen, 4, 11, 49–50, 52, 55, 70–90, 137, 146–8, 154, 221, 224, 321
coal, 2, 4, 12–13, 39, 49, 91–7, 101–21, 147, 157, 169, 247, 249, 253–5, 258, 261–97, 321, 325, 330, 334–5, 355
Coalbrookdale, 32, 101, 254, 269–72, 274, 278–80, 283, 285, 332
Cockburn, James, 195
Cockshull, John, 273
Cockshutt, John, 268
Cockworthy, William, 213
coke, 101, 262, 265, 269–72
colonial trade, 25, 39, 46, 74, 84, 89, 106, 143–53, 175–6, 195, 199, 267–9, 279, 287, 293, 298–340, 344–5, 368
colonies, 2–5, 13–14, 20, 35, 39–40, 48–52, 56, 77, 105, 114, 123–55, 176, 230–6, 298–340
coffee, 86, 230, 321
Commercial Society, 195–6
Company for Digging and Working Mines, 39
Company of Gunmakers, 166–7
Company of Gunmakers in Birmingham, 167
Company of Mineral Manufacturers, 108
Company of Royal Adventurers Trading into Africa, 34, 138
comparisons, 7
Congleton, 209–10, 344
Cope, John, 305
copper, 12–13, 15, 31, 49, 91–3, 101–11, 121, 137, 147–8, 154, 166, 231, 264–7, 269, 290, 328–9
Cornwall, 15, 66, 92, 102–3, 108, 110–11, 144, 199, 264–5, 282, 284, 294, 330–1
Corporation for the Linen Manufacture in England, 35
corporations, 19–20, 34–6
Cort, Henry, 280
Cotesworth, William, 114–22
Cotswolds, 71
cotton (raw), 1–4, 15, 125, 127, 149, 235, 237, 317–18, 332, 336, 341–75
County Durham, 96, 110, 114, 263, 283
Coventry, 25, 209, 359
Cranage, Thomas, 279–80
Crawshay, Richard, 278, 280–1
Crisp, Nicholas, 198–9
Cromford, 219, 348–9, 352
Crompton, Abraham, 356
Crompton, Samuel, 219, 349–50
Cromwell, Oliver, 124
Cropper, Arabella, 304
Crosley, William, 258
Crossley, Abraham, 221–2
Crossley, John, 221–2
Crouch, Nathanial, 125, 127
Crowley, Ambrose, 262–3
Cumberland, 92, 94, 105, 110, 147, 275
Cumberland, John, 28
Cunliffe, Ellis and Robert, 176
Cunningham, George, 326
Cyfarthfa works, 267, 273, 279–81

Dale, David, 219, 350
Dallas, Henry, 335–6
Darby, Abraham, 32, 101, 269–70
Darwin, Erasmus, 201
Davenport, William, 305, 307, 309, 334
Dawner, Steven, 148
Dawson, Nicholas, 37
Day, Edward, 86
Day, Peter, 144
Debaufre, Peter and John, 28
Defoe, Daniel, 37, 96, 163
de la Chaumette, Isaac, 190–1
Delavel, Thomas, 283–4
Delaware, 125
Denbighshire, 92
Denmark, 23, 74, 142, 154, 160, 163, 171, 246
Derby, 156, 207–9, 211, 213, 347–8, 351–2
Derbyshire, 92, 248, 350, 353

desalination, 33
Devon, 102
Dewsnap, John, 362
discipline, 81, 128–9, 134, 231, 235–6, 299, 358
Dissel, James, 148
Dobson, John, 332
Dominica, 124, 245
Donaldson, James, 63
Douglas, William, 349
Doville, John, 85
Dowlais, 272–3
Driver, Charles, 265
Dublin, 192, 199, 276
Dudley, 281
Duesbury, William, 213
Du Halde, Jean-Baptiste, 211–12
Duke of Bridgewater, 249
Duke of Hamilton, 113
Dundas, Henry, 253
Dupin, Nicholas, 35
Dutch *see* Netherlands and Dutch empire
duties, 21–2, 27, 45–51, 67, 141, 158, 207, 211, 223, 225, 275, 277, 300, 324, 344, 359–60, 366–7, 373
Dwight, John, 29
dyeing, 28, 72, 74, 83
dyes, 35, 74, 114, 125, 127, 199, 211, 214

Earle family, 305, 334, 372
East India Company, 20, 25, 34, 37–41, 86, 89, 109, 114, 145, 148, 157, 167, 172–3, 176, 178–82, 195, 209, 239–40, 294, 329, 341, 354, 374
economic frontiers, 3, 5, 35
economic output, 4–7
economic system, 3–4, 7–8, 14, 21
Edinburgh, 55, 113, 194–6, 203, 223, 242, 245, 326–7, 342, 350, 359
Edinburgh Society for Encouraging Arts, Sciences, Manufactures and Agriculture in Scotland, 196, 200
Edinburgh Sugar House Company, 326–7
Edmondson, Thomas, 244
Egypt, 52
Elizabeth I, queen, 99, 123
Ellis, Henry, 305–6
Elliston, Mathew, 132
Elton, Abraham, 146
engineering, 27, 175, 190, 203, 246–60, 261–97
environment, 13, 53–4, 91–2, 127–9, 133, 197, 146–60
Eryri, 55
Esgair Hir, 103–7
Essex, 41–2
Evans, Mary, 102
Evans, William, 372
Ewart, Peter, 368

factories, 1–3, 81, 165, 208, 341–75
Falkirk, 253
Fandell du Fresue, Francis, 29
Farmer, James, 170, 244, 289, 318
Farmer, Joseph, 168–70
Fatfield colliery, 96, 112
Feather, George, 222
Fens, 243
Fielden, Joshua, 222
Fielden, Samuel, 222
finance, 25, 33–6, 156–8, 183–4
Firth, John, 88
Fisher, Jabez, 203, 291
Fisher, Joseph and George, 220
fishing, 35, 52, 108, 149, 157, 195, 211, 333
Fitzgerald, Robert, 25
Flanders, 23, 46, 50, 74, 76
Fleet, John, 145
Fletcher, Andrew, 326
Foljambe, Joseph, 56
Forest, Thomas, 110
Forest of Dean, 92
Fowler, Edward, 38
Fox, Shadrach, 269
France, James, 317
France and French empire, 23, 25, 29, 41, 48, 50–2, 57, 74, 76, 82, 86, 124, 126, 148, 157, 159, 166, 172, 179–83, 192, 199, 204, 210, 223–5, 228–9, 250, 262, 299, 333, 337–8, 347, 359–60, 364, 366
Franklin, Benjamin, 198
Frodisham, William, 366
Frome, 81

Frye, Thomas, 212
Fulham, 29

Galton, Samuel, 170, 201, 244, 289, 318
Galton, Samuel junior, 185
Garbett, Samuel, 272, 276–8, 292–3
Gaskins, Joshua, 28, 83
Gateshead, 96, 114–15
Gavin, David, 245–6
George II, king, 158–9
Georgia, 154–5, 227–9, 235, 306, 371
Gerbier, Balthazar, 133
Germany, 25, 29–30, 40, 50, 74, 84, 94, 98–9, 108, 114, 154, 157, 159, 170, 200, 213, 223, 246, 265, 275, 302, 316, 327, 333, 373
Gibbons, William, 275, 278
Gibson, Benjamin, 360
Gildart, Richard, 149–50, 307–8
Gilpin, John, 144
Gladsmuir colliery, 282
Glamorgan, 110, 267
Glasgow, 4, 14, 149, 164, 223, 242, 253, 302, 313–16, 320, 322–3, 328, 350, 367, 369–71
Gloucester, 82
Gloucestershire, 66, 102, 110, 275
Gnoll, 102, 109
Golightly, Richard, 149–50
Goore, Charles, 307, 334
Goore, Elizabeth, 307, 317–18
Gordon, Robert, 25
Gourlay, Robert, 359
Gower, Earl 276, 278
Grace, Edward, 37
Graham, John, 326
grain, 59–66
Greenland, 35, 157
Greenwood, William, 244
Greg, Samuel, 244–5, 368, 374–5
Gregson family, 305
Grenada, 312, 314
Gresham College, 26
Grew, Nehemiah, 25, 132
Guadeloupe, 132, 183
Guericke, Otto von, 25
gunmakers, 165–72, 201, 218, 328
gunpowder, 15, 94, 96, 108, 146, 154, 158, 162, 166, 173–7, 184, 328, 332
Hackshaw, Robert, 39
Hadley, John, 25
Hale, Thomas, 30
Halifax, 85, 88, 146, 225, 321, 341
Hamilton, Robert, 315
Hanbury, John, 172
Hanson, Francis, 127, 136
Hardman, John, 150, 171
Hargreaves, James, 218, 347
Hartlib, Samuel, 24, 64, 189
Harvey, Robert, 224
Harvey, Thomas, 265
Haworth, Jonathan, 361
Hayes, John, 265
Hemming, Edmund, 29
Henry VIII, king, 123
Herd, David, 195
Herefordshire, 66
Herne, Joseph, 39
Heylin, Edward, 212
Heysham, Robert, 140
Heywood family, 176, 318, 336
Hibbert, Thomas, 232–3
Highs, Thomas, 219
Hill, Abraham, 51
Hill, Oliver, 25
Hilton, John, 366
Hindley, Henry, 250
Hoare, Richard, 105
Hobby, Mary, 38
Hobhouse, Isaac, 144
Hodgson, John, 313, 332, 333
Hodgson, Tom, 316
Hollow Sword Blade Company, 38
Home, Francis, 193, 196–7
Home, Henry, 326
Homfray, Samuel, 280
Hooke, Abraham, 176
Hooke, Robert, 25
Hopwood, Edward Gregg, 257
Horsfield, Thomas, 357–8, 363
Houghton, John, 66
Houlditch, Abraham, 140
Houston, Alexander, 313–16, 328, 371
Howard, Philip, 30
Hudson's Bay, 52, 137
Hughes, Thomas, 221–2
Hull, 74, 164, 248
Hume, David, 12, 192–3, 204

Hungary, 26, 98
Hunt, Peter, 313
Hutton, Harry, 316
Huygens, Christiaan, 25

import substitution, 10, 15, 26, 29, 35, 45–51, 80–3, 121, 165–72, 192–3, 199, 205–15, 276–80, 330, 342–3, 346, 354–5, 359–74
improvement, 10–11, 23–33, 45, 126–7
Incorporated Company of Hostmen, 113
India, 50, 74, 82–4, 87, 139, 148, 159, 172–3, 177–82, 209, 211, 235–40, 294, 312, 321, 341–2, 345–6, 354–5, 366
industrial revolution, 3–4, 9, 15
infrastructure, 8, 11–12, 14–15, 68, 114–15, 117–21, 151–2, 164, 197, 246–60, 278–9, 303, 319, 323–6, 332, 334, 336
Ingram, Francis, 334
institutions, 8–9, 19–20
investment, 1–2, 5, 8–9, 19–21, 33–9
Ipswich, 82
Ireland, 20, 25, 40, 49, 51–2, 74, 77, 123, 145, 147, 192, 225, 267, 275–6, 287, 302, 305, 308, 321, 323, 329, 331, 344
iron, 2, 12, 29, 32, 49, 52, 76, 91–3, 137, 142, 146, 148, 163, 166, 169–71, 176, 247, 254–5, 261–81, 286–95, 328, 332–3, 369
Italy, 23, 46, 74, 82–3, 88, 148, 170, 173, 192, 207, 209, 228, 262, 347–8, 368

Jacob, Samuel, 148
Jamaica, 127–39, 141, 149, 153–5, 172, 230–3, 236, 241, 303, 313, 317, 321, 324, 329
James I, king, 124
James II, king, 113
Johnson, Samuel, 184
Jonson, Derick, 80
Jordan, Edward, 170

Kay, John (flying shuttle), 218
Kay, John (spinning machinery), 218–19
Kaye, John, 305, 333
Keane, Michael, 232–3
Keir, James, 204
Kempson, William, 289
Kendall, 175
Kendall, Richard, 305
Kennedy, John, 1–3, 369
Kent, 75, 92
Kenyon, James, 372
Ker, James, 326
Keswick, 105
Ketley, 254
Kidderminster, 81
Killpatrick, James, 179
Kneller, Godfrey, 105
Knight, Edward, 272
knowledge exchange, 23–33, 39, 51, 57, 66, 94, 100–1, 107–8, 111–13, 128–9, 131–2, 189–225, 240–2, 272–4

Lace, Ambrose, 309, 334
Lancashire, 1, 218–19, 245, 270, 275, 341–75
Land Bank, 36, 39
Lane, John, 111
Lane, Ralph, 83
Lansdowne, Marquis of, 341
Law, Samuel and Robert, 221–2
lead, 30, 39, 92, 104, 106, 108, 148, 247–9, 261, 263, 265, 269, 274
Leake, John, 344
Leake, Samuel, 41–2
Lee, William, 48
Leeds, 86, 88, 203, 225, 250, 260, 280, 289, 325
Leeds and Liverpool Canal, 258, 260, 334–5
Leicester, 209, 359
Leicestershire, 66
Leominster, 218
Lewis, William, 273
Levant Company, 20, 118, 157, 209
Levett, Christopher, 161
Leyland, Thomas, 308, 312–13
Lidell, George, 118–19
Lister, Jeremy, 146–7
Lister, Samuel, 146–7
Lister, Thomas, 146–7

Liverpool, 4, 14, 77, 142, 145, 149–53, 164, 170–2, 174–6, 183, 200, 202, 247, 253–4, 256, 260, 274, 293, 301–11, 316–40, 358, 369, 372
Llanelli, 93
Lloyd, Samuel, 209
Lodwick, Francis, 46
Lombe, John, 207–8, 347–8, 352
Lombe, Thomas, 207–8, 228, 347–8, 352
London, 14, 42–3, 45, 48, 68, 74, 83, 92, 103, 113–15, 118, 123, 142, 144–5, 161, 166–7, 173, 185, 198, 203, 210, 250, 267–9, 286, 293, 301, 321, 324, 326, 331, 343–4, 351, 358–60, 365, 371
Longbotham, John, 258
Louverture, Toussaint, 338
Lowther, John, 147
Lumbutts, 220–1
Lunar Circle, 201–4, 214
Lydell, Robert, 108
Lynch, Thomas, 131–2
Lyon, Edward, 305

McCaul, John, 324
Macclesfield, 209–10, 321, 342, 344
McConnel, James, 1–3, 368
MacGregor, James, 367
McKell, Robert, 253
Mackworth, Humphry, 101–11
Mackworth family, 109
Maddock, John, 305
Maidstone, 82
Maltby, George, 224
Manchester, 1–4, 15, 82, 203, 209–10, 219, 247–9, 256–7, 260, 321, 328, 332, 341–75
manure, 45, 59, 61, 63–4, 130, 196, 230, 232, 240
Marshall, Ralph, 30, 84
Marsland, William, 265
Martin, Elias, 195
Martin, Joseph, 38
Martinique, 132, 183
Mary II, queen, 156
Mason, Henry William, 335
Massey, Ralph, 351
Massingberd, Margaret, 38
Masterson, Nicholas, 335
Maynard, Thomas, 265
Mayo, Edward, 29
Maxwell, Patrick, 315
Meagre, Leonard, 63
Mediterranean, 38–40, 74–5, 79, 106, 118, 207, 235, 324, 344
Melincryddan, 102–11
Mellor, 362
Merchants House (Glasgow), 253, 323
Merthyr Tydfil, 272–3, 280–1
metallurgy, 2, 12–13, 26, 29, 32–3, 49, 91–122, 144, 147–8, 165–72, 190, 201, 261–97, 355
Methuen, Paul, 80
Mexico, 52, 321
Midlands, 55, 63, 65, 102, 131, 166–72, 185, 201–2, 204, 209, 213, 254, 263–81, 284, 287–95
Milled Lead Company, 30–1
Million, Henry, 35
Million Bank, 36, 38
mills, 1–3, 71, 130–2, 174–5, 208, 216–25, 250, 252, 256–7, 262, 265, 333, 348
Mine Adventurers, 38, 101–11, 263
Mines Royal, 99
mining, 2, 12–13, 32, 35, 38–9, 49, 91–122, 252, 261–97, 334–5, 355
Mir Jafar, 182
Mir Qasim, 182
Mocha, 86–7, 294, 321
Modyford, Thomas, 129
Molineux family, 265
monocultures, 62–3, 230, 234, 237
monopolies, 20, 27, 32, 34, 40, 50, 73, 76, 99, 113–22, 116–19, 138–9, 166–7, 212, 239, 274–5, 318, 373
Montagu family, 118–19, 164
Montgomeryshire, 272
Montserrat, 132, 172
Morden, John, 38–9
Morgan, William, 110
Morris, John, 43–4, 69–70
Muscovy Company, 20
Mynydd Parys, 330–1
Mytholmroyd, 244

Nantwich, 259
naval stores, 23, 28, 49, 142, 149–50, 160–5
Neale, Thomas, 29
Neath, 102, 107–8, 271
Need, Samuel, 351
Needham, Robert, 245
Nelson, Robert, 105
Netherlands and Dutch empire, 25, 27, 29, 35, 39–40, 48, 50, 64, 66, 74, 76, 80–1, 86, 111, 125, 129, 148, 157, 159, 166, 169, 171, 211, 213, 246, 250, 302, 327, 348
networked capital, 8–9, 16, 19, 21, 39–40, 44–5, 58–9, 101, 110, 120, 129, 131, 140, 176, 189, 193, 201, 270, 304, 313, 319, 343, 350–1, 364
Nevis, 158, 268
New England, 39, 49, 124–5, 158, 161, 163
New England Company, 25, 161
New Hampshire, 162
New Jersey, 39
New Lanark, 219, 350
New York, 125, 158, 333
Newcastle, 92, 97, 108, 111–20, 157, 246, 248, 269, 271, 360
Newcomen, Thomas, 32, 281
Newdigate, Richard, 166
Newfoundland, 52
Nicholls, Richard, 125
Nicholson, Matthew, 303
Nicholson, Robert, 183, 303, 316–17
nitrogen, 64
Norfolk, 33, 39, 59, 63–5, 71, 78, 81–2
Norris, Robert, 322
North America, 14, 20, 35, 39–40, 46, 51–2, 77, 105–6, 124–6, 128, 139, 142–55, 161–5, 168, 170, 172, 183, 227, 229, 233–4, 267, 274, 279, 300–4, 306, 312–13, 322–3, 326, 333, 344, 371–2
Northampton, 191, 218
Northamptonshire, 198
Northumberland, 114, 284
Norway, 74, 142, 160, 163
Norwich, 82, 224, 274
Nottingham, 48, 209, 349, 351, 355
Ogilby, John, 68
Okill, John, 149–50
Oldham, 82
Oldknow, Samuel, 245, 335, 354–65
Ord, Thomas, 119
Ordnance Office, 165–72, 289
Osborne, Thomas, 105
Oswald, Richard, 246, 322–3
Otto Ephraim Robin John, 310
Ottoman empire, 23, 46, 83, 118, 344, 366
Oxford, 66
Oxley, Joseph, 283

Padmore, Richard, 372
Paine, Thomas, 320
Paisley, 223, 350, 370
Parke, Moses, 200
Parker, Robert, 358–60
Patchett, William, 244
patents, 10, 22, 25–34, 40, 44–7, 83–4, 132, 190, 208, 211–13, 270, 284, 348, 367
Paterson, John, 313
Paul, Lewis, 218, 247
Peel, Robert, 336, 349, 366
Pemberton, Peter, 150
Penn, William, 126–7
Pennines, 71
Pennsylvania, 268
Pequot, 124
Persia, 25, 29, 84, 180, 342
Petty, William, 26, 51
Philadelphia, 149, 201, 203
Phinn, John, 195
Pitt, George, 117
Planche, Andrew, 213
plantations, 2–3, 20, 33, 41, 114, 123–55, 190, 227, 229–37, 329, 344, 355
Plot, Robert, 66, 100
poisoning, arsenic, 116
Poland, 24
Pollard, John, 111
Polzunov, Ivan, 277
population, 5, 55, 67
Portugal and Portuguese empire, 39–40, 46, 50, 74, 79, 147, 154, 172, 225, 275, 321

potatoes, 132
Potosí, 103, 105, 330
pottery, 29, 146, 148, 201, 211–13
power, 3–4, 261–97
  animal, 56–7, 94, 98, 112, 131, 232, 271, 282–3, 352
  steam, 1–3, 13, 32, 94, 97, 113, 121, 203, 243, 251, 253, 258, 271–4, 281, 330, 335, 355, 362, 367–8
  water, 4, 25, 55, 57, 61, 71, 73, 84, 98, 109–10, 112, 131–2, 174–5, 200, 208, 210, 218–22, 232, 250–1, 253, 255, 262–3, 266, 271, 277, 291–2, 347–8, 350, 352, 355, 368
  wind, 57, 61, 131–2, 216, 232, 243, 251
Preston, 82, 351
Priestley, Joseph, 202–3, 214
productivity chain, 10, 45–52, 77, 83, 206, 248, 277
Pryce, William, 282
Pryse, Carbery, 103
pumps, 25, 97–8, 102–3, 112, 243, 252, 258, 281, 335

Raby, Alexander, 278
Ramsay, Allen, 193–4
Ramsay, William, 115
Rasbotham, Dornin, 352, 365
Rathbone family, 150, 202, 274, 318, 331–2, 372, 374
Ravensworth colliery, 112
Rawson, Christopher, 204
Red Sea, 86
Redbrook, 102
Rennie, John, 220, 243, 256, 335
rent, 43–4, 56, 115, 242, 246, 278
reputation, 36–7, 41–42, 44–5, 100, 129, 152, 192, 251, 311–18, 320, 358, 361
Reynolds, Richard, 254–5, 274, 275–6, 278, 297, 332
Reynolds, William, 202, 204, 254, 274, 280, 318, 332
Richards, Henry, 144
Richardson, John, 305, 333
Richmondshire, 92
Ridley, Richard, 116
Rigby, William, 372
rivers, 71, 102, 114, 117, 151–3, 164, 208–9, 219–20, 243–4, 247–8, 251–4, 266, 323, 325
Roberts, Lewes, 344
Robertson, Thomas, 242
Rochdale, 221
Rochdale Canal Company, 256–60
Roebuck, John, 272, 279, 284
Rotherham, 273
Royal African Company, 25, 35, 37–41, 52, 138–40, 166–7, 174
Royal Assurance Company, 38
Royal Lustring Company, 39, 207
Royal Navy, 30, 36, 41, 51–2, 77, 97, 115, 138, 150, 156, 158–62, 178, 180, 280, 318, 335
Royal Society, 24–6, 46, 51, 59, 66, 68, 92, 100, 105, 131–2, 190–1, 198, 216, 250
Rupert, prince, 99
Rushall, 169, 265
Russia, 23, 52, 170, 223, 272, 276–8, 368
Rutland, 66

sailing waggons, 103
St Kitts, 124, 127, 268
St Lucia, 132
Salisbury, 81
salt, 29, 115, 146–7, 247, 307
saltpetre, 127, 173–7
Sandford, Benjamin, 1
Sandford, William, 1
Saunders, Edmund, 141
Savery, Thomas, 32, 281
science, 3, 9–10, 22–5, 33, 100, 189–225, 277
Scotland, 1, 4, 54–5, 63, 112–13, 156, 164, 192–3, 219, 223, 242, 245, 251, 255, 272, 282, 284, 302, 304, 314, 322–3, 349–50, 361, 369
Searle, Edward, 140
Seel family, 307
Select Society, 193–5, 204
Shairp, Alexander, 149
sheep, 54–5, 59–60, 65–90, 127
Sheffield, 289, 290, 307, 333–4, 362
Shipley, William, 197–8
shipping, 29–31, 36, 49, 145, 149–53, 160–5, 302, 307

Shropshire, 2, 92, 101, 106, 110, 254, 265, 267, 272, 279
silk (raw), 83, 206–7, 228–9, 265, 351
silver, 104
Silvertop, Albert, 116–18
Simpson & Company, 372
Siraj-ud-Daulah, 178
Sisson, Thomas, 115
slavery and slave-trade, 2–4, 13–14, 20, 33–5, 40, 106, 108, 123–55, 167, 170–2, 176, 230–3, 245–6, 298–340, 344
Smalley, John, 351
Smeaton, John, 243, 250–3, 284
smelting, 33, 49, 102–11, 201, 261–81, 330
Smith, Adam, 192–3, 204, 357
Smith, Joseph, 366
Smith, Robert, 209
Snow, Thomas, 189–90
Society Appointed to Manage the British White Herring Fishery, 211
Society of Arts, 198–202, 273
Society for Promoting Christian Knowledge, 105
Society for the Propagation of the Gospel, 105
Soho, 284, 286, 291–2
Sorocold, George, 208
South America, 75
South Sea Company, 25, 33, 39, 108
Southampton, 37, 164
Spain and Spanish empire, 23, 46, 49–50, 66, 74, 79, 89, 98–9, 114, 126, 129, 154, 157, 159, 225, 275, 292, 299, 321, 338
Spark, Robert, 265
Spearman, Gilbert, 117
specialisation, 5
speculation, 35–7
Spedding, John, 94
Spencer, William, 268–9
spinning, 30, 70–2, 218–19
Staffordshire, 92, 213–15, 253–4, 278, 285, 303, 321
Stamford, Thomas, 351
standardisation, 44, 80, 168–9, 172, 177, 286, 291, 296, 311, 314, 354–65
Stanhope, Walter, 88
Staniforth, Thomas, 306–7, 317–18, 333–4
Stansfield, George, 85, 148
Stanyforth, Disney, 56
state committees for trade, 37, 46–7, 51–2, 77–8, 83, 126, 139, 157–9, 223–5, 294, 366
state support, 20–33, 45–52, 67, 75–6, 128, 138, 143, 158, 165–77, 211, 268–9, 274, 319, 341–4, 373
steel, 12, 29, 33, 171, 265, 290
Stockport, 209, 356–62, 369
Stour Valley, 272, 275
Stourbridge, 271
Stow-on-the-Wold, 82
Strathnaver, Lady, 326
Stroud Valley, 71, 81
Strutt, Jedediah, 350–4
Suffolk, 64, 75
sugar, 20, 23, 33, 114, 125, 127–37, 140–55, 176, 206, 230–3, 239–40, 302, 308, 315, 317, 321, 324, 326–9, 332
  refining, 37, 48, 144–5, 148, 233, 246, 326–8
sulphur, 173
Suriname, 129, 372
Sutcliffe, John, 220–1
Swansea, 111, 267, 344
Sweden, 23, 29–30, 49–52, 74, 99, 121, 142, 154, 160, 163, 170, 264–5, 272, 276, 287, 330, 333
Switzerland, 200
Sykes, Joseph, 369

Tailyour, John, 322–3
tariffs *see* duties
Tattersall, John, 222
Taylor, John, 133–4, 137, 290, 292
tea, 206, 321
Teshmaker, John Englebert, 30, 84
textiles *see* cloth
Thomas, John, 270
Thurlow, Edward, 274
tin, 91–2, 265, 294
tobacco, 52, 114, 125, 127, 141, 144, 147–8, 154, 158, 172, 195, 206, 233, 279, 308, 312, 321, 323

Todmorden, 221
Tomkyns, Thomas, 279
Tony, 135
Tourney, Anthony, 141
Trafford, Richard, 150
transport, 11, 66, 74, 97, 102–3, 107–8, 110, 112, 115–18, 209, 246–60, 278–9, 289–90, 293, 325, 334, 374
Triewald, Martin, 113
Tucker, Josiah, 184, 226–7
Tull, Jethro, 56
Turkey *see* Ottoman empire
Turnbull, Gordon, 241
Tyler, John, 270
Ty-llwyd, 111
Tylston, William, 317
Tyzacke, John, 28

universities, 26, 102, 111, 193–4, 203, 284
useful knowledge, 10, 25–6
Uttley, John, 220
Uttley, William, 222

van Tromp, Emerson, 148
Venables, Robert, 126–7
violence, 26, 35–6, 41, 52, 123–5, 134–6, 156–86, 309–11, 334, 364
Virginia, 20, 114, 124, 141, 144–8, 154, 157–8, 234–6, 268, 279, 303–4, 321, 333
Virginia Company, 124

wages, 5, 73, 96, 103, 159, 238–9, 298, 327–8, 349, 350, 354, 362, 366, 379
Waine, Gabriel, 29
Waite, James, 141
Wakefield, John, 176
Wales, 33, 35, 39, 55, 93, 101–11, 123, 131, 184, 226, 248, 265, 267, 269–72, 275, 294, 330–1, 349
Walker, Alexander, 236–9
Walker, John, 372
Walker, Samuel, 273
Waller, William, 104
Wapping, 28
Ward, Edward, 36–7
Ward, John, 39
Ward, Seth, 26
Washington, George, 235–6
Watson, Charles, 179–82
Watson, Francis, 30
Watt, James, 2–3, 13, 32, 201, 203, 254, 274, 280, 284–6, 330, 362
Watts, John, 268–9
weaponry, 26, 35–6, 125, 150, 157–8, 160, 165–72, 284, 289, 294, 312, 318, 321, 328
Weatherby, James, 116
weaving, 29, 35, 70, 72, 80–2
Webb, Mr, 236–9
Wedgwood, Josiah, 201, 213–15, 253, 291, 332
Weisehamer, Jeremiah, 132
West Bromwich, 279
Westmorland, 147
Whatley, George, 298
Whielden, Thomas, 214
Whitechurch, Sarah, 81
Whitehaven, 77, 144–5, 147, 267, 271
Wickham, 115
Wilkes, John, 184
Wilkinson, Isaac, 273–4
Wilkinson, John, 272–3, 284–5
Wilks, John, 28
William III, king, 46, 49, 156
Williamson, William, 150
Wilson, Alexander, 315
Wilson, Christopher, 176
Wilson, William, 209
Winter, Thomas, 132
Wirtz, Andrew, 200
Wolverhampton, 264–5, 272, 287–8, 293
women, 38, 71–2, 81, 102, 106, 127, 194, 210, 229, 319, 357
Wood, Charles, 267, 279–80
Wood, Francis, 267, 279
Wood, John, 267, 279
Wood, Sampson, 233, 236
Wood, William, 264–7
wool (raw), 4, 11, 50–2, 65–90

Woolatt, William, 351
Worcester, 81
Worlidge, John, 61
Wright, Robert, 117
Wright & Jesson, 279
Wyatt, John, 218, 347

Yerbury, Richard, 81
York, 222, 250
Yorkshire, 65, 76, 78–9, 84, 88, 92, 146–8, 220–2, 224, 248, 256, 263, 268, 289, 317, 362
Young, Arthur, 241
Young, William, 312

Zachary, John, 229
Ziegler, John Henry, 200, 274
zinc, 109